THIS WAY TO
YOUTH MINISTRY:
AN INTRODUCTION TO THE ADVENTURE

DUFFY ROBBINS

THIS WAY TO
YOUTH MINISTRY:
AN INTRODUCTION TO THE ADVENTURE

DUFFY ROBBINS

YOUTH
SPECIALTIES
ACADEMIC

ZONDERVAN™

WWW.ZONDERVAN.COM

YOUTH
SPECIALTIES
ACADEMIC

DEDICATION

This book is dedicated to my Mom, Mary P. Robbins (no longer on earth, but very much alive), and to my Dad, still on earth and one of the most alive people I know, and

to my brother Guy, whose love of research and study have provided for me a wonderful example of diligent scholarship, and

to Joe Modica and Chris Hall, two men who exemplify passionate scholarship combined with a passionate love for Christ, and who, beyond that, have been willing to share with me the journey of life with Jesus, and

to Darrell Pearson, Calenthia Dowdy, Eduardo Ramirez, Christine Parker, T.J. Foltz, and Jennifer Voloninno, coworkers in the Youth Ministry major at Eastern University, and trusted companions in the sometimes wild, sometimes exhausting, sometimes exhilarating odyssey we share, and

to Katie Robbins, and Erin and Peter Lima—and now, Henry (!)—whose laughter, love, and support always make life a fun and fascinating (and fascinating even when it is not always fun!) adventure, and especially, to Maggie, my wife and best friend who has shared the journey with me—good times and tough times—every step of the way, and who consistently lives out what it means to explore new frontiers in her relationship with Jesus.

But remember, sinner, it is not thy hold of Christ that saves thee—it is Christ; it is not thy joy in Christ that saves thee—it is Christ; it is not even faith in Christ, though that is the instrument—it is Christ's blood and merits; therefore, look not so much to thy hand with which thou art grasping Christ, as to Christ; look not to thy hope, but to Christ, the source of thy hope; look not to thy faith, but to Christ, the author and finisher of thy faith; and if thou dost that, ten thousand devils cannot throw thee down, but as long as thou lookest at thyself, the meanest of those evil spirits may tread thee beneath his feet . . . it is not faith, it is not our doings, it is not our feelings upon which we must rest, but upon Christ, and on Christ alone.

—Charles Spurgeon, in a sermon delivered August 24, 1856, New Park Street Chapel, Southwark, England

TABLE OF CONTENTS

UNIT ONE
INTRODUCTION

We are now ready to start on our way down the Great Unknown... We have an unknown distance yet to run; an unknown river yet to explore. What falls there are, we know not; what rocks beset the channel, we know not; what walls rise over the river, we know not... Jests are bandied about freely this morning; but to me the cheer is somber and the jests are ghastly . . . With some eagerness, and some anxiety, and some misgiving, we enter the canon [canyon] below.

—From the journal of John Wesley Powell, August 13, 1869, written at the junction of the Colorado River and the Little Colorado River, Arizona Territory

chapter one

DOWN THE GREAT UNKNOWN

Saddle up your horses, we've got a trail to blaze,
Through the wild blue yonder of God's amazing grace;
Let's follow our leader into the glorious unknown;
This is a life like no other; this is the great adventure
—Steven Curtis Chapman, "The Great Adventure"[1]

On your way! But be careful—this is hazardous work. You're like lambs in a wolf pack.
—Luke 10:3, *The Message*

---

[1] Steven Curtis Chapman, "The Great Adventure," words and music by Steven Curtis Chapman and Geoff Moore (Sparrow Song/Peach Hill Songs/BMI/Songs on the Hill/SESAC, 1992).

It had been three wet, miserable days since John Wesley Powell and his team of nine adventurers had crashed through the 14 miles and 35 rapids that make up the section of the Colorado River known as Marble Canyon. Powell and his crew were well into their fourth month of a grueling and dangerous attempt to navigate the entire course of river through the Grand Canyon. It was a journey that began on May 24, 1869, when four boats under Powell's command—the *Emma Dean*, the *Kitty Clyde's Sister*, the *Maid of the Canon*, and the *No Name*—were launched at Green River Station, Wyoming Territory. The opening quotation above was written on the morning of August 13, 1869, as the expedition team was ready to descend into the roaring water that would lead them into the steepest depths of the Grand Canyon—a journey of amazing adventure, or death, or perhaps both.[2]

Perhaps it seems strange that these should be the opening words in the opening chapter of an introduction to a youth ministry text. We do not commonly think of the classroom as a place of adventure: "The Quest for Calculus," "Journeys in Biochemistry," "Expeditions into Spanish Verbs." We are confronted in these opening paragraphs with words that might give pause to any reasonable person: words such as "depths," "dangerous," "death," and, that scariest of all words for college students, "morning." But it is good that we should begin here on the banks of a wild, beautiful, unpredictable river, because this book is about a launch into a grand adventure.

Risk, as we have seen, is indispensable to any significant life, nowhere more clearly than in the life of the spirit.
Dan Taylor, *The Myth of Certainty*

The spiritual life cannot be made suburban. It is always frontier and we who live it must accept and even rejoice that it remains untamed.
—Howard Macey, quoted in *Wild at Heart*

There are some very cautious, prudent, and entirely unadventurous 20-somethings who will never do anything wrong because they never do anything. Being an "old maid" in the following old poem is not a factor of gender; it is a factor of mindset:

Here lie the bones of Nancy Jones.
For her life held no terrors.
She lived an old maid,
She died an old maid,
No hits, no runs, no errors.
—Anonymous

---

[2] Edward Dolnick, *Down the Great Unknown* (New York: HarperCollins, 2001), 238, 239–240.

A Great Adventure

Every great story involves a quest. In J. R. R. Tolkien's *The Hobbit*, Bilbo Baggins ran from the door at a quarter til eleven without even so much as a pocket handkerchief and launched on an adventure that would change his life forever. Alice stepped through the looking glass into Wonderland; Lucy, Edmund, Susan, and Peter stumbled through the wardrobe into Narnia. Abraham left "his country, his people, and his father's household" to follow the most outlandish sort of promise from a God he had only just met, and he never came back. Jacob and his sons went to Egypt for some groceries and four hundred years later the nation of Israel pulled up stakes and headed for home. Peter, Andrew, James, and John all turned on a dime one day to follow the Master, their fishing nets heaped in a wet pile. The Sacred Romance involves for every soul a journey of heroic proportions. And while it may require for some a change of geography, for every soul it means a journey of the heart.

—*John Eldredge and Brent Curtis,* The Sacred Romance *(Nashville, Tenn.: Thomas Nelson, 1997), 143.*

The language of the journey—the quest, the adventure—has long been the language of the Christian life. At the very heart of the Bible, in the Book of Psalms, we find no fewer than 15 chapters of what might be described as "pilgrim songs" or "hiking songs," Psalms often referred to as Songs of Ascent.[3] In reading through these 15 gritty and earthy psalms, Psalm 120 to Psalm 134, we come to understand why Eugene Peterson characterizes the Christian life as "a long obedience in the same direction."[4] Life is marked "not so much by monuments as by footprints." It is a journey marked not by arrival, but by survival. The Christian life is about a quest, about pressing forward (Phil. 3:12–16, Col. 2:5, Heb. 12:1–3). It is about milestones, not tombstones. William Faulkner aptly sums up the idea this way: "A monument only says, 'At least I got this far,' while a footprint says, 'This is where I was when I moved again.'"[5]

So much of the drama of Scripture centers around journey, whether the study begins with that amazing call in Genesis, "The Lord had said to Abram, 'Leave your country, your people and your father's household and go to the land I will show you'" (Gen. 12:1), or that dramatic night, terrible and wonderful, when God led his people out of Egypt on a journey we call the Exodus. It is interesting to note

[3] Eugene Peterson, *A Long Obedience in the Same Direction* (Downers Grove, Ill.: InterVarsity Press, 1980), 13: "These fifteen psalms were likely sung, possibly in sequence, by Hebrew pilgrims as they went up to Jerusalem to the great worship festivals. Jerusalem was the highest city geographically in Palestine, and so all who traveled there spent much of their time ascending. But the ascent was not only literal, it was also a metaphor: the trip to Jerusalem acted out a life lived upward toward God, an existence that advanced from one level to another in developing maturity. What Paul described as 'the upward call of God in Christ Jesus' (Phil. 3:14) . . . Three times a year faithful Hebrews made that trip (Ex. 23:14–17, 34:22–24). The Hebrews were a people whose salvation had been accomplished in the exodus, whose identity had been defined at Sinai, and whose preservation had been assured in the forty years of wilderness wandering."

[4] Ibid. This is a phrase Peterson cites from Friedrick Nietzsche, *Beyond Good*. Here is the full quotation from Nietzsche: "The essential thing 'in heaven and earth' is . . . that there should be a long obedience in the same direction; there thereby results, and has always resulted in the long run, something which has made life worth living."

[5] Cited in ibid., 17. William Faulkner, quoted in Sam di Bonaventura's Program Notes to Elie Siegmeister's Symphony No. 5, Baltimore Symphony Concert, May 5, 1977.

In his introduction to one of Christendom's greatest literary classics, John Bunyan writes of his aspirations for *Pilgrim's Progress*:

This book will make a traveler of thee,
If by its counsel thou wilt ruled be;
It will direct thee to the Holy Land,
If thou wilt its directions understand:
Yea, it will make the slothful active be;
The blind also delightful things to see.

—John Bunyan, The Pilgrim's Progress *(Grand Rapids, Mich.: Zondervan, 1966), x.*

that while Israel sojourned in the wilderness, the Tabernacle—essentially a huge tent—was always set up in a sandy place; yet, even with all the ornate furnishings for the Tabernacle, there was never any effort to cover the sand. The priests could always feel the sand under their feet—God's subtle but vivid way of reminding his priests and his people that they were on a journey.[6]

In 1 Peter 2:11, followers of Christ are referred to as "strangers" and "pilgrims." Eugene Peterson notes that this designation as pilgrims[7]

tells us we are people who spend our lives going someplace, going to God, whose path for getting there is the way, Jesus Christ. We realize that "this world is not my home" and set out for the "Father's house." Abraham who "went out" is our archetype. Jesus answering Thomas' question, "Lord, we do not know where you are going; how can we know the way?" gives us direction: "I am the way, and the truth, and the life; no one comes to the Father except by me" (John 14:6). The letter to the Hebrews defines

By the time this letter reaches you, Ed and Pete and I and another fellow will have attempted with Nate a contact with the Aucas. We have prayed for this and prepared for several months.
. . . The contact is planned for Friday or Saturday, January 6 or 7 . . . I don't have to remind you that (the Aucas) . . . have never had any contact with white men other than killing. They do not have firearms, but kill with long chonta-wood knives . . . They have no word for God in their language, only for devils and spirits. I know you will pray. Our orders are "the gospel to every creature."—Your loving son and brother, Jim.
—Last letter written by Jim Elliot on December 28, 1955, to his parents before being killed by the Auca Indians of Ecuador.

---

[6] Stephen Olford, *Camping with God* (Neptune, N.J.: Loizeaux Brothers, 1971), 17. For more insight and understanding of the symbolism of the Tabernacle, and for deepening one's own sense of awe that God "pitched his tent among us" (John 1:14), this book is well worth reading.

[7] King James Version. The Greek word is *parepidomos*. See also Heb. 11:13.

Modern society, of course, has perfected the art of having nothing happen at all. There's nothing particularly wrong with this, except that for vast numbers of Americans, as life has become staggeringly easy, it has also become vaguely unfulfilling. Life in modern society is designed to eliminate as many unforeseen events as possible. And as inviting as that seems, it leaves us hopelessly underutilized. And that is where the idea of adventure comes in. The word is from the Latin, adventura *meaning "what must happen."*
Sebastian Junger, *Fire*

The life of faith is not a life of mounting up with wings [Isa. 40:28–31], but a life of walking and not fainting.
Oswald Chambers, *My Utmost for His Highest*

our program: "Therefore since we are surrounded by so great a cloud of witnesses, let us lay aside every weight, and sin which clings so closely, and let us run with perseverance the race that is set before us, looking to Jesus, the pioneer and perfecter of our faith" Heb. 12:1–2).[8]

Paul's words to the believers in 2 Corinthians 4:8–9 might just as well have come from the water logged journal of John Wesley Powell, staring up into distant sunlight from deep within canyon walls.

We are hard pressed on every side, but not crushed; perplexed, but not in despair; persecuted, but not abandoned; struck down, but not destroyed.

Adventure is inherent in the Christian life. In fact, it was that adventure of the Christian life that inspired J. R. R. Tolkien to pen his wonderfully creative tales of Middle Earth, with hobbits, elves, wizards, and perilous journeys in pursuit of the Ring.[9]

One writer, in commenting on Tolkien's work, noted

The Lord of the Rings is about a Quest... A Quest is any journey in which some difficult goal is to be achieved, some challenge must be met, some initiation has to be undergone, some place or object or person is to be discovered or won. The reasons for its perennial popularity is obvious enough. It is just such a Quest that gives meaning to our existence. We are not where (or whom) we wish to be: to get there it is necessary to travel . . . Each of us knows, deep down inside, that our life is not merely a mechanical process from cradle to grave; it is a search for something,

---

[8] Peterson, *A Long Obedience in the Same Direction,* 13–14.

[9] J. R. R. Tolkien, *The Lord of the Rings* (1968). In fact, as Ralph Wood observes, Tolkien made a distinction between adventure and quest: "An adventure, as Frodo explains, is a 'there-and-back-again' affair. One undertakes it largely as a matter of one's own desire—often from boredom and a lust for excitement. Once the treasure is found and the adventure is over, one circles back home essentially unchanged by the experience.

"A *quest,* by contrast is a fulfillment, not of one's desire but of one's calling. Frodo asks why he has been chosen for his dreadful task. His summons, moreover, is not to find a treasure, but to lose one—to cast the Ring back into the Cracks of Mount Doom. A quest is thus a vocation—an errand in the medieval sense, and its outcome entails something immensely larger and more important than one's happiness." Ralph Wood, "Hungry Eye: *The Two Towers* and the Seductiveness of Spectacle," *Books and Culture,* 9 (March/April 2003): 17.

"Is that why you stopped climbing mountains?"

Phil looked surprised. "I haven't stopped climbing mountains, I just happen to be doing reed boats at the moment. I guess I need some kind of adventure to feel alive. But you won't see me leaping up there on the mast. I learned what Mark never lived long enough to learn: use the fear."

"Actually, what's sad about it is that Mark had really matured a lot in the months before his death. He was just coming to the point where he knew fear. He'd had this weird experience on Aconcagua in Argentina, said he met God on the mountain—a kind of vision of Jesus—and it had changed his life. He couldn't say much about it. I guess it was kind of personal, but we all saw the effects of it."

The pink skies had faded, and the first stars had picked their way through the dark dome of heavens. I sat back in the silence, pondering . . . *He met God on the mountain.*

Wasn't that why anybody wandered into the wilderness, or onto the sea?

Wasn't that why we were all here?

—*Nick Thorpe,* Eight Men and a Duck: An Improbable Voyage by Reed Boat to Easter Island *(New York: Free Press, 2002), 181.*

for some elusive treasure. The same ultimate goal motivates us both in work and play. What the storyteller depends upon is a fact of human nature; that our imagination is always reaching out beyond the limits of the known and the evident towards the infinity of what is desired. The Quest activates our nostalgia for paradise lost, our

I knew that if I listened to this Jesus and followed him—if I, like the disciples, left my fishing and my tax collecting—he would lead me into treacherous territory, where every day would be an experience of danger and wonder at the same time: an adventure of dangerous wonder!
—**Michael Yaconelli,** ***Dangerous Wonder***

The mountains have done the spiritual side of me more good religiously, as well as in my body physically, than anything else in the world. No one knows who and what God is until he has seen some real mountaineering and climbing in the Alps.
—**Rev. F. T. Wethered, 1919 letter to the** ***Alpine Journal***

Eastward the dawn rose, ridge behind ridge into the morning, and vanished out of eyesight into guess; it was no more than a glimmer blending with the hem of the sky, but it spoke to them, out of memory and old tales, of the high and distant mountains.
—**J. R. R. Tolkien,** ***The Lord of the Rings***

To venture causes anxiety, but not to venture is to lose one's self… And to venture in the highest is precisely to become conscious of one's self.
—**Søren Kierkegaard, Danish philosopher, 1813–1855**

Some also have wished that the next way to their Father's House were here, that they might be troubled no more with either hills or mountains to go over: but the way is the way, and there is an end."
—**John Bunyan, *The Pilgrim's Progress***

yearning for the restoration or fulfillment to come.[10]

Eldredge reminds us, "Life is a desperate quest through dangerous country to a destination that is beyond our wildest hopes, indescribably good. Only by conceiving of our days in this manner can we find our way safely through."[11]

G. K. Chesterton argued that authentic adventure could only be known within the framework of a Christian worldview:

[The despair of pagan freedom] is this, that it does not really believe that there is any meaning in the universe; therefore it cannot expect to find any romance; its romances will have no plots. A man cannot expect to find any adventures in the land of anarchy. But a man can expect any number of adventures if he goes traveling in the land of authority. One can find no meanings in a jungle of skepticism; but the man will find more and more meanings who walks through a forest of doctrine and design. Here everything has a story tied to its tail, like the tools or pictures in my father's house; for it is my father's house. I end where I began—at the right end.[12]

To understand the adventure of youth ministry we need look no further than these words cited above by Stratford Caldecott, "A Quest is any journey in which some difficult goal is to be achieved, some challenge must be met, some initiation has to be undergone, some place or object or person is to be discovered or won."

[10] Stratford Caldecott, "Over the Chasm of Fire: Christian Heroism in *The Silmarillion* and *The Lord of the Rings*," in *Tolkien: A Celebration*, ed. Joseph Pearce (San Francisco: Ignatius Press, 1999), 20.

[11] John Eldredge, *Journey of Desire* (Nashville, Tenn.: Thomas Nelson Publishers, 2000), 164.

[12] G. K. Chesterton, *Orthodoxy: The Romance of Faith* (New York: Doubleday, 1990), 154.

This is a perfect definition of the youth-ministry adventure: It is all about facing difficult goals and pursuing real challenges; it is about persons—in this case teenagers—who literally are to be "discovered" and "won."[13] It is every bit a journey "down the great unknown."

That is not to say that youth ministry is always exciting, or that it will always feel as if you are engaged in a quest of epic importance. It will not. Edward Dolnick's account of Powell's journey through the Grand Canyon chronicles long days on the river—hot, hungry, grueling days:

> Inspection stickers used to have printed on the back "Drive carefully—the life you save may be your own." That is the wisdom of men in a nutshell.
> What God says, on the other hand, is "The life you save is the life you lose." In other words, the life you clutch, hoard, guard, and play safe with is in the end a life worth little to anybody, including yourself, and only a life given away for love's sake is a life worth living. To bring his point home, God shows us a man who gave his life away to the extent of dying a national disgrace without a penny in the bank or a friend to his name. In terms of men's wisdom, he was a Perfect Fool, and anybody who thinks he can follow him without making something like the same kind of a fool of himself is laboring under not a cross but a delusion.
>
> —Frederick Buechner, Wishful Thinking (New York: Harper and Row, 1973), 28.

> Journal of George Bradley, July 14, 1869: The river seemed almost still now—so much for gliding along—and the men had to row hard in the broiling heat. . .

Journal of John Sumner, August 8, 1869: Pulled out early and did a terrible hard work.

Journal of John Wesley Powell, August 8, 1869: It is with very great labor that we make progress, meeting with many obstructions, running rapids, letting down our boat with lines, from rock to rock, sometimes carrying boats and cargo around bad places.[14]

It was not all splash and thunder, river mists, and rugged vistas. Neither will be the expedition that begins with this book. There will always be those times in ministry when you feel as if you are ready for the river, rafts inflated, hopes pumped up, only to find that some person or circumstance (or test grade!) has punctured your boat and deflated your dreams. Be forewarned.

Somehow the notion of "adventure" seems very distant when sitting around the table at a church meeting. Pulling on the oars of a heaving boat careening through roaring rapids—that sounds like the stuff of adventure. Talking a 15-

---

[13] Caldecott, op. cit., 20.
[14] Dolnick, op. cit., 163, 215, 215.

year-old through the strong currents and dangerous waves of peer pressure—that just feels like a waste of time.

But understand this: Adventure is defined not just by story and landscape. It is defined by the heart of the adventurer. Herein is the grace that permeates every page of this youth ministry adventure story and binds it all together from cover to cover. God is at work in us, by his grace and mercy, and he gives us the will and the way to press on. "The one who calls you is faithful and he will do it" (1 Thes. 5:24).

A Gracious Adventure?

In the four verses of 2 Corinthians 5:18-20, the Apostle Paul uses no fewer than seven main verbs to describe the gracious adventure of ministry:

> All this is from God, who reconciled us to himself through Christ and gave us the ministry of reconciliation: that God was reconciling the world to himself in Christ, not counting men's sins against them. And he has committed to us the message of reconciliation. We are therefore Christ's ambassadors, as though God were making his appeal through us. We implore you on Christ's behalf: Be reconciled to God. God made him who had no sin to be sin for us, so that in him we might become the righteousness of God. (2 Cor. 5:18–21)

God *reconciled* us to himself (v. 18). God *committed* to us the ministry of reconciliation (v. 18). God was in Christ, *reconciling* the world to himself (v. 19), not *counting* men's sins against them (v. 19), and he has *committed* to us this amazing message of reconciliation. Even now, God is *making his appeal* through us (v. 20), an appeal based on the stunning fact that God *made* Christ—who himself had no sin—to be sin on our behalf.

(2 Cor. 5:18–20, summarized)

What is so striking is that all seven of those main verbs have as their subject none other than God alone. In the words of John R. W. Stott, "The whole source of our reconciliation is the grace of God the Father."[15]

What this means, in very simple terms, is that we are not in the boat alone. We are not the only ones pulling on the oar. Whether in rapids or flat water, good times or bad, the adventure of ministry, by God's grace and mercy, is a shared one. It is by grace that God ignites in us the taste for adventure. It is by grace that God equips us for the journey. It is by grace that Jesus goes before us as pioneer. It is by grace that Jesus travels beside us through the Holy Spirit (or *paracletos*, Greek for "called to the side of").

---

[15] John R. W. Stott, "Our Motives and Message," in *Change, Witness, Triumph*. A compendium of addresses from Urbana '64. (Downers Grove, Ill.: InterVarsity Press, 1964), 47–48.

It is by grace that we are allowed the privilege of inviting others to join the journey. From the day we start to the day we finish, it is a grace adventure.[16]

"Willie Juan," came the whisper once again.

"Y-yes? I'm here. I'm Willie Juan. Who are you?"

"To most I am known as Danger, Willie Juan. I make my presence known in water, wind, and fire. I am Spirit, without shape, form, or face. Those who seek safety try to summon me like a tame lapdog. They crave security instead of growth. They have no tolerance for mystery, certain that they can know everything knowable. The weak-kneed do not love Danger. They are afraid I will call them to become what they are not. They call me Comforter for all the wrong reasons and are surprised when no comfort comes to them . . . Your journey has begun in promise, Little Friend, but it could end in failure unless you are brave enough to risk the next step"[17]

---

[16] "Grace is behind and through all of this, our God giving himself freely, the Master, Jesus Christ, giving himself freely" (1 Thess. 1:12, *The Message*). To read a more thorough theological exposition of these truths, see the affirmations of the Second Council of Orange on Grace and Freedom. This council was a local gathering of bishops that took place in A.D. 529 in the southern Gallic city of Orange. The council issued 25 statements to refute the doctrine of Pelagianism. While the council certainly did that, it also offered robust and well-conceived statement of grace in the ministry of reconciliation.

[17] Brennan Manning, *The Boy Who Cried Abba* (Berkley, Calif.: Page Mill Press, 1997), 59–60.

JOURNEYING DEEPER: SWEET RELEASE

Meditations on the Way by Helen Musick

It is nine o'clock on a Wednesday evening, and you are at the library. Tomorrow you will endure your last and most difficult final of the semester. Images of a great, relaxing summer come to mind every so often, but you have to push them away. They are too distracting, and you desperately need to keep focused on your notes and textbooks. You are stressed out and tired, but you have several more hours to study before attempting to get some sleep before the early morning test. AAAAARGH! You just want it all to end.

You reach your bed at 2:00 a.m. Getting up at 6:45 a.m., you are tired—very tired—but determined to do your best. The test is exactly what you expected: there are no surprises, but it is intense. The exam is set to last at least two hours, and you know that you are going to need every minute. Your hand does not stop writing for even a brief moment. "Keep going, keep going, almost there!" You become your own personal cheerleader. Just as your professor calls time, you finish your last response. You hand in the test and walk out of the room. Stop! Take a deep breath. How do you feel? You are done! You are free! What a relief! Is there anything better than what you are feeling right now?

I ask you to imagine this scene, because I have a feeling that you know the sense of peace I am trying to portray. Walking out of that last final each semester is always so liberating. In these first moments of freedom, before we actually begin to wonder how we did, we take deep breaths; we revel in the peace; we may even dance down the hall. This type of peace comes once a semester, but what about all the other days? There is so much stress and so many burdens.

There are two words that seem to go hand in hand when it comes to college: tests and stress. But here is the question: How do we get beyond the stress to living in the peace that God talks about in Matthew 11:28–30?

Come to me, all you who are weary and burdened, and I will give you rest. Take my yoke upon you and learn from me, for I am gentle and humble in heart, and you will find rest for your souls. For my yoke is easy and my burden is light.

In this passage, Jesus promises rest to the weary and burdened. Notice that he does not define what the worries and burdens have to be for him to provide his rest. This means that it is available for you all the time, including the everyday stresses of school. The release after that last final can be yours every day.

How, you ask? Directions are found in the first three words: "Come to me." It is interesting to note that one of the most repeated phrases used by God in the Bible is, "Come to me."

How often do you come to Jesus? In the hustle and bustle of daily life, when do you let him in? As a student, life tends to revolve around due dates of papers and test preparation. The closer they get, the busier we become. When they are not luminous, we choose procrastination. I know this to be true. I was a student once too. Life is hectic, and we often choose to carry the burdens on our own. But daily rest and peace is ours if we simply come to Christ.

▶ What is it in your life that you are longing to allow Jesus to give you peace and rest in?

▶ What keeps you from coming to Jesus and leaving this with him?

▶ What is an incident in the past when you have truly asked God for peace and rest and you have experienced his presence and release?

chapter two

A JOURNEY MARKED BY "BLAZES"

In general, trails are maintained to provide a clear pathway . . . Some may offer rough and difficult passage. Most hiking trails are marked with paint on trees or rocks, or with axe blazes cut into trees. The trails that compose the Appalachian Trail through the White Mountains are marked with vertical rectangular white blazes throughout. Side trails off the Appalachian Trail are usually marked with blue paint.
—*1987 Appalachian Mountain Club Guidebook*

Visitors should remember that [bears], which seem so tame, are capable of inflicting serious injuries. Their prowess in terms of strength, agility and speed far exceeds that of man. The more bold individuals occasionally will "charge" at a visitor. This charge may be accompanied by snapping of teeth, a subtle groan, and "woofing". . . It is generally a bluff.
—Dick Murless and Constance Stallings, *Hikers Guide to the Smokies*[1]

Since personal destinies hinge upon its effectiveness, the care of persons deserves close study. Pastoral work does not proceed merely out of impulsive emotional hunches or simple intuition without intelligent effort. Pastoral care is, and has been for almost two millennia, a distinctive and well-defined discipline of study. It deserves the best reflective efforts of its practitioners. It is dangerous to the health of the church to enter ministry without preparing for it.
—Thomas Oden[2]

Most often youth workers—and especially youth pastors—are very pragmatic and oriented to the program: fun and games, Bible studies, camps, retreats, social activities, and such things. It is a little difficult to talk about philosophy and theology with youth workers in the morning when they know they are taking care of fifteen junior highers that same evening. Further, youth workers have a reputation not of being "thinkers" but doers, being more interested in how to do youth ministry than in the reasons and basis of it.
    But this is the problem. The tyranny of the immediate forces many to neglect the weightier matters of youth ministry.
—John Dettoni[3]

---

[1] Dick Murless and Constance Stallings, *Hiker's Guide to the Smokies* (San Francisco: Sierra Club Books, 1973), 36.

[2] Thomas Oden, *Classical Pastoral Care* (Grand Rapids, Mich.: Baker, 1987), 13.

[3] John Dettoni, *Introduction to Youth Ministry* (Grand Rapids, Mich.: Zondervan, 1993), 17.

In the beginning of almost every hiking guidebook is a brief word of introduction about the specific trail to be traveled. There will be discussion probably about elevation gain in the course of the journey and perhaps warnings about specific animals you might encounter along the way (everything from black bears to grizzly bears to snakes to wild boar). The guidebook might provide as well insight about the optimum time of year to travel the trail or a particular time of year when the trail is considered impassable. Almost certainly, a good guidebook will provide instructions about the potability of water you might find along the trail (that is, whether you can drink the water safely).

Most important of all, the guidebook will also identify for the hiker the specific signs that mark the trail. These marks, often called "blazes," are usually about six to eight inches long and about two to three inches wide. They are often painted in different colors so that hikers are not confused by trail junctions or two trails that for a time cover the same ground. These blazes are painted on trees or rocks along the trail to make certain that someone who traverses the trail is able to follow its twists and turns without getting lost. (Hence the double meaning of a phrase such as, "Where in the blazes are we?")

Before we set out on the journey described in this book, I must offer my guiding instructions—blazes that will mark out our course of study. Give these instructions some thought, because they will provide important information about the territory ahead. There are no warnings here about polluted water, extreme temperatures, or grizzlies and snakes (although I have had a few professors who were wild "bores"). The following guidelines will remind us of the danger spots and landmarks to watch for, and perhaps they will help us as well to find those special places of refreshment.

Youth Ministry Is Primarily a Theological Enterprise

When the turbulence of the twister finally subsided, and Dorothy's farmhouse finally dropped onto the land of Oz (and unfortunately onto the Wicked Witch of the East), the first phrase out of Dorothy's mouth was "Toto, I don't think we're in Kansas anymore." That was a wonderful triumph of understatement, but it also marked the beginning of an amazing adventure in a new place as Dorothy and her comrades began their sojourn down the yellow brick road. It may well be that you share that same sense of strangeness as you begin to work your way through this course and through this text.

Within a few short weeks, as you explore the terrain of youth ministry, it will become quite clear that this material is different from much of your previous academic experience. Unlike courses in accounting, biochemistry, Spanish, or computer programming, a holistic instruction in youth ministry moves beyond mere academic input to include matters of the soul.

Perhaps most of your previous education has been dominated by the Scarecrow's lament, "If I only had a brain." Now, in this new land of youth ministry preparation, there must be attention given to the yearnings of the Lion and the Tin Man. In youth ministry, a good brain must be joined by a courageous spirit and a warm heart. The reason for this distinct difference from most other academic disciplines is that youth ministry is primarily a theological enterprise. Or, to put it another way, the primary task of youth ministry is to focus on God.

> A sacrament is when something holy happens. It is transparent time, time which you can see through to something deep inside time ... In other words, at such milestone moments ... you are apt to catch a glimpse of the most unbearable preciousness and mystery of life ... If we weren't blind as bats, we might see that life itself is sacramental.
>
> *Frederick Buechner,* Wishful Thinking *(New York: Harper and Row, 1973), 82–83.*

In fact, biblically speaking, all of our pursuits, in whatever field of academic or professional endeavor, are at some level a theological enterprise.[4] The apostle Paul writes in Colossians 3:23–24, "Whatever you do, work at it with all your heart, as working for the Lord, not for men, since you know that you will receive an inheritance from the Lord as a reward. It is the Lord Christ you are serving."[5] In fact, when we do our work as unto the Lord, it becomes a sacrament. But there is a unique dimension to ministry preparation in this sense: while you should be an accountant or an astronomer or an historian to the glory of God, it is not essential to the respective fields.

A person might be an excellent accountant, astronomer, or historian without giving any thought to the glory of God. But to be a youth minister without regard to God's accompaniment and God's glory is a betrayal of calling. That is not to say it cannot be done. Sadly, it is done. But it is counter to the youth ministry calling itself in the same sense as, say, doctors who disregard the health of their patients or judges who ignore justice. Unlike biochemists or geologists whose work is more a factor of what they do, the work of youth ministers is largely a factor of who they are, and more specifically, who they are as an expression of their relationship with God.

---

[4]This approach to life—thoroughly biblical—is often described as a sacramental approach. It is an approach that sees all of life as a sacred place.

[5] Next time you are grinding away on that especially tedious lab assignment, remember this verse, and note especially verse 22. That "whatever you do" is fairly inclusive.

It is not that youth ministry is impossible without engaging the soul. Indeed, there is always the risk that some will attempt to do so. But this type of youth ministry is only possible in the sense that a prostitute engages in an act, designed for the deepest intimacy and communion, in a merely physical way. Youth ministry without theology—divorced from deep intimacy and communion with God—is little more than a vulgarity. It is, to use a more familiar phrase, "taking the Name of the Lord in vain." That is why William Willimon, dean of the Chapel of Duke University, says bluntly, "When ministerial education degenerates into the mere acquisition of skills, the inculcation of knowledge, and data and ideas, it is detrimental to the formation of pastors."[6] Youth ministry preparation that goes no further than acquisition of concepts is similar to a sex education course that only focuses on physiology. Such an approach neglects the deep and profound spiritual implications of Jesus's encounter with his bride, the church.[7]

What is so tragic about this approach is that it makes small the huge story that God, more than he desires to work *through* us, desires to work *in* us.[8] So powerful is this notion that Kenda Creasy Dean refers to youth ministry as "the God-bearing life":

> The Eastern Orthodox tradition calls Mary *Theotokos*, or "Godbearer," because she (quite literally) brought God into the world. In the biblical witness, God seems especially fond of calling on unlikely suspects for such missions. Young people— impetuous, improbable choices by all accounts—figure prominently among God's "chosen" in both the Hebrew Scriptures

Momentary inattention to trail markers, particularly arrows at sharp turns, or misinterpretation of signs or guidebook descriptions, can cause one to become separated from all but the most heavily traveled paths. So please remember that a guidebook is an aid to planning, not a substitute for observation and judgment.
—**AMC Mountain Guide**

It takes Almighty grace to take the next step when there is no vision and no spectator—the next step in devotion, the next step in your study, in your reading, in your kitchen; the next step in your duty, when there is no vision from God, no enthusiasm and no spectator.
—**Oswald Chambers**

---

[6] William Willimon, *Calling and Character* (Nashville, Tenn.: Abingdon, 2002), 44.

[7] "For this reason a man will leave his father and mother and be united to his wife, and the two will become one flesh.' This is a profound mystery—but I am talking about Christ and the church" (Eph. 5:31–32).

[8] See, for example, Hosea 1:1–2: "The word of the Lord that came *to* Hosea son of Beeri during the reigns of Uzziah, Jotham, Ahaz and Hezekiah, kings of Judah, and during the reign of Jeroboam son of Jehoash king of Israel: When the Lord began to speak *through* Hosea, the Lord said to him, '"Go, take to yourself an adulterous wife and children of unfaithfulness, because the land is guilty of the vilest adultery in departing from the Lord."' [Emphasis added]. Note that the word of the Lord came "to Hosea" (v. 1) before the word of the Lord spoke "through Hosea" (v. 2).

Scriptures and the New Testament. And while God does not ask any of us to bring Christ into the world as literally as did Mary, God calls each of us to become a Godbearer through whom God may enter the world again and again.[9]

You should not approach the study of youth ministry the way you approach other academic disciplines. Although it is true that youth ministry students will be required to process information, memorize concepts, wrestle with ideas, and comprehend theories, the heart of youth ministry is soul work. It is a theological enterprise. The following sections discuss two primary implications to this theological enterprise.

Content Cannot Be Divorced from Experience

It is virtually impossible to talk about youth ministry without talking about personal experience. Most of the best adventure stories are those stories woven from the pages of sweat-soaked, bloodstained, waterlogged diaries of the adventurers themselves. Who could not almost feel the mouth go dry in reading the words of Tim Cahill:

> It is like no night on the face of the earth: in this cave the darkness is palpable and it physically swallows the brightest light. The air underground smells clean, damp, curiously sterile. It feels thick, like freshly washed still-damp velvet, and I am about to rappel down a long single strand of rope into the heart of that heavy darkness. This is the second deepest cave pit in America: the drop is four hundred and forty feet, about what you'd experience at the top of a forty story building. If you took the shaft in a free fall, you'd accelerate to one hundred and some miles an hour and then—about six seconds into the experience—instantly decelerate to zero miles an hour. And die. Wah-hoo-hoo over and out. With six bad seconds to think about it.[10]

Note the power here of the first-person report.

There is actually a journal entry by Meriwether Lewis (who with his partner, William Clark, led an expedition exploring the land acquired in the Louisiana Purchase) in which Lewis recounts a conversation with a Native American named Cameahwait. Lewis asked whether there might be someone who knew a route across the Rocky Mountains as they appeared to be "inaccessible to man or horse." Cameahwait answered that he knew of an old man in his band who he thought might be able to describe such a route, and then added that, "he had understood from the Indians who inhabit this river below the rocky mountain that it ran a great way toward the setting sun and finally lost itself in a great lake of water which

[9] Kenda Creasy Dean, *The God-Bearing Life* (Nashville, Tenn.: Upper Room Books, 1998), 17–18.
[10] Tim Cahill, *A Wolverine Is Eating My Leg* (New York: Vintage Books, 1989), 241.

was illy taisted [sic]." Of this modest statement, the report of one man's personal experience, historian Stephen Ambrose writes, "That sentence linked the continent."[11]

There is great power in the words of those who by their personal stories can move us beyond geological concepts, botanical findings, and latitude and longitude and tell us what they saw on the journey. Yet this is not traditionally the formal academic approach, which is concerned (as it should be) that first-person anecdote might pollute the purity of the data. Parker Palmer writes,

> The question we most commonly ask is the "what" question—what subjects shall we teach?
>
> When the conversation goes a bit deeper, we ask the "how" question—what methods and techniques are required to teach well?
>
> Occasionally, when it goes deeper still, we ask the "why" question—for what purpose and to what ends do we teach?
>
> But seldom, if ever, do we ask the "who" question—who is the self that teaches? How does the quality of my selfhood form—or deform—the way I relate to my students, my subject, my colleagues, my world?[12]

Autobiography is rare in the academic environment. You do not expect to hear math professors reminisce about the first time they did expanded notation or English professors gush, "I'll never forget my first adverb." Personal references, in the strictest academic sense, are not considered to be good form. But teaching youth ministry without autobiography would be sterile and lifeless. The goal of any true theological enterprise, at least for those of us who are followers of Christ, is always to move beyond the "word become concept" to the "word become flesh." Anything else would be like describing a trek on the Appalachian Trail having only watched a video on the Discovery Channel.

Thus, you may expect your youth ministry professor to teach this material with personal references, not to obscure the material by just "telling war stories," but to ignite the material so that it offers real warmth and light. Indeed, as the author of this book, I have made a conscious decision to occasionally refer to my experience as a youth worker. This type of first-person writing is rare in an academic text, but it seems impossible to talk about matters of heart and soul without being willing to bare your own. I am eager to share this adventure because I am eager to live it. As Palmer puts it:

> We teach who we are . . . Teaching, like any truly human activity, emerges from one's inwardness, for better or worse. As I teach, I project the condi-

---

[11] Stephen Ambrose, *Undaunted Courage: Meriwether Lewis, Thomas Jefferson and the Opening of the American West* (New York: Touchstone, 1996), 272.
[12] Parker Palmer, *The Courage to Teach* (San Francisco: Jossey-Bass, 1998), 4.

Messy spirituality is a good term for the place where desperation meets Jesus.
—**Michael Yaconelli**

The entanglements I experience in the classroom are often no more or less than the convolutions of my inner life. Viewed from this angle, teaching holds a mirror to the soul. If I am willing to look in that mirror and not run from what I see, I have a chance to gain self-knowledge—and knowing myself is as crucial to good teaching as knowing my students and my subject.[13]

Material You Read Through and Pray Through

Of course, in youth ministry classes you will sometimes study mundane concepts and textbook theories. It may be that you mostly just pray that these theories will not be on the test. But there will also be issues that arise over the course of these chapters that require the serious work of prayer and reflection. Do not rush over these words.

Ask God to speak to you as you think through these ideas. Most students are unaccustomed to this type of "listening" in an academic setting ("God, speak to me through these Greek participles") because it is not required for the grade. But there are bigger issues at stake here. There is a grander story to be told than the one on the grade report. "Let him who has ears hear what the Spirit says . . . " (Rev. 2:7, 11, 17,29; 3:6,13,22; 13:9).

[13] Ibid, 2.

How vs why preaching idea
- who

Doing the Right Things Is More Important Than Doing Things Right

Chris Bender, 22 years old, was, by all accounts, one of the most conscientious workers in the Hamilton Standard Maintenance Facility at Rock Hill, South Carolina. His skill in doing the "taper bore work" on the aircraft propellers earned him the respect of his coworkers and supervisors. Meticulous and thoughtful, Bender often arrived early in the day so that he could do his most exacting work before afternoon fatigue set in. He was described as a mechanic who "followed instructions to the letter," a great trait to have—unless the instructions are wrong.

In fact, National Transportation Safety Board (NTSB) inspectors determined that it was precisely this factor that led to the deterioration of the left propeller blade on Atlantic Southeast Airline's Flight 590 on August 21, 1995. The twenty-six passengers, along with a crew of three, began to realize there was something wrong only a few minutes into the flight when they heard a loud bang and saw through the passenger windows the mangled and twisted propeller assembly that had chewed up most of the left wing. It would be a horrifying nine minutes and twenty seconds before the plane fell several thousand feet to the ground into a cornfield near Carrollton, Georgia. Ten people lost their lives in the crash, and almost everyone else received serious burns and injuries. The blade that caused the accident, blade serial number 861398, style 14RF9, had been inspected, prepped, and approved for flight by none other than Bender.

After a year-long investigation, however, the NTSB determined that the management policies of Hamilton Standard were to blame for the crash: "The fracture was caused by a fatigue crack from multiple corrosion pits that were not discovered by Hamilton Standard because of inadequate and ineffective corporate inspection and repair techniques, training, documentation, and communication." The board concluded its finding with this observation, "Although the sanding repair was inappropriate and had camouflaged a deeper crack in the propeller blade from being detected in the later inspection, Chris Bender had done essentially as he was instructed."[14]

It was a short sentence that told a sad story—the story of a conscientious young man[15] who performed as he was trained to perform,[16] but who had, in fact, been wrongly trained. It was not a failure of effort or technique. It was a failure of objective. The crash of Flight 529 was a tragic example that doing the *right* things is more important than doing *things* right.

---

[14] Gary Pomerantz, *Nine Minutes and Twenty Seconds: The Tragedy and Triumph of Flight 529* (New York: Simon and Schuster, 2001), audiotape, Disc 6 (Track 2) 1:30.

[15] Ibid., Disc 6 (Track 1). It is interesting to note that between the time of the crash and the time of the final NTSB hearings, Bender recommitted his life to Christ. He left Hamilton Standard on November 6, 1996, and moved to Tyler, Texas, where he trained for the mission field at the Youth With a Mission Training Center.

[16] Ibid., Disc 6 (Track 2) 3:15: "I was told if you had a rejected blade, and there was no damage or pitting, but if you had ridges, you could blend...That was told to me . . . by a multitude of people."

Youth ministry students, by and large, are an eager lot. They seem to be temperamentally predisposed to action. They walk into class on the first day with an overriding desire to learn *how*. This is not surprising in a culture infatuated with pragmatism and technology. But students must understand that *how* is not as important as *who, why,* and *what*. Doing wrong things, even if they are done with great care, creativity, and intention, can still lead to ministries and ministers that crash and burn.

Any youth ministry training that focuses on *how* without thinking about *why* is vapid and bankrupt. It is short-circuited by the same approach that assumes more books and magazines about sexual technique will breed deeper intimacy and greater sexual satisfaction. The assumption is that any talk about love or commitment is tedious and tangential. Unfortunately, it is precisely this sort of approach that has given us a culture in which marriages disintegrate with alarming frequency and sexual dissatisfaction seems to be far more prominent. We cannot be satisfied with training youth workers in general how to do nothing in particular. Doing nothing, creatively and effectively, is still doing nothing.[17]

This is why Eugene Peterson distinguishes between "a job" and "a profession or craft." He defines a job as what we do to complete an assignment. It is focused on execution. We learn what is expected by those to whom we are responsible and we do it. A profession, on the other hand, brings with it an obligation beyond pleasing somebody: "We are pursuing or shaping the very nature of reality, convinced that when we carry out our commitments we actually benefit people at a far deeper level than if we simply did what they asked of us." Here the emphasis turns to *why* and *what:*

> For physicians it is health (not merely making people feel good); with lawyers, justice (not helping people get their own way); with professors, learning (not merely cramming cranial cavities with information on tap for examinations). And with pastors [and youth pastors] it is God (not relieving anxiety, or giving comfort, or running a religious establishment)."[18]

Eugene Peterson does a good job of describing the "job preparation" approach to ministry training:

> For a long time I have been convinced that I could take a person with a high school education, give him or her a six-month trade school training, and provide a pastor who would be satisfactory to any discriminating American congregation. The curriculum would consist of four courses. *Course I:* Creative Plagiarism. I would put you in touch with a wide range of excellent and inspirational talks, show you how to alter them just enough to obscure their origins, and get you a reputation for wit and wisdom. *Course II:* Voice

[17] As recently as 1997, one could leaf through the catalogue of Youth Specialties' published materials and find fewer than five books in the entire listing that actually used traditional prose as a format. All of the information was reduced to an idea and a paragraph about how to execute the idea. There were whole books on melodramas, small group ideas, and games, but very little that went deeper than could be expressed in a one-paragraph statement. It is difficult to think about big ideas in little paragraphs.

[18] Eugene Peterson, *Working the Angles* (Grand Rapids, Mich.: Eerdmans, 1987), 7.

good people skills + pray well

Control for Prayer and Counseling. We would develop your own distinct style of Holy Joe intonation, acquiring the skill in resonance and modulation that conveys an unmistakable aura of sanctity. *Course III*: Efficient Office Management. There is nothing that parishioners admire more in their pastors [and youth pastors] than the capacity to run a tight ship administratively. If we return all telephone calls within twenty-four hours, answer all letters within a week, distributing enough (copies) to key people so that they know we are on top of things, and have just the right amount of clutter on our

— make it look like everything is smooth

desks—not too much or we appear inefficient, nor too little or we appear underemployed—we quickly get the reputation for efficiency that is far more important than anything that we actually do. *Course IV*: Image Projection. Here we would master the half-dozen well-known and easily implemented devices that create the impression that we are terrifically busy and widely sought after for counsel by influential people in the community.[19]

look good

> One of the great tragedies of the practice of contemporary professions like law and medicine *[and youth ministers?]* is that too many doctors and lawyers have so little to profess. They are primarily accountable to their clients or patients, rather than to jurisprudence or public health. The pastor professes God, and is accountable to more significant criteria than the praise even of the congregation ... Thus adequate theological training is an aspect of the clergy's peculiar vocation, an aspect of the service that we render to the church.
>
> — *Will Willimon*, Pastor *(Nashville, Tenn. : Abingdon, 2002), 20.*

Please understand that there is nothing wrong with doing any job. In fact, as Christians, we are called to do every job for the glory of God (Col. 3:17). In that sense, there is certainly a place for youth ministry training that focuses on technique.[20] But if we go no deeper, and no further, we have traded off our calling and our profession to be little more than technicians, fixer-uppers, and program planners. Unfortunately, if that is our approach, we begin to dumb down the prescription to fit the patient's diagnosis—we offer what they want rather than what they need.[21]

You will note in your studies then that many of the *how* questions of youth ministry may be postponed until later in your course work. Some of them will be addressed in the latter chapters of this book. But, much of the content in these

---

[19] Ibid., 5.

[20] I have personally benefited as a youth worker from many of the excellent products along these lines. As an author, I also have been part of the development of many such products.

[21] A few years ago I came across a youth ministry book that took an encyclopedic approach—listing a topic and then giving a brief word of comment. But this approach so diluted the material and dumbed it down as to make the book virtually useless. For example, under the topic, "Spiritual growth," there were only these two lines: "The kid that grows the fastest doesn't necessarily grow the deepest. Don't overlook the kid who grows slowly but steadily." Earlier in the book, however, the topic "Points" (as in attributing points for scoring in games), required about half a page with additional cross-references to two other topics, "Choosing Teams" and "Games." This misguided and cursory approach to youth ministry did not begin to provide the focus and depth needed.

early stages of the youth ministry adventure is about understanding the destination, getting to know the topography, and reflecting on what this journey will demand of us. Once we have oriented ourselves with the basic coordinates, then we can map out strategies for getting from point A to point B. There is no benefit in finding a great trail that takes us where we do not want to go. There is, as Bender knows all too well, no virtue in doing the wrong things, even if we do them well.

Effective Youth Ministry Is Informed by Other Academic Disciplines

The standard stereotype of people who pursue youth ministry study at the undergraduate level is that they are looking for an easy degree. Typically, this proves to be a bad stereotype and a bad strategy. But there is occasionally in the youth ministry classroom the plaintive cry, "What does this have to do with helping kids come to know Jesus?"

This is not a new phenomenon. Jim Elliot, who graduated from Wheaton College in the spring of 1949 and by January 8, 1956, had been killed along with four other missionaries trying to take the gospel to the Auca Indians of Ecuador, wrote these words in one of his first letters home as a young college freshman:

> The acquisition of academic knowledge (the "pride of life") is a wearing process, and I wonder if it is all worth while. The shiny paint laid on by curiosity's hand has worn off. What thing better can a man know but the love of Christ, which passes knowledge? Oh to be reveling in the knowledge of Him, rather than wallowing in the quagmire of inscrutable philosophy! My philosophy prof says I can't expect to learn much in his class—all he wants to do is to develop an inquiring mind in order to "make explicit and critically examine philosophical problems of the widest generality." Ho hum."[22]

Yet, Elliot, with all of his other extracurricular pursuits in competitive wrestling, ministry teams, and the Student Foreign Missions Fellowship, found time to maintain honors-level work and excel in Greek and Hebrew. He seems to have understood that discipline of the mind and the body was as important as discipline of the spirit. In a letter to his father in the second semester of his freshman year, he wrote:

> I begrudge myself an education, for at a time when my mind still functions quickly it is forced to work on subjects like René Descartes' rational epistemology or Laplace's nebular hypothesis, while I would so much more enjoy

---

[22] Elisabeth Elliot, *Shadow of the Almighty* (Grand Rapids, Mich.: Zondervan, 1958), 40.

studying on the things of God. Be that as it may, my Father knows best, and I am confident He has placed me here; my task is to labor quietly until the pillar-cloud removes and leads farther, working out God's purposes in God's time.[23]

You might ask yourself why you must spend time and effort on topics and issues that seem so foreign to the essential work of youth ministry. The answer is simple: because you will not learn in a youth ministry textbook all that you need to know to be effective in ministry.[24] Rigorous and well-rounded academic pursuit can play a vital part in preparation for ministry. What the church does not need is youth workers who neglect the life of the mind.[25] William Willimon, dean of the Chapel at Duke University, a prolific writer and thoughtful theologian, puts it this way:

> Although vocation is a primary matter for clergy, expertise is also required. Clergy must know the historic, orthodox, ecumenical faith of the church in order to bear witness to, and to interpret, that faith. Pastoral counseling, church administration, and biblical interpretation require competence. Thus adequate theological training is an aspect of the clergy's peculiar vocation, an aspect of the service that we render to the church. Careful preparation for pastoral leadership is a moral matter of the need for clergy to submit themselves to the leadership needs of the church. *A warm heart, and good intentions are not enough to fulfill the requisites of this vocation* [emphasis added].[26]

It is quite striking to observe the scholarship of many of the church's great saints. Surely

Sometimes seminarians complain that the seminary's expectations of them are too demanding, that the course is too difficult, or that it is placing academic burdens upon them that they cannot bear. Perhaps they feel that their sincerity and their sense of vocation are enough to sustain them in their ministry. They are wrong.

I remind them that I did not call them into the ministry. I am sorry if they have been misled, but the pastoral ministry is a very difficult way to earn a living, and our Master can be very demanding, despite his reassurance of a light burden and an easy yoke.
—**William Willimon**

---

[23] Ibid., 43.

[24] I have intentionally not identified a well-rounded education as a prerequisite for ministry because it clearly is not. When you consider the first 12 disciples, it becomes quite clear that Jesus was looking for something beyond academic and theological expertise.

[25] Columnist Hoover Rupert refers to a cartoon, drawn by his friend Jim Crane, that alludes to the fact that "Lord, I'll go anywhere for you" includes going to class! The cartoon portrays a person, obviously a college student, who is grappling with the meaning of his own life and what it would be for him to serve. In the series of four pictures, the character says, "Use me, Lord use me.—I'll go anywhere, do anything—suffer abject poverty, make any sacrifice, even martyrdom." Then, in the final picture the student, who is simply sitting there looking depressed, says, "Well, studying wasn't exactly what I had in mind". ("Not What I Had in Mind," *Presbyterian Outlook*, 162 (February 1980), 9.

[26] William Willimon, *Pastor* (Nashville, Tenn.: Abingdon, 2002), 20

no one would accuse John Wesley of having a cold heart and being dispassionate for lost souls. Yet, in just three weeks' of entries in his journal, we read these notes:

Monday, [Sept] 24 [1749].
I reached Kingswood in the evening; and the next day selected passages of Milton for the eldest children to transcribe and repeat weekly . . ."

Thursday, 27.
I went into the school and heard half the children their lessons and then selected passages of the *Moral and Sacred Poems* . . .

Saturday, 29.
I spent most of the day revising Kennet's *Antiquities*, and marking what was worth reading in the school.

Wednesday, October 3.
I revised for the use of the children, Archbishop Potter's *Green's Antiquities*; a dull, dry, heavy book.

Thursday, 4.
I revised Mr. Lewis' *Hebrew Antiquities*; something more entertaining than the other and abundantly more instructive.

Saturday, 6.
I nearly finished the abridgement of Dr. Cave's *Primitive Christianity*, a book written with as much learning and as little judgement [sic] as I remember to have read in my whole life.

Thursday, 11.
I prepared a short *History of England* for the use of the children; and on Friday a short Roman History, as an introduction to the Latin historians.

Monday, 15.
I read over Mr. Holme's *Latin Grammar* and extracted from it what was needful to perfect our own [grammar]."[27]

Bear in mind that these words were written by a man who often preached three to five times a day. It is quite clear that a big heart and an active mind can peacefully coexist in the same body. Indeed, for Tertullian, one of the fathers of the early church, "A great love for research and an even greater memory are *required* of a student who would gather, from the most accepted works of the philosophers, poets, and any other teachers of secular learning and wisdom, reasonable arguments for the truth of Christianity, in order to convict its rivals and persecutors by their own learned apparatus of error in themselves, and, thus, of their injustice toward us [emphasis added]."[28]

[27] John Wesley, *Journal of John Wesley* (Chicago: Moody Press, 1951), 181–182.

[2] Tertullian, Testimony of the Soul, *Fathers of the Church*, edited by R. J. Deferrari. 74 vols. to date. (Washington, D.C.: Catholic University Press, 1947ff), vol. 10, 131. Along these same lines, I would encourage students to consider the value of formal theological training in seminary as a complement to their undergraduate study in youth ministry. In his book, *Do You Mean Me, Lord?* (Philadelphia, Pa.: Westminster Press, 1985), 61, Robert Cox makes this very astute observation: "Although some of the more theoretical aspects of the seminary curriculum may not seem to be important to a local pastor, they can be vital as a foundation. Even though few people run up to a pastor and ask her or him to conjugate a Greek verb, it is nonetheless important for a pastor to understand the language and thought forms that color the New Testament. Similarly, systematic theology may not be considered a practical discipline, but when a pastor stands outside an emergency operating room with parents whose child is undergoing surgery, that pastor had better have some theological and pastoral competence."

Consider these "required readings" in the syllabus for ministry training offered by the Anglican Gilbert Burnet back in the late seventeenth century:

With the Study of the Scriptures, or rather as a part of it comes the Study of the Fathers, as far as one can go. In these their Apologies and Epistles are chiefly to be read, for they give us the best view of those Times. Basil's and Chrysostom's Sermons are by far the best. To these Studies, History comes in as a noble and pleasant Addition. It gives one broad perspectives on the Providence of God, the nature of Man, and the Conduct of the World. This is above no Man's Capacity. Admittedly some Histories are better than others, yet almost any Histories one can get one's hands on is better read than none at all. If one can find one's way through it, he ought to begin with the History of the Church, starting with Josephus, and go on with Eusebius, Socrates, and the other Historians. They are commonly bound together. Then go to other later Collectors of Ancient History, followed by the History of our own Church and Country; then the Ancient Greek and Roman History, and after that, as much History, Geography, and Books of Travels as can be had, will give an easy and useful Entertainment, and will furnish one with great variety of good Thoughts, and of pleasant as well as edifying Discourse. As for all other Studies, everyone must follow his Inclinations, his Capacities and that which he can procure to himself . . . The Study and Practice of Physick, [practical medicine] especially that which is safe and simple, puts the Clergy in a capacity of doing great acts of Charity, and of rendering both their Persons and Labors very acceptable to their People . . . These ought to be the chief Studies of the Clergy.[29]

> The work of the academy is important, but here is Richard Baxter's helpful balancing perspective:
>
> I confess I think NECESSITY should be the great disposer of a minister's course of study and labor. If we were sufficient for everything, we might attempt everything and take in order the whole Encyclopaedia: but life is short, and we are dull, and eternal things are necessary, and the souls that depend on our teaching are precious. I confess, necessity hath been the conductor of my studies and life. It chooseth what book I shall read, and tells me when, and how long. It chooseth my text, and makes my sermon.
>
> —*Richard Baxter,* The Reformed Pastor *(Grand Rapids, Mich.: Baker, 1987), 113.*

---

[29] Gilbert Burnet, *"Of the Pastoral Care,"* 85, cited in *The Curate of Souls,* edited by John R. H. Moorman, (London: SPCK), 1958.

It is fascinating to read Martin Luther's thoughts about what sort of books ought to be in one's personal library. His suggestions point to a keen and hungry mind:

> My advice is not to heap together all manner of books indiscriminately and think only of the number and size of the collection. I would make a judicious selection, for it is not necessary to have all the commentaries of the jurists, all the sentences of the theologians, all the *quaestiones* of the philosophers, and all the sermons of the monks. Indeed, I would discard all such dung, and furnish my library with the right sort of books, consulting with scholars as to my choice.
>
> First of all, there would be the Holy Scriptures, in Latin, Greek, Hebrew, and German, and any other language in which they might be found. Next the best commentaries, and, if I could find them, the most ancient, in Greek, Hebrew, and Latin. Then, books that would be helpful in learning the languages, such as the poets and orators, regardless of whether they were pagan or Christian, Greek or Latin, for it is from such books that one must learn grammar. After that would come books on the liberal arts, and all the other arts. Finally, there would be books of law and medicine; here too there should be careful choice among commentaries.
>
> Among the foremost would be the chronicles and histories, in whatever languages they are to be had. For they are a wonderful help in understanding and guiding the course of events, and especially for observing the marvelous works of God.

—*Martin Luther,* Luther's Works, *ed. I. Pelikan and H. T. Lehmann, 54 vols. (St. Louis: Concordia, 1953ff), 45: 375–376.*

I include this passage to show that this book, practically speaking, cannot give the whole story—that students who put their brains on automatic pilot until they walk into a youth ministry course are likely to be both stunted intellectually and ill-equipped for ministry. More to the point, one of the implicit expectations of a book such as this is that it will be read in tandem with other texts. For example, the chapters on adolescent development might be complemented with a course in adolescent psychology; the material on family ministry might be augmented by a course on sociology of the family. An English composition text, just because it is not a youth ministry text, is not irrelevant—"worldly wisdom" (1 Cor. 2:6–8) or the "many words" of a fool (Ecc. 5:3). This book nowhere refers to nouns and verbs or compositional style, but correct grammar comes in handy when preparing a talk or sending a letter home to parents.

Having said this, we need also to be reminded that one of the occupational hazards of scholarship is arrogance. No place is the danger more grave than in the study of theology. For good reason Paul writes, "Knowledge puffs up (1 Cor. 8:1). Helmut Thieleke, in his short tract, *A Little Exercise for Young Theologians*, warns of the dangers that come with having a little knowledge. He writes about the theology student who returns home after the first semester and attends a Bible study feeling smug and superior. Brimming with his newfound insights, his body language makes it clear that the teaching is primitive, "highly lay in character," clearly not informed by the latest findings of theological and biblical inquiry.

He says to his unlearned friend: "What you said was typically pietistic," or "typically orthodox," or maybe "Methodistic." He says to him: "You belong to the school of Osiander, which has not yet comprehended the forensic character of justification," and he patronizingly explains to him the strange learned words, which are the questionable by-products of his scientific study.[30]

> We cannot divorce Athens ["reason"] from Jerusalem ["faith"], for both stand under the sovereign Lordship of Christ in whom all things adhere and come together . . . It means that both library and chapel, both classroom and closet, are "holy of holies," in which we penetrate even deeper into the mystery of God revealed in Christ. It means that what we do in the classroom, in the study, in the library can be as "spiritual" as what we do on our knees; conversely what we do on our knees can be as "academic" as what we do in the classroom. A prayer spoken at the beginning of a class period does not necessarily make what goes on in the classroom more spiritual; nor is a half hour spent in Bible reading, meditation and prayer necessarily more spiritual than spending time in critical reflection on a problem in theology or exegeting a text in Romans for a class in New Testament theology.
>
> —Manfred Brauch, "Head and Heart Go to Seminary," Christianity Today (June 20, 1975), 11–12.

Then, in the *coup de grace*, Thieleke describes how the eager young theology superhero is asked if he might be willing to lead the Bible study—to share from his vast newfound wealth of biblical knowledge:

Under a considerable display of the apparatus of exegetical science and surrounded by the air of the initiated, he produces paralyzing and unhappy trivialities, and the inner muscular strength of a lively young Christian is horribly squeezed to death in a formal armor of abstract ideas. If something had been expected from the discussion afterward, even here, too, he develops an astounding talent for jabbing paralyzing injections of ideas into all lively, free, and easy conversation.[31]

It is understandable that many churches are not encouraged by such experiences to set great store by theology as taught at the university.

---

[30] Helmut Thieleke, *A Little Exercise for Young Theologians* (Grand Rapids, Mich.: Eerdmans, 1968), 7.
[31] Ibid., 8.

There is one additional dimension to be noted in describing the shape of this course material, and it concerns another type of arrogance. It is not an arrogance of breadth ("we needn't study any wider than the field of youth ministry"), nor an arrogance of depth ("those who do not know what I know are shallow, unlearned knaves"), it is an arrogance of novelty. It is the basic assumption that we can dismiss huge resources of thought and reflection simply because "they were written a long time ago." It is a mindset that automatically assumes old is bad and new is good.

We live in a culture that is infatuated with novelty—with anything new. Nowhere is that mindset more prevalent than in the world of youth ministry, where our "elder sages" are only in their fifties, and where most of our thinking and writing is done by "veterans" in their thirties and early forties who are targeting materials to people in their twenties and thirties. Our perspective can be limited by the lack of history and experience. The disadvantage to this limitation is twofold:

1. First of all, this type of arrogance limits the landscape of our experience. Adventurers who have never explored beyond Kansas might be astonished by the "mountain ranges" of Ohio and southern Indiana where peaks can shoot up sometimes to a height of 1,000 feet. But for the explorer who has traveled longer distances, either east or west, the "mountains" of Indiana seem like small lumps and rolling hills.

    The hiker who evaluates the entire Appalachian Trail based on the view from the southern terminus in Springer Mountain, Georgia, is apt to come to quite a different conclusion about the trail than the person who has hiked the entire length of the trail and has stood on Mt. Katahdin at the northern end. Those thru-hikers will have a much better perspective of the highs and the lows, and all the ground in between.

    So it is in learning about ministry. When we turn away from texts that were written long ago, we leave ourselves with a narrow frame of reference by which to discern and explore the landscape. This is one reason why church history can be such a profitable area of study, because it gives us a long view of what God is doing and has done in his church.

2. Second, this type of arrogance deprives us of the experiences of those who've gone before us. Mandatory reading in the huts and campsites along the Appalachian Trail that stretches 1900 miles from Maine to Georgia are the journals left by thru-hikers. There is an informal chain of information that occurs when a hiker going south writes up information in the journal that might be helpful to a hiker moving north: water sources, washed-out trails, bear warnings, etc. Beyond that, there are the printed trail guides that offer the experiences of those who have already made the trek, 200- to 300-page guidebooks that offer vital information about tricky trail junctions or difficult terrain. Both of these resources

offer something vital: the insight and lessons of those who have gone before.

To use a phrase from William Willimon, the reader will note that this book features the writing of a lot of dead people—people who have never heard of the Internet, data projectors, electronic music, instant messaging, or postmodernism. These are people who might find the current youth ministry landscape strange.

But what they offer is the voice of experience—the voice of those who have gone before. Despite what we may think, we are not the first people to deal with tough ministry issues. We are not the first people to reckon with opposition to the faith. We are not the first people to wrestle with what it means to be called. We are not the first people to struggle with what it means to be an agent of reconciliation in a hostile culture. We are not the first people to struggle with what it means to be the church. We are not the first people to explore the inner landscape of spiritual formation or the lofty heights of worship. These trails have been traveled before. While there will always be new routes to explore, there is much to be gained from those who have walked this way. Do not dismiss the antiquated and aged voices of writers such as Tertullian, Teresa of Avila, W. H. Griffith Thomas, Augustine, John Chrysostom, Amy Carmichael, Jim Elliot, Ambrose, Julian of Norwich, Origen, and Richard Baxter. They are not journeying beside us, but they can tell us much about the journey.

> It is possible ... theology makes the young theologian vain and so kindles in him something like gnostic pride. The chief reason for this is that in us men truth and love are seldom combined.
>
> —*Helmut Thieleke*, A Little Exercise for Young Theologians *(Grand Rapids, Mich.: Eerdmans, 1968), 16.*

Wisdom warns us about an approach to youth ministry training that is too short, too shallow, or too narrow. There is much to be learned beyond the covers of the latest youth ministry text, and we would do well to learn it.

We cannot do youth ministry without giving careful theological, psychological, and sociological thought to the world of adolescence.

One of the staples of Jay Leno's *Tonight Show* nightly routines is what is referred to as "crazy headlines and news stories"—a headline or news story that is either so misspelled or so poorly worded that it changes the meaning of the whole story. Consider these gems from misprinted stories from a police blotter:

▸ "Sent city police out at 11:38 a.m. to kick kids off the roof of a downtown furniture store."

33

> "Shortly after 8:30 a.m., Wednesday, Feb. 22, 1989, a Sikorsky S76A helicopter made an unscheduled crash a few yards off Rt. 19 at the Mansfield Rd. intersection"

Or these poorly worded headlines:

> One-Legged Man Competent to Stand Trial

> Man Says Body Is His Wife, But She Tells Police It Isn't

> Overnight, Second-Day Mail Will Be Delivered a Day Later

> Three Ambulances Carry Blast Victim to Hospital

> Bush Orders Army Troops to U.S. Virgins

And even these mistakes from the always dependable church bulletin:

> The Hampton United Methodist Church will sponsor a Harvest Supper on Saturday, October 1. The menu for the evening will be a traditional New England boiled sinner, rolls, homemade apple pie, coffee, tea, and cider.

> Hibben United Methodist Church will sponsor a barbecue chicken dinner on Saturday, March 2. Adults $4.50, children 12 and under, $2.50, children under five free if eaten in the dining room.[32]

It is mildly amusing to read this kind of stuff. But, in fact, these news stories and headlines point to an important truth—maybe one of the most basic truths of communication: the message is not about what you say, but about what they hear. It is quite possible to make a statement that is taken by others in a different way. What is important is how the message is received and translated by its hearer(s).

Missiologists James Engel and Wilbert H. Horton argue that one of the most common mistakes in ministry is being so focused on communicating the message widely that we neglect to ask if it is being heard accurately.[33] Or, to put it more simply, it is our mandate to preach the good news; we have a wonderful story to tell. But the first step in telling that story is giving serious thought about those to whom we will tell it.

We need to get the headlines right, but we also need to get into the heads of those who are going to hear the lines. In terms of youth ministry, this requires us to give thoughtful consideration to the adolescent experience. Who are these

---

[32] Jay Leno, *More Headlines* (New York: Warner Books, 1990), 8, 32, 33, 55, 59, 61, 94, 95.

[33] James Engel and Wilbert H. Norton, *What's Gone Wrong with the Harvest?* (Grand Rapids, Mich.: Zondervan, 1975), especially 20–30.

teenagers, and what is it like to live in their world? Our unwillingness to do this kind of careful thinking has left us rushing to press with youth ministry programs and strategies that simply do not fit the needs of our audience.

Chap Clark voices this concern precisely:

It is rare when a youth minister stops to ask some fundamental questions like, Just what is a *youth*? What kind of person am I trying to minister to? What are the distinctives between the students I work with in junior high and high school and the fifth graders who will be joining us? . . . Anyone who cares about children and adolescents has no choice but to take a new and careful look at how a postmodern, technological, and urbanized context affects the adolescent journey.[34]

Youth Ministry Can Be Taught in a Classroom, But It Cannot Be Fully Learned in a Classroom

One of the best ways to supplement formal youth ministry training is be involved as soon as possible, as much as possible, in a real live youth ministry of some type. There is simply no substitute for seeing these "kids" up close —talking with them, walking with them, and sharing the journey with them, the uphill and the down. Too often these kids are only represented in a classroom through the distant lens of concepts and statistics. Indeed, it is not until we are doing the field study that the sterile science of adolescence takes on the feel of an adventure. It is the difference between studying the map and walking the trail.

While writer Roy Oswald worked on his graduate theological degree he noted the drawbacks of pure academic study—warnings that are also relevant to those who study youth ministry at the undergraduate level:

There has been concern that while seminaries teach people to be good students, they do not necessarily train students to be professional ministers. Very often seminaries will train students more under an academic model than a professional one. "In the practice of ministry," writes Robert Kemper, "the greatest brain in the world is doomed to failure if that brain is not encased in a person with relational skills. As practitioners, we rise and fall not by our individual excellence, but by our interpersonal ministries within a community of faith."[35]

---

[34] Chap Clark, "The Changing Face of Adolescence: A Theological View of Human Development" in *Starting Right*, edited by Kenda Creasy Dean, Chap Clark, and Dave Rahn (Grand Rapids, Mich.: Zondervan, 2001), 42.

[35] Roy M. Oswald, *Crossing the Boundary: Between Seminary and Parish* (Washington, D.C.: Alban Institute, 1980), 1.

I don't think we should have people training for ministry who are not in ministry. The key to learning to minister is to minister, and I would think what this would translate into would be a local church connection in which a person is actually doing the things they're trying to learn to do well.
—Dallas Willard

You can get all A's and still flunk life.
—Walker Percy

What follows is an exchange of e-mails that took place between me and one of my youth ministry graduates. I had written to this student after hearing that one of his spiritual mentors had been involved in major moral failure. His response came a few days later just after the terrorist attacks of September 11, 2001:

I just wanted to share with you the issues I don't remember discussing in youth ministry classes that I have encountered since graduation. ☺:

1. What do you do and how do you feel when your youth pastor, a man that you have loved and modeled yourself after for years, is discovered to have been involved in multiple affairs?

2. How do you respond to the kid from a previous youth ministry position who you poured your life into and always fondly think, "Yeah, the other youth don't seem to have grown, but HE did"—e-mails you to tell you that he recently came out of the closet and he's gay?

3. How do you respond when you discover that one of your youth leaders is pregnant—BY ANOTHER one of your youth leaders?

4. How do you treat the family whose father is dying of AIDS and so these parents continually try (both directly and indirectly) to get you to parent their sons and keep setting you up to be the "bad guy" so that they don't have to be?

5. How do you walk with the youth group through your own personal pain, when two weeks after you announce to them that you are having a child, you have a miscarriage?

6. How do you help the 16-year-old in your

youth group who gets pregnant and whose parents want her to give the baby up for adoption but she wants to keep the baby?

7. What about when on a foreign mission trip, one of the students confesses to you that she has been sexually abused by her mother's boyfriend, with whom her mom is currently living?

> If you truly believe that you haven't begun to learn approximately 80 percent of what you need to be an effective pastor, you will begin parish ministry with a disposition that will get you through the first five years of ministry. If, on the other hand, you think you've about got it all together, and simply need to touch it up here and there with some firsthand experience, you are on the way to a major depression three years down the pike.
>
> —*Roy Oswald, cited in Robert G. Cox,* Do You Mean Me, Lord? *(Philadelphia: Westminster Press, 1985), 61.*

8. How do you handle it when another youth pastor from the same denomination calls you to tell you that one of your students (a guy who is in the small group that YOU are discipling) has been e-mailing one of his girls and recently told her that he was thinking of committing suicide?

9. How do you respond when the bubble of peace and prosperity that your students have grown up in is popped by the most horrible terrorist attacks that our nation has ever experienced?

9a. I don't remember discussing "Just War Theory" in YM 101.

9b. I don't remember discussing "The Providence of God and the Existence of Evil" in YM 101 either.

Just some food for thought as you plan future classes. ☺.

He was right, of course. There was much that we left uncovered in the classroom while he was there. It was only in agreement that I wrote back jokingly:

By the way, I have taken to heart the list of topics we never covered at Eastern and you'll be happy to know that we've changed the title of the Intro course to "Introduction to Youth Ministry, Geopolitical Crisis, Sexual Perversion, The Problem of Evil, Grief Counseling, and Pre-natal Ministry."

We do not seem to be attracting as many first-year students as in previous semesters. Let me know if you'd be interested in the on-line course. There are 73 required texts. Smirk.

Most of the great adventures begin because someone is unwilling to experience truth only as it can be found in the book or the classroom. Shackleton wanted to see firsthand what might be discovered in the interior of Antarctica. Lewis and Clark were determined to see with their eyes what had been described only in sketchy details by trappers and fur traders. John Wesley Powell could not be satisfied knowing there was a vast river called the Colorado; he wanted to ride it firsthand. It is possible to perform only clinical work in many areas of academic endeavor. It really is not possible with youth ministry. We can learn a lot about youth ministry in a classroom, but there is a lot that cannot be learned in a classroom.

Why is this so? Because youth ministry cannot be reduced to diagrams and philosophies, concepts and theological principles, overheads, and Power Point slides. Because youth ministry forces us to come to terms with the fact that most of our classroom answers do not fit real life out-of-the-classroom questions. It is much messier than that.

Our lives may be similar to the Peanuts cartoon Mike Yaconelli talks about in his book *Messy Spirituality*,[36] in which Lucy is standing at her five-cent psychology booth. Charlie Brown stops by hoping for words of counsel, advice about life. What he gets instead is Lucy's shrug and smug platitude, "Life is like a deck chair, Charlie Brown. On the cruise ship of life, some people place their chair at the rear of the ship so they can see where they've been. Others place their deck chair at the front of the ship so they can see where they're going." Looking at Charlie, she zooms in, "Which way is your deck chair facing?" Charlie Brown's blank face gives away his answer, and he says simply, "I can't even get my deck chair open."

> Both in history and in life it is a phenomenon by no means rare to meet with comparatively unlettered people who seem to have struck profound spiritual depths ... while there are many highly educated people for whom one feels that they are performing clever antics with their minds to cover a gaping hollowness that lies within.
>
> —*Herbert Butterfield*, Christianity and History *(New York: Scribner, 1949), 115.*

Somehow in Deck Furniture 101, it all seems so doable. When we are on the open sea of real life ministry, we are quick to learn that it does not unfold so easily. That is a reality we can escape from in the safe confines of a classroom. That is, no doubt, what moves William Willimon to write, "All ministerial formation worthy of the name consists of *various forms of apprenticeship* because the goal is the formation of consistent clerical character whose personification of gospel foolishness is strong enough to withstand merely worldly wisdom [emphasis added]."[37] In youth ministry, as with any other form of pastoral ministry, we simply cannot

---

[36] Michael Yaconelli, *Messy Spirituality*, (Grand Rapids, Mich.: Zondervan, 2002), 22.

[37] William Willimon, *Calling and Character*, (Nashville, Tenn.: Abingdon Press, 2000), 44.

> One cannot understand the meaning of preaching in the total work of the Church apart from direct personal hearing and proclamation of the gospel, nor know the character of worship, its direction, the requirements it makes on the self and its relations to proclamation and service unless one is a worshiper. How shall one understand Christian education in theory without engaging in it as teacher and student, or church administration without participation in the organized common life of a Christian community?
>
> —H. Richard Niebuhr, cited in Robert G. Cox, Do You Mean Me, Lord? (Philadelphia: Westminster Press, 1985), 72.

Anyone who is about to enter upon this walk of life needs to explore it all thoroughly beforehand and only then to undertake this ministry. And why? Because if he studies the difficulties beforehand he will at any rate have the advantage of not being taken by surprise when they crop up.
—**John Chrysostom**

just drive through the game preserve and stare through the window. We have to leave the safety of the car and risk an encounter in the wild.

But, of course, that is what makes the path so adventurous. That is what makes the unclimbed rock, the untamed wilderness, the unpaved road, the unmapped trail, the uncertain future so alluring. We do not know where the path will take us. It is, in every sense, a "journey down the great unknown."

What we *do* know as we launch on this messy journey of ministry is that we are led by him who knows the end from the beginning, and that we do not travel alone. That means we are guided both by "blazes" that mark the trail *and* by the One who led his people with "pillars of fire."[38]

"Therefore, since through God's mercy we have this ministry, we do not lose heart" (2 Cor. 4:1).

---

[38] "By day the Lord went ahead of them in a pillar of cloud to guide them on their way and by night in a pillar of fire to give them light, so that they could travel by day or night. Neither the pillar of cloud by day nor the pillar of fire by night left its place in front of the people" (Exod. 13:21–22).

Travel Log: Nigeria

Youth Worker Profiles by Paul Borthwick

Gideon Para-Mallam is a youth worker in Jos, Nigeria. Gideon is a veteran of more than 20 years of youth and student ministry in Africa's largest country. He is the outgoing director of the Nigeria Fellowship of Evangelical Students, the largest affiliate of the International Fellowship of Evangelical Students (IFES), a ministry that coordinates high school, college, and graduate student ministries in more than 120 countries. Gideon's next ministry will be training IFES workers across Africa.

Present Input/Future Output. What motivates Gideon to stay in youth ministry? "God's given me grace to stick it out through an irresistible inner motivation to serve young people, knowing that the fruits will somehow show later. The excitement I see in young people who are always eager to learn, even from their mistakes, and grow in their Christian faith excites me a lot. Helping young people discover their potential in Christ and helping them to use their gifts for maximum Kingdom impact compels me not to give up on young people easily."

Heads Up. Gideon's biggest youth ministry surprise? The amount of administration. Working in a para-church youth ministry, "I was surprised to discover how much time gets used up on administrative work. The administrative aspect of my work entails a lot of public relations work and fundraising to keep the vision of the work oiled for further service."

Great Story. "I once visited a big Church in Lagos, Nigeria's commercial capital. I found that 80 percent of the elders and deacons in this church were former students from our ministry. Most of them are now in the marketplace as witnesses for Jesus. The realization that the impact of what we do on campus reverberates in our churches, business boardrooms, governmental circles, and in society at large, generates a lot of internal fulfillment of life and ministry for me and my work."

Big Dream. "Change agents! Disciple makers! I love to see young people who are changed by God's power and live out the Scriptures in their workplaces the world over. I'd love to see them become mighty men and women of Scripture thereby becoming effective change-agents for the Master."

chapter three

THE CALL
OF THE WILD

There is nothing in this life, and especially in our own day, more easy and pleasant and acceptable to men than the office of bishop or priest or deacon, if its duties be discharged in a mechanical and sycophantic way; but nothing more worthless and deplorable and meet for chastisement in the sight of God . . . (A)nd, on the other hand, . . . there is nothing in this life, and especially in our own day, more difficult, toilsome, and hazardous than the office of bishop, elder or deacon; but nothing more blessed in the sight of God, if our service be in accordance with the Captain's orders.
—Augustine of Hippo (354–430 A.D.), in a letter written soon after his consecration[1]

In the evening, the men could watch the sun go down over the Missouri . . . They stared at that river, and talked about it, and thought about it. They were not daunted by it. Rather, they were drawn to it. What adventures awaited, what sights they would see, they knew they couldn't even guess, which only made them all the more eager to get going so they could find out.
—Stephen Ambrose, describing the Lewis and Clark party in the days just before their launch on the Missouri River to explore the massive wild expanse that was the western United States in 1803[2]

Think of what you were when you were called. Not many of you were wise by human standards; not many were influential; not many were of noble birth. But God chose the foolish things of the world to shame the wise; God chose the weak things of the world to shame the strong. He chose the lowly things of this world and the despised things—and the things that are not—to nullify the things that are, so that no one may boast before him.
—1 Corinthians 1:26–29

I know that my hopes and plans for myself could not be any better than He has arranged and fulfilled them. Thus, may we all find it, and know the truth of the Word which says, "He will be our guide even unto death."
—Jim Elliot[3]

[1] Augustine, cited in James Stitzinger, *Pastoral Ministry in History, Rediscovering Pastoral Ministry*, ed. John MacArthur Jr. (Dallas: Word, 1995), 44.

[2] Stephen E. Ambrose, *Undaunted Courage* (New York: Touchstone, 1996), 131.

[3] Quoted in Elisabeth Elliot, *Shadow of the Almighty* (Grand Rapids, Mich.: Zondervan, 1958), 249.

The college years are years of ever-looming questions:

▸ "What will I choose for a major?"

▸ "How will I get it all done in four years?"

▸ "What is God's will for my life?"

▸ "What is the minimum amount of sleep a human being needs to function at a level of moderate sanity?"

▸ "Will I ever pay off my student loans?"

▸ "Will I find a husband or wife before I graduate?"

▸ "Might I possibly find a husband or a wife who will help me pay off my student loans?"

And, of course:

▸ "Where is the nearest, cheapest place to buy pizza?"

Oh, yeah, and:

▸ "What is the meaning of life?"

And then, for those students pursuing undergraduate education in youth ministry, there are all of the questions related to discerning and sorting out a "call" to ministry:

▸ "What does it mean to be called to ministry?"

▸ "Am I fit for such a call?"

▸ "What are the demands and expectations of such a call?"

▸ "How do I know if I've been called?"

And finally:

▸ "If I pursue a call to youth ministry, will I ever be able to pay off my student loans?"[4]

---

[4] Perhaps you have heard your parents express these same concerns.

It was on a snowy Wednesday evening, January 13, 1892, that many of these same questions probed the heart of a young woman named Amy Carmichael. It had been four years earlier at the Keswick Bible Conference when she began to feel the nudging of God's call, and now it was clear she would receive no "rest from the cry of the heathen." She knew that she had to go; she was clearly being called by God. Sitting in her room that night, writing in her journal, that much was "inescapable, irresistible."[5]

But how could she? What about those she would be leaving behind—the "Dear Old Man" with whom she stayed and for whom she provided care and much comfort? What about the beautiful old house where she boarded, with its wonderful view of the river and the sloping mountains beyond? What about her mother? In this same journal Carmichael had earlier written, "My Precious Mother, have you given your child unreservedly to the Lord for whatever He wills? . . . O may He strengthen you to say YES to Him if He asks something which costs."

She [Carmichael] wrote of "those dying in the dark, 50,000 of them every-day,"of her own longing to tell them of Jesus, and her misgivings to do it because of the claims of home, and of how, only a few days before, she had written down for herself the reasons for not going: her mother's need of her, her "second father's" need, the possibility that by staying she might facilitate others' going, her poor health. Examining those reasons she wondered how God saw them. Were they good enough? She could not finish the letter. It was too excruciating. Next day she tried again.[6]

> I feel as though I had been stabbing someone I loved . . . Through all the keen sharp pain which has come since Wednesday, the certainty that it was His voice I heard has never wavered, though all my heart has shrunk from what it means, though I seem torn in two.[7]

Anyone who has seriously considered a call to ministry has wrestled with many of these same questions in some shape or fashion. These are good questions, honest questions, hard questions, and it is these questions that we must consider as we start out on this youth ministry adventure, because authentic ministry is an adventure that begins from the inside out.

---

[5] Elisabeth Elliot, *A Chance to Die: The Life and Legacy of Amy Carmichael* (Old Tappan, N.J.: Fleming H. Revell, 1987), 52, 54–55.

[6] Ibid., 52.

[7] Ibid. From the agonizing questions that searched her heart that night, Amy Carmichael went on to respond to God's call, venturing to Japan, China, Ceylon, and, finally, to India where she established the Dohnavur Fellowship, a ministry to children in moral danger, a ministry that she served for 53 years without a furlough. Her story—much of it taken from her own journals—is told powerfully in this biographical study.

A Pastoral Identity

No doubt, part of what makes it difficult to think through this issue of a ministry calling is that it leads us to uncomfortable stereotypes. There is the bumbling cleric, unaware and irrelevant, whom we often see caricatured in the media. There is the stern-faced party-pooper parson whose furrowed brow seems to disdain even the slightest hint of fun or freshness. There is the long-haired activist preacher, laughably hip, who does not seem to realize that the 1970s are over and it is time to put the beads away. There is the big-haired TV preacher who glares out from the screen with a phone number scrolling across the bottom of his chest. There is the earnest Generation-Xer with just the right amount of facial hair, trapped in what appears to be permanent discontent. We have seen them all: the comic, the conniving, the crooked, the caring, the charismatic. No matter how we look at these figures, we cannot really see ourselves. Even people "in the ministry" themselves are flattered when someone says, "You're not a typical preacher."

Perhaps it is a little like the notice posted around England toward the end of the 1930s, which called for everyone to register because of the war emergency. The sign read: "All persons in the above age groups are required to register for the national service except lunatics, the blind, and ministers of religion."[8] G. K. Chesterton wryly observed, "People pay ministers to be good, to show the rest of us it doesn't pay to be good."[9]

The embarrassment of these stereotypes was given full exposure in an award-winning 1990 play by David Hare called *Racing Demon*. The play portrays a team ministry of four Anglican clergy serving a South London parish, together with the diocesan bishop of Southwark and his

Those whom we designate as "ministers" are, in the New Testament, diakonoi, Paul's favorite title for Christian leaders, derived from the Greek word for "service" (1 Cor. 12:4–30). Significantly, it is the same word that is the root for "butler" and "waiter," terms that have a greater edge to them than "ministry." How odd of the church to designate its leaders by so mundane and lowly term. No pastor rises much higher than being a butler. Yet in the topsy-turvy ethics of the Kingdom, this is as high as anyone rises—a servant of the servants at the Lord's Table (see John 13).
—**William Willimon**

[8] Daniel Jenkins, *The Protestant Ministry* (New York: Doubleday, 1958), 7.
[9] G. K. Chesterton, quoted in Carnegie Samuel Calian, *Today's Pastor in Tomorrow's World* (Hawthorn Books, 1977), 75.

Advancement in the kingdom is not by climbing but by kneeling. Since the Lord has become Servant of all, any special calling in his name must be a calling to humility, to service. The stairway to the ministry is not a grand staircase but a back stairwell that leads down to the servants' quarters.
—**Edmund P. Clowney**

I will take the Ring, though I do not know the way.
—**J. R. R. Tolkien's character Frodo Baggins, in *The Lord of the Rings***

The name of *deacon* that is now appropriated to the lowest office in the church, was, in the time that the New Testament was written, used more promiscuously . . .

Generally in all those places where the word *minister* is in our translation, it is *deacon* in the Greek, which signifies properly a servant, or one who labors for another. Such persons are dedicated to the immediate service of God, and are appropriated to the offices and duties of the church . . .

The next order now is the name of *presbyter* or *elder*. Although at first it was applied not only to bishops, but to the apostles themselves, yet in the succeeding ages, it came to be appropriated to the second rank of the officers in the church. It either signifies a seniority of age, or of Christianity, in opposition to a neophyte or a novice, one newly converted to the faith . . . St. Paul divides this title either into two different ranks, or into two different performances of the duties of the same rank: those that rule well, and those that labor in word and doctrine (1 Tim. 5:17) . . .

The title of *bishop,* meaning *inspector* or *overseer*, is now by the custom of many ages, given to the highest function in the church. It implies a dignity in him, as the chief of those who labor, so it does likewise express his obligation to care and diligence, both in observing, and overseeing the whole flock, especially in inspecting the deportment and labors of his fellow workers who are subordinate to him in the constitution of the church, yet ought to be esteemed by him as his brothers, his fellow laborers, and fellow servants, in imitation of the apostles.

—*Bishop Gilbert Burnet, cited in Thomas Oden,* Classical Pastoral Care *(Grand Rapids, Mich.: Baker, 1987), 29–32.*

suffragan bishop of Kingston. Each of the men on the team has a different notion of their role and calling. John Stott describes it this way:

> To Lionel Espy, the gentle and largely ineffective team rector, "our job is mainly to learn from ordinary, working people. We should try to understand and serve them . . . Mostly, in fact, it's just being there and listening to the anger, and like a punch-bag absorbing it." In complete contrast, the young charismatic curate, Tony Ferris, is frighteningly self-confident. "I have this incredible power," he claims, which enables him to "spread confidence" around him, but he does it at the expense of other people. The other characters are more modest in their expectations. The diocesan bishop emphasizes the administration of holy communion. "Finally, that's what you're there for. As a priest you have only one duty. That's to put on a show." His suffragan, the episcopal diplomat *par excellence*, sees the heart of his job as "preventing problems growing into issues." To Donald Bacon ("Streaky"), who sings tenor, gets drunk, and describes himself as "a happy priest," there are no complications. "The whole thing's so clear. He's there. In people's happiness." Harry Henderson, the homosexual clergyman, is a trifle more ambitious. "There is people as they are. And there is people as they could be. The priest's job is to try and yank the two a little bit closer." Meanwhile, the sincere, agnostic girl Frances Parnell sees the ordained ministry as the "waste of a human being . . . always to be dreaming."[10]

> What a marvelous illustration fishing is, especially fishing with the net, and Jesus Christ told the disciples He would make them "fishers of men," catchers of men. Unless we have this divine passion for souls burning in us because of our personal love for Jesus Christ, we will quit the work before we are much older. It is an easy business to be a fisherman when you have all the enthusiasm of the catch, everybody then wants to be a fisherman. Just as everybody comes in with the shout and the "Hallelujah" when revival signs are abroad; but God is wanting those who through long nights, through difficult days of spiritual toil, have been trying to let down their nets to catch the fish. Oh, the skill, the patience, the gentleness and the endurance that are needed for this passion for souls: A sense that men are perishing won't do it; only one thing will do it, a blazing, passionate devotion to the Lord Jesus Christ, an all-consuming passion.
>
> —Oswald Chambers, Workmen of God *(London: Marshall, Morgan and Scott, 1937), 86.*

---

[10] John Stott, *The Contemporary Christian* (Downers Grove, Ill.: InterVarsity Press, 1992), 271–272.

Global Youth Ministry

By Paul Borthwick, Development Associates International

Need and Opportunity

Youth ministry needs to extend globally. Some estimate that half of the world's population is younger than 25. While the Western world ages, the non-Western world grows proportionately younger. Many of these young people live in places where the church is weak and youth ministry nonexistent. So, if we are to reach people for Jesus Christ during their most formative years, we need to go global.

As a result, a youth worker in the modern world has no worries about finding work (salary—yes, but work—never!).

▶ If your home church cannot employ you as youth pastor, you can always serve in South America, where the evangelical population grows at a rate estimated at four times the population—and most of these new believers are under age 25.

▶ If there is no work for you in your country as a youth evangelist, try China, where teenagers—most of whom know nothing about Jesus—number 300 million (that is more than the entire U.S. population).

▶ If you want to serve economically needy people, you can go to young people in the urban areas of the Western world, or you can exponentially increase your challenge by aiming at the thousands of street kids in Rio de Janeiro. Their poverty, drug problems, and vandalism have led to police being paid "bounty" for exterminating these kids as if they were vermin.

Around the world, the exportation of Western values, music, and lifestyles affects young people—most notably through the media—creating what some researchers call "global youth culture." Population growth, the impact of urbanization, and the "global village" have created one of the most exciting outreach opportunities facing the church of Jesus Christ around the world: global youth ministry!

But there is more to this global youth population than just an outreach opportunity. Once reached with the gospel, these youth represent perhaps the most energized population segment for reaching whole populations of people with the message of God's love through Jesus Christ. When mobilized, these youth can reach people we can never touch. They can change the world.

A recent conference for students in Nigeria (the most populous country in Africa) drew more than 6,000 young people—most of whom had become Christians in their high school or university years. They came together to focus on world missions. They met in spite of economic hardship and political unrest in their country. When the speakers challenged them to consider going out in cross-cultural service throughout Nigeria, Africa, and the world, more than 1,300 responded. When young people are presented with a vision of what God can do through them, they respond.

The need? Reaching the younger half of the world. The opportunity? To mobilize youthful energy for the Great Commission.

Go Equipped

But the question arises—how? How will these youth be reached? How will they be mobilized? Do I just pack my bag of youth ministry knowledge and skills and move overseas?

Some of our skills and knowledge about youth will be useful, but there are significant differences between U.S. youth ministry and youth ministry in other parts of the world. So how can a youth worker prepare?

Get Training in Cross-Cultural Ministry. In Sri Lanka, youth workers trained in American outreach methodologies used to begin their youth outreaches with "fun and games activities." Students from highly religious Buddhist and Hindu backgrounds found the fun and games to be disrespectful. The students thought a religious meeting should be serious. As the youth workers adapted their methods, they began their meetings with worship and prayer.

Incarnational youth ministry means understanding things such as language, culture, and society. While the media and globalization affect young people around the world, it is naive to assume that youth and youth culture are standardized. Each culture must be studied and understood to shape culturally relevant outreach and ministry.

Be Ready for New Definitions of What Is "Youth" Ministry. In most countries in Africa, Asia, and Latin America, a "youth" is generally anyone over age 12 and still unmarried. A youth group in Lebanon had a member who was 70; he had never married, so he stayed in the youth group! In Cuba, a "youth" retreat included anyone in the church under age 30.

Youth ministry definitions exceed issues of age. What youth ministry actually does needs redefining. It is not just discipleship groups, winter retreats, and an occasional outreach. Youth ministry in the townships of South Africa addresses issues of violence, unemployment, and a deep hopelessness in youth about their future. Youth ministry in Uganda and Thailand teaches young people a biblical response to people with HIV/AIDS. Youth ministry in Bosnia means addressing nontraditional youth ministry topics such as recovering from the traumas of war. Youth workers in Israel and Palestine try to exemplify forgiveness and reconciliation in the midst of a war-torn community.

Youth workers dedicated to wholistic ministry will find themselves in a cross-cultural context addressing sociological, economic, and even political issues that might never make it into the curriculum of their traditional concepts of youth ministry. They may also find themselves needing skills so that they can be self-supporting in the ministry because few of the greatest-need areas in youth work globally will provide the funding a youth worker needs.

Be Ready to Sacrifice. Most of the world's most challenging youth ministry opportunities exist in places that do not resemble American suburbia. It might be urban, poor, and crowded. Society and other world religions might passively or aggressively resist any efforts in outreach to their youth. Serving cross-culturally will mean sacrificing.

One speaker, addressing the challenges of reaching Muslims for Christ, remarked, "I think we've not been successful in reaching Muslims because we've not sent enough martyrs." In other words, if you really want to reach Muslims, you should also be ready to die.

Not all international youth workers will face the issue of martyrdom, but all must be ready to sacrifice. Youth workers dedicated to incarnational youth ministry and outreach to some of the 120 million street kids living in the slums of Nairobi, Manila, or Rio de Janeiro have died to many of the comforts and securities of their past. They live in the slums, walk the streets with their kids, and run the risk of dying alongside them.

Get Started

Jumping from where you are into global youth ministry does not mean an immediate trip to the airport to go somewhere else. It begins with awareness. Increase your vision for the world. Learn about youth in at least one other country. Go on a short-term mission trip. Start investigating where you might fit into the challenge and opportunity of global youth ministry.

Source: Lawrence O. Richards and Clyde Hoeldtke, A Theology of Church Leadership *(Grand Rapids, Mich.: Zondervan, 1980), 17.*

No wonder we stand at this trailhead, with its warning signs and vague promises of adventure, and wonder, "God, is this really the trail you want me to take?"[11]

Part of the problem is that the church in general, and youth ministry in particular, suffers from a weak *pastoral theology*. "Pastoral theology is that branch of Christian theology that deals with the office, gifts, and function of the pastor."[12] It is *theology* because it reflects on one means through which God has revealed himself in human history. It is *pastoral* because it considers how God's self-revelation affects the roles, tasks, duties, and work of the pastor. Its broad implications affect how we should think of youth workers, whether they serve in a parachurch ministry, such as Young Life or Youth for Christ, an innercity community center, a local congregation, or any place in between. Pastoral theology is an attempt to weave together a consistent way of thinking about ministry that gives attention to Scripture, the tradition of the Church, sociological and psychological insight, and practical experience.[13] These questions about leadership, calling, pastoral identity, and fitness for ministry are all questions subsumed in the realm of pastoral theology.[14]

Beginning with Basics: Leadership

There are several images Scripture gives us to describe a pastor's identity and work: *steward, herald, witness, father,* and *servant.*[15] (See Table 3-1 for a fuller explanation of the more prominent image.) Each of them tells us something significant about the role and responsibility of a pastor in general, and a youth pastor in particular. But the thread that weaves each of these images together is the thread of leadership responsibility. Each role highlights a different texture and tie-in, but the two main tasks of pastoral responsibility have always been feeding and leading.[16]

When we think of leadership, we think of Moses, Joshua, Peter, and Paul. Or maybe it is Margaret Thatcher, Winston Churchill, Abraham Lincoln, Stonewall

[11] Frederick Buechner notes our surprise at "the folly [of God] to choose for His holy work in the world . . . former lamebrains and misfits, nitpickers and . . . stuffed shirts and odd ducks and milquetoasts." Cited in David Roper, *A Burden Shared: Encouragement for Leaders* (Grand Rapids, Mich.: Discovery House Publishers, 1991), 66.

[12] Thomas C. Oden, *Pastoral Theology: Essentials of Ministry* (New York: HarperCollins, 1983), 311.

[13] Ibid. Oden continues, "As theology, pastoral theology seeks to reflect upon that self-disclosure of God witnessed to by Scripture, mediated through tradition, reflected upon by critical reason, and embodied in personal and social experience."

[14] Theology, properly understood, is always practical—it speaks to everyday issues that arise from the life and liturgy of the people of God. In fact, the old joke that "practical theology is an oxymoron" would have been lost on the early church where theology and practice were always wed together. "One did not study theology for three years, banking information about God and then, upon graduation, apply this in the field." R. Paul Stevens, *The Other Six Days* (Grand Rapids, Mich.: Eerdmans, 1999), 12. It was not until the twelfth century, when universities became more independent from the church and more narrow about the definition of scholarship, that theology came to be seen as an academic discipline apart from practical application and personal devotion. Luther said, "True theology is practical . . . speculative theology belongs to the devil in hell." Martin Luther, *Luther's Works*, ed. T.G. Tappert, 55 vols. (St. Louis Ill.: Concordia, 1955–1986), 22.

[15] John Stott uses the word *preacher* instead of *minister* and, while I am not uncomfortable with that word, it seems to already presume a certain role. On the other hand, the benefit of using such a term is that it prevents the confusion that might arise when we consider that all believers are called, at least in one sense, to be ministers. This material is informed by Stott's rich study of New Testament words, *The Preacher's Portrait* (Grand Rapids, Mich.: Eerdmans, 1961). James F Stitzinger identifies five terms that explicitly refer to the pastoral office: *elder* (Acts 15:6, 1 Tim. 5:17, James 5:14, 1 Pet. 5:1–4); *bishop* or *overseer* (Acts 20:28, Phil. 1:1, 1 Tim. 3:2–5, Titus 3 1:7); *shepherd* or *pastor* (Acts 20:28–31; Eph. 4:11; 1 Pet. 2:25; 5:2–3); *preacher* (Rom. 10:14, 1 Tim. 2:7, 2 Tim. 1:11); and *teacher* (1 Cor 12:28–29, 1 Tim 2:7;). See Stitzinger, *Pastoral Ministry in History*, 39. *Rediscovering Pastoral Ministry*, ed. John MacArthur, Jr. (Dallas: Word) 1995"

[16] We will focus more on the "feeding" dimension in later chapters of this book.

Table 3-1.
New Testament Images Used to Describe the Minister's Task

Leadership	Definition	Characteristic	Responsibility	Comment
Steward (Domestic metaphor); see 1 Cor. 4:1–2, Luke 16:1–9, Titus 1:7.	A trustee, a dispenser of another person's goods. "The manager of a household or of household affairs; especially a steward, manager, superintendent . . . to whom the head of the house or proprietor has entrusted the management of his affairs, the care of receipts and expenditures, and the duty of dealing out the proper portion to every servant and even to the children not yet of age." [1]	Must be trustworthy, faithful to the master of the household.	"Rightly dividing the Word" (2 Tim. 2:15). "The systematic preaching of the Word is impossible without the systematic study of it." [2]	A steward in the household of God is charged with rightly protecting and dispensing the "mysteries of God." (The Greek word *musterion* describes a truth that can be known only because God has made it known, that is God's revealed truth.)
Herald (Political metaphor); see 1 Cor. 1:21, 23.	A proclaimer, one who works not just within the household (steward), but outside in the public square, such as the town crier. "A messenger vested with public authority, who conveyed the official messages of kings, magistrates, princes, military commanders, or who gave a public summons on command." [3]	Must be self-controlled and bold, willing to deliver the message exactly as it was received. Must be faithful to the message.	Proclaiming the message of the gospel ("We preach Christ crucified," 1 Cor. 1:23), and making an appeal to those who hear that they might respond and believe.	Both proclamation and appeal are critical. Proclamation without appeal is a message with no heart, a town crier without tears. Appeal without proclamation is emotional manipulation, a call for decision without explaining the decision.
Witness (Legal metaphor); see Acts 22:15, 1 John 1:2, 4:14.	Witnesses bear testimony to what they have seen and heard.	First, we must have firsthand awareness of that to which we testify. Second, we must be able to give an accurate account of what we have seen and heard.	To be a witness "before the world" (Acts 1:8). "to the Son" (Rev. 12:17). "by the Father" (John 8:54, 17:1). through the Spirit" (John 16:13). "and the church" (Acts 5:32).	We cannot bear witness unless we have been witnesses. "It is quite futile saying to people 'Go to the Cross.' We must be able to say 'Come to the Cross.' " [4] A witness must be humble. We point to Christ and not to ourselves.
Father (Family metaphor); see 1 Thes. 2:7–12. [5]	Ministers care for their audience in the way a father cares for his child.	Loving, sincere concern. Gentle, steady care.	The first three metaphors speak of responsibility to the message. But this metaphor speaks of responsibility to the audience.	Not a father in terms of authority (see Matt. 23:9), but in terms of affection. "The tragedy of Christian ministry is that many who are in great need, many who seek an attentive ear, a word of support, a forgiving embrace, a firm hand, a tender smile, or even a stuttering confession of inability to do more, often find their ministers distant men who do not want to burn their fingers." [6]
Servant (Status metaphor); see 1 Cor. 3:5.	The servant (the Greek word *diakonos*) is one who executes the commands of another, especially the commands of his or her master.	Willingness to listen, and willingness to obey. Humility (see 1 Cor. 2:1–6, 4:10).	Obedience to the will of the Master, and submission so that the Master can work through his servant.	The servant plants and ploughs, but it is God who waters the crop and brings the fruitful harvest (1 Cor. 3:7).

[1] *A Greek-English Lexicon of the New Testament*, Rev. 2nd ed. (Edinburgh, Scotland: T. & T. Clark, 1892), 440–441.

[2] John Stott, *The Preacher's Portrait* (Grand Rapids, Mich.: Eerdmans, 1961), 31.

[3] *Greek-English Lexicon of the New Testament*, 346.

[4] William Temple, cited in Stott, *Preacher's Portrait*, 74.

[5] More important than the gender-specific imagery of fatherhood is the general imagery of a loving, caring parent ("like a mother caring for her little children," v. 7; see also Gal. 4:19).

[6] Henri Nouwen, *The Wounded Healer* (New York: Bantam Doubleday, 1979), 71. Nouwen adds, "No one can help anyone without becoming involved, without entering his whole person into the painful situation, without taking the risk of becoming hurt, wounded, or even destroyed in the process. The beginning and the end of all Christian leadership is to give your life for others. Thinking about martyrdom can be an escape unless we realize that real martyrdom means a witness that starts with the willingness to cry with those who cry, laugh with those who laugh, and to make one's own painful and joyful experiences available as sources of clarification and understanding" (72).

Jackson, Vince Lombardi, or Ernest Shackleton. Or, for others it may be Rudolph Giuliani, Bill Gates, Obi-Wan, Frodo, or former Minnesota governor Jesse Ventura.[17]

Obviously, there are numerous ways to define leadership. Management guru John Gardner defines it as "the process of persuasion or example by which an individual (or leadership team) induces a group to pursue objectives held by the leader or shared by the leader and his or her followers." James MacGregor Burns, in his Pulitzer Prize-winning study of leadership, summarized, "Leadership over human beings is exercised when persons with certain motives and purposes, mobilize, in competition or conflict with others, institutional, political, psychological and other resources so as to arouse, engage and satisfy the motives of followers." In his book *Leading Minds*, Howard Gardner explains that "Leaders are individuals who significantly influence the thoughts, behaviors, and/or feelings of others." Finally, describing leadership as adventure, James M. Kouzes and Barry Z. Posner comment, "Leaders are pioneers. They are people who venture into unexplored territory. They guide us to new and often unfamiliar destinations. People who take the lead are the foot soldiers in the campaigns for change . . . The unique reason for having leaders—their differentiating function—is to move us forward. Leaders get us going someplace."[18]

In the Old Testament, the Hebrew word *r'osh* (head) has a variety of meanings:

▸ the physical head of a person or animal,
▸ the chief priest (or nation or city) or head of a household,
▸ a position in the forefront (as at the front in the battle), or
▸ a qualitative meaning, as in *choicest* or *best*.[19]

It is quite clear from these definitions that, in the Old Testament, *headship* or leadership referred to a human authority that was judicial and authoritative (see Exod. 18:20–21, for example). However, by the time of the New Testament, there is a marked difference in the way the Greek equivalent, *kephale* (head), is understood. What is most significant is that out of the almost 75 occurrences of the word *kephale* or *head* in the New Testament, there is no indication that *headship* ever refers to leaders in the body of Christ. Why? Because Jesus is the head of the body, and the body has only one head.

Right away we are confronted with a fundamental truth about leadership in the body of Christ: it is a *leadership within the context of an organism and not leadership within the hierarchy of an institution.*[20] "A living organism can have only one head, and the function of the head can never be 'delegated' to other parts of the body. An insti-

---

[17] Guess which one of these names I threw in just for fun. Hint: think of large men in tight pants, living room "gladiators," and a guy who routinely goes on national television wearing a feather boa who refers to himself as "The Body." Another hint: Frodo and Obi-Wan have too much dignity for those types of stunts.

[18] Each of these quotations is cited in Burt Nanus, *Leaders Who Make a Difference* (San Francisco: Jossey-Bass, 1999), 7. Should the reader be interested in perusing the work of these writers, consider these titles: John W. Gardner, *On Leadership* (New York: Free Press, 1990); James MacGregor Burns, *Leadership* (New York: HarperCollins, 1978); Howard Gardner, *Leading Minds: An Anatomy of Leadership* (New York: Basic Books, 1995); and James M. Kouzes and Barry Z. Posner, *The Leadership Challenge* (San Francisco: Jossey-Bass, 1987).

[19] Lawrence O. Richards and Clyde Hoeldtke, *A Theology of Church Leadership* (Grand Rapids, Mich.: Zondervan, 1980), 16.

tution, on the other hand, having no organic relationship between its individual members and its head, must delegate authority and responsibility."[21]

Despite the fact that the *Random House Dictionary of the English Language* defines *headship* as "the position of head or chief; chief authority; leadership; supremacy,"[22] the New Testament notion of headship implies not position, but relationship. Every single person in the body of Christ is vitally connected to the Head, so any notion of top-down hierarchical leadership within the body of Christ misrepresents a biblical understanding of headship.[23] To portray the three most common models of headship, we might use the diagram[24] found in Figure 3–1.

Figure 3-1.
Three Different Notions of Headship

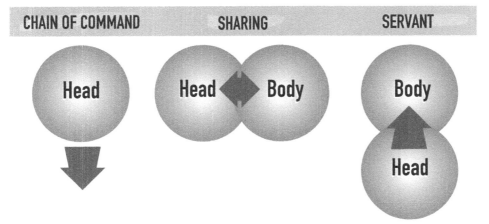

| CHAIN OF COMMAND | SHARING | SERVANT |

The first model in Figure 3-1, Chain of Command, represents the over/under notion typical of hierarchical structures. The emphasis within this model of leadership is authority, decision-making, and control from the top level. While the Chain of Command model typifies the way leadership and headship are commonly understood by most people, it clearly does not reflect the sort of leadership manifest in the life of Jesus (John 10:11–14, 13:1–17; Phil. 2:5–11).[25]

---

[20]This is not in any way to imply that hierarchical leadership within an institution is un-Christian or unbiblical. It is simply to point out that leadership within the church, the body of Christ, is substantially different from the sort of hierarchical leadership characteristic of corporate structures. That is because Christ's church is a corpus (body) and not a corporation.

[21]Richards and Hoeldtke, *A Theology of Church Leadership*, 17.

[22]Quoted in Richards and Hoeldtke, 21.

23See Ephesians 1:22, 4:15, 5:21–30; Colossians 1:18, 2:20, 2:19. In the slightly more complicated passage of 1 Corinthians 11ff, Bruce Powers, in *Growing Faith* (Nashville, Tenn.: Broadman, 1982), explains that headship refers to origin or source, and not hierarchical authority.

[24]Richards and Hoeldtke, *A Theology of Church Leadership*, 24. The diagram and related material is drawn from this helpful work.

[25]This is, of course, one reason why so many people found it hard to accept Jesus's claims to be the Messiah: they had one notion of headship, and he was working with a completely different model.

Unfortunately, the word *humility* is usually understood to signify a passive, dog-slinking attitude in the aggressive and often violent culture in which we live. The author of *The Cloud of Unknowing* [ed. James Walsh, *Classics of Western Spirituality* (New York: Paulist Press, 1981, 148)] viewed humility or meekness in a more positive way: "In itself, humility is nothing else but a [person's] true understanding and awareness of himself [or herself] as he [or she] really is." That is based on two realities: human sin and weakness, on one side, and "the superabundant love and worthiness of God," on the other. Proper self-esteem is crucial in . . . spiritual guidance.

—*E. Glenn Hinson,* Spiritual Preparation for Christian Leadership *(Nashville, Tenn.: Upper Room Books, 1999), 172.*

The second model, Sharing, suggests a side-by-side type of leadership in which the emphasis is on sharing and sustenance. This type of leadership, hinging more on a relationship than an institutional role, certainly reflects a Christ-like concern for people. On the other hand, this model obscures any sort of headship function. Perhaps that is why, in this egalitarian age, this is often seen as the more politically correct approach to leadership. Unfortunately, if the Chain of Command model gives us a head without concern for the body, the Sharing model gives us a body without any connection to a head.

The third model, Servant, turns the encounter upside down. Both leader and follower are closely intertwined through relationship. But now, the role of the leader is one of support and building up. At the heart of this model is the sacrificial headship that Paul refers to in Ephesians 5 wherein the husband, such as Jesus, subjects himself to the needs and developments of the wife in the relationship. This approach to leadership, taking seriously the "gave himself" language of Scripture, affirms the headship role—it does not deny that someone must lead (very important). But in emphasizing the support and nurture role of the leader, it defines the headship role quite differently from the Chain of Command or Sharing models.

Once we understand these three general models of headship, we can begin to predict how they will shape various approaches to leadership behavior. For example, Rollo May, in his book, *Power and Innocence*, talks about five kinds of power (or authority or headship):

- exploitative power—power that seeks to consume,
- manipulative power—power that seeks to control,
- competitive power—power that seeks to combat,
- integrative power—power that seeks to coordinate, and
- nutrient power—power that seeks to cultivate.[26]

[26] Rollo May, *Power and Innocence* (New York: Norton, 1972), 105ff.

Figure 3-2.
Use of Power in the Three Models of Headship

CHAIN OF COMMAND	SHARING	SERVANT

Exploitative Power	Manipulative Power	Competitive Power	Integrative Power	Nutrient Power

We can see how these various approaches to power play out when we think of them in relation to the three models of headship. Figure 3-2 illustrates where these five kinds of power fall in relation to the three models of headship.

Every person in youth ministry will be working for people and with people who exercise authority along the lines of one of these three headship models.[27] More to the point, all of us in youth ministry will ourselves exercise authority and headship by virtue of one of these three models. How we understand headship will determine the way we function as a leader. It will affect our response to students, volunteers, coworkers, parents, and our youth ministry peers. It will determine whether we tend to define our role primarily as managers or as leaders.[28] It will forge our priorities. It will likely affect even the way we approach our day-to-day activities.

Bernard Swain refers to this as leadership *style*, "the complex and varying patterns of behavior and relationship among ministerial leaders and between these leaders and other people."[29] Based on his research and consultation with a wide range of congregational and denominational bodies, Swain defines four leadership styles, each based on a unique *recipe* combining four ingredients (in different measure): degree and locus of authority, division of labor, delegation of responsibility, and joint performance (see Table 3-2). While most leaders would function in one style most of the time, an effective leader will likely operate within two or more of these styles depending on the circumstances. The key question for leaders is not, "Which style is the will of God?" but rather "How can we build a recipe for a leadership style that best fits our strengths, mission, and ministry context?"

[27] For a wonderful study in how you might respond to a pastor or employer who functions primarily in the Chain of Command mode, see Gene Edward's profound book, *A Tale of Three Kings* (Carol Stream, Ill.: Tyndale, 1992).

[28] This distinction is not merely semantic. In his book based on research examining leadership and its relationship to management, John Kotter argues that the delineation between leadership and management is crucial for an effective leader. Managers (1) plan and budget, (2) organize and staff for execution, and (3) control resources and solve problems. Leaders (1) establish direction, (2) align people through communication and equip to pursue the vision, and (3) motivate and inspire to maintain the pursuit. John Kotter, *A Force for Change: How Leadership Differs from Management* (New York: Free Press, 1990), 4–18.

Some of the literature casts this as a distinction between transactional leadership and transformational leadership. Bernard Bass characterizes transactional leaders as those who work within the situation, and transformational leaders as those who change the situation; those who talk about payoffs as opposed to those who talk about goals; those who define what we must do as opposed to those who motivate us to do more than we expected to do. Bernard Bass, *Leadership and Performance Beyond Expectations* (New York: Free Press, 1985), chaps. 1-2. For a theological and practical look at this style of leadership, see Leighton Ford, *Transformational Leadership* (Downers Grove, Ill.: InterVarsity Press, 1991).

[29] Bernard Swain, *Liberating Leadership* (San Francisco: Harper and Row, 1986), 30–31. Swain wants to make sure that we do not contrast this kind of style with substance, as with the familiar criticism, "more style than substance." In this understanding of style, style *is* the substance of leadership.

Table 3–2.
Swain's Four Leadership Styles Viewed in the Context of Youth Ministry

Leadership Style	Description	Values	Features
Sovereign	Example: Youth leader who operates as the "youth ministry guru in residence" and sees adult staff or interns as drones who do the "grunt work." Centralized authority. Marked by hierarchical structure, but not necessarily negative.	Someone must lead so there will be a sense of order. Professionalism: getting the job done right. Playing one's role without disrupting the system. Accountability for one's area of authority. Uniformity.	Authority is not shared or divided with anyone else. Or as the cliché puts it: "The buck stops here." Decision-making is highly centralized.
Parallel	Example: Youth worker who functions alongside a team of volunteers—some who teach Sunday School, some who do midweek programming, etc.—but makes no real effort to conjoin and coordinate everyone's efforts. Authority is vested in a team of people who work alongside each other, but not necessarily with each other. The team members understand their job, and individually do what they must to accomplish the task.	Places high value on division of labor and personal responsibility. Places high value on personal autonomy. Places high value on diversity: people doing their specific job in their personal way.	Allows energy to be focused on task rather than issues of authority and obedience. Has real delegation, as opposed to Sovereign style that only delegates the work, not the planning and method. In pure Parallel style, no one person has authority. Self-reliance.
Mutual	Example: Youth leader who wants to discern the gifts of others on the team so those gifts can be developed and deployed in a united effort. Teams are involved at all levels—planning, executing, and evaluating.	Stresses sharing: feelings, thoughts, ideas, and the work itself. Autonomy is absorbed in group identity. Stresses integration and fitting in with team.	Makes consensus a big part of decision-making process. Lots of interaction with others.
Semimutual	Example: Youth leader who has co-responsibility for youth group, alongside a team or committee—who seeks to share equal authority for the ministry while having the bulk of accountability for the ministry. A hybrid of Mutual and Parallel styles. Resembles relationship between youth pastor and youth leadership team—they work together but one or the other is probably in charge.	A division of labor (as with Parallel style), but not as pronounced and complete. Some joint accountability, but the emphasis is on autonomy.	Consensus about goals and objectives is more important than any one job. No joint responsibility for performance. There is interaction but it is not ongoing.

Leadership Style	Relationships	Strengths	Weaknesses
Sovereign	• Relationships are based primarily on authority (rank and position). • Volunteers and staff depend on the "paid youth worker." • Peerage is rare. People do not relate to each other as equals. • Relationships are based on institutional role rather than personal character.	• Efficiency. Simplified decision-making process. • Economical. Accomplishes work with minimal time and energy. • Provides control and structure. • Tries to take personality out of the equation (but often does not). Says, "We do it my way because I'm the youth pastor—not necessarily because you like me."	• Most people have a natural mistrust for authority. • Provides a weak base of delegation and synergy. • Discourages initiative and entrepreneurship. • Comes across as elitist and dictatorial. • Discourages body life.
Parallel	• Peerage or equality is created—in a strange way—by the fact that everybody is doing a piece of the project, so everyone is equally alone in the work, even though all are working on the same project. • Generates independence. • Requires little or no trust between leader and co-leaders and volunteers.	• It is simple—"lean and mean." Does not require a lot of organizational flowcharts. • Keeps too many cooks from "spoiling the broth." • Working alone allows people to work without distraction. • Neutralizes negative vibes regarding authority.	• Lack of communication. • Isolation can make people afraid to make decisions—because they do not want to take risks by themselves. • Loses benefits of collaboration. • Eliminating authority creates a body with no head.
Mutual	• Interdependence. • Authority is shared. • Trust is important, not just for character, but also for teammates' ability to do the job.	• Keeps one from being the "Lone Ranger." • Overcomes isolation. • Creates greater synergy: more people with more ideas mixing together in more ways. • Most people enjoy the interaction with other people.	• As the relationships go, so goes the work. • Expends a lot of resources just to build the team, before ever thinking about the youth program. • Complicates decision-making process.
Semimutual	• Moderate level of trust. • Can be stressful because of energy required to maintain balance in relationship. • Authority is vaguely defined: Is it the youth committee working with the youth pastor or the youth pastor working for the committee?	• Provides checks and balances. • More realistic, in that, unfortunately, this actually reflects the way people usually work together.	• Makes it tough to integrate planning and performance because it is not clear who plans and who performs. • Provides neither the clear authority of Sovereign style nor the relationships and peerage of the Mutual style.

Christian saw the picture of a very grave person hung up against the wall; and this was the fashion of it: it had eyes lifted up to heaven, the best of books in his hand, the law of truth was written upon his lips, the world was behind its back; it stood as if it pleaded with men, and a crown of gold did hang over its head.
—**John Bunyan**

Christian ministry is the worst of all trades, but the best of all professions.
—**John Newton**

Table 3–3.
Two Frameworks for Conceptualizing Leadership

Secular Authority: "Lord it over"	Servant Authority: "Servant among . . ."
Has power vested in strength.	Has power vested in love and concern.
Gives orders.	Follows orders.
Is unwilling to fail (discredits authority).	Is unafraid to fail (values learning over control).
Makes oneself necessary.	Works oneself out of a job.
Drives like a cowboy.	Leads like a shepherd.
Needs (institutional or personal) strength to control.	Compels allegiance through love and servanthood.
Is authoritarian.	Is steward of authority.
Has gold, makes rules.	Follows golden rule.
Seeks personal advancement.	Seeks to please master.
Expects to be served.	Expects to serve.

If we take all of these theories about kinds of power, models of headship and leadership style, what we are really left with is a portrait of leadership shaped by one of two broad frames: a secular model, or a servant model (see Table 3-3).[30]

Starting with the framework of the servant model, we can then begin to paint a specific portrait of youth ministry leadership.

Youth Pastor?

I remember the Sunday morning well. A large portion of the service was to be given over to celebrating the fact that we had paid off the mortgage on our church property. It was to be an affirmation of God's faithfulness and of the generosity of his people. This being a United

---

[30] George Mallone, *Furnace of Renewal* (Downers Grove, Ill.: InterVarsity Press, 1981), 86.

Methodist Church, the bishop had been invited to share in our celebration.[31] When I was introduced that morning to the bishop, I told him that I was the congregation's youth pastor. That's when the bishop replied, "Oh, so you're not *really* a minister then." It was an interesting moment. And a telling one, because the question that emerges almost immediately in our study of pastoral theology as it relates to youth ministry is simply this: In what sense is it theologically correct to refer to someone as a youth *pastor*? Is youth ministry *real* ministry? Can someone be *called to youth ministry*? Figure 3-3 provides a survey of how some youth workers view the calling to youth ministry.

What makes all of this a little confusing is that the New Testament does not provide us with a kind of clear-cut corporate flowchart. New Testament writers were far more concerned about faithful witness than they were about lining all the churches into ecclesiastical structures. From what we can observe in Paul's epistles,[32] it appears that some churches were led by bishops (*episcopoi* or overeseers),

Figure 3-3.
Survey of Youth Workers Reflecting on Specific Calling to Youth Ministry

Survey Item	Percentage of youth ministers who responded "strongly agree"	Percentage of youth ministers who responded "agree"	Percentage of youth ministers who responded "mildly agree"	Percentage of youth ministers who responded "mildly disagree"	Percentage of youth ministers who responded "disagree"	Percentage of youth ministers who responded "strongly disagree"
1. God called me to youth minstry.	67	22	8	2	1	0
2. God's call is my primary motivation for doing youth ministry.	63	27	7	2	1	0
3. I enjoy my work.	45	42	10	2	1	0
4. I want to be involved in the lives of youth.	56	37	6	1	0	0
5. Youth ministry should not be viewed as a stepping-stone position.	57	29	9	3	2	0

Source: Karen Jones, "Setting Ministry Goals: Personal and Interpersonal," in Karen Jones, Dave Rahn, and Merton Stommen, *Youth Ministry That Transforms* (Grand Rapids, Mich.: Zondervan, 2001), 214.

[31] I admit I found it intriguing that the bishop had not been able to visit us before this day, before we had paid off the mortgage. But now that we were paying off the mortgage, he was able to join us, to celebrate what "we (had) done together."
[32] William Willimon, *Pastor: The Theology and Practice of Ordained Ministry* (Nashville, Tenn.: Abingdon, 2002), 29–30.

What do we mean by pastor?

Drawing from the works of Gregory the Great (which strikes me as a name that would make it difficult to remain humble) (540–604 A.D.) and John Calvin (1509–1564), the term *pastor* can be understood to mean someone who is:

▸ a member of the body of Christ,

▸ called by God and the church,

▸ set apart by ordination to preach the Word,

▸ set apart to administer the sacraments, and

▸ able to guide and nurture the Christian community to full conformity to the image of Christ.

See John Calvin, Institutes of Christian Religion, *ed. J. T. McNeill, 2 vols., bk. 4, ch. 1, sec. 3; and Gregory the Great,* Pastoral Care *(591 A.D.), trans. by Henry Davis in* Ancient Christian Writers: The Works of the Fathers in Translation, *ed. J. Quasten, J. C. Plumpe, and W. Burghardt, 40 vols. (Westminster, Md.: Newman Press, 1946).*

sometimes also called *pastors* as well. Other churches appear to have been governed by a council of *elders (presbuteroi)* with different elders assuming various responsibilities within the congregation.

What in later centuries eventually emerged from this organic, patently untidy structure was a pattern with three different offices: bishops, who presided over a number of congregations; elders, who presided over a single church; and then, within each congregation, deacons *(diakonoi)* whose job it was to be the hands, eyes,[34] ears, and feet of the overseers and elders—sort of congregational social workers.[35] But, in the early centuries of the church's life, it simply was not so neat.[36] In fact, so fluid was the church's use of these various terms that John Calvin remarked that "in indiscriminately calling those who rule the church 'bishops,' 'presbyters,' 'pastors,' and 'ministers,' I did so according to the Scriptural usage, which interchanges these terms. For to all who carry out the industry of the Word it accords the title of 'bishops.' "[37]

[33] "The presbyter is only to teach, to offer, to baptize, to bless the people, and the deacon is to minister to the bishop, and to the presbyters." *Constitutions of the Holy Apostles*, bk. III, sec. XI, ANF VII, 432.

[34] "Let the deacons of the church, going about with intelligence, be as eyes to the bishop, carefully inquiring into the doings of each member of the church, ascertaining who is about to sin, in order that, being arrested with admonition by the president, he may perhaps not accomplish the sin. Let them check the disorderly, encouraging them not to forget to assemble to hear the discourses . . . Let the deacons keep an eye out for those who are suffering from illness, and let them bring them to the notice of the congregation who do not know of them, that they may visit them, and supply their wants." Clementina, *The Epistle of Clement to James*, cited in Thomas Oden, *Classical Pastoral Care* (Grand Rapids, Mich.: Baker, 1987), 120.

[35] The title *priest* (or *hieros*) is never used in the New Testament to refer to a Christian leader. In fact, the English word *priest* is a shortening of the Greek *presbuteros*, whose general meaning was elder, or presiding officer. John Stott provides a concise explanation of why the title *priest* as it is applied to human leaders is misleading and unacceptable. See John Stott, *The Contemporary Christian* (Downers Grove, Ill.: InterVarsity Press, 1992), 273.

[36] In Acts 20:17 and Titus 1:5–7, the terms *elder* and *bishop* appear to be synonymous. Likewise, in 1 Peter 5:1–2, both *elder* and *bishop* appear to be synonymous with the word *pastor*. This is the kind of evidence that leads J. B. Lightfoot to conclude that in biblical times, *elder* and *bishop* were synonymous terms. See J. B. Lightfoot, *The Christian Ministry*, in *St. Paul's Epistle to the Philippians* (Grand Rapids, Mich.: Zondervan, 1953), 196–201.

[37] John Calvin, *Institutes of Christian Religion, Book II* (Grand Rapids, Mich.: Eerdmans, 1972), 321.

Jonathan Edwards, following Calvin, adds, "'Tis a thousand pities that the world's church office and power should so tear the world to pieces and raise such a fog and dust about apostolic office, power, and succession, pope's, bishop's, and presbyter's power. It is not such a desperately difficult thing to know what power belongs to each of these, if we will let drop those words that are without fixed meanings [that is, meaning fixed by scriptures]."[38]

Our desire in present church life to organize, formalize, and homogenize these roles was not a priority in the early church. Obviously, there is no mention in the New Testament, nor in the writings of the church fathers, of the office of a youth pastor. Youth ministry, as we now know it, did not exist until the 1880s.[39] But the picture we are given, for example, in Acts 6:1–7 is a church that is quite willing to adapt and change, to create new structural forms of leadership to meet the changing needs of the churches. We hear this same openness to a variety of gifts and ministries in Paul's comment in 1 Corinthians 12:4–5: "There are different kinds of gifts, but the same Spirit. There are different kinds of service, but the same Lord." Indeed, one of the clearest principles we can infer from the New Testament regarding church offices is that the church seemed to recognize the possibility of a wide assortment of leadership gifts.[40]

Might we conclude then that it is proper to speak of a youth *pastor*? Perhaps, and perhaps not. What we can conclude is that to make such a clear distinction as did the good Bishop, between a *youth pastor* and a real minister, at least in terms of church office, is to draw a bold line where Scripture seems to draw a fuzzy one.[41] Of

The will of God is always a bigger thing than we bargained for.
—Jim Elliot

Have you been asking God what He is going to do? He will never tell you. God does not tell you what He is going to do; He reveals to you who He is.
—Oswald Chambers

I came here intending to devote my energies through life to the legal profession and the service of my country . . . But since I have been here I have not been contented with my plans and there has been a constant increasing impulse in me urging me to devote my whole life and talents to the service of Jesus.
—John R. Mott, missionary, one of the twentieth century's greatest student evangelists

---

[38] Jonathan Edwards's entry on "ministers" in *Miscellanies*, cited in *The Philosophy of Jonathan Edwards from His Private Notebooks*, ed. Harvey G. Townsend (Eugene, Ore: University of Oregon Press, 1955), 200.

[39] It was in 1881 that Francis Clark founded the first Christian Endeavor Society. Her work later spawned an international, interdenominational network of youth societies.

[40] Willimon, *Pastor*, 30.

[41] The reader will notice that I have used quotations and biblical guidelines that refer to the *pastor* as if they can be equally applied to the *youth pastor*. With the exception of a few rare cases, I am convinced that this is the case. If the role of youth pastor is to have any validity, it must take its shape and its basic requirements from the New Testament role of the pastor. Obviously, there are distinct differences in function between the two roles. But in essence, they are two stems that grow from the same root.

Pop Quiz: Multiple Choice

Circle one response before checking the answer below the list. *Laypersons* are:

1. Members of the people of God called to a total ministry of witness and service in the world.

2. Those who are ministered to by the clergy who are the true church.

3. People in part-time Christian service.

4. Nonordained Christians whose function is to help the clergy do the work of the church.

5. A person who sleeps all day (that is, your roomate).

In a survey that involved 12,000 members of the United Methodist Church, a solid 59.9 percent marked answer number four. The answer, however, is number one.

—*Georgia Harkness,* The Church and Its Laity, *cited in R. Paul Stevens,* The Other Six Days *(Grand Rapids, Mich.: Eerdmans, 1999), 25.*

the three offices generally identified within the New Testament church structure—such as it is—the one that comes closest to fitting "traditional" youth ministry is probably the role of the elder.[42]

Who Is Called to Be a Minister?

You may ask, "But isn't everybody called to be a minister?" Well, yes and no. Yes, all who are baptized into the body of Christ as believers are priests in the household of faith. "You also, like living stones, are being built into a spiritual house to be a holy priesthood, offering spiritual sacrifices acceptable to God through Jesus Christ . . . You are a chosen people, a royal priesthood, a holy nation, a people [*laos*] belonging to God, that you may declare the praises of him who called you out of darkness into his wonderful light" (1 Pet. 2:5,9).

Indeed, the common distinction we often hear today between "laity" and "clergy" was foreign to the New Testament writers. While the present-day church (depending on the specific denominational context) defines laity in terms of *function* (they do not administer the Word or sacraments), *status* (we do not put "Rev." in front of their name), *education* (they have not been to seminary or Bible college), *remuneration* (they do not get paid), or by *lifestyle* (more occupied with the secular than the sacred),[43] the New Testament church had only one people, the true *laos* (people) belonging to God.[44]

[42]I would definitely want to add some caveats to this statement. For example, I would probably be less comfortable using this terminology with someone who is involved in parachurch youth ministry—not because it is less legitimate, but because it is ministry exercised apart from a local church community, and this close community connection was a clear expectation of early church life. There are other issues as well, but they will emerge in more detail in the following pages.

[43] Notice that these traits are all negatives: what lay people do not do, do not have, do not know, and do not care about! No wonder we have not done a better job of mobilizing the people of God.

[44] Stevens, *Other Six Days*, 5,24–28. This Greek word *laos* originally meant "the crowd" or "the people as a nation." *Laos tou Theou* (people of God) is the universal term in the New Testament for the church. If the word *laos* stands alone (see Matt. 1:21) it usually refers to the nation or may just refer to a crowd of people (Acts 6:12), according to Ceslas Spicq in *Theological Lexicon of the New Testament*, trans. and ed. J. D. Ernest, Vol. II (Peabody, Mass.: Hendrickson, 1994), 371–374.

Os Guinness argues persuasively that the phrase, "full-time Christian service," used as a way of distinguishing between clergy and nonclergy, is completely inappropriate because every Christian is called to full-time Christian service in the same way every Christian is called to full-time Christianity. This is not a new confusion. One of the earliest and most prolific church historians, Eusebius, bishop of Caeserea, in his *Demonstration of the Gospel*, says that Christ gave "two ways of life": the *perfect life*, the spiritual life reserved for priests, monks, and nuns,

> ## You Might Be Rooming with a Bishop or Pope!
>
> Whoever comes out of the water of baptism can boast that he is already a consecrated priest, bishop, and pope, although of course it is not seemly that just anybody should exercise such office ... There is no true, basic difference between laymen and priests ... except for the sake of office and work, but not for the sake of status.
>
> —*Martin Luther,* To the Christian Nobility of the German Nation, *in* Luther's Works, *trans. Charles M. Jacobs and James Atkinson, vol. 44, (Philadelphia: Fortress Press, 1966), 129.*

and the *permitted life* that would be the normal course of daily labor, commerce, and family life followed by most nonclergy people. Obviously, any view of such a two-tiered calling, what Guinness refers to as *the Catholic error*, is completely foreign to Scripture. Equally troublesome, however, is what Guinness calls *the Protestant error*, the notion that any and every job could be pursued as a calling if pursued with devotion, enjoyment, and diligence.[45] This distortion misses the vital distinction between worshiping God and worshiping work—and people in ministry are particularly susceptible to such a distortion. That is why we can baptize our workaholism with phrases such as, "I'd rather burn out than rust out." Doing youth ministry just because "I love youth ministry" is not pursuing vocation; it is pursuing idolatry. Calling your work *ministry* because it is a full-time paid position is to misunderstand the full-time calling that God gives to every believer.[46]

Stevens observes, "While we observe in the church today two classes of people separated by education, ordination and intonation, we discover in the New Testament one ministering people for the work of the ministry (Eph. 4:11–12)."[47]

In that sense, all of us are called by God to do the work of ministry. As Marva Dawn puts it,

I am not an ordained clergy person—primarily because I have never been called to serve one local congregation since I finished my M.Div., but have

[45] This position is more widely referred to as the "Protestant work ethic."

[46] Os Guinness, *The Call* (Nashville, Tenn: Word, 1998), 32–33.

[47] Ibid., 30. Stevens argues passionately and with strong support that "Ordination as a rite or ceremony that conferred power or office simply did not exist in the New Testament." While I am not ready to come to that conclusion, it seems quite clear that our two-class system in the church with clergy doing the ministry and laity paying for it is simply an unbiblical and ineffective paradigm. Stevens's book is thorough, thoughtful, and frankly radical. His arguments are important and persuasive and worth further study.

> In recent years I have watched many people diminish the sacredness of God's specific call to be a shepherd to His people. We heard people say, "Everyone is called." But in the Scriptures, God specifically calls some to shepherd His people. The call and the enabling are special. Do not let anyone explain away your high calling, and make it common to all. It is not common!
>
> *—Henry Blackaby, Henry Brandt, and Kerry L. Skinner, The Power of the Call (Nashville, Tenn.: Broadman and Holman, 1997), 28.*

instead freelanced full time to serve the larger Church by speaking for various conferences and at seminaries and colleges. However, not to be ordained has been a great advantage for my goals of teaching because, if people ask, I respond that I was ordained when I was baptized at twenty-nine days old and welcomed into the Christian community as a called servant of God. Whether or not the denomination to which you belong advocates infant baptism, all of us who are God's saints can share our baptismal days as our ordination day into the priesthood of all believers."[48]

At the same time, it is undeniable that the church has historically tried for the sake of good order[49] (quality control, if you will) to call some from among the priesthood to serve as servants to the servants of God.[50] They might serve as *overseers* (bishops), or they might serve as *elders*, but it is these people we call *pastors*. Therefore, though all believers are called to minister, we are not all called to the role of *minister to the ministers*, and we are not all called to be *pastors*.

Two statements from Martin Luther provide clarification:

For although we are all priests, this does not mean that all of us can preach, teach, and rule. Certain ones of the multitude must be selected and separated for such an office . . . This is the way to distinguish between the office of preaching or the ministry, and the general priesthood of all baptized Christians. The preaching office is no more than a public service which happens to be conferred upon someone by the entire congregation, all the members of which are priests.[51]

Luther further notes,

It is true that all Christians are priests, but not all are pastors. For to be pastor one not only must be a Christian and a priest but must have an office and

---

[48] Marva Dawn and Eugene Peterson, *The Unnecessary Pastor: Rediscovering the Call* (Grand Rapids, Mich.: Eerdmans, 2000), 26.

[49] "As to the pastors, whom Scripture also sometimes calls elders and ministers, their office is to proclaim the Word of God, to instruct, admonish, exhort and censure, both in public and private, to administer the sacraments, and to enjoin brotherly corrections along with the elders and colleagues. *Now in order that nothing happen confusedly in the church, no one is to enter upon this office without a calling* [emphasis added]." John Calvin, *Draft Ecclesiastical Ordinances*, cited in Oden, *Classical Pastoral Care*, 95.

[50] How pastoral identity, this *priesthood among the priesthood*, has been defined over the years of the church's history has varied widely. With the pendulum swings so typical of human behavior, exaggerations or extremes of pastoral identity in one direction were often followed by exaggerations and extremes of pastoral identity in the other direction. For example, in the early church, the emphasis seemed to focus more on the pastoral person rather than the pastoral office. So we see much New Testament emphasis on the character of the person who might serve. In medieval years (476–1500), pastoral identity was shaped not by the one who held the office but more so by the office itself, a focus that gave way to moral hypocrisy and political corruption. This was precisely the error that John Huss (1373–1415) sought to address when he argued, "Not the office makes the priest, but the priest the office. Not every priest is a saint, but every saint is a priest." For a more thorough review of how the pastoral role has been viewed through church history, see Stitzinger, *Pastoral Ministry in History*, 34–63. See also Marshall Shelley, *The Character Question, Leadership Journal*, and Willimon, *Pastor*, 41–45.

[51] Martin Luther, "Commentary on Psalm 110," cited in Oden, *Classical Pastoral Care*, 83.

a field of work committed to him. This call and command makes pastors and "preachers."[52]

So, yes, we are called to Jesus. As Edmund Clowney observes, "There is no call to ministry that is not first a call to Christ. You dare not lift your hands to place God's name in blessing on his people until you have first clasped them in penitent petition for his grace. Until you have done that the issue you face is not really your call to the ministry. It is your call to Christ."[53] Yes, we are all called to serve, to do whatever we do as a service unto God for his glory (Col. 3:17–24). But no, we are not all called to serve in the same way. Those called to be pastors or youth pastors are called in a unique and wonderful way. Why? Because there is a vital distinction between *calling* and *career*.

Why do pastors have such a difficult time being pastors? Because we are awash in idolatry. Where two or three are gathered together and the name of God comes up, a committee is formed for making an idol. We want gods that are not gods, so we can "be as gods."

The idolatry to which pastors are conspicuously liable is not personal, but vocational, the idolatry of a religious career that we can take charge of and manage . . .

The pastoral vocation in America is embarrassingly banal. It is banal because it is pursued under the canons of job efficiency and career management. It is banal because it is reduced to the dimensions of a job description. It is banal because it is an idol—a call from God exchanged for an offer by the devil for work that can be measured and manipulated at the convenience of the worker. Holiness is not banal. Holiness is blazing . . .

Pastors commonly give lip service to the vocabulary of a holy vocation, but in our working lives we more commonly pursue careers . . ."

—*Eugene Peterson,* Under the Unpredictable Plant *(Grand Rapids, Mich.: Eerdmans, 1992), 4–5.*

Is Youth Ministry a Career?

The English word *career* comes from the French *carrèire*, meaning "a road" or "a highway."[54] Think of someone setting out on a road, map in hand, goal in sight, with stops marked along the way for food, lodging, and fuel. No wonder we often hear the word "career" coupled with the words "track" or "ladder." Both images suggest a well-marked course, a set itinerary, an expected schedule of travel. The traveler's choices are left solely to the dictates of the map.

---

[52] Martin Luther, "Exposition on Psalm 82," cited in Oden, 95. Willimon, in his excellent book, *Pastor* 16, comments: "Damage is done to the unique quality of the pastoral vocation when it is conflated with the vocation of all Christians to follow Jesus. Thus we have those who come to seminary not because they are called there to train to be pastors, but rather because they have received a call to be a more thoroughly committed Christian. Sadly, the church often does such a poor job of fostering the ministry of all Christians that there is nowhere to take a sense of vocation except to seminary. This is a judgment upon a church that seems not to know what to do with those who desire more faithful commitment to their baptism."

[53] Edmund P. Clowney, *Called to the Ministry* (Downers Grove, Ill.: InterVarsity Press, 1964), 4.

[54] Ben Patterson, *Is Ministry a Career? The Leadership Handbook of Management and Administration*, ed. James D. Berkley (Grand Rapids, Mich.: Baker Books with Christianity Today, 2000), 20–21.

The thing is to understand myself, to see what God really wants me to do; the thing is to find a truth which is true for me, to find the idea for which I can live and die.
—**Søren Kierkegaard**

For the secret of man's being is not only to live . . . but to live for something definite. Without a firm notion of what he is living for, man will not accept life and will rather destroy himself than remain on earth.
—**Fyodor Dostoevsky**

living into who you are

Everywhere Christian leaders... have become increasingly aware of the need for more specific training and formation. This need is realistic, and the desire for more professionalism in the ministry is understandable. But the danger is that instead of becoming free to let the spirit grow, the future minister may entangle himself in the complications of his own assumed competence and use his specialism as an excuse to avoid the much more difficult task of being compassionate ...; the danger is that his skillful diagnostic eye will become more like an eye for distant and detailed analysis than the eye of a compassionate partner ... More training and structure are just as necessary as more bread for the hungry. But just as bread given without love can bring war instead of peace, professionalism without compassion will turn forgiveness into a gimmick, and the kingdom to come into a blindfold.

—*Henri Nouwen,* The Wounded Healer *(New York: Image Books, 1979), 42.*

A *vocation* or *calling* is different (see Table 3-4). Derived from the Latin word *vocaré*,[55] it points neither to a map, nor a guidebook, but to the Guide himself. The emphasis here is not on following a course, but on responding to a voice—no schedule, no itinerary, no well-laid plans. As Patterson puts it, "The organ of faith is the ear, not the eye."[56] This is walking by faith and not by sight (2 Cor. 5:7). The whole enterprise depends on listening. From beginning to end, the key is maintaining an open, intimate relationship with the One who speaks (John 6:28–29)[57]. Guinness defines calling as "the truth that God calls us to himself so decisively that everything we are, everything we do, and everything we have is invested with a special

---

[55] Frederick Buechner, *Wishful Thinking: A Theological ABC* (New York: Harper and Row, 1973), 95.

[56] Patterson, *Is Ministry a Career?*, 21.

[57] Jonathan Grenz's research suggests that sometimes a posture of listening requires us to refine and reconfigure our calling before we find an opportunity that provides the best fit for our gifts. Although his research shows that the oft-quoted and never substantiated statistic about most youth ministers changing jobs every 18 months is false, he points out that one of the reasons emerging leaders seem more mobile during their twenties is because they are seeking to discover the best place to invest their gifts. Jonathan Grenz, "Factors Influencing Vocational Changes Among Youth Ministers," *Journal of Youth Ministry*, 1, no. 1 (Fall 2002): 73ff.

distinction by noting the difference between being called and being driven.[59] He notes that driven people are usually gratified only by the sense of accomplishment. Arrival is everything. You are what you do. The journey is not so much an opportunity for adventure as it is a requirement for advance. Of course, what makes this such a seductive danger is that by looking at ministry as a career, we gain a sense of professional identity. It helps us feel a little better about majoring in a field such as Youth Ministry, or planning to be something such as a Youth Pastor. Hansen explains it this way:

> It is easier to serve God without a vision, easier to work for God without a call, because then you are not bothered by what God requires; common sense is your guide, veneered over with Christian sentiment. You will be more prosperous and successful, more leisure-hearted, if you never realize the call of God. But if once you receive a commission from Jesus Christ, the memory of what God wants will always come like a goad; you will no longer be able to work for Him on the common-sense basis.
>
> —*Oswald Chambers*, My Utmost for His Highest *(Grand Rapids, Mich.: Discovery House Publishers, 1935), 64.*

> A surgeon is a person trained and authorized to perform surgery. A teacher is a person trained and authorized to teach school. A pastor is a person trained and authorized to carry out pastoral tasks. As a professional, I am a person with expertise. Experts have esoteric knowledge with powers to accomplish tasks. Such knowledge makes us valuable to society. It separates me from those around me. I become "distinguished."
>
> My ego loves the distance created by esoteric knowledge; it is the power of the witch doctor. But in the end the tragic distance created is within my own soul. When I move from being the lover of the soul to an expert on the soul, I objectify my own soul from myself. In the end my ego is warped; it goes on a rampage, climbing ladders to assert itself."[60]

That is why Marva Dawn and Eugene Peterson, in their book, *The Unnecessary Pastor*, warn of the powerful cultural forces determined to turn us, pastors, youth pastors, and leaders, "into kindly religious figures, men and women who provide guidance through difficult times, who dole out inspiration and good cheer on a weekly schedule, who provide smiling reassurance that 'God's in his heaven,'" all the while helping the youth follow Jesus just closely enough that they stay away from drugs and premarital sex, but not so closely that it actually affects their career choices, their grade average, or their free time.

[58]Guinness, *The Call*, 4.

[59]Gordon MacDonald, *Ordering Your Private World* (Nashville, Tenn.: Oliver-Nelson, 1984), 32–42, 55–62.

[60]David Hansen, *The Art of Pastoring* (Downers Grove, Ill.: InterVarsity Press, 1994), 20.

Table 3-4.
The Difference Between Career and Calling

Career	Calling (Vocation)
Lends itself to formulas and blueprints.	Is linked only to a relationship.
Can be pursued with a certain amount of personal detachment (just keep moving forward and stay on track).	Demands our attention, because it is hinged on response.
Requires activity.	Requires stillness and solitude.
Demands professional credentials.	Believes professional credential may be helpful, but the key credential is an ability to hear and a willingness to respond to the voice of God.
Is defined by what we do.	Is defined by who we are (and whose we are).
Fosters a growing sense of independence and competence.	Fosters a growing sense of dependence and need.
Is marked by ownership. ("I've got to work for what's coming to me").	Is marked by stewardship. ("I've got to make good use of what's been given me.")
Sees the steps of the journey as less important than the destination.	Understands that the journey is where vocation is lived out.
Is preoccupied with symbols of accomplishment (titles, office size and location, positions on flow charts, special perks).	Is preoccupied with the One who accompanies us on the journey.
Justifies the means by pointing to the ends.	Understands that the means is the way God accomplishes his ends.
Is predictable.	Is unpredictable.
Is called to a task.	Is called to a Master.

from drugs and premarital sex, but not so closely that it actually affects their career choices, their grade average, or their free time.

> And if they don't turn us into merely nice people, they turn us into replicas of our cultural leaders, seeking after power and influence and prestige. These insistent voices drum away at us, telling us pastors to go out and compete against the successful executives and entertainers who have made it to the top, so that we can put our churches on the map and make it big in the world.[61]

Little wonder that John Piper prays, "God deliver us from the professionalizers."[62] How can we at the same time be "child-like" and professional? How do we professionally "take up the cross"? How can we professionally be "fools for Christ's sake" (1 Cor. 4:10)? How can we be professionally "compelled by the love of Christ" (2 Cor. 5:14)?

Yet, while we must be on our guard against careerism and professionalism, there is a sense in which we *are* called to be *professionals*. The word, in fact, is born

[61] Dawn and Peterson, *The Unnecessary Pastor*, 1.
[62] Patterson, *Is Ministry a Career*, 20.

How may a young man know whether he is called or not? That is a weighty enquiry and I desire to treat it most solemnly. Oh for divine guidance in so doing! That hundreds have missed their way and stumbled against a pulpit is sorrowfully evident from the fruitless ministries and decaying churches which surround us. It is a fearful calamity to a man to miss his calling, and to the church upon whom he imposes himself. His mistake involves an affliction of the most grievous kind.

—*Charles Spurgeon,* Lectures to My Students *(Grand Rapids, Mich.: Zondervan, 1954), 25–34.*

I would have given the church my head, my heart, and my hand. She would not have them. She told me to go back to do crochet in my mother's drawing room; or marry and look well at the head of my husband's table.
—**Nineteenth-century missionary pioneer Florence Nightingale, who worked among the wounded in the Crimean War.**

out of the Latin *professaro* which means promise. That is why Peterson wants to emphasize the difference between a "job" and a "profession" (see chapter 2).[63] Those who do a job do only what is required of them by their employer. In other words, their commitment is to completing a task, and nothing more. For the professional, there is a reality, a value that is bigger than the task itself, and it is that greater value that is the motivator.

As a college professor, for example, my least favorite part of the job is grading. Not only is it difficult when it is done well; but it is a thankless task. If a student gets a good grade, she does not thank me for it (nor should she), because she feels she has earned it. But if the student gets a bad grade, well, of course, it is very much my fault.

Why did you give me an "F"?

Uh . . . well . . . because the school doesn't allow me to give "G's."

[63] Eugene Peterson, *Working the Angels* (Grand Rapids, Mich.: Eerdmans, 1987), 7

Until one is committed there is hesitancy, the chance to draw back, always ineffectiveness. Concerning all acts of initiative (and creation) there is one elementary truth, the ignorance of which kills countless ideas and splendid plans: that the moment one definitely commits oneself, then Providence moves, too. All sorts of things occur to help one that would never otherwise have occurred. A whole stream of events issues from the decision, raising in one's favor all manner of unforeseen incidents and meetings and material assistance, which no man could have dreamt would have come his way.
—**W. H. Murray**

Nevertheless, I take great pains in the grading process because I have made important promises: to my students, that I will give them my best effort, even if they do not want it; to my school, that I will be conscientious in the execution of my duties; to the Lord, that I will do my work as a professor not so that people can make good grades, but so that I can help people make better disciples. I could, no doubt, do the job of grading in a less conscientious way, giving everyone high marks, and it might garner higher student evaluations. But I cannot do that, because I have made a promise; I am a professional.

Youth ministry is crammed with just such decisions, and there is always the temptation to play to the crowd, the parents, the students, the elders, the culture, our youth ministry peers. We may well be lauded for the job we have accomplished. But to walk that course is to forsake our calling to a pursue a career. It is a vital distinction.

In fact, it was precisely this distinction that almost led Moses to forsake his calling. When God spoke to him in Exodus 3 from the burning bush, Moses responded as if this God were interviewing him about a career choice: he had been employed as a sheep-farmer; how would he like to consider moving into delivery work? Moses asked reasonable questions: Did God suppose he was really qualified for this kind of work? Did God really feel he had the proper experience, the right skills for such a task? Did God not know that he was a poor public speaker? Who was he supposed to tell people had sent him? What if the people did not follow him? What if they just thought he was some yahoo from the sticks, come to the big city with his hot rod? These were all reasonable questions if the issue were career choices.

Perhaps you have even heard yourself pose these same questions with regard to a possible call from God. That is why it is so important to recognize that becoming a youth pastor is not a career choice, it is a vocational response to the same Lord who told his disciples in John 15:16: "You did not choose me, but I chose you and appointed you to go and bear fruit—fruit that will last. Then the Father will give you whatever you ask in my name."

Beginning in the Heartland

When Sir Ernest Shackleton set out to find a crew for what turned out to be his ill-fated voyage to Antarctica back in 1915, he placed an ad in the *Times of London* which read: "Men wanted for hazardous journey. Small wages. Bitter cold. Long months of complete darkness. Constant danger. Safe return doubtful. Honor and recognition in case of success. Ernest Shackleton."[64] Amazingly, more than 5,000 men applied.

> The Road goes ever on and on
> Down from the door where it began.
> Now far ahead the Road has gone,
> And I must follow, if I can,
> Pursuing it with weary feet,
> Until it joins some larger way,
> Where many paths and errands meet.
> And whither then? I cannot say.
>
> —*J. R. R. Tolkien's character Frodo, from* The Fellowship of the Ring *(Boston: Houghton Mifflin, 1965), 82–83.*

A call to youth ministry can be no less daunting, and no less exhilarating, than Shackleton's ad placed almost a century ago—an invitation to adventures, risks, discoveries, and wonders untold. But how do we know if we are called to ministry in the special way that sets us apart as servants of the servants? Who would want to face the hazards, the times of darkness, the small wages, the dangers, the occasional seasons of bitter cold without a fairly certain sense that this is the will of God? How do we discern God's calling?

First and foremost, we must understand that the call of God moves from the inside out. It is an adventure that begins in the heartland.

The great theologian, H. Richard Niebuhr, talked about four different calls that come to the one who is set apart for pastoral ministry: (1) the call to be a Christian, (2) the secret call, (3) the providential call, and (4) the ecclesiastical call.[65] Let us look at each phase of the call more closely.

---

[64] "Shackleton's Voyage of Endurance," NOVA #2906 broadcast transcript, PBS Air date: March 26, 2002. Although this famous want ad is widely quoted, there is doubt as to whether it ever actually appeared in the Times. Morrell and Capparell point out that no copy of the ad has ever been found and that it "probably was the invention of someone amused by the long lines of men applying for such a horrific assignment." Margot Morell and Stephanie Capparell, *Shackleton's Way: Leadership Lessons from the Great Antarctic Explorer*, (New York: Penguin Books, 2001), 55.

[65] H. Richard Niebuhr, in collaboration with Daniel Day Williams and James F. Gustafson, *The Purpose of the Church and Its Ministry: Reflections on the Aims of Theological Education* (New York: Harper and Brothers, 1956), 46. The great expositor W. H. Griffith Thomas, early in the last century, suggested Isaiah's call (Isa. 6:1–11) as a prototype of how God forges one's sense of vocation: (1) A consciousness of God followed by a conviction of sin (vv. 1–5); (2) Confession of sin followed by cleansing from sin (vv. 5–7); (3) The call of God followed by consecration to God (v. 8); and (4) The commission of God followed by communion with God (vv. 9–11). W. H. Griffith Thomas, *The Work of the Ministry* (London: Hodder and Stoughton, c. 1910), 4–5.

The Leadership Style of Jesus

By Ajith Fernando, National Director, Youth for Christ, Sri Lanka

The first chapter of Mark gives a crisp and comprehensive picture of what Jesus's style of leadership was like. There are five major aspects of his leadership style.

Identifying with the People You Serve

Jesus's first public act was his baptism by John (v. 9), an act which was not necessary for him, but to which he subjected himself so that he could identify with the people he came to serve. He was the Lord of creation who took upon himself the form of a bondservant (Phil. 2:6-8). As part of his identification with his disciples he spent time in the home of Peter (vv. 29-31). He also visited homes of unbelievers and new believers. Because the home is the most important place in most people's lives, visiting homes is a great means of identifying with people. He walked at least 20 miles to the funeral of the brother of two of his female disciples and identified so much with their sorrow that, even though he was going to raise Lazarus from the dead, he wept (John 11:35).

When Jesus went to Peter's home he saw Peter's mother-in-law sick and healed her (vv. 30-31). Later he broke with custom to touch an "untouchable" leper when healing him (v. 41). Meeting needs was a key part of his ministry (vv. 23-35). When we identify with people, we see needs and adjust our ministry to meet those needs. Sometimes we do things we never dreamed we would do. As their servants (2 Cor. 4:5) our focus is on their needs and not our preferences.

I find that the older I get the harder I have to work at my talks to teenagers. I need to know what their questions are and see how we can give biblical answers to them. This takes a lot of time, and even though I have been speaking to youth for about 36 years, I am still quite nervous before I speak (much to the amusement of my younger colleagues). If we are to be good servants of youth, we will need to work hard at identifying with them, devoting for them what others may consider a waste of time and resources.

Getting Priorities Straight

Before Jesus started his public ministry we find that he got many priorities straightened out. The Spirit anointed him for his work (v. 10), and God affirmed him about his personal identity and call (v. 11). Then Jesus retreated into the wilderness to fast and pray, and to be tempted by Satan about the priority of being committed to God's will over all other attractions (vv. 12-13). After an extremely busy and exhausting Sabbath day, Jesus rose up early in the morning and went to a quiet place to pray (v. 35). Later we read many references to his spending time alone in prayer.

If Jesus needed to consciously concentrate on the priorities of his relationship with God and his will, how much more should we? Youth workers can get their primary identity and fulfillment from busy activity and from the people they minister to. Some often work themselves into spiritual deadness and burnout by not replenishing their spiritual lives. Some cling to their youth so closely that they cannot release them when they need to. Some concentrate more on the tie that the youth have with the youth program and the youth worker than they have with God and his Word, and in so doing fail to prepare them adequately to live for God in the world.

Three years ago, when I turned 50, I made a list of the biggest battles I have in life, and first on that list was finding adequate time to pray. Last year I celebrated 25 years in Youth for Christ and was asked to write an article for our prayer bulletin. I wrote about what I felt was the most important thing I have done as a youth worker. I said I did not think I did enough of it, but the little I did was the most important thing I did. I was talking about prayer. We must put first things first if we are to have effective long-term ministries.

Relying on Scriptures

All three answers that Jesus gave during his temptations came directly from the Scriptures. This signaled a pattern that he followed in his ministry. The New Testament records Jesus citing the Old Testament at least 90 times. While we need to be relevant to the needs of youth, our entire ministry must spring from the Scriptures. This is a discipline that demands hard work because youth workers could be satisfied by attracting crowds through relevant programs and fail to adequately equip youth with biblical principles to live healthy Christian lives in society.

Believing in Your Message

Mark summarizes the message Jesus preached as, "The time has come. The kingdom of God is near. Repent and believe the good news!" (v. 15). Jesus had a clear conviction that his was the message that the people had been eagerly waiting for. It was a message of such importance that it called for the radical response of repentance and faith.

However uninterested in or hostile to the gospel people may be, we go to them with the confidence that the gospel answers their aspirations, and that it is so important they are eternally lost without it. This confidence drives us to discover their felt needs and seek ways to communicate this message so that they would respond by giving their lives to Christ. If not for this conviction I would have despaired in our work of reaching youth from other faiths and gone to something easier. We face so much opposition! There is so much pain when parents find out that their children have given up the family religion. Of course, this means that we must work with the parents too. But the knowledge that this message is the most important news they can hear eliminates the option of giving up this work.

Ministering to Your Team Members

Right at the start of his public ministry Jesus selected a few disciples (vv. 16-20). The group expanded to a team of 12, and he spent his entire ministry in companionship with them. One of the most significant aspects of his work in the Gospels was being with and ministering to the Twelve and equipping them for ministry (Mark 3:14-15). Jesus taught them, went to their homes, washed their feet (John 13:5), prepared their meals (John 21:9-13), and prayed for them (John 17:6-26). Before leaving this world he fired them with a vision of the work they were to do by giving them his great commission at least seven times, each time focusing on a different aspect of it.

Similarly we too will encounter a few keen people who will become our primary ministry team. We will open up our lives to them and do our ministry through them. One of the most important tasks of leaders is to be servants of the teams they lead. However busy we are with public programs and urgent tasks, ministering to the team is one thing we cannot neglect. I see the tasks of praying for the teams I lead, spending relaxed time with them, and ministering to them as one of the most important features of my job description. Keeping this group united is a key priority (John 17:11) and, in my case, has been the most absorbing challenge that I have faced in ministry (Eph. 4:3).

The key to remedying the problem of lack of commitment in the church is for leaders to be committed to their people. The example of Jesus in giving his life for his friends was going to motivate these friends to give their lives for each other (John 15:12-13). Similarly when leaders show costly commitment to their people, the people will pay the price of commitment to the group to which they belong. We must not forget that in a majority of the times when the New Testament presents Jesus as an example to follow, he is also presented as an example of suffering.

Essentially, then, Jesus was sent by God with an urgent message to proclaim. He lived in communion with God while identifying with people, worked through a team, and adopted a lifestyle of costly servant-hood in his relationships with others. We may get other helpful principles of leadership from the corporate world, but these principles that our Lord exemplified remain the basic principles of Christian leadership.

For Further Study

Coleman, Robert E. *The Master Plan of Evangelism*. (Grand Rapids, Mich.: Fleming H. Revell, 1993).

Coleman, Robert E. *The Mind of the Master*. (Wheaton, Ill.: Harold Shaw, 2000).

Nouwen, Henri J. M. *In the Name of Jesus: Reflections on Christian Leadership*. (New York: Crossroad Publishing, 1993).

Hang on, God: Super–Us to the Rescue!

Probably the hardest thought of all for our natural egotism to entertain is that God does not need our help. We commonly represent him as a busy, eager, somewhat frustrated father hurrying about seeking help to carry out his benevolent plan to bring peace and salvation to the world . . . The God who worketh all things surely needs no help and no helpers.

Too many missionary appeals are based upon this fancied frustration of Almighty God. An effective speaker can easily excite pity in his hearers not only for the heathen but for the God who has tried so hard and so long to save them and has failed for want of support. I fear that thousands of young persons enter Christian service from no higher motive than to help deliver God from the embarrassing situation his love has gotten him into and his limited abilities seem unable to get him out of. Add to this a certain degree of commendable idealism and a fair amount of compassion for the underprivileged and you have the true drive behind much Christian activity today.

Again, God needs no defenders. He is the Eternal Undefended.

—*A. W. Tozer,* Knowledge of the Holy *(San Francisco: Harper, 1961), 41.*

The Call to Be a Christian

The call to be a Christian is a call to all people, though not all respond. It is the call to repentance and belief. It is fundamental and foundational. To respond to any other call from God without first responding to this call would be like a fireman charging into a burning building without any water or any gear. It is an attempt to give away what one does not possess.

Jesus told his disciples, "I am the Vine, you are the branches. When you're joined with me and I with you, the relation intimate and organic, the harvest is sure to be abundant. Separated, you can't produce a thing" (John 15:5, *The Message*). It is significant in Mark 3:14 that Jesus "appointed twelve—designating them apostles—that they might be with him and that he might send them out to preach." Note the order: first, "that they might be with him," and then, second, "that he might send them out." Oswald Chambers observes: "So many are devoted to causes and so few are devoted to Jesus Christ . . . If I am devoted to the cause of humanity only, I will soon be exhausted and come to the place where my love will falter; but if I can love Jesus personally and passionately, I can serve humanity though men treat me as a doormat. The secret of a disciple's life is devotion to Jesus Christ . . ."[66]

[66] Oswald Chambers, *My Utmost for His Highest* (Uhrichsville, Ohio: Barbour and Co, 1935), 171.

The Secret Call

Ben Patterson writes, "There is always a sense of compulsion, at times even a sense of violence, about God's call."[67] Jeremiah described it "like a burning fire shut up in my bones. I am weary of holding it in; indeed, I cannot" (Jer. 20:9). The Apostle Paul avowed, "Woe to me if I do not preach the gospel" (1 Cor. 9:16). These are those deep inner nudges of God's secret call to ministry.

Sometimes it cajoles us; sometimes it prods us; sometimes it reassures us; sometimes it pesters us. But it is an intangible, inexplicable sense that God is calling us into pastoral work and a growing sense of holy discontent with anything other than the pastoral vocation. Indeed, Charles Spurgeon, who saw this divine constraint as an important sign of a pastoral calling, encouraged his students *not* to pursue pastoral ministry if they felt they could be content doing anything else.[68]

In sensing this inner call, we need to begin to seek clarity and confirmation. If the inner nudge is only sporadic or occasional, we must not be too hasty in moving forward. The key is to be attentive and wait for stronger, more consistent prodding.

If it is a persistent—dare I say nagging?—sense, take the next logical baby step of obedience and be alert to where that leads you. Don't wait for the road map; start moving and let God lead.

As God explained to Moses, sometimes the confirmation of your call will only come *as you are obedient* to that call—not before you obey, but as you obey. In response to Moses's reluctant

No pay, no prospects, not much pleasure.
—**H.W. Tilman, from an ad placed in the London *Times*, encouraging climbers to join him on long sailboat journeys to far-off peaks.**

In order to climb properly on a big peak one must free oneself of fear. This means you must write yourself off before any big climb. You must say to yourself, "I may die here."
—**Doug Scott, world-class rock climber**

[67] Patterson, *Is Ministry a Career?*, 20–21.
[68] Ibid.

balking, "God said, 'I will be with you. *And this will be the sign to you that it is I who have sent you: When you have brought the people out of Egypt, you will worship God on this mountain*' [emphasis added]" (Exod. 3:12). The sign he was sent came as he went. Just as it is easier to steer a moving vehicle than a parked one, guidance comes more often to the one on his feet than the one on his seat! Waiting on the Lord is fine; but do not make him wait on you.

This phase of the call should also be marked by cautious, honest self-examination:

Are there obvious blockages or irreversible encumbrances? Is there severe physical incapacity or bodily limitation?

Be honest in asking yourself: Is my intellectual ability up to it? Can I . . . think critically? Speak intelligibly? Identify a leap in logic? No one can answer these questions for another. They must be answered candidly. It is God who does the calling, it is God who is listening.

The simplest questions one asks himself inwardly are often the toughest: Have I learned to pray? Have the means of grace (worship, sacraments, Scripture) begun to be deeply ingrained in my lifestyle? If unsure, one had best let these seeds grow, and ask this question about call to ministry later.[69]

One of the biggest misconceptions in sorting out this secret, inner sense of call is that God would never call us to do something that gives us great pleasure. There is an attitude: "God couldn't be leading me to do this because I like it too much." Not only does such a notion betray the goodness of God, it also betrays his wisdom. Sure there are calls to sacrifice, and certainly there are times when we must do in obedience what we do not want to do. But why would God not create us with a desire to do what he calls us to do?

In a sense, that is what makes vocation such a place of freedom. Thomas Merton saw this clearly:

A man [or woman] knows when he [or she] has found his [or her] vocation when he [or she] stops thinking about how to live and begins to live . . . When we are not living up to our true vocation, thought deadens our life or substitutes itself for life, or gives in to life so that our life drowns out our thinking and stifles the voice of conscience. When we find our vocation—thought and life are one.[70]

In commenting that much of his music is autobiographical, musician James Taylor once told an interviewer, "I have a unique job because I am myself for a living." It was an interesting observation. In truth, it could honestly be said about anyone pursuing a God-given vocation, because we are never more truly ourselves than when we are who God made us to be. It is this truth that led Buechner to

---

[69] Oden, *Pastoral Theology*, 18.

[70] Thomas Merton, *Thoughts in Solitude* (Garden City, N.Y.: Image Books, 1958), 85.

world's deep hunger meet."[71] This is not, "You are what you do;" this is "You do what you are"[72]

A second misconception, perhaps less critical, is that there is only one way to respond to a youth ministry calling, and that is to serve as a traditional local church youth pastor. The great news about youth ministry is that it is a field with an ever-expanding range of varied opportunities: curriculum design, publishing, drama, music ministry, sports ministry, street ministry, stage production, graphic design, software design, parachurch ministry, counseling ministry, prison ministry, camping ministry, and backpacking ministry.[73] Biblically, it would be difficult to characterize all of these types of ministries as pastoral work. But that does not make them any less legitimate as a place to invest one's gifts, and it certainly does not preclude the possibility of fruitful, fulfilling ministry in one of these related fields.[74]

> ## Am I Worthy?
>
> Saints are not extraordinary …"I knew nothing; I was nothing," one saint said about herself. "For this reason God picked me out."
>
> The world does not have many geniuses, but it can have many saints, for the life of a saint is open to all, even geniuses. What is required for a genius to become a saint is the same thing that is required of everyone, yielding to God. What matters is what God does with the capacities that people give over to God's use.
>
> —E. Glenn Hinson, Spiritual Preparation for Christian Leadership (Nashville, Tenn.: Upper Room Books, 1999), 184.

The Providential Call

This is that dimension of vocation based on the combination of circumstances, experiences, talents, and aptitudes. Rooted in the doctrine of God's sovereignty, and his providential rule in human affairs, this portion of God's call recognizes

---

[71] Buechner, Wishful Thinking, 95.

[72] Guinness, The Call, 46.

[73] For a taste of the wide buffet of options, go the Youth Specialties Web site and surf through some of the links at www.youthspecialties.com.

[74] Robert Cox observes, "A Joint Report in 1981 found that among every ten ministers of the Word and Sacrament in the Presbyterian Church (U.S.A.) there are approximately three who are engaged in what frequently are called specialized ministries. This same report says that 'at least fifty percent of all ordained ministers will serve in some form of specialized ministry prior to retirement' (p. N-47). If you're headed for the ordained ministry, you very well might be engaged in a specialized ministry at some point or even throughout your career. This is even more true if you happen to be female, since proportionately more women serve in specialized ministry." Robert Cox, Do You Mean Me, Lord? (Philadelphia: Westminster Press, 1985), 89.

A recent study by Auburn Theological Seminary in New York found that fewer than a third of entering seminary students intend to minister in congregations. One factor in their reluctance is that they often see the church as "a group of people speaking mostly to themselves—too isolated from their community and too concerned with their own institutional viability or growth." Andrew Black explains, "Many young Christians who display the spiritual and personal gifts normally associated with ministry—compassion, creativity, intellect and leadership—talk instead about how to best use those gifts for God's sake, the sake of the church, and their own integrity . . . Some lament that they must choose between the role of the missionary who leads others in mission to the world and the pastor who shepherds the flock of the saved." Andrew Black, "The Pastor Gap," available from www.Faithworks.com. Greg Warner adds that job insecurity is leaving some would-be pastors wary of working in the church. He notes that there is, if anything, an increasing number of folks interested in going into the ministry, "but that interest is focusing on parachurch organizations, social ministries, or other alternatives." Greg Warner, "Job Insecurity Leaves Young Ministers Wary," available from www.Faithworks.com.

and his providential rule in human affairs, this portion of God's call recognizes that God never calls us to do what he has not prepared us to do (see I Thes. 5:24). What makes this a little scary is that we cannot really appreciate the genius of God's providence until long after we have responded to his call. It is a bit like rewinding a video of a great mystery. When we saw it through the first time, it was tense and exciting because we did not know how the story would unfold. Now, as we watch it backwards, having seen how the plot played out, we can see all the pieces fall into place. What was not visible through the windshield is clearer in the rearview mirror.[75]

Having said this, there are these cautions to be made for this phase of the call:

1. **A providential call should not be weighed solely in the light of common sense.** God is not limited by our abilities, our inabilities or our circumstances. Scripture is filled with God doing the improbable through the unlikely.

   That being true, it is still reasonable to consider both abilities and circumstances in assessing one's calling. If, for example, someone is four feet tall, it would not take a whole night of prayer to discern that maybe God is not calling them to the NBA, except perhaps as an usher at the arena. If it is obvious that a person cannot carry a tune in a frying pan, God is probably not leading that person into a ministry of vocal performance. As Guinness reminds us, "God normally calls us along the lines of our giftedness, but the purpose of giftedness is stewardship and service, not selfishness."[76] It is a simple and reasonable question: Has God given me gifts, talents, experiences, aptitude, and temperament for ministry?

   If the pieces of the puzzle are not forming the picture we hoped for or expected, maybe we are looking at the picture on the wrong box, or maybe God will work outside the box. Common sense would have left David with the sheep, Peter with the fish, Billy Graham on the farm, and Amy Carmichael with her mother in Ireland. Common sense should not be silenced, but neither should it always have the last word.

2. **A providential call should not be assessed on the basis of stereotypes.** Aspiring youth workers often appraise their suitability for ministry by the standard of a stereotypical youth ministry personality: wild and crazy, gregarious and funny—we all know the type. In fact, there is no standard personality profile for the perfect youth minister. As Douglas Steere

---

[75] I see this at work very clearly in my own life as I look back at different experiences I had growing up, jobs I had, opportunities I was given, relationships I shared. A family where laughter was a consistent part of life, some key adult influences inside and outside of the faith, a four-year stint in broadcast journalism, playing in a rock-and-roll band, extensive travel, a kindergarten teacher mom whose love for creativity made learning fun—all of these are bits and pieces that, at the time, probably looked like fragments of colored glass. Now, I look back and see that each of these pieces had its place in the mosaic that is now my vocation.

[76] Guinness, *The Call*, 46.

points out, God uses all sorts of personalities in ministry:

A vacillating Peter; a mystically minded John; an authoritarian Jewish law-giver, Paul; strong, passionate, willful dispositions like those of Tertullian, Augustine, and Pascal; eclectic, balanced, rational natures like Clement of Alexandria, and Origen, Aquinas and Erasmus; poets . . . like Francis of Assisi and Jacopone da Todi, Henry Suso, Thomas Traherne and Francis Thompson; difficult personalities with naturally fragile and often disrupted psycho-physical dispositions, such as those of Catherine of Genoa, Teresa of Avila, or Søren Kierkegaard; a mother of many children and an eminently practical administrator like Bridget of Sweden; a German cobbler, Boehme; an English leatherworker, Fox; a New Jersey tailor, Woolman; an illiterate French peasant who could not pass his theological examinations and was so particularly deficient in moral theology that it was thought wise for years not to trust him to hear confessions, the Curé of Ars.[77]

The Ordination Ceremony

From Hippolytus's account of the ordination of a bishop in third-century Rome, we can detect a pattern for ordination rites that continues in the Western Church even up until today:

(1) The entire community and its presbyters choose the bishop.

(2) The candidate must respond in free will.

(3) The local congregation tests the faith of the person to be sure that his faith is apostolic.

(4) Episcopal laying on of hands with a prayer for the Holy Spirit shows that, though the community chooses, this is not solely a congregational choice.

(5) The new ministry is interpreted as a gift of the Holy Spirit, because of the choice of the community.

—*William Willimon,* Pastor: The Theology and Practice of Ordained Ministry *(Nashville, Tenn.: Abingdon, 2002), 20, 32.*

In addition to this fact, we should also be reminded that God is not limited by our self-evaluations of gifts, personality, or aptitude (see Exod. 3:4, Jer. 1:6–8). John Calvin described himself as "somewhat

---

[77] Douglas V. Steere, *On Beginning from Within* (New York: Harper Brothers, 1943), 43. Many readers may not be familiar with this last figure, but his academic struggles may give some of you needed encouragement.

unpolished and bashful, which led [him] always to love the shade and retirement." Although he confessed to preferring a work in "some secluded corner where [he] might be withdrawn from the public view," God put him in a place of very public ministry.[78] As Charles Keating noted, "Our basic personality is a starting point, not a jail."[79]

In fact, one of the advantages of the introverted personality is that it does not *need* people the way the extroverted personality does. Sometimes people go into ministry not because they have a love for people, but because they have a love for the *experience* of people. While a love for the experience of people can be quite beneficial in ministry, it is not essential ("I just get energized by potluck dinners, contact work, and sharing cabins and bathrooms on retreats"). Love for people is. One is a love that is played out in quiet conversations, sometimes painful, sometimes difficult. The other is a love that is played out front and center—in the front of the room, in the center of attention. There are obvious pitfalls for the youth worker who loves only the experience of people.[80]

3. Remember that God is a Redeemer; he does not waste any facet of one's life and experience. That means he can use both our strengths and our weaknesses, our victories and our defeats, our trophies and our scars. When God called Moses, he made it vivid: one man's snake on the ground is another man's rod in the hand (see Exod. 4:2–4). God can take our mistakes and mishaps and use them as the staff by which we lead trapped people out of the bondage of sin and into the promise of God. What may appear to us to be the jagged shards of bad decisions and deep regrets can be in the hands of God centerpieces of his vocational mosaic. Such is the wonder of God's providence.

The Ecclesiastical Call

In an affirmation of the secret call (internal) and recognition of the providential call (circumstantial), this ecclesiastical call is a confirmation by the Christian community that the call to pastoral ministry is genuine and recognized by the church. An extremely important phase of the call, this is by no means a rubber stamp.[81] Indeed, Socrates Scholasticus, in his *Ecclesiastical History*, describes the lament of Marcion, a bishop, whose regret in wrongly promoting a man named

---

[78] John Calvin, *Preface to Psalms*, in *Selected Works*, 26–28. In an article in the *Johns Hopkins Magazine*, psychologist Robert Hogan suggests that the key components of "the leadership personality" are anxiety, self-esteem, prudence, ambition, and likeability. Responding to this list, in which at least two of the elements are, at best, only marginally Christian virtues, Neil Hightower comments, "We must make sure our ambitions are entirely sanctified and subject to the control and direction of the Holy Spirit. In fact, each quality will be subject to the parameters of holy discipline described in the Word of God and established internally by the unfolding ministry of the indwelling Spirit of God." Neil Hightower, "Is There a Leadership Personality?" *Preacher's Magazine* (September/November 1983), 42–43.

[79] Charles J. Keating, *Who We Are Is How We Pray: Matching Personality and Spirituality* (Mystic, Conn.: Twenty-Third Publications, 1987), 118.

[80] Hansen, *The Art of Pastoring*, 36.

[81] "Some are enlisted in the ranks of the clergy to prevent their siding with the enemy, and others because of their bad character, to stop them causing a lot of trouble if they are overlooked! . . . They not merely choose the unworthy; they reject those who are suitable . . . For I think it is as bad to keep out the capable as to bring in the useless." John Chrysostom, *On the Priesthood*, cited in Oden, *Pastoral Theology*, 106.

Sabbatius to the role of presbyter was so acute that he commented "that it had been better for him to have laid his hands on thorns, than to have imposed them on Sabbatius."[82] The ecclesiastical call is a solemn responsibility for the church, and a critical affirmation for the called person.

The following are some of the criteria that the church has used down through history to evaluate the authenticity of an individual's call.[83]

Age. Traditionally, the candidate would have reached *canonical age* which for presbyters was fixed by the Council of Neocaeserea (314 A.D.) as 30 years. In later years, some portions of the church reduced the age to 25, and in some traditions the canonical age was as low as 21. The contemporary church tends not to use age as a criteria, basing this part of the assessment more on educational experience.[84]

Inner Sense of Calling. Candidates would have to be convinced that ordained ministry was the best way for them to respond to God's inner voice.

Demonstrated Gifts for Ministry. The church must consider whether the candidate has the gifts necessary for ministry of the Word. As well as gifts of preaching, teaching, evangelism, or counseling, the examining elders would also consider the candidate's people skills, emotional maturity, compassion, ability to work with a team, and a general respect for other people.

The Candidate Should Be in Good Health. Because of the demands of ministry and leadership, the church has traditionally

Climb if you will, but remember that courage and strength are nothing without prudence, and that a momentary negligence may destroy the happiness of a lifetime.
—**Edward Whymper, after his rope broke on the Matterhorn**

To have a great adventure, and survive, requires good judgment. Good judgment comes from experience. Experience, of course, is the result of poor judgment.
—**Geoff Tabin, mountaineering guide and climbing expert**

---

[82] Socrates Scholasticus, cited in Oden, *Pastoral Theology*, 103–104.

[83] Oden, *Pastoral Theology*, 22, based on conclusions of the Church Councils of Ephesus (A.D. 431) and Trullo (A.D. 692).

[84] Kierkegaard adds a good note of admonition when he warns that "would-be theologians . . . must be on their guard lest beginning too soon to preach they rather chatter themselves into Christianity than live themselves into it and find themselves at home there." Cited in Roper, *A Burden Shared*, 36.

limited ordination to those who are "reasonably free of disabling defects that would disproportionally encumber ministry."[85] We are a bit shocked (if not a little amused) by the comments of Charles Spurgeon, but his concern for physical fitness for ministry is consistent with church tradition:

> Application was received some short time ago from a young man who had a sort of rotary action of his jaw of the most painful sort to the beholder. His pastor commended him as a very holy young man, who had been the means of bringing some to Christ, and he expressed the hope that I would receive him, but I could not see the propriety of it. I could not have looked at him while preaching without laughter if all the gold of Tarshish had been my reward, and in all probability nine out of ten of his hearers would have been more sensitive than myself. A man with a big tongue which filled up his mouth and caused indistinctness, another without teeth, another who stammered, another who could not pronounce all the alphabet, I have had the pain of declining on the ground that God had not given them those physical appliances, which are as the prayer-book would put it, "generally necessary." [86]

Character. There was broad concern for the individual's character and reputation.

Doctrine. The candidate was to be examined for doctrinal knowledge, and for faithfulness to the teaching of Scripture. The church has an interest in vetting prospective pastors and youth pastors for their awareness of and faithfulness to biblical truth.

In a more abbreviated summary of the marks of pastoral calling, John Newton suggested three key elements in a genuine call to ministry:

▸ warm and earnest desire to be employed in God's service;

▸ the appearance of competence, sufficiency, knowledge—that is, apparent gifts for ministry;

▸ open doors of opportunity to do ministry—the assumption being that God will provide a place of service to those he calls to serve.[87]

What is absolutely clear in all of this is that neither Scripture nor tradition encourages lone individuals to simply declare themselves fit for ministry. In that sense, as Willimon points out, the call to ministry is *multivocal*. God calls *and the*

---

[85] Oden, *Pastoral Theology*, 23.

[86] Charles Spurgeon, *Lectures to My Students* (Grand Rapids, Mich.: Zondervan, 1954), 36–40.

[87] Ben Patterson, *Is Ministry a Career?*, 52–61. James George suggests the acrostic CALL as a summary of the four questions basic to the issue of calling: Confirmation (by the church), Abilities (gifts and skills for ministry), Longings (the sense of inner call), and Life (personal morality and character).

Pastors are often called *watchmen* (Ezek. 3:17), who used to stand on high towers, and were to give the alarm as they saw occasion for it. They were responsible for an attitude of constant attendance, watching in the night, as well as in the day. When this is applied to clergy, it suggests that they ought to be upon their watchtower observing what dangers their people are exposed to, either by their sins which provoke the judgments of God, or by the designs of their enemies. The watchman does no good if by a false sense of respect he allows the people to sleep and perish in their sins. He must be willing to enunciate the judgments of God to them, even if it incurs their displeasure by their freedom being imposed upon, rather than permit them to perish in their security.

St. Paul also calls churchmen by the name of *builders* and gives to the apostles the title of master-builders (1 Cor. 3:10). This implies both hard and painful labor, and great care and exactness in doing it. If the building lacks precision, it will be not only exposed to the injuries of weather, but will quickly tumble down. This suggests that those who carry this title ought to study well the great design by which they must carry on the interest of religion, that so they may build up their people in their most holy faith so as to be a building fitly framed together.

Clergy are also called *laborers* in God's *husbandry* (1 Cor. 3:9), laborers in his vineyard and harvest, who are to sow, plant, and water (Mt. 20:1, 9:37,38; 1 Cor. 3:6) and cultivate the soil of the church. This suggests a steady, continual return of daily and hard labor which is both painstaking and diligent.

—*Gilbert Burnet,* Discourse of the Pastoral Care *(Lewiston, N.Y.: Edwin Mellen Press, 1997), 29-32.*

church calls. It begins internally and is confirmed externally. It is not discerned in isolation.[88]

The means by which the church certifies this pastoral vocation is through the process and rite of *ordination.*

---

[88] "Churches are not all wise, neither do they all judge in the power of the Holy Ghost, but many of them judge after the flesh; yet I had sooner accept the opinion of a company of the Lord's people than my own upon so personal a subject as my own gifts and graces. At any rate, whether you value the verdict of the church or no, one thing is certain, that none of you can be pastors without the loving consent of the flock; and therefore this will be to you a practical indicator if not a correct one." Spurgeon, *Lectures to My Students,* 30.

Ordained or Ordinary: Does It Make a Difference?

The words *ordination* and *ordain* are never used in the New Testament. Rather, we see words like *chose* (Luke 6:13), *appointed* (Mark 3:14, Acts 14:23, I Cor. 12:28, Titus 1:5), *numbered* (Acts 1:26), and God *gave* (Eph. 4:11).[89] Yet some liturgical scholars are convinced that there are in the New Testament passages that suggest rites of ordination if only in embryonic form (Acts 6:3–8, 13:1–4; I Tim. 4:13; 2 Tim. 1:6).[90] Judging from 2 Timothy 1:6 and I Timothy 4:14, there was some sort of rite involved when people were called into ministry, and, apparently it involved the laying on of hands by one or more elders of the church.

> O Good Shepherd Jesus, good, gentle, tender Shepherd, behold a shepherd, poor and pitiful, a shepherd of your sheep indeed, but weak and clumsy and of little use, cries out to you. To you, I say, Good Shepherd, this shepherd, who is not good, makes his prayer. He cries to you, troubled upon his own account, and troubled for your sheep. For when in bitterness of soul I view my former life, it scares and frightens me that I should be called shepherd, for I am surely crazy if I do not know myself unworthy of the name.
>
> —Aelred of Rievaulx, The Pastoral Prayer, sec. 1–2, CFS 2, 105–106.

From those early roots, the church has come to see ordination as a way of saying something significant about people who are called to ministry leadership. Essentially, ordination is the way the church agrees:

▸ To *recognize* that a person has been called by God and gifted by his Spirit with gifts of leadership (I Cor. 12:28–31);

▸ To *set apart* this gifted person from normal responsibilities so that he or she can be focused on a particular work of ministry for which the church agrees that person is suited and to which the church agrees he or she is called;[91]

▸ To *empower* this person with responsibilities of leadership, discernment, and/or teaching. This is a solemn responsibility, not to be taken lightly, typically symbolized by the laying on of hands (see I Tim. 5:22);[92] and

---

[89] Darrell W. Johnson, *Ordination, The Leadership Handbook of Management and Administration*, ed. James D. Berkley (Grand Rapids, Mich.: Baker Books with Christianity Today, 2000), 18.

[90] Willimon notes these four passages suggested by Max Thurian. Willimon, *Pastor*, 341. The first full account of ordination rites for bishop, elder, and deacon come from a *Liturgy for the Ordination of Bishops* found in the *Apostolic Tradition* of Hippolytus, of the early third-century church in Rome. Ibid., 30–32.

[91] "We are all priests, and there is no difference between us; that is to say, we have the same power in respect to the Word and all the sacraments. However, *no one may make use of this power except by the consent of the community or by the call of a superior. For what is the common property of all, no individual may arrogate to himself, unless he be called.* And therefore this sacrament of ordination, if it have any meaning at all, is nothing else than a certain rite whereby one is called to the ministry of the Church. Furthermore, the priesthood is properly nothing but the ministry of the Word [emphasis added]." Martin Luther, *The Babylonian Captivity, Works of Martin Luther II*, 6 vols. (Philadelphia: Muhlenburg Press, 1943), 283.

[92] Typically, the ordination candidate is evaluated by five criteria: (1) authenticity of Christian experience, (2) acceptability of moral character, (3) genuineness of call, (4) correctness of doctrine, and (5) adequacy of preparation.

▶ To *hold accountable* this person to their ordination vows—typically, vows that promise faithfulness to Christian doctrine, fidelity to Christian standards of behavior, and faithful care of the flock for which they have charge.

Is pursuing ordination a necessity for someone who wants to pursue youth ministry? Definitely not. There are many effective youth pastors, highly respected by their congregations, who lack any ordination credentials. There is no clear reason why someone should be refused the role of pastor in the special biblical sense we have

> To be a minister is to be like a ballet dancer straining all muscles and energies into a daring leap only to find the partner not there to make the catch or steady the landing. To be a minister is to have learned one's role in a play well, to be committed to the message of the play and passionately geared for a performance, and to appear on stage to discover the rest of the cast in disarray, unprepared, or absent ... Most other professionals find their "clients" dependent on them; clients follow the rules and roles set by the lawyer, nurse, auto mechanic, or physician. But ministers are in a partnership. Their work depends on invitation and response from others. Lawyers and physicians and nurses and auto mechanics take charge. Ministers plant seeds.
>
> —*James E. Dittes*, Re-Calling Ministry *(St. Louis, Mo.: Chalice Press, 1999), 16–17.*

defined it just because they have not pursued a formal ordination procedure. In fact, if a congregation calls someone to come and minister as a youth pastor in their midst, there is a sense in which the call itself is an informal ordination of sorts.[93]

On the other hand, might ordination be a worthwhile pursuit? Definitely.

1. First of all, if this is God's call upon one's life, the greatest joy will always be in obedience. Whatever God leads us to do is a worthwhile pursuit!

2. There is great encouragement in knowing that one is set apart for the work and supported in the work by a local church community.

3. There is the added credibility within the congregation that follows the church's public recognition of gifts and calling for ministry, credibility that can be helpful (and is all too often lacking) for a youth minister.[94]

---

[93]Although "informal ordination," technically speaking, probably is an oxymoron!

[94] It is worth noting that the research of Strommen, Jones, and Rahn shows one out of ten youth workers are presently struggling with feeling unqualified for the job, and another 28 percent report they have felt that way at some point along the way. Merton Strommen, Karen E. Jones, and Dave Rahn, *Youth Ministry That Transforms* (Grand Rapids, Mich.: Zondervan, 2001), 100–104. While their findings do not report any correlation between ordination and a sense of adequacy (presumably, they did not explore this issue), there is an interesting correlation between seminary education and the sense of being well-qualified for the job. One wonders how many of these seminary-trained people might also be ordained.

4. There are the added privileges of administering the sacraments and officiating at weddings and funerals. This probably does not sound like big fun. But, in fact, for many in pastoral ministry, officiating and sharing in these significant lifetime landmarks is one of the highest privileges of ordained ministry. To be present in these intensely vivid and defining moments is to find oneself on stage and playing a pivotal role in real-life human dramas.[95]

Pastoral Ministry: "Mary Had a Little Lamb" Meets Braveheart

What is required of those in the pastoral role?

Much-tried Christian worker, you are not understanding what God is putting you through; perhaps this is what He is fitting you for, to teach you how to feed His sheep, to tend the flock of God . . . Take some time, Christian worker, over your Bible, and see what God has to say about shepherds, about hireling shepherds. This work of feeding and tending sheep is hard work, arduous work, and love for the sheep alone will not do it, you must have a consuming love for the great Shepherd, the Lord Jesus Christ; that is the point I want to leave impressed. Love for men as men will never stand the strain. In order to catch men for the Lord Jesus Christ, you must love Jesus Christ absolutely, beyond all others. You must have a consuming passion of love, then He will flow through you in a passion of love and yearning and draw men to Himself.[96]

We have not fully examined the pastoral role until we have thought through the task of the shepherd (*poimen*).[97] It was as a shepherd that our Lord consistently modeled and carefully explained his ministry.[98] Using Table 3-5, read carefully through John 10:1–18 and reflect on what it teaches us about the (youth) pastor's role as shepherd.

We should not too quickly read through John's description of the shepherd. We must not let childhood memories of nursery rhymes and fuzzy, cuddly toys lull us into an underestimation of the dangers in the shepherd's task. There are grave risks, steep precipices, eager wolves, and wandering sheep. It is not an adventure for the faint of heart. Why? Because the shepherd's job is to care, and caring never comes without great risk. C. S. Lewis was right: "To love at all is to be vul-

---

[95] There are also tax advantages that come with ordination. This is, of course, the last reason someone should pursue ministry. It would be like playing professional football because you like flat, green spaces. Flat green spaces are nice, but there are less painful, less demanding ways to enjoy them. The tax benefits of ordination are nice, but there are myriad other easier ways to pad the bank account.

[96] Oswald Chambers, *Workmen of God* (London: Marshall, Morgan and Scott, 1937), 88.

[97] This is why pastoral theology is technically referred to as *poimenics*.

[98] John 10:1–18.

Jesus: The Good Shepherd or the Good Subversive?

While the shepherd imagery is often used in Scripture to describe the pastoral role, Eugene Peterson suggests that we might also consider the *subversive*.[1] The subversive is someone who takes on the coloration of the culture, as far as everyone else can see, but he is not a part of that culture. Subversives work quietly, patiently—powerful not because of how visible they are, but because they are willing to remain invisible. The subversive is one who understands that small, apparently insignificant acts that draw little attention can often have a much greater impact than big high-profile events that draw a lot of attention.

Peterson notes that Jesus was a master at subversion. Until the end of his ministry, everyone, including his own disciples, called him "Rabbi" or "Teacher." They had no idea that the Creator himself had infiltrated behind enemy lines. On those occasions when suspicions were aroused that he might be more than a profound but relatively harmless teacher, Jesus tried to keep it quiet—"Tell no one," he would say. In fact, it was his rejection of pomp and pageantry that led Jews to conclude he could not be the *real* Messiah.

Subversives after the order of Christ understand that:

▶ The status quo is wrong and must be overthrown if the world is going to be livable. Indeed, it is so deeply wrong that repair work is futile.

▶ There is another world to come that is livable. Although it is not visible, it is most certainly real. It is not a fairy tale. In fact, it is far more real than what most people consider to be the real world—more real than the *Real World* on MTV, more real than the hallways of the high school, more real than the cold statistics of drug use, teenage pregnancy and juvenile violence. It is not some kind of utopian dream. It is not some kind of never-never land. It is called the Kingdom of God.

▶ We have neither the necessary military power nor the needed political power to usher in this real "real world" through conventional means. It is going to have to happen another way.

It is a radical vision; but it was a vision that, over the course of three short years, enabled Jesus to forge a movement that changed human history.

Maybe what we need are youth pastors who are one part shepherd and one part subversive. Karl Marx taught his disciples that revolution comes through three steps: *penetrate* (figure out a way to be among the culture), *indoctrinate* (teach a small group within that culture), and then finally, *subvert* (influence the culture with small acts that make a big impact). We will never know if Marx got this from another source, but it sounds vaguely familiar: Step 1, infiltration through incarnation (John 1:14); Step 2, train 12 disciples (Mark 3:14); Step 3, be like salt (Matt. 5:13).

[1] Eugene Peterson, *The Contemplative Pastor* (Dallas: Word Publishing, 1989), 35ff.

Table 3-5.
Observations and Implications of John 10:1–18

Observations	Implications for Youth Ministry
The shepherd intimately knows the sheep.	
The shepherd knows the sheep by name.	
The shepherd does not enter the sheep pen through some underhanded means, as does a thief or robber, but is fully authorized to care for the flock.	
The sheep recognize and respond to the shepherd's voice.	
The shepherd leads the flock to the pastures where they can be adequately fed and watered.	
The shepherd is characteristically "out ahead" of the flock, watching for danger, guiding, protecting.	
The shepherd is willing to lay down his life for the sheep.	
The good shepherd, unlike the hireling who is apt to run away in the presence of danger or hardship, is committed to the welfare of the flock.	

nerable. Love anything and your heart will certainly be wrung, and possibly broken . . . The only place outside heaven where you can be perfectly safe from the perturbations of love is Hell."[99]

David Hansen talks about standing before his ordination examining committee, and finding out to his horror that one of the examining elders was the great theologian Bernard Ramm. But his horror turned to bewilderment when, upon being invited to question the candidate, Ramm asked him only one question, and it had nothing to do with theological expertise. In a low, growling voice, the renowned theologian asked simply, "Have you ever suffered?"[100]

Henri Nouwen, in his marvelous book, *The Wounded Healer,* asks, "Who can save a child from a burning house without the risk of being hurt by the flames? Who can listen to a story of loneliness and despair without taking the risk of experiencing

---

[99] Cited in John Ortburg, *Love Beyond Reason* (Grand Rapids, Mich.: Zondervan, 1998), 48.
[100] Hansen, *The Art of Pastoring,* 35.

similar pains in his own heart and even losing his precious peace of mind? In short: 'Who can take away suffering without entering it?'"[101]

Are there traits to be cultivated in pursuit of such a role? What is required of the person who pursues the shepherd's task? And what are the risks of falling short? Those we will explore in the next chapter.

[101] Henri Nouwen, *The Wounded Healer* (New York: Bantam Doubleday, 1979), 23.

LORD OF THE RING

Meditations on the Way by Helen Musick

Last month I was talking with a student about God's provision. She was quick to show me a silver ring, which she wore on her left ring finger. The ring had nothing to do with an engagement or marriage commitment. It was a commitment ring to the Lord—a token of remembrance that caused her to recall God's provision in her life, as well as a reminder of her personal commitments to him regarding holiness and purity. As a bride of Christ, she wanted to be reminded daily of her pledges to him. She wanted to remember his provision for her everyday.

There is great biblical significance in remembrance. Take Joshua 4:1–9:

When the whole nation had finished crossing the Jordan, the Lord said to Joshua, "Choose twelve men from among the people, one from each tribe, and tell them to take up twelve stones from the middle of the Jordan from right where the priests stood and to carry them over with you and put them down at the place where you stay tonight." So Joshua called together the twelve men he had appointed from the Israelites, one from each tribe, and said to them, "Over before the ark of the Lord your God into the middle of the Jordan. Each of you is to take up a stone on his shoulder, according to the number of the tribes of the Israelites, to serve as a sign among you. In the future, when your children ask you, 'What do these stones mean?' tell them that the flow of the Jordan was cut off before the ark of the covenant of the Lord. When it crossed the Jordan, the waters of the Jordan were cut off. These stones are to be a memorial to the people of Israel forever." So the Israelites did as Joshua commanded them. They took twelve stones from the middle of the Jordan, according to the number of the tribes of the Israelites, as the Lord had told Joshua; and they carried them over with them to their camp, where they put them down. Joshua set up the twelve stones that had been in the middle of the Jordan at the spot where the priests who carried the ark of the covenant had stood. And they are there to this day.

Before this passage, we read about the miraculous crossing of the Israelites through the Jordan River. The crossing of this river was full of significance. Perhaps of utmost importance was that the journey brought the Israelites ever closer to the Promised Land, which had been promised through Abraham (Gen. 12:2–3) and for which they had been seeking throughout their wanderings in the desert for four decades (Josh. 5:6). The promise was being fulfilled, and the miracle of crossing the Jordan on dry ground set God apart as the power behind the promise.

Consider the following points as you read the passage. First, the initial command to build an altar came directly from God. He knows the human mind he created it. We are so prone to forget the great works of his hands as we go through life. Second, note the immediate obedience of Joshua to God, as well as the people to Joshua. No sooner had God finished speaking than Joshua began to instruct the people. No sooner had Joshua instructed the people than the twelve men began to seek and carry out the stones from the midst of the Jordan. The altar would never have been constructed without this twofold display of obedience. Third, the physical appearance of the altar itself was a symbol of unity. Twelve stones chosen by twelve men to represent the twelve tribes of Israel. Thus the altar had special meaning and connection to each person who had crossed the Jordan. Fourth, the memorial had a specific purpose beyond the present moment. It would become an educational tool in the future—an instigator of personal testimony of God's provision.

This miracle was not forgotten. There is power in remembering, and God calls us to do just that. God calls us to remember how he we pursued us, how he has provided for us, and the great promises he has made to us. We could probably maintain several memorials to proclaim God's provision, but perhaps God will call you to one like the student's ring I described above that will continue to abound with meaning and testimony throughout your life.

▸ **What are you teaching others regarding God's working in your life?**

▸ **How do you intentionally remember God's goodness?**

▸ **Is there anything in your life that praises his provision?**

chapter four

THROUGH MANY DANGERS, TOILS, AND SNARES

It's a dangerous business, Frodo, going out of your door . . . You step into the Road, and if you don't keep your feet, there is no knowing where you might be swept off to. Do you realize that this is the very path that goes through Mirkwood, and that if you let it, it might take you to the Lonely Mountain or even further and to worse places?
—J. R. R. Tolkien's character Frodo, reminiscing about the warnings of Bilbo the Hobbit[1]

Dangers face us all through our ministry. Constant use of Bible and Prayer Book words, constant association with religious people, constant service in Church affairs tend to spiritual formality, dryness, and even deadness which must assuredly affect the spiritual quality of our ministry if not at once and wholly altered. And herein lies the solemnity for students and clergymen of the Psalmist's words which call us to face these issues with ourselves, and never to rest until we can look up to God and feel perfectly sure that we are not among the false prophets, or even in danger of traveling on the way thither [in that direction].
—W. H. Griffith Thomas[2]

I trust you will have a pleasant and profitable time in Germany. I know you will apply hard to German; but do not forget the culture of the inner man,—I mean of the heart. How diligently the cavalry officer keeps his sabre sharp and clean; every stain he rubs off with the greatest care. Remember you are God's sword,—His instrument,—I trust a chosen vessel unto Him to bear His name. In great measure, according to the purity and perfections of the instrument, will be the success. It is not great talents God blesses so much as great likeness to Jesus. A holy minister is an awful weapon in the hand of God.
—From a letter written by Robert Murray McCheyne to the Rev. Dan Edwards on October 2, 1840, after his ordination as a missionary to Jews in Germany.[3]

Strike the shepherd, and the sheep will be scattered.
—Zechariah 13:7

---

[1] J. R. R. Tolkien, *Fellowship of the Ring* (Boston: Houghton Mifflin, 1965), 82–83.

[2] W. H. Griffith Thomas, *The Work of the Ministry* (London: Hodder and Stoughton, c. 1910), 20–21.

[3] Andrew Bonar, *Memoir and Remains of R. M. McCheyne* (London: Oliphant, Anderson and Ferrier, 1892), 282.

Young Life founder Jim Rayburn was one of those people who inspired the allegiance of those who knew him. Fellow staffers and coworkers speak of him in glowing terms:[4]

> I'd heard a lot of people pray, but when I heard Jim pray, I knew that everything I'd heard before was suspect. I was awed; when I'd hear him talk to God, I felt that I was standing before God, too.

> I've never met a person with so much charisma . . . He was an amazing man; I think most of us would have followed him to the edge of hell.

> As a speaker he was the best I ever heard. I'd laugh so hard I'd feel drained, and then I'd weep as Jim took us to the feet of Jesus Christ.

> Jim was a man's man, a man with courage, a man with guts, a man who'd lay his life on the line for what he believed. I've never met a person with so many God-given gifts.

Yet, notwithstanding his youth ministry skills, the glowing accolades, and the huge impact he made for the kingdom of God through the movement he founded, Jim Rayburn's story is marred by failure and tragedy. Told in painful, personal detail in the book *Dance, Children, Dance*, authored by his son, we see a man whose considerable strengths and gifts could not help him to overcome his many demons:

> As the tumultuous sixties rolled around, things collapsed on Jim. His cross had been heavy, and he'd carried it a lot of miles. Since October 27, 1937, the day something snapped inside the pretty young girl he'd married, life had been a difficult road. A quarter century had passed and . . . [his wife] Maxine remained a crippled victim of narcotics. Finding a solution seemed hopeless, and Jim was near the end of his rope . . . Unable to sleep well, digest food properly, or decrease the migraine attacks, Jim turned to sleeping pills to help him rest. His stomach seldom dissolved the pills when they were needed. At numerous public appearances his speech was slurred and his message disoriented. On one such occasion in a leading Methodist church, he could not speak at all. In front of a packed house, Jim rose to speak and could not do so; he began to weep, turned to take his seat, and collapsed . . . As word of these public failures spread, feelings of anger, confusion, and doubt rose to the surface throughout Young Life . . . As the full extent of his exile began to dawn upon him, Jim's emotions broke down. Within months, the man's health was at an all-time low; he was visibly suffering, slowly dying from a broken heart. In early August, his two sons-in-law visited him in Colorado Springs. Jim wanted them to see the new headquarters building of which he'd been proud, so he sent them over with his key, as he was not allowed to go

---

[4] Jim Rayburn III, *Dance, Children, Dance* (Wheaton, Ill.: Tyndale, 1984), 159-160.

himself. That's when I found out they had changed all the locks so that I couldn't get into the building. This was a very low time for me—the ultimate humiliation.[5]

The moral of this story is all too clear: a person may have a great reputation, superior abilities, visionary leadership, and remarkable charisma, but none of that offers an automatic pass through the pitfalls and perils of the ministry adventure. The real test of Christian leadership is not about those who start well; it is about those who finish strong.[6]

Some Really Disgusting Habits to Avoid

Some personal habits [are] so very offensive, that it is difficult to speak of them ... audible and uncovered eructation;—picking the nose, and the ears, not in a guarded and delicate manner, with the handkerchief, but with the finger, and with full exposure to view; blowing the nose in a loud and disgusting manner;—looking into the handkerchief, after blowing the nose, as if finding some threatening appearance in the secretion inspected;—sneezing frequently without breaking the force or the noise of the blast by the application of the handkerchief; holding the handkerchief at a distance from the mouth and spitting into it, instead of silently and covertly wiping the saliva from the lips;—snuffing up the nose with an offensive frequency;—the habit of hemming, and clearing the throat very loudly and frequently, and in a disgusting manner as if labouring (sic) under some organick (sic) obstruction.

—*Samuel Miller,* Letters on Clerical Manners and Habits Addressed to a Student in the Theological Seminary at Princeton, NJ *(New York: G&C Carvill, 1827), 81–82.*

Suited for Perilous Work

It was back in the middle of the thirteenth century that Bonaventure found himself the newly elected governor general of the Franciscans, an order originally founded by St Francis of Assisi. But in 1256 the Franciscan movement was deeply divided and floundering.[7] It was a tough test for the young leader, but under Bonaventure's leadership the movement not only survived, it flourished. In reflecting on the essential traits that would suit someone for a calling in Christian leadership, Bonaventure identified six virtues—what he described as The Six Wings of the Seraph: (1) zeal for righteousness, (2) brotherly love, (3) patience, (4) good example, (5) good judgment, and (6) devotion to God.[8]

---

[5] Ibid., 161, 168.

[6] Steve Farrar provides another haunting example of this sad story in recounting the life and ministry of Chuck Templeton, a Youth for Christ (YFC) evangelist who in 1945, still in his mid-20s, was described by one seminary president as "the most gifted and talented young man in America today for preaching." He was a man of striking appearance and stunning giftedness who had a profound impact on thousands who heard him minister. In fact, in 1946, when the National Association of Evangelicals published an article on men who were "best used of God" in the fledgling organization's five-year existence, it was Templeton who received the spotlight. Remarkably, the article never mentioned his fellow YFC evangelist, a young North Carolina native named Billy Graham. Yet, by 1950, Templeton had left the ministry altogether and had completely disavowed his once bold faith in Christ. Steve Farrar, *Finishing Strong* (Grand Rapids, Mich.: Zondervan, 1997), 3–5.

[7] The dissension largely involved those in the order who wanted to keep to the austere (strict) disciplines of St Francis, and those who were seeking to relax some of the stricter elements of the Franciscan vows (that is, allowing the monks to wear shorts, pierce their ears, keep their sideburns, and hold on to the Walkmans even while they were on the retreat).

[8] "Tests of a Leader's Character," *Leadership* (Fall 1993).

Six centuries later, students at Princeton Theological Seminary, when considering traits appropriate to those in Christian leadership, were provided a slightly different slant on the topic by Samuel Miller, their professor of Ecclesiastical History and Church Government. Hoping to exhort his students to consider their personal conduct, Miller prepared for them a document creatively titled *Letters on Clerical Manners and Habits Addressed to a Student in the Theological Seminary at Princeton, NJ.*[9] It was in a latter section of that document that Miller provided a list of 16 offensive personal habits:

(1) **Spitting on the floors and carpets** . . . If it be asked, how those who spit much shall manage; I answer, if possible, let them instantly discontinue all those practices which lead to the secretion of an excess of saliva.

(2) **Excessive use of tobacco, in any form** . . .

(3) **Habitual use of ardent spirits** . . .

(4) **Manifesting or cherishing an excessive fondness for luxurious eating** . . . Eat slowly; gently; without that smacking of the lips, and that noisy motion of the mouth, which are expressive either of extreme hunger, or vulgarity, or both . . . And finally, eat without talking much about eating . . .

(5) **Guard against loud or boisterous laughter** . . . The laughter of a polished man, and especially of a clergyman, however hearty, ought never to be obstreperous, and seldom audible.

(6) **Do not be among those who take liberty in public to pare their nails; or, if they have been sufficiently pared before, to scrape, or polish, or clean them.**

(7) **Picking at the skin of their hands** . . .

(8) **Combing the hair in company** . . . I have known many candidates for the ministry, and even ministers, [to] do this without reserve; and what is more, wiping off what had accumulated on the comb in the course of the operation, and scattering it at their feet.

(9) **The practice of yawning in company ought, as far as possible, to be avoided** . . . And when it does involuntarily occur in company, hide it as much as you can by the delicate use of your handkerchief.

(10) **Coughing in company** . . . The practice in which many vulgar people indulge, of coughing, yawning or sneezing over the dishes placed in their immediate neighborhood, is intolerable, and has driven many a delicate individual from the table.

(11) **Picking your teeth at the table** . . . As to picking your teeth with the fork

[9] Samuel Miller, *Letters on Clerical Manners and Habits Addressed to a Student in the Theological Seminary at Princeton, NJ* (New York: G&C Carvill, 1827), 60–87.

which you employ in eating, (which I have sometimes witnessed) I presume your own sense of propriety will instinctively revolt from it, as peculiarly offensive.

(12) **Leaning with your elbows on the table** . . .

(13) **The mode of sitting in company, is a point concerning which no little indecorum is often indulged. The offences against propriety in this respect are numerous** . . . lifting up one or both feet and placing them on a neighboring chair . . . Others, if they can get a place on a sofa or settee, lay their bodies upon it at full length . . . A third class, the moment they fix themselves upon any kind of seat, appear to be searching for something to lean or recline upon . . . While a fourth class, though they have only a single chair to occupy, thrust out their feet as far as possible, and throw their persons as near to the horizontal posture as they can, as if the object were to cover the largest practicable space on the floor, and to subject those who have occasion to pass before them to the risk every moment, of stumbling over their feet . . .

(14) **Tilting your chair back, while you are sitting upon it, so as to rest only on its two hinder feet** . . .

(15) **Many persons, the moment they seat themselves in company, and especially when they become engaged in conversation, if there be a screw, a knob, or small fixture of any kind within their reach, which admits of being turned or handled, are incessantly engaged in performing this operation** . . . Try to learn the art of sitting still while you are conversing, without pulling and tugging at the furniture around you; without playing with any part of your own dress or person; without incessantly stretching and cracking the joints of your fingers; without pulling out your watch every half minute, and twirling the chain in every direction, &c . . .

(16) **Avoid all slovenly habits of whatever kind.** When you quit your bed in the morning, lay up the bed-clothes decently, so that no visitant be offended by the appearance of things. When you wash yourself, especially in the house of a friend, do it with gentleness and neatness, without wetting the carpet or floor, without bespattering the wall or furniture in the immediate vicinity of the basin.

Perhaps as you read through this list of admonitions you found yourself thinking, "Oh, how quaint." Or perhaps you found yourself thinking, "How could I get this list into the hands of my roommate?" Or, perhaps, you found yourself wondering, "Maybe I really should stop picking my teeth at the table and spitting on the floor in the library."[10] In any case, whether it be Bonaventure's Six

---

[10] Here is a study break idea: Go through the list of 16 items, and grade yourself on each item with a score of 1 (This is disgusting and I never do it) to 5 (This is disgusting, and I do this a lot). Total your score and use this chart to test your Personal Indecency Grade (P.I.G.): 0–15 Welcome to Mr. Rogers's neighborhood; 16–30 Charmingly gross; 31–40 Mildly offensive; 41–50 Consistently disgusting; 51–60 You are strongly urged to consider ministry with middle-school males!; 61–70 You *are* a middle school male; 71–80 Gross! Go wash your hands before you turn even one more page in this book!

Wings of the Seraph or Miller's Sixteen Habits of a Slacker, what clearly emerges is a basic principle of ministry: neither Scripture nor tradition allows us to compartmentalize life so that we can separate calling from conduct. Accordingly, the way we live our personal, everyday lives is a matter of grave importance for those of us in ministry. This is a recurring theme of the Epistles, coming into clear focus with Peter's admonition, "Be examples to the flock" (I Pet. 5:3).[11]

No doubt, this is why Paul cites specific guidelines of lifestyle and character for those who aspire to the role of elder (see I Tim. 3:1–13, Titus 1:5–9).[12] Twice in the Titus passage, in describing the qualifications for eldership/leadership, Paul uses the Greek word *anengkletos* (not to be called in), which the NIV translates as "blameless." Paul is saying quite clearly that as stewards of the gospel, Christian leaders must live a life of "unimpeachable virtue"[13] "Since an overseer is entrusted with God's work, he must be blameless . . ." (Titus 1:7).

The media have helped us by uncovering our sexual and financial scandals, by shining their flashlights under our covers, leafing through our IRS returns, publicizing our behind-closed-door deals, and broadcasting our hypocrisies. Some of us used to think we could indulge in private immoralities (alcohol or drug abuse, sexual misconduct, financial malfeasance) as long as we took a strong stand on public issues (poverty, racism, war). Some of us thought the reverse—that a little racism or sexism was no big deal as long as we stayed in the right bed. Too many of us thought we could do just about anything as long as we said the right things and didn't get exposed. But the media have virtually fulfilled Jesus's prophecy about things said and done in secret being broadcast from the housetops (see Matt. 10:26–27). They have taught us what we had ignored in our great Christian moral tradition: that we need to integrate both public morality and private morality to have something called "integrity."

The lawyers then stopped by to help us in a second way. As lawsuits were filed dealing with clergy pedophilia and clergy sexual harassment (whether hetero- or homosexual in orientation), churches had no choice but to get serious about at least their leaders returning to Ten Commandments-style morality, for legal and public-relations reasons if not for moral conviction. And if the leaders must become more traditionally moral, the people in their congregations probably will, too. Isn't it interesting how history has a way of being self-correcting? And think of it: the media and lawyers, like a rewriting of the Balaam story.*

—*Brian McLaren,* The Church on the Other Side *(Grand Rapids, Mich.: Zondervan, 2000), 61–62.*

See Numbers 22:21-30 if you do not catch the humor here.

---

[11] This is a charge that is directly quoted in most rites of ordination.

[12] For a more thorough review of these qualifications and disqualifications cited by Paul, see John MacArthur, "The Character of a Pastor," in *Rediscovering Pastoral Ministry*, ed. John MacArthur Jr. (Dallas: Word, 1995), 87–101.

[13] J. B. Phillips, *The New Testament in Modern English* (London: Geoffrey Bles, 1967), 449.

Women in Youth Ministry

By Kara Eckman Powell

If you are a woman in youth ministry, you probably are accustomed to meetings where there is more testosterone than estrogen. While you share a passion to see students' lives changed by Christ to change the world, you cannot help but notice that the way you go about that is a little different from your male colleagues.

According to Patricia Aburdene and John Naisbitt in *Megatrends for Women*, women in most Western cultures have reached "critical mass." If your understanding of physics is a little rusty, "critical mass" is the point at which a process becomes self-sustaining and builds momentum. It is when a rockslide becomes an avalanche, a trend becomes a mega-trend. Aburdene and Naisbitt argue that we are living in a time of unprecedented choices for women in the fields of politics, sports, medicine, and fashion.

What about youth ministry? There is some evidence that critical mass has been reached for women in youth ministry.

1. **There are more women in youth ministry than ever before.** In a 1998 multidenominational survey of 2,416 full-time U.S. youth workers conducted by the Link Institute, 29.8 percent of respondents were women. While there was quite a bit of variance based on denomination (ranging from 5 percent of Assembly of God youth workers to 60 percent of Presbyterian youth workers), women are sprinkled throughout the youth ministry work force in greater numbers than many might expect.

2. **There are more jobs for women in youth ministry.** Many churches, parachurch ministries, and nonprofit organizations are specifically looking to hire women for key leadership positions. These churches and organizations might already have a male area director, or a male junior high pastor, so they wisely recognize that the more than 50 percent of their students who are female would benefit from having a female role model.

Furthermore, camps, seminars, and conferences are often proactively seeking women to include in their buffet of speakers. Although some claim this is "tokenism," maybe it is better to have a "token woman" than no woman at all.

There remain several quagmires women must sidestep on the trail to critical mass and full acceptance. While there is no recent empirical investigation of obstacles women face, a recent multidenominational gathering of church and parachurch women at the 2002 National Network of Youth Ministries Forum revealed the following challenges and recommended responses:

1. **Lack of theological understanding of women in leadership.** In the Link Institute survey described above, men expressed a significantly greater satisfaction with their theological grounding than women. While 52 percent of males report having seminary training, only 39 percent of females indicate the same. This difference may be especially problematic as women try to define biblically derived boundaries for women in leadership. Significant theological questions related to women in leadership include:

    Are spiritual gifts equally available for both genders?

    ▸ What did Paul mean in 1 Timothy 2:12 when he wrote, "I do not permit a woman to teach or to have authority over a man; she must be silent?"

    ▸ Given 1 Timothy 3:2 that specifies that an overseer must be "the husband of but one wife," can women be elders and deacons in a church?

    ▸ Why would Paul write in 1 Corinthians 14:34 that "women should remain silent in the churches" while two chapters earlier he commands women who are praying and prophesying in worship services to do so with their heads covered?

    ▸ What is the influence of first-century historical and cultural factors in all of the above?

    While my theological research has led me to rather broad boundaries for women in leadership, my advice for men and women alike is to do the hard work of wrestling with these questions until they've pinned down some answers.

2. **Deficit of mentors.** The first known "mentor" was a youth worker. In the Greek epic *The Odyssey*, a character named Mentor is hired to groom the junior high son of King Odysseus. While its origins are derived from a myth, women in youth ministry continue to swallow a dangerous second myth that could choke their ability to find mentors: that one mentor will guide them in all areas of their personal and ministry lives. The reality is that while women may not know the "perfect guru" to help them with everything from marshmallow crowd-breakers to sermon preparation, they have men and women perhaps divinely placed in their lives to mold them. Instead of just having one mentor, many wise women in youth ministry are choosing to proactively learn from a constellation of empowering relationships. Personally, I have never met some of my greatest mentors. Many of them are even dead, but as I have read their biographies, their character and convictions leap out of the page and into my life.

3. **Feeling isolated.** Youth workers in general tend to feel isolated and alone. It could be suggested that female youth workers, who often end up serving in smaller churches, might be prone to greater feelings of isolation. Even women who are blessed to be embedded in a multiple staff team still feel "different" from their male counterparts. To help overcome these feelings of isolation, women in youth ministry are gathering together in formal and informal networks across the nation. In 1996, a ministry called the Women's Youth Network began with the mission of equipping, encouraging, and connecting women in youth ministry. One of its primary methods is to set up networks for women in youth ministry in strategic cities. The anecdotal evidence of the effectiveness of these networks is encouraging. As one woman shared at one Women's Youth Network meeting with tears in her eyes, "I've been praying for something like this." For more information about how to start a network in your area, see www.womensyouthnetwork.org.

4. **Feeling inadequate.** Many women feel more than just "different." They feel unqualified. Women often seem to fall on two ends of a continuum. On one end are those women whose spiritual gifts and talents remain underused and hidden, primarily because of their gender. On the other end are women who have been granted enormous opportunities, placed in the spotlight, and labeled as a model for other women to follow. Either extreme, and those who fall somewhere in between, often seem to leave women feeling inadequate.

A fundamental question for women in youth ministry is that of calling. While that question is important for all believers, women who are plagued with feelings of inadequacy may find their only cure in realizing that when God calls, he always equips and provides.

5. **Different leadership styles.** Secular management theorists have often proposed two types of leadership styles: a more "masculine" style that is focused on tasks, and a more "feminine" style that prioritizes relationships. While it is inappropriate to label all women as "feminine" leaders and all men as "masculine" leaders, perhaps there is some overlap. The advantage for women in our culture is that they are able, and expected, to nurture and encourage those they supervise. The disadvantage is evident in research conducted by Deborah Tannen. Tannen found that women who were assertive in stating their ideas were disliked by others in the workforce, even if they were not being confrontational.

I recommend that women draw from the best of the polarities and strive for the leadership style that Jesus modeled: gentle strength. Jesus wept with compassion and yet he overturned tables in the Temple. He publicly mourned over the death of his friend, but he also taught with fiery conviction. While Jesus's model of gentle strength applies to men and women, it is likely a little more relevant for women in leadership because of the expectations they face. Churches often either expect them to overemphasize gentleness and end up rather weak or to swing the other direction so that they overemphasize strength and are somewhat domineering.

6. **Women need men to open doors of opportunity for them.** Because men occupy the majority of positions of influence in the youth ministry community, women are still dependent on men for career advancement. If you are a woman, seek to work alongside men who help you develop your gifts and stretch you beyond your comfort zone. If you are a man, identify one or more women who would benefit from new challenges and do everything you can to help them succeed.

Source: Joe E. Trull and James E. Carter, Ministerial Ethics: Being a Good Minister (Nashville, Tenn.: Broadman and Holman, 1999).

If God's threatenings be true, why do not you yourselves fear them? If they be false, why do you needlessly trouble men with them, and put them into such frights without a cause? . . . You who teach others, shall you not be taught yourselves? You who say that others should not commit adultery, or be drunk, or covetous, are you such yourselves? You who make your boast of the law, do you through breaking the law dishonor God? What! Shall the same tongue speak evil that speaks against evil?
—**Richard Baxter**

It doesn't take many years in this business to realize that we can conduct a fairly respectable pastoral ministry without giving much more than ceremonial attention to God.
—**Eugene Peterson**

Thinking About "Blamelessness"

In Titus 1:9 Paul explains *what* an overseer is to do. But in Titus 1:6–8, the apostle gives very clear guidelines about *who* the overseer is to be. Paul's sketch of the leader's character is colored by three broad emphases: sexual morality (v. 6a),[14] proven family leadership (v. 6b), and purity of attitude and conduct (vv. 7–8). While these passages raise as many questions as they answer,[15] what is beyond dispute is that Paul takes seriously the character and lifestyle of those in Christian leadership. In his quick sketch of those qualities that adorn the Christian leader Paul mentions five negative qualities (what we should not be) and six positive qualities (what we should be).[16]

The Negatives

The Christian leader must not be:

1. **Self-willed** (stubborn or headstrong), see 2 Peter 2:10 and Matthew 20:25–26;

2. **Quick-tempered** (a smoldering anger that is quick to ignite), see 2 Timothy 2:24 and James 1:20;

3. Not **addicted to wine or strong drink**, see Romans 14:19–21, 1 Corinthians 8, Timothy 3:3;[17]

4. **Nonviolent** (*The Message* renders this phrase "not a bully, someone who

---

[14] The literal translation of the Greek phrase Paul uses is *"a one-woman man'"*.

[15] Some important questions are beyond the scope of this book: Are divorced people disqualified from ministry? What about women in ministry? If a Christian leader has a child who forsakes the faith, does that mean the leader has mismanaged his or her family? For a broader look at this passage, see MacArthur, *Rediscovering Pastoral Ministry*, 88ff. For a very thorough look at the question of women in ministry, see Bonnidell Clouse and Robert G. Clouse, eds., *Four Views on Women in Ministry* (Downers Grove, Ill.: InterVarsity Press, 1989); Andreas J. Kostenberger, Thomas R. Schreiner, and H. Baldwin, eds., *Women in the Church: A Fresh Analysis of 1 Timothy 2:9–15* (Grand Rapids, Mich.: Baker, 1995); Stanley J. Grenz and Denise Muir Kjesbo, *Women in the Church: A Biblical Theology of Women in Ministry* (Downers Grove, Ill.: InterVarsity Press, 1995); and Diane Elliot and Ginny Olson, eds., *Breaking the Gender Barrier in Youth Ministry* (Wheaton, Ill.: Victor Books, 1995).

[16] The main source I am drawing from here is MacArthur, *Rediscovering Pastoral Ministry*, 94–101.

[17] This passage addresses a different issue, but the same basic principle is at stake.

resorts to force—physical, emotional, or political to enforce leadership)"[18]; and

5. **Not pursuing dishonest gain** (not money-hungry, *The Message*).

The Positives

The Christian leader should be:

1. **Hospitable** (from the Greek, meaning "a lover of strangers"), see Luke 14:12–14, Romans 12:13, Hebrews 13:2;

2. **Love what is good**, see Philippians 4:8;

3. **Thoughtful** (discreet, J. B. Phillips)[19];

4. **Fair (or just)**;

5. **Holy** (pure, unpolluted by sin); and

6. **Self-controlled.**

Admittedly, after reading through a list such as this, any honest person would say, "Ah, 'unpolluted by sin'—no problem . . . I'll just drop this youth ministry course and find some kind of work better suited to sinful wretches . . . such as politics or the stock market." Yet, obviously, what God is calling us to here as leaders is not sinless perfection. Were that the case, no human being would ever be qualified for Christian leadership. Anyone arrogant enough to read through this Titus passage and think, "Hey, that's me!" would be disqualified by their deceit.

But this does not in any sense dumb down the potency of Paul's pastoral words to Titus. He clearly means us to regard this as a high standard. It is, after all, a standard rooted in the unique calling of *all* God's people to be a reflection of his glory and his values on this planet. Walter Brueggemann observes that as far back as the Old Testament, Israel's ethical identity was anchored in "a distinct, self-conscious theological-ideological perspective."[20] So it was in the New Testament church as well (Rom. 12:1, I Pet. 1:15–16; 2:9).

To be sure, the history of the church reflects some awkwardness in working out just what this distinct ethical identity might mean for its leaders. There were those such as Cyprian who so strongly emphasized the higher moral standard of

---

[18] The ancient voice of John Climacus (c. A.D. 600) reminds us, "It is not right for a lion to pasture sheep, and it is not safe for one still tyrannized by the passions to rule over passionate men. A fox found in the company of hens is an unseemly sight, but nothing is more unseemly than an enraged shepherd. The former agitates and destroys the hens, while the latter agitates and destroys rational souls. See that you are not an exacting investigator of trifling sins, thus showing yourself not to be an imitator of God." John Climacus, *To the Shepherd*, sec. 47–49, cited in Thomas Oden, *Classical Pastoral Care* (Grand Rapids, Mich.: Baker, 1987), 12.

[19] In Greek, literally "one who saves his thoughts".

[20] Walter Brueggemann in Michael L. Budde and Robert W. Brimlow, eds., *The Church as Counterculture* (Albany, N.Y.: State University of New York Press, 2000), 40.

the clergy that he seemed to suggest a two-tiered Christian ethic, one for those in leadership and the other for normal believers.[21] On the other hand, there were those such as Luther who responded that Cyprian placed too much stress on the character of the clergy and too little on the truth that "the office is not ours but the Lord Jesus Christ's." Luther felt that even the ministry of a low-life could have sacramental value, because Christ ministers even through those who represent him poorly.[22]

There are, even today, those who express similar concerns. One of the popular buzzwords currently making the rounds in youth ministry is the word *authenticity*. What does *authenticity* mean with relationship to holiness of lifestyle and character? Is it not true that what most teenagers are looking for in their youth leader is honesty and authenticity more so than righteousness? How can we expect students to share with us their temptations, doubts, and struggles, if they feel that we are so much more holy than they? Might we not be better able to understand their struggles if we ourselves have experienced some of these same failures? In his book *Ministry in the New Testament*,[23] David Bartlett remarked, "One must ask about the definition of ordination that presupposes a kind of two-tiered Christianity: the relatively moral lay people and the astonishingly moral clergy. Especially for those for whom the gospel consists centrally in the proclamation of God's choice to justify the ungodly, it becomes odd to define that by the heroic godliness of the preacher."

But there are several points to be made here:

▶ **Is it not true that what most teenagers are looking for in their youth leader is honesty and authenticity more so than righteousness?** Absolutely, we must be leaders who are transparent, honest, and authentic about our questions and struggles. Having said that, though, it must be said that the crux of the issue is not what teenagers expect of us, but what God expects of us. It is just possible that what teenagers are most looking for in their youth leader is someone who will provide free beer to minors. That does not make it right.[24]

▶ **How can we expect students to share with us their temptations, doubts, and struggles, if they feel that we are so much more holy than they?** We cannot expect that. One of the risks of ministry is transparency, allowing

[21] Cyprian, the Bishop of Carthage, (A.D. 248–258), martyred for his faith, said, "The conduct of a prelate should so far surpass the conduct of the people as the life of a pastor sets him apart from the flock. For one who is so regarded that the people are called his flock must carefully consider how necessary it is for him to maintain a life of rectitude. It is necessary, therefore, that one should be pure in thought, exemplary in conduct, discreet in keeping silence, profitable in speech, in sympathy a near neighbor to everyone, in contemplation exalted above all others, a humble companion to those who lead good lives, erect in zeal for righteousness against the vices of sinners. One must not be remiss in the care for the inner life by preoccupation with the external; nor must one, in solicitude for what is internal, fail to give attention to the external." Quoted in William Willimon, *Pastor: The Theology and Practice of Ordained Ministry* (Nashville, Tenn.: Abingdon, 2002), 29–30.

[22] Willimon, 29–30.

[23] David Bartlett, *Ministry in the New Testament* (Philadelphia: Fortress Press, 1993), 183.

[24] Derek Phillips comments that one of the faults of many modern therapeutic methodologies is that "all restrictions and inhibitions are to be eliminated, all in the name of realizing authenticity . . . Whereas the moral life begins with renunciation (*Thou shalt not*), the therapeutic life begins with the renunciation of renunciation ('Thou shalt not commit a *thou shalt not*')." The problem with making authenticity the principal virtue is that it can lead to very unprincipled behavior. "Since such persons view social relationships as reducible to individual desires or to a calculation of means and ends, *moral discourse* does not exist for them . . . Because there is no moral foundation for their actions, they cannot be expected to act on the basis of something other than their own desires and impulses." Derek L. Phillips, "Authority or Morality?" in *The Virtues: Contemporary Essays on Moral Character* (Belmont, Calif.: Wadsworth, 1987), 23–35.

The Dangers of Transparency

What do students *really* see when we think they are seeing the real us?

Transparency, if it is healthy, will always be bound by common sense, prudence, propriety, and the awareness that there is a fine line between transparency and exhibitionism.

▸ **Healthy transparency allows students to hear what they need to know; unhealthy transparency tells them more than they wanted to hear.** It is completely appropriate, for example, for the students in my youth group to know that I struggle with lust. On the other hand, if I continue by saying, "In fact, Sally, your mom is a fox, and you're not bad either!" that sort of feels like it crosses a line!

▸ **Healthy transparency allows students to trust the messenger; unhealthy transparency distracts students from the message.** If I begin my Bible study lesson by confessing, "I'm battling an awful case of diarrhea tonight, and I may have to quickly end the Bible study," my authenticity may be admirable. But human nature suggests that after my touching revelation, some of the students will spend more time wondering about my bug than about my Bible study. Garrison Keillor, host of National Public Radio's *A Prairie Home Companion*, is right when he relates: "As soon as the pastor stands up in the service and says, 'I'm a human being just like you,' the immediate conclusion of everyone in the congregation is that he must have committed adultery. And then, the next question on their minds is *Who was she?* And *For how long?* Sure, I want them to understand that I struggle with real issues. That's being authentic. That gives me credibility when I teach and speak. But there is a point at which the sharing of my dark emotions begins making it *harder* for them to hear!"

▸ **Healthy transparency is heard as honest confession; unhealthy transparency is heard as implicit permission.** It is appropriate for students to understand that my high school years were not free from mistakes and bad choices. But I must also understand that what I meant as confession will likely be heard by some of my students as permission. Some of them will think, "Well, if he did it—he's doing okay and he's got a good life—I'll play now and worry about confession later." In my mind, I am looking back on my bad decisions as signposts of God's protection and mercy. But when my students hear too vividly about those same decisions, they interpret them as signs that all the dire warnings about sin's consequences are perhaps a bit overblown.

These considerations must not frighten us away from transparency. But they probably ought to temper and shape our confession. Remember communication is not what we say; it is what someone else hears.

"Well, Didn't You Do Any of This Stuff When You Were a Kid?"

Every now and then, a student may just point blank ask you if you were involved in certain behaviors when you were a teenager, or before you became a Christian. When asked that question, you might be wise to offer the following response: "If I answer that it's none of your business and the answer is between me and God, there's a pretty good chance you'll hear that as a 'yes.' If I answer 'yes' to your question, there's a pretty good chance that you'll take that as permission to make the same mistakes that I've made. If, on the other hand, I say 'no,' there's a good possibility that you might reason then that I couldn't possibly understand what you're facing or what you're going through right now. So, what that question amounts to is a lose-lose proposition for both of us, and I'm not willing to put us in that position, so I'm not going to answer it."

students to see our hearts—the good, the bad, and the ugly. It is an essential element of credibility. In his book, *Being Holy, Being Human*, Jay Kesler writes, "We're to be spiritual examples, yes. People watch us. But that's not reason to hide our faults; it's reason to admit them. If people watch closely enough and long enough, either they'll discover what we try to hide, or else we'll crack under the strain of trying to keep it from view."[25]

On the other hand, should we really expect students to seek counsel from a youth worker whose life is in shambles? Using that same logic, we would buy diets from fat people, hair growth products from bald people, and sexual abstinence advice from former presidents. As Ambrose, Bishop of Milan (A.D. 374–397), so vividly put it:

"Who seeks for a spring in the mud? Who wants to drink from muddy water? . . . Who will think a man to be useful to another's cause whom he sees to be useless in his own life? . . . Am I to suppose that he is fit to give me advice who never takes it for himself . . ."[26]

▸ **Might we not be better able to understand their struggles if we ourselves have experienced some of these same failures?** This kind of thinking, common in today's therapeutic culture, suggests that we cannot fully understand someone's pain or struggle unless we have felt it ourselves. Surely, there is a kernel of truth in this notion. As Paul himself pointed out, the comfort we receive from Christ in our troubles allows us to better comfort others in their troubles (2 Cor. 1:4).

[25] Jay Kesler, *Being Holy, Being Human* (Dallas: Word, 1988), 40.
[26] Ambrose in *A Select Library of Nicene and Post-Nicene Fathers of the Christian Church*, ed. H. Wace and Phillip Schaff, vol. 2. (New York: Christian, 1897–1892), 53.

Guidelines for Transparency:
Honest Disclosure Without Indecent Exposure

Here are some simple guidelines that can help us understand the shape of healthy transparency:

1. **Self-exposure must have a purpose.** Transparency is not just about saying everything we feel or think. The front of a youth group is no place for a leader to work out his or her issues. We do not speak just to get something "off our chest." The goal must be edification, not self-expression.

   William Willimon reminds us, "It is not my task primarily to 'share myself' with my people, certainly not to heed the facile advice of those who say, 'Just be yourself.' As Mark Twain said, 'About the worst advice one can give anybody is, 'Just be yourself.' Fortunately, as I enter into the struggles of my people, I have considerably more to offer than myself. I have the witness of the saints, the faith of the church, the wisdom of the ages.'"

2. **Make sure that every confession of failure is joined with a clear intention to do better.** The glory of the gospel is that by the death of Jesus *for* us we are saved "just as we are." But, at least as glorious is the fact that by the life of Jesus *in* us we are not bound to stay as we are (Rom. 5:9–10, 8:8–17).

   It is obvious to everyone that the baby has dirty diapers. When the child is honest enough and aware enough to admit that, that is certainly progress. But, when the child is once again cleaned up and embraced by the father, *the greater progress still is that the child exercises enough self-control to stop making the mess.* We should be honest enough to admit, to use Mike Yaconelli's phrase, that ours is a "messy spirituality." But the great news of God's sanctifying Spirit is that little by little he helps us to clean up our mess. It's true: God loves us as we are, but he doesn't intend to leave us as we are.

3. **Our transparency must point students to Christ.** We do not share our problems so people will notice how much we have given up, how wild we were, how humble we are, how honest we are willing to be. The nature of real transparency is that it allows students to see *through* us so that they can more clearly see Christ.

4. **Some confessions simply are not suited for public consumption.** Talk to your prayer group of peers. Talk to your pastor. Talk to your counselor. Talk to your spiritual director. But do not dump on a youth group a load they shouldn't be asked to bear.

Adapted from Jay Kesler, Being Holy, Being Human *(Dallas: Word, 1988), 45–48. Quotations taken from William Willimon,* Pastor: The Theology and Practice of Ordained Ministry *(Nashville, Tenn.: Abingdon, 2002), 21.*

In retrospect, I now believe that it would have been much easier—and the right thing to do—to have confessed to Tammy Faye right after it happened and accepted the consequences. I believe she could have handled it, and we would have been able to work through it.
—**Jim Bakker**

Charisma without character leads to catastrophe.
—**Peter Kuzmic**

On the other hand, this type of reasoning is close to suggesting that ideally lifeguards must experience a shark attack before they can mount a rescue, or that firemen must be horribly burned before they respond to the alarm. This is, indeed, a strange path to enlightenment, to suggest that the shepherd must be dismembered by the wolves before he is fully capable of tending the sheep. The notion that somehow those who succumb to temptation are better able to understand temptation than those who resist it is like arguing that the person who dropped out of the race in the first mile better understands the struggle of the race than those who go the distance. It is an argument made all the more remarkable when we consider clear biblical teaching that even though Jesus himself was perfectly sinless, he is able to understand our frailties. "For we do not have a high priest who is unable to sympathize with our weaknesses, but we have one who has been tempted in every way, just as we are—yet was without sin" (Heb. 4:15).

Authentically Holy and Healthy: "Great Gifts Mean Great Responsibilities"

While it probably makes us feel a bit uncomfortable—Jesus had the bluntness to describe it like bearing a cross (Luke 14:27)—the bulk of biblical evidence and church tradition points to a higher standard, a raised bar, for those in leadership. Even Luther remarked, "These are the two causes of offense to hearers: doctrine and life. If a man leads a good life but preaches bad doctrine, this is a great offense, because he should not be believed. If, on the other hand, he teaches good doctrine but leads a bad life, people say: If what he teaches were true, he himself would live it."[27]

[27] Martin Luther, "Sermon on John 8:46–50, 1528," in *What Luther Says*, ed. E. Plass (St. Louis, Ill.: Concordia, 1959), 1123.

Richard Baxter, author of the classic *The Reformed Pastor*, underlined this point in pleading that those in ministry must measure themselves by a higher standard than those who are not in positions of leadership:

> Great works as ours require greater grace . . . Do not think that a heedless, careless course will accomplish so great a work as this. You must look to come off with greater shame and deeper wounds of conscience than if you had lived a common life . . . We have seen some private Christians of good esteem, who, having thought too highly of their parts, and thrust themselves into the ministerial office, have proved weak and empty men, and have become greater burdens to the Church than some whom we endeavored to cast out. They might have done God more service in the higher rank of private men . . . As you may render God more service, so you may do him more disservice than others. The nearer men stand to God, the greater dishonor God has by their miscarriages.[28]

Why is this so important? Because water—even *living water*—that flows through polluted pipes could inflict serious damage to those who depend on the pipes for refreshment.

Leadership Is a Privilege, Not a Right

Along with privilege always comes responsibility (Luke 12:48). Some have protested that when we severely discipline fallen leaders, we are communicating to the watching world a message of condemnation when we should be communicating a message of grace.[29] The stock phrase typically used is, "The Christian army is the only army in the world that shoots its wounded." While discipline must always be exercised with grace and support (which, granted, does not always happen), this criticism is based on two flaws:

▸ **All sin is equal in the sight of God, but clearly, all sin does not have equal consequences.**[30] When a leader falls, the consequences are much greater, in part at least, because they are so much more visible.[31] There is no question: it is important for the church to be seen as gracious toward those who sin. But it is equally important that the church be seen as faithful and obedient to the God who calls us to holiness.[32]

---

[28] Richard Baxter, *The Reformed Pastor* (Grand Rapids, Mich.: Christian Classics Ethereal Library; 1974), 23.

[29] Anyone who makes such a remark should consider the witness of the Roman Catholic Church in the first decade of this new millennium. Has disregard for sin in the priesthood helped or hurt its witness to the watching world?

[30] This is the point Richard Baxter is making when he warns, "Take heed to yourselves, lest your example contradict your doctrine,... lest you unsay with your lives, what you say with your tongues . . . He that means as he speaks, will surely do as he speaks. One proud, surly, lordly word, one needless contention, one covetous action, may cut the throat of many a sermon, and blast the fruit of all that you have been doing." Baxter, *Reformed Pastor*, 63.

[31] "Henry Lyons, former president of the National Baptist Convention, U.S.A., embarrassed his entire denomination by being convicted of various forms of thievery, while blaming his crimes on the media and white racism. Allan Boesak, who inspired so many of us with his stirring words of resistance to racial apartheid [in South Africa], was sent to jail for misappropriation of funds that were given to help the poor, claiming that he was a victim of European cultural imperialism." Willimon, *Pastor*, 29–30.

[32] "One might object that these are private matters, incidental to the quality of ministry, and the rights of privacy should apply to ministers as well as any other citizen. But that objection assumes that we are dealing essentially with a civil right. The privilege and calling of ministry is not a civil right, because only states can grant civil rights, but no state can ordain canonically to ministry. The minister who voluntarily affirms the call to ministry and takes up the task of teaching Christian faith and practice, cannot appeal to the right of privacy when his behavior fails to correspond with his teaching." Oden, *Classical Pastoral Care*, 187.

▸ **Disciplining a fallen leader is not about shooting the wounded.** It is about taking seriously the wounds of that fallen leader and admitting that serious wounds (especially a malfunction of the heart) impede one's ability to lead troops into battle.[33]

Youth Ministry Is Primarily for the Students

Youth ministry is not a tool for therapy by which we can heal needy adults, or a means by which some wounded adult can be made to feel special. The primary question to ask about the leadership is "what is best for the sheep," not "what is best for the shepherd." Jesus was clear about the dire danger of bad leadership (Matt. 7:15–20). Elton Trueblood reminds us that even great skill cannot be allowed to trump simple integrity:

> It is hard to think of any job in which the moral element is lacking. The skill of the dentist is wholly irrelevant, if he is unprincipled and irresponsible. There is little, in that case, to keep him from withdrawing teeth unnecessarily, because the patient is usually in a helpless situation. It is easy to see the harm that can be done by an unprincipled lawyer. Indeed, *such a man is far more dangerous if he is skilled than if he is not skilled.*[34]

The Key to Ministerial Ethics: How Will It Affect the Body?

Ministerial ethics tends to be intensely communal, corporate, and congregational in nature, not only because pastors are called to upbuild the Christian community, but also because Christian ethics is by nature communitarian ... In most of Paul's letters, ethics is intrachurch ethics. Time and again his test for the ethical appropriateness of a given practice is, *Does this edify the body?* The foundational Pauline metaphor for the church is the body, "Now you are the body of Christ and individually members of it" (1 Cor. 12:27). He even evaluates worship practices like the Lord's Supper and speaking in tongues on the basis of how well worship builds up the body. In the letter in which Paul evokes most strongly the image of the church as the body, he writes twice, "All things are lawful, but not all things are beneficial" (1 Cor. 6:12; 10:23a).

William Willimon, Pastor: The Theology and Practice of Ordained Ministry *(Nashville, Tenn.: Abingdon, 2002), 310.*

---

[33] We can love someone, forgive someone, and continue to value someone without necessarily keeping that person in a leadership role. Moving someone out of leadership is not moving that person out of the kingdom.

[34] Elton Trueblood, *Your Other Vocation* (New York: Harper and Row, 1952) cited in Gordon MacDonald, *Facing Turbulent Times* (Wheaton, Ill.: Tyndale, 1981), 93.

The gods have given me almost everything, but I let myself be lured into long spells of senseless and sensual ease. Tired of being on the heights, I deliberately went to the depths in search of a new sensation. What paradox was to me in the sphere of thought, perversity became to me in the sphere of passion. I grew careless of the lives of other people. I took pleasure where it pleased me, and passed on. And I forgot that every little action of the common day makes or unmakes character. And that therefore, what one has done in the secret chamber, one has someday to cry aloud from the housetop. I ceased to be lord over myself. I was no longer the captain of my soul, and I did not know it. I allowed pleasure to dominate me, and I ended in horrible disgrace.

Oscar Wilde, gifted Irish poet. Cited in Steve Farrar, Finishing Strong (Grand Rapids, Mich.: Zondervan, 1997), 138–139.

The Christian Life Cannot Be Compartmentalized

In *Ministerial Ethics*, Trull and Carter identify three key elements that make up pastoral ethics: character—who we are; conduct—what we do; and moral vision—the "true north" that provides a reference point and guiding light for our moral choices. Integrity is the integration of these three elements into an organic whole. (See Figure 4-1).

We cannot say of a Christian leader, "He is immoral, but he is a great worship leader, so let's keep using him." Worship is not just what happens on Sunday morning. It is a whole life, whole-hearted expression to God. Doing that is not combined with being is empty and phony. James speaks forthrightly about this:

We preached so many sermons of Christ, while we neglected him; of the Spirit, while we resisted him; of faith, while we did not ourselves believe; of repentance and conversion, while we continued in an impenitent and unconverted state; God is no respecter of persons; he saveth no men for their coats or callings; a holy calling will not save an unholy man.
—**Richard Baxter**

You cannot read too much in Scripture; and what you read you cannot read too carefully, and what you read carefully you cannot understand too well, and what you understand well you cannot teach too well, and what you teach well you cannot live too well.
—**Martin Luther**

Figure 4-1.
Integrity

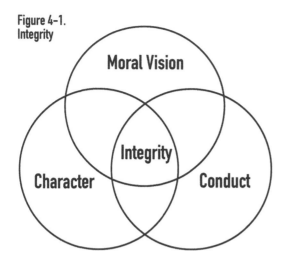

Source: Joe E. Trull and James E. Carter, *Ministerial Ethics: Being a Good Minister* (Nashville, Tenn.: Broadman and Holman, 1999).

A spring doesn't gush fresh water one day and brackish the next, does it? Apple trees don't bear strawberries, do they? Raspberry bushes don't bear apples, do they? You're not going to dip into a polluted mud hole and get a cup of clear, cool water, are you? Do you want to be counted wise, to build a reputation for wisdom? Here's what you do: Live well, live wisely, live humbly. It's the way you live, not the way you talk, that counts (James 3:11-13, *The Message*).

No Place for a Guilty Conscience

The best ministry leadership is leadership unencumbered by a guilty conscience. There are hardships and trials enough in ministry without having to face also the strain of a heavy conscience. Not only does it sap our strength physically and emotionally (see Ps. 32), but it restricts our access to the reservoir of God's resources so critical for effective youth ministry. One can hear the peace that a clear conscience offers even in tough times in the journal of Mary Slessor.

Mary Slessor was a young woman who left Scotland at the turn of the century to go to a part of Africa that was infested with disease and incredible danger. Once,

You Make the Call—Case I

Jane is a youth minister. Her reputation for creativity and sensitivity has made her a widely respected and much loved member of the First Church staff. But now it looks as if all of that will come to a sharp stop. Jane has admitted that she has had a sexual relationship with one of the guys in the single-adult ministry. They are talking about getting married. Everyone knew they were dating. But nobody could believe it when she announced that she was pregnant. She wants to stay on in her job. Many of the kids want her to stay. They say she is only human. There are parents on both sides of the issue, and emotions are strong from all quarters. The pastor has announced that the elders will be making a decision about Jane within the next week. You are an elder. What do you decide to do?

after a particularly draining day, she found herself trying to sleep in a crude jungle hut (reminiscent of last summer's camp experience?). Of that night she wrote: "I am not very particular about my bed these days, but as I lay on a few dirty sticks laid across and covered with a litter of dirty corn-shells, with plenty of rats and insects, three women and an infant three days old alongside, and over a dozen sheep and goats and cows outside, you don't wonder that I slept little. But I had such a comfortable quiet night *in my own heart* (emphasis added)".[35]

Research has consistently demonstrated what we all know intuitively to be true: "We may speak long and hard with our lips, but we speak loud and clear with our lives."[36] We simply cannot divorce our role as leaders from our lives as disciples.

You Make the Call—Case 2

John is studying for what he hopes will be a fruitful and fulfilling ministry working with youth. He is 24-years-old, and he feels that he has a lot to offer. He admittedly has made some serious mistakes already in his young life. Although John became a Christian during his senior year of high school, he has had a rocky road. He has already been through a hastily arranged marriage that lasted less than a year. He attempted to start his own business, but had to declare bankruptcy when creditors questioned his integrity and business practices, preventing him from getting a necessary line of credit. John is popular with high school and junior high students. He is funny. He is a good athlete, and he has a good sense of how to get along with kids. His internship in the youth ministry major has shown him to be a charismatic leader with students. But now, just before he graduates, you find yourself in a bit of a dilemma as his professor of youth ministry. A church has called you to vouch for John's character. They take their kids seriously and they want a godly youth minister for their church. They want to know if you can give them a recommendation for John's ministry. How do you answer?

Potholes and Dangerous Falls

In the 2001 edition of *Accidents in North American Mountaineering*, there are the usual reports of ice accidents and climbing falls, hypothermia and heat stroke, avalanches and surprise blizzards. But in the opening paragraphs of the report are these sobering words: "The accidents that could have been prevented, and can

---

[35] James Buchan, *The Indomitable Mary Slessor* (New York: Seabury, 1981), 86.

[36] Robert G. Cox, *Do You Mean Me, Lord?* (Philadelphia: Westminister Press, 1985), 24–30. Cox cites the research of Merton Strommen and others for the "Readiness for Ministry" project. They undertook an extensive study of what laity and clergy value in those who are leaving seminary and joining the ranks of the ordained ministry. Summarizing their findings, Strommen, Schuller, and Brekke noted that the value rated the highest is "an open affirming style. A style of ministry that reflects a minister who is positive, open, flexible; who behaves responsibly to persons as well as to tasks."

They went on to conclude that effective ministry demands an approach to life in which one maintains "personal integrity despite pressures to compromise." It is an approach that places style in the foreground and function in the background. In other words, their findings suggest that "while the expectation of ministry or priesthood in North America includes competence in functions, *it is also highly sensitive to the character and spirit of the person who carries out these functions* (emphasis added)."

Youth Ministry Trouble Spots

Beth Slevcove, a spiritual director and retreat leader, helps us to see how these issues are manifest in the everyday life and ministry of youth workers:

▸ Instead of nurturing spiritual intimacy, many youth workers display a compulsiveness to do more, work harder, and be better. Exhaustion and despair are inevitably the result.

▸ Often, there is little or no awareness that intimacy with Christ, a sense of being deeply loved, a lasting peace, and the fruits that come from communion with him are even possible.

▸ Many lack a safe place to wrestle with issues, a safe person to be honest with and accountable to (preferably outside of the church in which they are ministering).

▸ Often there is a belief that they should be strong enough Christians to do it on their own and that sharing or asking for help is weakness.

▸ Many fail to see that God provides other members of the body of Christ to assist each of us in our journeys of faith.

▸ Most have little sense of the importance of the concept of Sabbath, that constant productivity is not required of us, but resting in God is.

▸ Many carry the false belief that *What I do = Who I am*. Thus, their sense of self worth is often deeply wed to their job, which results in a need to be liked, praised, popular, and successful.

▸ Many are striving to live up to the stereotypical, fun, charismatic, extroverted, cool youth worker, instead of recognizing their own giftedness and ministering in their own unique way.

—Introduction to Spiritual Direction *seminar, presented at the National Youth Workers Convention, Sacramento, Calif., October 3–7, 2002.*

therefore be learned from, include: solo climbing, climbing in poor conditions, using inadequate belay and rappel stations, and using poor judgment in route selection based on unfavorable conditions or ability."[37]

There are in the world of youth ministry several notorious trouble spots—places on the adventure where arrogance, ignorance, bad judgment, and inadequate safety procedures can cause a serious fall—potholes on the road of long-term youth ministry that lead to blow-out, burnout, fallout, dropout, and early retirement. In their extensive research of almost 2,500 youth workers, Strommen, Jones, and Rahn determined six common concerns on the minds of

---

[37] *Accidents in North American Mountaineering*—2001 (Golden, Colo.: American Alpine Club, 2001), 1.

youth workers—issues they describe in their study as "six perils that can sink a career":[38]

> ▸ Feelings of personal inadequacy.

> ▸ Strained family relationships.

> ▸ A growing loss of confidence.

> ▸ Feeling unqualified for the job.

> ▸ Disorganization in one's work habits.

> ▸ Burnout.

Youth ministry can indeed be perilous work. There are steep climbs, quick descents, deep valleys, and hidden chasms. Prudence requires that we give some thought to the places where others have fallen so that we can learn from their mistakes.

1st Danger Area: Phony Persona

Youth ministry requires us to function sometimes within what psychotherapist Carl Jung called the *persona*, referring to a mask that was sometimes worn in an ancient Greek tragedy. For Jung, the persona is that psychological mask that we put over our real inner feelings so that we can better relate to others. When a kid confesses to us his sin, the persona is what keeps us from saying, "Wow, you're sick!" Or, when a parent worries about a son who has a pierced ear, the persona is what keeps us from saying, "You've got to be kidding!" Or, when a youth pastor shares the disappointment of a tenth grade girl who has lost a boyfriend, even if he never really felt good about the relationship, that is persona. He is not being phony. He is putting on a persona and putting aside his personal feelings to accomplish the greater good of caring for the student.

All good athletes train hard. They do it for a gold medal that tarnishes and fades. You're after one that's gold eternally. I don't know about you, but I'm running hard for the finish line. I'm giving it everything I've got. No sloppy living for me! I'm staying alert and in top condition. I'm not going to get caught napping, telling everyone else all about it and then missing out myself.

–1 Corinthians 9:25–27 (The Message)

---

[38] Cox, *Do You Mean Me, Lord?*, 20–21.

Oh how curiously have I heard some preach; and how carelessly have I seen them live! . . . Those who seemed most impatient of barbarisms, solecisms, and paralogisms in a sermon, seemed to easily tolerate them in their life and conversation . . . We must study as hard how to live well, as how to preach well.
—**Richard Baxter**

Air-brushed adventurers are rarely as interesting as ordinary humans who find themselves in deep water.
—**Nick Thorpe**

I don't know of any other profession in which it is quite as easy to fake it as in ours. By adopting a reverential demeanor, cultivating a stained-glass voice, slipping occasional words like "eschatology" into conversation and [other theological terms] into our discourse—not often enough actually to confuse people but enough to keep them aware that our habitual train of thought is a cut above the pew level—we are trusted, without any questions asked, as stewards of the mysteries. Most people, at least the ones that we are with most of the time, know that we are in fact surrounded by enormous mysteries: birth and death, good and evil, suffering and joy, grace, mercy, forgiveness. It takes only a hint here and a gesture there, an empathetic sigh, or a compassionate touch to convey that we are at home and expert in these deep matters. Even when in occasional fits of humility or honesty we disclaim sanctity, we are not believed. People have a need to be reassured that someone is in touch with the ultimate things. If we provide a bare bones outline of pretense, they take it as the real thing and run with it, imputing to us clean hands and pure hearts.

—*Eugene Peterson,* Working the Angles *(Grand Rapids, Mich.: Eerdmans, 1987), 4.*

But, as William Willimon points out, herein lies a problem:

Too many pastors deny themselves an opportunity to "de-role." They are always pastors . . . They go through their entire lives feeling as if they are delicately balancing themselves on a pedestal, desperately attempting to fulfill an impossible ideal. This leads to a life of posturing, suppression of true feelings, and loss of touch with our real selves . . . When too much energy

Figure 4-2.
The Four Ministerial Selves

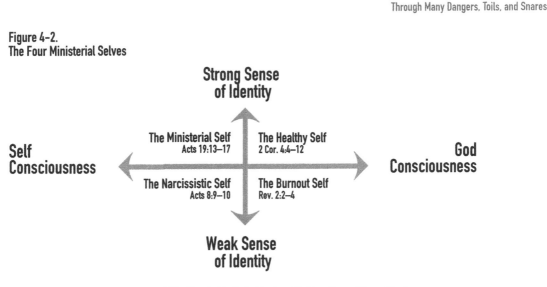

Source: Michael Cavanagh, *The Effective Minister: Psychological and Social Considerations* (New York: Harper and Row, 1986), 76.

is expended in keeping up this mask, when there is no chance to move out of the role, take off the mask, and let down our image, there is a fundamental disjunction between who we are and the role that we play.[39]

One way to think about this notion of phony persona is to recognize that, as Michael Cavanagh describes it in *The Effective Minister*, there are four selves that can operate within a Christian leader (see Figure 4-2)[40]:

1. **The Ministerial Self**: I will act the way ministers or youth ministers are supposed to act.

2. **The Narcissistic Self**: I will act in whatever way brings me the greatest success, favor, and admiration.

3. **The Burnout Self**: I will act because I cannot feel, because I am too busy trying to please God to stop and feel.

4. **The Healthy Self**: I will not act. I will be who I am called to be in Christ, even if sometimes it may seem "nonministerial," may occasionally cost me favor and success, and may require me to reduce my doing so that I can fully experience being.

It may be helpful to think of these four selves as four different quadrants on a grid with two variables: (1) sense of identity, and (2) sense of intimacy. All of us

[39] Willimon, *Pastor*, 29–30. James Dittes makes this same point in warning of the dangers of "the empty yes": "The empty yes is the routine yes, the rootless yes, the routeless yes, the yes that goes nowhere, the bodiless yes, the thin yes, the cosmetic yes, the yes that washes away at first test, the yes that crumbles at first touch and leaves the heartbreaking no." James Dittes, *Re-Calling Ministry* (St. Louis, Mo.: Chalice Press, 1999), 42–44.

[40] Michael Cavanagh, *The Effective Minister: Psychological and Social Considerations* (New York: Harper and Row, 1986), 76ff.

Table 4-1.
The Four Ministerial Selves

Self	Defining Feature	Behavior Characterizations	Results
The Ministerial Self	The Ministerial Self, consciously or unconsciously, is programmed to fit the youth worker's perception of what a youth minister is like. Youth workers who operate in this self spend more time acting like youth workers than being human beings who serve as youth workers. The Ministerial Self is more often adopted by senior pastors than youth pastors.	• Youth workers who function out of the Ministerial Self believe they should only feel and communicate "youth minister emotions" (enthusiasm and happiness, or cynicism and coolness) and not feel other emotions (fear, loneliness, anger, disappointment, seriousness) even when those emotions could be appropriate. • They feel that because they are ministers, they should always have a religious sentiment to offer in every situation. • They feel they should always be "nice," even when it would be more honest to express disagreement or confrontation. • Some youth workers use a different tone of voice when they preach and pray; they tend to use words and inflection they would not use in normal conversation so they have a tone of gravitas and spirituality.	• When we function out of the Ministerial Self, we exhaust ourselves trying to be something we are not. For all the exhaustion and effort, our reward is the mistrust of others who are suspicious that we are not who we appear to be. • This is probably one of the reasons that so many youth workers burn out: being someone you are not is exhausting work! • This Ministerial Self also makes intimacy difficult because the more intimate the relationship, the more difficult the facade.
The Narcissistic Self	The Narcissistic Self makes youth workers self-conscious of being liked, being admired, considered cool, and thought successful.	• Youth workers who function out of the Narcissistic Self feel they must always be funny, outgoing, gregarious, wild and crazy; they feel the need to make frequent comic references to body functions, and often throw in some profanity. • They must always be "on," must always project the appearance of being really "up." • They focus more on how they are doing in relating to the student than on how the student in the relationship is doing. • They find subtle ways to remind everyone of all they gave up to follow Jesus, how utterly committed they are. • They tend to be unduly energized by success; very attuned to numbers. • They overreact to frustration, failure, and criticism because ego is at stake.	• When we function out of the Narcissistic Self, we eventually end up using ministry to meet our needs rather than doing ministry to meet other's needs. • The Narcissistic Self leads to disillusionment because we are trying to fill a broken cup. Although we work harder and harder, we still feel unsuccessful and empty. • The Narcissistic Self breeds jealousy when we see other youth workers succeed.

Self	Defining Feature	Behavior Characterizations	Results
The Burnout Self	The Burnout Self probably began as the Ministerial Self or the Narcissistic Self, but this self has pushed so hard and so fast for so long without refreshment and refueling that it simply cannot continue to move forward.	• Youth workers who function out of the Burnout Self tend to see students and their families no longer as people, but as "clients," jobs to be handled and dealt with. • That cell phone ring that used to mean opportunity now produces dread and resentment. • Relationships that do not directly help to accomplish a task are bypassed as an unnecessary drain of time and energy. • Days off become not so much a time of refreshment, refocus, or reconnection, as a time of "shut down"—mostly sleeping, eating, or watching TV or videos. • Doing for people has replaced being with people—tasks take priority over relationships. • There is no rhythm to life, no "space" for prayer, quiet, solitude, reading Scripture. • They suffer lost capacity for dreaming and vision; everything has been reduced to hand-to-hand, hour-to-hour "combat." • Youth workers often use cynicism and sarcasm to disguise deep disappointment with life and with God.	• The central problem with the Burnout Self is that it puts us in a vicious cycle. We cannot slow down, because we have become what we do, and the noise of business drowns out the ache of meaninglessness. • The more we sink into the Burnout Self, the more those around us see its effects. The more those around us see its effects, the more negative feedback we get. The more negative feedback we get, the harder we work to reverse the mood. But the harder we work, the more we get burned out.
The Healthy Self	The Healthy Self is healthy principally because it is not contaminated by the other selves. The simple (although, admittedly, it is not always so simple) guiding principle for the Healthy Self is a growing Christ-consciousness leading to a diminished self-consciousness.	• Youth workers who function out of the Healthy Self operate on the principle: "Who you see is who I am." They have a realistic sense of themselves and others—their potential for sinfulness and the rich potential for holiness through Christ. The good news of the gospel is that they can say, "Who you see is who I am, but by Christ's power at work in me, who you see today does not have to be all and forever what I am." • They are secure enough and self-contained enough to feel they are okay even without the expressed approval of a 14-year-old, her parents, or the church board. • This security allows them to set realistic boundaries and limits. • They continue to cultivate a part of their lives that is not public—in other words, there is more to them than the job. • Youth workers can appreciate the joy of small blessings and small successes because they are not being driven by an insatiable thirst for recognition. • This allows them to facilitate and celebrate the gifts of others.	• Functioning out of the Healthy Self is no guarantee of a conflict-free, trouble-free ministry. The key is that when we operate out of the Healthy Self, we tend to grow around and through adversity. • Because we are being ourselves, we can enjoy greater longevity in ministry: we never get too old to be ourselves. • The Healthy Self will likely result in healthier family relationships because the pressure is off to prove oneself by overachievement and overinvolvement. • The Healthy Self also frees up other people (staff colleagues and volunteers) to function out of a healthy sense of self.

are fully capable of operating on the basis of any of these selves at any given time depending on the circumstances. But most of us function a majority of the time as one of these four selves, and these selves begin to expose themselves in predictable patterns of behavior (see Table 4-1).

Basic Principle of Healthy Ministry Leadership:
To thine own Lord be true (Ps. 139:1–6).

The Central Question for Christian Leaders

It is not enough for the priests and ministers of the future to be moral people, well trained, eager to help their fellow humans, and able to respond creatively to the burning issues of their time. All of that is very valuable and important, but it is not the heart of Christian leadership. The central question is, are the leaders of the future truly men and women of God, people with an ardent desire to dwell in God's presence, to listen to God's voice, to look at God's beauty, to touch God's incarnate Word and to taste fully God's infinite goodness?

—*Henri Nouwen,* In the Name of Jesus: Reflections on Christian Leadership *(New York: Crossroad, 1993), 29–30.*

Authentic holiness happens when (1) a youth leader honestly identifies the self in which he or she operates; and (2) a youth leader begins, by God's power, to take steps intentionally to become more often that authentically holy and healthy self God made him or her to be.

2nd Danger Area: Professional Holiness

The French have an expression, *déformation professionnelle*, which means literally, "the unraveling of one's job."[41] The phrase describes what happens when one does one's job with the head but not the heart. Imagine a food critic who previously came to the table for taste and delight but now comes only to write an article about eating; or the professional golfer who originally played the sport because of a love for the game but has long since forgotten what it was like to think of golf as a game; or the gardener who used to believe in the beauty of gardening but now only thinks in terms of dreary tasks such as filling pots with dirt. It is the difference between doing a job with passion and doing a job for pay.

One of the grave dangers of ministry is professional holiness, falling into the habit of what John Henry Jowett, one of the great preachers of the early twentieth century, called the "deadening familiarity with the sublime." Henri Nouwen described it as "that dead-end street . . . where all the words [are] already spoken,

---

[41] Knute Larson in *In Need of a Good Reputation, Measuring Up*, ed. Stuart Briscoe, Knute Larson, and Larry Osborne (Sisters, Ore.: Multnomah Books, 1993), 28.

Marks of Professional Holiness

What in youth ministry are the marks of professional holiness? Here are a few:

▸ Spending more time talking about prayer than actually praying.

▸ Private prayers beginning to sound like "nice" public prayers (prayers before the banquet, prayers before the game, prayers before the offering).

▸ Reading the Bible only when preparing a message or Bible study.

▸ Living a life so fast and so cluttered there is no time for cultivating the inner life that people don't see.

▸ "Third-person reading": reading not for what God can say to you, but for what you can say when you speak to students.

▸ Inner exhaustion that leads to outer crankiness and cynicism.

▸ A loss of wonder.

The only way to survive in ministry is to steadfastly refuse to be interested in ministry and to be interested only in Jesus Christ.
—**Oswald Chambers**

A public man, though he is necessarily available at many times, must learn to hide. If he is always available, he is not worth enough when he is available.
—**Elton Trueblood**

all events [have] already taken place, and all the people [have] already been met."[42]

You will not have been long in the ministry before you discover that it is possible to be fussily busy about the Holy Place and yet to lose the wondering sense of the Holy Lord. We may have much to do with religion and yet not be religious. We may become mere guideposts when we were intended to be guides. We may indicate the way, and yet

[42] Henri Nouwen, *The Wounded Healer* (New York: Image Books, 1979), 74.

not be found in it. We may be professors but not pilgrims. Our studies may be workshops instead of "upper rooms." Our share in the table-provisions may be that of analysts rather than guests. We may become so absorbed in words that we forget to eat the Word. And the consummation of the subtle peril may be this: we may come to assume that fine talk is fine living, that expository skill is deep piety, and while we are fondly hugging the non-essentials, the veritable essence escapes. I think this is one of the most insidious, and perhaps the predominant peril in a preacher's life.[43]

> I want to give one word of warning to workers for God, especially Sunday-school teachers and preachers of the Gospel—beware of the snare of putting anything first in your mind but Jesus Christ. If you put the needs of your people first, there is something between you and the power of God. Face Jesus Christ steadily, and allow nothing, no work and no person, to come between you and Him.
>
> —Oswald Chambers, Workmen of God, (London: Marshall, Morgan and Scott, 1937), 21.

The danger is especially real in ministry because our work for the kingdom can so easily overshadow our fellowship with the King. The work seems so right, so compelling. The novelty and romance of youth ministry is so engaging; we sense God's presence in the work. But then little by little, we become so absorbed in the work that we no longer sense God's presence.

It is not a new story in ministry. Countless studies have demonstrated that sometimes those of us who talk *about* God the most talk *to* God the least. One survey of 572 pastors across America found that:

> "Do not rejoice that the demons are subject to you," said Jesus; "but rather rejoice, because your names are written in heaven." God grant we may understand that the mainspring of our passion for souls must be a personal, passionate devotion to the Lord Jesus Christ.
>
> —Oswald Chambers, Workmen of God, (London: Marshall, Morgan and Scott, 1937), 21.

▸ The pastors spend an average of 22 minutes per day in prayer.

▸ 57 percent spend less than 20 minutes a day in prayer.

▸ 34 percent spend between 20 minutes and one hour a day in prayer.

▸ 9 percent pray for an hour or longer daily.[44]

---

[43] Gerald Kennedy, ed., *The Best of John Henry Jowett* (New York: Harper and Bros, 1948), 146f.

[44] Peter Wagner, cited in H. B. London and Neil B. Wiseman, *Pastors at Risk* (Wheaton, Ill.: Victor Books, 1993), 179. In 1993, Paul Borthwick published an article in *Youthworker* that explored youth workers' responses to a survey on personal spirituality. While the sample was very small (only 58 out of 400-plus surveys were returned, approximately 15 percent), Borthwick draws the conclusion that "measuring spiritual health by the disciplines of prayer, Bible study, and devotional reading suggests a general weakness in youth minister's inner lives." Paul Borthwick, "When Spirituality is Your Job," *Youthworker* (Spring 1993), 75.

Figure 4–3.
Working the Angles

Source: Eugene Peterson, *Working the Angles* (Grand Rapids, Mich.: Eerdmans, 1987), 2–5.

Basic Principle of Healthy Ministry Leadership:
Keep working the angles; keep the main thing the main thing (Luke 10:27).

There is only one way across this cold tundra of professional holiness: consistent, intentional pursuit of intimacy with God. Eugene Peterson describes it as "working the angles."[45] (See Figure 4-3.) There are three tasks essential for those of us in any sort of ministry, and as with the proverbial three-legged stool, the absence of any of these tasks leaves us unbalanced. The three tasks are:

1. Prayer: focusing on what God is doing in one's life.

2. Scripture reading: focusing on how God has worked in the lives of his people over the centuries.

3. Spiritual direction (mentoring, discipleship): focusing on what God is doing in the life of another person.

It is no coincidence that each of these acts has at its heart a focus on God. This is always the central task of ministry—listening to God.

Unfortunately, there are three elements of this task that are typically foreign to youth workers.

First of all, it requires quiet, and youth workers tend to be a loud bunch. As a professional group, youth workers seem collectively to suffer from attention

[45] Eugene Peterson, *Working the Angles* (Grand Rapids, Mich.: Eerdmans, 1987), 2–5.

*It is the momentary careless-
ness in easy places, the lapsed
attention, or the wandering
look that is the usual parent of
disaster.*
—**Albert F. Mummery**

*Come hither,
you that walk along the way;
See how the pilgrims fare that
go astray!
They catched are in an
entangling net,
'Cause they good counsel
lightly did forget.
'Tis true they rescued were;
but yet you see,
They're scourged to boot.
Let this your caution be.*
—**John Bunyan**

Sobering Facts

▸ 90 percent of pastors work more than 46 hours a week;

▸ 75 percent reported a significant stress-related crisis at least once in ministry;

▸ 50 percent felt unable to meet the demands of the job;

▸ 90 percent felt they were inadequately trained to meet the demands of the ministry;

▸ 70 percent said they had lower self-esteem than when they started in ministry;

▸ 40 percent reported a serious conflict with a parishioner at least once a month;

▸ 37 percent confessed having been inappropriately involved in sexual behavior with someone in their church;

▸ 70 percent do not have someone they consider a close friend.

From 1991 Survey of Pastors, *from the study by Fuller Institute for Church of Growth, cited by H. B. London and Neil Wiseman,* Pastors at Risk *(Wheaton, Ill.: Victor Books, 1993), 22.*

deficit disorder. We are doers and movers, and listening to God requires stillness and quiet.

Secondly, none of these three acts—prayer, Scripture reading, and spiritual direction—are best practiced in public (in the front of the room). They require silence and solitude—two elements typically foreign to youth ministry.[46]

> What have we our time and strength for, but to lay them out for God? What is a candle made for but to burn? Burned and wasted we must be; but is it not fitter it should be in lighting men to heaven and in working for God than in living in the flesh?
>
> *Richard Baxter,* The Reformed Pastor, *cited in William Willimon,* Clergy and Laity Burnout *(Nashville. Tenn.: Abingdon, 1989), 13.*

Third, because none of these acts is public, it is easy to cheat. No one knows whether we are doing in private what we talk about in public. In fact, that is what makes the risk so acute. Most of our students assume we are so spiritual and so "in touch with God" that they give us the benefit of all doubt. If we are not very, very careful, we will accept their appraisal of us as true, even when we know it's not.

3rd Danger Area: Consuming Activity

On January 30, 1962, the Flying Wallendas tightrope troupe was performing its signature feat, "The Seven," at the State Fair Coliseum in Detroit. It was an amazing 4-2-1 pyramid of tightrope walkers all moving together across a wire suspended high above the ground (with no safety net), the woman at the top of the pyramid standing precariously in a chair perched on the wire. As the audience sat in spellbound silence, the performers began making their way across the wire when the front man on the wire faltered and fell to the wire, leading to the pyramid's collapse. There were a number of extremely serious injuries. Two performers died from their falls; a third was paralyzed from the waist down. Miraculously, the girl in the chair suffered only a concussion because she was caught by Karl Wallenda, the family patriarch, who managed to hold on to the girl after she fell to the wire on top of him. Those who witnessed the incident can still recall the haunting words of the front man who, just before he dropped to the wire, cried out in German, "I cannot hold on any longer!"

Research and experience suggest that many in youth ministry know the feeling.[47] We perform on the high wire of leadership, week after week, year after year, standing in the spotlight of ministry. Then one day comes a collapse, a fall,

---

[46] If you do not think these two elements are typically foreign to youth ministry, take some time to watch and listen to a gathering of youth workers. What is frightening is that part of what makes youth workers such a fun and fascinating species is what could also well cause the species to become extinct.

[47] There are a number of studies documenting the perceived stress level of those in ministry. According to the Alban Institute, an estimated 20 percent of the nation's 300,000 clergy suffer from long-term stress. In one year, "when the Southern Baptist Convention paid out $64 million in medical benefits for pastor's claims, stress-related illnesses were second in dollar amount only to maternity benefits." *Current Thoughts and Trends* (December 1992), cited in London and Wiseman, *Pastors at Risk*, 166. "Some research shows that as many as 75 percent of the clergy report experiencing periods of major distress, while 33 percent feel it so acutely, they have considered leaving the ministry." Malony and Hunt, *The Psychology of Clergy*, cited in London and Wiseman, *Pastors at Risk*, 163. William Moore's study of 341 clergy from 36 denominations and 43 states showed that unrealistic expectations are a major factor in pastoral burnout. Malony and Hunt, *The Psychology of Clergy*, cited in London and Wiseman, *Pastors at Risk*, 58.

In Herman Melville's *Moby Dick*, there is a turbulent scene in which a whaleboat scuds across a frothing ocean in pursuit of the great, white whale, Moby Dick. The sailors are laboring fiercely, every muscle taut, all attention and energy concentrated on the task. The cosmic conflict between good and evil is joined; chaotic sea and demonic sea monster versus the morally outraged man, Captain Ahab. In this boat, however, there is one man who does nothing. He doesn't hold an oar; he doesn't perspire; he doesn't shout . . . This man is the harpooner, quiet and poised, waiting. And then this sentence: "To ensure the greatest efficiency in the dart, the harpooners of this world must start to their feet out of idleness, and not out of toil."

The metaphors Jesus used for the life of ministry are frequently images of the single, the small, and the quiet, which have effects far in excess of their appearance: salt, leaven, seed. Our culture publicizes the opposite emphasis: the big, the multitudinous, the noisy. It is, then, a strategic necessity that pastors deliberately ally themselves with the quiet, poised harpooners, and not leap, frenzied, to the oars. There is far more need that we develop the skills of the harpooner than the muscles of the oarsman. It is far more biblical to learn quietness and attentiveness before God than to be overtaken by what John Oman named the twin perils of ministry, "flurry and worry." For flurry dissipates energy, and worry constipates it.

—*Eugene Peterson,* The Contemplative Pastor *(Dallas: Word Publishing, 1989), 33.*

because we simply do not feel we can hold on any longer. What results is dropout, fallout, and burnout.

"Burnout," explains John Sanford, "is a word we use when a person has become exhausted with his or her profession or life activity."[48] While Sanford argues that it may not result as much from a loss of energy as from a loss of meaning, typically, it is marked by stagnation, frustration, and apathy.[49] Unfortunately, it flags a serious danger spot for youth workers.

[48] John Sanford, *Ministry Burnout* (New York: Paulist Press, 1982), 1.

[49] Jerry Edelwich, *Burnout: Stages of Disillusionment in the Helping Professions* (New York: Human Sciences Press, 1980), 28–29. Edelwich describes a five-stage process: enthusiasm, stagnation, frustration, apathy, and intervention (which ideally breaks the cycle). Willimon comments: "I was never happy with the metaphor of 'burnout' as a description of why some pastors call it quits. 'Burnout' implies that our problem as pastors, is a lack of energy . . . From what I observe, our pastoral problem of constancy is more a matter of 'blackout' or 'brownout', the gradual dissipation of meaning in ministry, a blurring of vision." Willimon, *Pastor*, 326.

Why? For a number of reasons:[50]

1. In youth ministry, the job is never finished. No matter how much we do, there will always be much left undone—students we did not get to talk to, letters we did not get to write, phone calls we didn't get to make, students we still have not reached. When is a farmer finished with the field? When is a shepherd done with the flock?

2. There are often conflicting expectations for the youth minister. The church board has one set of expectations, the pastor another, the students another, and parents yet another.

3. We are working with sinners (like ourselves), and sinners have the unfortunate habit of occasionally acting sinful—petty, jealous, selfish, insensitive, being purveyors of gossip and discontent.

4. Ministry is messy. Willimon quotes the advice of a pastoral counselor who, after 15 years of listening to the problems of pastors and their spouses, concluded that "the essential personality requisite for happiness in the pastoral ministry was 'a high tolerance for ambiguity.'"

   Personalities who put a premium on neatness, exactitude, and order are miserable in ministry. Life is messy, people are mysterious, and few people—once one really gets to know them—fit our labels. No one should become a pastor who has been in business as a printer or a photographer! . . . Printers, who must be exact, whose goal is neatness and legibility, will find that parish life is messy. And if your idea of life is limited to what you can see through a small hole, with all the action focused and frozen, a church can drive you crazy.[51]

5. Lack of professional respect, both outside and inside the church.

6. Ministry is hard. In his great book, *Workmen of God*, Oswald Chambers says realistically, "Now both the fisherman's art and the shepherd's art sound poetical until you have tried them! When you have to carry across your shoulders a dirty old [lamb] and bring it down the mountainside, you will soon know whether shepherding is poetry or not; you will soon know whether it is not the most taxing, the most exhausting and the most exasperating work . . ."

Rahn, Jones, and Strommen, in their survey of almost 2,500 youth workers, suggest that youth worker burnout clusters around these types of concerns:

▸ I lack the enthusiasm I had when starting the ministry.

---

[50] This list is an abbreviation and adaptation of material provided in Willimon, *Pastor*, 316–325.
[51] Ibid., 324.

▸ I grow increasingly wary of spending time with youth.

▸ I consider leaving the profession of youth ministry.

▸ I fear I am not remaining faithful to God's calling.

▸ I feel like a babysitter.

▸ I struggle to keep my vision alive.[52]

There are two factors that make us vulnerable to burnout—two factors especially prominent among youth workers.

1. **Vanity.** As youth workers who are often undervalued and undervalidated we are especially vulnerable here.[53] Nouwen articulates three main temptations of ministry leadership, all of them born of vanity: the temptation to be relevant, the temptation to be spectacular, the temptation to be powerful.[54] It is significant that they loosely parallel John's words in 1 John 2:16, what some have described as "The Devil's Triangle":

   "For everything in the world—the cravings of sinful man, the lust of his eyes and the boasting of what he has and does—comes not from the Father but from the world."

   We want to feel important, necessary.[55] "We don't like being wallflowers at the world's party."[56] So we say yes when we should say no. It is not enough to simply lead a Young Life club or serve as a youth pastor. There must be something beyond the pastoral task that gives us importance. We fill our Day-Timers and Palm Pilots with appointments and activities so that there can be no question that God really needs us and kids really need us and "doggone it, we're loveable." We seek validation by getting invited to speak outside of our normal sphere of ministry, or by pursuing opportunities to write, or by participating on boards and commissions—all of which are valid and important opportunities, but opportunities nonetheless which take us away from our central task of discipling the same group of kids week after week—opportunities which consume us with activity.

2. **Slothfulness.** Just as important, but perhaps a little more insidious, is our tendency toward what the Scripture calls *slothfulness* (see Pro. 18:9,

---

[52] Merton Strommen, Karen E. Jones, and Dave Rahn, *Youth Ministry That Transforms* (Grand Rapids, Mich.: Zondervan, 2001), 109–110.

[53] It is no surprise that psychiatrist Louis McBurney cites low self-esteem as the number one problem pastors face. "We are in a high-demand, low-stroke profession in a culture that does not value our product or our work. We labor among people with unrealistic expectations, and deep inside we expect far more from ourselves and the church . . . McBurney's study identified depression as the second most identified pastoral problem." David Fisher, *The 21st Century Pastor* (Grand Rapids, Mich.: Zondervan, 1996), 7–9.

[54] For a full discussion and excellent treatment of these unique temptations of ministry leadership, see Henri Nouwen, *In the Name of Jesus,* (New York: Crossroad, 1991). Gordon Smith refers to these as the three classic sins: "(1) the desire for power, (2) the desire for material security and comfort, and (3) the desire for fame and prestige." Gordon Smith, *Courage and Calling* (Downers Grove, Ill.: InterVarsity Press, 2002), 102.

[55] For an excellent discussion of this phenomenon, see Eugene Peterson and Marva Dawn, *The Unnecessary Pastor* (Grand Rapids, Mich.: Eerdmans, 2000).

[56] Eugene Peterson, *The Contemplative Pastor* (Dallas: Word Publishing and Carol Stream, Ill.: Christianity Today, 1989), 45.

Eccles. 10:18). The sloth is a tropical mammal that lives much of its life hanging upside-down from tree branches. On the rare occasion each day when it descends from the tree, it crawls along at a blistering 10 feet per minute. Or, for the sports-minded, a sloth can run "a hundred" in just under nine hours. Most notable is the sloth's reputation for sluggishness and inactivity. Building no nests and seeking no shelter, even for its young, the sloth prefers to sleep, typically anywhere from 15 to 22 hours a day. When it does finally awaken in late afternoon, it is to eat whatever leaves may be close at hand.

It may strike some as ironic that slothfulness would be identified as a cause of consuming activity. Yet, as C. S. Lewis was fond of pointing out, lazy people are those that often work the hardest, because when we have not done the hard work of setting goals and priorities, saying "yes" to some activities and "no" to others, the task is left to other people. When that happens, we find ourselves frantic and weary, seeking to serve the many last-minute masters who make demands on our time.

Slothfulness then, as John Ortberg reminds us, is not the absence of activity. It is "the failure to do what needs to be done when it needs to be done," like the kamikaze pilot who flew 17 missions![57] He was extremely busy, but he was not doing what he supposed to do when he was supposed to do it. That is why slothful people are often consumed by increasing activity coupled with diminishing contentment. Buechner comments:

To the untrained eye, selfish or ego climbing and selfless climbing may appear identical. Both kinds of climber place one foot in front of the other. Both breathe in and out at the same rate. Both stop when tired. Both go forward when rested. But what a difference! The ego climber is like an instrument that's out of adjustment. He puts his foot down an instant too soon or late. He's likely to miss a beautiful passage of sunlight through the trees. He goes on when the sloppiness of his step says he's tired. He rests at odd times. He looks up the trail trying to see what's ahead even when he knows what's ahead because he just looked a second before. He goes too fast or too slow for the conditions and when he talks his talk is forever about something else. He's here but he's not here.
—**Robert Pirsig**

57 John Ortberg, "Confessions of a Lazy Pastor," in *Dangers, Toils, and Snares*, ed. Richard Exley, Mark Galli, and John Ortberg (Sisters, Ore.: Multnomah, 1994), 52–53. I am indebted to Ortberg's article for much of this material on slothfulness.

A slothful man . . . may be a very busy man. He is a man who goes through the motions, who flies on automatic pilot. Like a man with a bad head cold, he has mostly lost his sense of taste and smell. He knows something's wrong with him, but not enough to do anything about it. Other people come and go, but through glazed eyes he hardly notices them. He is letting things run their course. He is getting through his life . . . [58]

**Basic Principle of Healthy Ministry Leadership:
Live on purpose; be fully present in the moment.**

Live on Purpose. Stephen Covey identifies four quadrants (see Figure 4-4) in which all of our daily activities can be divided/ arranged/ organized/ ordered:[59]

Quadrant 1: Those activities that are urgent and important (for example: a woman in labor needing a doctor; a firefighter rushing to a house fire).

Quadrant 2: Those activities that are important, but not urgent (for example: exercising; sleeping; spending time with God; nurturing relationships with students, staff, and family members).

Quadrant 3: Those activities that feel urgent but are not important (for example: attending meetings; working under report deadlines; purchasing the newest electronic gadget).

Quadrant 4: Those activities that are neither urgent nor important (for example: surfing the web; watching TV).

Figure 4-4.
Covey's Four Quadrants

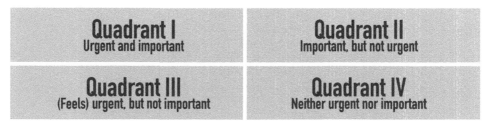

Quadrant I Urgent and important	**Quadrant II** Important, but not urgent
Quadrant III (Feels) urgent, but not important	**Quadrant IV** Neither urgent nor important

Source: Stephen Covey, *The Seven Habits of Highly Effective People* (New York: Simon and Schuster, 1989), 149–156.

[58] Frederick Buechner, *Wishful Thinking* (New York: Harper and Row, 1973), 89–90.
[59] Stephen Covey, *The Seven Habits of Highly Effective People* (New York: Simon and Schuster, 1989), 149–156.

Covey's insights remind us that one way to combat the endless stream of activities threatening to consume us is to order our lives so we mostly spend our time on those activities in Quadrant II. It is impossible (and probably not even desirable) to live such a purposeful life that we exclude all activities in Quadrants III and IV. There are certain elements of every job that require us to do those tasks that in the grand scheme of our main mission we perhaps consider nonessential (reports to the board, fund-raising, promotion and publicity, record-keeping, and so on), and there are certainly times when recreation and leisure are appropriate (even if that means playing a computer game, throwing a frisbee, shopping with a friend, or watching a TV marathon of your favorite show). The key is not feverish activity. The key is purposeful activity.

> ## Coffee Break Discussion: How Does Willimon's Comment Apply to Youth Ministry, or Does It?
>
> Almost any Christian could be a pastor, almost anywhere, for a few years. But to remain a vital servant of God—lively, loving, and life-giving over the long haul—that requires the discipline of constancy. Some church observers believe that the most productive year in a pastorate comes about the sixth year. I agree. It takes awhile for a pastor to gain the trust of his or her people, to communicate a vision that is required for effective ministry. I also might add that it takes about six years for your pastoral chickens to come home to roost, for you to be confronted by your failures, for your program of ministry to require rejuvenation and growth. Long pastorates generally make wonderfully grounded and centered pastors, while a series of short pastorates are often an indication of a pastor who has not had to develop the resources for maturation of ministry.
>
> —*William Willimon,* Pastor: The Theology and Practice of Ordained Ministry *(Nashville, Tenn.: Abingdon, 2002), 315.*

Be Fully Present in the Moment. Another key to fending off the fatigue of consuming activity is simply to be fully present in the moment. Sometimes we rob our pleasure of the present because we are living too much in the past or in the future. Psychologist David Burns asks this question: Suppose that every time you sat down to eat, you thought about all the food you would have to consume over the course of your lifetime? "Yeah, I love steak; but, man, by the time I die I'm going to have to eat several hundred more pounds of beef!" Just the thought of it would make you sick. The secret is to consume one meal at a time, one bite at a time.[60] Jesus said in Matthew 6:34: "Therefore do not worry about tomorrow, for tomorrow will worry about itself. Each day has enough trouble of its own."[61]

---

[60] Ortberg, "Confessions of a Lazy Pastor," 59.

[61] Note that Jesus did not say, "Do not think about tomorrow, or do not plan or prepare for tomorrow." He simply made the point that we shouldn't waste today's energy worrying about tomorrow's challenge.

Beating the Burnout Trap

1. **Be more than your job.** If your whole life is defined by work, it can make for a very small cage. Develop relationships outside of youth ministry. Read books, magazines, and articles that take you beyond youth ministry. Practice hobbies not directly related to being a more effective youth worker: sports, cooking, art, music.

2. **Maintain stability without stagnation.** Stability in ministry is important. It is a quality that speaks of consistency—an ability to maintain a trail through good terrain and bad. Stagnation, on the other hand, is when stability grows into predictability and routine. It is walking the same trail so much that we no longer notice the scenery or hear the noises of the wilderness. One is a willingness to keep climbing the peak, the other is an unwillingness (because of fear, habit, ignorance, lack of imagination) ever to consider taking a different trail to see what it might offer. The implications could be anything from driving to work a different way each day to getting a new haircut, to taking some part-time graduate courses, to doing a short-term mission project outside of youth ministry.

3. **Live a whole life.** Establish life practices that maintain a lively mind, body, and spirit.

4. **Learn to say "no."** Understand that every "yes" that is important to you (God, family, health, intellectual growth) will need to be protected by some "no's" that may be important to someone else.

5. **Remember that you are not the Messiah.** A preacher once paraphrased Isaiah 26:3 as "God will keep him in perfect peace whose imagination stops with God." The world will not cave in if you take a 20-minute nap, or do 30 minutes of exercise, or leave the office for an hour to have a surprise Coke snack with your child after school.

6. **Cultivate your sense of play.** Whether it is the basketball goal hanging over the trash can or the electronic parrot that greets visitors entering your office, do not forget to take fun seriously.

7. **Keep the Sabbath.** And keep it wholly, weekly!

8. **Do not take yourself too seriously.**

9. **Remember not to let your job get in the way of your calling.** Your primary calling is to God, not youth ministry (see John 6:28-29).

10. **Never step on the scale of comparison.** Any time you compare yourself with another youth worker, or your ministry with another youth ministry, you will always weigh yourself on a bogus scale. Those kinds of

comparisons almost always amount to you comparing the bad things you know about yourself or your ministry with the good things you know about someone else or his or her ministry. It is a great way to get discouraged.

11. **Recognize that even the best farmer faces seasons of slow growth.** People walked away from Jesus. Audiences turned their backs on the apostles. There was a reason Jesus told the parable of the soils (Mark 4:1-4) and then took great pains to make sure it was understood by his disciples (Mark 4:13-32).

12. **Keep coming back to where you want to end up (Prov. 28:19).** A task without a vision leads to drudgery; a vision without a task leads nowhere; but a vision with a task makes for purposeful life and ministry.

Adapted from Les Parrott, Helping the Struggling Adolescent: A Counseling Guide *(Grand Rapids, Mich.: Zondervan, 1993), 32.*

4th Danger Area: Dishonest Intimacy

Although not by necessity or by doctrine, there has long been an uncomfortable relationship between ministry and sexuality. As early as the fourth and fifth century saints such as Jerome and Augustine of Hippo espoused the view that sex interferes with devotion to God, and therefore, the truest devotion demands a vow of celibacy.[62] Indeed, it was out of devotion that Origen, an influential theologian of the early third century, castrated himself[63] to become a "eunuch for the kingdom's sake" (a fairly heavy-duty abstinence pledge). Both Jerome and Augustine[64] wrote that true devotion, especially of Christian leaders, depended on a complete renunciation of sex. What makes this a little more ironic is that Augustine of Hippo is well known for his struggles and failures in the area of sexual restraint.[65]

Since those early days of Christian history, there have been many sons and daughters of Augustine who have struggled with lust: youth workers who succumb to pornography, fornication, adultery, molestation, and compulsive masturbation. Just how real this issue is in the realm of ministry is verified by numerous studies. Although, as Grenz and Bell point out, only a small percentage of abuse cases come to light, it is quite clear that ministry provides no immunization against sexual temptation.[66] Ministers of all ages, both genders, ordained and nonordained, old and young, married and unmarried, leaders in every conceivable ministry context—none are exempt from sexual temptation.

---

[62] Early on Christian authorities prohibited sex before Communion, considering it somewhere between a diversion and a defilement, a disdain that carried over to menstruation as well. Beginning as early as the late second century, many Christians were convinced that the only appropriate reason for sexual intercourse was for procreation.

[63] Which may be why pictures of Origen often show him frowning and looking a bit traumatized.

[64] E. Glenn Hinson, *Spiritual Preparation for Christian Leadership* (Nashville, Tenn.: Upper Room Books, 1999), 118–120.

[65] Although he never names the mother in his journals, it is quite clear that as an unmarried 18-year-old he fathered a child, a son who was named Adeodatus, "given by God."

[66] Stanley Grenz and Roy D. Bell, *Betrayal of Trust* (Downers Grove, Ill.: InterVarsity Press, 1995), 20–23. "A recent study of the Manitoba Branch of the Canadian Mental Health Association discovered that out of 82 cases of professional abuse, only 24 of the victims had reported the situation to police or other professionals. And, only four were convinced that their complaints had been taken seriously."

Within the Roman Catholic Church,

according to David Rice, "almost one quarter of the active priests in the world" have left the ministry largely for sexual and marital reasons. Richard Sipe maintains that "about 20 percent of priests vowed to celibacy . . . are at one time involved either in a more or less stable sexual relationship with a woman or, alternatively, with sequential women in an identifiable pattern of behavior. An additional 8 to 10 percent of priests are at a stage of heterosexual exploration that often involves incidental sexual contacts."[67]

Among Protestants, the record is equally upsetting: officials of the United Church of Canada, observe that "women are more likely to get sexually harassed in the church than in the workplace" and that "clergy were sexually exploiting their parishioners at twice the rate of secular therapists." A 1984 survey of 300 ministers in the United States indicated almost four out of ten had sexual contact with a congregant, and over one out of ten reported actual sexual intercourse with a congregant. Not surprisingly, over three quarters of the respondents were aware of ministers who had engaged in sexual intercourse with a congregant. Three years later, in a *Christianity Today* survey, some 23 percent of clergy responded that since entering local church ministry they had engaged in some form of sexual behavior they considered inappropriate. Another 12 percent confessed to having extra-marital sex.[68]

One of the gravest dangers to backcountry adventure is the avalanche. On February 20, 2001, 27-year-old Toma Vracarich, who was skiing an off-trail area on the northeast side of Wright Peak in the Adirondacks High Peaks, was killed when the side of the mountain gave way and plowed downhill. Although Vracarich was the only fatality, five other skiers were also injured, three badly enough to require hospitalization.[69] As is typically the case with avalanche injury, the victim was skiing in an unstable area, and when the slide started, he was unable to arrest his fall. It is a tragedy that mirrors all too well the circumstances that sweep incautious youth workers into a disastrous moral fall.

Although it provides no excuse, the word *intimacy* itself gives us some clue as to why this danger area is so troublesome. Etymologically, *intimacy* comes from the Latin word *intus*, meaning "inside," thus, the Latin word *intimus*, which can also mean "best friend." The whole force of the Latin root suggests depth and interiority, a sharing of one's insides with another.[70] Which is why intimacy is such a wonderful gift, and a clear and present danger in youth ministry: we are all about making friends, and getting folks to share their insides. Problems arise when we allow these relationships in places that are out of bounds where instability can give way to a tragic slide.

---

[67] Ibid., 21.

[68] Ibid., 22–23.

[69] *Accidents in North American Mountaineering*, 71.

[70] Donald R. Hands and Wayne L. Fehr, *Spiritual Wholeness for Clergy: A New Psychology of Intimacy with God, Self, and Others* (Bethesda, Md.: Alban Institute, 1993), 37.

Unfortunately, what makes this issue so risky is that we do not often recognize the unstable conditions until it is too late. Perhaps we thought we were only showing affirmation or providing a friendly hug. But for a young man or woman whose context of affection has never been anything other than sexual, *agapé*[71] is mistaken for *eros*.[72] As Paul points out in 1 Corinthians 2:14, those who live in the context of carnality will interpret actions and words in the context of that carnality.[73]

> We have been dealing with the worker for the cure of souls, now I want to deal with the prevention which is better than cure. How can a man or woman become a workman approved unto God? Read 1 Timothy iv. 16, "Take heed to thyself, and to thy teaching." If you forget everything else, do not forget that verse. The word "heed" occurs again in Acts iii. 5 and xx. 28. It means to concentrate, to screw your mind down, fix it, limit it, curb it, confine it, rivet it on yourself and on your teaching. It is a strong word, a powerful word, a word that grips, a rousing word. That is what we have to do if we are going to be workmen approved unto God.
>
> Oswald Chambers, Workmen of God *(London: Marshall, Morgan and Scott, 1937), 93.*

Even if intentions are clear, that does not preclude the fact that caring, nurturing love is attractive. A listening ear is seductive. When we experience exposure to this kind of intimacy, it is quite natural to desire greater exposure and greater intimacy still. We must also be honest enough to own the fact that those of us in ministry leadership have a *power of office* that often leads those around us to grant us inordinate amounts of respect, trust, and vulnerability. Add to all of this the normal sexual attractions inherent in being a human being, the close relationships in which ministry places us, and a ministry schedule that places stress on even the best marriages, and what we have is a moral avalanche waiting to happen.[74] And when the slide occurs, there will be many victims, many parties injured. It was a well-known saying in the Middle East, "Strike the shepherd and the sheep will be scattered" (see Zech. 13:7).

That is why Thomas à Kempis counseled in *The Imitation of Christ*, "The only time to stop temptation is at the first point of recognition. If one begins to argue and engage in a hand-to-hand combat, temptation almost always wins the day." Walter Wangerin calls this first point of recognition "the moment of maybe." In his book *As For Me and My House*, he observes:

---

[71] Vine notes that agapé love is a love that "values and esteems." It "is not an impulse from the feelings, it does not run away with natural inclinations, nor does it spend itself only upon those for whom some affinity is discovered." W. E. Vine, *An Expository Dictionary of New Testament Words* (Old Tappan, N.J.: Fleming Revell, 1966), bk. III, 21–22.

[72] The word from which we derive our word *erotic*. This refers to a more sexual affection.

[73] This is why Youth for Christ veteran Jack Crabtree advises, "Discretion must be used in dealing with all students, especially regarding physical contact. Innocent behavior can be misinterpreted. A hug around the shoulders is not sexual abuse, but a full "body-to-body hug," stroking, massaging, or an affectionate kiss raises questions. Any overt display of affection should be made in a public setting in front of other group members, if at all." Jack Crabtree, *Play it Safe: Keeping Your Kids and Your Ministry Alive* (Wheaton, Ill.: Victor Books, 1993), 60–61.

[74] According to a August 1989 Newsweek article written by Kenneth Woodward with Patricia King, the minister who strays sexually is typically "middle-aged, disillusioned with his calling, neglecting his own marriage, and a lone ranger who is isolated from his clerical colleagues." Cited in Joe E. Trull and James E. Carter, *Ministerial Ethics: Being a Good Minister* (Nashville, Tenn.: Broadman and Holman, 1999), 83.

When a desire is born in us, we have a choice. When it exists still in its infancy, we have a choice. We can carefully refuse its existence altogether, since it needs our complicity to exist . . . Or else we can attend to it, think about it, fantasize into greater existence—feed it! . . . But if we do the latter, if we give it attention in our souls, soon we will be giving it our souls. We've lost free will and the opportunity to choose. The desire itself overpowers us, commanding action, demanding satisfaction.[75]

How then might we guard ourselves from traversing those places of instability so that risk does not turn into avalanche, and slide does not turn into fall? There is, of course, Origen's approach ("True Love Castrates"), but I would imagine prayer and self-control to be less painful. A proactive approach to sure-footed resistance will involve intentional thoughtfulness about setting strict boundaries for ourselves with regard to personal time with students (regardless of gender):

▸ One-to-one counseling with a student should always occur in a public place—never alone or behind closed doors.

▸ Being alone with a student (particularly a student of the opposite sex) should be avoided. [76]

▸ Avoid even the appearance of evil; do not give the devil an opportunity (see I Tim. 5:14).

Basic Principle of Healthy Ministry Leadership:
Better to flee than to fall.

Joseph's hasty retreat from seduction (Gen. 39:7–12) by Potiphar's wife may have been clumsy and awkward. We know it cost him a good coat. But as one preacher put it, "It's better to lose a good coat than a godly conscience." Paul counseled his young protégé, Timothy, "Flee the evil desires of youth . . . "(2 Tim. 2:22) Caution is almost always the wisest posture when dealing with temptation. That is why counselor Archibald Hart admonishes: "What you may do and what you should do are two different things."

It's a strange paradox in Christian ministry: we can be supersensitive to sin and immoral behaviors, but we are often oblivious to the need for ethical

---

[75]Walter Wangerin, Jr., *As for Me & My House* (Nashville, Tenn.: Thomas Nelson, 1990), 195.

[76] Crabtree cautions, "If it is necessary to drive or ride alone with a teen, special care is to be taken with a student of the opposite sex:
·Don't sit close to one another in the car;
·No physical contact;
·Do not stop the car to talk;
·If you must stop, turn on the inside light of the car;
·Avoid physical contact when saying good-bye (hugs and kisses)."

Some youth workers suggest calling the student's home on a cell phone en route to notify parents of the situation. At the very least, a youth worker should note the circumstances, time, and date in a journal or log in case accusations are ever made.

boundaries. This partially accounts for the fall of upright, spiritual and well-intentioned pastors [and youth pastors]. Christian leaders can be so preoccupied with discerning whether something is sinful that they ignore the trickier question: Is this action a stepping stone to sin, even though it may not be sin in and of itself? . . . This is why morality isn't always enough.[77]

Lest we underestimate just how gradual and deceitful is the downward slope of sexual sin, psychologist and counselor Earl Wilson identifies six slippery spots that can lead to a fall:[78]

1. **Minimization:** "I don't see what all the big deal is about; it was nothing more than . . . " This is often done with euphemism or exaggerated humor so that anyone who holds us accountable can be made to feel prudish or unsophisticated about "the real world."

2. **Rationalization:** "Look, a lot of these kids never get any attention at all. How are we going to communicate God's love if we treat them like untouchables and lepers?"

3. **Denial:** Denial can be complicated because it can range from outright deceit of another (see stage 1 below) to the more subtle deceit of ourselves (see stage 9 below). In between, as Wilson reminds us, it can take many forms.

   1. It didn't happen.
   2. If it did happen, people shouldn't be hurt.
   3. I didn't do it.
   4. I didn't mean to do it.
   5. It only happened once.
   6. It's not my fault.
   7. I didn't hurt anyone but myself.
   8. I don't know why everyone has to make such a big deal about this.
   9. I've stopped doing it so it's no big deal.[79]

4. **Relabeling:** "Okay, I'll admit the movie had some crude stuff in it, but I wouldn't call it porn, and it's what all my kids are watching, and it was so incredibly funny."

5. **Justification:** "Look, I don't claim to be perfect; I'm just trying to be honest, and besides, it's not like I'm overwhelmed by passion at home."

6. **Spiritual Rationalization:** "God gave me this man/woman as a soul mate. I can't believe that God would give me this relationship and then ask me to give it up."

---

[77] Archibald D. Hart, "Being Moral Isn't Always Enough," *Leadership* (Spring 1988), 24ff.

[78] Earl D. Wilson, *Steering Clear* (Downers Grove, Ill.: InterVarsity Press, 2002), 65–75. Wilson rightly explains these slippery spots in terms not limited by any means to just sexual sin. This same slippery slope leads to other destructive habits like lying, stealing, cheating, alcoholism, and workaholism.

[79] Ibid., 69.

None of us is self-aware enough to fully guard our own souls. The rationalizations and justifications are just too slick. One of the statements often repeated in backcountry accident reports is "Victim was climbing alone."[80] In protecting ourselves from the delusions of sin, one of the best assets is a friend or ministry colleague who will hold us accountable and ask the hard questions.

Basic Principle of Healthy Ministry Leadership:
Better to be roped to a climbing partner than to be hung by your own deceit.

In a study of 246 men in full-time ministry who experienced moral failure over a two-month period, Howard Hendricks[81] was able to discover four correlations between the fallen leaders:

▸ None were involved in any accountability group.

▸ Each had ceased to invest in daily time of prayer, Scripture reading, and worship.

▸ Eighty percent were involved with another woman as a result of counseling the woman (that is, a close personal emotional relationship with a woman to whom they were not married).

▸ All were convinced "it will never happen to me."

5th Danger Area: Neglected Relationships

A few years ago at the National Youthworker Convention, I heard a different story each day about someone in youth ministry whose marriage was falling apart. It was really quite staggering—six people who obviously, at one point, had been very much in love, but for one reason or another, had now left the fire untended long enough that the coals of the relationship had virtually burned out.

It is no longer an uncommon story.

The following article appeared in one of the earliest editions of *The Wittenberg Door*. I read it at least once a year, and I never fail to be chilled by its warning.

My husband is a full-time youth minister. He is extremely dedicated and spends between 50 and 70 hours a week with young people.

---

[80] This report, for example, from the Warden Service at Jasper National Park, Jasper, Alberta, Canada, documents the death of Drambuie Deamon who died at an ice fall on December 16, 2001: "Fall on ice, climbing alone and unroped." *Accidents in North American Mountaineering* 2001, 14.

[81] Cited in Farrar, *Finishing Strong*, 27.

I think the reason he is so successful with kids is that he is always available to them, always ready to help when they need him.

That may be the reason why the attendance has more than doubled in the past year. He really knows how to talk their language. This past year, he would be out two and three nights a week talking with kids until midnight. He's always taking them to camps and ski-trips and overnight campouts. If he isn't with the kids, he's thinking about them and preparing for his next encounter with them.

And, if he has any time left after that, he is speaking or attending a conference where he can share with others what God is doing through him. When it comes to youth work, my husband has always been 100 percent.

I guess that's why I left him.

There isn't much left after 100 percent.

Frankly, I just couldn't compete with "God." I say that because my husband always had a way of reminding me that this was God's work, and he must minister where and when God called him. Young people desperately needed help, and God had called him to help them. When a young person needed him, he had to respond or he would be letting God and the young person down.

When I did ask my husband to spend some time with the kids or me, it was always tentative, and if I became pushy about it, I was "nagging," "trying to get him out of God's work," "behaving selfishly," or I was revealing a "spiritual problem."

Honestly, I never wanted anything but God's will for my husband, but I never could get him to consider that maybe his family was part of that will.

It didn't matter how many discussions we had about his schedule, he would always end with "Okay, I'll get out of the ministry if that's what you want." Of course, I didn't want that, so we would continue as always until another discussion.

You can only ask for so long. There is a limit to how long you can be ignored and put off. You threaten to leave without meaning it until you keep the threat. You consider all the unpleasant consequences until they don't seem unpleasant anymore. You decide that nothing could be more unpleasant than being alone and feeling worthless.

You finally make up your mind that you are a person with real worth as an individual. You assert your ego and join womanhood again.

That's what I did.

I wanted to be more than a housekeeper, diaper changer, and sex partner.

I wanted to be free from the deep bitterness and guilt that slowly ate at my spiritual and psychological sanity.

Deep inside there was something making me dislike not only my husband, but everything he did or touched.

His "I love you" became meaningless to me because he didn't act like it. His gifts were evidence to me of his guilt because he didn't spend more time with me. His sexual advances were met with a frigidity that frustrated both of us and deepened the gap between us.

All I wanted was to feel as though he really wanted to be with me. But, no matter how hard I tried, I always felt like I was keeping him from something. He had a way of making me feel guilty because I had forced him to spend his valuable time with the kids and myself.

Just once I wish he would have canceled something for us instead of canceling us.

You don't have to believe this, but I really loved him and his ministry once. I never wanted him to work an eight-to-five job. Nor did I expect him to be home every night. I tried to believe every promise he made me, honestly hoping things would change, but they never did.

All of a sudden I woke up one day and realized that I had become a terribly bitter person. I not only resented my husband and his work, but I was beginning to despise myself. In desperation to save myself, our children, and I guess, even my husband and his ministry, I left him.

I don't think he really believed I'd leave him. I guess I never really believed I'd leave him either.

But I did.[82]

It was the great eighteenth-century evangelist George Whitefield who once wrote in his journal, "I believe it is God's will that I should marry . . . I pray God that I may not have a wife till I can live as though I had none."[83]

---

[82] Anonymous, "Diary of a Mad Housewife," *The Wittenberg Door* (June 1971).

[83] Briscoe, Larson, and Osborne, *In Need of a Good Reputation*, 83–84.

It sounded good—admirable and deeply spiritual, and when they were written, the words were no doubt, well-intentioned. But to Whitefield's wife, Elizabeth, during their week-long honeymoon in the bride's home, when he left twice a day for preaching missions in the surrounding countryside, it probably felt less like godliness and spirituality and more like a messiah complex. When he left his wife at home in London while he conducted his many trans-Atlantic travels (13 trips across the Atlantic to be precise)—once for as long as two years—it probably seemed less like godly devotion and more like marital desertion. When Whitefield's four-month-old son died, and Whitefield stayed away to preach three more services before he returned home for the funeral, it probably did not feel like Christ-like love, it probably just felt like distance and betrayal. No wonder she felt that she was "nothing but a load and burden to him."

Marriage and ministry can be a mix of absolutely wonderful and frustratingly difficult. In one study of professional clergy by the Fuller Institute for Church Growth:[84]

▶ 94 percent feel pressured to have an ideal family.

▶ 33 percent of pastors are dissatisfied with the level of sexual intimacy in their marriages; and pastors report 16 percent of their spouses are dissatisfied, which 69 percent blame on their busy schedule, and 35 percent on frequent church night meetings.

▶ 80 percent believed that pastoral ministry affected their families negatively.

▶ 33 percent said that being in ministry was an outright hazard to their family.

Data provided by Jones, Rahn, and Strommen echo some of these same concerns. In their sample of 2,416 youth ministers, 81 percent of whom are married, respondents expressed concern that "their job as ministers and excessive time involvement creates conflict between spouses."[85] The cluster of issues that surround this matter of neglected relationships was characterized by the following statements:

▶ I often experience conflict at home over my job.

▶ My spouse has difficulty understanding my ministry.

▶ Conflicts often arise over how much time I spend at home and at work.

▶ My family gets only leftovers of my time.[86]

Why does this happen? There are no easy answers. But, from my own personal experience, a number of factors come to mind:

---

[84] 1991 Survey of Pastors, Fuller Institute of Church Growth, cited in London and Wiseman, *Pastors at Risk*, 22.

[85] Jones, Rahn, and Strommen, *Youth Ministry That Transforms*, 91.

[86] Ibid., 93.

A Victim's Plea

By Julie Prey-Harbaugh

When I was a teenager, I loved my youth group. The group's activities were my social life, and I spent hours every week involved in the youth program at my church. During my third year in youth group, I felt called to be a youth pastor myself. The admiration and respect I felt for my youth pastor were tantamount to hero worship. When she said she wanted to mentor me, I was delighted. My parents and I hoped that the relationship to which she invited me would be one that would form and shape my life.

Unfortunately, in ways that I never would have imagined, that is just what it did. You see, my youth pastor used her relationship with me not as an opportunity to help me grow in Christ, but as an opportunity to sexually and emotionally exploit me.

Under the guise of a discipling relationship, my youth pastor/perpetrator invited me to stay over at her house after youth events and to go on weekend excursions. Any day trip or outing alone together was an opportunity for her to touch me or to unload her worries on me. As a teenager, all alone with this secret, I was left with the abusive role of bearing my youth pastor's adult burdens, and trying to comfort her adult loneliness and pain.

It is important to understand that sexual abuse is about power; it is not about sex. Sexual contact is a tool of manipulation, a manifestation of the abuse of the incredible amount of access and influence church leaders have in the lives of their people. My youth pastor "crossed the line" before she ever kissed me. She broke down the boundaries between professional and personal when she began to plot how she could use me to meet her own needs, rather than to think of what would be in my best interest.

As a youth pastor, you will have amazing power in the lives of young people and their families. If you intend to follow through on your call to ministry with integrity, I would you encourage you to heed the following suggestions.

Know Yourself and Be Known

As a pastor, you have the sacred job of tending souls. This is exhausting, emotional work. Most individuals who perpetrate are emotionally immature and socially disconnected. Go out of your way to make sure you have all the healthy care and support you need. You need all the help you can get to do your work well.

Have a life outside of youth group.

> ‣ Make time to interact with adults as peers (that is, join a small group that you do not lead).

> ‣ Create a support network of like-minded clergy.

Have a life outside of the church.

> ‣ Join a bowling league, go horseback riding, take up martial arts.

> ‣ Be in therapy. Helpers need help.

Recognize the power you have with children and families and respect boundaries.

You Are Part Shepherd and Part Watchdog

Guard your church's children and youth.

> ‣ Make a child protection plan—your number one priority! To go without a plan is unthinkable in other child-serving agencies. If you do not have a plan in place, your church is wide open to perpetrators.

> ‣ Screen, train, and observe volunteers and other staff. No child protection plan is worth anything if these protections are not in place. Your commitment is essential. At a minimum, require at

least three references and conduct background checks: state child abuse and criminal records.

▸ Review this area of training at least once a year; supervise closely.

▸ Trust your gut. If it seems bad, it probably is.

Act wisely when handling abuse cases.

▸ Believe the victims. Very few allegations are false. It takes incredible courage to come forward to tell the truth about abuse. You are better to err on the side of standing with the less powerful person in the situation. This is what Jesus did, and what almost no one in the church does for victims of sexual violence, especially those abused by clergy.

▸ Confront child abuse (by staff, volunteers, parents, or others) right away and report it to the authorities. Know your state's child abuse laws and your denominational and congregational policies about dealing with situations of abuse, and follow them to the letter.

All of this takes courage. To stand up to prevent child abuse and to support victims will be risky to you—especially if a case of abuse does arise in your congregation. It will be difficult and, at best, complicated for you to do the right thing. Systems in trauma move quickly toward closure. Silencing is the number one tool to preserve the so-called "peace" of the church. Be brave. Be a hero. Break the silence.

For Further Study

Crabtree, Jack. *Play It Safe* (Wheaton, Ill.: Victor Books) 1994.

Geoly, James C. "The Law on Sexual Harassment," *Leadership Journal* (summer 1995).

Lansing, Carl F. *Legal Defense Handbook for Christians in Ministry* (Colorado Springs, Colo: NavPress) 1993.

Mazur, Cynthia S., and Ronald K. Bullis. *Legal Guide for Day-to-Day Church Matters* (Cleveland, Ohio: United Church Press) 1994.

Ruth, Kibbie. "*How to Develop a Church Policy on Sexual Harassment,*" Leadership Journal (summer 1995).

Somebody Told. Videotape. VideoNet, P.O. Box 70525, Seattle, Wash. 98107 (Helpful—although dated and poorly acted—video resource for talking about issues of sexual abuse and molestation. Can be used for staff training.)

1. Family life is not in the job description. To begin with, we are usually not rewarded or affirmed for spending time with our families. We are affirmed for spending extra nights out, "always being there" when someone needs us, and "being a team player," even if it means forfeiting family plans to do so.

2. Family life is not as easy as youth ministry. To be frank, it is much easier to be a good youth worker than it is to be a good father and husband or a good mother and wife. I can give the youth group kids all kinds of counsel about all kinds of topics, but when the situation turns dirty, I have the option of walking away from the problem. I can plead that the situation has grown beyond my expertise or responsibility. Not so with my family.

    It is always easier to work through other people's problems than it is to work through my own. It's sort of like the old maxim: Minor surgery is when they operate on you; major surgery is when they operate on me.

3. Family problems are not always so easily resolved. If push comes to shove, we could just tell a problem student that he is not allowed to come to youth group for a while. It is a bit more awkward to tell your child she cannot come to dinner for the next three weeks.

    Sometimes with a youth group student, when all else seems to be failing, we at least have the consolation that sooner or later this kid is going to graduate from the youth program. It may take a few years, but there is light at the end of the tunnel. Marriage doesn't offer us that easy out. We have got to work through the problems. We cannot just wait for our spouse to "graduate" and move on.

    Even if things turn nasty in the youth group, we know that we have six days to recuperate before the next round on Sunday night. Family living does not offer us that kind of breather. The problem that you left behind when you drove to the church on Sunday afternoon is going to be waiting right there when you come back through that door on Sunday night.

4. Family life does not always stroke the ego like youth group does. I have met youth workers who are deemed courageous and sacrificial because of the great amount of time they spend with their students. And that's great. But I am not so sure how sacrificial it is. Back home at the house, there are diapers to be changed (rarely demanded of us by students at youth group), garbage to be taken out, and toilets to be unclogged (we have custodians who do that stuff at church).

One might question whether it is all that sacrificial to hang around teenage girls and guys who look up to us and tell us it has "been a wonderful night." When we give a great talk at youth group, the students applaud and tell us how great we are. When we give that same talk at home, people have a way of expecting us to live up to our words. That is not quite as invigorating.

5. Youth ministry just naturally entails unique demands on our time. If we want to spend time with teenagers, we must do it after school or on weekends. We cannot as easily work their schedule around a normal workday schedule or a normal family schedule. They need our time, and the only hours of the day when we can meet that need is during what might have been prime time for the family.

6. Youth ministry requires us to straddle two cultures and two roles with different demands. It is not so easy to walk back and forth between two different cultures everyday. The culture of teenagers and the culture of adulthood are quite different. I have met more than a few youth ministers who could not seem to stop being youth ministers long enough to be husbands and dads, wives and moms.

But ministry does not have to be toxic to family life. It can be a shared adventure that brings unique challenges and unique advantages, such as the following:

▸ Flexible hours, especially during the day when young children are awake and ready for action;

▸ The joy of involving the whole family in shared ministry;

▸ The privilege of providing for a youth worker's children an extended family of several dozen big brothers and sisters (who babysit for free!);

▸ By involving spouse and children in the ministry, youth ministry allows us to creatively integrate family time with "work" time (much more difficult in a traditional secular job);

▸ A seasonal schedule that offers a friendlier and more varied rhythm than the standard 50 weeks of work and two weeks of vacation afforded by most jobs.

Basic Principle of Healthy Ministry Leadership:
Remember that every genuine "yes" must be protected by genuine "no's."

What it all comes down to is the realization that priorities must be protect-ed—that every yes we really mean to say will have to be protected by a no we really mean. What that means, practically speaking, will vary from marriage to marriage and family to family. But the following questions might help us to consider how we can say a wholehearted "yes" to youth ministry without saying an implied "no" to vital family relationships.

1. Am I taking a day off and "keeping it holy"? God made the world and held things together for several thousand years before he had the benefit of our help. We need to understand that he can maintain this solo performance for at least one day a week without our assistance, and that there will be no serious damage to the kingdom. No cheating. No bringing work home. No phone calls. Just undivided attention to family for 24 hours.

2. Who am I holding responsible for my family's schedule? For the most part, the average congregation will blindly affirm the youth minister who is out away from home eight nights a week: "What a commitment!" "What a great youth minister!" "What a zeal for youth ministry!" Until finally all of those nights away from home add up to a broken marriage. Then that same congregation will be saying, "What? A divorce? We're sorry, but we cannot really allow a divorced person to serve on our staff."

   It is not that anyone means wrong. It is just that we should not assume someone else is watching out for the welfare of our families. That is no one's responsibility but our own. We can blame the elders, the students, the pastor. But when it is all said and done, your family is your responsi-bility before God.

3. What am I doing to let my family members know that they are as special as the students in my youth program? Some of us go to great pains to show youth group kids how special they are. We send birthday cards and short notes. We attend athletic events and music recitals. We take them to meals and go to movies together.

   But at the same time, we forget those birthday and anniversary dates so important in our own family. Or we are so busy watching the high school soccer team practice that we do not have time to go to our son's third grade play. It is true our families may understand and forgive us for these over-sights—but should they have to?

4. Do I invest as much creative effort to make my family a fun and special place as I invest in the youth group at church? Or has home become humdrum? We have to make youth group attractive or kids will not come. What are the consequences of an unattractive home life on our own children?

5. Am I giving my students a biblical model of a healthy marriage and effective parenting? A tragically high number of teenagers will never get an up-close picture of a healthy family. It may well be that the closest they ever come to one is in our living rooms. Far more convincing than any Bible study or talk about the biblical guidelines for love and sexuality is a youth worker and spouse who are transparently and passionately in love with each other.

Families Know That Sacrifice Is by Definition What Ministry Is

The immediate contextual factor of the pastor's household environment extends into issues of career-path trajectories, financial limitations of the ministry, and the fact that one is called to sacrifice in ministry. Approximately 44 percent of spouses reported that they find it necessary to work to make ends meet. By and large, families know that this sacrifice is by definition what ministry is and are willing to make appropriate personal sacrifices, including the need for spouses to work. By contrast, an effort to try ministry because it is something different and has humanitarian value through assisting people in their various needs is a decision based on spurious vocational considerations. Missing is an understanding of the sacrificial nature of ministry . . . The more carefully and thoroughly the pastor understands that ministry is a spiritual call primarily between the pastor and God, the more secure the marriage. We have shown that when theological and familial issues have been openly discussed among family members, the pastor and the family will experience less stress than those who ignore or take lightly either spiritual or family commitments.

—Paul A. Mickey and Ginny W. Ashmore, Clergy Families: Is Normal Life Possible? (Grand Rapids, Mich.: Zondervan, 1991), 73. Mickey and Ashmore provide several interesting findings in this book based on the responses of about 750 pastors from across the country representing 11 Protestant denominations.

To watch a lot of youth workers, one might suppose that our goal is to model how to be a cool teenager. On the contrary, what they desperately need for us to model is fulfilled, contented adulthood—a mom who enjoys being a mom, a husband who enjoys being a husband. Most teenagers don't believe there is life or passion after the age of 20. A healthy model can teach them both.

"Mirror, Mirror on the Wall, Who Am I to Sense a Call?"

A chapter such as this one that forces us to look at ourselves in the mirror of some tough issues can make us second guess God's calling. Thinking through these kinds of questions can almost be like going to the doctor for a physical—we know we are going to have to step on the scales, we are going to experience what might be some awkward moments of exposure, we may even feel a little pain. But we keep the appointment because we understand the value of good health. Maintaining a lifestyle of healthy leadership requires us to consider the tough issues in this chapter. The fact that some of these issues make us feel uncomfortable is not an altogether bad sign.

C. S. Lewis makes the point that "When a man is getting better, he understands more and more clearly the evil that is still left in him. When a man is getting worse, he understands his own badness less and less."[87] When I get dressed early in the morning, I do not notice as readily that my shirt clashes with my sweater and my pants make my tie look weird. But by the time I get to my classroom when the sun is up, the lights are on, and students are offering to pray for my color-blindness, the fashion sin is all too obvious. It was there all the time, of course, but it was only exposed by the greater light. The closer we are to the blazing light of Christ's holiness, the more we will be aware that we fall pitifully short of his righteous standard.[88] Even a man as godly as John Wesley, when giving instructions about the epitaph for his tombstone, ordered that if there be any epitaph at all, it must include these words: "Here lieth the body of John Wesley, a brand plucked out of the burning: . . . God be merciful to me, an unprofitable servant!"[89]

[87] Cited in Kesler, *Being Holy*, 13.

[88] Note Paul's confession in I Timothy 1:15–16. This awareness of one's sin can be quite healthy to a point. The Puritan preacher of colonial times, Thomas Goodwin, observes, "When I was threatening to become cold in my ministry, and when I felt the Sabbath morning coming, and my heart not filled with amazement at the grace of God, or when I was making ready to dispense the Lord's Supper, do you know what I used to do? I used to take a turn up and down among the sins of my past life, and I always came down with a broken and contrite heart, ready to preach, as it was preached in the beginning, the forgiveness of sins . . . Many a Sabbath morning, when my soul had been cold and dry for the lack of prayer during the week, a turn up and down in my past life before I went into the pulpit always broke my heart, and made me close with the gospel for my own soul before I began to preach." Cited in Gordon MacDonald, *Ordering Your Private World* (Nashville, Tenn.: Oliver-Nelson, 1984), 143.

[89] Percy Livingston Parker, ed., *Journal of John Wesley* (Chicago: Moody Press, 1951), 198.

May we prayerfully consider the danger areas and troubling questions posed by this chapter as we sort out the call of God on our lives. May we do so with the knowledge that in the midst of it all there is a Great Physician who probes us only so he can prepare us and protect us for the adventures and perils that await us.

Travel Log: Lebanon

Youth Worker Profiles by Paul Borthwick

John Sagherian is national director of Youth for Christ (YFC) in Beirut, Lebanon. John and his wife Nancy started in youth ministry in July 1971. They continued working in Lebanon during the nation's long-running civil war. Bombs damaged their house and offices. When the danger was greatest, they had many opportunities to leave and pursue ministry elsewhere. They stayed.

Pump Me Up. What gets John most excited in youth ministry? "Hearing young people tell me something I had shared (sometimes years ago) affected their lives, or better still, led them eventually to commit their lives to Christ." An even greater excitement? "Seeing a young person I have led to the Lord, or done follow-up with, lead someone else to the Lord."

Great Moment. John describes a moment recently when he thought to himself, "This is an awesome job! This is why I do youth ministry!"

This past summer I was attending a conference in Armenia for the Armenian Evangelical Youth from around the world. I had been asked by the group of leaders to be the director of the conference and one evening I gave an appeal to the 235 young people present to commit themselves to live all out for the Lord. Many of them stood up, some making first-time commitments. Being used by the Lord like that was a great and humbling experience!

The Call. "When I was first asked to go full-time into youth ministry (through YFC) it seemed a natural progression of my involvement up to that point and I felt the Lord was in it. I think confirmation has come many times since then as I have been able to communicate the gospel, and see young people respond; as I have motivated others to join us as volunteers; as I've been able to put youth programs and activities together. I realize that 'success,' as the world defines it, is not necessarily the best proof of being in the Lord's will. But I believe the Lord allows us to see success every now and then to encourage us and help us to keep going."

One Thing to Tell Youth Workers? "People count more than programs, however 'successful' those programs appear to be."

Fill in the Blank. How would John complete this sentence: "Apart from the grace of God, the key to whatever success I have had thus far in youth ministry is———"

"I persisted. I didn't give up."

OPEN WIDE

Meditations on the Way by Helen Musick

I recently sat in a comfortable dentist chair to receive a not-so-comfortable dental procedure—the dreaded root canal. I thought to myself, "I can do this. People live through this every day." I got situated in the chair and opened wide. In a short time I was completely numb on the right side of my face. "This is going to be just fine. I'm not going to feel a thing." The drilling began.

Apart from the noise, I was great—until the drill struck a nerve. Instantly, the peace I had received from the Novocain was gone. In the blink of an eye I was seven years old again—I flashed back to my days in Brazil when I went to dentists who never used numbing agents. These were terrible memories of fear and trepidation, as my small, fragile mouth was put in the hands of a man who seemed to care nothing about the tears I shed or the agony I suffered. Surely he knew how hard it was to sit in that chair. Why did he show no care toward me? Surely he had once been through this pain. Why did he not acknowledge mine? Surely he could see my tears. Why did he not attempt to soothe my pain?

When we are hurting, we long for someone to acknowledge our pain, for someone to notice. There is nothing worse than hurting alone. In Mark 5:24–34, we get a glimpse of the hopelessness, desperation, and fear that can form in the heart of a lonely sufferer—a woman whose ailment had cost her everything. After 12 years of suffering, she was now an outcast, living in seclusion. Yet she knew about Jesus. She sought out his healing in secret. Her touch of faith brought immediate healing.

Jesus knew that this woman needed more than just physical healing. In many respects, the physical healing was the easiest to give. However, he did not stop there—for to do so would have kept her anonymous lonely. He causes her to confront her fears of being known; he acknowledges her as "daughter"; he confirms her faith; he proclaims her freedom (v. 34). Jesus restores wholeness. The woman emerges accepted and healed for all to see.

Do you see the difference between the dentist and the Messiah? More importantly, do you see a contrast between you and Jesus? We do not have the advantage of Jesus walking within our towns. Today he walks within our hearts. This means that we need to be Jesus to the hemorrhaging people in our own lives. When it comes to suffering, we see that Jesus's response is one of compassion and holistic healing.

We must realize that not everyone who needs a divine touch will be as bold as the woman in Mark 5. Many need to be invited as they cry out secretly inside.

▸ Does your life allow people to reach out and touch?

▸ Is your life an invitation into the faith-developing, healing power of Jesus?

▸ How can God use you to bring freedom from suffering?

▸ Where is someone reaching out to you in your world?

UNIT TWO
UNDERSTANDING THE TERRAIN

The opaque glance and the pimples. The fancy new nakedness they're all dressed up in with no place to go. The eyes full of secrets they have a strong hunch everybody is on to. The shadowed brow. Being not quite a child and not quite a grown-up either is hard work, and they look it. Living in two worlds at once is no picnic.

—Frederick Buechner[1]

[1] Frederick Buechner, *Whistling in the Dark* (San Francisco: Harper, 1993), 2.

chapter five

CHANGING PLACES:
ADVENTURES IN THE "LAND OF THERE BUT NOT THERE"

[Adolescence is] . . . a stage between infancy and adultery.
—Ambrose Bierce[2]

Adults tend to treat adolescents as "big kids" or "little adults." They are neither. Yet they are both. Adults must work to respect and honor the unique challenges and opportunities of this age "between the times."
—Richard Dunn[3]

In the evening, the men could watch the sun go down over the Missouri [River]. Surely, as they sipped their whiskey ration at the end of the day, they stared at that river, and talked about it, and thought about it. They were not daunted by it. Rather, they were drawn to it. What adventures awaited, what sights they would see, they knew they couldn't even guess, which only made them all the more eager to get going—so they could find out.
—Stephen E. Ambrose, describing the scene in camp (late March 1804) just days before the launch of the Lewis and Clark expedition.[4]

And Jesus grew in wisdom and stature, and in favor with God and men.
—Luke 2:52

Whoever dares venture into this canyon will never come out alive . . .
—Newspaper editor Samuel Bowles[5]

---

[2] Cited in Wesley D. Camp, *Camp's Unfamiliar Quotations from 2000 BC to the Present* (Englewood Cliffs, N.J.: Prentice-Hall, 1990), 2.

[3] Richard R. Dunn, "Putting Youth Ministry in Perspective," in *Reaching a Generation for Christ*, ed. Richard Dunn and Mark Senter III (Chicago: Moody Press, 1997), 36.

[4] Stephen Ambrose, *Undaunted Courage: Meriwether Lewis, Thomas Jefferson and the Opening of the American West* (New York: Touchstone-Simon and Schuster, 1996), 131.

[5] Edward Dolnick, *Down the Great Unknown* (New York: HarperCollins, 2001), 19. This quotation, so far as we know, does not refer explicitly to adolescence. In fact, this was a prediction Bowles made to his readers after hearing of Powell's attempt to run the Colorado River the entire length of the Grand Canyon.

Anyone who has walked the trails of a mountain range knows the frustration of being fooled by a "moving horizon." The peak in the distance ranges above closer summits, but it looks reachable. Perhaps it is 20 miles or less, a two-day hike if the pace is consistent. But with every hour of hiking, the peak seems no closer.

You might ask, "Could the mountain be moving?"

Just when the trail seemed to promise a final notch before the final ridge before the final climb, the trail heads down again. Yet another valley. More elevation lost—elevation that was hard won through hours of switchbacks and sweat, and elevation that has to be gained again before the trail reaches its promised terminus.

"How can we not be there?"

Trail guides speak often of these "false summits" that seem to congratulate hikers on their newfound view by showing them still more trail to climb. It is a high-country curse, expecting to look down on a trail traversed only to be still looking up at trail yet climbed.

This is surely part of what makes the adolescent adventure such a combination of hopefulness and restlessness, quick starts and sudden stops, setbacks and switchbacks. Adolescence, as we now know it, is an amazing trail of awesome discovery and false summits. One day it is the airy heights of adulthood and the next day it is back into the valley of childhood, with limited views and loss of ground gained. It is a schizophrenic time of life that says, "You're grown up—except that you're not grown up."

Sociologist Gwen Neville provides an apt description:

In the literature of education and religious education the term *youth* has come to refer to a particular stage of life and to be widely used in the labeling of church educational programs and printed materials. The term is elusive, however. Does it refer to people between the ages 13 and 21, 15 and 24, to the same phenomena that goes by the label *teenage*? Is it the same as adolescence as defined by the psychologists, or does it come somewhere after adolescence? Is it a physical condition or is it a social affliction? In the educational program of churches, youth refers roughly to all those people who are between elementary school and "young adult"; it comes after the confirmation class, during it, or before-during-and-after it until one reaches the "young couples' class" or the "young adult singles class." In the evening it becomes "youth group," "youth fellowship," "young people" or is marked by some particular denominational marker such as "M. Y. F. ," "Luther League," or for older youth "Westminster Fellowship" or "Wesley Foundation." In the summer, the term is found in connection with youth conference, youth camp, and youth triennium. One young person told me that youth "begins at the beginning of junior high and ends when the person has been out of school a few years or gets married—if they don't get married too young." Legally, when a young couple marries they are plummeted into adulthood under the law, no matter what their ages, and in some states a youngster can apply to a judge to have his or her youth removed by gaining "emancipation" and being declared an adult.[6]

How are we to understand such an amazing journey?

In "the Land of There but Not There"

We begin our study of adolescence with definition: What is it? When does it begin? What part does it play in the developmental process of a human being created in the image of God? The root word for adolescence is the Latin word *adulescens*, "young man or woman," from the verb *adolescere*, "to grow up, increase; burn." The past participle *adultus*, " grown up" gives us the English word *adult*.[7]

Historically, both the pacing and the process of that growth—even the phenomenon of adolescence itself—has been the subject of much discussion.[8] As far back as the writings of Aristotle (fourth century B.C.), human growth was discussed in "stratified" terms that attempted to understand human development in terms of stages of maturity (physical, intellectual, or otherwise). For example, Aristotle described three stages of human development: "(1) infancy—the first 7 years of life; (2) boyhood—age 7 to puberty; and (3) young manhood—puberty to age 21."[9] This notion of stratification was further affirmed by the eighteenth-century enlightenment philosopher, Jean-Jacques Rousseau, who argued that treating children like miniature adults was potentially harmful, and that children should be allowed to live their first 12 or so years of life as children—free to explore and experience life without the strictures of adult expectation and responsibility. While the stratified notion of development (the notion that development happens in stages) was fairly common, there has been consistent debate about this specific stage of development we today know as adolescence.

It is an issue of "moving mountains" and "false summits." The question essentially is this: Is adolescence the end of childhood and the beginning of adulthood, or, is adolescence a period of development that is no longer childhood, *but not yet* adulthood? To put it another way, does the onset of puberty mark the beginning of adulthood, or does it mark the last stage of a prolonged child-

---

[6] Linda Nielsen, *Adolescence: A Contemporary View* (Philadelphia: Harcourt Brace, 1996), 3.

[7] *Collins Latin Gem Dictionary*, s.v. *adolescere, adulescens, adultus*. An *adulescens* was between 15 and 30 years old.

[8] For this historical overview, I have drawn from the work of John Santrock, *Adolescence* (Dubuque, Iowa: Brown and Benchmark, 1996), 8–10.

[9] Ibid., 9. Aristotle felt that the second stage—what we would probably refer to as the adolescent stage—is the stage at which young people develop the ability to choose, a skill he singled out as the hallmark of maturity. Plato, also writing in fourth century B.C. described three facets of human development: desire, spirit, and reason. The highest of these, reason, first appears according to Plato in what we would today typically describe as the adolescent years.

hood? The word *puberty* comes from the Latin *pubertas*, which means "adulthood."[10] But today most people think of puberty not as the beginning of adulthood—we do not think of 12- and 13-year-olds as adults. Typically, in the lexicon of modern life we think of puberty as the beginning of adolescence—a stage of life that *concludes* with adulthood. This raises a question with important implications for society at large and youth ministry in particular. Are teenagers old children, or young adults, or are they somewhere in between, neither child nor adult?

What we can observe as we look back from a historical perspective is that seeing adolescence as an "in-between" time—a "no-longer-child, not-yet adult" stage of life—seems to be a relatively recent invention. It was G. Stanley Hall,[11] a scientist heavily influenced by the work of Charles Darwin, who did the most to explore adolescence as a unique stage of life. Hall characterized adolescence as a stage of "storm-and-stress" marked by oscillations "between conceit and humility, good and temptation, happiness and sadness," rude to a peer at one moment and kind the next, desiring in one moment to be alone and in the next to have company. While Hall believed that much of the script for human development is written by genetically determined physiological factors, he acknowledged that environment played some part in the process, an increasing part as the child grew into the teenage years. Although his research methods were suspect, Hall is recognized by many as "the father of adolescent psychology," because it was he who began to systematically and scientifically study adolescence as a distinct stage of life.

Jesus was once a teenager, but he was never an adolescent.
—**Donald Joy**

The third age, which is called adolescence . . . ends in the twenty-first year . . . and it can go on till thirty or thirty-five. The age is called adolescence because the person is big enough to beget children. In this age the limbs are soft and able to grow and receive strength and vigor from natural heat.
—*Le grand propriétaire*, **written in 1556**

Adolescence begins in biology . . . and ends in culture.
—**Chap Clark**

---

[10] Ronald Koteskey, "Adolescence as a Cultural Invention," in *Handbook of Youth Ministry*, ed. Donald Ratcliff and James Davies (Birmingham, Ala.: Religious Education Press, 1991), 42–43. John Santrock defines puberty as "a rapid change to physical maturation involving hormonal and bodily changes that occur primarily during early adolescence." Santrock, *Adolescence*, 87. What exactly triggers this change is uncertain. It appears to be a function of nutrition, health, genetics, and body mass. Research has demonstrated a correlation in females between the onset of puberty and body fat. Santrock summarizes, "Menarche occurs at a relatively consistent weight in girls. A body weight approximating 106 plus or minus 3 pounds can trigger menarche and the end of the pubertal growth spurt. For menarche to begin and continue, fat must make up 17 percent of the girl's body weight." Santrock, *Adolescence*, 88. Interestingly, Linda Nielsen observes that "teenagers living in higher altitudes and those from small families enter puberty sooner than children living in lower altitudes and those from large families. Even the seasons might have some bearing on how fast we mature—fewer girls start to menstruate in the spring than in any other season." Linda Nielsen, *Adolescence: A Contemporary View* (Philadelphia: Harcourt Brace, 1996), 28.

[11] Hall's two-volume *Adolescence* (New York: D. Appleton, 1904) was the first major textbook on adolescent psychology.

Until Hall began his research, there was little notice taken of adolescence as the stage of life we know it today. Nielsen observes that even as recently as the 1950s and 1960s in professional journals devoted to the science of human behavior, less than two percent of the articles published were articles written about adolescence.[12] "The concept of adolescence, as generally understood and applied, did not exist before the last two decades of the nineteenth century. One could almost call it an invention of that period."[13]

That is to say, there have always been 13- to 17-year-olds throughout human history. That much has not changed. But, until the latter half of the nineteenth century, 13- to 17-year-olds were seen as "little adults," capable of learning a trade, bearing responsibility, even starting a family.

Fourteen Years Old and Still Not Married!

Ronald Koteskey notes that under Hebrew law there was an unabashed intention that young people should be married as soon after puberty as possible—in some cases, even earlier. In Talmudic commentary on Leviticus 19:29, "Do not degrade your daughter by making her a prostitute," Rabbi Akiba warned that postponing the marriage of a pubescent daughter (a *bogareth*) might tempt her to become unchaste (Sanhedrin 76a).[14] Indeed, the thrust of rabbinic teaching was that one should first study Torah (the first five books of the Bible) beginning at least by the age of five. Then, ideally, by the age of 13 one would become subject to the commandments (a "son of the law" or *bar mitzvah*), by the age of 15 study the Talmud, and by the ripe old age of 18 be ready "for the bridal canopy" (Aboth 5).[15] This would have coincided with the average age of the onset of puberty at that time—around 18 years old.

The central concern was that delaying marriage for too long after the onset of puberty would lead to sexual misconduct and sexual fantasy. It is intriguing that there were even exceptions made for those who found love's fires burning too hot to restrain: "If one has to study Torah and to marry a wife, he should first study and then marry. *But, if he cannot live without a wife, he should first marry and then study*" (emphasis added) (Aboth V, Kiddushin 29b).[16] Rabbi Huna even warned gravely that anyone not married by the age of 20 would spend all of his days in sinful

[12] Nielsen, *Adolescence*, 3.

[13] John Demos and Virginia Demos, cited in Ronald Koteskey, *Understanding Adolescence* (Wheaton, Ill.: Victor Books, 1987), 16.

[14] Koteskey, *Understanding Adolescence*, 14.

[15] Koteskey, "Adolescence as a Cultural Invention," 42–43. Compare with Prov. 5:18: "May your fountain be blessed, and may you rejoice in the wife of your youth." See also Prov. 2:16–17.

[16] Koteskey, *Understanding Adolescence*, 14. One wonders how many readers of this textbook are even now wondering if these are the words of guidance for which they have been personally praying? "Eureka! That's it! Marry first, then study! Wait 'til we tell our parents!"

thoughts (Kiddushin 29b).[17] One Rabbi Hisda claimed that his early marriage at the age of 16 made him superior to other rabbis who continued to be haunted by impure thoughts until age 18 or 19. Indeed, in a rare display of rabbinic trash-talking, he added that it would have been better if he had been married by the age of 14 so that he "could have said to Satan, 'An arrow in your eye'" (Kiddushin 29b–30a).[18]

Roman law provided the same kinds of social boundaries. Young women were permitted to marry by the age of 12, young men by the age of 14. Should a young woman still not be married by the age of 13, the parents began to actively seek for her a husband. If by the age of 19, there were no takers, she was considered "distinctly an old maid."[19]

This same pattern of early adulthood was reflected under English law as well, whereby the legal age of marriage for men was 14, and for women 12. Kostesky observes that "early marriages were common into the eighteenth century. Any man of fourteen and woman of twelve could marry, without their parents' consent . . . In 1882 Parliament raised the age of consent from twelve to thirteen, but an attempt to raise it to sixteen failed."[20] Not surprisingly, early colonial law, modeled as it was on English law, showed this same bias toward early marriage. "In 1704 Madam Knight wrote that Connecticut youth usually married very young, that men were more likely to marry under the age of twenty than over, and that women often married at sixteen or under. Old maids were ridiculed, and they became 'antient (ancient)' maids at twenty-five . . . Others noted that a woman single at twenty was a 'stale maid.'"[21]

This way of thinking about postpubescent teenagers as adults was translated into every facet of life. Under Roman law, and into the Middle Ages, children were expected to learn a trade—typically from their fathers. Under Hebrew law, neglect of this fatherly responsibility was held to encourage one's son to become a thief.[22] A child born to Puritan parents in early colonial America was expected to be working by the age of six, although it was not until the age of 14 that his father would choose for him a calling. This early age of responsibility and employment was reflected in labor laws in the United States that allowed children to work full days with full responsibility. It was not until the 1890s that states began enacting laws that were aimed at putting limits on child and teenage employment and requiring children and teenagers to attend further schooling. What all this points to (see Figure 5-1) is a different way of thinking about the teenage years—seeing them not as the final stages of childhood but as the early stages of adulthood.

[17] Ibid., 14. Yes, if you are reading these words, and you are under 20 and unmarried, this means you! Put on some Christian music in your dorm room right now, and get your mind back on your studies.

[18] Koteskey, "Adolescence as a Cultural Invention," 44.

[19] Ibid., 44–45. Roman law required that parents could not force a daughter to marry against her will. But, unless she openly refused her parents, it was assumed she would marry the chosen mate. Interestingly, the pattern of self-initiated courtship that is so prominent today in Western culture appears to have been unknown at the time. There were no Latin words corresponding to our English language words, *to court* or *to woo*.

[20] Ibid., 45.

[21] Ibid.

[22] Ibid., 46.

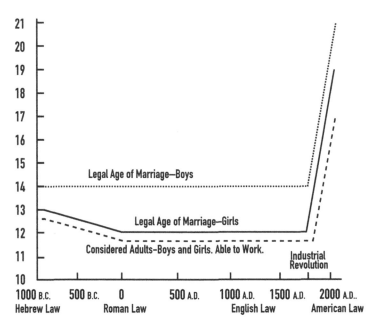

Figure 5-1.
Legal Ages for Work and Marriage During the Past 3,000 Years

Source: Ron Koteskey, "Growing Up Too Late, Too Soon" *Christianity Today*, March 13, 1981, 26.

Was Jesus Ever an Adolescent?

Even a cursory survey of the historical information leads us to ask an important question. We know that Jesus was a teenager. We know that he was at some point in his life 12 years old, 14 years old, 16 years old. But was Jesus ever an adolescent?

We know, for example, that in other biographical portraits given to us in Scripture, we see very little of an apparent adolescence as we now know it today.

▸ In Exodus 2:9–10, we read about Moses as a nursing infant. Exodus 2:11, just one verse later, describes him as "grown up."

▸ Timothy, Paul's young disciple in the faith, is given an extraordinary amount of "adult" responsibility even as a "young" person.[23] While we are never given his exact age, it appears that Paul recruited him as a missionary companion sometime in his late teens or early twenties. It is likely that his

---

[23] In Paul's commissioning exhortation of 1 Timothy 4:11–5:1ff, he refers to "younger men" who Timothy is to treat as "brothers" and to "younger women" who Timothy is to treat as "sisters." But clearly, Timothy himself is a "young" man. Indeed, Paul warns Timothy in his second letter (2 Tim. 2:22) to "shun *youthful* passions"(emphasis added)."

increasing role in church leadership did not come to full fruition until perhaps 15 years later when he was in his mid- to early 30s. While the term "young" probably did not mean in Paul's usage what it does today,[24] it is quite clear that Timothy's apprenticeship to Paul began at an early age. Perhaps this helps to explain his timidity and shyness (see 1 Cor. 16:10–11; 2 Tim. 1:7–8; 2:1,3; 3:12; 4:5).

▸ When the apostle Paul alludes to his growing-up years (1 Cor. 13:11), he writes, "When I was a child, I talked like a child, I thought like a child, I reasoned like a child. When I became a man, I put childish ways behind me." Notice that Paul refers only to years of childhood or years of adulthood. There is no hint of an interim period of growth: "When I was a teenager, I thought like a yahoo" or "When I was an adolescent, I stopped thinking altogether" or "When I was neither a child nor an adult, I reasoned as an adolescent." He was either a child or an adult. There was no allusion to an adolescent time of life in between.

▸ When the apostle John exhorted the early church to turn away from darkness and live in the light (1 John 2:12–14), he addressed the church as three distinct groups: "children," "young men," and "fathers." Perhaps we would assume that his reference to "young men" is a reference to adolescence, but commentator John Stott notes, "[T]here were only two recognized standards of age to the Greek or Roman, *neos* and *geron*, *juvenis* and *senex*, and the former of these conveyed no such juvenile implication as our term *youngster*. It was employed of adults in the full vigor of life and of soldiers of military age to the verge of forty."[25] What this demonstrates, again, is that one moved from childhood directly into adulthood. There was no exhortation to "children," "young men," "fathers," and "*adolescents*."

▸ Donald Joy observes that Jesus's visit to the Jerusalem Temple in Luke 2:41–52 gives us what is perhaps the most convincing look at how differently adolescents were viewed in biblical times:

> Every year his parents went to Jerusalem for the Feast of the Passover. When he was twelve years old, they went up to the Feast, according to the custom. After the Feast was over, while his parents were returning home, the boy Jesus stayed behind in Jerusalem, but they were unaware of it. Thinking he was in their company, they traveled on for a day. Then they began looking for him among their relatives and friends. When they did not find him, they went back to Jerusalem to look for him. After three days they found him in the temple courts, sitting among the teachers, listening to them and asking them questions. Everyone who heard him was amazed at his understanding and his answers. When his parents saw him, they were astonished. His

---

[24] John Stott comments: "We do not know his precise age. If he had been about 20 years old when Paul enrolled him as a missionary associate, he would be in his mid-30s now . . . Certainly the 30s would be a young age for such church leadership as had been committed to Timothy." John Stott, *Guard the Gospel* (Downers Grove, Ill.: InterVarsity Press, 1973), 19–20.

[25] Ibid.

The real solution is not to keep (children) from growing up, but to give back their role in adult society. Children should be allowed to be children, but adults expected to be adults (emphasis added).
—Ronald Koteskey

Adolescence has become a waiting period of enforced leisure with few responsibilities and little or no meaningful contact with adults.
—From "Adolescent Rolelessness in Modern Society," a report of the Carnegie Council on Adolescent Development

mother said to him, "Son, why have you treated us like this? Your father and I have been anxiously searching for you."

"Why were you searching for me?" he asked. "Didn't you know I had to be in my Father's house?" But they did not understand what he was saying to them. Then he went down to Nazareth with them and was obedient to them. But his mother treasured all these things in her heart. And Jesus grew in wisdom and stature, and in favor with God and men.

Reflecting on this passage, Joy comments that it would not have been so unusual for the women traveling with their families in cross-country caravans to leave early and travel ahead of the men. Typically, the men would leave just in time to overtake the women before sundown and set up sleeping arrangements for the overnight stay. Perhaps Mary was thinking that Jesus was traveling with the men, or Joseph might have assumed that Jesus was traveling with his mother. It was fairly traditional at that time for children to travel with the women's caravan.

What is noteworthy is that Jesus, at age 12, is allowed the freedom and responsibility for making his own decision about which caravan he will travel with. He is left with adult-like options. Having been deemed responsible enough to make such a decision for himself, Jesus is apparently left behind by both caravans, all alone in the big city.

Joy poses the obvious questions: "What would you think and do if your child had been missing for three days and nights before you finally found him? What would you do with him? To him? Today we would be inclined to report Mary and Joseph to Social Services or to the police for child abuse or negligence."[26]

[26] Donald Joy, *Parents, Kids and Sexual Integrity* (Waco, Texas: Word Books, 1988), 33–34.

In some ways, it almost seems shocking that Mary and Joseph would allow such latitude for a child of only 12 years. For example, they do not appear to feel the need to keep constant check on him while in Jerusalem. They assume he can make sound judgments regarding his health and safety, and they apparently have complete trust that he will meet up with the caravan by the appointed time of departure. Even more stunning, three days pass before they began to wonder where he might be. That seems an amazingly long time before one parent says to another, "Have you seen our son?" "Well, now that you mention it, no; I haven't seen him since three days ago when we left Jerusalem."

We might be tempted just to resolve our surprise by explaining, "Well, if my child were God I might be willing to let him stay out a little later too." But what if in fact, this familiar narrative says something not just about Jesus in particular, but about 12-year-olds in general, and how they were viewed in New Testament times? The picture that emerges is a culture in which a child might well be a teenager but be treated as an adult.

In summary, it seems to be true: adolescence as the period of prolonged childhood that we think of today is a relatively recent invention. Donald Bakan, writing in the journal of the American Academy of Arts and Sciences, summarizes his survey of the historical landscape of adolescence with these words: "The idea of adolescence as an intermediary period of life starting at puberty . . . is the product of modern times . . . [It developed] in the latter half of the nineteenth century and the early twentieth century . . . to prolong the years of childhood."[27]

The question remains, why has it happened?

"All Grown Up and No Place to Go"

In defining adolescence as we have come to know it over the past 100 years, we are confronted with this indisputable fact: adolescence is a time of mixed signals, of an almost schizophrenic rotation between the "adultish" child, and the childish adult. To a large extent, this relatively recent invention of adolescence is due to two key factors: biology and sociology.

Biology

During the past century, something remarkable has been happening with regard to the age of the onset of puberty in both boys and girls. It has been declining.

---

[27] David Bakan, "Adolescence in America: From Idea to Social Fact," *Daedalus* 100 (1971): 979–995. Bakan has written extensively about the emergence of adolescence as a social fact of life in the United States.

Grace Wyshak and Rose Frisch of Harvard Medical School and Harvard's Center for Population Studies reviewed more than 200 studies including more than 200,000 women between 1795 and 1981.[28] They found not a single one of the 65 studies done before 1880 pinpointed an average age of first menstruation (*menarche*) below the age of 14 and a half. Indeed, a number of the studies showed the average age of menarche to be 17 years or higher. Taken together, the studies show that, before 1850, the average age of menarche was 16 years old. Contrast that finding with the fact that by 1950 the average age of first menstruation had dropped "down to about twelve and a half or thirteen."[29]

> It should be noted that puberty is not an actual one-time event that can be neatly captured in a moment: "Dear Diary: Reached puberty this afternoon about 4:37. I am, like, soooo growing breasts."
>
> As John Santrock points out, there are several physical manifestations to puberty, and they do not just happen in one day. For girls, the onset of the first menstrual cycle may be easy enough to pinpoint in time, but the pubertal sequence also includes growth in height, breast growth, and growth of pubic hair. Obviously, these changes take place over time. For boys, "the pubertal sequence may begin as early as 10 years of age or as late as 13 ... It may end as early as 13 years or as late as 17 years."
>
> *John Santrock,* Adolescence *(Dubuque, Iowa: Brown and Benchmark, 1996), 92–93.*

Parallel studies in men that survey the average age for the onset of puberty are more difficult to find.[30] But there is anecdotal evidence that the decline is observable in adolescent males as well. For example, "when Bach was choirmaster at St. Thomas Church in Leipzig 200 years ago, boys often sang soprano until they were seventeen. Tenors and basses were men whose voices had already changed. Altos were those whose voices were changing." In 1744, Bach had 10 altos: the youngest was 15 and the oldest was 19.[31] In Bach's day, 17 was the average age for a young man's voice to begin changing. That age is now "about 13 or 14."[32]

Indeed, this decline in the average age of the onset of puberty (see Figure 5-2) has been observed consistently during the past several decades, averaging a decline of about four months every 10 years during the past century. Santrock speculates that if such a rate of decline continues into future decades, by the year 2250 we could see "a three year old girl with fully developed breasts or a boy just slightly older with a deep male voice."[33] While we're not likely, even in the year 2250, to see ads for personal hygiene products on Saturday morning cartoon

[28] Grace Wyshak and Rose Frisch, "Evidence for Secular Trend in Age of Menarche," *New England Journal of Medicine*, April 29, 1982, 1033–1035.

[29] Koteskey, *Understanding Adolescence*, 12.

[30] This is, in part, because of the fact that puberty's onset is a little tougher to pinpoint in males. Some define its onset as the appearance of the first facial whisker (not easy to notice) or the first wet dream (seldom reported).

[31] Try to imagine one of your male 18-year-old classmates chirping in sweet soprano or alto song, and you begin to get a sense of how dramatic has been the decrease in the age of male puberty.

[32] J. M. Tanner, *A History of the Study of Human Growth*, cited in Koteskey, *Understanding Adolescence*, 13.

[33] Santrock, *Adolescence*, 87. He does not suggest this will happen, of course, but he uses the illustration to make the point that the decline in the average age of the onset of puberty has been rather steep.

Figure 5-2.
The Decline of Age at Menarche in Five Nations

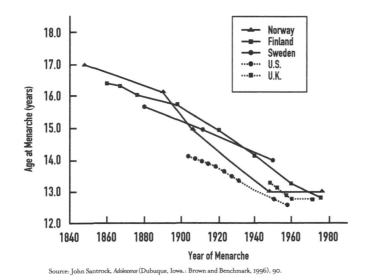

Source: John Santrock, *Adolescence* (Dubuque, Iowa.: Brown and Benchmark, 1996), 90.

shows, this information helps us to make an important observation. The later age at which puberty occurred in earlier cultures (Jewish, Roman, early American) more closely coincided with the legal age at which marriage was allowed in those cultures. To that extent, our invention of adolescence is partially biological.

Sociology

Nielsen points to three societal factors that have changed the way we think about adolescence: "industrialization, compulsory education—and the post-war baby boom."[34] The first two factors—industrialization and compulsory education are functions of an observation we made earlier in this chapter about the upward trend in expectations regarding the age of employment and economic responsibility from Old Testament times into Roman culture and even into early American colonial life. The third factor that shapes our newly invented adolescence, the post-war baby boom, grew out of the sheer increase in the numbers of adolescents in the 1960s and 1970s. During that 20-year span of time, the total number of American teenagers catapulted to an all-time high of 52 percent of the total population—a demographic factor that demanded the attention of advertisers, businesses, and manufacturers, who began to target their wares specifically

[34] Nielsen, *Adolescence*, 4.

There are several theories about why this biological shift in the age of puberty's onset has occurred. Pointing to the correlation between body weight (and percentage of body fat) and the onset of puberty, and the fact that children from richer families—and therefore, those that have typically better diets—tend to mature earlier than malnourished children, Linda Nielsen suggests that this downward shift might be because of better nutrition during the past 150 years. Donald Joy suggests additional factors might be climate or light. Joy even goes on to advance the notion of adolescence as a "crucible"—a God-given time during which a young person can develop the moral muscle to thrive in an immoral culture:"I want to offer another perspective. It is this: the stressing of sexual maturity against postponed privileges and responsibilities is essential to produce moral giants whose wisdom is needed to sustain human values and to protect the exploding human race with its capabilities of annihilating itself with its technological inventions."

Linda Nielsen, Adolescence: A Contemporary View *(Philadelphia: Harcourt Brace, 1996), 28. Donald Joy,* Parents, Kids and Sexual Integrity *(Waco, Texas: Word Books, 1988), 39, 64.*

for this group of people. When these factors are coupled with the dramatic changes that have taken place with regard to the rising age at which people marry and are legally permitted to marry, we can begin to see how adolescence came to be the cultural invention that it is.

Donald Joy has charted the onset of aspects of adulthood through history (see Figure 5-3). Joy is the first to admit that his chart is highly stylized, but it shows well the interplay between three key factors that have led to the invention of adolescence: the age of legal responsibility (economic independence), the age of marriage, and the age of the onset of puberty.

There are other sociological factors to add into the mix. As amply documented in the work of David Elkind,[35] there seems to be a cultural impulse (at least in the Western Hemisphere) to move children out of childhood and into adulthood at an early age. Whether it be highly organized sports for five-year-olds, explicit sexual programming readily accessible to seven-year-olds, or "proms" and dances for 10- and 11-year-olds, Elkind observes an unfortunate loss of childhood innocence. The story is told of two young boys walking down the street one day, when one says to the other, "I found a condom on the patio." His little friend, intrigued, asks, "Really? What's a patio?"

Today's children have seen more, heard more, done more, and been exposed to more than any generation before their own. One might suggest then that perhaps this is a return to an earlier way of thinking about older children as "little

[35] See these works by David Elkind: *The Hurried Child: Growing Up Too Fast Too Soon* (Reading, Mass.: Addison-Wesley, 1984); *The Disappearance of Childhood* (New York: Dell Books, 1984); and *All Grown Up and No Place to Go: Teenagers in Crisis* (Reading, Mass.: Addison-Wesley, 1984).

adults." But one might rather describe it as an unhealthy way of thinking of little children as older adults.[36] The end result of these mixed messages is a hodge-podge of confusion, precocity, and pseudo-sophistication. It is a culture that says it is okay to provide birth control counseling to high school students but requires them to seek parental permission if they need to get aspirin from the school nurse. It is a culture that says teenagers can make choices about sexual behavior as early as middle school but should not be allowed to smoke or use alcohol until age 21. It is parents who expect their sons and daughters to be well-behaved children while allowing them to leave the house dressed as seductive adults. It is a dad who says, "Grow up! Act like an adult!" and then gets mad when the child makes an adult decision to return home 45 minutes after curfew on Friday night. It is a church board that says, "These young people should be worshiping with the rest of the members of the congregation," but sees no reason to involve them in decision-making facets of congregational life.

It is, in simple terms, a moving horizon—an odyssey that seems to begin earlier than we might hope and last longer than we might expect. The adolescent adventure is an adventure in the "Land of There but Not There."

Two Views of Adolescence: Fear and Wonder

There are many ways of thinking about this confluence of pressures, forces, and waves that blow across the life of a young person as he or she moves into adolescence. Is it a time of inevitable turmoil, or is it a time of amazing discovery? Or is it a little of both? It was with a sense of astonishment that David wrote those familiar words in Psalm 139:14, "I am fearfully and wonderfully made . . ." But which word best captures the drama of adolescence: *fearful* or *wonderful*? Or is adolescence an era of both wonder and fear?

View Number One: The Perfect Storm

Late at night on October 28, 1991, the six-man crew of the sword-fishing boat *Andrea Gail* desperately tried to navigate their 72-foot steel-hulled boat[37] in seas that were stirred by 120-mile-per-hour winds, with waves that were 10 stories high. The battleground for Captain Billy Tyne and his crew from Gloucester, Massachusetts, was a stretch of stormy sea somewhere north of data buoy #44139 near the Sable Island Shoals in the North Atlantic.[38] No one knows for sure what happened in what must certainly have been horrible hours following the *Andrea Gail's* last radio contact at 6:00 p.m. that evening. All that is known for certain is

---

[36] Koteskey argues that the remedy to this situation is not to treat little children as adults, nor to treat teenagers as little children. "Children should be allowed to be children, but adults should be *expected* to be adults (emphasis added)." Koteskey, "Adolescence as a Cultural Invention," 51.

[37] Sebastian Junger, *The Perfect Storm* (New York: Harper Torch, 1997), 35.

[38] Ibid., 168.

Figure 5-3.
Joy Chart on Adulthood in History

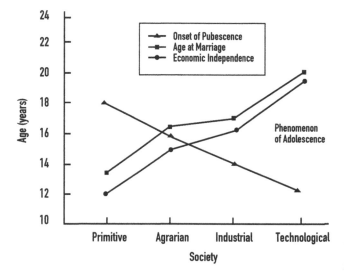

that Tyne and crew lost their battle with the sea, and neither boat nor crew were ever seen again.

In describing the epic storm that swallowed the *Andrea Gail* that night—a magnificent tempest that resulted from the confluence of three massive storm systems, one of which was a hurricane—Bob Raguso of *Weathernews New York* reported that it "ranked as one of the five most intense storms 1899–1991. It had the highest significant wave heights either arrived at by measurements or calculation. Some scientists termed it the hundred year storm."[39] For Bob Case, a meteorologist with the National Weather Service office in Boston, surveying the monster storm from the vantage point of his computer models and satellite imagery, there was only one way to describe the nightmare unfolding a couple hundred miles to his east. "My God," thought Case, "this is the perfect storm."[40]

It was G. Stanley Hall who first described adolescence as a period of *Sturm und Drang* storm and stress—"a turbulent time of life charged with conflict and mood swings."[41] To be sure, the rapidly changing body, the surging hormones, the ever-changing winds of culture, and the increasing pressures of peer relationships can all make for turbulent seas. For those who observe the collision of these genetic, social, spiritual, and hormonal forces it might indeed be described as "the perfect storm."

But is there another way to think about the barometric changes of life that happen during the teenage years? Might adolescence be viewed as a gift, as an adventure to be lived rather than a storm to be circumnavigated and possibly survived? Does it really have to be "batten down the hatches"? Or could it be "hoist the sails"? It is easy to make broad generalizations about this adventure of adolescence by looking at the storm charts, by listening to the "May Day" alarms of popular pundits, and by noting where lives were lost. But surely there is another way to think of this voyage.

[39] Ibid., 146.
[40] Ibid., 191.
[41] Santrock, *Adolescence*, 10.

View Number Two: The Mighty River

In late July 1805, William Clark took a small party on an overland expedition in a desperate search for Native Americans who might help him find a way over the Continental Divide and into the Columbia River's drainage system into the Pacific. Fatigued and under almost constant assault from a "trio of pests" described as mosquitoes, eye gnats, and prickly pears (a type of cactus with spines that pierced through moccasins), the party was discouraged. Every time the mountains broke to offer a view, the men were disheartened to see only the "sight of lofty summits all covered with snow, standing between the expedition and its goal."[42]

On July 27, his colleague, Meriwether Lewis, and the remaining members of the party set out early on the boats. At about 9:00 a.m., as they cleared a bend in the river, they were confronted with a "smoth (smooth) extensive green meadow of grass . . . a distant range of lofty mountains" and the confluence of three rivers (which Lewis named the Gallatin, the Madison, and the Jefferson). It was a moment of high drama and great relief; Lewis was convinced that the coming together of these three rivers, at what is today termed the Three Forks area, was "an essential point in the geography of this western part of the Continent."[43] It was a significant milestone, but fraught with the frustration that they had yet to find a way through to the Columbia River, and the concern that the mountains that continued to loom on the horizon never seemed to allow them a true summit. There was a sense of wonder: they were now moving into a significant and exciting part of the journey. But it was wonder mixed with some

Of course, long before you mature, most of you will be eaten.
—Caption to Gary Larson's illustration of the warning offered to young praying mantis students by their praying mantis instructor

Adolescents are, more than anything else, growing up. They do not do it quietly. They do not stay in their rooms and grow up in isolation; they do not restrict their growing to the times when they are safely among peers. Their growing spills out, unsystematically, all over the place. In this way adolescents energetically modeling and constantly stimulating growth, are God's gift to parents who are in danger of being arrested in their own growth.
—Eugene Peterson

All the days ordained for me were written in your book before one of them came to be.
—Psalm 139:16

[42] Ambrose, *Undaunted Courage*, 253.
[43] Ibid., 257–258.

real concerns. It must have felt as if they were in some sense in the "Land of There but Not There."

Studying the development of young people as they make their journey through childhood into adulthood is not unlike the experience of Lewis and Clark that day in the high country of Montana. Puberty has about it the feel of a significant milestone, "a main event." Indeed, it has been described as such by Erikson (1968), Freud (1958), Hall (1904), and Rousseau (1762).[44] It is, in some sense, a continental divide of life. Accompanying the physical changes of puberty are dramatic changes on the whole landscape of life—changes in self-conception, changes in cognitive capacities, changes in moral reasoning, and changes in the way one looks at family and friendship. It is as if, at adolescence, one finds oneself caught up in the confluence of several mighty rivers that usher one into a new channel and a new current altogether. It is a point in the journey where one could be fearful about what is left to explore—or wide-eyed with wonder about what is yet to be experienced.

Too often, when youth workers, parents, or academics talk about adolescence, the conversation unfolds with all the optimism and hopefulness of people viewing the scene of a traffic accident. Let us be clear in discussing adolescent development that the teenage years are *not* an accident. It may be the *scene* of some accidents, and it certainly offers its share of flashing lights and near misses. It may well be that the shifting lanes of culture and the accelerating drives of early puberty have made the journey more difficult. But this process of growing from childhood to adulthood is *not* an accident. When we talk about the way people mature, the process of "growing up," we are talking about nothing less than the work of God.[45] This is very important.

Nobody is pretending adolescence is purely a pleasure cruise. This is not one of those declarations that "your teenage years are the best years of life!" It is simply noting that somewhere between the *Yellow Submarine* and the *Titanic* is a truer story. It is a reminder that when we talk about adolescence we are speaking of human beings made in the image of God, and that this process of maturing, this growing into "full personhood" (Eph. 4:13) is by his design, a design that is "very good" (Gen. 1:31). We are "fearfully and wonderfully made" (Ps. 139:14). As Eugene Peterson puts it,

> Adolescence is a gift, God's gift, and it must not be squandered in complaints or stoic resistance. There is a strong Christian conviction, substantiated by centuries of devout thinking and faithful living, that everything given to us in our bodies and in our world is the raw material for holiness. Nature is

[44] Santrock, *Adolescence*, 95. Only in the past 20 years have empirical studies explored the attitudes toward and adaptations by young people to these pubertal changes. For example, in one study (Brooks-Gunn and Ruble, 1982) of 639 adolescent girls the reactions to menarche ranged widely from "a little upsetting" to "a little surprising" to "a little exciting." Of the 120 fifth- and sixth-graders in this study who were telephoned to obtain more detailed information, the most frequent tone of response was positive.

[45] This is not to say that "adolescence as a cultural invention" is God's perfect plan. It may be, as Koteskey argues, that adolescence as we now know it is in fact a hindrance to healthy growth and development. But what we can affirm for certain is that God created us as human beings who experience pubertal changes as a normal part of growing up, and that God created us as human beings who change in the ways that we process information. These changes were likely experienced as well by Jesus, who, although he was fully God, was also fully human (see Luke 2:52). Koteskey, *Understanding Adolescence*.

brought to maturity by grace and only by grace. Nothing in nature—nothing in our muscles and emotions, nothing in our geography and our genes—is exempt from this activity of grace. And adolescence is not exempt.[46]

He suggests three texts to frame our thought:[47]

▸ "And the child grew and became strong in spirit; he lived in the desert until he appeared publicly to Israel" (Luke 1:80).

▸ "And Jesus grew in wisdom and stature, and in favor with God and men" (Luke 2:52).

▸ "...until we all reach unity in the faith and in the knowledge of the Son of God and become mature, attaining to the whole measure of the fullness of Christ. Then we will no longer be infants, tossed back and forth by the waves, and blown here and there by every wind of teaching and by the cunning and craftiness of men in their deceitful scheming" (Eph. 4:13–14).

All of us grow up, and all of us *are* growing up. John, before he was John the Baptist, was John the baby and John the boy (Luke 1:80). Jesus, before he showed himself to be the Son of Man and the Son of God, was simply known as the son of Joseph and the son of Mary (Luke 2:52). Even those of us who have moved well beyond the childhood years are still growing into mature personhood, our supreme goal to "grow up into him who is the Head, that is, Christ" (Eph. 4:15).

Growth is a work of God's grace in our lives. As youth workers, parents of teenagers or perhaps, even teenagers ourselves, we can approach the voyage as either a sail into "the perfect storm"—a result of colliding systems likely to end in disaster, or an adventure on "a mighty river"—riding convergent currents to a place of new horizons. Risk and potential hardship are a part of both stories. But I prefer the latter story because it allows us to make the journey with a sense of hope, and it reminds us that adolescence is not an accident waiting to happen.

> Where can I go from your Spirit? Where can I flee from your presence? If I go up to the heavens, you are there; if I make my bed in the depths, you are there. If I rise on the wings of the dawn, if I settle on the far side of the sea, even there your hand will guide me, your right hand will hold me fast. If I say, "Surely the darkness will hide me and the light become night around me," even the darkness will not be dark to you; the night will shine like the day, for darkness is as light to you. For you created my inmost being; you knit me together in my mother's womb. I praise you because I am fearfully and wonderfully made; *your works are wonderful, I know that full well.* (Ps. 139:7-14, emphasis added)

---

[46] Eugene Peterson, *Like Dew Your Youth: Growing Up With Your Teenager* (Grand Rapids, Mich.: Eerdmans, 1994), 5.
[47] Ibid., 4.

A DAY WE ALL REMEMBER

Meditations on the Way by Helen Musick

September 11, 2001—where were you? You will probably never forget. Instantly, life stopped, and the deepest concerns of the day meant absolutely nothing. Watching more than 3,000 people enter death's door on the local news truly has a way of bringing perspective to everyday life. What did that perspective look like for you? Perhaps the importance of getting an A on your upcoming midterm was no longer a motivating factor to study. Maybe the realization of the true gift of life was enough to mend a broken relationship. Possibly, you cancelled plans to go out shopping for "the perfect outfit," choosing instead to attend a quickly planned prayer vigil. Whatever happened in your life sphere, I have no doubt that you stopped—you thought—you prayed—maybe you cried.

The terrorism of 9/11 did more than rock our world—it rocked our very souls. In many ways it helped us realize that we really do not have control over the events of life—over our daily routine. While we are on this earth, there are really no certainties. However, as Christians awaiting a heavenly home, one thing is for sure—in the end, the victory is our Lord's. There will be a time when we will dwell in complete love, joy, and peace.

This great place is beautifully described in Revelation 21:1–4. This passage refers to it as "the New Jerusalem"—a "Holy City coming down from heaven." Typically, when we talk about heaven, we think about it with a human mindset. It is a place of hope and reunification—where we will see our fellow believers whom we love. It is a place of joy and relief—where all pain, agony, and suffering are obliterated. Yet our biblical picture here goes much further than our own thoughts. Revelation shows us that heaven is not just a kingdom in the sky. It is a Promised Land that will make its way down to earth at a certain appointed time!

By way of description, we read that this place is "the dwelling of God" (v. 3). It will be a place of security with a guarantee of God's presence and the certainty of our role as "his people." It will be a place free from death, mourning, crying, and pain (v. 4a). Why? Because the way of life as we know it now will "pass away," creating a new life similar to the new life that every married couple embarks upon on their wedding day. As inhabitants of that peaceful, holy city we are "as a bride beautifully dressed for her husband" (v. 2b). What an awesome picture! The terror in our lives will be gone. The anguish of destruction will be free from memory. The heartless terrorists in our society will no longer have power over us. We will be God's people, and he will be our God. What a great promise of eternal peace.

▶ **Most of us, at some point, are terrorized by ways far more subtle than bombs and threats. What are some of the fears that rob your peace? Are they fears about your future? About your present? What are the uncertainties that haunt you from time to time?**

▶ **In the midst of the fear that rocks our soul is a certainty that calms our fear. Have you allowed the certainty of God's promise to drip down deep into your soul? How would your thinking be changed if you truly embraced these promises?**

▶ **Why not stop right now and pray that God would meet you in your place of fear? Ask God to stand with you before the rubble of a terror-past, or the prospect of a terror-future, and ask him to give you the confidence that he wants to build in your life a place of peace and promise.**

chapter six

CONVERGING CURRENTS:
EXPLORING ADOLESCENT DEVELOPMENT

Have I been skipping too much from one subject to another? I can't help it. I feel that Spring is coming. I feel it in my whole body and soul. I feel utterly confused. I am longing . . . so longing . . . for everything . . . for friends . . . for someone to talk to . . . . someone who understands . . . someone young, who feels as I do . . .
—**Anne Frank**[1]

Sometimes I'm convinced confidence is ungraspable. Other times I seem to have an unending supply. But nearly always there is a little part of me saying, "You're not good enough, you don't fit." Thank God it is a little part, easily stifled and easily covered up.
—**Jennifer Teschler, sophomore, El Cajon High School, California**[2]

If asked to identify the most significant transformation in adolescence, most adults would select physical changes . . . However, another important transformation is the adolescent's new way of thinking . . . This fateful change has been described as "thinking in a new key."
—**Gary L. Sapp**[3]

The teenager's mind sometimes freezes up, not because he cannot think of anything to say, but because he is thinking of too many things to say. This is what David Elkind calls "pseudostupidity."
—**Wesley Black**[4]

Even today, the big rapids on the Green and the Colorado [Rivers] are the stuff of dry mouths and pounding hearts. For amateurs seeing them for the first time, the rapids must have been a revelation, a rumbling heaving nightmare.
—**Edward Dolnick**[5]

---

[1] *Diary of Anne Frank*, dramatized by Frances Goodrich and Albert Hackett (New York: Random House, 1956), 132.

[2] Quoted in Susannah Meadows, "In Defense of Gamma Girls," *Newsweek*, June 3, 2002, 50.

[3] Gary L. Sapp, "Adolescent Thinking and Understanding," in *Handbook of Youth Ministry*, ed. Donald Ratcliffe and James A. Davies, (Birmingham, Ala.: Religious Education Press, 1991), 52.

[4] Wesley Black, *An Introduction to Youth Ministry* (Nashville, Tenn.: Broadman and Holman, 1991), 103., citing David Elkind, "Understanding the Younger Adolescent," *Adolescence 13* (spring 1978), 128.

[5] Edward Dolnick, *Down the Great Unknown* (New York: HarperCollins, 2001), 5.

This river called "adolescence" is one of fast turns, deep troughs, amazing vistas, churning rapids, and stretches of flat water punctuated by dangerous whirlpools and high adventure. Understanding these converging currents, and how they can shape the flow of a young person's life, is the intent of a field of study known as developmental psychology. Although this may sound like a subject way too academic to reach into the world of youth ministry, it is, in fact, a field of study that is as close to youth ministry as the kids in a youth group or Young Life club.

Steve Patty suggests that we can best understand this field of investigation by seeing it through "four essential developmental assumptions."[6]

Figure 6-1.
Quantitative and Qualitative Mental Growth

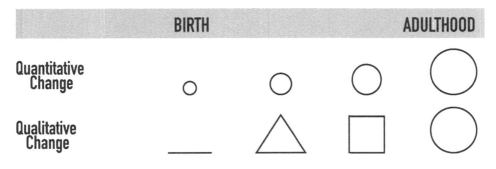

Source: Ronald Habermas and Klaus Issler, *Teaching for Reconciliation* (Grand Rapids, Mich.: Baker Books, 1992), 81.

1. **Qualitative Growth.** At the heart of developmental theory is a notion that "growth is not merely quantitative, but qualitative as well." What that means in very plain terms is that teenagers do not just collect more information as they mature through childhood into young adulthood (quantity); they actually change in the ways they think about that information they have collected (quality). This qualitative shift in adolescent development can be illustrated by a simple diagram shown in Figure 6-1.[7]

It is this advance from quantitative thinking to qualitative thinking that allows us, for example, to read *The Chronicles of Narnia* as a child and hear in its pages a wonderful story of childhood adventure, and then, read it again years later and hear in its pages remarkable lessons about faith and the Christian life. So a sixth-grader listening to your lesson about David and Goliath hears a story about a shepherd boy killing a giant. An eleventh grader studies that same passage and hears in it a lesson about God's power to help the weak overcome the strong, or to help good overcome evil. It is

---

[6] Steve Patty, "A Developmental Framework for Doing Youth Ministry" in *Reaching a Generation for Christ*, ed. Rick Dunn and Mark Senter III (Chicago: Moody Press, 1997), 71–74.

[7] Ronald Habermas and Klaus Issler, *Teaching for Reconciliation* (Grand Rapids, Mich.: Baker Books, 1992), 81.

not just grasping more information: it is adding new ways of processing the information.

2. **Structured Wholes.** A second assumption of developmental theory is that growth is more than a merely genetic process, something that happens in isolation from one's surroundings. Human beings, beginning in childhood, engage in a lifelong process of "constantly interpreting their world and fitting the pieces of their understanding together in increasingly complex structures."[8] For example, Sally, the ninth grader in your high school group, does not simply develop her sense of identity as a passive receptor. She develops it in response to feedback that comes to her through interaction with her everyday surroundings. As interpreter of this feedback—sometimes accurately, sometimes perhaps not—she develops more and more complex ways of understanding herself and making sense of her world.

In the developmental view, this ongoing process of "making sense" of the world is called "equilibration"—a desire to harmonize new experiences and information with previously held assumptions about reality. This rethinking or restructuring happens when there is some new experience, or new information, or new way of thinking about old information that causes disequilibration. Sometimes in everyday discourse, we might say, "It just rocked my world." What we are talking about actually is disequilibration.

For example, Sally thought the Darth Vader tattoo on her right cheek would really make a great Mother's Day present for her mother. Her mother's response really "rocked her world" (disequilibration). In debriefing her mother's reaction, Sally will rearrange her assumptions about what pleases her mother. She will restructure some of her assumptions about reality and parent-teen relationships in an effort to reestablish equilibration. She will also try to get removed the Father's Day gift that is tattooed across her entire back.

3. **Invariant Sequence.** A third underlying assumption of developmental theory is that stages of maturity always appear in order. While the rate of advance may vary widely, the pathways of advance will not. There is no "Advance to Boardwalk" card in the process of development. Every young person will have to move through the various stages of maturity in sequence.

4. **Hierarchical Integration.** A fourth tenet of developmental theory is that with each step into a more advanced stage of maturity a person reconfigures and restructures some of the qualitative changes of earlier stages. In other words, each stage is essential in the process of moving to the next stage.

[8] Patty, "A Developmental Framework," 73.

Having said that, it would be wrong to think of these stages as stepping stones, used once for a particular crossing in the journey, and then no longer important. In fact a more appropriate image is that of scaffolding upon which one builds and continues to make use of while moving to higher levels. Perhaps a more helpful metaphor is to think of these stages as a base camp system that a climbing team builds on, and continues to draw from, while moving to higher levels of the climb. When climbers mount an assault on a high peak, they accomplish it in stages, ferrying gear and food from camps at lower elevations to camps at higher elevations. This allows the climbers to set the trail, prepare tie-ins for the climb ahead, pack supplies they will need for later in the journey, and adjust gradually (acclimatize) to the thinning atmosphere of higher altitudes.

In terms of developmental theory, we can think of these camps as advanced stages and levels of maturity. The basic assumption is that each level in the developmental climb must be fully established and explored (*horizontal exploration*) before one can move to a higher elevation or higher stage in the climb (*vertical integration*). Developmental theory suggests that we must, in a sense, "acclimatize" at one level before we can move to the next level. That is what we mean by *hierarchical integration*. It is not possible to just skip the lower levels of the climb in our zeal to grow and reach higher levels of maturity.[9]

But, while skipping ahead does not happen, slipping backward occasionally does. It is not uncommon to see a

"You come of the Lord Adam and the Lady Eve," said Aslan. "And that is both honor enough to erect the head of the poorest beggar, and shame enough to bow the shoulders of the greatest emperor on earth."
—**C. S. Lewis's character Aslan the Lion in *Prince Caspian***

---

[9] In fact, if a climber were to ascend too high too fast, without allowing time to acclimatize at the new elevation, the result might well be a condition known as hypoxia, the starvation of oxygen in the brain.

student who, having gained the capacity to function at a higher level of maturity, in a particular circumstance functions at a lower level of maturity (*stage regression*). These two ideas, *invariant sequence* and *hierarchical integration*, are, of course, particularly relevant to youth ministry. There are many youth workers who have been needlessly discouraged because for some reason they expected a seventh grade guy to act like a high school junior (that is, skip to a higher level of maturity that is uncharacteristic of seventh graders) and got frustrated when a high school senior in a given situation acted more like a seventh grader (*stage regression*).[10]

Donald Miller,[11] who has done a great deal of reflection on developmental theory from the vantage point of a Christian educator, suggests two additional, perhaps more subtle, "presumptions" to a foundational perspective. They serve as bookends to developmental thought.

5. **A Pre-Existent Structure.** There is inherent in developmental theory the notion of order and design. This is not to suggest that all developmentalists embrace a doctrine of God as Creator. They do not. But there is implicit in developmental theory the notion that human development, with all of its myriad complexities, cultural differences, and historical contexts, follows a predictable, discernible pattern.

6. **An End Goal.** The other common feature of every developmental theory is an implied goal—an understanding that development doesn't just terminate but it "moves towards a final level of integration which is usually referred to as maturity."[12] This is the uppermost point of the climb, the terminus of the trail.

The Scientific and the Sacred: Beyond a Human Point of View

Tim Flannery, a biologist and principal research scientist at the Australian Museum, is sometimes referred to as "the Indiana Jones of Science." In writing about his research adventures in the jungles of New Guinea, he speaks with passion and warmth about creatures that most people would find disgusting. However, Flannery, with his passion for conservation and wildlife, sees these creatures through a different lens.

We found that the innumerable tiny trackways running through the tussocks were made by two species of small rat. The more common was a drab little thing with a distinctive mousy odor . . . the Moss-forest Rat . . . The other

---

[10] This is occasionally referred to as obnoxia and it tends to cause hypoxia in youth workers.

[11] Donald E. Miller, "The Developmental Approach to Christian Education," in *Contemporary Approaches to Christian Education*, ed. Jack L. Seymour and Donald Miller (Nashville, Tenn.: Abingdon, 1982), 76–77.

[12] Robert W. Pazmino, *Foundational Issues in Christian Education* (Grand Rapids, Mich.: Baker Books, 1997), 215.

rat was beautiful, an inoffensive little red creature known as the Mountain Melomys (*Melomys rubex*). I became very fond of these mice as the days wore on. It was always a pleasure to feel their soft red fur, and to smell their pleasant scent after opening a trap, when the ten [traps] before had held only the more olfactorally [sic] challenging Moss-forest Rat.[13]

We need to be careful about drawing any parallel between adolescents and jungle rats. But Flannery's rhapsody about a jungle rat reminds us that *how* we think about adolescents will have some real bearing on *who* and *what* we see as we study adolescence.

The lens through which we as Christians examine adolescence is cut and contoured by a biblical perspective. As Paul put it, "For Christ's love compels us, because we are convinced that one died for all, and therefore all died. And he died for all, that those who live should no longer live for themselves but for him who died for them and was raised again. *So from now on we regard no one from a worldly point of view. Though we once regarded Christ in this way, we do so no longer* (emphasis added)" (2 Cor. 5:14–16). That means we bring to our study of adolescence some critical assumptions:[14]

1. We believe that all human beings were created in the image of God, and that all human beings, thereby, have intrinsic worth and value—quite apart from their physical beauty, athletic prowess, intellectual acumen, net financial worth or any other factor—even the eighth-grade guy in Sunday School class who has many of the mannerisms of a jungle rat, but without the charm. We understand that even the complexities of psychological, intellectual, social, and physical development reflect the wonder and genius of this creative God (Gen. 1:26–28, Ps. 8:3–5, 139:1–18, Luke 2:52).

2. We believe that this image of God has been horribly marred by sin, and that this "fall" has marked every facet of our being, both personally (as individuals) and corporately (as families, societies, and nations) (Gen. 2:6–19; Rom. 1:18–32, 8:19–22).

3. We believe that it is possible through the redeeming work of Christ's cross to be recreated into a new creature ("the old has gone, the new has come"), made whole again by God's grace and transformed by his power (Rom. 8:1–11, 12:1–3; 2 Cor. 5:17; Col. 1:21–27).

4. We believe that God's desire is to continue in us the work he begins at redemption, and that through his Holy Spirit he continues to restore us and renew us into the person (and people) he created us to be (Rom. 8:9–17, Phil. 1:6, Col. 3:10).

[13] Tim Flannery, *Throwim way leg: Adventures in the Jungles of New Guinea* (London: Weidenfeld and Nicholson, 1998), 32.

[14] These assumptions are an adaptation of material from Pazmino, *Foundational Issues in Christian Education*, 192–193.

5. We believe that as persons created in the image of God, we are more than water, body fat, muscle, and bones—"we are spirit/souls as well as bodies,"[15] and that every living human being is an embodied soul.[16] We believe that any attempt to understand humanity apart from this fundamental truth will be flawed,[17] like trying to study our shadow without understanding light.

6. We believe that "persons are moral, aesthetic, and creative individuals,"[18] that as people created in God's image, we are ourselves capable of free choices, creative expressions, and appreciation of that which is good, lovely, true, noble, right, and pure.[19]

7. We believe that persons cannot be fully understood apart from the "historical, cultural, economic, political, and social"[20] networks that define and sustain them.

Sally's family has been ripped apart by divorce. Ben is one of five children in a blended family. Ahmed is of the first generation in his family to be born in America. Hank lives with his aunt in a federally subsidized housing complex. Two of Jill's best friends are cutting themselves. For Joe's buddies, everything is about skateboarding. In the same way that Tim Flannery has to understand the jungle to understand the jungle rat, we cannot fully understand any of these students apart from the human networks in which they live. To do so would be like trying to understand the branch of a tree without considering its trunk, its leaves, and the ecosystem in which it grows.

If we begin to think about adolescent development without giving full consideration to these seven key theological presuppositions, we might just as well be studying some "olfactorally challenging" jungle rodent. We end up studying "stats and stages" instead of real live people—trying to come to terms with concepts and systems instead of reflecting on God's amazing and complex work in the lives of human beings. Perhaps the best way to focus the lens through which we look at adolescence is to reflect on these words from C. S. Lewis's sermon "The Weight of Glory":

It may be possible for each to think too much of his own potential glory hereafter; it is hardly possible for him to think too often or too deeply about that of his neighbor. The load, or weight, or burden of my neighbor's glory

[15] Ibid., 192.

[16] "God made the inner person; he molded the outer. 'Molding' is suitable for clay, but 'making' is [fitting] for an image. So, on the one hand, he 'molded' flesh; but on the other, he 'made' the soul." Gregory of Nyssa, "On the Origin of Man," cited in Ancient Christian Commentary on the Scriptures, Vol. I, Genesis, ed. Andrew Louth (Downers Grove, Ill.: InterVarsity Press, 2001), 51.

[17] "Therefore the soul is not blood, because blood is of the flesh; nor is the soul a harmony, because harmony of this sort is also of the flesh; neither is the soul air, because blown breath is one thing and the soul something else. The soul is not fire, nor is the soul actuality, but the soul is living, for 'Adam became a living soul,' since the soul rules and gives life to the body which is without life or feeling." Isaac Ambrose, "On the Soul," Fathers of the Church: A New Translation (Washington, D.C.: Catholic University Press, 1947), cited in Ancient Christian Commentary, ed. Andrew Louth, 51.

[18] Ibid., 193.

[19] Philippians 4:8.

[20] Louth, Ancient Christian Commentary, 192.

should be laid daily on my back, a load so heavy that only humility can carry it, and the backs of the proud will be broken. It is a serious thing to live in a society of possible gods and goddesses, to remember that the dullest and most uninteresting person you talk to may one day be a creature which, if you saw it now, you would be strongly tempted to worship, or else a horror and a corruption such as you now meet, if at all, only in a nightmare. All day long we are, in some degree, helping each other to one or other of these destinations. It is in the light of these overwhelming possibilities, it is with the awe and circumspection proper to them, that we should conduct all our dealings

> If psychology offers insights which will sharpen our counseling skills and increase our effectiveness, we want to know them. If all problems are at core spiritual matters we don't want to neglect the critically necessary resources available through the Lord by a wrong emphasis on psychological theory ... The problem facing evangelical Christians who are wrestling with integration is straightforward enough to describe. There is a body of revealed truth in propositional form to which all evangelicals are committed as the inerrant, inspired Word of God. There is another vast literature which represents the diverse, sometimes contradictory, theories and observations which we can call simply secular psychology. Let each be symbolized by a circle ... The question before us who want to meaningfully tussle with integration—what is the relationship between the two circles?
>
> —*Lawrence J. Crabb*, Effective Biblical Counseling: A Model for Helping Caring Christians Become Capable Counselors *(Grand Rapids, Mich.: Zondervan, 1977), 37.*

with one another, all friendships, all loves, all play, all politics. There are no ordinary people. You have never talked to a mere mortal. Nations, cultures, arts, civilization—these are mortal, and their life is to ours as the life of a gnat. But it is immortals whom we joke with, work with, marry, snub, and exploit—immortal horrors or everlasting splendors. This does not mean that we are to be perpetually solemn. We must play. But our merriment must be of that kind (and it is, in fact, the merriest kind) which exists between people who have, from the outset, taken each other seriously—no flippancy, no superiority, no presumption. And our charity must be a real and costly love, with deep feeling for the sins in spite of which we love the sinner—no mere tolerance or indulgence which parodies love as flippancy parodies merriment. Next to the Blessed Sacrament itself, your neighbor is the holiest object presented to your senses. If he is your Christian neighbor he is holy in almost the same way, for in him also Christ *vere latitat*—the glorifier and the glorified, Glory Himself—is truly hidden.[21]

---

[21] C. S. Lewis, *The Weight of Glory* (Grand Rapids, Mich.: Eerdmans, 1973), 14–15.

An Accurate Focus

How then do we take this theological lens and focus it so that it helps us to think rightly about what we observe in the data laid before us by psychological, cultural, and sociological thought? How do we integrate our theological perspective with the insights and findings on adolescence in current research literature? Christian psychologist Larry Crabb suggests four possible approaches,[22] best explained by thinking of the two sighting pieces on a pair of binoculars. Think of one eyepiece as insight provided by clinical scientific (psychological, sociological, anthropological) research, and the other eyepiece as insight that comes to us through our theological presuppositions.

> We must therefore move with extreme caution in accepting the conclusions of secular psychology into our Christian thinking. We may be absorbing ideas which subtly contradict our biblical position. Again, let me insist that psychology does offer real help to the Christian endeavoring to understand and solve personal problems. However, the first priority of responsible integration efforts is to develop a strategy for evaluating secular psychology in the light of Scripture.
>
> —*Lawrence J. Crabb,* Effective Biblical Counseling: A Model for Helping Caring Christians Become Capable Counselors *(Grand Rapids, Mich.: Zondervan, 1977).*

▸ **Approach Number One:** One Eye Blind. This approach supposes that the only lens necessary is the theological eyepiece, that it is possible to gain full understanding of human development and behavior by using "nothing but" the Bible. Crabb describes this as the "nothing-buttery" approach. Not only does this approach leave the lens cap on one side of the binoculars, but it seems to fear its removal for what might be seen.

▸ **Approach Number Two:** One Eye Bland. The basic supposition of this approach is that the two eyepieces provide legitimate perspectives, but that they are unrelated. This approach suggests both lenses are valid, but instead of using both eyepieces simultaneously, this approach looks with one eye at a time so that neither eyepiece can bring depth and texture to the other. And typically, it is the theological eyepiece that ends up getting neglected altogether.

▸ **Approach Number Three:** One Eye Blend. This approach, often described as an integrated approach that brings together the two perspectives, actually leads to such a radical adjustment of the lens that the whole view changes altogether. In this approach, the theological dimension is so "psychologized" that terms such as faith, grace, sin, and guilt lose any clear Christian meaning. Think "Oprah-scopic"—a kaleidoscope of psychologi-

[22] Lawrence J. Crabb, *Effective Biblical Counseling: A Model for Helping Caring Christians Become Capable Counselors* (Grand Rapids, Mich.: Zondervan, 1977), 31–56.

cal and religious concepts that are blended together to offer a more inspiring (unfortunately, not more accurate) view.

▸ **Approach Number Four:** Both Eyes Blessed. This approach begins with the affirmation that we should embrace truth—if it really is truth—whenever and from whatever source it comes, because the ultimate author of all truth is God.[23] Therefore, both eyepieces should be used together to provide a view of the greatest possible depth and clarity. Christian educator Robert Pazmino offers a biblical example: "As the Israelites used the vessels and ornaments of gold and silver offered by the Egyptians to adorn the tabernacle in the wilderness (see Exod. 12:33–36, 35:30–36:38), so Christian educators must use the wisdom gained from psychology to enrich and embellish their thought and practice to the end that God might be glorified."[24]

Having said this, we also must understand that this approach requires discernment. Samuel Rowen's warning is a good one: "The church along with other social institutions has too often uncritically accepted theoretical formulations and applied them to her life . . . A past executive of General Motors reported that 'GM's solutions of five years ago are its problems of today.'"[25] What that means is that in getting the binoculars properly focused, we must begin with the theological eyepiece (revealed truth) and then bring into focus the scientific eyepiece (discovered truth). If we begin without sighting through the biblical-theological eyepiece, we will skew our focus and perspective.[26]

> One theme that consistently runs throughout the New Testament is that the Holy Spirit works by renewing our mind (see Rom. 12:2, Eph. 4:23, 1 Pet. 1:13). We are expected to analyze, to collect information, to measure effectiveness—in short, to be effective managers of the resources God has given us.
>
> *James Engel and W. W. Norton,* What's Gone Wrong With the Harvest? *(Grand Rapids, Mich.: Zondervan, 1975), 40.*

Once we have affirmed the importance and preeminence of the theological eyepiece, we can then add in assumptions that come to us through the scientific eyepiece. Pazmino proposes the following:

---

[23] "All truth is from God; and consequently if wicked men have said anything that is true and just we ought not to reject it, for it has come from God." John Calvin, *Commentary on the Epistles to Timothy, Titus and Philemon*, trans. T.A. Smail on Titus 1:12 (Grand Rapids, Mich.: Eerdmans, 2001), 300–301.

"Therefore, in reading profane [secular] authors, the admirable light of truth displayed in them should remind us that the human mind, however much fallen and perverted from its original integrity, is still adorned and invested with admirable gifts from its Creator. If we reflect that the Spirit of God is the only fountain of truth, we will be careful, as we would avoid offering insult to him, not to reject or condemn truth wherever it appears. In despising the gifts, we insult the Giver." John Calvin, *Institutes of the Christian Religion*, Vol. II (Grand Rapids, Mich.: Eerdmans, 1972), 236.

[24] Pazmino, *Foundational Issues in Christian Education*, 193.

[25] Samuel Rower, "Testing Validity: Moral Development and Biblical Faith," in *Moral Development Foundations*, ed. Donald Joy (Nashville, Tenn.: Abingdon, 1983), 111–112.

[26] Romans 1:18–25, 2 Corinthians 4:4–6.

1. **"Persons have bodies and we must attend to their physical nature, sexuality, gender, and their activity or behavior in the natural world."** Think, for example, just about how the reality of these factors alone affects the way we plan a high school retreat: everything from site selection, to housing arrangements, to length of sessions, to the schedule itself. If we do not consider these factors, all the theological presuppositions—God loves these students, students need to hear about Christ, etc.—simply will not matter.

2. **"Persons have minds, and we must consider their thinking and reasoning. Both the structure and content of cognitive processes must be considered."** A question that sparks lengthy discussion among tenth-grade girls falls flat in a group of seventh-grade guys—not necessarily because of the question itself, but because of the cognitive and reasoning powers of those who heard the question.

3. **"Persons have feelings and the affective dimension of their lives is important. We must recognize and be sensitive to feelings, motivations, and attitudes in teaching."** This means we must consider room design, music, seating arrangement, lighting—all of these are factors that affect the learning environment in a Bible Study or youth group.

4. **"Persons have wills and make decisions in various areas of their lives."** We must recognize the intentions, judgments, and decisions of persons upon which they act. Such intentions and decisions become the basis for our inquiry into matters of responsibility, accountability, and integrity.

5. **"Persons are in community and we consider their relationships with other persons, groups, institutions, and social structures.** Networks of care and responsibility must be discerned in ministry with persons along with concerns for righteousness and justice in corporate life.

6. **"Persons have intuition and aspects of character, personality, imagination, and values which transcend our analytical categories."** To every student in a youth group or Campus Life club, there is much more than meets the eye—be it the analytical eye of the researcher or the watchful eye of the youth worker. "We are called to recognize the individuality or uniqueness of persons."[27]

It will be important as we reflect on the various theories of adolescent development that we use both lenses of the binoculars. There is much ground to cover in this youth ministry adventure and the landscape of our study is broad. We need always to use discernment in our study—to never lose the "true north" of the biblical compass. On the other hand, maps and guidebooks, as long as they are properly oriented, can be helpful whether they be written by people of faith or not.

---

[27] Pazmino, *Foundational Issues in Christian Education*, 193.

Different Accounts of the Same Journey

Like divergent trails that climb the same peak, different developmental theorists have taken pains to document the varied routes of ascent to maturity. Some theorists focus more on the cognitive ascent, taking note of the stages of development with reference to cognitive (thinking, reasoning) capabilities. Others focus more on moral development or faith development. Still others describe the pathways by which we develop a sense of personal identity. To fully understand the adolescent journey, we need the voices of these different accounts.

> And the brethren immediately sent away Paul and Silas by night unto Berea: who coming thither went into the synagogue of the Jews. These were more noble than those in Thessalonica, in that they received the word with all readiness of mind, and *searched the scriptures daily, whether those things were so (emphasis added).*
>
> —Acts 17:10–11

In a sense, it is like reading from the journals of different expedition members giving their personal accounts of the same adventure. In documenting the journey of those first men to raft through the Grand Canyon under the leadership of John Wesley Powell in 1869, Edward Dolnick[28] had access to the journals of three different men who had been on the trip: Jack Sumner, George Bradley, and Powell himself. While, by Dolnick's measure, "the various versions corroborate one another in places, contradict one another in places, and leave a host of questions unresolved," still "the overall contour of the story line seems fairly certain."[29] Such is the way we should understand the various theories of developmental theory. It is appropriate to think of them as complementary accounts of the same journey—the journey toward maturity. Needless to say, there are numerous approaches to developmental theory. Our purpose in the pages that follow will be to gain an overview of some of the most basic and widely discussed developmental frameworks.

Exploring the Headlands: Cognitive Development

While there are many and varied accounts of the developmental process, it is cognitive development that seems to shape the "overall contour of the story line." The word cognitive comes from the Latin *cognoscere*, which means "to become acquainted with, to know."[30] Research in cognitive development focuses on how we process information, and on how those processes change as we grow from

---

[28] Dolnick, *Down the Great Unknown*, 30–33.

[29] Ibid., 329.

[30] Merriam-Webster's Collegiate Dictionary, 10th ed., s.v. *cognition*.

In a way, it's a good thing adults don't know much about teens. If they knew all about us, they'd puke.
—14-year-old student quoted in the *Chicago Tribune*

Most of us are like, blonde. When we walk into a room we let people know we're there. We always have to look so cute. We match. We wear cool stuff? Like shirts and capris? We all have cute cars?
—Wendi, a high school sophomore, talking about her "crowd" to *Newsweek*

infancy into childhood and from preteen years into late adolescence and adulthood.[31] The leading researcher in this field of study has been the Swiss psychologist Jean Piaget.

Piaget's findings are based on the notion that the human mind is driven by an innate desire to make sense of the world it encounters. This process, referred to by Piaget as *organizing*, is the mind's attempt to form into a cohesive picture the mosaic pieces of thought, feelings, and experiences to which it is exposed. These emerging pictures of reality Piaget described as *schema* or *schemata*[32]—patterns of understanding that allow the mind to store old information so we can draw from it to process new information. This process of making sense of new information is called *assimilation*. It is the process whereby the mind draws on schemata to filter and interpret new knowledge, feelings, or experiences so we can make sense of it, and use it to update our mosaic picture of reality.

On occasion, it happens that the new tiles of data simply do not fit into the mosaic as we have laid it out, and this new information leaves us a with a feeling of imbalance or uneasiness described by Piaget as *cognitive dissonance (or cognitive disequilibrium)*. It is not unlike what happens on Sunday morning when two women sing that lovely offertory duet together and one of them is a shade off key. I have actually witnessed this from the platform in the front of the sanctuary: all over the congregation, people begin looking up and visibly raising their head as if by conjoined effort the congregation could nudge one of the singers back on key and bring the notes into harmony. It is a natural response to the dissonance in sound, and it is analogous to the way the mind works when it receives new information that cannot be harmonized with old information. It requires us to reshape and reorganize our schemata so that they harmonize with

---

[31] Sometimes, in the strange netherworld of a college student's mind, the best way to remember an idea is to associate it with another idea. In terms of *cognition*, it might be useful—albeit completely unscientific—to think of cognitive theory as the study of the way "the cogs" turn in the brain. But if you ever write that on an exam, we will deny that you read it here.

[32] A *schema* is defined as a "conceptual model of how to operate in terms of a future project or how to organize something already in existence." Raymond J. Corsini, *The Dictionary of Psychology* (Philadelphia: Bunner/Mazel, 1999), 864. In terms of Piaget's work, it can also be, as in the case of the sensorimotor stage "an organized pattern of behavior." *Schemata* is simply the plural form of the term.

with the new information. Piaget referred to this process as *accommodation*.

Imagine that, for you and every student in your youth group, life is like working on a jigsaw puzzle. The picture that guides you doesn't come from the puzzle box. Instead, it's one that comes to you from many sources: your family, your friends, the media, your church, your intuitions, and even God. Just when you think you are figuring out how the puzzle fits together, life hands you another piece to the puzzle. Maybe it comes through disappointment, or through success, or through an encounter with a person or an idea. Now of course the question: What is to be done with this new piece of the puzzle?

Perhaps the new piece goes well with the picture you are already building; all you need to do is fit it into its place, and it actually allows the picture to become a bit clearer. That's assimilation.

Cognitive Disequilibrium

Another way to understand dissonance uses a slightly different metaphor. Imagine the sidewalk outside of the classroom where I teach many of my classes. It is gently sloped and poses no threat to safe passage most of the time. But when winter comes, the sidewalk gets icy, and students are warned to use the handrail placed conveniently by my college next to the walkway. In my informal, unscientific study, I have noticed that the collegiate male appears congenitally disinclined to use this handrail in icy conditions. Perhaps it is a matter of pride or some macho instinct; perhaps it is fear of social disease.

But I have noticed that there is one circumstance when even the manliest male is likely to reach for that handrail, and that is in midfall. All of a sudden, without exception, as the feet begin to slip, the body senses the imbalance, and the arms to flail wildly—*then* comes the keen desire to use the handrail. It is change of thinking initiated, rather awkwardly perhaps, by disequilibrium. Cognitive disequilibrium happens when new information throws us off balance, when the old familiar cognitive walkway leaves us feeling off balance.

But what if the new piece does not fit? Do you cut it down to size so it will fit the picture as you understand it? Do you make space for it by throwing out one or more of the existing pieces? If so, that's still assimilation. But what if you consider that there might be new ways to put all the pieces together that may yield a complete different picture? That's *accommodation*. In a sense, this is how cognitive disequilibrium allows (and sometimes forces) a teenager to construct and reconstruct his or her sense of reality.

It is through this process of accommodation that we move from one level of cognitive development to a higher level. No doubt this is why Jesus, the master

Obviously, Piaget was aware that people do not always accommodate the new data they receive even when the new data are dissonant with their old schemata. That is why we find adults, adolescents, even children reasoning at a lower level than we might expect for someone their age. That is why Pharaoh, for example, was unmoved by nine awful plagues (Exod. 7:14–12:33) and required ten before he finally released the people of Israel (and then tried again to recapture them). There was dissonance to be sure—the boils, the frogs, the Nile River turning blood red: all of it must have led Pharaoh into a kind of cognitive disequilibrium. But he kept finding alternative explanations for what he was experiencing (that is, the fact that his wizards could reproduce some of the plagues: blood, frogs, and gnats), and so his mind simply refused to accommodate this new information.

There are several ways to account for this failure of accommodation. A Freudian explanation might suggest that some sort of defense mechanism deceives us into thinking that there are reasons other than our own error for the apparent contradictions between what we think is true and what appears to be true. The most likely culprit goes under a variety of names—denial, defensiveness, closed-mindedness—which, biblically speaking, boil down to pride (see Prov. 14:12, Obad. 1:3). The Scripture refers to this condition as "hardness of heart."

For this reason they could not believe, because, as Isaiah says elsewhere: "He has blinded their eyes and deadened their hearts, so *they can neither see with their eyes, nor understand with their hearts, nor turn*—and I would heal them (emphasis added)" (John 12:39–40).

In an episode from *The Chronicles of Narnia*, C.S. Lewis relates the attempt of Aslan the Lion (a Christ figure) to rescue a character, Uncle Andrew, from his doom. But instead of seeing the Lion as loving, Uncle Andrew sees the Lion as ferocious, something to be feared. "And the longer and more beautifully the Lion sang, the harder Uncle Andrew *tried to make himself believe that he could hear nothing but roaring. Now the trouble with trying to make yourself stupider than you really are is that you very often succeed. Uncle Andrew did. Soon he couldn't have heard anything else if he wanted to (emphasis added)."

It is little wonder that the Scriptures speak so much about being deceived by the hardness of heart (see Heb. 3:7–15). One of the main consequences of the Fall was a catastrophic deterioration of our ability to think clearly (see Rom. 1:18ff), and one of the essential steps to restoration of sound thinking is repentance (*metanoia*—which means literally *to think again*), and letting Christ transform us by the renewing of our minds (Rom. 12:2).

teacher, made frequent use of cognitive dissonance and cognitive disequilibrium in his own teaching: "You have heard that it was said, 'Love your neighbor and hate your enemy.' But I tell you: Love your enemies and pray for those who persecute you . . ." (Matt. 5:43–44).[33] He understood that sometimes people have to be puzzled before they are willing to rethink the way they picture reality. Sometimes the only way to nudge people into a new way of thinking is to introduce new ideas that are dissonant with their old ways of thinking.

Piaget's Stages of Cognitive Development

What then are the stages identified by Piaget? There are four:

▶ **Stage One:** Sensorimotor Stage (birth–18 months). In this first and most basic stage of cognitive development, the mind is capable of only generalized responses to the people and objects it encounters through sensory perceptions and motor activities. All of reality is defined by what only can be immediately felt, heard, tasted, seen, and smelled. This is what Piaget referred to as "practical intelligence." During these early years a child develops some rudimentary elements of cognition (that is, cause and effect, a sense of self), and communication (verbal and nonverbal). One of the most important advances of this stage is in acquiring the concept of *object permanence*—the ability to recognize that objects or people still exist even when they are no longer in the field of view (that is, Mom still exists even though she has walked out of the room.)

▶ **Stage Two:** Preoperational Stage (2–7 years). Mental skills begin to advance as the child develops the ability to think and speak on a symbolic level (that is, drawings, dreams, make-believe play, toys—dolls, stuffed animals, model trains—are symbols for reality). Children learn about the world by imitating the activities of those around them. Concepts are still fuzzy and somewhat confused—as Piaget says, "semilogical." While the intellect is now advanced enough to move beyond the boundaries of the senses, it is still bordered by what Piaget referred to as *egocentrism*—the inability of the child to perceive an experience from any perspective other than his own.

This type of egocentrism is not to be confused with the concept of pride or arrogant self-centeredness.[34] This is more a matter of limitation. For example, five-year-old children presented with the pieces of a jigsaw puzzle spread out upside down on a table would likely not be able to assemble

---

[33] See also, for example, Matthew 5:2–10, or Matthew 5:20–48.

[34] While pride and arrogance may be manifest in a type of egocentrism, this type of egocentrism is less the fruit of pride than it is of limited experience. When we think about arrogance we are thinking about the pilot who ignores every other jet on the radar as if his is the only jet that needs the runway. But when we think of this type of egocentrism, we should imagine a pilot whose radar is simply not powerful enough or sophisticated enough to pick up and transpond to the incoming signals of other aircraft. That is not pride; that is incapacity.

the pieces together—even if they have completed the puzzle several times before when the pieces were facing up. These children's egocentric thinking leaves them unable to visualize the pieces of the puzzle from a perspective other than their own.[35]

▸ **Stage Three:** Concrete Operational Stage (7–11 years). The years of later childhood are characterized by thinking that is less egocentric. The child develops a growing repertoire of cognitive skills that allow for more logical thinking, basic math operations, and tools of organization and classification. Among these skills of logical thought is the *rule of equivalence*: the notion that, if A equals B and B equals C, then A equals C.

We can begin to appreciate how this advancing cognitive ability translates into ministry application. For example, a child at this age can begin to reason: "God loves all people. I am a person. Therefore, God loves me." Children, at this stage, can begin to comprehend concepts like associativity, the notion that an object or a person might belong to several different categories at the same time. Dad is also someone's son. Mom might be someone's sister. The child begins to grasp that she can be a member of her family at home, and at the same time be a member of the larger family of her local church, and on a still broader level be a member of the family of God.

▸ **Stage Four:** Formal Operational Stage (12–15 years). Finally, the last utensils of cognitive intake are placed on the table as the student develops increasing abilities in abstract thought—not just thinking, but thinking *about* thinking—not just concrete objects, but abstract ideas and hypotheses. The adolescent now has the mental capacity to understand more complex concepts like irony, parody, metaphor, and satire, which helps us as youth workers to better appreciate the power of story, symbolism, liturgy, and art.

A person's sense of humor becomes more adept and refined with the development of formal operational abilities. That is why humor can be such a great bridge for communication with teenagers.[36] With this advanced stage of thinking, we can also respect the positive impact of good questions and open-ended discussions.

Jamal as a seven-year-old was able to comprehend the simple equivalence "God loves all people. I am a person. Therefore, God loves me." At age 17 he now begins to wonder, "But why, if God loves me, did he let my mom and dad get a divorce?" "Why did he make me look like this?" "Why

---

[35] Linda Nielsen, *Adolescence: A Contemporary View* (Philadelphia: Harcourt Brace, 1996), 81.

[36] Anybody who spends much time around teenagers will not be surprised that there are clinical findings (in addition to television's Nielsen ratings) that substantiate adolescents' appreciation of satire. See K. W. Fischer and A. Lazerson, *Human Development* (San Francisco: Freeman, 1984), cited in Sapp, "Adolescent Thinking and Understanding," 76. David Elkind, in his book, *All Grown Up and No Place to Grow* (New York: Addison-Wesley, 1984) suggests that adolescents so enjoy word play because it allows them to practice their new linguistic abilities and make observations about the world in ways that are not as vulnerable to the scrutiny and concerns of adults. See also Sapp, "Adolescent Thinking and Understanding," 76.

Table 6-1.
Piaget's Stages of Cognitive Development

Stage	Level	Age Range	Description
I	Sensorimotor Stage	Birth–18 months	Child's cognitive horizon is limited to what can be experienced through the five senses—thinking is not so much reflective as reflexive. One key change is acquisition of the concept of object permanence.
II	Preoperational Stage	2–7 years	Child begins to acquire basic tools of symbolic thought—developing language and writing skills. Child is still egocentric in perspective.
III	Concrete Operational Stage	7–11 years	Improved skills in problem solving. Child is still limited to literal thinking—not yet capable of abstract thought.
IV	Formal Operational Stage	12–15 years	Young teenager becomes less egocentric in perspective. Able to think in abstract terms. Begins to acquire skills of critical thinking.

didn't he make me smarter in school?" It is not as if Jamal's old concrete answers are no longer valid; it is just that they do not always fit Jamal's new questions very well. These new ways of thinking provide adolescents with lots of novel possibilities and new avenues for pursuing fresh answers—some good, some not so good.

Another important facet of the formal operational stage is the fact that we become much more self-conscious. We not only become aware that there are perspectives beyond our own when viewing an issue or an idea, but there are other perspectives besides our own in terms of how people see us. We not only accrue the ability to think about thinking, but we begin to think about how people are thinking about us. Piaget described this as a *second egocentrism*.[37] More specifically, developmental psychologist David Elkind defines this phenomena as *adolescent egocentrism*, a phrase he uses in referring to the adolescent's obsession with how he or she is being seen by other people. In Elkind's words, teenagers are playing to an *imaginary audience*—they seem to feel somehow that everyone is taking notice of how they look, what they do, and how they are dressed.

As a personal observation, I recall recently sitting in the parking lot of a fast-food restaurant when a car pulled up next to mine. Inside the car appeared to be a father and a mother and their teenage son, all apparently stopping for an all-American dinner of burgers and fries. When only the parents got out of the car and walked into the restaurant, I was intrigued to see why the son remained in the car. I watched as he leaned over the back seat, grabbed the rear view mirror and adjusted it so it could be used from his vantage point in the back seat. He had more pressing matters to attend to before dinner. He spent a few minutes care-

---

[37] Sapp, "Adolescent Thinking and Understanding," 78.

As a parent of teenagers, I often found amusing this phenomenon of "imaginary audience." One of the many memorable conversations I can recall from my years of raising two teenage daughters was a conversation that began when my oldest daughter asked me if I could remember whether she had worn a certain outfit in the previous week. Being, probably, a typical dad, I had no clue.

"No, pal, I can't remember whether you wore that blouse with those pants last week. Why does it matter?"

"Because I can't remember, and Mom can't remember either."

"Okay, but why is that important?"

"Because I don't want people to wonder why I wear the same clothes to school every week, like I only own one shirt."

"Okay, I understand that. But if you can't remember what you wore last week, and I can't remember what you wore last week, and Mom can't remember what you wore last week, who at your school do you think is keeping a record of this stuff? I'll bet most of the people at your school are giving very little thought to your repertoire of clothing from week to week. Maybe that's bad news? But I'm guessing most people aren't taking careful notice. Relax and wear what you want."

fully styling his hair and checking his "look" before he got out of the car. His parents seemed to be not the least surprised at this delay. They understood that this was routine preparation for their son's appearance before an eager public. In some ways it was a telling gesture and a perfect example of imaginary audience. This teenage guy was not just going for a hamburger, he was preparing to step on to a fast-food stage. While it might appear that all attention is focused on quarter-pounders and Happy Meals, he knew better and he did not want to let his audience down!

In her book *Teenage Romance or How to Die of Embarrassment,* Delia Ephron reminds us that this adolescent egocentrism can make daily life a troublesome and worrisome proposition, a bumpy ride in a risky rapid. Here are her facetious "guidelines" for adolescents on "How to Worry":

> Worry that if you (make out) too much you'll get mononucleosis.
> Worry that if you masturbate, you'll get pimples.
> Worry that if you masturbate, you'll get brain damage.

Worry that if you masturbate, you'll go blind.
Worry that, while making out, you ought to be talking too, saying encouraging things like "Oh, baby."
Worry that in a long kiss, you'll have to breathe through your nose and your nose will be stopped up.
Worry that your breath smells.
Worry that you have BO.
Worry that everyone is in on the joke but you.
Worry that there's a right way to kiss and you don't know it.
Worry that there's a right way to make out and you don't know it.
Worry that your date will be able to tell that you don't know it.
If you are a girl, worry that your breasts are too round.
Worry that your breasts are too pointed.
Worry that the nipples are the wrong color.
Worry that your breasts point in different directions.
If you are a boy, worry that you will get breasts.
Worry that your nose is too fat.
Worry that your nose is too long.
Worry that your neck is too fat.
Worry that your lips are too fat.
Worry that your rear end is too fat.
Worry that your ears stick out.
Worry that your eyebrows are too close together.
If you are a boy, worry that you'll never be able to grow a moustache.
If you are a girl, worry that you have a moustache.
Worry that you will eat too much food at other people's houses.
Worry that when you go to the bathroom, people will hear.
Worry that the lock on the door doesn't work. Worry that someone will walk in.
Worry that everyone hates you.
Worry that everyone thinks you're stupid.
Worry that you have ugly toes.[38]

The other dimension of adolescent egocentrism identified by Elkind is *personal fable*,[39] the deep-seated belief in one's uniqueness. Teenagers tend to assume not only that they are important to many people (imaginary audience), but that their personal feelings are unique only to themselves. No one can possibly understand the depths of their depression or the heights of their joy; no one can fully appreciate what it is like to be them. This personal fable mindset probably also accounts for the sense of great injustice most teenagers feel they must suffer on a daily basis:

▶ If they do poorly on a test, the teacher was unfair.

▶ If they run out of money, it is because of unexpected expense.

[38] Delia Ephron, *Teenage Romance or How to Die of Embarrassment* (New York: Ballantine Books, 1981), 113–116.
[39] Elkind, *All Grown Up and No Place to Go*, 36–38.

▸ If their parents will not give them additional allowance, it is because "My parents are so uptight about money."

▸ If there appears to be the slightest inequality with other siblings, "That's not fair."

▸ If they are treated the same as other siblings, parents are reminded, "But I'm not her (or him)." "But I'm older than her (or him)."

▸ If they are not allowed the freedom they desire, they want to be treated like an adult.

▸ If they are treated like an adult when it comes to work and responsibility around the house, they remind parents, "You're treating me like some kind of grown-up; can't I just enjoy being a kid?"

Some, such as Sapp and Elkind, have even suggested that this sense of over-wrought uniqueness may account for higher risk behaviors along adolescents.[40] Adolescents simply cannot imagine anything like death or debilitating injury happening to them.[41]

The upside of this kind of egocentrism is that it probably makes teenagers more open to the gospel.[42] Their longings and disappointments are closer to the surface. Their sense of injustice in the world is more real. Their loneliness is more stark. Even the notion of one's specialness before God is perhaps more believable. Edwin Starbuck, who back in the late nineteenth century extensively researched Christian conversion, discovered that the age at which a person experienced religious conversion averaged 15.6 years. Later studies have verified his finding. Starbuck also listed eight primary motivating factors in a teenager's spiritual commitment: (1) fears, (2) other self-regarding motives, (3) altruistic motives, (4) following out a moral ideal, (5) remorse for and conviction of sin, (6) response to teaching, (7) example and imitation, and (8) urging and social pressure. Much of this is the fruit of adolescent egocentrism.[43] Little wonder then that Sapp observes, "The egocentric assumptions of adolescence, then, are not to be scornfully rejected, for they may serve as an underlying motivation for movement toward a mature productive faith."[44]

Piaget's insights on cognitive development are neither to be too readily dismissed nor too readily embraced but they are important. Whether we are working with middle school students just entering into the stage of formal operations, or

[40] See Sapp, "Adolescent Thinking and Understanding" and Elkind, *All Grown Up and No Place to Go.*

[41] Sapp, "Adolescent Thinking and Understanding," 80.

[42] Data from the Barna Research Group indicate that 77 percent of the adolescents in their survey sample cited "having a clear purpose for living" as something they very much desired; 71 percent responded the same way to "living with a high degree of integrity"; and 66 percent responded very desirable for the value "having a close relationship with God." George Barna, *Real Teens* (Ventura, Calif.: Regal Books, 2001), 84–85. I present this data here not to substantiate a correlation between Elkind's *personal fable* and an openness to spirituality as much as to demonstrate that, for whatever reasons, there seems to be among adolescents an openness to spiritual things.

[43] Larry Poston, "The Adult Gospel," *Christianity Today*, 34, no. 11 (August 20, 1990): 23–25.

[44] Sapp, "Adolescent Thinking and Understanding," 80.

working with high school students capable of exercising advanced skills like critical reasoning, Piaget's framework can help us as youth workers shape Bible studies, messages, and illustrations so that they are better suited to our particular audience.

Piaget and Cognitive Stage Theory: A Critique

Of course, central to the discussion of any theory is the question of validity. So often in youth ministry circles, Piaget's theories are embraced as if they are absolute certainty. No doubt, at one level, Piaget's insights ring true to experience. However, here are some questions we might consider in relation to Piaget's theories:[45]

1. How trustworthy is Piaget's methodology? Many who have faulted Piaget's methodology are quick to note that his conclusions were drawn, at least in part, from observing his own children.[46] Although most of us would agree, on the face of it, that this approach is a little suspect, that does not mean the conclusions are false. It just means his methodology is questionable.

2. Is it really qualitative change? Some critics have argued that at times adults keep relying on concrete operational thought long after Piaget's theory predicts they would do so, and that children seem to use formal operational thought long before the theory predicts they will. If this is true, then maybe the issue in cognitive development is not one of advancing stages, but of simply acquiring more experience and knowledge with age. If that is the case, then cognitive changes are perhaps more quantitative than Piaget suggests.

3. How much do our experiences affect our cognitive development? We know, for example, that college students seem to use more advanced reasoning skills than those of the same age who have not attended college. Research also informs us that in countries where formal operational thinking is not as valued as it is in more industrialized countries, adults use concrete operational thinking more often than adults in the industrialized nations.[47] This suggests that Piaget was wrong in thinking that culture would have little effect on the processes of cognitive development.[48]

[45] Adapted from Nielsen, *Adolescence*, 86–87.

[46] D. Keating, "Adolescent Thinking," in *At the Threshold*, ed. S. Feldman and G. Elliot (Cambridge, Mass.: Harvard University Press), 1990.

[47] "A majority of adolescents in the United States do not think in formal operational ways when presented with scientific reasoning problems, but in developing countries, an even smaller proportion of adolescents and adults do . . .Cultural experiences play a much stronger role in formal operational thought than Piaget envisioned." John Santrock, *Adolescence* (Dubuque, Iowa: Brown and Benchmark, 1996), 117.

[48] This notion is broadly described as *cognitive socialization*. It simply suggests that our interactions in childhood—the conversations we have with parents and with people outside the family circle—can have a very strong influence in shaping our cognitive development. Despite Piaget's insistence that the cognitive process is completely innate, this approach suggests that environment comes into play as well. Research has shown, for example, that "adolescents who participate in high school courses where they are regularly required to participate in small group discussions develop higher order thinking skills." Cited in Nielsen, *Adolescence*, 90. That being so, there are important implications for the way we think about the influence of church on cognitive socialization, and particularly programming that encourages intergenerational and family interaction. It also reminds us of the importance of providing opportunities for discussion and small groups, especially with high school age youth and older. For more information, see Santrock, *Adolescence*, 118f, or Nielsen, *Adolescence*, 90f.

4. Does more formal operational reasoning make us more reasonable? Research in social psychology reminds us that our intuitions and illusions often pollute our logical thinking. It is true, we are able to think more abstractly, but sometimes those abstractions allow us to better see what is not there. Our ability to think of possibilities can obscure our ability to embrace actualities. It might be described as the difference between increased intellectual capacity (formal operations) and good, common "horse sense" (concrete operations).

5. How much is increased capacity for formal operational thought simply a function of age and experience? Piaget seems to suggest that all of the cognitive pistons are firing by the age of 17. On the other hand, while we are told not to disrespect youth, the Scripture seems to suggest that real wisdom, if it ever comes at all, comes much later in life (see Lev. 19:32).

6. To what degree is cognitive capacity a function of gender or innate (inborn) disposition? Keating's 1990 research suggests that people who are more perceptive and insightful as adolescents might have been that way from birth.[49] This would suggest that cognitive development is not just a matter of advancing stages, but a process that is influenced, perhaps, by gender and genes.

7. Most important of all, how does Piaget's theory comport with a biblical worldview? Piaget spoke of maturity and cognitive development only in terms of the advancing capabilities of reason. While within a biblical framework this is certainly a consideration, it overlooks some serious issues:

   ▶ The impact of the Fall on human reasoning. The apostle Paul is quite vivid in Romans 1:18–31 in his outline of the effects of sin on human reasoning. Piaget, writing as a humanist and scientific naturalist, seems to assume the fundamental goodness of humankind—that as we advance to higher levels of reasoning, we also become more whole and more mature. In fact, sometimes our higher reasoning can allow us even more sophisticated ways to obscure the truth and rationalize untruth. "Thinking ourselves to be wise, we become fools" (see Rom. 1:22).

   ▶ Piaget's theory of development focuses solely on reasoning as a measure of maturity. But, informed by Scripture, we can understand the need to factor in other intangibles such as motivation, feelings, morality, and behavior. Most people consider Adolf Hitler to be one of the darkest figures in human history, and yet his was not a failure of intellect, reason, or imagination. Surely there must be a better measurement of maturity.

[49] Nielsen, *Adolescence*, 87.

▶ Piaget's definitions of higher reasoning are defined with no reference to biblical standards of right and wrong, righteousness and sin. By his standard, growth and maturity are matters of restructuring one's perceptions and *creating one's own emerging reality*. In fact, some adherents of Piaget have even suggested that instruction in biblical ethics might impede the cognitive process because it does not allow students to draw their own conclusions (through assimilation and accommodation). As Christians, we can believe that the processes of assimilation and accommodation are important, but we also understand that without the guiding and correcting word of Scripture our reasoning can lead us to make unreasonable decisions (see 2 Tim. 3:16). Scripture makes it quite clear that we can never be fully mature in our thinking until we respond to God's invitation, "Come now, let us reason *together* . . ."

> Ah, sinful nation, a people loaded with guilt, a brood of evil-doers, children given to corruption! They have forsaken the Lord; they have spurned the Holy One of Israel and turned their backs on him. Why should you be beaten anymore? Why do you persist in rebellion? Your whole head is injured, your whole heart afflicted. From the sole of your foot to the top of your head there is no soundness—only wounds and welts and open sores, not cleansed or bandaged or soothed with oil. Your country is desolate, your cities burned with fire; your fields are being stripped by foreigners right before you, laid waste as when overthrown by strangers . . . *Come now, let us reason together, says the Lord*. Though your sins are like scarlet, they shall be as white as snow; though they are red as crimson, they shall be like wool. If you are willing and obedient, you will eat the best from the land; but if you resist and rebel, you will be devoured by the sword (emphasis added).[50]

Moral Development and the Influence of the Cognitive Current

This discussion of Jean Piaget and his exploration of cognitive development sheds light on one of the major currents of the adolescent river. But how do these developing cognitive abilities affect other areas of adolescent development? How, for example, does cognitive growth affect our capacity for moral reasoning? How does cognitive development affect the ways we determine right and wrong? In what ways does cognitive development influence the formulation of our personal identity? Surely, in the realm of youth ministry, with our desire to help teenagers shape clear and wise moral choices, to become whole and authentic persons committed to Jesus Christ, we are concerned with such questions. Which leads us to explore still further the inner passages of adolescent development.

[50] Isaiah 1:4–7, 18–20.

Travel Log: Costa Rica

Youth Worker Profiles by Paul Borthwick

Bob Sabean has been serving in youth ministry and youth
ministry leadership since being a youth counselor at a
children's camp when he was 14 years old. In 1969, he
embarked to serve in Costa Rica through a Latin American
mission, and he's served there ever since. Youth work
has taken him into high school ministry, discipleship
classes, and most notably, the development of youth
camps. This last item led Bob to become the Latin
American director of Christian Camping International in
San Jose in 1987. He serves as a trainer of youth workers, a professor of recreational ministry, and an
encourager to younger leaders.

Getting Started. Many Americans do not realize that
youth ministry is fairly new in the world of Latin
America. Bob helped introduce it to Costa Rica in 1965.
"I arrived in Costa Rica at age 29. My goal was student
ministry (high school and university). With a coworker,
we developed an indigenous program akin to Young Life.
We began by advertising a camp for high schoolers. At
camp (activity-based, small-group oriented, counselor-
centered) decisions were made. These young people were
invited to a meeting in the city. We planned follow-up
activities, such as roller-skating, and then we inaugu-
rated weekly meetings of inspiration. Then discipleship
courses (basics of the Christian life, etc.) continued
the process. And for those who chose it, we made one-on-
one discipleship relationships available."

Favorite Memory. Reaching out across the Catholic-
Protestant divide in those days was big stuff—especially
in Latin America. "We were a group of Protestant missionaries invited to hold weekly 'clubs' in both private

and public high schools. We showed Moody Films in schools all over the country including private Catholic schools. High school guidance directors invited our team members to provide counseling to some of the more difficult students. Parent-teacher meetings were opened to us to provide advice on parenting teenagers. The schools often gave us permission to give away New Testaments. The student bodies received information on our camps during vacation periods, which in turn brought new students into the ongoing ministry of our New Youth Christian Movement. Catholic high schools, at their traditional retreat at the end of the senior year, invited us to work with their priests in directing the retreats.

"With the outbreak of the charismatic movement, hordes of young people, both Protestant and Catholic, met weekly in homes, in both Catholic and Protestant churches—and wherever the word got out that the meeting would take place. For a couple of years it was like one ongoing prayer and praise meeting."

Fruit That Remains. "The New Youth Christian Movement (NYCM) still exists today, and the leadership is committed to ministering to both Protestant and Catholic youth. They emphasize evangelism and discipleship, with no call to convert to Protestantism. The most outstanding Catholic youth evangelist in Latin America—Martin Valverde, a Costa Rican residing in Mexico, is a product of NYCM. And several priests and Catholic youth workers in Costa Rica always turn to this team to train their own youth and camp workers.

"Otto Garrido came to camp at age eight. He came from a home abandoned by his father, with an alcoholic mother. He was VERY incorrigible as a camper for a couple of years. But in time, he became a member of the counselor staff, and later program director of one of our Costa Rican camps, Camp Roblealto, as a paid position. As a student of physical education, he took my 'Introduction to Recreation' course. Today, as a physical education teacher at a secular private high school in Costa Rica, he organizes camps as a pre-evangelism tool with excellence. And has a strong commitment to evangelism in his position as a high school teacher."

Changing Roles and Expanding Impact. "While building the Costa Rica youth movement in those early years, I was also building the Association of Christian Camps Latin America. We had already put together two all Latin America conventions in 1972 and 1978. But in the 80s and 90s, we became more concentrated on training youth leadership. While the context was usually 'camps,' everything could be easily adapted to overall youth outreach.

"During those years, I traveled to Mexico, all Central American countries, and most of the countries of South America, leading seminars, workshops, conventions, training camps, and institutes. We wanted to expand the impact of the 'youth camp' idea by putting the tools needed for effective ministry into the hands of youth leaders: administrative, programming, theological, recreational, and biblical tools. We also multiplied the ministry by creating training manuals on topics like camp administration, basic Bible study guides, and spiritual health for Christian leaders (the camp counselors)."

Entrusting the Future to Faithful Others. If the goal of ministry is to equip others to do their own ministry, Bob can feel satisfied as he faces a pending retirement: "All high school ministry in Costa Rica is now led by Costa Ricans—including Camp Roblealto. The same is true for Christian Camping International (CCI). The director of CCI Latin America is from Panama, and all our national associations throughout these Spanish-speaking countries are under national leadership.

"Bessy Macotto was 14 when she went to camp in Honduras. Her parents were not Christians, but she was going to a Methodist school, and the school camp brought her to Christ. At age 16, she attended her first convention in Honduras. After high school, she inherited the family business. She runs two hardware stores, and a depot of cement and sand supplies. She is on the national board of the Methodist schools in Honduras. She trains a group of youth leaders and takes them out on weekends to the far reaches of Honduras to run camps with kids from off the street. She has been on the board of CCI Latin America for seven years, and this year took over the presidency of CCI Latin America for two years. In the words of the apostle John, I have no greater joy than to hear and see Bessy walking in the truth and affecting the lives of the next generation."

chapter seven

EXPLORING THE INNER PASSAGES OF ADOLESCENCE: MORAL CHOICES AND EMERGING IDENTITY

Live among human facts. Thank God He has given the majority of us the surroundings of real, definite, sordid human beings; there is no pretense about them, the people we live among and come in contact with are not theories, they are facts. That is the kind of thing God wants us to keep among.
—**Oswald Chambers**[1]

Kohlberg . . . either is a blind optimist and regards all men as intrinsically good, or has given insufficient attention to "immoral development." My reading of his work suggests chiefly the latter.
—**Donald M. Joy**[2]

[1] Oswald Chambers, *Workmen of God* (London: Marshall, Morgan and Scott, 1937), 20.

[2] Donald M. Joy, "Kohlberg Revisited: A Supra-Naturalist Speaks His Mind," in *Moral Development Foundations*, ed. Donald M. Joy (Nashville, Tenn.: Abingdon, 1983), 52.

It's a rainy morning in the Veronga Volcanoes of central equatorial Africa, and I'm crawling along on my hands and knees, nearly certain that somewhere up ahead I'll intercept a family of 12 mountain gorillas. I'll want to move slowly now, carefully. Blundering into the midst of them is so aggressively impolite that the dominant male might feel obliged to charge. I don't want to provoke a charge because I'd be disrupting the animal's lives. And I want to be sensitive about this—delicate. Also, in the event of a charge, I would have to do something very difficult indeed. I would have to stand rock-steady in the face of 500 pounds of rampaging, implacable rage. I would have to stand there stupidly staring down a silverback because 20 years of research indicates that a gorilla almost never makes contact with a human that holds his ground. On the other hand, if there's a forest elephant at the end of the trail, I should be prepared to run. I've been informed that elephants, unlike gorillas, seldom come pounding after a running man. Mostly, I don't want to encounter a forest buffalo. It's early for these guys. They don't usually get too rambunctious until about two hours before sundown. But you never know. The scientists and game wardens have told me that it does no good to hold your ground before forest buffalo because they will gore and stomp and kill you. Unfortunately, they also have a tendency to run down retreating humans, whom they gore and stomp and kill. Climb a tree and they will knock it down so they can gore and stomp and kill you. Some few humans have survived a buffalo attack by playing dead. They were merely gored and stomped in a playful, nonlethal way.[3]

For teenagers making their way through the jungle of adolescence there are options and choices, dangers and snares, risks and adventures. Like the excerpt above from Tim Cahill's journey through central equatorial Africa, the right choices are not always so clear, the possible options not always so appealing. Part of successfully navigating that journey is understanding the factors and dynamics that affect a teenager's moral reasoning.

In chapter 6, with Jean Piaget and his exploration of cognitive development, we considered one of the major currents of the adolescent river. But how do these developing cognitive abilities affect other areas of adolescent development? How, for example, does cognitive growth affect our capacity for moral reasoning? How does cognitive development affect the ways we determine right and wrong? Again, in the realm of youth ministry, with our desire to help teenagers make clear and wise moral choices, we are concerned with such questions. This leads us to explore the streams and currents of moral development.

[3] Tim Cahill, *A Wolverine is Eating My Leg* (New York: Vintage Books, 1989), 142.

Table 7-1.
Kohlberg's Levels of Moral Reasoning

Levels	Stages	Characteristics of Moral Reasoning
I	**Preconventional Reasoning (ages 4–10)** Child's only real guideline for making choices is an orientation toward pleasure and away from pain; there is no internalization of moral values. Sole consideration is external rewards and punishment.	**Stage One: Punishment-Obedience Orientation** Only factor in moral reasoning is which behavior will help to avoid punishment. **Stage Two: Instrument-Relativist Orientation** Child determines right or wrong by reasoning whether the actions are instrumental in satisfying his or her wants and desires.
II	**Conventional Reasoning (ages 10–13)** Focus extends beyond one's personal wishes. Young person becomes aware of external factors in making moral judgments (family, school, government, societal expectations). Early adolescents begin forming their moral convictions, but at this level, these convictions are more "inherited" than they are internal.	**Stage Three: "Good Boy" – "Nice Girl" Orientation** Right and wrong is determined by the desire to gain approval and acceptance by others. **Stage Four: Law and Order Orientation** Early adolescents place a high emphasis on law and order; right or wrong correspond to doing one's duty.
III	**Postconventional Reasoning (ages 13–young adult)** Highest level of moral reasoning; moral choices are based on internalized values.	**Stage Five: Social Contract-Legalistic Orientation** Young adolescents realize law is for the benefit of the common good, and therefore to be taken seriously. Yet laws have been determined by societal consent, and they can be changed. Laws are not absolute and irrevocable. **Stage Six: Universal Ethical Principle Orientation** Person uses universal principles to determine morality of personal acts. That means there are rare occasions when it may be necessary to "bend" or "break" the law to abide by a higher moral standard.

Lawrence Kohlberg, "Moral Stages and Moralization: The Cognitive-Developmental Approach" in *Moral Development and Behavior*, ed. Thomas Lickona (New York: Holy, Rhinehart and Winston, 1976), 37–38.

Lawrence Kohlberg and Moral Development

While there are many researchers in the field of moral development, none has been as influential as Lawrence Kohlberg.[4] Building on the work of Piaget, Kohlberg researched how cognitive changes affect moral choices. At the risk of

[4] Again, there are numerous ways of accounting for moral development, just as there are for cognitive development. Sigmund Freud, from his psychoanalytic perspective, wrote of morality largely in terms of the feelings generated: guilt, inferiority, or shame. Those who advocate a social learning approach to moral development emphasize the distinction between the adolescent's moral *competence*, the ability to comprehend and construct moral behaviors (which is more a factor of cognitive development), and moral *performance*, or behavior in a given situation (which is based more on social influences—rewards and incentives to act in a certain way). Piaget, from his perspective as a cognitive stage theorist, suggested a two-level framework in which moral development advances from an attitude of *heteronomy* (morality shaped by the constraints and rules of adults and authority figures) to *autonomy* (morality shaped by internal values of justice or equality quite apart from the threat of penalty or punishment from external forces). For more on these theories, see Sigmund Freud, *A General Introduction to Psychoanalysis* (New York: Washington Square Press, 1917); D. K. Lapsley, R. D. Enright, and R. C. Serlin, "Moral and Social Education," in *Adolescent Development: Issues in Education*, ed. J. Worrell and F. Danner (New York: Academic Press, 1986); and Jean Piaget, *The Moral Judgment of the Child* (New York: Harcourt Brace Jovanovich, 1932). For a brief summary and overview of these theories and others consult also Michael Anthony, *Foundations of Ministry: An Introduction to Christian Education for a New Generation* (Wheaton, Ill.: Bridgepoint Books/Victor Books, 1992), 115–125; and John Santrock, *Adolescence* (Dubuque, Iowa: Brown and Benchmark, 1996), 420ff. For a more in-depth survey of the literature, see Daniel Lapsley, *Moral Psychology* (Boulder, Colo.: Westview Press, 1996). Lapsley's evaluation of Kohlberg is especially comprehensive. While Kohlberg's work is something of a flagship, I am particularly intrigued by the research being done by William Damon about how morality develops in childhood. Although this work is beyond the scope of this chapter and this book, it is well worth investigation. See William Damon, *The Moral Child* (New York: Free Press, 1988).

oversimplifying Kohlberg, it might be helpful to describe his understanding of moral maturity as a sequential (stage-like) growth of one's understanding of justice.[5] Because of his allegiance to cognitive-development theory, Kohlberg's focus is more on the form and process than on the content of thought. Kohlberg based his research on evaluations of people's responses to stories in which the characters face various moral dilemmas.[6]

Specific questions of right and wrong were not Kohlberg's concern. He was more interested in how people at various stages of cognitive growth arrived at their conclusions of right and wrong. One of his main areas of attention was what Kohlberg described as *internalization*—the developmental change that occurs when one's moral choices are shaped less by external factors (fear of parental punishment, respect for law and order, societal expectations) and more by internal factors (an inner compass that is set on universal ethical principles).[7] Kohlberg's framework (summarized in Table 7-1) posits a process of moral growth that develops through three levels, each level consisting of two stages:

▶ **Level One: Preconventional Reasoning (ages 4–10).** In the earliest stages of moral reasoning, the child's only real guideline for making choices is an orientation toward pleasure and away from pain—no internalization of moral values. The sole consideration in moral reasoning is external rewards and punishment.

> *Stage One: Punishment-Obedience Orientation.* At this lowest of all the stages of moral reasoning the only factor in moral reasoning is *which behavior will help the child to avoid punishment*. For example, a five-year-old child does not reason, "I mustn't draw with permanent ink on the walls of the living room, because that grieves Mommy, and it lowers our home's resale value, which causes Daddy stress." Rather, the child reasons, "I did this once before and I got spanked for it. That hurt. Therefore, I will not draw any more murals of biblical imagery on the walls of the living room."

> *Stage Two: Instrument-Relativist Orientation.* At this stage of moral reasoning, the child determines right or wrong by reasoning *whether the actions are instrumental in satisfying his or her wants and desires*. The needs and feelings of others are not really an issue, nor are any larger moral principles. The "right" choice is that choice which will provide the best advantage in any given situation. The moral choice itself is little more than an instrument—a means to an end, and that choice is *relative* to any particular situation. For example, a

---

[5] This word *justice* is probably too narrow to fully encompass what Kohlberg means by moral maturity, but he is certainly concerned about rights and responsibilities in relationship to society. Indeed, he defines his highest stage of moral maturity as a morality based on universal human rights. For further discussion of this question, see Lapsley, *Moral Psychology*, 76.

[6] The most widely known of these moral dilemmas is the following: "In Europe, a woman was near death from a rare type of cancer. There was one drug that the doctors thought might save her. It was a form of radium that a druggist in the same town had recently discovered. The drug was expensive to make, but the druggist was charging ten times what the drug cost him to make. He spent $200 for the radium and charged $2,000 for a small dose of the drug. The sick woman's husband, Heinz, went to everyone he knew to borrow the money, but he could only get together $1,000, which is half of what it cost. He told the druggist that his wife was dying and asked him to sell it cheaper or let him pay later. But the druggist said, 'No, I discovered the drug and I'm going to make money from it.' So Heinz got desperate and broke into the man's store and stole the drug for his wife." Taken from Lawrence Kohlberg, "Moral Stages and Moralization: The Cognitive-Developmental Approach," in *Moral Development and Behavior*, ed. Thomas Lickona (New York: Holt, Rinehart and Winston, 1976), 41–42.

[7] Kohlberg, "Moral Stages and Moralization," 37–38.

For those of us who are quite sure that spiritual reality is neither a product of, nor entirely described by, data on moral development, it is stimulating to reflect on a matter of basic consensus . . . : that the spiritual essence of human- kind is not defined by nor can it be explained in the naturalistic terms of cognitive development and stages of moral growth. It is something else!
—**Ted Ward**

seven-year-old child cleans up toys left in the family room, not just to avoid spanking (punishment), and not really to please father (internal value), but because "if I clean up, Daddy (external value) will let me play with his high-tech Sharper Image Lazy Boy recliner (reward)."

▸ **Level Two: Conventional Reasoning (ages 10–13).** The focus of this second level extends beyond one's personal wishes. The young person becomes aware of external factors in making moral judgments (family, school, government, societal expectations). Initial (internal) moral standards are formed, but they are formed primarily through loyalty and conformity to external influences. Early adolescents begin forming their moral convictions, but at this level, these convictions are more "inherited" than they are internal. Obviously, this says something about the importance of good moral influence in the family, and about the formative power of positive (or negative) group structures (youth groups, clubs, teams, etc).

Stage Three: "Good Boy"–"Nice Girl" Orientation. Right and wrong is *determined by the desire to gain approval and acceptance of others.* Moral choices are based on what will win the praise of authority figures (parents, teachers, camp counselor, coach—or gang leader). It is no longer solely a fear of the negative (punishment) as much as it is a desire for the positive ("Good boy," "Nice girl"). But still the locus of moral motivation is external. For example, a child responds positively to traditional parental tricks such as, "Hey, Johnny, show Daddy how fast you can run to take that garbage out to the street." Johnny is not motivated by a deep sense of servanthood as much as he is eager to hear Dad say, "Nice job, Johnny. Very fast! Daddy will help you practice again tomorrow night when we have more trash."

Stage Four: Law and Order Orientation. The young person at this level places *high emphasis on law and order. Right or wrong correspond to doing one's duty.* Instead of making moral choices based on a desire for approval, moral reasoning is based on a growing appreciation for the fact that everyone's life is better when there are basic rules of conduct, and some sense of law and order. This is moral reasoning based on doing one's duty (based on rules, laws, or conventions)—nothing less and nothing more. For example, a 12-year-old guy agrees to pick up the trash he left near the lakefront at camp not because he wants to "maintain the beauty of God's creation," but because he knows he threw the trash there. If he threw it down, it is his duty to pick it up. (He probably would not pick up the gum wrapper and paper cup next to his trash, because "It's not my trash—I didn't leave it there.")

▸ **Level Three: Postconventional Reasoning (ages 13—young adult).** At this highest level of moral reasoning, moral choices are based on internalized values. The emerging adolescent evaluates and considers various moral courses, and begins to develop a personal internalized moral compass. Behavior is no longer shaped solely by conventional expectations or requirements (hence Kohlberg's term *postconventional*).

Stage Five: Social Contract-Legalistic Orientation. The young adolescent realizes that law is for the benefit of the common good, and therefore to be taken seriously. Inherent in this perspective, however, is the knowledge that these laws have been determined by societal consent and *they can be changed* through legislative action and advocacy. They are not to be disregarded lightly, but *neither are they absolute and irrevocable.* For example, 17-year-old Sally discovers that almost one third of her meager paycheck from the Gap each week is going toward state and federal taxes. She reports the income and pays her taxes as a responsible citizen, but she also joins the Young Republican Club at her high school and works to elect officials who will cut taxes and work to decrease government spending.

Stage Six: Universal Ethical Principle Orientation. The person at this highest stage of moral reasoning uses universal principles to determine the morality of personal actions. They understand that law is still important, but there are higher values that deserve human allegiance. It is these higher values that must be respected even above civic statutes and legal requirements. That means there are rare occasions when it may be necessary to "bend" or "break" the law to abide by a higher moral standard. For example, Sally, who only recently received her learner's permit, is racing to the hospital, ignoring speed limits and stop lights. She reasons this is the right decision because her mother is in the backseat of the car in the latter stages of labor. Sally understands traffic laws are important and knows that they are for the good of society. She understands that we cannot speed everywhere we want to go. On the other hand, this is a scenario not covered in driver's education class. Her mother's health and the baby's may be at stake, and unpleasant sounds from the back seat indicate mom is uncomfortable and a little stressed that Sally's father is out of town.[8]

While the nomenclature for Kohlberg's stages and levels can be confusing, what is most important in Kohlberg's theory is to observe the locus of moral reasoning as it evolves from a place of complete egocentrism (totally self-centered) through a place of external influence (shaped by others' expectations) to a place of internal influence (shaped by personal moral convictions). Cathy Stonehouse's simplified summary of Kohlberg's levels is illustrated in Table 7-2.[9]

Table 7-2.
Stonehouse's Process of Moral Development

Levels	Source of Authority	Justice	Motivation to Moral Action
Level One	Primary concern is with the self.	Justice is doing what adults and authority figures have commanded.	Fear of being punished; desire to receive reward.
Level Two	Primary concern is with how others might respond to one's moral choices (legal, societal, family, expectations); there are external standards—models and rules.	Justice is defined by the conventional standards of society (that is, if abortion is legal under the law, it is just).	Desire to meet expectations of family, society; a sense of duty.
Level Three	Primary concern is with internal principles.	Justice is giving all parties and individuals equal consideration.	To be true to one's own moral principles, regardless of the expectations of conventional thinking.

Source: Adapted from Cathy Stonehouse, "Moral Development: The Process and the Pattern," cited in Charles Shelton, *Adolescent Spirituality* (Chicago: Loyola University Press, 1983), 45.

---

[8] Another, perhaps more inspiring, example of this stage of moral reasoning is Martin Luther's courageous stand against the corruption of polity and doctrine within the Roman Catholic Church in 1517. When he posted his "Ninety-Five Theses" on the door of the castle church in Wittenberg, Germany, he was not suggesting that order in the church is unimportant or unnecessary. Indeed, he took this step of protest with great trepidation. But, when brought to trial before the church hierarchy in the Diet of Worms, his "Here I stand; I can do no other . . ." was based on higher principles than those legislated in Rome by any human authority. The sole authority of God's Word (*sola scriptura*) was the universal principle that guided his reasoning.

[9] Adapted from Cathy Stonehouse, "Moral Development: The Process and the Pattern," cited in Charles Shelton, *Adolescent Spirituality* (Chicago: Loyola University Press, 1983), 45.

Table 7-3.
Selman's Five Stages of Perspective-Taking

Stage	Perspective-Taking Stage	Ages	Description
0	Egocentric	3–6	Child is unable to understand that others have feelings or thoughts and is aware only of "what matters to me."
1	Social-informational	6–8	Child begins to comprehend that others may see an issue differently but tends still to focus on only one perspective—not really attempting to integrate various viewpoints.
2	Self-reflective	8–10	Child can now understand and appreciate that there are other perspectives; children are able to put themselves in the place of another: "I might respond the same way if I were in the same situation."
3	Mutual	10–12	Early adolescents begin to comprehend that both self and other can view each other with mutuality—and step back to view exchange of ideas from perspective of third person, "Both of us are trying to wrestle with this issue, and both of us may have something to offer."
4	Social and conventional	12–15	Teenager recognizes that individuals will not always agree with or even fully understand each other's perspectives, but individuals can still show respect to others. Individual perspectives may be different, but for society to function effectively, we may have to learn to disagree agreeably.

Source: Robert Selman, *The Growth of Interpersonal Understanding: Clinical and Developmental Analyses*, cited in John Santrock, *Adolescence* (Dubuque, Iowa: Brown and Benchmark, 1996), 122–123.

Robert Selman's Stages of "Perspective-Taking"

Kohlberg's theory is far from the only way to define moral maturity. Robert Selman,[10] in an extension of Piaget's concept of adolescent egocentrism, described moral development in terms of *perspective-taking*—the ability to think about an issue or a question from a perspective other than one's own. In short, it is moving beyond the narrow world of egocentrism. Selman's research, developed by analyzing children's and adolescents' responses to case studies, demonstrated strong support for the kind of sequential growth that parallels cognitive maturity. Based on his findings, Selman offered that perspective-taking evolves through a series of five stages (see Table 7-3), beginning around three years of age and continuing into adolescence.

In sum, Kohlberg has indeed contributed to our understanding of moral development. A discerning youth worker will be able to retool some of Kohlberg's insights and make use of them in thinking about how to nurture biblical moral development. Kohlberg's three levels provide concepts that deserve to be included in the lexicon of moral instruction. But from a Christian perspective his primary assumptions about morality and the human condition evince a faulty beginning point for his work (see chapter 6). As Donald Joy observes, "Kohlberg . . .

[10] Robert Selman, *The Growth of Interpersonal Understanding: Clinical and Development Analyses* (New York: Academic Press, 1980), cited in John Santrock, *Adolescence*

either is a blind optimist and regards all men as intrinsically good, or has given insufficient attention to 'immoral development.' My reading of his work suggests chiefly the latter."[11]

Kohlberg and Moral Development: Critique

In reviewing Kohlberg's framework for moral development, we are presented with a range of questions. Let's begin with what in Kohlberg can be affirmed by those who operate from within a Christian worldview.[12]

1. Kohlberg's approach to moral development is hinged on the notion that justice is the core of morality. But is this perspective big enough to include the whole picture? Kohlberg argues that, aside from justice, the only general principle for moral reasoning seriously advanced by philosophers is some vaguely defined benevolence. Indeed, Kohlberg's emphasis on justice as a core of moral reasoning is resonant with the words of the Old Testament prophets and their frequent calls to justice.

   Having said that, one might reply that while an emphasis on justice is certainly important, an exclusive focus on it truncates all the biblical teaching about interpersonal relationships into a very small package. Doug Sholl has offered a seven-fold pattern of Christian relational content that seems to unfold more broadly the fabric of biblical morality: "love and justice, truth and faithfulness, forbearance and patience, forgiveness and repentance, edification and encouragement, humility and submission, and prayer and praise."[13]

   Trying to tie up all of these important dynamics into one prescribed package called "justice" seems to overestimate the size of the box. We can affirm with Kohlberg the importance of justice without affirming that it is the "core of morality."

2. Kohlberg does not fully explore the relationship between reasoning what is right to do and actually *doing* what one has reasoned. We all know from experience that moral reasoning is easier than moral doing. We know also from research that the former is by no means a guarantee of the latter.[14] But defining moral reasoning simply in terms of a cognitive process

---

[11] Joy, "Kohlberg Revisited," 52.

[12] For a full expression of this common ground between Kohlberg and Christian thought, see ibid., 49–53. Bonnidell Clouse provides a biblically based model that goes further still and, in fact, incorporates some elements of truth from each of the four main approaches to moral development. According to Clouse, morality springs from conflict (psychoanalytic—Freud), morality springs from action (behavioral/conditioning—B. F. Skinner), morality springs from knowledge (cognitive/moral reasoning—Piaget/Kohlberg), and morality springs from innate human potential (moral potential—Carl Rogers and Abraham Maslow, humanist psychologists). Clouse writes, "Each of the major psychologies . . . emphasizes one of the four expressions of morality: conflict, action, knowledge, and potential. By contrast, the Bible stresses all of them, thus presenting a more complete picture of what it means to be a moral person." But there are some important issues to be raised. Bonnidell Clouse, *Teaching for Moral Growth* (Wheaton, Ill.: Victor/Bridgepoint, 1993), 35–49.

[13] Robert W. Pazmino, *Foundational Issues in Christian Education* (Grand Rapids, Mich.: Baker Books, 1997), 205. While he applauds the emphasis on justice, particularly in our unjust world, Pazmino criticizes Fowler at this point for focusing too narrowly on justice as the essence of all moral reasoning.

[14] Anthony, *Foundations of Ministry*, 124. This is a complaint that has been well articulated by Nicholas Wolterstorff in *Educating for Responsible Action* (Grand Rapids, Mich.: Eerdmans, 1980), 79–100.

seems to stop too short. It is almost like asking, "Do you know what time it is?" and someone answers simply, "Yes." We want more. We are not just interested in the cognitive ability to comprehend chronology and read a clock. Indeed, from a biblical standpoint, knowing what is right to do, and not doing it, is explicitly unreasonable (see James 1:23–25).

In short, Kohlberg's definition of moral reasoning is too simplistic. As Pazmino observes, "Moral development includes more than moral reasoning. Moral behavior can be seen to encompass moral judgment, the situation and its pressures, individual motives, and emotions, and a sense of the will. Moral judgment entails both moral reasoning (Kohlberg's primary emphasis) and moral content. Thus, moral reasoning is more complex than Kohlberg believes it to be."[15]

Study Group Crowd-Breaker Idea

Take a break from trying to memorize developmental stages by trying to make up some of your own cool-sounding Kohlberg and Piaget-type stages. Suggestions (make up your definitions for each stage):

For Piaget:
(1) sensual motor stage,
(2) collegiate optional stage,
(3) postcrematorial stage,
(4) post toastial stage,
(5) precelestial stage, and
(6) concrete premillennial stage.

For Kohlberg:
(1) preconfessional level,
(2) unconventional level,
(3) Youth Specialties Conventional level,
(4) congressional-delusional stage,
(5) pejorative-restrictive stage, and
(6) ethical-invisible stage.

3. Kohlberg's work does not do enough to account for gender differences in moral reasoning. Do these processes happen the same in men and women? Most of the developmental theorists suggest that the various stages of maturity are universal, not only across time and culture, but across gender as well.

The research of Carol Gilligan, however, offers evidence that female moral reasoning generally looks quite different from moral reasoning in males.[16] She asserts that female moral reasoning tends to be less self-centered and more empathic than males. When a teenage male is seeking to arrive at a good moral choice he may more likely consider issues such as justice, fairness, and self-reliance. In contrast, a teenage female might

---

[15] Pazmino, *Foundational Issues in Christian Education*, 204.

[16] Carol Gilligan, *In a Different Voice: Psychological Theory and Women's Development* (Cambridge, Mass.: Harvard University Press, 1982), cited in Linda Nielsen, *Adolescence: A Contemporary View* (Philadelphia: Harcourt Brace, 1996), 221. For a balanced appraisal of these issues, and how Kohlberg responds to these criticisms, see Lapsley, *Moral Psychology*, 132–147.

view that same decision from the standpoint of developing intimacy, maintaining harmony, and working toward cooperation. From the vantage point, then, of Kohlberg's model, the women are reasoning at a conventional level (Level Two) because they are influenced, at least in part, by the needs and wishes of others. Meanwhile, the men are reasoning at a postconventional level because they appear to operating on the basis of more universal principles. Gilligan asks, is this really a different *level* of moral reasoning, or just a different *way* of doing moral reasoning? It is an interesting observation, and if it does nothing else, it demonstrates that "stage theory" does not always fit reality as cleanly as we might wish.

4. Kohlberg's focus on autonomy (literally, "self rule" or "making one's own laws") does not do justice to the influence of relationships in moral development. Even at the postconventional level, Kohlberg still defines moral reasoning as a function of one's appraisal of what is truly just and right. But that leaves out of the process any dependence on God or interdependence on a nurturing community. Both omissions are serious flaws. The lack of connection to community, from a pragmatic standpoint, is an especially serious issue for youth work because it undercuts the importance of family, church community, and the youth group in formulating moral maturity. In Pazmino's words, "Rather than a stance of autonomy, the Christian faith involves a theonomy, where persons are dependent upon God and interdependent with others within the Christian and human community."[17]

   The flaw in this approach of making children into *autonomous* moral thinkers is observable in work done by Samuel and Pearl Oliner through their extensive study of individuals who rescued Jews in Nazi-occupied Europe. Their study, reported in the book *The Altruistic Personality*, showed that only a small minority of the rescuers were motivated by "autonomous" or "principled" ethics—the type of moral reasoning that Kohlberg identifies as the highest level of moral maturity. Much more frequently, the rescuers accounted for their behavior by referring to moral principles by which they were brought up, to the example of parents, or to the influence of religion. The Oliners take great pains to make the point that these people were not "moral heroes, arriving at their own conclusions about right and wrong after internal struggle, guided primarily by intellect and rationality." On the contrary, "what most distinguished them were their connection with others in relationships of commitment and care."[18]

5. Kohlberg's emphasis on cognitive process blurs the distinction between good thinking and what might be described as "right" thinking. Kohlberg divorces moral reasoning from moral content. From the standpoint of youth ministry this error is particularly grievous, because it assumes that teaching teenagers how to think reasonably will lead them to reason morally. This is a mistake that results from bad theology and faulty pedagogy.

---

[17] Pazmino, *Foundational Issues in Christian Education*, 204.

[18] Cited by William Kilpatrick, *Why Johnny Can't Tell Right From Wrong* (New York: Touchstone-Simon and Schuster, 1973), 112–114.

Theologically, Kohlberg's theory overlooks the disastrous effects of sin on human judgment (Prov. 3:5–6, 14:12). Craig Dykstra has made this point convincingly:

One of the critical problems with Kohlberg's theory of moral development stems from the fact that he does not take human sinfulness seriously. This is a problem, not because I expect or even hope that people who write about the moral life will deal explicitly with theological categories,

> Looking at Stonehouse's simplification of Kohlberg, it is striking how closely it parallels (in reverse order) an unpretentious little acrostic sometimes taught to children in Vacation Bible School—and, I might add, one of the few lessons I remember from Sunday School. It was based on the word joy: J-Jesus, O-others, Y-yourself. A modest ethic, perhaps, for a day of complicated moral choices, but it provided clear instruction that good moral reasoning begins by asking first, "How could I please Jesus?" Second, "How could I serve others?" And third, and last, "How can I please myself?"

but because I think Kohlberg in particular completely misses an important *empirical fact* about human beings to which the doctrine of sin points. Moreover, he constructs his theory in such a way to hide that fact from view and thus misrepresents what moral growth involves and leads us astray educationally. In other words, what he proposes does not add up to good science, philosophy, or theology.[19]

What is this fact about human nature that Kohlberg misses or hides from view? It is the fact that people, as they strive to be moral, consistently find it impossible to *think* their way into goodness. Reasoning power does not translate into moral power.

Just because a car has an engine that is well-tuned does not mean it will take us in the right direction, and just because a mind is capable of the highest levels of moral reasoning does not mean it will reason its way to high moral principles.

Educationally, Kohlberg's presuppositions lead to a pedagogy that is far too passive. This confusion is one of the reasons that most "moral education" is severely impoverished. William Kilpatrick, in his provocative book *Why Johnny Can't Tell Right From Wrong*, puts it this way:

[19] Craig Dykstra, "What Are People Like? An Alternative to Kohlberg's View," in *Moral Development Foundations*, ed. Donald M. Joy (Nashville, Tenn.: Abingdon, 1983), 153. See also Romans 7:14–24. Dykstra, in his extremely helpful and thoughtful article, also comments that Kohlberg himself has responded to this kind of criticism by saying that he understands that logical reasoning does not necessarily translate into moral reasoning, and that moral reasoning does not necessarily lead to moral behavior. But he does assert that the essence of the moral life is moral reason, "and that when moral reason is fully developed in all its aspects we have what can be called morally mature people." Joy, "Kohlberg Revisited," 154.

> One of the basic problems in moral education is to find the proper balance between content and process. Where should the emphasis be placed: on the content of the Judeo-Christian-Western moral heritage, as was done in the past, or on independent thinking processes, as Kohlberg . . . and others would have it? The stress in recent decades has, of course, been on the second. Like the Cheshire cat [in *Alice in Wonderland*], moral content has been in the process of disappearing from moral education. Not much of substance is left except, perhaps, for a ghostly smile.[20]

Youth workers should not just assume that opportunities for moral reflection will lead to biblical or even moral reasoning. That is why instruction in biblical content is so critical and profitable for "teaching, rebuking, correcting and training in righteousness" (2 Tim. 3:16). Wolterstorff suggests that the best way to help children internalize Christian values and act out the values they have internalized is for a person (someone who will show love and concern for that child) to act "lovingly toward the child to combine discipline and modeling *with the enunciation of a moral standard* which the child perceives to fit the situations and on which he or she is willing to act (emphasis added)."

As we conclude our discussion of moral development and consider its source in cognitive development, it is quite clear that as an individual grows up what emerges is a complex and unique individual. These students sitting on the floor and laughing at a skit, meeting in small groups to think about a question, sharing in a building project for a third-world congregation, listening together to a Bible study, singing intently as they gather for worship—these are human beings coming to be. As they move through this journey, in each of them there is the wonder of a developing sense of self. To round out our discussion of adolescent development, we must take a closer look at how that self develops.

Erik Erikson and the Search for Identity

> This brings us to the most one-sided contest of all—heavy hydraulics. This colorful expression is usually reserved not for big waves (although on western desert rivers waves can be gigantic) but for powerful current effects, reversals, whirlpools, boiling and unstable eddies, giant holes, and so forth which occur with some frequency on the biggest rivers, and even on much smaller rivers at high water and flood stages.[21]

One of the most notorious traits of this river called adolescence is its frequent changes in course, following sometimes the contour of previous channels,

---

[20] Kilpatrick, *Why Johnny Can't Tell Right From Wrong*, 116.

[21] Lito Tejada-Flores, *Wildwater: The Sierra Club Guide to Whitewater Boating* (San Francisco: Sierra Club Books, 1978), 185.

sometimes sluicing off into new directions, and sometimes overflowing old boundaries altogether. At times a torrent and at times a stream, nowhere is the surging, probing, expanding current of adolescence more strong than in the search for identity.

Attempting to map this changing current is not precise work. The growing self does not fit neatly onto a chart. It is like trying to take a photograph of a moving river. The loops and bends, the standing waves, the hidden boulders just beneath the surface that the camera records in one moment are changed in the next moment. If we are looking only at the surface water in a teenager's life, it is not so easy to tell. But, just beneath the surface, there are coursing, cutting, conflicting currents that continually reshape the river that was.

There are many who have sought to map this flow, but few who have been more influential than a Harvard University professor of developmental psychology, Erik Erikson. It was Erikson, building on and revising the work of Sigmund Freud, who attempted to describe this search for identity in *psychoanalytic* terms.[22] He agreed with Freud that our personalities as teenagers and adults are shaped by the experiences and

In fairness to Kohlberg, he appeared to have had second thoughts about his complete mistrust of what he described as "indoctrination." In a 1978 article, "Revisions in the Theory and Practice of Moral Development," Kohlberg admits, "Some years of active involvement with the practice of moral education have led me to realize that my notion that moral stages were the basis for moral education, rather than a partial guide to the moral educator, was mistaken ... I thought indoctrination invalid philosophically because the value content was taught culturally and personally relative and because teaching value content was a violation of the child's rights ... I no longer hold these negative views of indoctrinative moral education, and I now believe that the concepts guiding moral education must be partly 'indoctrinative.' This is true by necessity in a world in which children engage in stealing, cheating, and aggression and in which one cannot wait until children reach the fifth stage in order to deal directly with their moral behavior." Still, even in this article, Kohlberg asserts that "indoctrinative" moral instruction will violate the child's rights unless "teacher advocacy is democratic (or subject to the constraints of recognizing student participation in the rule-making and value-upholding process)." So, while he had come to believe that indoctrinative moral instruction could be valid philosophically, he still maintained that the content itself was relative, "subject to the constraints of recognizing student participation in the rule-making and value-upholding process."

Lawrence Kohlberg, "Revisions in the Theory and Practice of Moral Development" in New Directions for Child Development: Moral Development, *ed. William Damon (San Francisco: Jossey-Bass, 1978), 84–85, Robert W. Pazmino,* Foundational Issues in Christian Education *(Grand Rapids, Mich.: Baker Books, 1997), 208.*

---

[22] Psychoanalytic theories of personality are rooted in the notion that our behavior as teenagers and adults is shaped by environmental factors, specifically those in early childhood. Traditionally, psychoanalytic theorists focused particularly on the relationship between child and mother.

> *Psychosocial* is a term Erikson explains this way: "in discussing identity, as we now see, we cannot separate personal growth and communal change, nor can we separate ... the identity crisis in historical development because the two help to define each other and are truly relative to each other. In fact, the whole interplay between the psychological and the social, the developmental and the historical, could be conceptualized as a kind of *psychosocial* relativity.
>
> Erik Erikson, Identity: Youth and Crisis *(New York: Norton, 1968), 23.*

relationships we have as children. Erikson also agreed that the personality tends to mature and develop through specific stages. But, while Freud's theory defined these stages in *psychosexual* terms[23] and suggested that the personality is, for the most part, developed in the first five years, Erikson explained these stages in *psychosocial* terms, arguing that personality development is a lifelong process that encompasses more than just sexuality. For Erikson, this process of growth is characterized by movement through eight stages, each marked by a *psychosocial crisis*. What Erikson meant by crisis was not necessarily some life catastrophe, but a place of inner conflict to be faced and mastered, "a crucial period of increased vulnerability and heightened potential, and therefore, the ontogenetic[24] source of generational strength and maladjustment."[25] In Erikson's words, these are conflicts "inner and outer, which the vital personality weathers, re-emerging from each crisis with an increased sense of inner unity, with an increase of good judgment, and an increase in the capacity 'to do well' according to his own standards and to the standards of those who are significant to him."[26] One's responses to these eight life crises—mastery and adjustment versus confusion and maladjustment—are the formative factors, positive or negative, in future stages of personality development.[27]

Erikson was firmly convinced that growth should be understood in epigenetic terms, which is to say that it grows out of a "ground plan, and that out of this ground plan the parts arise, each part having its own time of special ascendancy, until all parts have arisen to form a functioning whole." Erikson portrayed the eight stages of the "ground plan" in the following terms (see summary in Table 7-4):

[23] Freud believed that many significant childhood experiences are laden with sexual feelings—feelings that often breed a mixture of tensions, emotions, and satisfactions. He theorized that each stage of personality development is shaped by five main pleasure-giving parts of the body—what he termed the *"erogenous zones,"* parts of the human anatomy that offer strong pleasure-giving sensations at each stage of development. Personalities are contoured by how one responds to the conflict between these various sources of pleasure and the demands of reality.

[24] A cool word, used occasionally in biology and psychology to describe what grows out of an event, and shapes what follows as a result of that event. Think of *genetic* as "giving birth," and *onto* as what follows, what we "move on to." This privilege of making up words is one of the great benefits of academia and scholarship. Unfortunately, it can be abused (see Kohlberg).

[25] Erik Erikson, *Identity: Youth and Crisis* (New York: Norton, 1968), 16f.

[26] Erik Erikson, "The Life Cycle Epigenesis of Identity/Identity Confusion in Life History and Case History," in *Social and Personality Development: Essays on the Growth of the Child,* ed. William Damon (New York: Norton, 1983), 410. This material was actually excerpted from Erikson's landmark work, *Identity: Youth and Crisis* (New York: Norton, 1968), 409.

[27] Pazmino describes this as a lifelong process of "conflict-resolution." Pazmino, *Foundational Issues in Christian Education,* 200.

Table 7-4.
Erikson's Stages of Psychosocial Development

Stage	Life Period	Radius of Significant Persons[1]	Age	Crisis	Rudiments of Ego Strength[2]
1	Infancy	Mother	0–2	Trust vs. mistrust	Hope
2	Early Childhood (toddler)	Paternal person	2–3	Autonomy vs. fear	Will
3	Childhood (preschool)	Basic family	4–5	Initiative vs. guilt	Purpose
4	School Age	Neighborhood and school	6–11	Initiative vs. inferiority	Competence
5	Adolescence	Peer groups, models of leadership	12–18	Identity vs. identity confusion	Fidelity
6	Young Adulthood	Partners in friendship, sex, competition, cooperation.	19–28	Intimacy vs. isolation	Love
7	Adulthood	Divided labor and shared household	28–50	Generativity vs. stagnation or self-absorption[3]	Care
8	Later Adulthood	Humankind, "my kind"	51+	Integrity vs. despair	Wisdom

Source: Erik Erikson, *Identity: Youth and Crisis* (New York: Norton, 1968).
1. This is a category that Pazmino adds to his table showing the Erikson model. I am using his terminology and wording. Robert W. Pazmino, *Foundational Issues in Christian Education* (Grand Rapids, Mich.: Baker Books, 1997), 201.
2. Again, this is a category used by Pazmino in describing Erikson's model.
3. This is the term used by Michael Anthony to describe this stage and I prefer it to the term "stagnation." Michael Anthony, *Foundations of Ministry* (Wheaton, Ill.: Bridgepoint Books/Victor Books, 1992), 81.

▸ **Stage One: Trust versus Mistrust (0–2 years).** Erikson pointed to trust as the most "fundamental prerequisite of mental vitality."[28] If an infant is cared for by a primary caretaker who meets his or her physical and emotional needs, the infant begins to develop a sense of[29] well-being and safety, a sense that the world is a hospitable place. If the child is deprived of that sort of nurture, the stage is set for mistrust, a sense of fear and apprehension about the world.

▸ **Stage Two: Autonomy versus Fear (2–3 years).** As toddlers grow into early childhood, they begin to develop a sense of independence. Having gained trust in their caregivers, and thereby gaining a sense of trust for the world that surrounds them, they become a bit more willing to explore, a bit more outgoing—hence, the increasing sense of autonomy, what Erikson describes as "the will to be oneself."[30] If children are restrained too tight-

---

[28] Erikson, *Identity*, 412.

[29] Erikson uses the phrase "a sense of" to describe three dimensions of personality: "a conscious experience," "a way of behaving, observable by others," and "an inner state verifiable only by testing a psychoanalytic interpretation." Ibid., 412.

[30] Ibid.

ly, or pushed too quickly, they are likely to develop a sense of fear and doubt, or perhaps, even a sense of shame:

> Only parental firmness can protect him against the consequences of his as yet untrained discrimination and introspection and circumspection. But his environment must also back him up in his desire "to stand on his own feet," while also protecting him against the now newly emerging pair of estrangements, namely, that sense of having exposed himself prematurely and foolishly which we call shame or that secondary mistrust, that "double take," which we call doubt . . . [31]

▶ **Stage Three: Initiative versus Guilt (4–5 years).** Now that the child has developed the sense that he or she is a person on his or her own, the child begins to deal with the question, "What *kind* of person might I become?" Children begin to develop growing competencies in language and locomotion that allow them to attempt to complete more tasks—playing with toys, activities with pets, personal hygiene—without direct parental assistance. Taking the initiative in this way helps children develop a sense of responsibility. If parents are overly critical at this point, children may feel a sense of guilt at having tried and failed to do too much too soon.

▶ **Stage Four: Industry versus Inferiority (6–12 years).** Bolstered by a growing sense of self-worth, rooted in the mastery of stage three, the child now moves into stage four with confidence, eager to learn and to meet and grasp the many new competencies that confront a child during the elementary school years. The danger at this point is that the enthusiasm will be dampened by poor grades, or unsupportive parents and teachers who do not realize the importance of nurturing in the child this sense of self-confidence and competence. Not only will this loss of confidence undermine the sense of adventure and self-reliance that is important for healthy progress into adolescence, it will leave the child with unsteady footing for those already uncertain early steps into puberty.

▶ **Stage Five: Identity versus Identity Confusion (13–18 years).** It is here in adolescence that we begin to see most clearly the epigenetic nature of personality development as Erikson describes it, because it is in stage four that we begin to see the fruits of seeds planted in earlier stages of development. Erikson puts it this way:

> If the earliest stage bequeathed to the identity crisis is an important need for trust in oneself and others, then clearly the adolescent looks

[31] Ibid.

most fervently for men and ideas to have faith in. At the same time, the adolescent fears a foolish, all too trusting commitment, and will, paradoxically, express his need for faith in loud and cynical mistrust.

If the second stage established the necessity of being defined by what one can will freely, then the adolescent now looks for an opportunity to decide with free assent on one of the available or unavoidable avenues of duty and service, and at the same time is mortally afraid of being forced into activities in which he would feel exposed to ridicule or self-doubt.

If an unlimited *imagination* as to what one might become is the heritage of the play age, then the adolescent's willingness to put his trust in those peers and leading, or misleading, elders who will give imaginative, if not illusory, scope to his aspirations is all too obvious . . .

Finally, if the desire to make something work, and to make it work well, is the gain of the school age, then the choice of an occupation assumes a significance beyond the question of remuneration and status.[32]

What Erikson is describing here in these paragraphs is what Chap Clark describes as "the primary and most basic goal of adolescence"—*individuation*. It is the process, begun in childhood, by which one grows into an individual with an identity apart from one's family. When this process is healthy, one continues to embrace one's family, even though choosing perhaps not to embrace all of the ideals, convictions, and feelings that one was raised with as a member of that family. This process of individuation requires a person to come to terms with three key questions:

▸ "Who am I?"—the question of *identity*.
▸ "Where am I going with my life?"—the question of *autonomy* (literally, *self-rule*), taking responsibility for one's choices.
▸ "How do I—how should I—relate to other people?"—the question of *intimacy*: "I am a separate (adjective) person from my other family members and my peers, but how can I maintain that 'separateness' without having to separate (verb) from these significant relationships?"

Clark[33] adds, and rightly so, an additional question undergirding these three:

▸ "How do I know these things, and how can I know that I know?"—the question of *epistemology*: on what basis does one pursue or conclude the answer to these life questions? Embedded, of course, in this question is perhaps the biggest question of all: "What is truth?"

---

[32] Ibid., 418; emphasis in original.

[33] Chap Clark, "The Changing Face of Adolescence: A Theological View of Human Development" in *Starting Right*, ed. Chap Clark, Kenda Dean, and Dave Rahn (Grand Rapids, Mich.: Youth Specialties/Zondervan, 2001), 55.

Erikson understood and conceded the importance of all of these issues. However, he felt that the question of identity stirred the major crisis of adolescence. When this crisis of identity is not met and mastered effectively, a young person will quite likely lack the kind of self-reliance and self-definition needed to seek out answers to the other key questions.

▸ **Stage Six: Intimacy versus Isolation (18–28 years).** The main crisis of stage six centers around the ability to establish and nurture intimate relationships. Intimacy is much broader and deeper than sexual relations. Erikson describes intimacy as finding oneself yet losing oneself in another.[34] For Erikson, it is unthinkable that individuals would be able to know someone else intimately until they have, first of all, begun to understand themselves. "It is only when identity formation is well on its way that true intimacy—which is really a counterpointing as well as a fusing of identities—is possible."[35] Those words, "I love you," are hollow if we are strangers to either the "you" or the "I."

▸ **Stage Seven: Generativity versus Self-absorption (28–50 years).** As we mature into midlife, the real question, or, to use Erikson's term, the real crisis, is whether we have made any significant contribution to benefit those who follow. Has there been any contribution made through one's life to help the next generation (generativity), or has the focus been simply on one's affairs (self-absorption or stagnation)?

▸ **Stage Eight: Integrity versus Despair (51-plus years).** In this final stage of life, with more than a half century of choices, relationships, passions, and investments, Erikson posits that our personalities are shaped by the backward look: Have we been faithful to our values and convictions? Have we shown consistency in the way we have integrated these values in the life we have lived?

Erikson and the Developing Adolescent Identity: A Critique

Erikson's work has been so influential for so many years that his phrase "identity crisis" has become a part of the everyday lexicon for youth ministry. His contributions are to be respected. At the same time, there are some questions that we might pose about his work:[36]

1. Do Erikson's predetermined stages leave room for God? This is a question we have raised before. As we have already noted with Piaget and Kohlberg, Erikson's work hinges on basic assumptions. One of those

---

[34] Santrock, *Adolescence*, 47. See also Erikson, *Identity*, 135–138.

[35] Erikson, *Identity*, 135.

[36] I have adapted this material from Pazmino, *Foundational Issues in Christian Education*, 201–202.

assumptions is that the human personality develops according to a pattern of predetermined steps—each of which is defined by an ever widening range of social interactions. "Personality, therefore, can be said to develop according to steps predetermined in the human organism's readiness to be driven toward, to be aware of, and to interact with a widening radius of significant individuals and institutions."[37] From a biblical perspective, there is certainly nothing wrong with such a notion. But what it lacks is the recognition that God can come into a teenager's life, into a child's life, into a family's or society's collective life, in unexpected ways. Somehow, the rigidity of the stage framework seems too inflexible, as if "predetermined stages" could cage in the Lion of Judah.

What makes this question so important is that a rigid determinism removes the hope factor in the life equation. It can be discouraging to think about developmental crises that were not mastered well, or the stages of growth that were particularly painful—that lessons were learned but the emotional tuition was too high. Or when thinking about attachment theory and the determinant impact of family, again it would be dispiriting to think that the basic plot of one's life story—good or bad—is written well before a teenager ever gets through adolescence. The great news of God's power is that our Master can redeem and heal those crises and stages that we were not able to accomplish. No matter what was written in the previous chapters of one's life, God can change the remainder of the story. Any predeterminism that excludes this fact is, to borrow J. B. Phillips' phrase, based on a God who is too small.

2. Does Erikson's theory account for the fact that individuals, in their relationship to society, can be actors as well as reactors? One assumption of Erikson is an implicit partnership between the individual and the community whereby, sometimes with support and sometimes with a challenge, the community of surrounding relationships will nudge the individual to grow to a new stage of development. Pazmino observes, "Erikson assumes that society, in principle, tends to be so constituted as to meet and invite this succession of potentialities for interaction and attempts to safeguard and to encourage the proper rate and sequence of their enfolding. Thus Erikson views the relationship between individuals and society as properly cooperative and mutually supportive provided there is a proper resolution of each of the successive crises."[38]

But that presupposition raises two objections.

▸ First of all, there are clearly societies in which healthy growth and development is not fostered, societies in which one's personal growth and development might come only in opposition to the society's expecta-

---

[37] Erikson, *Identity*, 93. "Personality, therefore, can be said to develop according to steps predetermined in the human organism's readiness to be driven toward, to be aware of, and to interact with a widening radius of significant individuals and institutions."

[38] Pazmino, *Foundational Issues in Christian Education*, 202.

[39] One might wonder if, in fact, Western culture is coming to be similarly inhospitable to that which is truly authentic and human.

tions.[39] Erikson allows, of course, for the fact that there may be negative resolution at each stage and that the residue of these negative resolutions can impair our development in later stages. But what about the society itself that is an impairment? What about, for example, the society in which a young woman is forced to have a clitoridectomy[40] to lessen her sexual enjoyment so that she can be exempt from sexual impurity? What if it is by such negative societal practices that identity is defined? What does it mean to interact and respond positively in such a society?

▸ Second, we might object to this presupposition because, while it recognizes the impact of society on the individual, it does not give proper recognition to the potential impact of individuals on society. A central tenet of the gospel is the mandate to be "salt" (Matt. 5:13), even the opportunity to be "salt." While it is certainly true that we are transformed and changed by the ever-widening community of relationships, our legacy as followers of Christ is that we ourselves are to be agents of transformation. By God's power, individuals are not just the "transformees," we can be the transformers.

3. Is ongoing growth limited to the dynamic interactions that occur in everyday life—the everyday responses to stress, challenge, and relationships? The key word here is "limited." Erikson understood that growth is not so much achieved as it is pursued. This is certainly in accord with any biblical notion of Christian maturity (see Col. 2:6-7). Paul writes in Philippians 3:12–16:

> Not that I have already obtained all this, or have already been made perfect, but I press on to take hold of that for which Christ Jesus took hold of me. Brothers, I do not consider myself yet to have taken hold of it. But one thing I do: Forgetting what is behind and straining toward what is ahead, I press on toward the goal to win the prize for which God has called me heavenward in Christ Jesus. All of us who are mature should take such a view of things. And if on some point you think differently, that too God will make clear to you. *Only let us live up to what we have already attained* (emphasis added).

Within Erikson's framework, this continuous pursuit unfolds as an ongoing tension between the stresses, challenges, and relationships of everyday life, and whether we meet them with positive or negative resolutions. Personality is never a finished product.

What Erikson did not address—did not, of course, even attempt to address—is the role of the Holy Spirit in this ongoing process of transformation. For Erikson, the elements in the equations of growth are historical and cultural, not supernatural. Although he recognized the role of

---

[40] Genital mutilation that some groups in Africa believe "helps insure a girl's virginity before marriage and fidelity afterward by reducing sex to a marital obligation. Often, people follow the custom simply because it has always been done." See http://wakingbear.com/africa1.htm.

religion as an institution concerned with engendering hope for the human condition, he did not seriously consider what would be described in theological terms as the sanctifying work of the Holy Spirit in a believer's life. From a biblical perspective, this is a serious flaw. As Christians and as youth workers, we must understand that it is the Spirit's ongoing work that sustains and catalyzes any new growth (see Phil. 1:6).[41]

4. Erikson, along with his Freudian colleagues, underestimates the role of the father in healthy ego development. It has become the stuff of comedy now, the psychoanalytic emphasis on the role of the mother in child development: "the mother was overbearing," "the child felt betrayed by the mother's early weaning from breast-feeding," "the child felt abandoned by the mother's lack of exuberance in toilet training," or "the child was traumatized by the mother's insistence that he wear bow ties to school." As Nielsen points out, critics have accused psychoanalytic theorists of "either blaming or praising mothers for everything and letting the fathers off the hook completely."[42]

What has been observed, especially in more recent research, is that the role of the father is far more critical than Erikson supposed. Although we noted some of this research in the previous chapter, it bears emphasis. Fathers who are as actively involved as mothers in parenting their infants and toddlers produce children who:[43]

▸ tend to be more outgoing, cry less, be less overly dependent on their mothers, and explore their surroundings more eagerly;

▸ tend to be more at ease around strangers, more mature socially, more self-controlled, and more empathic; and

▸ tend to carry these benefits into the teenage years.

We might add that these benefits of early bonding appear to be greater for boys than for girls. In any case, this emphasis on the role of involved fathers is critical. As youth workers, and as potential parents ourselves, it is a reminder that raising healthy teenagers begins in infancy, and it is not just the mother's task.

Attachment Theory

This discussion of how family relationships play into the developing identity

[41] Philippians 1:6:" . . . being confident of this, that he who began a good work in you will carry it on to completion until the day of Christ Jesus."
[42] Nielsen, *Adolescence*, 124.
[43] Ibid., 124.

affords us an opportunity to reflect on one of the key areas of adolescent development that grows out of this process of individuation. This is the area of *attachment*. Attachment theory is based on the notion that healthy individuation and ego development result from healthy relationships between parent and child in early childhood.[44] One major attachment theorist, John Bowlby, sums up this field of thought:

> The family experience of those who grow up anxious and fearful is found to be characterized not only by uncertainty about parental support but often also by covert yet strongly distorting parental pressures . . . Similarly, the family experience of those who grow up to become relatively stable and self-reliant is characterized not only by unfailing parental support when called upon but also by a steady yet timely encouragement toward increasing autonomy, and by the frank communication by parents of working models—of themselves, of child, and of others—that are not only tolerably valid but are open to be questioned and revised . . .

> Because in all these respects children tend unwittingly to identify with parents and therefore, to adopt, when they become parents, the same patterns of behavior toward children that they themselves have experienced during their own childhood, patterns of interaction are transmitted, more or less faithfully, from one generation to another. Thus the inheritance of mental health and of mental ill health through the medium of family microculture is certainly no less important than is their inheritance through the medium of genes.[45]

> Research by attachment theorists suggests that roughly 70 percent of us are in a place of healthy attachment in childhood. We feel loved and supported by parents, but not so overly protected or overly dependent that it impedes our growth into self-reliant, self-confident individuals.[46]

Perhaps it seems ironic, but the work of attachment theorists points to the notion that healthy parent-child attachment (a good relationship with parents) leads to healthy autonomy (a healthy sense of self and independence apart from parents). It is not unlike what happens in rock climbing when one climber is making her way up the face of the rock, and another climber is standing on the top of the rock in what is known as a belay position.[47] It is the responsibility of this lead climber to feed her partner enough rope so that she is free to pick her route up the face of the rock. If the rope is too tight, she will not have room to maneuver. On the other hand, the lead climber also has a responsibility to maintain enough tension in the rope so that if her partner loses her grip or falls, she will not fall more than a few feet before the rope arrests her fall.

---

[44] "There is a strong case for believing that an unthinking confidence in the unfailing accessibility and support of attachment figures is the bedrock on which stable and self-reliant personality is built." John Bowlby, *Attachment and Loss*, vol. 2 (New York: Basic Books, 1973), 322.

[45] Ibid., 323.

[46] Nielsen, *Adolescence*, 123.

[47] Tom Lyman and Bill Riviere, *The Field Book of Mountaineering and Rock Climbing* (New York: Winchester Press, 1976), 203–204.

When there is adequate tension in the rope, the climber can enjoy the challenge of the climb and enjoy the view from the newly gained heights. Every new challenge posed by the rock face is met with a growing sense of confidence and self-reliance. It is a picture of healthy individuation. On the other hand, if the belay line is too tight, the climber might feel she is being hoisted or hurried up the climb without being given the chance to choose her own footing. If the belay line is too loose, however, the climber might feel the lead climber is not giving her enough support. Neither feeling engenders a sense of climber security!

Parents who fear the tension of this combination of dependence and independence may offer too much slack in the parental rope. Others, who fear the consequences of a fall, may offer too little. In any case, the unhealthy attachment can lead to real problems as the teenager grows older. Some teenagers, giving in to the pull of the rope, just stop climbing and surrender to the tug of their parents. That can result in deep resentment. More often, in protest against a line too tight, they just cut the rope altogether—an act of rebellion. A "free" climber, without a rope (*parental detachment*), is at risk of serious injury with even the slightest misstep or lost hand-hold.

Indeed, the research on this is quite clear. Teenagers who have that feeling of closeness and connection with their parents are significantly less likely to be involved in risky behaviors.[48] For example, boys who are deprived of a good relationship with their fathers in early childhood are more likely to manifest delinquency behaviors and engage in more overstated forms of masculinity, such as aggression, violence, defiance, and lawlessness.[49] While at one time the conventional wisdom might have been summarized by the notion that teenagers have to make a "break" from their parents if they are to become their own persons, the vast majority of more recent research suggests precisely the contrary.

The first slack in the rope of healthy attachment comes even in early childhood (somewhere between six months and three years), when the child learns to walk and begins to learn basic self-reliant behaviors. According to attachment theorists, this process, described by Margaret S. Mahler as "the psychological birth of the human infant," is crucial in laying the groundwork for healthy autonomy later in life.[50] But what a number of more recent writers are suggesting is that something similar happens a second time in adolescence,[51] something

---

[48] For a good summary of the evidence regarding father attachment, see Clark, "The Changing Face of Adolescence," 59. He cites research that demonstrates a positive correlation between healthy father-child attachment and "reduced risk-taking behaviors," "greater interpersonal competence," "greater self-esteem," "increased likelihood of identity formation," "greater social competence," "greater career self-efficacy," and "increased problem-solving ability." Nielsen also provides a very thorough summary of the research findings, *Adolescence*, 300–322.

[49] Nielsen, *Adolescence*, 296, 302. Adolescents of both genders show problems in getting along with peers and performing well in school when they have been underfathered or poorly fathered.

[50] The process of separation and individuation takes about 30 months for the average infant. The baby gradually begins to 'hatch' from mother's existence into an 'I' and 'not I' relationship. A loving caretaker gently pushes her infant away toward greater independence." J. O. Lugo, *Infant Development, Encyclopedia of Psychology*, vol. 2, ed. Raymond J. Corsini (New York: John Wiley and Sons, 1984), 204–206.

[51] J. Belsky and J. Cassidy, "Attachment: Theory and Evidence" in *Developmental Principles and Clinical Issues in Psychology and Psychiatry* (Oxford: Blackwell, 1994). See also C. Parkes, J. Stevenson-Hinde, and P. Marris, *Attachment Across the Life Cycle* (New York: Tavistock/Routledge, 1991).

[52] Peter Blos, "The Second Individuation Process of Adolescence," in *The Adolescence Passage*, ed. Peter Blos (New York: International Universities Press, 1979), 142, first published in *The Psychoanalytic Study of the Child* (New York: International University Pres, 1967), 162–186. Blos sounds this same theme, although with less focus, in his earlier work, *The Adolescent Personality* (New York: D. Appleton-Century Co, 1941), 5ff.

described by Peter Blos as the *second separation-individuation phase*.[52] It is this second separation-individuation phase that we have described as a process of climbing with a healthy combination of attachment and independence.[53]

Sometimes when a rock face is particularly high, it may be necessary to set belay lines in two stages, or two "pitches"[54]—one line offering security to the top of stage one, and a second line offering security for the climb up stage two. In a sense, this image of a two-pitch climb provides a helpful metaphor as we consider these two phases of separation-individuation. The mother plays the more important role in the early years of the climb, and the father plays the more important role in the adolescent years.[55]

Chap Clark has portrayed this two-phase process of separation-individuation with a diagram of a tightrope—signifying the sometimes scary, sometimes exciting adventure of moving from childhood to adulthood (see Figure 7-1). The diagram illustrates the importance of the maternal support leading into the early years of adolescence by showing one end of the tightrope clearly supported by that relationship. Then, as the child begins to walk the tightrope of those years, the father attachment becomes the undergirding safety net. The mother's supporting role is still important, but the father's role becomes more critical in terms of helping the child move with safety and security from early adolescence into adulthood.

This is a critical insight for folks in youth ministry, because it reminds us

Figure 7-1.
Clark's Tightrope of Adolescence with Attachment

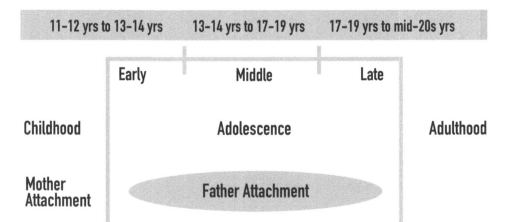

Source: Chap Clark, "The Changing Face of Adolescence: A Theological View of Human Development" in *Starting Right*, ed. Chap Clark, Kenda Dean, and Dave Rahn (Grand Rapids, Mich.: Youth Specialties/Zondervan, 2001).

[53] Santrock notes that the expectations regarding the timing of this second separation-individuation phase can vary depending on ethnic and racial background, as well as the marital status of the teenager's parents (single parents or married parents).

[54] Lyman and Riviere, *Field Book of Mountaineering*, 206.

[55] This is true regardless of the child's gender. Nielsen, *Adolescence*, 304.

again of the absolutely essential role of parents in the healthy development of a teenager. Youth ministry is not about helping teenagers cut the rope of attachment and become free climbers. At its best, youth ministry is about helping the parties at both ends of the rope to maintain and strengthen their grip, and perhaps even trying to provide them with the proper equipment for the climb. But what it surely is not about is youth workers trying to offer teenagers an alternative rope, or an alternative route for the climb. Everyone understands that there are families in which the relationships are unhealthy, that sometimes parents themselves do not have secure enough footing to offer a safe line of support. But effective youth ministers will do whatever they can to facilitate this healthy process even when the climb looks steep, and climbers look weak. Ignoring the family relationships that so deeply impact a teenager is like a farmer planting a crop without giving any thought to the soil out of which it grows.[56]

Adolescent Development: A Binocular Assessment

Having surveyed the convergent currents of development that form the river we call adolescence, it is important that we ask some questions with regard to the developmental assumptions that we have explored. These assumptions come to us as the product of research and experience. But to be faithful to the presuppositions of orthodox Christianity, we need to examine them as well under the lens of biblical truth ("both eyes blessed"). These are some of the general questions we might suggest for reflection:

▸ Is it really possible to capture the infinite possibilities of God's intricately creative work in a four-, five-, or six-stage model? Is a human being, created in the image of God, so wonderfully complex, and so unique from every other human creature, really so easily summarized and explained as the developmentalists portray? Even if we could propose a model to fit Western culture in the current millennium, what about other cultures so different from our own? Or what about peoples in the first half of the previous millennium? Did these same stages apply to them as well?

Before we answer too quickly—in either the negative or the affirmative—we must agree that Christians have always affirmed the obvious structure and form that is apparent in creation. Even with the endless variety of plant life, we still find that most growing plants follow a predictable process in growing toward maturity. This appears to be true without regard to time and place. Is it so farfetched to believe it could be so in the human order of God's creation?

Also, to be fair, while Piaget, Kohlberg, and other "stage-theorists" are frequently criticized for "locking people in boxes," the consistent imagery used by these

[56] For more reading in this area, see Mark Devries, *Family-Based Youth Ministry* (Downers Grove, Ill.: InterVarsity Press, 1994).

Figure 7-2.
Joy's Development of the Logocentric Mind

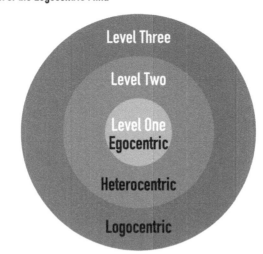

Source: Adapted from Donald M. Joy, "Kohlberg Revisited: A Supra-Naturalist Speaks His Mind," in *Moral Development Foundations*, ed. Donald M. Joy (Nashville, Tenn.: Abingdon, 1983).

developmental theorists is that of a "flow." In fact, Piaget takes pains to stipulate that there are no abrupt jumps from one level to the next. Donald Joy, certainly one who would want to be described as theocentric in his understanding of moral develop-ment, has likened these stages to concentric circles, like ripples in a pond. It is not really possible to tell where one ripple ends and another begins. His diagram, great-ly simplified in Figure 7-2, helps us to see how the ripples start with an *egocentric* mind set ("*mine is the only view*") and then develop, as Kohlberg and Selman suggest, into a *heterocentric* view ("*there are ways of viewing other than my own*"), which by God's grace—some-times through unmet longings, sometimes through tragedy, sometimes through the power of love—can grow into a theocentric or, more precisely, a *logocentric* way of viewing the world (based on the revelation of God and his Word).

  ▸ It might be said that developmental theory, as far as it goes, is in accord with a biblical worldview. But does it go far enough? The presupposition of developmentalism appears to neglect the supernatural work of God intruding in our everyday lives—bringing experiences and truths into our environment in a way that has no reference to anything that has gone before. In other words, God puts in place scaffolding that is not built upon any previous experience.

Pazmino (1997) comments: "Interaction with the environment must include the supernatural environment where God's presence and/or work may intrude upon development to bring out a result that is not directly attributable to what has gone before. This recognizes the place of transformation and conversion through the sovereign operation of the Holy Spirit. The work of the Holy Spirit may build upon and/or negate existing elements of development in ways that bring a creative and dynamic integration which otherwise was not possible."[57]

While the concept of "invariable sequence" might tie a nice knot around the developmental package, it also seems philosophically to tie the hands of God in the process. As Christians who affirm the radical transformation that can happen in a life touched by God, might we argue that developmental theory leaves us with a shrunken god? James Loder, whose study of human transformation has wrestled with precisely these questions, coins the phrase, "the knight's move"[58] as a chess metaphor to remind us that God's movements are not confined to the normal "rules." Not only is he not a pawn, he is the king, the queen, the bishop, and the rook all rolled into One! God can do what he wishes, when he wishes, and Scripture assures us that he is not trapped by "invariant sequences."

One of the pleasant advantages of thinking of moral growth with this image of expanding ripples is that it underlines the growing impact we can have when we are willing to allow God to expand our horizons. More sobering perhaps is the fact that this diagram also reminds us of the biblical principle that an expanded life begins with a crucified self.

The ripple metaphor also provides a vivid picture of the simple fact that an egocentric life is a life lived small. In our culture, we typically think of a life lived in pursuit of pleasure and wealth as "living large." In fact, it is just the opposite. It is a shrinking life, a life that continues to shrink until there is no life at all. This was a favorite theme of C. S. Lewis.

See C. S. Lewis, The Great Divorce *(New York: Touchstone-Simon and Schuster, 1996). See especially chapter 13.*

▸ Each of these developmental theories pose an end goal, a highest level of development appropriate to the respective area of maturation. But are these goals in accord with the biblical notion of completion or fulfillment (Greek: *teleiosis*)?[59] Who does the completing work? Pazmino asks, for example, "Is it God's will that all persons be at stage six of Kohlberg's . . . schemes?"[60]

---

[57] Robert Pazmino, *Foundational Issues in Christian Education* (Grand Rapids: Baker Books, 1997), 216.

[58] James E. Loder and and W. Jim Neidhardt, *The Knight's Move: The Relational Logic of the Spirit in Theology and Science* (Colorado Springs, Colo.: Helmers and Howard, 1992), 2.

[59] See Ephesians 4:13, Philippians 1:6, and Hebrews 6:1.

[60] Pazmino, *Foundational Issues in Christian Education*, 217.

The writer of Hebrews alludes (Heb. 5:12–61) to a journey from being a child in the faith, to becoming an adult in the faith, to becoming one who is mature in the faith. But the ultimate goal of a Christian is to grow into the likeness of Jesus (Rom. 8:29), and the focus in that process is on Christ's regenerating work in the heart of believers. It is not primarily a story of believers working through stages and levels. Although it may appear to happen in stages, it is primarily a story of Jesus Christ, "the author and the *finisher* of our faith," (Heb. 12:2, emphasis added), working through and in believers.

▶ In what sense is it possible to speak of moral reasoning without any reference to moral absolutes? Even the briefest review of Kohlberg or Selman's work can attest that it has some merit. Surely, there is a sense in which moral development involves a movement away from an egocentric (self-centered) way of viewing the world. But it is also readily evident that Selman's approach is completely anthropocentric (human-centered); his whole scheme for thinking about moral development is developed without any reference to God. In fact, were we to push Selman, we might question how he chose perspective-taking as the key element of moral development. Why not sacrifice, or service, or generosity? Why not kindness to large farm animals, or demonstrations of affection toward bald people or slightly nerdy college professors or slightly nerdy and bald college professors? Is it not a bit arbitrary to say this one trait or that is the backbone that supports the growing body of moral development?

From a biblical standpoint, Scripture speaks with resounding clarity: we cannot think about morality apart from God. We may listen and learn from the likes of Kohlberg, Selman, and others. We may even find their insights helpful and instructive, but it is always God who has the first and last word. God's moral guidelines as originally laid out in the Decalogue (the Ten Commandments, Exod. 20:1–17) speak with eloquent simplicity. Morality is explained, first of all, in terms of obedience to God, and secondly, in terms of our relationship with fellow human beings created by God. Jesus said as much in Matthew 22:37–39 when he said, "'Love the Lord your God with all your heart and with all your soul and with all your mind.' This is the first and greatest commandment. And the second is like it: 'Love your neighbor as yourself.'" Indeed, in his prosecution of human guilt in Romans 1:18–32, Paul begins by delineating humanity's alienation from God (vv. 18–23), and then demonstrating how this has been manifest in man's alienation from his neighbor (vv. 24–32). There is a sense in which any system of thinking about moral development is bankrupt unless it begins with God. Biblical morality is theocentric ("God-centered"). It begins with caring about God, and it extends to caring about whatever and whoever God cares about.

Developmental Theory and Youth Ministry

What are we to say then about developmental theory? Can it be of use to us in youth ministry? How can we benefit from its contributions? Should we just post a big chart in the youth room with the various stages and levels of cognitive, moral, and faith development, and write students' names in the appropriate places?

In his thorough work, *Foundations of Ministry: An Introduction to Christian Education for a New Generation*,[61] Michael Anthony suggests a number of ways that the insights of developmental psychology can help those of us in ministry. What follows is an adaptation of his remarks.

1. Developmental psychology can provide for us cues about which issues and which questions might be best addressed at critical times in the lives of our students. What developmental theorists help us understand is that life itself raises questions as we move through its various stages. We could expect, for example, that a discussion on "why bad things happen to good people" might not be as effective with eight-year-old concrete thinkers as it would be with 16-year-olds who are stretching the muscles of abstract thought. When we take into consideration the insights of developmental thought we can better shape our ministries and our curricula so we actually scratch where people itch.

2. Developmental psychology provides direction that shapes programming and methodology. Dunn and Senter[62] demonstrate this vividly in their discussion of developmental psychology and its implications. Specifically, they consider how programming at three different adolescent life stages might shape three common elements of youth ministry: a one-on-one contact, a Bible study, and a retreat. Their illustration is so practical and so helpful that I provide it here in its entirety:

   Early Adolescents: Stage two is not a wrongfully immature place to be for a sixth or seventh grader. The concrete is necessary and appropriate. Relationships and logic are a crucial part of stage two, but they are mediated through the concrete event.

   ▸ "For example, in a *one-on-one time* with a stage two student, it is difficult to sit for an hour over a soft drink and talk meaningfully about how life is going. The contact is too intense. But to toss the football and talk, take a hike and talk, or go to the store and talk helps smooth the way for meaningful mentoring."

[61] Anthony, *Foundations of Ministry*, 84–85.
[62] Steven Patty, *A Developmental Framework for Doing Youth Ministry, Reaching a Generation for Christ*, ed. Richard Dunn and Mark Senter III (Chicago: Moody Press, 1997), 81–83.

▸ "*A Bible study* about faith with a small group of stage two students should incorporate—even revolve around—something concrete and tangible. For instance, an inductive exploration of the adventure stories of Hebrews 11 or having the students prepare an ongoing notebook in which they describe three specific ways healthy faith will make this week different will help to move the abstract to the concrete."

▸ "*A retreat* designed for stage two students should have clear, well-planned activities. The young adolescent will be asking of the retreat, 'What will we be doing?' The event is important to stage two ministry."

Middle Adolescents: Following the precedent of stage two, a stage three student has not outgrown the impact of significant events, nor is she immune to the power of logical thought. Rather, her way of making meaning is mediated through relationships.

▸ "A *one-on-one contact time* with a stage three student needs far less supporting structure than would be the case with a stage two student. Meaningful interaction can usually occur anytime and at any place, with only a little courageous initiative exercised by the youth minister. The student wants to know, however, 'Are you talking to me because you like me and really care about me?' The social antenna is highly tuned to authenticity of motive."

▸ "*A Bible study* with a small group of stage three students would do well to encourage the exploration of the thoughts, feelings, and interrelationships of a life that is exercising faith. 'How does this affect our relationships?' and 'How do our friends and family affect our faith?' would be profitable tracks of reflection. At this stage the implicit messages and the silent metaphors of godly living are potent. Hence the sharing of what faith looks like, feels like, and tastes like in daily living establishes a tacit standard."

▸ *A retreat* for stage three students should create space for meaningful interaction. Relationships are critical for stage three ministry. Retreats should not be overscheduled or filled with large-group experiences only. Time should be allowed for students to hang out."

Late Adolescents: A stage four student loves meaningful activities and is highly motivated by relationships, but equally concerned, if not more, about how systems of reality fit together. This idea-interestedness does not imply an idea-fixation: Stage four students commonly act illogically. However, they are adept at using their formal operational reasoning abilities to define and evaluate the stuff of life.

▸ "For example, a *one-on-one contact time* with a stage four adolescent is potentially stimulating even prior to establishing relational closeness. Stage four students seek out those they not only enjoy, but respect. Hence, a college professor with whom a student is barely acquainted can have a profound personal effect by way of the presentation of ideas."

▸ "*A Bible study* consisting of a small group of stage four students needs to regularly master information and develop explicit systems of beliefs into which both life experiences and Scriptural truth can fit. Questions must go beyond surface formation to explore the meaning of God's Word in the complexity of life."

▸ "*For a retreat*, instead of asking the stage three question, 'Who's going to be there?' a stage four student will often ask, 'Why are we doing this?' or 'What will we accomplish this weekend?' The emphasis of leading stage four students should be on the development of a Christian synthesis, a putting of the parts together into a coherent whole. Meaningful thinking is essential for stage four ministry."

3. Developmental psychology gives a more holistic, more realistic, and therefore more biblical, portrait of human growth. Human beings are not just spiritual beings (whatever we take that to mean). Habermas and Issler remind us that the human creature is a complex combination of many *domains*[63] (see Figure 7-3), some of them structural (genetic, hereditary traits),[64] and some of them functional (volitional, "related to the will"). If we are not conversant with the insights of developmental psychology, we might not appreciate the fact that growth in one area is related to growth in another area. Personality development, for example, as we have seen, is related to growth in social development. Likewise, moral growth is related to cognitive capacity. Misunderstanding this complexity oversimplifies holistic Christian growth and discipleship. It is like tuning one cylinder of an eight cylinder automobile and thinking the task is done.

4. Developmental psychology reminds us that, as with other areas of human experience, the development of faith is affected by growth and maturity in other domains. We see this manifest, for example, in Paul's comment, "When I was a child, I talked like a child, I thought like a child, I reasoned like a child. When I became a man, I put childish ways behind me" (1 Cor. 13:11). His observation demonstrates a clear connection between cognitive maturity and spiritual maturity.[65]

[63] Ronald Habermas and Klaus Issler, *Teaching for Reconciliation* (Grand Rapids, Mich.: Baker, 1992), 76–77.

[64] Habermas and Issler liken the structural domains (physical, cognitive, personality) to the superstructure of a building. These are the raw genetic materials we are born with. The functional domains (moral, social, vocational, faith) refer to what we do with that raw material. If the structural domains refer to superstructure of the building, the functional domains refer to how we design, decorate, and use the building. Ibid., 76.

[65] That is not to say that cognitive maturity will necessarily cause spiritual maturity. Manifestly, it will not. Sometimes indeed, as we have already noted, we become so impressed with our powers of reasoning that we think ourselves wiser than God. "Thinking ourselves to be wise, we become fools" (paraphrase Rom. 1:22). But, it is equally true that growth in grace (a factor of faith development) is coupled with growth in knowledge (a factor of cognitive development) of our Lord Jesus Christ (2 Pet. 3:18).

Figure 7-3.
The Seven Domains of Human Growth

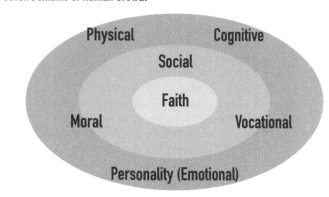

Source: Ronald Habermas and Klaus Issler, *Teaching for Reconciliation* (Grand Rapids, Mich.: Baker, 1992), 76–77.

5. Developmental psychology points us to the biblical truth that spiritual maturity comes through reflection—and not just the accumulation of data. One of the clear lessons of cognitive development is that as we move into more formal ways of reasoning we are more apt to embrace that which we have thought through ourselves. Take the one word *consider*. In Paul's epistles alone there are at least four instances in which he exhorts believers to *consider* (reflect on) truths so they might grow in their understanding and obedience.

6. Not only does developmental psychology offer us insight about which issues are especially germane to particular stages of life, it also offers us guidance about how we might actually provide instruction on those issues at various stages of life. The 30-minute small group discussion planned for the third graders: bad idea. The one-hour lecture instructing the middle-schoolers about the doctrine of the Trinity: bad idea. The coloring book exercise designed to help the high school group reflect on sexual choices: *really* bad idea.

   If our presentation of biblical truth is too simplistic for the age group we are teaching, it will not be regarded as authentic. On the other hand, if in our desire to uncover all the facets of some biblical truth we are too complicated and over the head of the age group we are teaching, it will not be understood. Developmental psychology reminds us that people can absorb truth at virtually any age. But what kinds of truths they can absorb, and how they absorb them—that changes over the course of the life span. This seems to be the implication of Paul's comment, "I gave you milk, not solid food, for you were not yet ready for it. Indeed, you are still not ready" (1 Cor. 3:2).[66]

7. Developmental psychology underlines the role of community and relationships for healthy growth. One of the recurring themes of develop-

[66] For other examples of this see Hebrews 5:12–13, and 1 Peter 2:2.

mental research is the impact of relationships on virtually every area of development. This truth needs to be woven into the fabric of our entire approach to ministry. *Relationships are key*: parent to child, leader to student, student to youth group, youth group to congregation, and so on. Our doctrine of God is shaped by three beings in relationship, a union of three persons in one. Relationships are fundamental to the growth and nurture of Christian disciples.

> *Consider* therefore the kindness and sternness of God: sternness to those who fell, but kindness to you, provided that you continue in his kindness. Otherwise, you also will be cut off. (Rom. 11:22)
>
> *Consider* the people of Israel: Do not those who eat the sacrifices participate in the altar? (1 Cor. 10:18)
>
> You are looking only on the surface of things. If anyone is confident that he belongs to Christ, he should *consider* again that we belong to Christ just as much as he. (2 Cor. 10:7)

Conclusion

Perhaps in working through the material of these last two chapters—with Kohlberg's levels of this and Piaget's stages of that—you began to think to yourself, "Shakespeare was right: 'All the world's a stage!'" What is important overall is this: human beings are created in the image of God, marvelous in our possibility, wonderful in our complexity, and sometimes stunning in our simplicity ("Oh, so you mean being loved and nurtured by both a father and mother is important, huh? What a bombshell!") If Tim Flannery can endure the jungles of New Guinea to delight in the study of forest rats, surely we can afford the effort that is required to appreciate adolescents and the mysteries of their development. To a large extent, this chapter and the one preceding it are little more than terms and jargon. As a merely academic exercise, laboring over such words have little lasting value. But if these terms and this jargon can help us to better understand, better love, better communicate with, and better minister to human beings in general and teenagers in particular, then it is more than worth our while.

> For Christ's love compels us, because we are convinced that one died for all, and therefore all died. And he died for all, that those who live should no longer live for themselves but for him who died for them and was raised again. *So from now on we regard no one from a worldly point of view.* (2 Cor. 5:14-16, emphasis added)

JOURNEYING DEEPER: FIRST DATE

Meditations on the Way by Helen Musick

Jimmy Parish, a name I will forever remember. Jimmy was my first date. I spent all day getting ready. I even used a special hair conditioning treatment to make my hair extra silky. I had great hopes for a night that, to this point, had only existed in my "Someday My Prince Will Come" world of teenage fantasy.

The doorbell rang. I remember my mother calling to my room, "Helen, Jimmy is here." My heart was pounding. I took one last look in the mirror and walked with bated breath to meet him.

"Here, I got this for you." Jimmy handed me an oversized corsage for my dress.

"Thank you, it's really pretty," I said, thinking all the time that it really didn't match my well-thought-through outfit. And things went downhill from there.

Jimmy never had a chance. I had dreamed up a fantasy that only God himself could have fulfilled! I had created in my mind a picture of exactly how he was supposed to be instead of giving him the freedom to uncover for me who he really was.

We serve a God who does not look at the perfect outfits we wear or the personal expectations about which we dream. Praise the Lord! Our God looks at the heart. Look with me at 1 Samuel 16:1–7. At this stage in Israel's history, God rejected King Saul, because he had chosen to disobey him on more than one occasion (see 1 Sam. 13:7b–14 and 15:7–26). With each disobedient act, Saul's true heart was exposed, and God grieved. Now the prophet Samuel was on a divine mission to anoint a new king.

Samuel found David. He was not as handsome as his brothers, but that does not matter! God saw his heart and was pleased. Even Samuel, God's prophet, assumed incorrectly, thinking the height and appearance of Eliab (David's older brother) should make him king. What is God's response? "The Lord does not look at the things man looks at. Man looks at the outward appearance, but the Lord looks at the heart" (v. 7).

As a teenager, destined for self-discovery, I was convinced that my first date with "Mr. 6' 4", car owner" would be perfect. Yet his first mistake (an oversized corsage) cost him everything. I was instantly turned off. But after looking at 1 Samuel 16:1–7, an important question emerges. What is our motivation in relationships? Is it pleasing ourselves or looking at others' hearts? Teenagers are not the only ones who struggle with the relationship scene—we all do! It seems to me that, if we long to work with youth (or anyone, for that matter), we need to have our priorities straight. Every relationship is an opportunity to model God's love. Let us learn to see beyond the corsages and into each other's hearts.

▸ In my relationships with others do I strive to make them what I want or do I accept them for who they are?

▸ Think of a people you find yourself living in judgment with. No matter what they do you seem always to find fault with them. Now, ask yourself, "Why?" What is it about those people that pushes those buttons in you?

▸ Ask God, "What do you want to do in me through these relationships? What are you trying to teach me about myself and about your provision?

chapter eight

READING THE WATER:
THINKING ABOUT CULTURE

One of the most valuable skills for fishermen is to learn to "read" the water . . . If you know the direction a fish is facing, then you will know where to place the fly. Otherwise you can cast all day with perfectly good flies and catch nothing.
—**Myrlene L. J. Hamilton**[1]

An understanding of culture is basic to Christian youthwork . . . Communication of any sort therefore involves some appreciation of this cultural world . . . Youth ministry is shaped by youth culture, but it is also shaped by the culture of the church. This means that Christian youthworkers also must be culturally bilingual.
—**Pete Ward**[2]

To understand the world of youth is to feel the cutting edge of cultural change. Each new kind of music, new fad, and new advertising pitch is a challenge to those who would understand the beauties and pitfalls of our culture and the ups and downs of adolescent years. To do theology in youth culture forces one to be in touch with the spirit of the age and the trends of the times . . . Fidelity to Scripture and creeds, relevance to the times, and integrity of self are the threefold responsibilities of Christian theology.
—**Dean Borgman**[3]

[1] Myrlene L. J. Hamilton, *All I Needed to Know About Ministry I Learned from Fly Fishing* (Valley Forge, Penn.: Judson Press, 2001), 11.

[2] Pete Ward, *God at the Mall* (Peabody, Mass.: Hendrickson, 1999), 80.

[3] Dean Borgman, *When Kumbayah Is Not Enough* (Peabody, Mass.: Hendrickson, 1997), 13.

In her fascinating little book, *All I Needed to Know About Ministry I Learned from Fly Fishing*, Myrlene Hamilton observes:

> One of the most valuable skills for fishermen is to learn to "read" the water. Trout like to hide behind big rocks and below undercut banks with overhanging tree roots. At the head of a pool, they are likely to position themselves on either side of the current, or under the current, where the water slows a bit, in order to have the best vantage point for watching the bugs that are being swept along. They like deep, clear, weedless pools, where they can easily see their prey, and they often hang out in eddies, where food is plentiful. It helps, too, to know that trout face upstream, with their noses into the current. If you know the direction a fish is facing, then you will know where to place the fly. Otherwise you can cast all day with perfectly good flies and catch nothing.[4]

> Matthew records three different back-to-back parables in the thirteenth chapter of his Gospel. While each parable reveals a different facet of truth, the implicit message of all three parables is that the soil is absolutely critical. For example, in what is commonly known as Jesus's Parable of the Soils (Matt. 13:4–23), Jesus seems to be saying that there are three key components in the process of God's work: the seed, which is the Word; the sower, the one who sows the seed; and the soil, which is the world, or culture. He makes this even more explicit in verse 38.

As disciples of Jesus, our heritage and mandate is to be "fishers of men" (see Matt. 4:19). It is a mandate that calls us from the safety and comfort of the shoreline and invites us out into that place where the fish swim. It is a place of adventure, and a place perhaps of some risk. But if we are to be wise in this calling, we need to learn to read the rivers and know the pools of adolescence. We need to give careful thought to which way the fish are facing, what their habits are, and where they like to swim. In short, if we want to reach teenagers with the gospel of Christ, we need to understand the culture in which those teenagers live. To put off considering the culture where ministry plays out because of the hard questions it raises would be like a farmer refusing to consider the soil in which he intends to sow his seed because he does not want to get dirty. Culture is where ministry happens.

> "Gospel and culture" is not a purely academic interest. On the contrary, it is the burning practical concern of every missionary, every preacher, every Christian witness. For it is literally impossible to evangelize in a cultural vacuum. Nobody can reduce the biblical gospel to a few culture-free axioms which are universally intelligible. This is because the mindset of all human beings has been formed by the culture in which they have been brought up.

---

[4] Hamilton, *All I Needed to Know About Ministry*, 11.

Their presuppositions, their value systems, the ways in which they think, and the degree of their receptivity and resistance to new ideas are all largely determined by their cultural inheritance and are filters through which they listen and evaluate.

The overriding reason why we should take other people's cultures seriously is that God has taken ours seriously. God is the supreme communicator. His Word came to us in an extremely particularized form. Whether spoken or written, it was addressed to particular people in particular cultures using the particular thought-forms, syntax, and vocabulary with which they were familiar. Then, when God's Word actually "became flesh," the "flesh" he became was that of a first-century, male, Palestinian Jew. Thus both Inspiration and Incarnation—two fundamental evangelical truths—are models of sensitive cross-cultural communication and summon us to follow suit.[5]

Defining Culture

The study of culture is not an isolated pursuit. In fact, it is a natural complement to the discussions in previous chapters on adolescent development. One area of study tells us about how the "fish" think and mature; the other area tells us about where they feed, swim, and live. The renowned missionary anthropologist Paul Hiebert reminds us that this integrated approach gives us a better look at the complete picture. Hiebert's integrated approach is illustrated in Figure 8-1.

The term *culture* conjures for us a wide range of images and ideas. For some, it refers to the fine arts— an evening of ballet, a night at the opera, or a trip to the art museum. For others, maybe it is the textures, smells, and tastes of the village in a strange new travel destination. For a few of us, the word *culture* perhaps brings

Figure 8-1.
An Integrated Approach to Understanding Adolescence

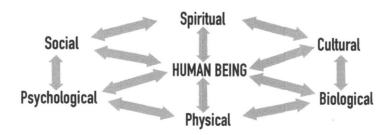

---

[5] John Stott, *Down to Earth: Studies in Christianity and Culture* (Grand Rapids, Mich.: Eerdmans, 1980), vii-viii.

back memories of biology lab—or little fuzzy stuff that appears on the surface of food items pushed into the back corners of the refrigerator. Culture is relevant to ministry with teenagers because it gives us a way of thinking about "integrated systems of ideas, feelings, and values and their associated patterns of behavior and products shared by a group of people who organize and regulate what they think, feel, and do."[6] To put it in a phrase, culture is defined by what people do and what they produce.

British youth worker and youth ministry thinker Pete Ward explains culture as "human knowledge, belief, art, morals, law, custom, economic relationships, myths and stories, sexual behavior, in fact any aspect of human life which is common to members of a society . . . "[7] Think of culture as a human mosaic, with tiles marked by religion, art, social and political institutions, common symbols (oral and written), and common meanings.[8]

The smallest units of these mosaic tiles are referred to as *culture traits*[9]—individual acts such as a smile, for example, or a high five, or what one youth worker refers to as the "head bob."[10] Clusters of related traits are referred to as *cluster complexes*—a sequence or cluster of traits that combine into a single unit. For example, when someone approaches with a smile, a wave, and a pointed index finger (a combination of three culture traits), this forms a culture complex most teenagers would construe as a friendly greeting (as in "You da man"). However, if the person approaches with no smile or wave and holding up the middle finger (a different combination of culture traits), this forms a culture complex widely recognized as a not-so-friendly greeting. Learning these traits and complexes is an important part of "reading the waters."

[6] Paul Hiebert, *Anthropological Insights for Missionaries* (Grand Rapids, Mich.: Baker, 1985), 30.

[7] Ward, *God at the Mall*, 82. While Ward attributes some of this material to other sources, I believe it is an adaptation of a statement originally made by the pioneer British anthropologist Sir Edward Tyler, who defined culture as "that complex whole which includes knowledge, belief, art, morals, law, custom, and any other capabilities and habits acquired by man as a member of society." Edward Tyler, *Primitive Culture* (London: J. Murray, 1971).

[8] "Culture is all learned behavior that is acquired socially. It includes language, values, beliefs, artifacts, technology, mores, norms, and styles. By 'culture' then we mean all that is learned and passed on from generation to generation. Culture is our human environment, family, education, marketing and economics, entertainment (including recreation and athletics), politics and religion are its institutions." Borgman, *When Kumbayah Is Not Enough*, 65.

Bruce Nicholls comments, "To understand culture involves understanding the total 'design for living' of a people. It means perceiving the worldview (which may be consciously or unconsciously expressed) and the religious and spiritual elements that are normally the dominant factors in any cultural framework. Culture is a way of behaving and thinking that includes value systems and social institutions (family, law, education, etc.). Because culture is the sum total of behavioral patterns learned by instruction, observation, and imitation, it is constantly changing; therefore the task of relating the gospel to a particular culture is always a continuing one." Bruce Nicholls, "Towards a Theology of Gospel and Culture," in *Down to Earth: Studies of Christianity and Culture*, ed. Robert Coote and John Stott (Grand Rapids, Mich.: Eerdmans, 1980), 49–50.

There are disagreements about what should be included within the definition of culture, but the intent here is to provide a working definition. For a discussion of other views, see Robert W. Pazmino, *Foundational Issues in Christian Education* (Grand Rapids, Mich.: Baker Books, 1997), 163 (especially sources mentioned in his footnotes).

[9] Stephen A. Grunlan and Marvin K. Mayers, *Cultural Anthropology: A Christian Perspective* (Grand Rapids, Mich.: Zondervan, 1988), 39.

[10] The following are definitions of "head bob" (verb): 1. The slight (approximately five to ten degrees) forward movement of the head, typically a greeting. 2. A nonverbal way of saying "How ya' doin'?" 3. When head is tilted an additional 40 degrees and remains in that position for some time, this is a physical gesture indicating "I would like us not to make eye contact because I don't like you."

A Life Lens: Understanding Worldview

The central adhesive factor that holds these mosaic tiles of culture in place is what is termed a *worldview*. This is not something that is separate from culture. It is the structuring of basic deep-seated presuppositions that undergird the culture. While a culture's dominant worldview may certainly be shaped by religion, it is really misleading to use the two words interchangeably.[11] As with culture, worldview does not do anything, but worldview provides the cultural basis for what *people do*.[12]

> Missiologist Lloyd Kwast explains:
>
> At the very heart of any culture is its worldview, answering the most basic question: "What is real?" This area of culture concerns itself with the great ultimate questions of reality . . . Who are they? Where did they come from? Is there anything or anyone else occupying reality that should be taken into consideration? Is what they see really all there is, or is there something else, or something more? Is right now the only time that is important? Or do events in the past and the future significantly impact their present experience?[13]

In the same way that a computer translates electronic bits of data into the pixels on a computer screen to provide a coherent picture, one's worldview functions as a processor.[14] Forgive the pun, but in that sense, understanding teenager's worldview gives us *windows* into their minds and hearts.

A Worldview Is a Foundation. For example, understanding teenagers' worldview can help us to better comprehend what anthropologists refer to as those teenagers' *cognitive foundations*—the bedrock assumptions they make about the world, and on which they build their beliefs and values. A young person makes certain assumptions about the way the world works (worldview), and if one begins with those assumptions, then other beliefs and behaviors make sense—at least to the young person. Take, for example, a premise widely held within the worldview of adolescence that *"you are how you look"*—that physical beauty is just about the most important facet of who you are. If one starts with that assumption, then lots of other rationalizations and beliefs make sense: the importance of being thin even if it means starving oneself, the importance of having the right look, the notion that beautiful people have the best lives, the conviction that all of one's clothing should feature small polo logos or display the name "Abercrombie."

---

[11] Charles H. Kraft, *Anthropology for Christian Witness* (Maryknoll, N.Y.: Orbis Books, 1996), 53. There is "a tendency, still apparent in the writings of many anthropologists and non-specialists alike, to confuse the core of a culture (worldview) with a people's religion. Increasingly, though, it is being recognized that even in 'supernaturalistically-oriented' societies there appear to be deep-level, core assumptions that are not easily labeled 'religious.' Furthermore, as greater attention is being given to cultures whose core assumptions are largely non- (even anti-) supernatural (e.g., Western), it is becoming obvious that the term religion as the designation for the core of culture is misleading."

[12] Here is Kraft's definition of worldview: " . . . the culturally structured assumption, values, and commitment/allegiances underlying a people's perception of reality and their responses to those perceptions." Kraft, *Anthropology for Christian Witness*, 52.

[13] Lloyd Kwast, "Understanding Culture," in *Perspectives on the Christian World Movement*, ed. R. D. Winter and S. C. Hawthorne (Pasadena, Calif.: William Carey Library, 1981), 363.

[14] These concepts about worldview are adaptations of material from Hiebert, *Anthropological Insights for Missionaries*, 48. For additional explanation, and a more thorough discussion of characteristics of worldview, functions of worldview, and universals of worldview, see Kraft, *Anthropology for Christian Witness*, 55–65.

A Worldview Offers Validation. The worldview of teenagers serves to validate the norms of their culture. It is through the lens of that worldview that they interpret their experiences and discern their choices. When we as youth workers understand that worldview we can begin to make sense of the road map our students are working with as they make decisions and evaluate options. It may be a lousy map with north down and south up, but if we can at least understand the map teenagers are working with, we have a better chance of understanding where they might get lost and how to help them "get found."[15]

A Worldview Offers Integration. Teenagers move through a myriad of thoughts and feelings in the course of a day. It is by way of their worldview that they are able to organize and integrate all of these experiences. It is a way, more or less, of maintaining in one's life a unified sense of reality. But, as anthropologist Charles Kraft points out, that teenager's worldview not only helps to integrate new experi-

The following is Arthur Holmes's description of what a Christian worldview might look like. Note that his essential characteristics are equally true of any other worldview:

1. It is *holistic*. It enables those within the culture to hold together all the various mosaics of the culture in an integrated fashion.

2. It is *perspectival*. Like sunglasses, a worldview changes the way people see reality.

3. It is an *exploratory* process in that it helps people within a culture probe the relationship of one element of cultural life with another. For example, when we see a movie, our worldview helps us to explore how that film is related to other areas of life, religion, relationships, politics, and so on.

4. It is *pluralistic*. It can be articulated in varied terms without losing the basic core beliefs.

5. It has *action outcomes* in that our worldview influences our behavior.

Arthur Holmes, The Making of a Christian Mind: A Christian World-View and the Academic Enterprise, *(Downers Grove, Ill.: InterVarsity Press, 1985), 17.*

ences and ideas, it also serves as a monitor that sifts out new ideas and concepts that might cause change.[16] That is precisely where we youth workers, as people called to communicate biblical truth in an adolescent culture rife with deceit, face our challenge. This is something of what Paul was talking about in Romans 12:2, "Do not conform any longer to the pattern of this world, but be transformed by the renewing of your mind. Then you will be able to test and approve what God's will is—his good, pleasing and perfect will."

[15] Hiebert comments that "our worldview provides us with a map of reality and also serves as a map for guiding our lives." Worldviews serve both predictive and prescriptive functions. Hiebert, *Anthropological Insights for Missionaries*, 48.

[16] Charles Kraft, *Christianity in Culture* (Maryknoll, N.Y.: Orbis, 1979), cited in Hiebert, *Anthropological Insights for Missionaries*, 49.

Figure 8-2.
Understanding Worldview Is Key to Understanding the Culture

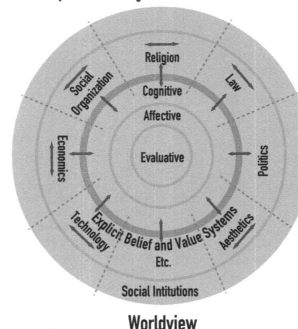

Worldview

Another way of describing this concept of worldview is that it serves three basic functions:[17]

▸ The *evaluative dimension*: it defines one's values and allegiances—what is "cool" and what is "lame," what is right and what is wrong, what is appropriate behavior and what is inappropriate.

▸ The *affective dimension*: it defines how we feel: "notions of beauty, tastes in food and dress, likes and dislikes and ways of enjoying ourselves or experiencing sorrow." It is this affective dimension of worldview that is manifest in what anthropologists call "expressive culture," dance, music, art, literature, drama.[18] Of course, in the adolescent world, media is the great conveyor of the affective dimension of the predominant worldview.

> To give this idea of worldview some further thought, take a passage of Scripture—for example, John 5:1–18, where Jesus heals a man who had been paralyzed for 38 years—and work through Table 8-1. Use the biblical evidence to reflect on what might have been the worldview of the Jews who were so outraged and befuddled by this miraculous healing.

---

[17] Hiebert, *Anthropological Insights for Missionaries*, 30–34.

[18] Ever noticed, for example, how all of the "alternative" kids dress exactly alike? They are all "alternative" in the same way. This is a reflection of the affective dimension of a particular worldview.

Table 8-1.
Observations on Teenagers' Worldview

Dimension	Evaluative Dimension (Values and allegiances)	Affective Dimension (How they feel)	Cognitive Dimension (Shared knowledge, the common wisdom, what they believe to be true about reality)
Questions to Think About	• What are some of the core values that are implicit in their worldview? • How do they determine right and wrong? What is moral and what is immoral?	• What are some of the characteristics of their art, their music, their dance? • How do they express anger or grief? • How do they show appreciation or affection?	• What are some of the commonly accepted beliefs? • What are some of the shared assumptions about reality?
Your Observations			
Examples of Observations	"Physical beauty is one of their highest core values."	"They hang out together on weekends."	"Sex is one of the most important things in life."

▶ The *cognitive dimension*: it defines our shared knowledge, our common wisdom, what we believe to be true about reality and the nature of the world.

In short, every dimension of a teenager's life and culture is affected by that teenager's worldview (Figure 8-2).[19] One cannot help but wonder how often our efforts to communicate the gospel to adolescents have been less than effective because we have not given adequate attention to how they might be shaped by and attentive to each of these dimensions of adolescent reality. It might be helpful to take a few minutes right now and sketch out some of your own observations about the worldview of teenagers you might like to work with. Do not think of it as a portrait. Just think of it as a quick sketch. Use Table 8-1.

Types of Cultures

Spend one lunch period in the cafeteria of any high school and it becomes readily apparent that a wide range of cultures is represented in that one room.[20] Borgman describes four types of cultures, which are illustrated in Table

---

[19] Hiebert, *Anthropological Insights for Missionaries*, 46.

[20] George Barna, in his research work among American teenagers born between 1984 and 2002 (what Barna describes as the "Mosaic Generation"), identifies and names some 20 different teenage subcultures. For a fascinating overview and description of these subcultures, see George Barna, *Real Teens* (Ventura, Calif.: Regal Books, 2001), 41–42.

Table 8-2.
Observations on Types of Culture

Culture Type	Description	Observations on Groups (or People) from Your High School Experience
Dominant Culture	• Inherited from traditional ways and beliefs. • Produced by the economically or politically dominant. • Accepted throughout society as common knowledge. • Transmitted in urban societies by mass media.	
Subcultures	• Do not challenge but negotiate optional styles. • Youth subculture may disdain adult responsibilities, tastes, beliefs, and restraints. • Working-class subculture may disdain higher education and professionalism."	
Contracultures	• Seek not to replace but simply to contest dominant values. • May exhibit truancy, vandalism, and drugs, etc.	
Countercultures	• Go beyond defiance and seek to change values and institutions." • Communes may replace families; play and hustling may replace work; love or protest may replace war.	

Excerpts taken from Dean Borgman, *When Kumbayah Is Not Enough* (Peabody, Mass.: Hendrickson Publishers, 1997).

8-2.[21] As you read through the descriptions in the table, think about your high school experience. Can you think of specific people clusters, cluster complexes, art forms, ideas, styles, stories, or understandings for each respective type of culture? Maybe they were not all represented in your high school. But if you were paying attention, you may even remember which types of cultures were represented in different sections of the lunch hour landscape. (Who sat at which tables? Did some groups leave campus at lunch? Did they eat outside the cafeteria at a specific location?)

Why Is Culture Important?

When we pay attention to the cultural landscape, when we take time to explore the individual tiles of the mosaic, we will have a much better sense of the complete human picture. For example, when we see a young teenage guy walking through the mall with his pants hanging down low over his rear end, the crotch of the pants slipping down to just above knee level, we can begin to understand that this choice

---

[21] Borgman, *When Kumbayah Is Not Enough*, 71. Borgman attributes this material to Kenneth Roberts, *Youth and Leisure* (London: Routledge, 1985).

Figure 8-3.
Surface Traits Have Deeper Roots in Core Traits

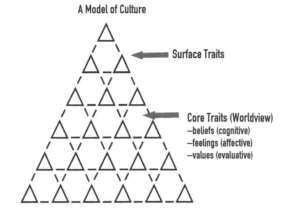

Paul Heibert, *Anthropological Insights for Missionaries* (Grand Rapids, Mich.: Baker, 1985).

is not primarily dictated by physical comfort![22] There are fundamental perceptions at work here—perceptions that are cognitive, affective, and evaluative.
Rather than just dismissing this as a fashion trend and whispering a silent "Thank
you, Lord, for belts," we can begin to appreciate these cues as indicators of worldview and culture. Hiebert reminds us that these surface manifestations are rooted in deeper places of the heart and mind (see Figure 8-3).[23]

There are at least three crucial reasons why any local youth ministry could be
sharpened and aided by a more thorough understanding of the local youth culture.

Understanding Needs, Hopes, and Assets

Giving heed to the culture gives us a better sense of the needs, the hopes, and the
assets of the students we want so much to reach. Teenagers, as human beings, want
to feel valued. They want to feel heard. They wish to be taken seriously. To be
sure, one of the ways that we communicate care and concern to other people is by
listening and paying attention to their life situations.

In John 9:1 there is an amazing narrative about Jesus healing a man born
blind, and it is made all the more amazing by virtue of the method Jesus used: a
mud-and-spit concoction smeared on sightless eyes. This startling episode of
healing simply grew out of Jesus's habit of being attentive to need—taking time to
look and to listen. Jesus "saw a man blind from birth." Had Jesus not seen the
man's blindness we might have had a completely different story. Suppose Jesus

[22] If you are not sure about this, drop your pants to down around your ankles and try walking around. If you are reading this
in the library or another public place, it might be prudent to wait until later to research this.
[23] Paul G. Hiebert, *Anthropological Tools for Missionaries* (Singapore: Haggai Institute, 1983), 4.

had been less attentive and mistook the man's affliction for a sore throat. That would have made the mud-and-spit therapy even more awkward than we can assume it already was.

Russell Hale, who almost a quarter of a century ago did a massive study of unchurched people in America, summarized his findings with this insight: "The overwhelming experience my conversations with the unchurched conveyed to me was that those outside the church *want and need to be heard . . .*"(emphasis added).[24]

Does anyone reading these words suppose that it is any different today? Or that it will be any different 50 years from now? Dietrich Bonhoeffer crystallizes the mandate here:

> The first service that one owes to others . . . consists in listening to them . . . Many people are looking for an ear that will listen. They do not find it among Christians, because these Christians are talking when they should be listening . . . Christians have forgotten that the ministry of listening has been committed to them by Him who is Himself the great listener and whose work they would share. We should listen with the ears of God that we may speak the Word of God.[25]

Being Relevant

Understanding youth culture can help us reflect on how to be culturally relevant without being biblically relativistic. Or to put it another way, understanding youth culture can help us, and our students, to live out Jesus' prayer that we might be "in the world" without being "of the world" (John 17:15–16). "Cultural anthropology makes it easier for us to enter other cultures and realize that the eternal truths and intents of the Scripture, under the guidance of the Holy Spirit, may take different forms from those in our own culture or the biblical cultures."[26]

Youth ministry is a cross-cultural ministry. It requires people of one culture (adults)—with one set of values and mores regarding fashion, leisure, volume of music, and so on—to cross over into the world of another culture (teenagers) with its distinct language, customs, arts, and preferences. Sometimes this gulf is wider and sometimes narrower, but the gulf always exists. The danger is that we will cross that cultural gap with a message shaped more by culture than by Scripture. This trap, called *ethnocentrism,* is defined as "the practice of interpreting and evaluating behavior and objects by reference to one's own culture rather than by those of the culture to which they belong."[27] Ethnocentrism happens all the time in youth ministry: adult youth workers or church leaders who in one form or another suggest that matters of musical style, musical volume, musical instruments, tat-

[24] J. Russell Hale, *Who Are the Unchurched? An Exploratory Study* (Washington, D.C.: Glenmary Research Center, 1977), cited in Harvie M. Conn, *Evangelism: Doing Justice and Preaching Grace* (Grand Rapids, Mich.: Zondervan, 1982), 20.

[25] Dietrich Bonhoeffer, *Life Together,* trans. John W. Boberstein (New York: Harper and Bros, 1954), 97–99.

[26] Grunlan and Mayers, *Cultural Anthropology,* 272.

[27] J. Himes, *The Study of Sociology* (Glenview, Ill.: Scott, 1968), cited in Grunlan and Mayers, *Cultural Anthropology,* 24. William Graham Sumner, author of *Folkways* (Boston: Ginn, 1906), defines ethnocentrism as the "view of things in which one's own group is the center of everything, and all others are scaled and rated with reference to it." Cited in Grunlan and Mayers, *Cultural Anthropology,* 252.

toos, body piercings, clothing styles, hair length, and so on are less a matter of personal taste and more a matter of scriptural mandate. Obviously, when we speak so forcefully where God is silent, we blur the essential message of the gospel.

Were anyone among you to be a youth pastor among the Lani people, a large tribal group who live in the West Baliem River Valley of New Guinea, you might have more than tattoos and body piercings to contend with. Take note of these words from zoologist Tim Flannery:

> On landing we were immediately surrounded by a small crowd of Lani youths, which quickly swelled as we unloaded our cargo. Almost all of them were dressed traditionally, wearing short, very broad penis gourds, and hair nets . . . Many older Lani men wear extraordinarily long [gourds], which are in some cases so extreme that they threaten to poke the wearer in the eye. Youths, on the other hand, prefer the short, broad gourd I came to think of as a "sporting model."[28]

Suppose one of your guys walked into youth group wearing one of those next Sunday night? Obviously—hopefully, prayerfully—this will not happen. But the point remains, youth workers face issues every week that force them to consider the question: Is this something that God in his Word describes as sinful, or is it just something that the culture has defined for us as distasteful?

The challenge is to do cross-cultural ministry in such a way that we communicate across the culture the message of the Cross and not the message of a culture. Missiologists refer to this area of theological thought as *ethnotheology*—the interface between theology and culture. It is

As we study humans as social beings, as well as spiritual beings, we learn more about God, because people were created in the image of God.
—**Stephen Grunlan and Marvin Mayers**

Without culture, Christianity is an abstraction unrelated to human life.
—**Robert Pazmino**

---

[28] Tim Flannery, *Throwim way leg: Adventures in the Jungles of New Guinea* (London: Weidenfeld and Nicholson, 1998), 229. Flannery goes on to add: "There is a functional reason for these preferences. The gourd worn by the younger men serves as a pouch. They remove the plug of fur or cloth at its end, and retrieve from it tobacco, matches, or other small knick-knacks. Being broad, it has a considerable capacity. Being short, it does not get entangled during a dash through the forest in pursuit of a possum. Such an accident, by the way, could be rather painful, considering the string that ties the gourd at its base to one testicle."

based on the simple notion that because we learn theology within a culture it is easy to just assume that our own learned cultural behavior is in fact the most truly "Christian" behavior.

Clearly Paul was wrestling with something like this in Romans 14:1–3 when he instructed the church regarding dietary restrictions: "Accept him whose faith is weak, without passing judgment on disputable matters. One man's faith allows him to eat everything, but another man, whose faith is weak, eats only vegetables. The man who eats everything must not look down on him who does not, and the man who does not eat everything must not condemn the man who does, for God has accepted him."[29]

There have been those who argue with real justification that, in fact, this separation between theology and culture is not really possible. To begin with, some have observed that the notion of cultural relativity is itself ethnocentric because it deems all cultures equally good and equally valid, equality itself being a cultural value. Others have questioned whether it is even possible for us to be fully and authentically culture-free, claiming that our cultural values will always sabotage the process of evaluating what is good or appropriate.[30] There is certainly merit to these concerns. We know too well our capacities for self-deception to think that we will always be able to prepare Bible studies and give talks that speak to teenagers about God's concerns without occasionally polluting the message with some of our own. "Am I teaching on this topic because it breaks God's heart, or because it gets on *my* nerves?"

In light of this concern, Dean Borgman suggests it is imperative that we do what he describes as *holistic exegesis* of the biblical text.[31] This entails our honest and faithful attention to three kinds of exegesis:

▸ The exegesis of Scripture—this is taking pains to make certain that we understand what was the original message of the biblical text that God intended us to hear.

▸ The exegesis of (youth) culture—this is making the effort to listen carefully before we speak to make sure that we communicate with relevance and sensitivity; "*How does this text speak* to the needs of my students in their world, and *how will they hear* the message of this text?"

▸ The exegesis of self and community—this is taking time to reflect thoughtfully about how my own culture and background might lead me to misrepresent, distort, taint, or otherwise miscommunicate what God wants these students to hear from this text.[32]

[29] See also 1 Corinthians 8:4–13.

[30] For further explanation of these and other concerns regarding cultural relativity, see Grunlan and Mayers, *Cultural Anthropology*, 252–253 and 258–259 where he twice reiterates some of the key issues.

[31] Borgman, *When Kumbayah Is Not Enough*, xvii.

[32] The full description of this threefold exegetical process is beyond the scope of this work. However, there is simply no better practical explanation of this process than that which Borgman provides. Ibid., 37–44. James I. Packer also offers some excellent insights about how "culturally conditioned assumptions can hinder communication." See "The Gospel: Its Content and Communication—A Theological Perspective" in *Down to Earth*, ed. John R. W. Stott (Grand Rapids, Mich.: Eerdmans, 1980), 100ff.

Surveying the Local Ground: Exegeting Your Community

1. What sort of people live within the sphere of our church's influence? What is their ethnic makeup? Which nationalities, religions, and cultures are represented? Which radio stations do they listen to? What proportions are there of traditional families, single-parent families, single people, senior citizens, young people? What are the area's main social needs in terms of housing, employment, poverty, education, afterschool programs?

2. Where do the local students go to school? Are there any private schools that need to be factored into the picture? Are there any local colleges or universities?

3. What places of business are found in this area? Factories, farms, offices, shops, or studios? Is there significant unemployment?

4. Where do the people live? Do they occupy houses or flats, and do they own or rent them? Are there any hotels, hostels, student residences, apartment blocks, or homes for senior citizens?

5. Where do people congregate in their free time? Coffee shops or restaurants, pubs or clubs, shopping malls, concert halls, theaters or cinemas, public parks, or street corners?

6. What public services are situated locally? Police, fire department, prison, hospital, public library, other social services?

7. Are there other religious buildings—church or chapel, synagogue, mosque, temple, or Christian Science Reading Room? Are there other ministries in the area that target teenagers?

8. Has the community changed in the last 10 years, and what changes can be forecast during the next 10 years?

This material is adapted from John R. Stott, The Contemporary Christian *(Downers Grove, Ill.: InterVarsity Press, 1992), 247–248.*

Marvin Mayers suggests these four questions for interpreting and evaluating culturally normative behaviors:

1. What is the cultural norm? This is the expression of cultural relativity.

2. Is the norm in keeping with biblical principles? This is the expression of biblical authority.

3. Is the action in keeping with the norm? This defines the situation.

4. Does the action violate either the norm or biblical principles? This is the integration of biblical authority and cultural relativity.

Marvin Mayers, Christianity Confronts Culture (Grand Rapids, Mich.: Zondervan, 1987), 255.

The critical balance is maintaining an atmosphere of grace, openness, and *cultural relativity*,[33] while maintaining the reality of biblical authority. Jesus called us to be "salt" in the culture (Matt. 5: 13) and warned us in grave terms that salt, if it loses its flavor is virtually useless. We do not want to preach a gospel that is not seasoned with salt; but we want to make sure we are not adding any other seasonings into the mix just because it fits our personal taste. What usually happens in churches, and among youth leaders, is some imbalance between these two dynamics of biblical authority and cultural relativity that breeds something short of biblical Christianity. This can best be illustrated by thinking of a paradigm with four possible combinations (Figure 8-4), each described in terms of relativism and absolutism:[34] (1) biblical relativism and cultural absolutism; (2) biblical relativism and cultural relativism; (3) biblical absolutism and cultural absolutism; (4) biblical absolutism and cultural relativism.

Eugene Nida, the respected missiologist and anthropologist, suggests that the most accurate way to describe this balance would be in terms of *relative relativisim*:

In contrast with the absolute relativity of some contemporary social scientists, the biblical position may be described as a "relative relativism," for the Bible clearly recognizes that different cultures have different standards and that these differences are recognized by God as having different values. The relativism of the Bible is relative to three principal factors: (1) the endowment and the opportunities of people, (2) the extent of revelation, and (3) the cultural patterns of the society in question.[35]

Nida cites passages such as Luke 12:47–48 as evidence that rewards and judgments are relative to what people know:

[33] Cultural relativity is "the practice of interpreting and evaluating behavior and objects by reference to the normative and value standards of the culture to which the behavior or objects belong." Himes, cited in Grunlan and Mayers, *Cultural Anthropology*, 24. "In other words, cultural relativity is the position that ideas, actions, and objects should be evaluated by the norms and values of the culture in which they are found rather than by another culture's norms and values." Ibid., 252.

[34] Or relativity and authority.

[35] Eugene Nida, *Customs and Cultures* (New York: Harper & Row, 1954), 282.

Figure 8-4.
Maintaining the Balance Between Biblical Authority and Cultural Relativity

Biblical

	Relativism	Absolutism
Cultural Absolutism	The culture sets the rules and Scripture's teaching is watered down to fit the culture's values. **RESULT: Situational Ethics**	Scripture sets the rules, but cultural traditions are embraced as if they had biblical authority. **RESULT: Traditionalism**
Relativism	Neither the culture nor the Scripture is considered authoritative. Everyone does as they wish. **RESULT: "Might makes right," anything goes**	The Scripture speaks with authority and may therefore reject cultural norm, but where the Scripture is silent, respect is given to the cultural norms. **RESULT: Mutual Respect**

Source: Stephen A. Grunlan and Marvin K. Mayers, *Cultural Anthropology: A Christian Perspective* (Grand Rapids, Mich.: Zondervan, 1988), 256.

That servant who knows his master's will and does not get ready or does not do what his master wants will be beaten with many blows. But the one who does not know and does things deserving punishment will be beaten with few blows. From everyone who has been given much, much will be demanded; and from the one who has been entrusted with much, much more will be asked.

In other words, if we are working with completely unchurched teenagers, we might be inclined to evaluate their behavior differently from that of a student who has been raised in the church. Smoking in the church parking lot, wearing a Hooters T-shirt that is inappropriately graphic, using profanity, or yelling at another student when they get angry in a game—while we understand Scripture to speak to matters of personal health, lustful thoughts, and untamed tongues, we might recognize that, given the cultural context of our work, we have to look beyond some of these issues to get the Cross from church culture (or adult culture, or white middle-class culture) over to adolescent culture. At the same time, in response to the authority of biblical teaching, there will come a time when we will want to offer clear instruction about Christian behavior. We cannot just go on forever excusing sub-Christian behavior as "the way everybody is."

The apostle Paul puts it this way:

To the Jews I became like a Jew, to win the Jews. To those under the law I became like one under the law (though I myself am not under the law), so as to win those under the law. To those not having the law I became like one not having the law (though I am not free from God's law but am under Christ's law), so as to win those not having the law." (I Cor. 9:20–21)

Acting as a Bridge

Understanding youth culture can help us to move more effectively in and out of that culture. God became human because he sought to reach humans. This movement into our world as a human—who lived in a specific culture, as a member of a specific ethnic group, who supported himself in the carpentry trade—gave Jesus the distinct advantage of fully comprehending what it meant to be human.

The writer of Hebrews could say, "For we do not have a high priest who is unable to sympathize with our weaknesses, but we have one who has been tempted in every way, just as we are—yet was without sin. Let us then approach the throne of grace with confidence, so that we may receive mercy and find grace to help us in our time of need" (Heb. 4:15–16).

Jesus understood every dimension of human experience from loneliness to sweat, to physical labor, to paying taxes. These experiences gave him a natural bridge into the culture of humanity. He was able to draw from a rich reservoir of everyday life in his illustrations, his rebukes against injustice, his knowledge of social customs. In the same way, our knowledge of the local adolescent culture will help us to understand better their needs, their frustrations, their temptations, their dreams, their social conventions, even just the way kids use language.

For example, one year I worked at a summer camp where a missionary came to share with the kids and acted as a sort of a "missionary in residence." One morning he was talking to the students about his life as a missionary in Brazil, and about how there was so much rain in that tropical climate. That is when he commented, "We would never think of leaving the house without putting on rubbers!" Of course, what he meant to communicate is that he would never leave his house without proper footwear. But, that is *not* what the students heard when he talked about "putting on rubbers." In fact, immediately, hands began shooting up to volunteer for mission work in Brazil. Just kidding. But, it was a classic example of a well-meaning adult who had not taken the time to listen before he spoke.

To some degree, teenagers develop a natural suspicion about adults. Sometimes even the smallest violation of social convention might be all that is necessary to lose one's credibility. We all know that often when the messenger loses credibility, the message is not considered credible either. The apostle Paul was enough aware of the culture of his audience in Athens (Acts 17:16ff) that he was able to quote to them the words of their own poets. That knowledge of Greek culture probably bought his initial hearing among those people. A thoughtful youth worker who wants to walk the bridge into adolescent culture will give some thought to adolescent tastes, styles, and presuppositions.

That might mean losing the big, black 40-pound "Weightlifter's Bible." It might mean trying to stay abreast of topics that would be of interest to teenagers.

It might mean knowing where teenagers in a given community hang out. It might mean losing the necktie, or the bow tie, or the cool souvenir gourd you brought back from your trip to New Guinea.

What If We Don't Like What We See? Preaching Good News in a Bad News Culture

There remains then the basic question of how Christians, in general, are to respond to culture. We know that Scripture calls us to "not love the world or anything in the world" (1 John 2: 15), and yet we know that "God so loved the world" (John 3:16). We know that we are called to "become blameless and pure, children of God without fault in a crooked and depraved generation" (Phil. 2:15) and yet we are also warned, "Do not be yoked together with unbelievers. For what do righteousness and wickedness have in common? Or what fellowship can light have with darkness?" (2 Cor. 6:14). What is the proper response of Christianity to culture? Are we to salt the culture, or assault the culture? Are we subversive agents trying to overthrow a fallen system, or agents of reconciliation trying to heal a broken world? Do we declare holy war, or just declare that the whole thing is none of our business? Is our response supposed to be *jihad* or "Gee, whatever you guys think"?

In his classic work *Christ and Culture*, H. Richard Niebuhr suggests five possible ways (summarized in Figure 8-5) of thinking about the relationship between Christ and the culture:[36]

I. **Christ of Culture.** This position is on the opposite end of the spectrum from the first one. Its basic assumption is that the differences between the Christian system and the culture of the world are differences in quality, not in kind. Through the lens of this position Jesus is more of a role model or a cultural hero. The best culture is the one that conforms most nearly to the traits and values of Jesus.

By way of further explanation, Niebuhr defends this position: "If it is an error to interpret [Jesus] as a wise man teaching a secular wisdom, or a reformer concerned with the reconstruction of a social institution, such interpretations serve at least to balance the opposite mistakes of presenting him as a person who had no interest in the principles men used to guide their present life in a damned society because his eye was fixed on the Jerusalem that was to come down from heaven."[38]

---

[36] H. Richard Niebuhr, *Christ and Culture* (New York: Harper and Row, 1956), 45–229. I have also incorporated here material from Borgman, *When Kumbayah Is Not Enough*, 79–80, and Robert W. Pazmino, *Foundational Issues in Christian Education* (Grand Rapids, Mich.: Baker Books, 1997), 65–66.

[37] See Matthew 6:24 and Ephesians. 5:11–12.

Figure 8-5.
Christ and Culture: Five Views

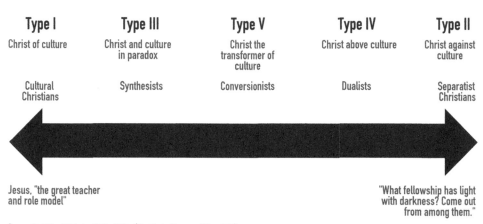

Source: H. Richard Niebuhr, *Christ and Culture* (New York: Harper and Row, 1956).

II. **Christ Against Culture.** This response stands on the notion that Christ is the sole authority and therefore believers are bound only by his claims. Any claims by culture on the allegiance of believers is deceptive and untrue.[37]

III. **Christ and Culture in Paradox.** Advocates of this position begin with the fact that God is the source of both our sense of sin and the promise of grace. It is a fact that confronts us at the same time with a profound awareness of both God's judgment on our sin and God's grace in the midst of our need. For that reason, Niebuhr describes this position as a "dualist" view that "the whole edifice of culture is cracked and madly askew; the work of self-contradicting builders, erecting towers that aspire to heaven on a fault in the earth's crust."[41]

This is the paradox: that we are called to be good citizens of two cities, the city of humanity and the city of God. But these two cities, one dominated by sin and law and the other dominated by holiness and grace, are almost always at war with one another. So our response to culture must be one of living in tension, "rendering unto Caesar the things that are Caesar's, and rendering unto God the things that are God's," understanding all the while that, quite often, the claims of Caesar are in direct contradiction to the claims of God.

IV. **Christ Above Culture.** This position begins with the presupposition that because God is the creator of this world, and it is inherently good and

---

[38] Niebuhr, *Christ and Culture*, 106.

[39] See also Matthew. 5:17–19, 22:21, 23:2.

[40] Niebuhr, *Christ and Culture*, 127.

rightly ordered by God, it is wrong to think of Christ in opposition to culture. To think of culture merely as a realm of godlessness—because culture exists only by God's design and rule—ignores the fact that culture is a product of both God and man, both holy and sinful. We cannot talk in terms of "*either* Christ *or* culture" because God is at work through both. We must take both seriously.

Proponents of this position point to passages such as Romans 13:1,6: "Everyone must submit himself to the governing authorities, for there is no authority except that which God has established. The authorities that exist have been established by God . . . This is also why you pay taxes, for the authorities are God's servants, who give their full time to governing."[39]

Christ is not against culture, but "uses its best products as instruments in his work of bestowing on men what they cannot achieve by their own efforts."[40]

V. **Christ the Transformer of Culture.** This position is rooted in the theological notion of redemption, the notion that Christ is the great healer and gracious forgiver. Christ does his redemptive work "not simply by offering ideas, counsel, and laws; but by living with men in great humility, enduring death for their sakes, and rising again from the grave in a demonstration of God's grace rather than an argument about it."[42] This position recognizes that any effort at cultural improvement anchored in humanity's sense of self-sufficiency is bankrupt and lies under the judgment of God. But proponents of this position "believe also that such culture is under God's sovereign rule, and that the Christian must carry on cultural work in obedience to the Lord"[43]—that we do this work as a continuation of God's creative, redeeming, healing purposes in the world (see Col. 1:16).

In evaluating Niebuhr's five responses, it is important to recognize that these categories are not necessarily antagonistic in every case. Each position brings its own strengths and inherent dangers. David Hesselgrave, whose own contributions in terms of missionary anthropology and cross-cultural communication have gained him wide respect, suggests that Niebuhr's categories I, IV, V, and "quite possibly" III, each provide some valuable emphases.[44] Evangelical Christians have typically been characterized by a type I, IV, or V approach.[45] The danger of opting for the personal piety of Niebuhr's type I or II is that we short-circuit the impact that we as Christians might have on the culture—or (were we humble enough to admit it) that the culture might have on us. We maintain our

---

[41] Ibid., 156.
[42] Ibid., 191.
[43] Ibid.
[44] Hesselgrave, *Contextualization, Meanings, Methods and Models*, ed. David Hesselgrave (Grand Rapids, Mich.: Baker, 1989), 80.
[45] Pazmino, *Foundational Issues in Christian Education*, 66.

Jesus Christ is the captive of no culture and the master of all cultures.
—**Leighton Ford, in an *Hour of Decision* radio broadcast**

According to Scripture, culture has much to do with faith; it is part of being "fearfully and wonderfully made" in the image of God (Psalm 139:14). Culture represents human responses to God's first foundational command: "Be fruitful and increase in number; fill the earth and subdue it" (Gen. 1:28). God entrusts ordinary human beings like you and me with the continuing process of creation . . . An understanding of what the Bible says about culture provides a justification for Christian engagement with popular art and also a basis for both production and criticism.
—**William D. Romanowski**

"saltiness," but we never get "out of the salt-shaker."[46] The danger of adopting a type IV response is that we view the church and wider society as complementary—"We're okay; they're okay." Too often this posture just maintains the status quo—so we're out of the salt-shaker, but we never land in the food.

Avery Dulles provides what may be a simpler way of thinking about the relationship between Christ's church and the culture of the state. In Dulles's scheme there are four key positions,[47] illustrated in Figure 8-6. Each of these positions pledge trust in the church and/or the state in varying degrees.

Youth Pastors and River Scouts: How to Read a River

Rafter Lido Tejada-Flores reminds us that the goal of a good river guide is not just reading the river: it is having the talent for good navigation. "The first function of river reading is to help you avoid obstacles; the second is to pick the right route."[48] But, practically speaking, how are youth ministers to pick "the right route" in the churning, changing currents of postmodern culture? Do we follow the main current? Do we attempt to raft upstream? Do we pick the course of least resistance? Which fork of the river offers the best choice? It is not enough just to scout the cultural current. Ultimately, our desire is to chart a course that avoids the pitfalls and deep holes but allows us still to maintain our biblical mandate.

The challenge of taking seriously both culture and biblical truth is worked out through the hard work of what missiologists refer to as *contextualization*. As explained by Stephen Knapp, con-

---

46 To borrow a phrase from Rebecca Pippert, *Out of the Salt-Shaker* (Downers Grove, Ill.: InterVarsity Press, 1979).
47 Kreeft, *C. S. Lewis for the Third Millennium*, 35–36.
48 Ibid., 156.

Figure 8-6.
Dulles's Four Positions Between Church and State Culture

The Church

Radicalism "A plague on both your houses!" This view suggests that the culture and the church are so intertwined that neither can be trusted. An example would be people like the Amish, who form alternative cultures within the culture.	**Traditionalism** Trusts in the church but not in the state—not in the present state of society Suggests that the real battle is spiritual and that even the church's victories in the public or cultural arenas are hollow, temporary victories. The only way to impact a sick and sinful culture is through Christ's work in individual hearts and minds.
Liberalism Trusts in the state but not the church; not traditional Christianity This would be representative of those who believe that the church should stay out of the public arena. Let the government deal with cultural/social problems because the church will muddy the water with religious issues. Some refer to this as "the secular Left."	**Neo-conservatism** Wants to work with both the church and the state This would be representative of what is commonly referred to as "the Christian Right." This is the notion that Chistians must exercise their faith in the public square and the salt of collective Christian witness in the culture can make a difference.

The State "Culture" *(row label at left)*

Source: Peter Kreeft, *C. S. Lewis for the Third Millennium* (San Francisco: Ignatius Press, 1994), 35–36.

textualization is the "dynamic process through which the church continually challenges or incorporates—transforms—elements of the cultural and social milieu of which it is an integral part in its daily struggle to be obedient to the Lord Jesus Christ in its life and mission in the world."[49]

Maintaining the Balance of Context and Content

The first function of [a] river [guide] is to help you avoid obstacles; the second is to pick the right route. [50]

Practically speaking, how might a youth worker maintain this equally important balance of content and context? Ericson offers the following four categories of cross-cultural communication (summarized in Figure 8-7) with each successive category of communication allowing for greater flexibility and variation:[51]

▸ **Stage One:** The Core. This is the revelation and salvation that is mediated through Jesus Christ alone. Because this is a finished work by Christ himself, it is not open for variation.

[49] Stephen Knapp, "Contextualization and Its Implications for U.S. Evangelical Church and Missions," cited in Pazmino, *Foundational Issues in Christian Education*, 169. To gain a fuller sense of the practical outworkings of contextualization, see the article, *Working out Contextualization with Fear and Trembling* in the Companion Guide to this book, *This Way to Youth Ministry Companion Guide: Readings, Case Studies, Resources to Begin the Journey* by Robbins and Kageler (Grand Rapids, MI: Zondervan, 2004).

[50] Pazmino, *Foundational Issues in Christian Education*, 156.

[51] Norman R. Ericson, "Implications from the New Testament for Culturalization," *Contextualization, Meanings, Methods and Models*, ed. David Hesselgrave (Grand Rapids, Mich.: Baker, 1989), 83.

▸ **Stage Two:** The Substance. This is the gospel tradition that comes to us through apostolic transmission in the Bible. We dare not alter this message in substance. *But we can shape the way we communicate it* so that its unaltered message wrapped in a different cultural and historical context can be better understood by teenagers in today's cultural and historical context.

▸ **Stage Three:** The Application. The various applications of unchanging biblical truth will differ depending on the audience. The application will be shaped, for example, by life situations, level of spiritual commitment, amount of biblical knowledge—even, perhaps, the intent of the specific ministry situation (outreach, nurture, community-building).

Figure 8-7.
Ericson's Categories of Acceptable Variation for Cross-cultural Communication

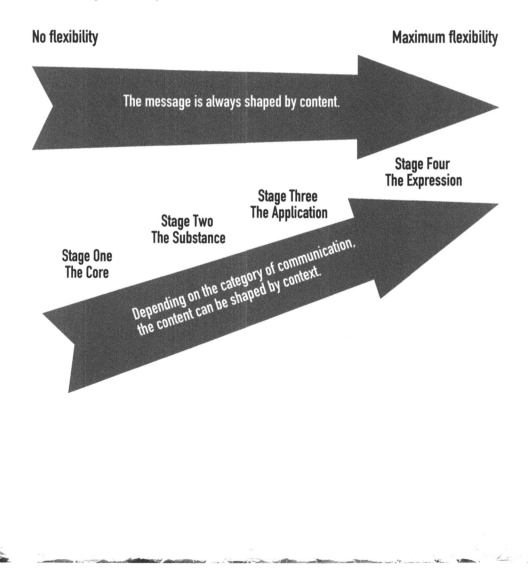

No flexibility   Maximum flexibility

The message is always shaped by content.

Stage Four
The Expression

Stage Three
The Application

Stage Two
The Substance

Stage One
The Core

Depending on the category of communication, the content can be shaped by context.

▶ **Stage Four:** The Expression. How obedience to the biblical truth will be played out will again depend on the particular audience. Are they middle-schoolers or high schoolers? Where do they live: inner city, suburban, Northeast metropolis, rural Midwest, deep South? The expression is shaped by their particular cultural setting. If Stage Three is how I apply the truth to my students' lives in general, Stage Four is how the students apply the truth to their own lives in particular.

There is, perhaps, a word of warning to us in Ericson's categories: sometimes in our efforts to be "seeker-sensitive" we dilute the message of the God's Word. No one

> But the greatest triumph of all is to elevate this horror of the Same Old Thing into a philosophy so that nonsense in the intellect may reinforce corruption in the will. It is here that the general Evolutionary or Historical character of modern European thought (partly our work) comes in so usefully. The Enemy loves platitudes. Of a proposed course of action he wants men, so far as I can see, to ask very simple questions: Is it righteous? Is it prudent? Is it possible? Now, if we can keep men asking: "Is it in accordance with the general movement of our time? Is it progressive or reactionary? Is this the way that History is going?" they will neglect the relevant questions. And the questions they do ask are, of course, unanswerable; for they do not know the future, and what the future will be depends very largely on just those choices which they now invoke the future to help them to make.
>
> *C. S. Lewis's demon character Wormwood, offering instruction to his rookie nephew Screwtape in* The Screwtape Letters *(New York: MacMillan, 1959), 118.*

denies, for example, that the message of human sinfulness is less popular than the message of abundant life, but neither can anyone reasonably deny that the message of human sinfulness is integral to the apostolic message. That means that leaving out that message or ignoring it is not an option if we wish to be faithful to Scripture.

Several years ago I was to speak at a large denominational gathering for high school youth out in the Rocky Mountains. About two weeks before the event, I received a phone call from one of the members on the design team who simply "wanted to go over a few last-minute details before the weekend." We discussed a few logistical issues before I was shocked by this request: "Also, we've been talking a bit on the design team, and we wanted to ask you, when you give your talks, would you mind please not mentioning Jesus's name? We don't mind if you talk about God; but if you could just be sensitive, some of our students might be offended if we start ramming Jesus down their throats." At first I thought I was hearing things, then I tried to keep an even voice in my reply. I explained that not mentioning Jesus would be difficult for me because I tend to think of Jesus as God, and that, speaking as often as I do with reference to the Bible, I have probably slipped into

We might add that contextualization is not just what can be *drawn from* a culture to make the gospel relevant in that culture. It is also a willingness to *lay aside* certain elements of one's culture and allow one's understanding and experience of the gospel to develop in the light of the host culture. In other words, it is not just drawing from a host culture to find ways of nurturing their faith; it is drawing from a host culture and discovering new ways that we can nurture our own faith. It is easy to get stuck on the assumption that one's own cultural expression of the Christian faith is the most faithful expression of "Christian culture."

something of a habit of referring to Jesus by name—though I have no intention of "ramming" anything down anyone's throat . . . I went on to offer that, if the mere mention of the name of Jesus would be troublesome for them, I would be happy to release them from any contractual obligation. At this point, the voice on the other end began to stammer and stutter, "No, we want you to come—we'd just like to ask you to be sensitive."

I did actually speak at that event, and I did mention the name of Jesus (a little more than normal). But the episode reminds us that we always face the risk of being so sensitive to the audience that we cease being sensitive to the text—and sensitive to the Spirit of God who inspired it. In Ericson's Stages Three and Four, we have much room to be seeker-sensitive. In Stages One and Two, however, we are listening not for the voice of the audience, but for the voice of the Word.

We need to be honest about how our personal tastes and allegiances shade our gospel presentation. There is a fine line between propagation and propaganda. Drawing from C. S Lewis, Peter Kreeft observes, "'Propagation is old birds teaching young birds to fly.' Propaganda is programming parrots."[52] Propagation is the faithful transmission of biblical truth. Propaganda is allowing God's Word to be muddled by our own words. We can see then that contextualization is not just some concept from an academic never-never land. It is an integral part of the youth worker's task of massaging the message into the aches, hopes, life-questions, and issues of youth culture.

Ericson's four stages of cross-cultural communication force us to ask: How, and how much, should our presentation of the gospel be shaped by the culture around us? How much can we change for the sake of understanding the gospel before we are at risk of undermining the gospel? On the playing field of youth ministry—in the bumps and bruises and dirt of live action—these principles of culturalization and cross-cultural communication will not call the play for us, but they can help us to be mindful of both the boundaries and the goal.

[52] Peter Kreeft, *C. S. Lewis for the Third Millennium* (San Francisco: Ignatius Press, 1994), 49.

Tracing the Broad Brush Strokes of Societal Context

If culture is indeed a "mosaic," we will better understand that mosaic not by moving in too close but by pulling a step or two back.[53] This is scouting the river as a social observer—not just watching for the ripples made by the latest media splash, but *asking how the surrounding landscape has changed over the years, and considering how that has changed the river.* How about the resort community built 10 miles upstream? What effect did that have on the river? What about the runoff of fertilizers from nearby farm lands? What were the consequences of a riverside brush fire that scorched the shoreline?[54]

When Mark Twain was learning how to pilot a river boat on the Mississippi River—a river that is constantly changing, a river that looks so different in the daylight from in the dark—his tough, experienced teacher told him that the key was to master "the shape of the river." Twain wrote, "Two things seemed pretty apparent to me. One was that in order to be a pilot a man had got to learn more than any one man ought to be allowed to know; and the other was, that he must learn it all over again in a different way every twenty-four hours."[55]

Consider, for example, how societal changes in the past four decades have affected the lives of adolescents. How has the changing landscape of American life shaped the flow of adolescent culture?[56]

It's become clearer and clearer to me that if families just let the culture happen to them, they end up fat, addicted, broke, with a house full of junk and no time.
—**Mary Pipher**

So at the crux of a Christian conception of culture is that it belongs inescapably to the task of being human, is cosmic in scope, and is actually performed as a service of reconciliation and praise or as a wasteful, fruitless attempt to regain paradise for ourselves.
—**Calvin Seerveld**

[53] In the movie *Clueless*, Cher (played by Alicia Silverstone) is asked by a friend, "What's a Monet?" Her answer: "It's like a painting, see? From far away, it's okay, but up close it's a big old mess."

[54] Much of the discussion in this section is drawn from the work of sociologist Robert Wuthnow in his article, "Youth and Culture in American Society: The Social Context of Ministry to Teenagers" in *Christ and the Adolescent: A Theological Approach to Youth Ministry* (Princeton, N.J.: Institute for Youth Ministry, 1996). In his article, Wuthnow actually uses the phrase *social context.* This can be misleading, however, because this same terminology is used, as I did in the preceding section on social exegesis, to describe the relational patterns within a group of people. See, for example, Dave Rahn, "A Sociological Framework for Doing Youth Ministry," in *Reaching a Generation for Christ*, ed. Rick Dunn and Mark Senter (Chicago: Moody, 1997), 97. So, in the interest of maintaining the distinction between the *relational dynamics within a subculture* and the larger *sociological dynamics that might impact that subculture from the outside*, I have opted to use the phrase societal context instead.

[55] Mark Twain, "Old Times on the Mississippi," *Atlantic Monthly* (March 1875): 283–284, cited in William Willimon, *Pastor: The Theology and Practice of Ordained Ministry* (Nashville, Tenn.: Abingdon, 2002), 279–280.

[56] Also helpful, and providing the same sort of broad-stroke portrait of youth culture as Wuthnow, is the work of William Romanowski, Quentin Schultze, Roy Anker, James Bratt, John Worst, and Lambert Zuidervaart in their book, *Dancing in the Dark* (Grand Rapids, Mich.: Eerdmans, 1991), 3–11. In this impressive book they take the reader on a tour of five "sites" that help define the topography of adolescent culture.

1. **Neighborhoods have been replaced by networks.** The average American, for example, moves every three years. There is no longer a sense of connectedness either to place or to neighbor. "Most people still have friends, but these friends are people at work [or at school], or in some other town or state, rather than their neighbors . . . For young people it becomes harder to settle in. Your church friends, if you have any, are generally different from your friends at school. You feel like a transient . . ."[57]

2. **People are working longer hours.** "At present, nearly forty percent of all men in the U.S. labor force put in more than forty hours a week at their jobs and a quarter put in more than fifty hours. Among women the numbers are still somewhat lower, but at least one woman in five works outside the home more than the standard forty hours..."[58]

   Someone has commented that the complaint of teenagers in the 1960s and 1970s was, "It's *my* life!" and the complaint of teenagers in this first decade of the new millennium is "It's *my* life!" The difference is that in the 1960s and 1970s, it was a statement of rebellion. Now, it is a statement of *fact*. Many children and teenagers are simply growing up alone—kept in touch by cell phones and pagers instead of mothers and fathers. While nine out of ten teenagers in one survey rated their families as "healthy and functional," the most frequently cited change they would like to see in their relationships with their fathers was "to spend more time together."[59]

   For young people, the results are likely to range from not having parents to help with the youth group at church, to the problems of latchkey children staying at home unattended and getting into trouble, to picking up signals from their role models that it is better to pick up a part-time job after school in order to buy new clothes and CDs than to spend time doing volunteer work at the church.[60]

3. **The nuclear family is proving to be persistent but precarious.** Wuthnow notes that since the 1950s, there has been a steady decline in the number of families with a mother and father married and living with each other. The number of unmarried couples living together in the United States in 1970 was just 523,000. That number climbed to 1.3 million by 1979, and between 1960 and 1979 the proportion of all white families who lived together as married units declined from 76 percent to 64 percent. Households headed by single males increased from 7 percent to 12 percent, and the number of those headed by single females increased from 17 percent to 24 percent. These declines were even more stark in the African

---

[57] Wuthnow, "Youth and Culture in American Society," 68. This concern has been given a much broader and deeper treatment in Robert Bellah's important work, *Habits of the Heart: Individualism and Commitment in American Life* (New York: Harper and Row, 1985). Bellah wants to call attention to the degree to which Americans have become ethically individualistic ("What I do is my own private business"), and how this has been exaggerated by a culture that increasingly presses people to become at the same time more individualistic and more conformist. Bellah observes the decline of those institutions and practices in our culture that breed and nurture genuine community. Put this one on your list of "Books-to-read-when-I-finish-reading-books-I'm-required-to-read."

[58] Ibid., 68–69.

[59] Barna, *Real Teens*, 71.

[60] Wuthnow, "Youth and Culture in American Society," 68–69.

American community where the percentage of households with both mother and father married and living together has dropped from 60 percent to 40 percent. Families in the African American community headed by a single male rose from 11 percent to 15 percent, and for single females the increase was from 29 percent to 41 percent of the total.

Based on research we reviewed in earlier chapters, we can readily understand that changes in the landscape of the family will have an acute impact on the flow and current of adolescent lives. Wuthnow observes:

> At present, there is much talk about the social ill effects of divorce, of single-parent families and absentee fathers. Those problems, of course, directly influence American young people . . . But there is a broader implication as well. American churches have always drawn close connections between God and the home [naming God as "Father"], probably to the good, insofar as the connection reinforces the value of families. Yet, we are no longer as confident of this imagery as we once were.[61]

Expanding Buffet of Spiritual Resources

Robert N. Nash provides several examples of how the search for spiritual enlightenment has expanded well beyond church institutions, even in mainstream American culture:

▶ The PTO president at the elementary school my children attend opened a recent meeting with a devotional reading from *A Cherokee Feast of Days*, a book about Native American spirituality.

▶ The first two Muslim chaplains were recently appointed for ministry to U.S. military personnel.

▶ The Buddhist Churches of America now include some 60 independent churches and 40 branches scattered from California to New York. Their Sunday School department publishes study guides, lessons, and children's books for use in local Buddhist churches.

▶ A recent commercial on television portrayed a "politically correct" football locker room in which a line of priests and preachers and monks and bhagwans offered a prayer for the team.

Robert N. Nash, Jr., An 8-Track Church in a CD World (Macon, Ga.: Smyth and Helwys, 2001), 8.

4. **Organized religion no longer has a monopoly on religion and/or spiritual life in America.** Between the years 1870 and 1914, the number of

---

[61] Ibid., 70.

local churches in the United States grew from 70,000 to 225,000, and the number of church buildings grew from 63,000 to 203,000. By the end of World War I, there was a higher percentage of church attendance than at any other time in this country's history.[62] In the 1800s, fewer than half of all Americans held church membership. By the 1950s, studies showed that three quarters of all Americans had some affiliation with a local church. Indeed, one study conducted in 1956 put the figure at 80 percent. Church membership is still relatively high—the present rate is about 60 percent, and about 30 percent of all Americans say they attend some house of worship each week.

What is striking in all of this is that while church participation is relatively high, the church no longer holds a monopoly as people seek out spiritual inspiration.[63] They are just as likely to seek spiritual awareness through a holistic health cohort, or travel to "sacred places," or chanting lessons, or seminars in alternative spirituality as through some traditional church-affiliated Christian house of worship. Remarkably, in fact, they are quite likely to be seeking spiritual inspiration through these unorthodox means *and* attending some Christian service of worship. For example, Wuthnow observes that in one recent 12-month period, 5 million people purchased books about angels, none of which were published by Christian publishers or written by Christian clergy.

In his book, *Soul Tsunami*, seminary professor Leonard Sweet highlights this trend:

> Phyllis Tickle, editor-at-large for *Publisher's Weekly*, reveals that spirituality has been "the fastest-growing segment in adult publishing the last two years." Slurp your way through one of the easy-to-sip *Chicken Soup for the Soul* books, and lick your lips at the fortunes being made in this literary franchise. Sales of religious publishers topped $1 billion in 1996, with more than 150 million book units sold. Sales of New Age books went from an astonishing 5.6 million copies in 1992 to an unbelievable 9.7 million three years later . . .
>
> Since 1995, nearly 1,000 books with the word "soul" in the title or subtitle have been published. Seven of the top 10 books on the New York *Times* bestseller list in the spring of 1998 were about spirituality and personal growth.[64]

---

[62] Historians tell us that even in the colonial era, church attendance was between 15 and 20 percent. Wuthnow, "Youth and Culture in American Society," 71.

[63] Polls show that a majority of Americans have confidence in organized religion. But in 1988, according to Gallup, 44 percent of Americans were unchurched (people who said they were not members of any church or had not attended services in the previous six months other than for special religious holidays, weddings, funerals, or the like). That figure amounted to about 78 million adults. Gallup found that overwhelming majorities, churched and unchurched, agreed that people "should arrive at their religious beliefs independent of any church or synagogue," and that one can be a good Christian or Jew without attending a church or synagogue. Gallup discovered in polls taken in 1992 and 1995 that confidence in the clergy was at 54 percent of the populace, down from 67 percent in 1985. "When asked why they attended church less often, few of those interviewed gave reasons that reflected a deep animosity toward organized religion. Only eight percent said they disagreed with policies and teachings. A mere five percent said they were atheists or agnostics. For many, going to church just did not seem that important [a point to which we shall return]. Leading the list were 34 percent who said they were "too busy." Thomas Reeves, *The Empty Church* (New York: Simon and Schuster, 1996), 61.

[64] Leonard Sweet, *Soul Tsunami* (Grand Rapids, Mich.: Zondervan, 1999), 414.

Spirituality is typically associated less with church life and more with a do-it-yourself pursuit. This major trend in the cultural landscape—this perception of an open "spiritual marketplace"—has a profound influence on the way teenagers think about the authority and exclusivity of the claims of the church in particular, and the Christian faith in general.

5. We live in an increasingly multicultural society.[65]

In 1950, 89 percent of the [United States] population was white, 10 percent was black, and the remaining 1 percent was mostly Asian, and the Hispanic population was not counted separately from the white Anglo population. By 1990, the white population had decreased from 89 percent to 80 percent; the black population had increased from 10 percent to 12 percent; the Asian American population had risen from less than 1 percent to 3 percent; other races now made up 4 percent of the population; and the Hispanic population, when considered separately, was 9 percent. Another way to grasp the changes taking place is to compare the growth rates of various groups between 1980 and 1990. During that decade, the white population grew by a mere 6 percent; the black population by 13 percent; the Hispanic population by 53 percent; and the Asian American population by 108 percent. What does that suggest? It suggests that about one quarter of the population is not white Anglo—and that proportion is getting larger all the time . . . *But multiculturalism is about values, even more than it is about demographics* (emphasis added)[66]

On this point we must take notice: *mutliculturalism is not just about changing demographics; it is about changing values.*[67] For those of us in youth ministry, the implications of this fact are huge:

▸ More teenagers tend to conclude that they are simply Christians as a circumstance of birth and nationality. *They are more apt to see the exclusive truth claims of Christianity as a type of cultural imperialism.*[68] In Wuthnow's words, "they are likely to regard Christianity as just one of many ways to establish a relationship with God; it ceases to be THE TRUTH."[69]

▸ As the culture becomes more and more diverse, teenagers are immersed in the notion that multiculturalism should be valued *for its own sake*—that diversity should be embraced *for its own sake*. The problem with this is that *it is a short downhill trip from saying that "all beliefs are*

---

[65] Neil Howe and William Strauss, *Millennials Rising* (New York: Vintage Books, 2000), 15.

[66] Wuthnow, "Youth and Culture in American Society," 72–73.

[67] Richard Bernstein argues convincingly that multiculturalism, as it is currently understood, "is a code word for an expanded concept of moral and cultural relativism." Richard Bernstein, *Dictatorship of Virtue: Multiculturalism and the Battle for America's Future* (New York: Knopf, 1994), 9.

[68] It must be admitted that sometimes the Christian message has been and still is perverted and blurred by a very real type of cultural imperialism. This is not just the mistake of pith-helmeted missionaries who sought to get local populations to put down their "pagan drums" and sing instead to the "heavenly sounds of a pipe organ as God intended." This is the type of cultural imperialism that still happens today in many of our churches and youth groups. All the more reason why we must do the hard work of thinking through issues like *contextualization* (earlier in this chapter), if we are to be effective and faithful messengers of the gospel.

[69] Wuthnow, "Youth and Culture in American Society," 73.

to be respected" to saying that *"all beliefs are equally valid."* As Stanley J. Grenz points out in his book *A Primer to Postmodernism*, there is the widespread and growing perception that "truth is relative to the community in which a person participates. And since there are many human communities, there are necessarily many different truths."[70]

▸ As teenagers are indoctrinated with the notion that diversity is good *in and of itself, they are more likely to believe that Christianity is fine, but eclecticism is better.* If one is to really get the full picture of spirituality, one must mine the truths (with a small "t") of other religions, and then mix and match to come up with a personal spirituality that best "fits" one's understanding.

▸ Finally, in this kind of cultural environment, there is *the grave danger— a different kind of danger—that those of us within the church will become so alarmed about the surrounding culture that we seek to make the church a refuge of homogeneity*—a place where our students can seek out others who think just like they do. This kind of parochialism not only leaves us out of touch with the wider world, it starves us of the questions and challenges— the iron sharpening iron (Prov. 27:17)—of those who do not think precisely like we do.

6. **"The sexual revolution has come and gone—almost."**[71] It has now been more than three decades since the birth control pill made its way into the lexicon of modern life. Since that time, whatever cultural taboos existed about premarital and extramarital sexual behavior have been almost entirely eliminated. With the widespread threat of AIDS and the increasing questions being raised about homosexual behavior adding new textures of complexity to the issues, there is no question that today's adolescent deals with questions of sexuality in a world quite different from that of generations past. As one writer put it, "It used to be that 'sex' and 'sacred' went together; now it's 'sex' and 'scared,' and maybe even, I would add, 'scarred.'"[72]

7. **Technology is an emerging revolution.** It is hard to fathom the magnitude of change that has come about in the past two decades as a result of advances in digital technology. Sweet remarks, "The digital watch you now wear on your wrist contains more computing power than existed in the entire world before 1961."[73] When our grandparents said, "Log on," they were talking about replenishing the fuel supply. Now it is a phrase that marks a gateway into a virtual world that was unknown even two decades ago.

The French writer Paul Virilio argues that Western culture has been shaped by "three industrial revolutions." In the first revolution, the Industrial Revolution, machines gave us muscle and power, but the

---

[70] Stanley Grenz, *Primer to Postmodernism* (Grand Rapids, Mich.: Eerdmans, 1996), 14.

[71] Wuthnow, "Youth and Culture in American Society," 73.

[72] Sweet, *Soul Tsunami*, 422.

[73] Ibid., 84.

Diversity for Diversity's Sake

It is this notion that is particularly troublesome—that there is value in diversity simply for the sake of diversity. The implication is that we should celebrate every idea or belief or culture just because it is different. Yet surely no one would suggest that we should celebrate the culture of the Ku Klux Klan, or the culture of Nazi anti-Semites, or the culture of the child molester, or the culture of the slave traders of west Africa. No one seems to be particularly interested in celebrating diverse viewpoints when it comes to landing an airplane or performing brain surgery. Once we begin to separate out one type of diversity as bad and others as good, we have already moved away from the notion of *diversity for the sake of diversity*.

It is true, although it is difficult to practice, that our disdain for these cultures does not allow us license to be disrespectful or cruel. But our respect for those who hold these notions does not have to extend to the ideas they embrace. We value all people because they are created in the image of God. But, all ideas and cultural ideals are not created in the image of God (and certainly, this includes many of the ideas and ideals of everyday Western culture and American life). To embrace *all peoples and their cultures* with equal respect is critical. To embrace *all ideas and values* with equal respect, and without critical evaluation, is to surrender moral responsibility. This is not a new idea. The landscape of history is littered with the broken nations and ruined lives of cultures before our own that uncritically embraced all ideas and values. Respect must not be the same as approval.

Efrem Smith, a veteran urban youth pastor and leader in thinking about some of these issues, suggests that we should not be celebrating multiculturalism as much as we should be celebrating multiethnicism. One celebrates a diversity of *ideas*; the other celebrates a diversity of *peoples* (see Rev. 5:9).

For an excellent and more expanded treatment of this idea, see Stan Gaede, When Tolerance Is No Virtue: Political Correctness, Multiculturalism, and the Future of Truth and Justice *(Downers Grove, Ill.: InterVarsity Press, 1994).*

Industrial Revolution, machines gave us muscle and power, but the machines could only operate by the intelligence of human brains. In the second revolution, the Information Revolution, the machines joined muscles and power with intelligence and senses. *Newsweek,* in an issue that was devoted entirely to "the Big Bang of our time," called this revolution "the Bit Bang." If the sound of the first industrial revolution was clanging steel, the sound of the second industrial revolution was clicking keyboards.

One weekday edition of the *New York Times* includes more information than the average person encountered in his entire lifetime in 17th century England. The average consumer will see or hear one million messages a year. That's almost 3,000 per day.

—*Leonard Sweet,* Soul Tsunami *(Grand Rapids, Mich.: Zondervan, 1999), 113.*

Now, we are on the cusp of a third industrial revolution that brings together brains and biology. Biophysicists at the Naval Research Laboratory in Washington, working collaboratively with scientists at the National Institute of Health and at the University of California—Irvine, have reported that they have taken a "key first step toward creating electronic microchips that use living brain cells," according to the *Wall Street Journal*. DNA (which stores information) and microchips (which process information) are now being combined, with the flow of information going from one to the other."[74]

Research by George Barna demonstrates just how pervasive this virtual culture has become in adolescent life. Table 8-3 shows how teenagers' use of the Internet has changed during just the last few years.[75]

Obviously it is impossible to think about youth culture without taking changes of this magnitude into consideration. Certainly, the ramifications of this virtual reality are neither all positive or all negative. But it would be naive to assume that the advances in technology are neutral. Leonard Sweet tells the true story about people who, unaware that the material they had found was radioactive, smeared it all over themselves and their families because they liked the blue glow it gave to their appearance.[76] It is a parable that serves a prudent warning. It is unlikely that smearing our lives with advancing technologies will kill us, but there is little doubt that it will change the way we look and the way we look at each other, and we may well find it changes us in ways that are unhealthy.

As trenchant as these seven observations listed above are, one of the problems with even the broad societal portraits of adolescent culture is that they are given to change. Because culture is so all-encompassing, it is difficult to see or foresee these changes.[77] Trying to make observations about the broad societal landscape is like trying to mark the precise moment of the day that "it got dark." Even if we were to agree that the decisive moment of darkness occurred at sunset, we would

---

[74] Ibid., 245.

[75] Barna, *Real Teens*, 35.

[76] Sweet, *Soul Tsunami*, 34.

[77] Rapid cultural change—even in the broad societal landscape—can make any book out of date. In *Millennials Rising*, published about youth culture in September 2000, Strauss and Howe offer a table comparing and contrasting the childhood cultural environments for the Boomer Generation (1945–1965), the Xer Generation (1965–1985), and the Millennial Generation (1985–present). In the category of "Confrontations Abroad," their description for the Millennial Generation reads, "the wars . . . Iraq to Kosovo." Of course, the terrorist attacks of September 11, 2001, and the subsequent U.S.-fought wars, have made dramatic changes throughout our cultural environment.

Table 8-3.
Teenage Usage of Internet, 1998–2000

Internet Application	Percentage Using in 1998	Percentage Using in 2000	Percentage Change
Find information	93%	93%	–
Check out new music or videos	56%	64%	+14%
Participate in chat rooms	51%	46%	-10%
Maintain existing relationships	28%	42%	+50%
Play video games	33%	38%	+15%
Make new friends	34%	35%	+3%
Buy products	7%	29%	+314%
Find spiritual or religious experiences	4%	12%	+200%

Adapted from George Barna, *Real Teens: A Contemporary Snapshot of Youth Culture* (Ventura, Calif.: Regal Books, 2001), 35.

still have to contend with the fact that the hour of sunset in one location is "an hour more of daylight" in another location and "an hour past darkness" in yet another, and in still another location it is a new morning altogether. Mark Twain's comments about piloting a riverboat are equally true of youth pastors who want to keep up with cultural change: "Two things seemed pretty apparent to me. One was, that in order to be a pilot a man had got to learn more than any one ought to be allowed to know; and the other was, that he must learn it all over again in a different way every twenty-four hours."[78]

Wade in the Water

Youth workers cannot avoid culture any more than those who fish can avoid water. It is where students live. Thomas P. "Tip" O'Neill, the Democratic representative from Massachusetts and powerful Speaker of the House during the late 1970s and 1980s, supposedly based his entire political life on a simple principle: "All politics is local." In other words, even the big questions get played out on the small stage of individual lives, in the small local theater of family, workplace, neighborhood, and school. So it is in youth ministry. Biblically speaking, grand theological concepts are shaped in part by just those kinds of real-life cultural realities, youth groups, campuses, families, and individual lives. Eugene Peterson, drawing on his study in the Book of Jonah, observes:

> Jonah yoked the polarities: geography and eschatology.[79] Either without its biblical partner falsifies the pastoral vocation. Both are necessary—equally yoked.

[78] Willimon, *Pastor*, 280.

[79] *Eschatology*: literally "the study of last things," it includes big ideas like heaven and hell, the kingdom of God and the kingdom of humanity, and what God's long-term intentions are for this planet on which we live.

Geography without eschatology becomes mere religious landscaping, growing a few flowers, mowing the lawn, pulling out crabgrass, making life as comfortable as possible under the circumstances. It takes considerable delight in what is there, but only in what is there.

Eschatology without geography degenerates into religious science fiction . . .[80]

Peterson continued:

Pastoral work is local: Nineveh. The difficulty in carrying it out is that we have a universal gospel but are distressingly limited by time and space . . .

When Jonah began his proper work, he went a day's journey into Nineveh. He didn't stand at the edge and preach at them; he entered into the midst of their living — heard what they were saying, smelled the cooking, picked up the colloquialisms, lived "on the economy," not aloof from it, not superior to it (emphasis added).[81]

Let us travel then, in the next chapter, "a day's journey into Nineveh" to see what we might hear, see, and smell.

---

[80] Eugene Peterson, *Under the Unpredictable Plant* (Grand Rapids, Mich.: Eerdmans, 1992), 148.
[81] Ibid., 129.

Thinking Theologically About Culture

By Dean Borgman

Once upon a time people thought theologically by taking their biblical knowledge to the philosophical library and coming up with an Augustinian, Thomistic, or Calvinistic type of theology. Their theological questions came from the philosophers, and it was in terms of philosophy that they wrestled with those theological questions, and expressed answers to those questions. It could almost be expressed in terms of a formula: *theology = Bible + philosophy*.

All that has changed—or should have. In fact, too many are still doing medieval theology. For theology to be relevant, we need biblical principles and current information from the social sciences. Keep in mind what theology is. Theology is a translation of the eternal Word of God in any contemporary cultural scene. Culture sets the stage, or the context, and asks the questions. Accepting God's divine revelation, in nature and people generally, and in the Bible and Jesus Christ more specifically, we enter culture. It takes a thorough knowledge of the Word and collaboration within the body of Christ to come up with answers. We are humbled by two facts: much of divine truth is mystery (Deut. 29:29), and many of today's questions are so complicated as to deny black and white, or absolute, answers. Theology, then, is an attempt to deal with the human situation from God's perspective.

Next, we must be clear about culture. So pervasively does culture surround us, it often goes unnoticed. Culture is everything between the physical universe and the spiritual world. No one can become, or be, human without it—as babies raised by animals have proven. Culture is everything we have ever learned, from eating, walking, and talking to computer skills. It is everything human beings have ever invented, developed, or conceived. It is our social life-breath. It influences us through family, community, schools, the media, peers, church, and more.

If you want to be even more effective in long-term youth ministry than you are, it is important for you to consider theologically who you are and who the distinct group of young people you serve is. As has often been said, every Christian is a theologian. Just as you must think culturally, you are called as a follower of Jesus to think theologically— from a distinctly divine perspective. Whether it is easy for you to admit it or not, your cultural heritage and identity affects you in many conscious and subconscious ways. You react according to whether you are upper-, middle-, or lower-class in socioeconomic terms. Your thinking is influenced by being black or white, Euro-American, African American, Asian American, Native American, Hispanic, or whatever. Each culture treats gender differently, but even your perspective as a woman or man is part of who you are and how you think theologically. You are probably also culturally influenced by your generation. Whether you accept the labels or not, and whether you go along with or react to current styles, you may be approaching life and youth ministry in terms of responses more like Generation X or the Millennials.

Good theology needs three kinds of exegesis or efforts at interpretation. Followers of Jesus, in our complex and rapidly changing culture, must exegete or interpret (1) themselves, (2) their culture, and (3) the Scriptures. Know yourself, understand what is happening in society, and take that to your interpretation and application of the Word of God.

To think theologically about culture, then, will take you to the mall as well as to the library. You will not only study the Bible, you will turn on the TV. Along with sermons, you will take in some good movies. If you have given attention to your cultural identity and how growing up these days has affected us all, you will perceive how easy it is for you to compartmentalize your spiritual and cultural intake. Your TV, movie, and music compartments may not reflect your theological, church, or Jesus compartments. You will appreciate the fact that you must exert real effort to integrate your cultural and spiritual thinking.

You will find help in significant books by Walt Mueller (*Understanding Youth Culture*), William Romanowski (*Eyes Wide Open*), Mark Pinsky (*The Gospel According to The Simpsons*), and Robert Johnston (*Reel Spirituality*). My own *When Kumbaya Is Not Enough* may encourage you to think theologically about culture.

When it comes to thinking theologically about youth cultures in specific terms, we are being led first not to the library or even to the mall but to the bedrooms of boys and girls! At least that is what those in the realm of market research are doing, and these are people who work hard to stay in touch with teenagers. Besides being on the streets and hosting critical focus groups of informed insiders, advertisers have found young people most at home, most open, in their newly equipped castles, their bedrooms. There they watch TV, listen to music, do homework, play with the computer, and respond to instant messages all at the same time! More isolated and fragmented than any other generation in history, they live too much in virtual community, staying in touch by means of virtual communication.

Part of your challenge is not only to think theologically about culture yourself, but to help young people do the same. That is what happens when we bring in magazine ads, movies, or television clips and ask our students: "How does this help you understand yourself?" "What issues does this raise?" "What does Jesus think about this, and how does God respond?" and finally, "What kind of people, then, ought we to be?"

What is written here is meant to encourage your theological understanding of today's youth culture. No one has it figured out. You have already realized the challenge this Net Generation poses. You are responding to their need for real community and communication. You believe the human heart always demands affirmation from a supportive group, that your students want and need caring older mentors. You have realized there are positive as well as negative aspects in all their music and entertainment. Now our response to these needs as youth workers is to look carefully, listen thoughtfully, and think theologically about the world in which they live so that we can better communicate to them the love and message of Jesus Christ.

Travel Log: Zimbabwe

Youth Worker Profiles by Paul Borthwick

After Femi Adeleye's conversion at age 13, he started reading biographies of various people who had committed their lives to Christ at a young age. These included people such as Charles Spurgeon, Jonathan Edwards, Charles Finney, and Billy Graham. "Reading about them convinced me that young people were special in the heart of God. I felt challenged to commit my own life to serving God as much as possible while I was young. This desire intensified as I grew older. I wanted to invest a significant part of my life reaching out to young people and mobilizing them for kingdom service."

After years of service in his native Nigeria, Femi and his family moved to Harare, Zimbabwe. "My wife Affy and I are now missionaries with International Fellowship of Evangelical Students (IFES) and provide leadership for IFES ministry to college and university students in 22 English- and Portuguese-speaking countries of sub-Saharan Africa."

Grass-Roots Foundations. "After becoming a Christian at age 13, I began sharing the gospel with my friends and colleagues on campus while still a student. I was also involved in cross-cultural evangelism as a student under the auspices of the Nigeria Fellowship of Evangelical Students (NIFES), leading teams of students on mission trips to rural communities in Northern [Muslim] Nigeria. With other students, we soon began crossing borders to do evangelistic outreaches in Niger and Guinea Republics. From Zaria, and later Kano where I studied, we also went on preaching stations to various high schools to challenge students to Christ."

Motivated to Endure. Femi and Affy's vision is for new Christian leadership for Africa, where more than 50 percent of the population is under age 20. "We desire to challenge students to integrate faith with life on campus and in the public arena in such a way that they can be change agents. Our strongest desire is to use campus groups and national student movements as a catalyst for building a new generation of leaders for Africa, a continent that suffers too often from inept leadership in government and the public."

Eyes on the Future of His Students. "My dream is to see them rise up to fulfill God's purpose for them in their generation, to see them emerge as a new generation of credible leaders for the continent of Africa."

chapter nine

READING THE WATER: SCOUTING THE RIVER

One of the ongoing charms of whitewater sport is the way a river, even the same stretch of river, is always changing, always different, always new.
—**Lito Tejada-Flores**[1]

In considering a Christian worldview, however, we must keep in mind that a Christian does not and cannot think in a closet, uninfluenced by other than biblical input alone. The Bible, after all, is not an exhaustive revelation about everything we might need to consider: there is simply not a decisive text for each issue we face today or in any other age. Yet, we must learn to think biblically about the contributions of philosophy and psychology and art, and about values to pursue in the political and economic arenas. This means drawing on the overall framework of belief and moral principles which the biblical writers brought to a multitude of different situations in different cultural and historical settings.
—**Arthur F. Holmes**[2]

Then I saw in my Dream, that when they were got out of the Wilderness, they presently saw a Town before them, and the name of that town is Vanity; and at the Town there is a Fair kept, called Vanity Fair: It is kept all the year long; it beareth the name of Vanity Fair, because the Town where 'tis kept is lighter than Vanity; and also because all that is there sold, or that cometh thither, is Vanity. As is the saying of the wise, "All that cometh is Vanity."
    . . . Now, as I said, the way to the Celestial City lies just through this Town where this lusty Fair is kept; and he that will go to this City, and yet not go through this Town, must needs go out of the world . . . This Fair, therefore, is an ancient thing, of long standing, and a very great Fair.
—**John Bunyan**[3]

---

[1] Lito Tejada-Flores, *Wildwater: The Sierra Club Guide to Kayaking and Whitewater Rafting* (San Francisco, Calif.: Sierra Club Books, 1978), 146.

[2] Arthur F. Holmes, "Toward a Christian View of Things," in *The Making of a Christian Mind*, ed. Arthur F. Holmes (Downers Grove, Ill.: InterVarsity Press, 1985), 13–14.

[3] John Bunyan, *Pilgrim's Progress* (New York: Dutton, 1910), 89–90.

In his book, *Wildwater*, whitewater rafting instructor Lito Tejada-Flores writes, "Reading the water is an art, and like any art it takes time to master. Experience and patient observation will teach you far more than [can be outlined] in a few pages. But there are some general patterns that can help you make sense out of your first experiences."[4]

Our challenge in taking the message of Christ and him crucified to teenagers is discerning the general patterns we can observe that will help us to read the waters of adolescent culture. Tejada-Flores offers a simple strategy for rafters who want to chart a course through bumpy waters. It consists of three important steps:

1. Watch the surface movement. "You should become sensitive to the movement of the surface water all around you. This is easy to see and can tell you a lot about the currents beneath . . . "[5]

2. Focus on the river, but not on the rapids. Looking at the surface water will give some general impressions that are helpful. But the key to good navigation is looking "more carefully at the surface of the river ahead of you to spot evidence of submerged rocks."[6]

3. Everything looks different from the bank of the river. "The river is always the best teacher. And for most of us, most of the time, playing in whitewater is the best and most enjoyable way to tune in to all it can teach us."[7]

In this chapter, we are going to use this same three-step approach to scout the waters of adolescent culture.

Part I: Watch the Surface Movement

There are usually a lot of lines, ripples, mini-waves, wind ruffles, and so forth on the surface; a river is far from the undifferentiated mass of flowing water. Look for the tiny line of bubbles and swirls . . . Look for patches of moving surface water—a kind of river within the river—that will tell you where some current is flowing through the pool.[8]

There are numerous approaches to exploring the rapids and waves of youth culture. Each of them gives us different ways of being "sensitive to the movement of surface water all around . . ."

---

[4] Tejada-Flores, *Wildwater*, 146.

[5] Ibid., 155.

[6] Ibid.

[7] Ibid., 182.

[8] Ibid., 155.

Looking Through the Lens of Popular Culture

Probably the most common way of attempting to gain insight into youth culture is by surveying the various elements of electronic and print media.[9] Taking time to reflect on popular culture can provide clues about adolescent "maps of meaning."[10] Dean Borgman observes that "pop art must be understood from a psychological and social perspective" because if we look and listen carefully, we will hear in these various forms of media:

▶ Clues to adolescent rites of passage: What in adolescent culture are the markers of maturity, adulthood, or autonomy?

▶ Ideas about religion: What are their notions about God and spirituality?

▶ Descriptions of their idols: Who are their heroes, their role models, their fantasy love objects?

▶ Portraits of tribal affiliation: How does a teenager identify herself as a member of a certain group or subculture, and what is the glue that holds that group together?

▶ Their patterns of escape: How do they numb down, run away, or drown out their pains and fears?

▶ Interesting forms of social elixir: How do movies and songs move kids to aspire, create, come together?

▶ Teenagers' statements of self-definition, protest, or plea: What are these electronic stories telling us about teenagers that we have not taken the time to hear *them* tell us?

▶ Expressions of protest and proclamation about justice and injustice, right and wrong, good and evil: What are some of the notions that trace adolescents' collective ideas of what the world should look like?

▶ Assumptions about what teenagers consider to be fun and funny.[11]

[9] Some very helpful resources to consider in this regard: Walt Mueller, *Understanding Today's Youth Culture* (Wheaton, Ill.: Tyndale, 1994); William Romanowski, *Dancing in the Dark: Youth, Popular Culture and the Electronic Media* (Grand Rapids, Mich.: Eerdmans, 1991); William Romanowski, *Eyes Wide Open: Looking for God in Popular Culture* (Grand Rapids, Mich.: Brazos Press, 2001); Robert K. Johnston, *Reel Spirituality: Theology and Film in Dialogue* (Grand Rapids, Mich.: Baker, 2000); and Reynolds Ekstrom, *Access Guide to Pop Culture* (New Rochelle, N.Y.: Salesian Society, 1989).

[10] Tracey Skelton and Gill Valentine, *Cool Places: Geographies of Youth Culture* (London: Rutledge, 1998), 155.

[11] Dean Borgman, *When Kumbayah Is Not Enough* (Peabody, Mass.: Hendrickson, 1997), 128. Charles Arn makes the point that understanding these pop culture stories is a critical facet of evangelism: "There are four stages to postmodern storytelling and evangelism: (1) reckoning, (2) drafting, (3) piloting, and (4) sailing. In the reckoning phase there is listening, observing, learning, identifying, and interpreting the stories that are already being told. What stories are important to your audience? Perhaps even use interviews and questionnaires to find what issues they take seriously. In the drafting stage, one puts forward some biblical stories that connect with their own context and models stories that match with their experience. Get people to respond to a variety of approaches. In the piloting phase, one builds on what one has garnered from the first two stages to implement a storytelling strategy and test its validity and reliability. In the sailing stage, one continues to refine and refocus what one is doing, trusting the Spirit to lead and guide and bring the person home." Charles Arn, "The Growth Report," *Ministry Advantage* (July–Aug 1994), 9, quoted in Leonard Sweet, *Soul Tsunami* (Grand Rapids, Mich.: Zondervan, 1999), 427.

Anthropologists have long understood the impact that stories have on a culture. Neil Postman, in his provocative work *Amusing Ourselves to Death*,[12] talks about Northrop Frye's concept of resonance. Frye observes, "Through resonance, a particular context acquires a universal significance."[13]

In addressing the question of the source of resonance, Frye concludes that *metaphor is the generative force—that is, the power of a phrase, a book, a character, or a history to unify and invest with meaning a variety of attitudes or experiences* (emphasis added).

In other words, for someone to say, "it's only a story; it's not real" is to miss a vital factor in reading the cultural waters: our stories, our phrases, our characters, and our images create for us a reality. This is precisely the point made by Carl Sandburg:

I meet people occasionally who think motion pictures, the product Hollywood makes, is merely entertainment, has nothing to do with education. That's one of the darndest fool fallacies that is current . . . Anything that brings you to tears by way of drama does something to the deepest roots of our personality. All movies, good or bad, are educational and Hollywood is the foremost educational institution on earth. What, Hollywood more important than Harvard? The answer is not as

Resource and Tools for Staying Current with the Ever-Changing Currents of Culture

Print Periodicals Although phone numbers have been provided for further inquiry, most of these resources have fully functioning Internet sites as well.:

Books and Culture (800-523-7964)
Echoes (804-924-7705)
First Things (800-783-4903)
National Review (815-734-1232)
Rolling Stone (303-604-1465)
Utne Reader (800-736-8863)
Wilson Quarterly (800-829-5108)
Wired (800-769-4733)

Audio Resources:

Mars Hill Tapes (800-331-6407)

Internet Resources:

Books and Culture,
www.christianity.net/B&C
Center for Parent/Youth Understanding,
www.cpyu.org (numerous links at this site)
Center for Youth, www.centerforyouth.org,
www.cys-community.org
Mind Over Media, www.ministrymedia.com
Parentingteenagers.org, www.parenting
teenagers.org
Teenink.com, www.teenink.com
Youth Specialties, www.youthspecialties.com
(Also many helpful links through this site)
Youthworker journal, www.youthworker.com/links

---

[12] Neil Postman, *Amusing Ourselves to Death* (New York: Viking Penguin, 1985), 17.

[13] Northrop Frye, *The Great Code: The Bible and Literature* (Toronto: Academic Press, 1981), 217, cited in Postman, *Amusing Ourselves to Death*, 17.

[14] Originally quoted by Robert G. Konzelman, *Marquee Ministry: The Movie Theater as Church and Community Forum* (New York: Harper and Row, 1971), 13, and cited by Robert K. Johnston, *Reel Spirituality* (Grand Rapids, Mich.: Baker, 2000), 19–20. There will be those from various circles of media influence who would suggest that this is a "chicken and egg" question. They would argue that it is not a question of movies and music *creating* reality as it is a question of movies and music *reflecting* reality. For a very vivid and passionate argument against this position, see Michael Medved, *Hollywood vs. America* (New York: HarperCollins, 1992).

Pop Art Cartography

Reading the maps of meaning is not always so simple. Too often adult criticism of pop art is driven by a dislike of the genre itself: "too loud guitars are the 'devil's harp,'" or "it didn't say anything about God." On the other hand, teenagers too often evaluate pop art on terms that are too shallow: "I liked it because you can dance to it," "The special effects were awesome," and "The babe was really hot." Dean Borgman suggests *three basic criteria for pop culture cartography—characteristics that we can use as youth workers and suggest to our youth and adults as we evaluate the value of pop culture:*

▸ Skill, an unusual ability to convey beauty and truth through a given medium;

▸ Insight, providing unusual reflections on our life condition, its meaning, and the human drama; and

▸ Integrity, a faithful linking together of skill and insight into genuine personal and social experience."

Dean Borgman, When Kumbayah Is Not Enough (Peabody, Mass.: Hendrickson, 1997), 138. Borgman's book has some very helpful material in this area, and it should be considered by anyone who wants to take pop culture and pop artistry seriously.

clean as Harvard, but nevertheless far reaching.[14]

One of the reasons that media has such potency is because of what behavioral psychologists refer to as *social norming*—the theory that adolescent behavior is often shaped by what they perceive to be the normal behavior of their peers.[15] If most teenagers think that their peers are getting high, having sex, or cheating in school, they will be more likely to exhibit those same behaviors. Clearly, this could produce something of a "snowball effect" in a culture. As perceptions are developed, behaviors adjust, and as behaviors adjust, perceptions develop.

Although social norming as a concept has become prominent as a factor in addressing drug and alcohol abuse,[16] obviously it has implications for other realms of adolescent behavior as well. This is akin to what Reynolds Ekstorm calls *mimicry*, "the imitative feature in life, by which persons tend to reproduce in themselves patterns of behavior they have beheld in others."[17] This helps us to understand, for example, why all of the girls in the high school group wear their shirts just short enough to expose the "Brittany Belly," or why all of the "alternative" kids are alternative in precisely the same way.

Sociologist Todd Gitlin puts it this way:

Popular culture is the very oxygen of our collective life. It circulates the mate-

[15] Karen Thomas, "The Kids Are Alright: Social Norming May Be the Way to Keep Them That Way," *USA Today*, May 28, 2002, 1D–2D.

[16] Lydia Gerzel Scott, one of the first counselors to apply this principle to high school students, attempted to create an environment in which she could "norm" a decrease in alcohol abuse. Her program, used in two Dekalb County, Georgia high schools, has seen drinking and smoking drop significantly faster than national health trends. Ibid., 2D.

[17] Ekstrom, *Access Guide to Pop Culture*, 10.

rials with which people splice together identities. It forms the imagescape and soundtrack through which we think and feel about who we are, or—as film critic Robert Warshow put it—who we wish to be and fear we might become.[18]

Any wise youth worker will want to become an observer of the culture because it tells us a great deal about the adolescent river. Its images so vivid, its presence so pervasive, its impact so universal—it simply cannot be ignored.

On the other hand, popular art brings with it this disadvantage: it is constantly changing. Romanowski talks about short-lived cultural phenomena that are "the glue of the month."[19] It is a little like a rafter's guidebook that describes the course by pointing out "the log that has washed up against a rock 40 feet down river from the carcass of the dead fish along the shoreline." All of these landmarks are quite vivid—until the next high water comes along. Then the guidebook has to be rewritten. Which is why sometimes we gain more by looking at the broad features of the cultural landscapes than the ones flickering across the screen of pop culture.

Let's Rescue Gilligan and the Skipper!

Sherwood Schwartz wrote and produced a number of popular television series, including *Gilligan's Island*, a comedy originated in the 1960s in which a zany group of castaways manages to survive not only a shipwreck but each other. In 1964, after six or seven episodes of *Gilligan's Island* had aired, Schwartz received a visit from a Commander Doyle of the U.S. Coast Guard. Commander Doyle presented Schwartz with a batch of telegrams, some addressed to Hickam Field in Honolulu, some to Vandenberg Air Force Base in central California, some to other military bases.

While the wording of the telegrams varied, they all in substance said the same thing: "For several weeks now, we have seen Americans stranded on some Pacific island. We spend millions in foreign aid. Why not send one destroyer to rescue those poor people before they starve to death?" The telegrams were not jokes. They came from concerned citizens.

Schwartz commented on this "most extreme case of suspension of belief I ever heard of. Who did these viewers think was filming the castaways on that island? There was even a laugh track on the show. Who was laughing at the survivors of the *S.S. Minnow*? It boggled my mind!"

Sherwood Schwartz, "Send Help Before It's Too Late," cited by Reynolds Ekstrom, Access Guide to Pop Culture (New Rochelle, N.Y.: Salesian Society, 1989), 32.

[18] Sociologist Todd Gitlin, quoted in Romanowski, *Eyes Wide Open*, 61.
[19] Ibid.

The Ear Persuades the Eye and Shades the Mind

Just how much could an image or a vivid phrase really reshape our perceptions of reality? We already have some sense of this, drawing from the simple fact that eyewitnesses to the same event often report conflicting testimony of what actually happened. University of Washington psychologists Elizabeth Loftus and John Palmer conducted a series of experiments demonstrating that our current perceptions are shaped by past impressions.

Loftus and Palmer showed people a film of a traffic accident and then proceeded to ask the audience-subjects questions about what they had seen. The audience was divided into two groups, each of whom was asked about the movie using a slight variation of the same question. One group was asked, "How fast were the cars going when they smashed into each other?" The other group was asked, "How fast were the cars going when they hit each other?" Which group do you suppose reported the higher impact speed?

Those in the group asked the first question, using the word "smashed" gave consistently higher estimates of the impact speed than those in the group asked the question using the word "hit." In fact, one week later, when the subjects in both groups were asked whether they recalled seeing any broken glass, they found the same effect. Even though there was no broken glass in the accident, those who were asked the question using the word "smashed" were more than twice as likely to report broken glass than those who were asked the question using the word "hit."

If one word, changed in this way, can so affect our perceptions of reality, how much could our perception of reality be shaped by an entire song full of words? Or, an entire song full of words coupled with a video? Or a vivid film? How does the phrase "make love" affect teenagers' perceptions about sexual intercourse? How do the typical media caricatures of Christians, using in some combination the four "B's" (bumbling, backward, bigoted, buffoons) color teenagers' perceptions about Christianity?

Source: David Myers, The Human Connection *(Downers Grove, Ill.: InterVarsity Press).*

Global Weirding: Climate Changes That Affect the Culture

These sights and sounds of pop culture, as intriguing as they are, are merely atmospheric signs pointing to significant climate changes in the way western culture defines itself. In his excellent book *Deliver Us from Evil*, Ravi Zacharias comments:

> The greatest scrutiny must be paid to how and why we make our individual and societal decisions . . . When those reasons are examined, they often prove to be unblushingly spurious and would result in chaos if everyone operated by the same principles. The implications of our choices carry over into what we call *lifestyles*. Individually they may seem to be insignificant, but when the mindset of a whole culture is altered in accordance with those choices, the ramifications are staggering.[20]

In an effort to understand youth culture, we need to give thought to some of the climate changes that have made adolescent culture so stormy. Zacharias suggests three: secularism, pluralism, and privatism.

Secularism

Secularism is a worldview that assumes that this world—the material world—is all there is. Any romantic notions about a reality beyond that can be accessed through our five senses may be a pleasant illusion, but it simply is not true.[21] The process by which this worldview takes root

What people learn best is not what their teachers think they teach, or what their preachers think they preach, but what their cultures in fact cultivate.
—**George Gerbner**

Scottish patriot Andrew Fletcher once said that if he were permitted to write all the ballads, he did not care who makes the laws of a nation. Ballads, songs, tales, gestures, and images make up the unique design of the human environment.
—**"Viewer's Declaration of Independence," Founding Convention of the Cultural Environment Movement, St. Louis, Missouri, USA, 17 March 1996**

---

[20] Ravi Zacharias, *Deliver Us from Evil: Restoring the Soul in a Disintegrating Culture* (Waco, Texas: Word Books, 1996), 17. Part of the material that follows is drawn from this book.

[21] Ibid., 23. These poignant lines from James Taylor's "Up from Your Life" (*Hourglass*, CD recording, Sony Music, 1997) capture the thought and the despair in secularism:

So much for your moment of prayer,
God's not at home, there is no there there
Lost in the stars, That's what you are
Left here on your own
You can only hope to live on this earth
This here is it, for all it's worth
Nothing else awaits you, no second birth
No starry crown . . .

Norming

The language we use as youth workers, the films we talk about, the examples we offer in speech and in our behavior all suggest something to our students about what is *normal*—and not just *normal for anybody*, but *normal for Christians*: Christians they admire, Christians they would like to emulate. This new research about how *norming* can have positive impacts on negative behaviors (that is, if college students realize that, in fact, most of their friends are not getting totally wasted over the weekend, they will themselves decide not to get totally wasted) also suggests something about negative impacts on negative behaviors. One wonders how many teenagers are now sexually active because they have heard the prophets of Planned Parenthood lament the fact that "all these kids are sexually active,"[1] and have therefore assumed that they were in the oddball minority who were chaste. As others have commented, this is, no doubt, one reason for the coarsening of behavior that is so obvious on the broader cultural landscape (increase of profanity, violent behavior, loss of civility, road rage, air rage, Brittany Spears rage). This is a sobering concept for those of us in youth ministry because it makes a powerful statement about the power of our own example. But coupled with this sobering thought is the hopeful statement it makes about the potential impact of positive stories, positive examples, positive mimicry, positive norming.

[1] Of course, when the prophets of Planned Parenthood sound the alarm about rising rates of teenage sexual activity, there are increased donations to organizations who claim to help prevent teen pregnancy. Which, intriguingly, increases the donations to . . . Planned Parenthood. An interesting coincidence. For more on this, see George Grant, *The Grand Illusion: The Legacy of Planned Parenthood* (Brentwood, Tenn.: Wolgemuth & Hyatt, 1989).

in the consciousness and public policy of a culture is called *secularization*. Secularization might be manifest in a number of ways. But essentially it is marked by the removal of sectors of society and culture from the domination of religious institutions and symbols. It is defined by Os Guiness as "the process by which religious ideas, institutions, and interpretations [lose] their significance."[22]

For example, in July 2002, a panel of the U.S. Court of Appeals ruled in a 2–1 decision that the words "under God," when recited in the Pledge of Allegiance to the U.S. flag, were unconstitutional and amounted to breach of the Constitution's First Amendment guarantee of separation between church and state. While the decision was quickly reversed by a larger court panel, the ultimate legality of the two words in the pledge remains in question and is destined for a Supreme Court ruling. The initial decision itself, however, is indicative of a secularist pattern in American culture that includes previous court rulings banning

[22] Zacharias, *Deliver Us from Evil*, 24.

prayer at school graduations or even student-led invocations at public high school football games.[23]

It is a trend observed with wry humor by William Simon in the following verse:

Now I sit me down in school, where praying is against the rule;

For this great nation under God, finds public mention of Him odd;

Any prayer a class recites now violates the Bill of Rights;

The law is specific, the law is precise, praying aloud is no longer nice;

Praying aloud in a public hall upsets believers in nothing-at-all;

In silence alone we can meditate, and if God should be reached, well that's just great;

This rule, however, has one gimmick in it, you'll have to be finished in under a minute;

So all I'll ask is a minute of quiet, and if I feel like praying then maybe I'll try it;

If not, O Lord, this plea I make: Should I be knifed in school, my soul you'll take.[24]

Without commenting on all of the legal questions surrounding these issues, it is quite clear that the implications of this seismic shift are significant. Perhaps the best way to explain those implications is to go back to a philosophical notion among the ancient Greek Sophists that "Man is the measure of all things."[25] It was a worldview that proclaimed individuals free from responsibility to any transcendent moral authority for their actions and choices.

It marked a significant shift, because even among a majority of nonreligious peoples there had been a presupposition of Aristotelian teaching that offered three principal reasons for knowledge: Truth, Morality, and Technique, *in that order*.[26] Now with the deterioration of any transcendent notion of Truth, there would be no basis for Morality, and the only remaining rationale for knowledge was Technique. In other words, with *Who?* or *What?* off the table, *Why?* becomes a matter of personal opinion. The only real question of import then becomes simply *How?*[27]

---

[23] Howard Fineman, "One Nation Under Who?" *Newsweek* (July 8, 2002): 23–24. In a court ruling regarding the possible mention of the name of Jesus in a prayer offered at a high school graduation, Judge Samuel B. Kent of the U.S. District Court for the Southern District of Texas ruled that any student mentioning the name of Jesus would be sentenced to a six-month jail term. The following excerpt is taken directly from court papers dated May 5, 1995, in which Judge Kent issued the following warning: "And make no mistake, the court is going to have a United States marshal in attendance at the graduation. If any student offends this court, that student will be summarily arrested and will face up to six months incarceration in the Galveston County Jail for contempt of court. Anyone who thinks I'm kidding about this order . . . [or] expressing any weakness or lack of resolve in that spirit of compromise had better think again. Anyone who violates these orders, no kidding, is going to wish that he or she had died as a child when this court gets through with it." Cited in Josh McDowell, *The New Tolerance* (Wheaton, Ill.: Tyndale, 1998), 53.

[24] William Simon, "The Missing Issue," *National Review* (March 15, 1993), 21.

[25] Zacharias, *Deliver Us from Evil*, 37–38.

[26] The Greek philosopher Aristotle taught that there were three principal reasons for knowledge. The first is Truth: we gain knowledge so that we might learn truth. The second is Morality: we gain knowledge so that we might know how to live better lives. The third is Technique (or technology): we gain knowledge so that we might know better how to live. Kreeft comments, "The modern world has simply turned this hierarchy exactly upside down, as it has turned man upside down." Peter Kreeft, *C. S. Lewis for the Third Millennium* (San Francisco: Ignatius Press, 1994), 22.

[27] Here is an experiment: Just to show how saturated our culture has become with this enthronement of Technique over Truth, listen to comments students make after a Bible study or sermon. Nine times out of ten, the evaluation will be on the basis of entertainment value (Technique): "It was funny"; "It was boring"; "The hand puppets scared me." Seldom will there be any evaluation based on the lesson itself (Truth): "I didn't agree"; "I think he overstated the case"; "I thought she made too big a leap from what the Bible says to how she felt it should be applied."

William Romanowski points out at least five ways that popular art plays a role in our cultural self-definition. As you read through this list, think back to movies, videos, or songs that have served these purposes for you:

1. "The popular arts can enlighten us in the sense that they furnish knowledge and offer insight into our lives and culture." Sometimes they make us laugh at ourselves; sometimes they make us ashamed, but they often show us something about ourselves that we might not have otherwise seen.

2. They provide a means of cultural communication. "They are one way that we convey and examine cultural ideals, beliefs, values, and assumptions."

3. They provide social and cultural criticism.

4. The popular arts provide us with a kind of social unity. Mass media, because it is *mass* media, has the capacity to bring together a population of widely diverse ethnic, racial, and religious peoples. Total strangers hug each other in the sports bar when the home team scores. The devout Muslim, the New England WASP, and the new age Californian all laugh at the same *Friends* episodes and cry at the same scene when *E.T.* finally goes home.

5. The popular arts provide for us a collective memory. Like the petroglyphic drawings of cavemen, the popular arts provide for us electronic sketches on the digital walls of our collective experience. They document for us where we have been, what we have been through, what we've faced and conquered together.

William Romanowski, Eyes Wide Open: Looking for God in Popular Culture *(Grand Rapids, Mich.: Brazos Press, 2001), 59-63.*

Purpose and performance had to be tied together. But purpose had been lost, and technique and pleasure had replaced truth and morality... Under the debris of the pillars and the stones is not just the story of a civilization destroyed by internecine wars but of a people who would not acknowledge the wretchedness and evil pent up within the human heart and the absolute necessity that man find a measure outside himself.[28]

When Technique overshadows Truth and Morality, the greatest loss is one of context. Context is everything. For example, if I look closely at a map of South Dakota but have no sense of context—that is, I cannot recognize any key city that can help me orient myself—it will be easy for me to get lost. I cannot know where to go if I do not know where I am. Even if I am an excellent map reader (Technique), I can still be massively confused by a lack of context (Truth). Unfortunately, Technique without Truth is now the norm of culture, and we do not seem to understand the consequences of being in such a state. Interestingly, as Richard Corliss observes, MTV "is all about the death

---

[28] Zacharias, *Deliver Us from Evil,* 39. Reynolds Ekstrom reminds us of Jacques Ellul's concept of the Technique described in his book *Propaganda* (New York: Knopf, 1965): "*The Technique* is not a particular propagandist with a point of view. It is a method of solving problems, and thus is completely amoral. It only asks how best to get this done, how to solve this particular problem at this time. *It does not ask what is true, or what is just or what is right* (emphasis added)." Ekstrom, *Access Guide to Pop Culture,* 34.

of context. It is the shotgun annulment of character from narrative, the anaesthetizing of violence through chic, the erasing of the past and the triumph of the new."[29]

The most serious fallout of such a position is that, on such terms, any choice, any decision, can be defended as the *right* choice. If there is no transcendent compass, then any trail in any direction is the right way to go. One's *commitment* to a belief is the only rationale necessary to validate the belief. But if that is the case, then where are the limits to human evil? All moral choices are reduced to simple pragmatism—if "it works for me," it must be right.[30] Unfortunately, the bankruptcy of secularism has left our cultural landscape littered with ruined lives, broken families, scarred hearts, horrible violence, and brash selfishness. As the profound social prophet Malcolm Muggeridge put it, "the great moral fallacy of our time [is] that collective virtue may be pursued without reference to personal behavior."[31]

Reynolds Ekstrom suggests that adults in general, and youth workers in particular, should:

▸ Pay attention to what youths pay attention to;

▸ Educate young people (make them aware) about messages and values in their rock songs and rock art;

▸ Help parents and other interested adults to watch and listen to the world of music (songs, videos, concerts, radio, MTV) with youth, dialoguing with them about the empty search and desperate pursuit of the American "good life";

▸ Read more and become generally more aware of the music industry and all pop culture entertainment;

▸ Enable youth to recognize who profits, who pays, and who gets cut out of financial help whenever we consume without Christian limits and responsibility; and

▸ Help them engage in discerning and living out gospel values, rather than accepting the passive, materialistic, illiterate life urged on us by electronic media.

Reynolds Ekstrom, Access Guide to Pop Culture *(New Rochelle, N.Y.: Salesian Society, 1989, 51.*

In a recent conversation with a group of Christian teenagers, one girl mentioned that she had just been to a concert by one of the hottest pop female vocalists of the moment. I commented that a friend of mine had gone to the same concert with her young preteen daughter, but they had to leave the concert out of disgust with the blatant (actually, "crude" is the way she put it) sexual dancing and

---

[29] Richard Corliss, "The Medium Is the Message," *Film Comment* (July–August, 1983): 34, cited in Romanowski, *Dancing in the Dark*, 207.

[30] We see this played out, for example, in the realm of sexual ethics where the rationale for discretion is not morality, but safety. Because teenagers cannot be told what is *right* to do, the ethics of sexual behavior are based on what is *safe* to do. See Zacharias, *Deliver Us from Evil*, 58.

[31] Thomas Reeves, *The Empty Church* (New York: Free Press, 1996), 74. For other work related to the moral decline of culture, see also James Davison Hunter's *The Death of Character: Moral Education in an Age Without Good or Evil* (New York: Basic Books, 2000), 15ff; and William J. Bennett's *Devaluing of America: The Fight for Our Culture and Our Children* (New York: Summit Books, 1992).

We have moved away from the historic experience of mankind. Children used to grow up in a home where parents told most of the stories. Today television tells most of the stories to most of the people most of the time.
—**George Gerbner**

monologue from the stage. The teenage girl who had been to the concert was shocked. "Oh, I thought she did a great job! It was a really amazing show!" Sounding like an aging prude, I said, "I'm not saying it wasn't a good show. I'm just curious if you think Jesus would have been pleased had he been there in the audience." At which point, a gallant young lad defended the befuddled damsel by saying, "Sure! I'm sure that Jesus would have thought, 'If she's comfortable with her body, and everybody's having fun, then that's just fine.'"

Two thoughts came to me as I reflected on the conversation. First, the girl's evaluation of the show was solely based on technique. The truth of the message—or, for that matter, the message itself—never came into question. Secondly, the noble young man stepping in to the rescue clearly articulated a morality that is rampant in an increasingly secularized church: "If I feel okay about it, it must be fine with Jesus." Welcome to secularism in everyday life.

Pluralism

The natural outgrowth of a secularism that says "there is no such thing as Truth" is a pluralism that says, "there is no such thing as false." As G. K. Chesterton put it, "the trouble with someone who does not believe in God is not that he will end up believing in nothing; it is that he will end up believing in anything."[32] When secularism turns a culture from God, that does not mean we will believe in nothing; that means we will believe in everything. Pluralism is "the existence and availability of a number of worldviews, each vying for the allegiance of individuals, with no single worldview dominant."[33] After all, if all truth is created by humans, and all humans are created equal; then doesn't it make sense that all viewpoints are equally true?[34]

[32] Richard John Neuhaus, "While We're at It," *First Things* (June–July 1995): 58–76.

[33] Zacharias, *Deliver Us from Evil*, 70–71.

[34] This new definition of tolerance has even now been codified by the American legal system. Judge Daniel Boggs, of the U.S. Circuit Court of Appeals for the Sixth Circuit, argued in a ruling regarding homosexual marriages that not only do "adherents of all faiths deserve equal rights as citizens, '*all faiths are equally valid as religions.*' Stephen Bates, "Religious Diversity and the Schools," *American Enterprise* 4, no. 5 (Sept/Oct, 1993): 18, cited in McDowell, *The New Tolerance*, 19.

Table 9-1.
Have You Heard These Phrases?

Phrase	I've Heard People Use the Phrase	I've Heard the Phrase in the Last Two Weeks	What Was the Context? The Issue Being Discussed?
"It's not right for us to force our morality on someone else."			
"Who are we to say that someone else is doing something sinful?"			
"We do not have the right to judge other people."			
"It's not for us to say that somebody else is involved in sin"			
"We need to be careful about being judgmental."			
"I don't think we have the right to condemn other people."			
"The Bible says not to judge."			
"We need to be tolerant of people who do not share the same values we do."			
"None of us really has the right to question someone else's moral choices; it's a personal decision."			
"It's not right for us to say someone else is wrong. Christians get a bad name because they lack tolerance."			

Read through the chart in Table 9-1 and try to track the last time you heard each of the phrases listed.

Much of the time, when we hear one of the well-worn phrases in Table 9-1, we are tasting the fruit of a pluralistic culture. Its basic premise is that "we can tolerate everything but intolerance." Alan Wolfe's account of the moral outlook of the American suburban middle-class in his book *One Nation, After All*, provides an apt depiction of the degree to which many people have now gravitated toward what is often referred to in the media as the "sensible center." As Wolfe puts it, "Middle-class Americans have added an Eleventh Commandment: . . . 'Thou Shalt Not Judge.'"[35]

[35] Alan Wolfe, *One Nation, After All* (New York: Putnam Penguin Books, 1998), 54. Wolfe's findings are based on 60- to 90-minute interviews with a relatively small sample (rather than a series of short-answer questions posed to a large sample). But in general he seems scrupulously cautious in his conclusions, and he went out of his way to include places in the South and West that might not be as predictably liberal-minded as the Northeast.

George Hunter talks about symbols recognized around the world: "Just a few years ago, a London marketing firm asked seven thousand people in Australia, Germany, India, Japan, Great Britain, and the United States to identify nine well-known symbols, among them were the cross, the Olympic rings, and the logos of Shell Oil and McDonald's. Guess which one was recognized by the most people? Ninety-two percent of those surveyed recognized the Olympic rings. The company logos of Shell and McDonald's were recognized by 88 percent. The cross was recognized by 54 percent.

"One of the results of the death of Christendom is that a large segment of our population is 'ignostic.'" Hunter distinguishes *ignostics* from both atheists and agnostics. Atheists are people who say they do not believe in God. Agnostics are people who say they are on not sure what they believe. But ignostics are people who have no idea of what we are talking about because they themselves have no Christian memory.

George Hunter, How to Reach Secular People *(Nashville, Tenn.: Abingdon Press, 1995), 41.*

Especially telling is the comment of Barbara Tompkins, the daughter of a Southern Baptist minister, who lives in Tulsa, Oklahoma. When told by Wolfe, in her interview, of another interviewee who disapproved of homosexuality, she countered: "He cannot make a broad statement that that's wrong . . . Why is it wrong for them? I mean, do we all have to have the same color hair?" She goes on to explain, "I think everyone inside has their own persona of God. You don't have to accept anybody's dogma whole. Live with the concept of God as you perceive it."[36]

There are two glaring flaws in this kind of pluralism: (1) All ideas are not created equal, and exercising good judgment is all that stands between human beings and beasts; (2) quite often, people who consider themselves pluralistic can be narrow-minded toward those who disagree with them. Or to put it differently, every opinion is equally valid, *except* for the opinion that every opinion is *not* equally valid (as, for example, Tompkins's comment: "He cannot say that that's wrong.")

In any case, teenagers immersed in this kind of cultural environment are not comfortable with exclusive truth claims, whether they be religious or moral in nature. It is not so much that they would dispute the validity of the claims. They would simply dispute their equal validity for all people. It is not likely the response would be, "It isn't true." More likely, it would be, "That may be true for you, but it's not true for me."[37]

[36] This is an interesting comment because one wonders if Tompkins would have demonstrated the same openness and generosity had she been told of a terrorist interviewed in the neighborhood whose sincere belief was that all Southern Baptists (particularly those from Tulsa) are enemies of Allah, and that his mission was to kidnap them and sell them as slaves to be card dealers and dancers in Las Vegas.

[37] Alan Wolfe reports, "Americans take their religion seriously. But very few of them take it so seriously that they believe that religion should be the sole, or even the most important, guide for establishing rules about how other people should live. And some . . . also would distrust such rules for providing guidelines about how they personally should live." Wolfe, *One Nation, After All,* 55.

Thank God for Hitler?

Dostoyevsky wrote, "If God does not exist, everything is permissible." History shows far more people, both atheists and theists, on Dostoyevsky's side than on Plato's here. For Sartre, "there can be no eternal truth since there is no infinite and perfect consciousness to think it." For Nietzsche, the consequence of the new gospel that "God is dead" is a "transvaluation of all values." Like Milton's Satan, he says, in effect, "Evil, be thou my good." He declares love, compassion, mercy, justice, impartiality, and democracy to be weak and therefore evil; cruelty, ruthlessness, war, competition, and selfishness are good. For from the natural struggle of selfishnesses emerges the strongest, the Superman.

Please do not be horrified, but I am often tempted to thank God for Hitler. For if one big Hitler and one big Holocaust had not scared the hell out of us, we might be living in a worldwide Hitler-Holocaust-Hell right now. God rubbed our face in it—we have seen the pure logical consequences of "the death of God" in the fires of Auschwitz. Yet most of us in the West still have not learned the old and simple lesson (scandalous to modern intellectuals simply because it is simple and old) that "unless the Lord build the house, they labor in vain who build it." No one in our time has ever faced and answered the question: If there is no God, why shouldn't I do as I please if I can get away with it? Because it's not "acceptable," nice, humane, human, democratic, fair, just, community-building, helpful, survival-enhancing, practical, and approved? But suppose I don't want to be "acceptable," nice, humane, human, democratic, fair, just, community-building, helpful, survival-enhancing, practical, or approved?

Taken from Peter Kreeft, C. S. Lewis for the Third Millennium *(San Francisco: Ignatius Press, 1994).*

It needs to be said that pluralism is not, in and of itself, a bad thing. Holmes comments: "Pluralism can be extremely beneficial. Its very presence offsets lop-sided emphases, counters premature dogmatism, encourages self-criticism, aids the improvement of understanding, and provides alternate avenues to explore. It reminds us of our finiteness, our creatureliness, our humanity; without that awareness a worldview could not be Christian at all."[38]

The problem is when pluralism gives birth to relativism; that is too high a price to pay. No matter how open-minded we wish to be, if there is no difference between boat and water, those on board the ship are in trouble.[39] "If the loss of shame was the child of secularization, the loss of reason is the child of pluraliza-tion."[40]

Privatism

"Secularization left society without shame and with no point of reference for decency, and pluralization left society without reason and with no point of refer-ence for rationality. Privatization—born from the union of the other two—has left people without meaning and with no point of reference for life's coherence."[41]

When we wed secularism and pluralism, the first-born child is privatism, the socially required and legally enforced separation of our private lives from our public lives. Wolfe refers to this as *quiet faith*, the belief that if one applies any moral conclusions to the lives of others or to public policy in any way, one is commit-ting an offense of insensitivity and unfairness.[42] Because allowing one's moral or religious beliefs to intrude into the arena of public life might offend or exclude another person with

---

[38] Holmes, "Toward a Christian View of Things," 16.

[39] An example, laughable if it were not so tragic: According to a profile in the *Los Angeles Times* the "mission statement" of the Simi Valley United Church of Christ declares: "For us the Bible is a record of faith journeys to be taken seriously but not always literally . . . Our church seeks to be multicultural, respecting and learning from traditions which differ from our own." Needless to say, the *Times* was duly impressed with the openness of such a "mission statement." But the most positive note in the story was reserved for the news that the church is so "open-minded" that it has an atheist teaching Sunday school. "'Stuart,' says the pastor, the Rev. Bill Greene, 'is a caring, bright, perceptive, inclusive kind of person who has a strong sense of justice . . . Here is this incredibly fine man, with honesty and passion for justice, who is in our church. And that's a bless-ing for us, and for all our kids.'"

And here is a pluralism where boat and water are one, a "mission statement" that skulks away from the embarrassment of "the way, the truth, and the life" and adds the correction that can only come from "traditions which differ from our own." Even if that means affirming atheism. Reported by Neuhaus, "While We're At It," 82.

[40] Ibid., 95. Peter Kreeft notes that C. S. Lewis refutes no less than 20 different moral heresies that grow out of subjective pluralism: subjectivism, emotivism, positivism, cultural relativism, historicism, utilitarianism, instinctualism, hedonism, ego-tism, pragmatism, optimistic humanism, cynicism, pop-psychobabble, moral philistinism, rationalism, Calvinism, secular-ism, pantheism, moralism, and Nietzscheanism. Kreeft then goes on to provide an excellent recap of Lewis's arguments with regard to each of these moral heresies. Very helpful stuff. Kreeft, *C. S. Lewis for the Third Millennium*. For additional thoughts regarding an effective apologetic in a pluralistic culture, I would also recommend Brian McLaren's design for a "new apolo-getic" in *The Church on the Other Side* (Grand Rapids, Mich.: Zondervan, 2000), 78–85.

[41] Ibid., 108.

[42] Social critic Jonah Goldberg uses different terminology—he describes this as cultural libertarianism—but his description is perfectly fitting. "Cultural libertarianism basically says that whatever ideology, religion, cult, belief, creed, fad, hobby, or per-sonal fantasy you like is just fine so long as you don't impose it on anybody else, especially with the government. You want to be a Klingon? Great! Attend the Church of Satan? Hey man, if that does it for ya, go for it. You want to be a 'Buddhist for Jesus'? Sure, mix and match, man; we don't care. Hell, you can even be an observant Jew, a devout Catholic or a faithful Baptist, or a lifelong heroin addict—they're all the same, in the eyes of a cultural libertarian. Just remember: keep it to your-self if you can. Don't claim that being a Lutheran is any better than being a member of the Hale-Bopp cult, and never use the government to advance your view. If you can do that, then—whatever floats your boat." Cited by Neuhaus, "While We're At It," 86–87.

different moral or religious beliefs, the appropriate response is self-censorship.

What it really boils down to is a mandate that issues of ultimate meaning must be relegated to the sphere of private life. At first glance, in fact, it seems fair and objective. But it is a concept hinged on the spurious assumption that people who are dishonorable and immoral in private will somehow be moral and honorable in public. The irony of this mindset is that when these same people turn out also to be dishonest and immoral in the public arena, we respond with outrage. We are indignant that politicians lie and disgrace us. We are livid that corporate CEOs cheat the system and juggle the numbers. Yet our collective opinion is supposedly that personal morality cannot invade the arena of everyday life. It is a reminder of Chesterton's insightful comment: "We laugh at honor, but are shocked when there are thieves in our midst."

The culmination of these three cultural climate changes is producing what some consider to be a completely new paradigm of cultural thought. That new paradigm of cultural thinking is called *postmodernism*.

The Loss of Shame

One of the casualties of secularization is our culture's disdain for shame. Why, after all, should anyone ever feel shame, if there is no right or wrong? But we have underestimated the cost of losing any sense of shame. Zacharias comments:

> Shame is to the moral health of a society what pain is to the body. It is the sense of shame that provides an indicator to the mind. There is a powerful analogy even from the physical world of the materialist. It comes to us from the scanner theory of cancer causation. This theory propounds that an incurable cancer is not ultimately caused by the cancer itself as much as by a detection system that has broken down. According to this hypothesis, healthy cells in the body routinely become cancerous. But built into the body is a system of detection and a mechanism that comes into play to identify the cancerous cells and destroy them before they take over. It is not the cancer but the breakdown of the detection system that proves fatal.
>
> How pitiful is the condition we have reached if we smother that sense of shame that was part of society's scanner system to detect wrongdoing and deal with it. Is it any wonder that our news journals are filled with page after page of incidents that continually shock us and are steadily bleeding decency out of life's mainstream?

Ravi Zacharias, Deliver Us from Evil: Restoring the Soul in a Disintegrating Culture *(Waco, Texas: Word Books, 1996), 64–65.*

Introduction to Postmodernism

C. S. Lewis writes about an experience he had one day while standing in the dark of his toolshed:

> The sun was shining outside and through the crack at the top of the door there came a sunbeam. From where I stood that beam of light, with the specks of dust floating in it, was the most striking thing in the place. Everything else was almost pitch black. I was seeing the beam, not seeing things *by* it.
>
> Then I moved so that the whole beam fell on my eyes. Instantly the whole previous picture vanished. I saw no toolshed, and (above all) no beam. Instead I saw, framed in the irregular cranny at the top of the door, green leaves moving on the branches of a tree outside and beyond that, ninety-odd million miles away, the sun. Looking along the beam, and looking at the beam are very different experiences.
>
> But this is only a simple example of the difference between looking at and looking along. A young man meets a girl. The whole world looks different when he meets her. Her voice reminds him of something he has been trying to remember all his life, and ten minutes' casual chat with her is more precious than all the favors that all other women in the world could grant. He is, as they say, "in love." Now comes a scientist and describes this young man's genes and a recognized biological stimulus. That is the difference between looking *along* and looking *at* . . .
>
> As soon as you have grasped this simple distinction, it raises a question. You get one experience of a thing when you look along it and another when you look at it. Which is the "true" or "valid" experience?[43]

Obviously, as the name suggests, if it does not mean anything else, *postmodernism* is the quest to move beyond modernism. Postmodernity seeks, first of all, to move beyond the notion that *looking at* is somehow more valid than *looking along*. It is an affirmation that could readily be affirmed by any thoughtful orthodox Christian. Lewis himself, although certainly not a postmodernist, rejected modernity's claim to trump all other kinds of knowing simply because it was based on rational, objective knowing (*looking at*). "The people who look *at* things have had it all their own way; the people who look *along* things have simply been browbeaten. It has even come to be taken for granted that the external account of a thing somehow refutes or 'debunks' the account given from inside . . . "[44]

That, Lewis argues, would be as short-sighted as a physiologist who has studied pain—the way various stimuli affect various body chemicals that affect various

---

[43] C. S. Lewis, quoted in *The Business of Heaven: Daily Readings from C. S. Lewis*, ed. Walter Hooper (New York: Harcourt, Brace and Company, 1984), 196-197 (emphasis added).

[44] Lewis, *The Business of Heaven*, 197.

Changing Paradigms: Traditionalism to Modernism to Postmodernism

Various authors have offered ways to understand the changing paradigms from traditionalism (what might be called premodernism) to modernism to postmodernism.

For example, Bob Fryling offers three pictures: (1) "The robed priest represents traditional culture, bound together by the priesthood's divine authority, revealed beliefs, sanctioned customs, absolute rules, accepted rituals, and meaningful holidays." (2) The scientist clad in white lab coat represents modern culture, feeling both skeptical of and superior to traditional culture. Her way of knowing is through tough-minded, objective research and empirical observation: (3) "The rock musician, clad in almost anything, represents the postmodern culture. He, or she, is disappointed with, disillusioned with, and suspicious of both priest and scientist. He, or she, doesn't stand, but rather slouches, gyrates, or dances with uneasy energy."

Ihab Hassan offers a set of antitheses: modernism emphasizes purpose and design, postmodernism emphasizes play and chance; modernism lives by hierarchy, postmodernism nurtures anarchy; modernism seeks the underlying meaning of the universe, postmodernism eschews any metameaning to the universe; modernist art focuses on the art as a self-contained, finished work, postmodernist art focuses more on the performance, the process of art; modernism values selection and boundaries, postmodernism values combinations and interconnections; modernism emphasizes form, postmodernism cultivates antiform.

For those of you for whom this kind of antithetical, philosophical dialectic just makes your head hurt, try this comparison and see if it better fits your intellectual style: Stanley Grenz says that modernism is the original *Star Trek* (think Spock), postmodernism is *Star Trek: The Next Generation*.

Bob Fryling, Being Faithful in This Generation: The Gospel and Student Culture at the End of the 20th Century *(Downers Grove, Ill.: InterVarsity Press, 1995); Ihab Hassan, "The Culture of Postmodernism,"* Theology, Culture and Society, *2 (1985), 123–124; Stanley Grenz,* Primer on Postmodernism *(Grand Rapids, Mich.: Eerdmans, 1996), 88.*

nerve endings—and therefore is convinced he knows all there is to know about pain. In fact, "the word *pain* would have no meaning for him unless he had 'been inside' by actually suffering. If he had never looked *along* the pain, he simply wouldn't know what he was looking at."[45] Or, to put it another way, understanding must be complemented by standing under.

> This case is not likely to occur, because every man has felt pain. But it is perfectly easy to go on all your life giving explanations of religion, love, morality, honor and the like, without ever having been inside any of them. And, if you do that, you are simply playing with counters. You go on explaining a thing without knowing what it is . . . [46]

If we begin with this distinction, *looking at* (modernism) versus *looking along* (postmodernism), we have a good basis for understanding these defining tenets of postmodernism:

1. **Postmodernity rejects the notion of objectivity.** We cannot speak objectively about reality because we all see reality differently. To use Leonard Sweet's phrase, none of us can claim "immaculate perception."[47]

   Let us keep the example of *pain*. We cannot speak objectively about something like pain because all of us are conditioned to think about pain in different ways. The athlete, for example, thinks, "no pain, no gain—pain is good." Others, whose preferred form of physical activity is "pumping biscuits" and "remote control lifting," think, "no pain, no pain; why should I hurt myself?—pain is bad." We think one way about the pain of a doctor's visit: "This is painful, but it's necessary." We think another way about the pain of smashing our thumb with a hammer: "This is painful, and it's not particularly helpful." We think one way about pain when we're young: "It's a growing pain in my legs." We think another way about pain when we're old: "It's a gnawing pain in my knees."

   In fact, not only are we unable to speak objectively about pain itself, we must admit that we are unable to speak objectively even about the experience of pain. What is a minor annoyance to one person is a throbbing menace to another. What is slight cramping to one is a monumental curse to another. What is only a scratch to the tough-guy cowboy is a bullet wound just above the left eye for the rest of us.

   Postmodernism posits that objective knowledge is impossible—and, furthermore, that when we try to objectify knowledge and say, "This is what we know," we are, consciously or unconsciously, using knowledge as a means of oppression.

---

[45] Ibid., 198.
[46] Ibid., 199.
[47] Sweet, *Soul Tsunami*, 28.

2. **Knowledge is uncertain.** If objectivity is an impossibility, then all knowledge is subjective. Postmodernism, therefore, rejects the notion that there is some sort of foundational knowledge, absolute enough and solid enough, to build upon it the assumption of certainty.

3. **All-inclusive systems of explanation are suspect.** Referred to as *metanarratives*, these all-inclusive ways of understanding life—whether historical, scientific or metaphysical (spiritual)—must be based on subjective presuppositions. At best, these big stories are subjective and mistaken attempts to make sense of all of our "little stories" (national histories, everyday occurrences, life stories). At worst, they are oppressive attempts to change the way we think about our little stories by forcing us to see them through the lens of one big story.[48]

4. **Knowledge is not inherently good.** Postmodernists reject as naive the idea that more knowledge is always a good thing. Because science has been so successful in conquering disease, discomfort, and distance, there is an aura of immortality and authority about it. But we have come to see that, unfortunately, the technology that provides us better machines cannot produce better people to run them. The myth of human progress has been overcome by the reality of human history.

5. **Truth is defined by, and for, the community.** Postmodernism rejects the modernist model of the isolated knower in favor of discerning truth through a community-based approach. As individuals, our reasoning is hopelessly tainted by the constructs of our society, telling us what to believe, telling us how to interpret reality, forcing us to embrace predetermined universal metanarratives. Modernism's promise is a reality that can be known through careful objective methodology, and that exists independently of any individual knower. In other words, it is truth whether or not one believes it. But the postmodern answer to "where are we?" is "we are in a reality we have constructed."[49]

Therefore, we can know only by deconstructing the myths and collectively redefining ourselves and our history.

Since there is no objective truth, history may be rewritten according to the needs of a particular group. If history is nothing more than a "network of . . . language games," then any alternative "language game" that advances a particular agenda, that meets "success" in countering institutional power, can pass as legitimate history. "Performance, not truth" is the only criterion. Truth does not have to get in the way.[50]

---

[48] The comments of neo-Marxist Terry Eagleton underscore this point: "Post-modernism signals the death of such 'metanarratives' whose secretly terroristic function was to ground and legitimate the illusion of a 'universal' human history. We are now in the process of wakening from the nightmare of modernity, with its manipulative reason and fetish of the totality, into the laid back pluralism of the post-modern, the heterogeneous range of lifestyles and language games which has renounced the nostalgic urge to totalize and legitimate itself . . . Science and philosophy must jettison their grandiose metaphysical claims and view themselves more modestly as just another set of narratives." David Harvey, *Condition of Postmodernity* (Cambridge, Mass.: Basil Blackwell, 1989), 9, cited in Kreeft, *C. S. Lewis for the Third Millennium*, 49.

[49] J. Richard Middleton and Brian J. Walsh, *Truth Is Stranger Than It Used to Be: Biblical Faith in a Postmodern Age* (Downers Grove, Ill.: InterVarsity Press, 1995), 30–31.

[50] Gene Edward Veith, *Postmodern Times: A Christian Guide to Contemporary Thought and Culture* (Wheaton, Ill.: Crossway Books, 1994), 50. Note, here again, that Technique is placed above Truth. Veith goes on to cite examples of this revisionist redefinition: the villainizing of Christopher Columbus and other American heroes, the attempt to demonstrate that the American heritage is one not of freedom, but of oppression. "They decry the bias of 'Euro-centric' scholarship and curricula, only to substitute aggressively 'Afro-centric' scholarship and curricula. Histories are rewritten and whole disciplines are revised in accordance with feminine or gay agendas."

Some have described this facet of postmodernism by telling an old joke attributed to Walter Truett Anderson. One umpire says, "There's balls and there's strikes, and I call 'em the way they are." He is the naive realist. He represents modernism's belief in objective truth that exists apart from the knower, and the belief that careful methodology and objective observation can determine that truth.[51]

The second umpire says, "There's balls and there's strikes, and I call 'em the way I see 'em." He is a modernist in that he believes there really is a reality called *balls and strikes*. But he realizes that what he calls *balls and strikes* may not be seen that way by someone else. He must simply call them as he sees them. *Balls and strikes* are relative to perspective.

Then, the third umpire, who represents the viewpoint of the postmodernist, says, "There's balls and there's strikes, and they ain't nothin' until I call 'em." This is the skepticism of any truth or reality that exists beyond our judgments, "because we simply do not have access to 'reality' apart from the concepts and language by which we represent that reality. We can never get outside our knowledge to know reality in some direct fashion. It is always mediated to us by our linguistic and conceptual constructions."[52]

6. **We can only begin to arrive at the meaning of a text or an idea through the process of deconstruction.**[53] Postmodernists argue that whatever meanings words have has been vested in them by the surrounding culture. Therefore, the true meaning of a text can only be gained as the reader or hearer takes on the role of an interpreter, entering into dialogue with the text—an approach that yields as many meanings of the text as there are readers and hearers. One might even add, there are as many meanings to the text as there are readings, since the same text may have different meanings each time we visit it.[54]

From that premise, the deconstruction of literary criticism evolved into:

> . . . an all-encompassing theory of knowledge and reality of the world as a whole. Just as there is no inherent meaning in texts, which the reader attempts to discover and extract, so also reality as a whole does

---

[51] Assuming, of course, that he is a good and honest umpire!

[52] Millard J. Erickson, *Postmodernizing the Faith* (Grand Rapids, Mich.: Baker, 1998), 106.

[53] The French philosopher Jacques Derrida said that the true meaning of a text can only be understood (or, at least partially understood) through the following steps of deconstruction:
  •Look first at the author's intention (Is there subtle manipulation or power being used here?).
  •Expose the author's assumptions (What metanarratives form the author's assumptions?).
  •Analyze what has been left out of the text (What has not been said, and why has it been excluded?).
  •Look beneath the author's words to discern the intended meaning (What is really being said here?).
  •Juggle the center of authority by balancing the author's agenda with the agenda of those who might have been excluded or marginalized by the text.
Chuck Smith, Jr. *The End of the World As We Know It* (Colorado Springs, Colo: Waterbrook Press, 2001), 57.

[54] Erickson, *Postmoderninzing the Faith*, 86.

not contain an objective meaning. Reality can be read differently by different observers. The meaning of reality is dependent on the knower, and each knower has a somewhat different perspective he or she brings to the knowing experience. There is no one meaning of the world, no transcendent center to reality as a whole. *In the final analysis, the world is only an arena of one person's interpretation against another's* (emphasis added).[55]

7. **Postmodernism believes that there is more than one way to know.** Modernism's overdependence on reason and outright dismissal of other means of knowing unjustly rejects the possibility that we might gain knowledge by intuition, metaphor, story, feeling, and experience.

Imagine trying to experience a cake by only the objective study of food chemistry (the proportions of sugar, flour, food coloring, eggs, etc., in the recipe), and rejecting the senses of taste, smell, or sight as too subjective. Not only would such an approach to cake appreciation "marginalize" children who cannot read or understand food ingredients, it would assume that little children cannot possibly know anything about cake because they cannot objectively comprehend its content. In fact, one might argue that children are *better* able to appreciate cake than those who are able to read sugar content and calculate the costs in calories. Postmodernism argues that there is more than one way to know reality and that objective rational thinking is not necessarily the superior way.

Modernism and Postmodernism Side by Side

To summarize the contrasting values of these two prevailing moods of thought, Millard Erickson uses this parable from the world of music:[56]

1930 Define rhythm.

1960 The movement of music in time, including tempo and meter, is called _____.

1990 The movement of music in time, including tempo and meter is called:
   a. melody
   b. harmony
   c. rhythm
   d. interval

---

[55] Ibid. Smith comments, "In 1933, Alfred Korzybski argued that people tend to use language in a sloppy way, their language is not technically precise, and they do not try hard enough to distinguish between the real world and their perceptions of the world . . . At the heart of the problem lies the word *is*. We say 'the sky is blue,' but we mean the sky appears blue." Smith, *The End of the World as We Know It*, 53. President Bill Clinton used precisely this defense in trying to stave off a charge of perjury when asked about his lying about adultery. When subpoenaed to appear before a grand jury, he was asked if certain charges about him were true. His famous defense was, "That depends on what the meaning of *is* is."

[56] Erickson, *Postmoderninzing the Faith*, 14.

2000 The movement of music in time, commonly called *rhythm*, **makes you feel:**
  a. I don't understand the question.
  b. I think this is an unfair question.
  c. I don't know what the word *rhythm* means.
  d. It doesn't matter how I feel, as long as it is my own authentic feeling.

In 1930, there was one correct answer to the question (modernism). In 1960, there was one correct answer, but you had to figure that out for yourself (modernism under the influence of individualism).[57] In 1990, the question has become multiple choice. There is not one absolutely true answer (modernism, blurred by relativism and pluralism). In 2000, the answer is up for grabs; but perhaps the more important question is why such a question is even being asked (postmodernism).

Is Truth Stranger Than It Used to Be?[58]
A Limited Critique

When youth workers talk about postmodernism, it tends to be in terms of resignation, admiration, intimidation, or, in some cases, damnation.[59] In fact, amorphous as it is, postmodernism is difficult to either fully embrace or fully assail. But sound youth ministry requires us to carefully examine its premises because, as Zacharias reminds us, those premises ". . . often prove to be unblushingly spurious and would result in chaos if everyone operated by the same principles."[60]

What Good Is Postmodernism?

There are, in fact, some facets of postmodernism that can be affirmed by Orthodox Christianity.

1. Orthodox Christians[61] agree with postmodernism that human reasoning alone cannot be trusted to lead us always to reality.

First of all, the Bible makes it quite clear that human reasoning is flawed. "Although they claimed to be wise, they became fools" (Rom. 1:22).[62] Our prejudices, biases, affections, and hormones lead us to make unreasonable, unwise choices in everyday life, and inaccurate assessments of objective reality. Indeed, it was precisely this arrogance that led to the Fall. We think we see well, but our minds are darkened (2 Cor. 4:4).

---

[57] Typically, this was done under the glow of black lights, while listening to Hendrix and wearing beads, bell bottoms, and tie-dyed clothing.

[58] This is a phrase I've borrowed from Middleton and Walsh, *Truth Is Stranger Than It Used to Be*, 4.

[59] For an excellent overview of six different examples of evangelical response to postmodernism, see Erickson, *Postmodernizing the Faith*. Erickson places each of the six views on a spectrum ranging from a position of complete repudiation (David Wells) on one end to a warm (though not total) embrace (Keith Putt) on the other end.

[60] Zacharias, *Deliver Us From Evil*, 17.

[61] I am using "orthodox Christian" in the way that it was defined by G. K. Chesterton, "it means the Apostles' Creed, as understood by everyone calling himself a Christian until a very short time ago, and the general historic conduct of those who hold such a creed." *Orthodoxy* (London: Bodley Head, 1957), 8.

[62] See also Isaiah 1:3–6.

2. Orthodox Christians agree with postmodernism that knowledge is not the panacea modernism thinks it to be.

One of the basic doctrines of Christian orthodoxy has been the inherent sinfulness of human nature—a sinfulness belying any notion that people who know more will act better. Every advancement for potential good seems to be canceled by its possibility for potential evil. History has been quite clear in its verdict that greater knowledge will not necessarily lead to a better world.

3. Orthodox Christians agree with postmodernism: there is no reason to believe in the inevitability of human progress.

We are, for the most part, healthier, better fed, better educated, more technologically advanced than we have ever been. But, for all our sophistication and learning, we are still threatened by the same enemies that have always plagued humanity: disease, loneliness, isolation, hatred, poverty, bigotry, greed, hunger for power, laziness, and ecological disaster, to name but just a few. We need not be cynical or despairing to observe that humanity's plight is getting worse, not better.

4. Orthodox Christians can affirm postmodernism's insistence that there is more than one way to know.

Scripture teaches us that there is simply more to reality than can be grasped through objective, rational thought. The writer of Hebrews describes faith as "the substance of things hoped for, the evidence of things not seen" (Heb. 11:1). It is the difference between "looking at" and "looking along." Along with many postmodernist thinkers, we embrace the concept of myth, the importance of story, the value of metaphor. Indeed, it was one of C. S. Lewis's favorite themes: "Myth is thus like

These are the two points I want to make. First, that human beings, all over the earth, have this curious idea that they ought to behave in a certain way, and cannot really get rid of it. Secondly, they do not in fact behave that way. They know the law of nature; they break it. These two facts are the foundation of all clear thinking about ourselves and the universe we live in.
—C. S. Lewis

manna; it is to each man a different dish and to each the dish he needs. It does not grow old nor stick at frontiers racial, sexual, or philosophic; and even from the same man at the same moment it can elicit different responses at different levels . . . "[63]

Tolkien explained that "the story of Christ is simply a true myth: a myth working in us in the same way as the others, but with this tremendous difference that it really happened: and one must be content to accept it in the same way."[64]

5. Orthodox Christians can affirm postmodernism's emphasis on experience.

The Psalmist writes, "Taste and see that the Lord is good" (Ps. 34:8), not "Learn theological concepts and see that the Lord is good." In fact, we can discover much about God's goodness through the learning of theological concepts, but there is a learning process more existential as well. It is the difference between learning about love from a psychology text, and learning about love from one you love. It is possible to learn, and to be misled, by both. But neither means of learning by itself can teach all that there is to know.

6. Orthodox Christians can affirm postmodernism's emphasis on community.

Community was a central element of life in the New Testament church (see Acts 2:42–47). The disconnectedness of modern life is neither healthier nor more biblical. While Christianity affirms individual responsibility, it also affirms the individual's responsibility to the community. This sense of connectedness and accountability has been lost in the privatism that now permeates even church life.

Problems of Postmodernism

"Often the obvious line or main current through the rapid is split by a big boulder partway down . . . In this situation you will want to look ahead."[65]

While there are elements of postmodernism that can be embraced by orthodox Christians, we need to be alert for those spots where this significant current of cultural thought might lead us into trouble. Among several issues that might be addressed,[66] perhaps the biggest boulder of postmodernism is its antifoundationalism—its rejection of Truth, or any sort of universal metanarrative.

Even without raising theological objections, the subjectivist uncertainty of postmodernism—the rejection of any universal metanarrative—makes meaning impossible and leaves us with a gnawing emptiness we seek to fill through pursuit, possession, profession, pleasure, passion, and perversity. David Harvey cites four

[63] C. S. Lewis, *Rehabilitations and Other Essays*, cited in Clyde S. Kilby, *A Mind Awake: An Anthology of C. S. Lewis* (New York: Harcourt, Brace and World, 1968), 216.

[64] J. R. R. Tolkien, cited in Richard John Neuhaus, "C. S. Lewis in the Public Square," in *Ancient and Postmodern Christianity: Paleo-Orthodoxy in the 21st Century*, ed. Christopher A. Hall and Kenneth Tanner (Downers Grove, Ill.: InterVarsity Press, 2002), 271.

[65] Tejada-Flores, *Wildwater*, 156.

[66] Again, for a very thorough review of the spectrum of opinion, see Erickson, *Postmodernizing the Faith*.

possible ways of responding to the absence of metanarratives, and all four ways are clearly visible in adolescent culture:

- ▶ Deny complexity. Try not to think deeply about life. Take refuge in fashion, superficiality, and triviality. Television's "reality" shows and "my neighbor-got-my-mother-pregnant-while-having-an-affair-with-me" shows provide a ready venue for this type of escape.

- ▶ Settle for limited action. Concentrate on your own little reality. If there are no big causes that matter, settle for creating small causes that matter: getting the right outfit, buying the right car, finding a boyfriend or girlfriend, being a cheerleader, playing in a band.

- ▶ Construct your own language and thus command it. In its mildest form, this would be anything from taking on a Goth identity, to being in a gang, to spending time online in some virtual "community." In its harshest form, this is called schizophrenia.[67]

- ▶ Accept the meaninglessness. Embrace it with what Allan Bloom in *The Closing of the American Mind* refers to as "debonair nihilism."[68] Pretend that the loss of meaning does not mean anything. C. S. Lewis, in *The Abolition of Man*, makes a remarkable observation:

> But you cannot go on "explaining away" for ever: you will find that you have explained explanation itself away. You cannot go on "seeing through" things for ever. The whole point of seeing through something is to see something through it. It is good that the whole window should be transparent, because the street or garden beyond it is opaque. How if you saw through the garden too? It is no use trying to "see through" first principles. If you see through everything, then everything is transparent. But a wholly transparent world is an invisible world. To "see through" all things is the same as not to see.[69]

It has been said by some, even those who greatly admire Lewis, that today's postmodernists would not find such an argument compelling—that they might simply respond, "But, of course, you old fogey; this is what we've been saying all along. Except that it would be more accurate to say that when one sees through all things, and sees clearly, one sees nothing, which is precisely what is there—nothing."

Neuhaus comments that this kind of "debonair nihilism"—reveling in the meaninglessness of life and language and thought—reminds him of precocious children trying to get attention by standing near the edge of a drop-off and saying, "Look, Mommy, I'm going to jump." Neuhaus continues, "Soon it becomes tiresome. 'Yes, my dear,' one is inclined to say, 'we see you playing on the edge of the abyss. Now either jump or come away and let's get on with the conversation.

---

[67] David Harvey, *Condition of Postmodernity* (Cambridge, Mass.: Basil Blackwell, 1989), 351–352.
[68] Neuhaus, "C. S. Lewis in the Public Square," 269.
[69] Ibid.

Much Ado About Nothing

The irony was not lost on the announcer for National Public Radio's *All Things Considered* on the afternoon of July 2, 2002, when he reported that a lawsuit had been filed by the avant-garde postmodern musician John Cage. Cage's postmodernist leanings were verified when a few decades ago he "composed" a four-minute, 33-second piece called *Silence*. The piece was striking because it was nothing but, well, silence—not one note of audible music.

Now if that were all there were to the story, it would just be another pseudo-artistic example of postmodern logic. What made the story laughable was that the lawsuit filed by Cage accused English musician Michael Batt of copyright violation.

It seems that Batt had recorded a one-minute version of *Silence* without giving Cage the recognition (and royalties) he so richly deserved.

Batt said that at first he thought the complaint was a joke. But the letter representing the copyrighting agency made clear that Cage took this very seriously—no language games, no clever wordplay about the fact that there is no such thing as objective reality. The "debonair cynicism" was gone.

All of a sudden Cage was acting much like an objective thinker. He knew *Silence* when he heard it, and Michael Batt had stolen his *Silence*. Like a good postmodernist, Cage probably felt that nothing could make him think like an objectivist. And, as it turns out, it took about 60 seconds of nothing to get him to do just that.

It is really most annoying when you keep interrupting by announcing your discovery of nothing. Everything is, or is not nothing; and if it is, it is nothing. So whatever you may say, you really cannot have discovered it.'"[70]

In my opinion, this fourth response, the embrace of meaninglessness, is the option least attractive to teenagers whose youthful search for meaning keeps them from surrendering so young to complete cynicism. It is, however, noteworthy that one MTV study concluded "nearly half of all 'concept' (that is, nonperformance) videos depict nihilistic images such as sacrifices, murders, self-destruction, brutality, theft, drug use, and skin punctures—images that suggest a surrender to meaninglessness."[71]

Factoring in the theological damage done by this kind of antifoundationalism only adds to the concern. There simply is not much room in John 14:6 ("I am the way, the truth, and the life, no one comes to the Father except by me") for a pluralism that rejects foundational Truth. Stanley Grenz, who argues persuasively that evangelicals need to take seriously (and favorably) many of the emphases of postmodernism, is quite clear in his concern that orthodox Christians

---

[70] Ibid., 270.

[71] Donald M. David, "Nihilism in Music Television," cited in Romanowski, *Dancing in the Dark*, 209.

simply cannot go so far as to embrace a philosophy that rejects Truth. "This rejection . . . not only leads to a skepticism that undercuts the idea of objective truth in general; it also undermines the Christian claims that our doctrinal formulations state objective truth . . . "[72]

The fact is, postmodernists cannot even live by their own nonrule "rules."[73] For example, in light of postmodernism's burden for deconstruction of language, postmodernist Jean-François Lyotard claims that using the word *we* is "a form of grammatical violence." He goes on to say, that the use of *we*

> aims to deny and obliterate the specificity of the "you" and the "she" of other cultures through the false premise of incorporation within a universal humanity. We must therefore wean ourselves away from the word

Having Some Fun with Postmodernist Gibberish

One could be forgiven for thinking that some postmodern rhetoric is nothing more than gibberish. Physicist Alan Sokal proved that with the right postmodernist buzz words he could say anything, and have it received as a profound *something*. In his article, "Transgressing the Boundaries: Toward a Transformative Hermeneutics of Quantum Gravity," Sokal argued that recent advances in quantum physics support the idea that physical reality is nothing more than a social construct.

Social Text, the respected academic journal of cultural studies, published his article in 1996 as an important perspective from an established scholar. The editors later admitted that they did not actually follow much of the science in the article, but in light of Sokal's scholarly credentials, the article demanded to be heard. Unfortunately, Sokal's whole article was a sham, a hoax—nothing more than a demonstration of postmodernist academic pretense. In revealing his hoax, Sokal invited those who believe the laws of physics are cultural conventions to test them from his twenty-first-floor window.

Thomas Hayden, "Gotcha," U.S. News and World Report *(August 26, 2002), 36.*

---

[72] Stanley Grenz, *Primer on Postmodernism* (Grand Rapids, Mich.: Eerdmans, 1996), 163. Lest we become arrogant about the truthfulness of "our doctrinal formulations," we should perhaps balance our certainties with an honest embrace of our uncertainties. McLaren suggests three different ways of saying it: "A. I believe Christianity is true, but I do not believe my version (or yours, for that matter) of the Faith is completely true. (In other words, I believe that all versions are incomplete in some ways, weighed down with extra baggage, and marred by impurities, biases, misconceptions and gaps.) B. I believe Jesus is true, but I don't believe Christianity in any of our versions is true. (In other words, we know in part and prophesy in part; we have not yet reached that unity and maturity of faith and knowledge that will come when we know as we are known.) C. I believe there is no completely true version of Christianity anywhere except, of course, in the mind of God. (In other words, incompleteness and error are part of the reality of being human.)" McLaren, *The Church on the Other Side*, 172–173.

[73] Peter Kreeft (*C. S. Lewis for the Third Millennium*, 43–44) makes an interesting observation along these lines:

Why would someone want to deny objective truth? Who's afraid of the Law of Non-Contradiction? What's behind the insane attempt to soften up the very structures of sanity? I think it is not logical, mathematical, or metaphysical truths that threaten them, but moral truths. If there were permanent moral truths, that would mean that morality is no longer about nice, warm, fuzzy, vague, soft, negotiable things called "values" but about hard, unyielding, uncompromising, uncomfortable, nonnegotiable things called "laws."

And their fear of permanent, objective moral laws is amazingly selective. It almost always comes down to just one area: sex.

In my experience, students, like professors, bluff a lot and do adroit intellectual dancing. But I would bet a wad of money that if only the sixth commandment were made optional, nearly all hatred and fear of the Church would vanish. Saint Augustine was one of the few honest enough to admit his obsession. After puffing great philosophical profundities about the intellectual problems that kept him back from the Church, he finally admits in the *Confessions*, "The plain fact was, I thought I should be impossibly miserable without the embraces of a mistress." If that profoundly philosophical motive was what held back one of the most honest, truth-seeking wisdom-lovers in history, do you really hope that nobler ideals motivate the spiritual children of Woodstock? Thus, much more crucial than permanent truths are permanent values, or rather, permanent moral laws, laws as objective and unchangeable as the laws of mathematics. Applying these laws may be uncertain and changeable, but [the laws themselves] are not. Applying the law of mathematics is also sometimes uncertain and changeable, e.g. when you try to measure the exact length of a live alligator.

we, that grammatico-political category that can never exist except as legitimating myth . . . Instead we must embrace and promote every form of cultural diversity, without recourse to universal principles.[74]

Now, what is striking about the statement above is that it is stated as if it is absolute truth. But, of course, postmodernists say there is no such thing. And then, even more befuddling, here is a paragraph in which the reader is urged to stop using the word *we*, and twice in the paragraph the author uses the word *we*![75]

One of the most flagrant examples of the untenability of actually and fully living out postmodernism was an article by the godfather of postmodernism, Jacques Derrida, in response to an article written by John Searle criticizing and challenging some of Derrida's concepts. In rebuttal to Searle's 11-page article, Derrida wrote a 93-page reply in which he objected that Searle had *misunderstood* and *misstated* his position, even asserting at one point that the meaning of his arguments *should have been clear and obvious* to Searle.[76] This from a figure who has argued that language is meaningless! All of a sudden the nihilist is not debonair anymore.

Perhaps the fairest, and certainly the most charitable, way of summarizing postmodernism is with the assumption that all but the most hard-core postmodernist would admit that there really is such a thing as objective truth. In those famous words from *The X-Files*, "the truth is out there." The real question is in our capability to know it. Brian McLaren may well be right when he suggests, "What most postmodern people tend to reject is not absolute truth, but absolute knowledge . . . "[77] Perhaps what most postmodernists really mean to say in response to the question "Do you believe in absolute truth?" is this: "Well, of course, there is absolute truth out there. I don't doubt that. I just doubt your ability, or my own for that matter, to apprehend that truth, and comprehend it and remember it and encode it in language and communicate it to others and have them understand it in an absolutely accurate way."[78]

How then does an understanding of postmodernism guide us in effective youth ministry? Largely, what it does is provide for us a context for accounting for much of what we see in adolescent culture:

1. the suspicion of any universal statement of truth or falsehood, right or wrong;

---

[74] Jean-François Lyotard, as summarized by Steven Connor, *Postmodernist Culture: An Introduction to Theories of the Contemporary* (Oxford: Basil Blackwell, 1989), 37.

[75] It is reminiscent of Tony Jones's comment in *Postmodern Youth Ministry* that if we are to get a grip on postmodern cultural patterns we should, among other things, "Never make lists!" Yet it is the fifth suggestion he makes in what he describes as a "list of postmodern credos." Or, the ironic comment, also by Jones, "The premise of postmodernism is, then, to question all premises." But if postmodernism embraces the premise that all premises are invalid then it must reject the very premise upon which it is based.

[76] The two articles are John Searle, "Reiterating the Differences: Reply to Derrida," *Glyph* 1 (1977): 198–208; and Jacques Derrida, "Limited, Inc, abc," *Glyph* 2 (1977): 162–254, cited in Erickson, *Postmoderninzing the Faith*, 156.

[77] McLaren, *The Church on the Other Side*, 166.

[78] Ibid. McLaren offers this rather eloquent analogy to take us inside the postmodern mind: "Imagine a line of people trying to pass a handful of sand from one end to the other. With each passing, some sand is lost. Now imagine that the truth is not just a handful of sand, but rather all the sand on all the beaches of the world. How can we claim to hold the truth and pass it on, when our hands not only lose so much but grasp so little?"

2. the amazing influence and power of story;

3. the passionate desire to experience Truth as well as hear it;

4. the decreased effectiveness of a Christian apologetic based solely on "evidence that demands a verdict";

5. the power and influence of authentic Christian community (note the importance of small groups); and

6. the need, perhaps, to "look along" the Christian faith before being willing to "look at" it.

Part II: Everything Looks Different from the Banks of the River

There is "an optical effect which makes whitewater look even fiercer from above (the same way a cliff looks steeper from the top) . . . Although you may indeed spot the best route through from up there, you may also scare yourself to the point where you tip over from sheer nervousness . . . You should mentally adjust for the fact that everything looks a little harder from the bank [of the river]."[79]

From a distance, the whitewater of adolescent culture looks scary. Wading into a high school cafeteria, diving into the stands at a football game, jumping with both feet into a group of middle school kids—especially for people just beginning to launch into youth ministry—can be a frightening proposition. But the method of God is undeniable. God's message is always to be preached in the presence. It is always a "word become flesh."

God's commission to Jeremiah was clear: "Do not say, 'I am only a child.' You must go to everyone I send you to and say whatever I command you. Do not be afraid of them, for I am with you and will rescue you," declares the Lord" (Jer. 1:7–8). "*Go to* . . . *and say*."

Jonah's instructions were explicit: "Go to the great city of Nineveh and preach against it, because its wickedness has come up before me" (Jon. 1:2). "*Go to* . . . *and preach*."

Paul's approach was simple: "We were . . . among you . . . while we preached the gospel of God to you" (1 Thes. 2:7–9). "*Among you* . . . *while we preached*."

[79] Tejada-Flores, *Wildwater*, 157.

Jesus's model was obvious: "The Word became flesh and made his dwelling among us" (John 1:14). "The Word became flesh . . . *among us*."

Trying to understand youth culture without being around teenagers is like a weatherman trying to gauge the temperature by looking through a window, or a doctor trying to do a physical by looking at someone's photograph. The best way to understand youth culture is to be there, to be among kids, to move beyond the theoretical to the geographical.

We begin by asking a simple question: where do teenagers hang out in your community—what are the spaces that become a defining part of a group of students? Is it a particular park, a particular place in the mall, or a particular parking lot? Is it a street corner, a playground, or a club?[80]

A geographical approach to understanding a local youth culture might entail simply spending some time where students congregate, and then doing, in perhaps a less formal way, what anthropologists call *ethnographic research*. Typically based on *participant observation*,[81] this is the practice of intentionally observing and describing the various behaviors, styles of dress and adornment (tattoos, earrings, leather, chains, safety pins), social relations, and artifacts (comic books, languages, skateboard designs) of the teenagers in that particular space. It is more or less a way of understanding the *who* by taking the time to observe the *what* with an emphasis on the *where*. For example, one youth worker wrote about the significance of a single Burger King restaurant in the adolescent geography where he once did youth ministry—referred to by local students as the "BK Lounge."[82]

How we interpret those findings will vary. For example, The Center for Contemporary Cultural Studies, in connection with the University of Birmingham in the United Kingdom, has done some interesting work in this area of study. *Cool Places: Geographies of Youth Culture* edited by Tracey Skelton and Gill Valentine, argues that much of what we observe in terms of adolescent geography is undergirded by a power struggle between youth and adult populations.[83] They found:

> that public space is produced as an adult space. Studies on teenagers suggest that the space of the street is often the only autonomous space that young people are able to carve out for themselves and that hanging around, and larking about, on the streets, in parks and in shopping malls, is one form of youth resistance (conscious and unconscious) to adult power.

You do not need to be a trained anthropologist to do simple geographical study of a youth population in your community—what some have characterized as

---

[80] "To date there is a small but growing body of work by Geographers (i.e. with a capital G) and academics from related disciplines who are interested in spatiality (geographies with small *g*)." From Tracey Skelton and Gill Valentine, *Cool Places: Geographies of Youth Culture* (London: Rutledge, 1998), 7.

[81] Sort of an academic approach to "people-watching."

[82] Dave Rahn, "A Sociological Framework for Doing Youth Ministry," *Reaching a Generation for Christ*, ed. Rick Dunn and Mark Senter (Chicago: Moody, 1997), 97.

[83] Their special area of interest has been in the area of *structural anthropology*, looking at how the worldview of individual teenagers enters into, and takes its meaning from, the shared worldview of the group as a whole. In other words, they looked for properties of collective conscience that transcend and cannot be explained wholly in terms of the minds of individual teenagers within the group. For example, how does the collective mindset of the teenagers who regularly hang out in a Burger King parking lot influence the individual worldview and identity of those students?

Geographical Study: Mapping Out the Local Terrain

Use the chart below as a guide and see what you discover. Remember to be discreet about this: you are not Jane Goodall and these are not mountain gorillas. The students' behavior may well change if they sense they are being watched like orangutans in a habitat.

Table 9-2.
Mapping Out the Local Terrain

Place:		Day:	Time:
Is there a particular time or day of the week that students gather here?			
Is there a particular racial or ethnic makeup?			
What behaviors do you observe (sitting and talking, skateboarding, playing basketball, etc.)?			
Can you discern certain styles of dress that appear to be the "uniform of the day"?			
Are there common forms of adornment (tattoos, earrings, leather, chains, safety pins, hats, pants worn low, trench coats, makeup, etc.)?			
Social relations	Is the group largely single gender or coed?		
	Are there groups within the group? What are they?		
	Can you discern any student(s) who seem to be "leading" the others?		
	If someone new shows up, what is the response of the regulars?		
Do you notice any common artifacts (hand gestures, comic books, shorthand language—common phrases, skateboard designs, T-shirt art)?			
Any other common behaviors (smoking, dancing, flirting, roughhousing, etc.)?			
After you have learned what you can through observation, why not try also to initiate some conversation?[1]			

1. "Any time a leader enjoys a casual conversation with a student where something previously unknown is discovered that leader is engaging in a form of research. Over time, and through a number of such conversations, leaders cannot help forming some impressions about adolescent social patterns in their communities. Arming themselves with questions that will fill in knowledge gaps does not turn youth ministers into lab coat technicians. Neither does the process of seeking conversational opportunities with key kids. In truth, an increasingly natural curiosity to learn about the world a teen lives in is a great way to extend the unconditional love of Jesus to young people." Dave Rahn, "A Sociological Framework for Doing Youth Ministry," *Reaching a Generation for Christ*, ed. Rick Dunn and Mark Senter (Chicago: Moody, 1997), 97.

exegesis of the social context or social exegesis.[84] What mainly is required is a commitment of intention, some time, and attentive eyes and ears. In its most basic form it consists of three simple questions:

1. What can be observed? "The first step is to gather as much cold, hard data pertaining to teenage social life as possible . . . The question guiding inquiry is, 'What are the facts of teenage social life in this community that can be verified?'"[85] Think of this as a photographer snapping some mental images of teenage life.

2. What does it mean? This is looking back through the snapshots and taking time to reflect:

   ▶ What is going on here?

   ▶ What is this space about?

   ▶ Why do these kids gather here?

   ▶ What are they looking for here?

   ▶ What have they found here?

3. What could it mean for my youth ministry?

   ▶ Does this help us better shape an outreach strategy?

   ▶ Does this suggest some issues or topics that need to be addressed in our youth group?

   ▶ Do we have any students who have a connection to this group through whom we could begin to build a bridge or connection with this group?

In addition to these simple steps, there is the informal research available to any youth worker:

1. Talk to the kids themselves. Sure, there is the likelihood that answers will be seasoned to make them a little more tasteful to an adult outsider, but it is better than nothing. When teenagers know we are going to take them seriously, they can be amazingly open. A youth pastor might want to supplement this information with written surveys (short, easy to complete) that will provide teenagers with anonymity as they talk about some of these issues.

---

[84] Rahn, "A Sociological Framework for Doing Youth Ministry," 91.
[85] Ibid.

2. Talk to other youth pastors and youth workers in the community. When people are going to fish a spot they have never fished before, they talk to the locals. They stop at a nearby bait and tackle shop to see what the fish are biting. They take advantage of insights offered by anglers who fish the same stretch of water. Obviously, you will want to talk to local youth workers. But do not neglect to interview school officials, principals, counselors, coaches as well. Talk to people at the local drug or crisis pregnancy center.

3. Talk to the parents. Just being a youth worker does not mean you are the local guru on adolescent culture. Parents see a side of their teenagers not so readily visible from any other angle.

The best part of being among teenagers is not just the information it gives us, but the relationships it offers us. Like so many creatures, teenagers are harder to love from a distance. Once we begin to develop relationships, the fear diminishes and the joy of ministry kicks in.

For example, most of us would not be naturally attracted to the female Long-beaked Echidna[86]—a fairly large egg-laying mammal with dense fur and an extended, down-curved beak. At first sighting, we might even find it threatening, or just plain disgusting. Even at the very best, it is not an animal that people feel drawn to cuddle.[87] Yet one zoologist recalls with deep appreciation an occasion, while involved in night time research, when an Echidna he had been working with sneaked up on him for a surprise greeting.

The first I knew of my old friend's approach was a wet, worm-like thing entering my boot. Then, I felt a great, curved beak plunge down almost to my sole, so that the extraordinarily long pink tongue could tickle my toes.

The Echidna and I were soon on terms of considerable intimacy, a state doubtless precluded during our earlier association by her fright . . . Long-beaked Echidnas really are the most remarkably intelligent and affectionate animals. Their bird-like faces allow no show of emotion. But they can show their feelings in other ways.[88]

We probably will not learn to love teenagers from a distance. It is easy to be put off by their appearance, or the apparent lack of emotion, or the ways they communicate their feelings. But, as those of us know who have invested our lives in youth ministry, they really can be "the most remarkably intelligent and affectionate animals." It is "perfect love [that] drives out fear . . ." (1 John 4:18). In order to get to know teenagers, we need to be in their natural habitat.

---

[86] *Zaglossis bruijnii*, for those of you who are double-majoring in a natural science.

[87] For example, you almost never see Long-beaked Echidnas as stuffed animals or Beanie Babies.

[88] Tim Flannery, *Throwim way leg: Adventures in the Jungles of New Guinea* (London: Weidenfeld and Nicholson, 1998), 32.

Whitewater instructor and river guide Lito Tejada-Flores puts it best, "The river is always the best teacher. And for most of us, most of the time, playing in whitewater is the best and most enjoyable way to tune in to all it can teach us."[89]

Part III: Focus on the River, Not on the Rapids

One of the keys in reading river rapids is learning how to recognize the features below the surface of the water. "Rocks just below the surface produce a humping-up or pillow of water on top of themselves and a shallow depression in the water just downstream. If the overall surface of the water is somewhat rippled or choppy, then a smooth or glassy patch can be a tell-tale sign of a large flat rock just beneath the surface. While any rafting guide can appreciate the value of reading the behavior of surface water, the real skill in reading a river is in understanding the features beneath the surface of the water."

Sometimes the risk in youth ministry is that we become so preoccupied with the splashes, waves, and dips of culture that we lose sight of the basic features of human experience that are deeper down beneath the surface. That is why it is so important that *we focus on the river, and not on the rapids.*

One of the most crucial facts to bear in mind about teenagers is that *"people are more alike than cultures."*[90] Despite the rapidity and variety of cultural change, it is quite striking to realize how much of what today's teenager feels and questions was felt and questioned by teenagers even four or five decades ago. There is, for example, an abundance of anthropological evidence to suggest that people of vastly different cultures and widely diverse societies have much in common—evidence that points to the simple fact that human beings, in all places and in all times, were created in the image of God, and that all peoples, *in all places and in all times, share basic yearnings and longings.*

In an environment where it is popular to talk about "how much has changed," it's easy to lose sight of how much *has not* changed.[91] This distortion often leads us to overemphasize the cracks and fissures on the surface of the cultural landscape instead of observing the deep, more permanent features beneath the surface.[92]

---

[89] Tejada-Flores, *Wildwater*, 182.

[90] Walter Goldschmidt, *Comparative Functionalism* (Berkeley, Calif.: University of California Press, 1966), 134.

[91] This myopia may result from a secular worldview of sociologists and anthropologists unwilling to reckon that God is our Creator. Or perhaps it results from a debate over the influence of nature or nurture: are we all born with these yearnings, or are they bred in us by family and society?

[92] Donald Brown, *Human Universals* (Philadelphia: Temple University Press, 1991), 154.

Many Cultures— Same Questions

In thinking about the universal experience of humanity, the British anthropologist Bronislaw Malinowski demonstrated seven biological and psychological needs observable in every human culture:

1. Metabolism. The need for oxygen, liquid, and food.

2. Reproduction. This is the need to replenish the society; it includes, but goes beyond, the sex drive.

3. Bodily comforts. This is the need to maintain a range of temperature, humidity, etc., to sustain physiological processes such as circulation and digestion.

4. Safety. Prevention of bodily harm, accidental or otherwise.

5. Movement. Activity is necessary to all organisms, and all human activity is instrumental; that is, it is directed toward the satisfaction of other needs.

6. Growth. Not only is this the need for growth itself, but the needs related to growth, that is, nurture, advice, example, even physical care, etc.

7. Health. This is the maintenance and repair of one's body, personal hygiene, etc.

Bronislaw Malinowski, A Scientific Theory of Culture and Other Essays, *cited in Stephen A. Grunlan and Marvin K. Mayers,* Cultural Anthropology: A Christian Perspective *(Grand Rapids, Mich.: Zondervan, 1988), 41–49.*

To put it in simple terms: many things we have discussed in the preceding pages—everything from changing patterns of relationships, to varieties of style and dress, to digital forms of communication—are the changing features of a massive river that continues to roll forward in time. Over time, those features change, the landscape shifts, the river carves its course. But what has not changed over time are the questions that people of all ages, in all times, and in all places have posed in response to the human situation throughout human history.[93]

The real key to understanding culture is learning how to read those submerged features of the human landscape that often cause the ripples, whirlpools, and depressions of adolescent life. This is a view that values depth over breadth.

What this means is that while we cannot afford to ignore culture, sometimes we make the opposite mistake of taking it way too seriously.

---

[93] "[Anthropologists] have dwelt on the differences between peoples while saying too little about the similarities . . . At the same time, anthropologists have exaggerated the importance of social and cultural conditioning, and have, in effect, projected an image of humanity marked by little more than empty but programmable minds. These are distortions that not only affect the way we look at and treat the rest of the world's peoples, but also profoundly affect our thoughts about ourselves and the conduct of our own affairs." From Charles Kraft, *Anthropology for Christian Witness* (Maryknoll, N.Y.: Orbis Books, 1996), 118.

The teenagers I know are both cynical and harshly passionate. What they want is so big, it's hard to get your eye around it at first. Who would've thought that teenagers talking about sex would end up talking about their souls? For that's what they're talking about, isn't it? Not body heat, but life everlasting. Not the adventure of skin on skin, but a dinner table in the skies.

They have none of our ambivalence—independence vs. love, distinction vs. belonging. Their struggle is with the world— will it let them lose their loneliness? And how? They want something bigger than themselves to live for, something steadier and stronger than one-on-one love, something I long for and loathe, something eradicating—a 'we' in their lives; a family feast that never ends, a tribe of friends, God's will.

—Kathy Dobie, associate editor at Pacific News Service

The sharp differences and sweeping changes of culture can blind us to the simple fact that teenagers today—at least under the surface, in the deepest places of life—have the same basic longings and questions that teenagers (and human beings of all ages) have been asking from the beginning of time.

Eugene Nida, widely recognized as one of the foremost missiological anthropologists, insists that "the similarities that unite mankind as a cultural 'species' are much greater than the differences that separate."[94] What Nida was largely referring to are the common quests that stir the heart and mind of virtually every human being—quests that are right at the heart of adolescence.

What are those questions? Essentially, there are four big questions (summarized in Table 9-2).[95]

1. **Intimacy.** This is the quest for *community*. All human beings have a basic longing to love and be loved. At our core, we long to be both loveable and love*able*. Every statistic about sexual promiscuity, every story about broken families and scarred lives, every teenage clique and cluster—all of it is rooted in a deep, God-given desire to know and be known. Ultimately, it is a desire to know and be known by God himself. In his poignant lyrics, singer David Wilcox captures the power of this deep universal longing:

---

[94] Ronald Habermas and Klaus Issler, *Teaching for Reconciliation* (Grand Rapids, Mich.: Baker, 1992), 64.

[95] Erik Erikson's psychosocial theory cites these first three as: (1) Intimacy, (2) Industry, and (3) Integrity, as cited in Habermas and Issler, *Teaching for Reconciliation*, 66. More recently, Clegg and Bird articulate three basic needs: (1) Transcendence, (2) Significance, and (3) Community. Tom Clegg and Warren Bird, *Lost in America: How You and Your Church Can Impact the World Next Door* (Loveland, Colo.: Group Books, 2001).

Table 9-3.
Universal Human Quests

Quest	Questions	Answers
Longing to know and be known (Ps. 139, 1 Cor. 13:1–8a)	• How can I love and be loved? • How do I relate to other people?	Community Intimacy
Longing to know who I am (Jer. 1:4–10, 1 Tim. 4:12)	• Who am I and who do I want to be?	Character Integrity
Longing to know why I am here (Eccles. 1:2–10)	• What will I do with my life? • Do I want my life to count for something?	Calling Initiative
Longing to know God (Ps. 42:1–11)	• Is there a God, and does he care about me?	Communion Immanence

The depth of your dreams, the height of your wishes, the length of your vision to see,

The hope of your heart is much bigger than this because it's made out of what might be.

Picture your hope, your heart's desire as a castle that you must keep,

with all of its splendor, it's drafty with lonely, this hearth is too hard to heat.

When I get lonely, that's usually a sign,

some room is empty, but that room is there by design.

If I feel hollow, that's just my proof that there's more for me to follow,

that's what the lonely is for.

Is it a curse or a blessing, this palace of promise, when the empty chill makes you weep?

with only the thin fire of romance to warm you, these halls are too tall to heat.

When I get lonely, that's surely a sign,

some room is empty, that room is there by design.

If I feel hollow, that's just my proof that there's more for me to follow;

that's what the lonely is for.

You can seal up the pain, build walls in the hallways, close off a small room to live in,

but those walls will remain, and keep you there always,

and you'll never know why you were given the lonely.[96]

2. **Identity.** The quest for *character*. Erik Erikson's word for this was *integrity*[97] — a uniquely human desire to integrate the parts with the whole, the inner person with the outer, the private with the public, the world outside the heart and mind with the world inside—integrating the aspirations of who we think we are, or who we wish we could become, with the reality of who we know ourselves to be.

---

[96] David Wilcox, "That's What the Lonely Is for," *The Very Best of David Wilcox*, CD recording, A&M Records, 2001.

[97] Habermas and Issler, *Teaching for Reconciliation*, 66. This is probably the longing most closely related to Abraham Maslow's notion of *self-actualization*. For a very thorough study of what psychologist Paul Vitz calls selfism, see Paul Vitz, *Psychology as Religion* (Grand Rapids, Mich.: Eerdmans, 1977).

In his book *The Wounded Healer*, Henri Nouwen writes:

> Many young people are convinced that there is something terribly wrong with the world in which they live and that cooperation with existing models of living would constitute betrayal of themselves. Everywhere we see a restless and nervous people, unable to concentrate and often suffering from a growing sense of depression. They know that what is shouldn't be the way it is, but they see no workable alternative. Thus, they are saddled with frustration, which often expresses itself in undirected violence which destroys without clear purpose, or in suicidal withdrawal from the world, both of which are signs more of protest than the results of a new-found ideal.[98]

While not all cultures are as individualistic in approach as western cultures,[99] there is a universal sense in which we ask *who am I?* Unfortunately, the problem with this longing for the true self is that we are sabotaged by our very pursuit, as when we try so hard to fall asleep that we lie awake wondering why it hasn't yet happened. In *The Pilgrim's Regress*, C. S. Lewis describes our dilemma this way:

> *Their labor-saving devices multiply drudgery,*
> *Their aphrodisiacs make them impotent,*
> *Their amusements bore them,*
> *Their rapid production of food leaves half of them starving,*
> *And their devices for saving time have banished leisure from their country.*

Jesus put it more simply: "For whoever wants to save his life will lose it, but whoever loses his life for me will save it" (Luke 9:24).

3. **Initiative.** The quest for *calling*. Standing beside the grave of his mother, Forrest Gump in the movie with the same name said longingly, "I don't know if we each have a destiny, or if we're all just floating around accident-like on the breeze."[100] With those simple words, he struck a chord that resonated deeply with all of us who have in one way or another asked, "Does my life really matter?"

> Our problem is that most of us live our lives like a movie we've arrived at twenty minutes late. The action is well under way and we haven't a clue what's happening. Who are these people? Who are the good guys and who are the bad guys? Why are they doing that? What's going on? We sense that something really important, perhaps even glorious, is taking place, and yet it all seems so random.[101]

[98] Henri Nouwen, *The Wounded Healer* (New York: Image Books, 1979), 34.

[99] For example, in some cultures, more communal and less individualistic, the question "Who am I?" is defined by the question "Who are we?" The question *who?* is still very real; but there is a difference in the way that question is pursued. Hiebert notes, "In many tribes and in the Orient, the basic building block of the society is not the individual person but a group. People do not see themselves as autonomous, but as members of the group to which they belong . . . The search for identity is largely foreign in societies where the basic reference point is the group, not the individual. A person is born into a group and therefore has an identity within the society." Paul Hiebert, *Anthropological Insights for Missionaries* (Grand Rapids, Mich.: Baker, 1985), 122–123.

[100] Cited in Brent Curtis and John Eldredge, *The Sacred Romance* (Nashville, Tenn.: Thomas Nelson, 1997), 30.

[101] Ibid., 35.

Deep at our core is a desire for a calling, a part to play, a role in the story of life. At the end of the day, we need to feel that it mattered we were here. We try to construct these stories out of recognition, accomplishment, wealth, and ability, shrinking big hearts to fit into small stories, but we are left with a hunger for meaning.

4. **Immanence.**[102] The quest for *communion*. It was Blaise Pascal, the French physicist and mathematician, who said:

> What else does this craving, and this helplessness, proclaim but that there was once in man a true happiness, of which all that now remains is an empty print and trace? This he tries in vain to fill with everything around him, seeking in things that are not there the help he cannot find in those that are, though none can help, since this infinite abyss can be filled only with an infinite and immutable object; in other words, by God himself. God alone is man's true good.[103]

> John Stott defines this quest for transcendence as "the search for ultimate reality beyond the universe."[104]

The most basic of all humanity's longings is a longing for God. As Augustine put it, "The thought of you (God) stirs [mankind] so deeply that he cannot be content unless he praises you, because you made us for yourself and *our hearts find no peace until they rest in you.*"[105] The multiple expressions of this longing are rampant. Whether it be in the latest Hollywood blockbuster about life after death, or the seminar that promises "spirituality coaching," or the Oprah author whose book promises that "faith can make a difference," or the crystal dangling from the rearview mirror, or the mask and magic ritual of some tribal ceremony—human beings are inherently seekers.

To some extent, the increasing noise of spirituality is a bad sign. People do not go around talking constantly about their lungs unless the air quality is bad. The popularity of spiritual conversation is a symptom of a deep sickness in western culture.[106] On the other hand, this spiritual awakening offers to the church an amazing window of opportunity. There is a genuine thirst in the human spirit, a universal longing to be near to God—whoever or whatever that god might be. And at this moment in time, although often misguided and wrong-headed, there seems to be an acute awareness of that thirst. This is surely, as David put it, "a dry and weary land where there is no water" (Ps. 63:1).

---

[102] I'm using this word in the sense of nearness, drawing near.

[103] Blaise Pascal, *Pensée 428*. In Peter Kreeft, *Christianity for Modern Pagans (Pascal's Pensée(s) Edited Outlined and Explained)* (San Francisco: Ignatius, 1993)

[104] John Stott, "The World's Challenge to the Church," cited in Habermas and Issler, *Teaching for Reconciliation*, 66.

[105] Emphasis added. St. Augustine of Hippo, *Confessions*, Book I, trans. and edited by R. S. Pine Coffin. (New York: Penguin Books, 1961), sec. I, 21.

[106] Eugene Peterson makes this point persuasively and forcefully in his collection of articles, *Subversive Spirituality* (Grand Rapids, Mich.: Eerdmans, 1997), 32ff. To study more about spirituality as it is defined in the lexicon of current western culture, I suggest these resources: Chuck Smith, *The End of the World as We Know It*, particularly chap. 5; Robert K. Johnston, *Reel Spirituality* (Grand Rapids, Mich.: Baker, 2000); and Tom Beaudoin, *Virtual Faith* (San Francisco: Jossey-Bass, 1998). Also especially helpful is the Mars Hill 1999 audiotape series "Best-Selling Spirituality: American Cultural Change and the New Shape of Faith."

What an incredible moment in history to be able to say,

> Come, all you who are thirsty, come to the waters; and you who have no money, come, buy and eat! Come, buy wine and milk without money and without cost. Why spend money on what is not bread, and your labor on what does not satisfy? Listen, listen to me, and eat what is good, and your soul will delight in the richest of fare. Give ear and come to me; hear me, that your soul may live. (Isa. 55:1–3)

Keep Your Eye on the Subject

Antonio Mendez served for 27 years as an agent of the Central Intelligence Agency. In his book *Master of Disguise*[107] he describes how, as a new recruit, he was taking part in a reconnaissance training exercise. He was to pursue his subject through a busy downtown area without losing contact and without being seen. It was not going to be easy. But Mendez, young and cocky, knew he could do it, and he did—for about five minutes, after which the subject disappeared into a store and ducked out of a separate entrance, leaving Mendez and his partner red-faced and humble. In debriefing the operation, his instructor remarked that the biggest mistake agents make in doing "recon" work is they focus too much on the surrounding scene. "Stay focused on your man," he was told. Do not get distracted by the terrain he walks through or the clothing he wears. Stay focused on the person.

Having been in youth ministry for many years, I am occasionally asked, "How have kids changed

Pleasure is *The Enemy's* Territory

"Never forget that when we are dealing with any pleasure in its healthy and normal and satisfying form, we are, in a sense, on the Enemy's ground. I know we have won many a soul through pleasure. All the same, it is His invention, not ours. He made the pleasures: all our research so far has not enabled us to produce one. All we can do is to encourage the humans to take the pleasures which our Enemy has produced, at times, or in ways, or in degrees, which He has forbidden. Hence we always try to work away from the natural condition of any pleasure to that in which it is least natural, least redolent of its Maker, and least pleasurable. An ever-increasing craving for an ever-diminishing pleasure is the formula. It is more certain; and it's better style. To get the man's soul and give *him nothing* in return—that is what really gladdens our Father's heart."

C. S. Lewis character Screwtape instructing his rookie nephew, Wormwood, in The Screwtape Letters

---

[107] Antonio Mendez, *Master of Disguise* (New York: Perennial-Harper Collins, 2000).

from when you first started out in ministry?" Of course, in answering I allude to the many changes that we have noted in this chapter. But then I give what has to be the world's most boring response: "They haven't changed much." People are still people, and teenagers are still teenagers. Kids still need to know Christ, and they still need to know they are loved. Sometimes we are so distracted by the changing terrain of culture that we forget to focus on people.

J. R. W. Stott quotes a missionary's conversation with Bakht Singh, the Indian evangelist. Singh was asked how he could do ministry in a culture that seemed so inhospitable to Christianity.

"Do you preach to them about the love of God?"

"No," he said, "the Indian mind is so polluted that if you talk to them about love they think mainly of sex."

"Well," the missionary said, "Do you talk to them about the wrath and judgment of God?"

"No, they are used to that," he replied. "All the gods are mad anyway. It makes no difference to them if there is one more who is angry."

"About what do you talk to them? Do you preach on the crucified Christ?' the missionary guessed.

What All Societies and Cultures Everywhere Have in Common

Various lists of elements found in all societies have been developed. Perhaps the most famous of these is that by George Peter Murdock. This is not a complete list, but about seventy-three categories of human ways listed alphabetically are mentioned. Here is the list:

Age-grading, athletic sports, bodily adornment, calendar, cleanliness training, community organization, cooking, cooperative labor, cosmology, courtship, dancing, decorative art, divination, division of labor, dream interpretation, education, eschatology, ethics, ethnobotany, etiquette, faith healing, family, feasting, firemaking, folklore, food taboos, funeral rites, games, gestures, gift-giving, government, greeting, hair styles, hospitality, housing, hygiene, incest taboos, inheritance rules, joking, kin-groups, kinship nomenclature, language, law, luck superstition, magic, marriage, mealtimes, medicine, modesty concerning natural functions, mourning, music, mythology, numerals, obstetrics, penal sanctions, personal names, population policy, post-natal care, pregnancy usages, property rights, propitiation of supernatural beings, puberty customs, religious ritual, residence rules, sexual restrictions, soul concepts, status differentiation, surgery, toolmaking trade, visiting, weaning, and weather control.

—*Charles Kraft*, Anthropology for Christian Witness *(Maryknoll, N.Y.: Orbis Books, 1996), 118.*

"No, they would think of him as a poor martyr who helplessly died."

"Then what is your emphasis? Eternal life?"

"Not so," he said, "if you talk about eternal life the Indian thinks of trans-migration. He wants to get away from it."

"What then is your message?"

And here Stott summons us to pay attention:

"I have never yet failed to get a hearing if I talk to them about the forgiveness of sins and peace and rest. That's the product that sells well. Soon they ask me how they can get it, and *then I lead them to the Savior who alone can meet their deepest longings.*"[108]

That is not meant to oversimplify cultural issues, or to make a black and white glossy out of a color photo. It is simply to observe that there will never be a time in ministry or a place of ministry, no cultural shift or sociological trend,[109] that will alter the fact that people deep down in one form or another are wrestling with these questions: "Does anybody love me?" "Does life have meaning?" "Will my life count for anything?" and "Does God exist, and how can I know him?"

Final (and Somewhat Personal) Observations About Youth Ministry and Culture

Despite the "sky is falling" rhetoric that sells books and packs seminars, wisdom demands that we be cautious when making sweeping judgments about culture in general, or youth culture in particular.

The crisis of the present moment, like the nearest telephone pole, will always loom largest. Isn't there a danger that our great, permanent, objective necessities—often more important—may get crowded out? While the moderns [and postmoderns?—DR] have been pressing forward to conquer new territories of consciousness, the old territory, in which alone man can live, has been left unguarded, and we are in danger of finding our enemy in our rear.[110]

Sometimes when I hear youth workers talk about cultural trends, or even ministry trends, it sounds to me like people who have just arrived on the beach

---

[108] George W. Peters, "Is Missions Homesteading or Moving?" *Mennonite Brethren Herald*, April 15, 1977, cited in John Stott, *Down to Earth: Studies in Christianity and Culture* (Grand Rapids, :Mich.: Eerdmans, 1980), 120-121.

[109] That does not mean, in any sense, that culture can be ignored. Peter Ward warns (and it is a valid concern) that sometimes an anthropological approach "flattens out the subtle divisions between youth subculture, racial groups, the impact of the media and a mass popular culture, and indeed the presence of a vibrant church subculture." Pete Ward, *God at the Mall* (Peabody, Mass.: Hendrickson, 1999), 83.

[110] C. S. Lewis, *A Preface to "Paradise Lost,"* cited in Kreeft, *C. S. Lewis for the Third Millennium*, 14.

and are witnessing their first high tide. Their immediate assumption is that everything will be flooded: "We need to move everything, rebuild the church in a different location or it will be ruined!"

Not to sound either stodgy or arrogant, but you know what? We need to remember that tides rise and fall; this has happened before and it will happen again. One of the significant elements of a culture saturated in mass media is that stories get internationalized, magnified, and ratified quickly—sometimes way out of proportion. Ideas are broadcast more widely, catchphrases are picked up more quickly, fashions are entrenched more readily, conventional wisdom becomes conventional too hastily. Yes, tidal movement is important; it's foolish to set sail without taking it into account. And, it may be, as Leonard Sweet suggests, that postmodernism is not just a high tide, but a cultural "tsunami." But we need to be careful about relocating and rebuilding the church every time the water rises.

> ## Study Group Recreation Idea
>
> Brainstorm together about movies that speak to each of these four big questions: "Does anybody love me?" "Does life have meaning?" "Will my life count for anything?" and "Does God exist, and how can I know him?" You get ten points for every movie you can list. Scoring: 0–20 points = Uh ... er ... you need to get out a little more; 30–70 points = If you could just have this kind of recall for actual stuff that, you know, really matters; 80–120 points = Be honest. Do you really think *Shrek* is a movie about the meaning of life?; and 130 points or higher—Time to consider joining another study group before these slackers get back from the theater.

No Universal Consensus About Reality

The prevailing worldview is neither *all* modernism nor all postmodernism. Talk with teenagers in one part of the country and you would swear that postmodernism has swept the countryside. Go to another part of the country, or perhaps even another part of the same town, and you will hear kids who sound very much like modernists. Or talk to the same students on two different occasions, and you are likely to notice that, depending on the situation, sometimes they think like modernists, and sometimes they think like postmodernists. Without the advantage of a broader view, it is easy to draw conclusions about teenagers in one area and extrapolate that this is how teenagers are everywhere.

What astonishes me as I travel all over the world to speak to teenagers is how remarkably similar they are—not just to each other but to their peers from 15 or 20 years ago. They respond to the same themes, the same issues, the same promises,

Mountaineering guidebooks for glacial terrain face a unique challenge. First of all, on a landscape where there is little or no vegetation, and nothing but ice and snow, it is a little tough to find a natural landmark: "Go three miles north where there will be an angry polar bear, then proceed quickly in the opposite direction."

Secondly, any features on the glacier—crevasses, ice towers, streams of ice melt—are in constant flux, rising up, breaking apart, crashing down. Both factors make it tricky to map a trail in alpine tundra.

To some degree, it is that same problem we face in trying to map out the terrain of teenage culture. The features change so fast, upheaval is so frequent, that no sooner is it in the guidebook than it is off the landscape. For that reason, sometimes the best approach to understanding adolescent landscape is to look beyond the more visible ice towers of media culture that rise up and crash down, or the sociological changes that appear on the horizon and then pass from the scene. We need to know these features of the landscape exist and we might well encounter them. We need to understand the features to watch for and how they might affect our journey. But there is little wisdom in mapping out a ministry vision or a ministry plan solely on the basis of something as changing as the face of a glacier.

the same hopes. I have even seen them respond to the same illustrations.[III]

I am always a little amused at youth workers who predict long term trends when they themselves have only been on the job 10 years or less. A few years ago at the National Youthworker Convention, I remember hearing a youth worker breathlessly describe PowerPoint™ and computer graphics as the next huge wave in the church. Of course digital media and creative graphics have made massive leaps forward in recent years. But this youth worker was probably too young to remember that people used to talk this way about the overhead projector, and before that, video, and before that, 16mm films, and before that, slide shows, and before that, film strips, and before that, cave drawings, and *in the beginning* were flannelgraphs.

Trust the Truth

The old expression is still true: God is not looking for lawyers to plead his case; he is looking for witnesses to bear testimony. What makes the stories of writers such as Dostoyevsky, Lewis, Tolkien, and L'Engle so popular, even to this day, is that their stories stir within us deep longings. They take us to places that somehow we recognize even though we are not aware that we have ever been there before. We read their stories and discover that they are somehow about us. Their writings continually draw us in by asking, "Is it not true?" Do you not find it to be so?"

[III] Okay, I know I am not supposed to admit that I use the same illustration more than once; but let me just assure you unequivocally that I do. If an illustration helps kids to understand a biblical truth once, I will use it twice; and if it works twice, I will use it again and again until I find something better.

It is a question that points to both our certainty and our strategy in a post-modern context. Without surrendering the importance of Truth, or the grand gospel metanarrative, we can lay aside that certainty long enough to address the postmodern thinker this way: "Okay, let's assume that there are many different ways of looking at reality—many metanarratives that could be true. But don't you agree that, when it's all said and done, the gospel metanarrative best fits both the world as we know it to be and life as we wish it could be? Is it not true? Do you not find it to be so?" And if the answer is "no" right now, we need to be patient, be consistent, and be who we're called to be.

> One keeps at this in the confidence that there is such an irrepressible thing as human nature, and people may at some point be shamed into not denying—or maybe even admitting—the obvious. Or at some point they may be faced by a question of great personal consequence that requires a yes-or-no, true-or-false, answer. Or, best of all, they may be weary of trashing their own dignity as creatures endowed with the divine gift of reason.[112]

Human beings are hard-wired to search for truth, and life has a way of exposing our false assumptions. Even cynics cannot be debonair forever. As Richard John Neuhaus observes,

> We should tell better stories that winsomely, even seductively, reintroduce the great Story; being confident . . . that the pagans now and then, in the fine phrase of Edward Norton, got it "broadly right." We must help them to tell their story, for whether they know it or not their story is the story of God's ways with his creatures, the story of salvation.[113]

Don't Surrender to Despair

Like the prophet Jonah, we have been called to Nineveh (Jon. 1:1). Like Jonah, we may well be convinced that the prospects are unpromising. Indeed, even God's message to Nineveh seemed to portend doom and destruction (Jon. 3:4). But a funny thing happened on the way to disaster: Nineveh turned around. From the palace to the marketplace there was confession and repentance. God saved the land. "When God saw what they did and how they turned from their evil ways, he had compassion and did not bring upon them the destruction he had threatened" (Jon. 3:10).

Peter Kreeft writes of what he calls "the skin of our teeth principle," and while his creation story does not precisely parallel the Genesis account, it does parallel its promise of a sovereign Creator:

> Humanity always seems to survive by the skin of our teeth. If any one of a thousand chances had gone just slightly the other way, none of us would be

---

[112] Neuhaus, "C. S. Lewis and the Public Square," 270.
[113] Ibid., 274.

here now. If the temperature of the primeval fireball had been a trillionth of a degree hotter or colder three seconds after the Big Bang, no life could have evolved anywhere in the universe. If the cosmic rays had not bombarded the primeval slime at just the right angle, protein molecules would never have come out of the stew. If Europe had not invented ale before the Black Death had polluted the water supply, most of our ancestors would have died. If Hitler had gotten the atom bomb, he would have destroyed the world. If your grandfather hadn't turned his head right instead of left one day and noticed your grandmother on the trolley, he would never have dated her, married her, and begat you. If one Egyptian tailor hadn't cheated on the threads of Joseph's mantle, Potiphar's wife would never have been able to tear it, present it as evidence to Potiphar that Joseph attacked her, gotten him thrown into prison, and let him be in a position to interpret Pharaoh's dream, win his confidence, advise him to store seven years of grain, save his family, the original seventy Jews from whom Jesus came. We owe our salvation to a cheap Egyptian tailor.[114]

More precisely, we owe our salvation to the fact that God can work his plans even through the hands of a cheap Egyptian tailor.

Culture is a human fabric woven from many varied threads, some good and some not so good. The biggest mistake we could make is to become so obsessed with the fabric of that cloth that we forget the rule and dominion of the God behind the cloth. One of the passages in Tolkien's *Lord of the Rings* records a conversation in which Eomer has an unexpected meeting with Aragorn, and says:

"It is hard to be sure of anything among so many marvels. The world is all grown strange. Elf and Dwarf in company walk in our daily fields; and folk speak with the Lady of the Wood and yet live; and the Sword comes back to war that was broken . . . How shall a man judge what to do in such times?"

"As he ever has judged," said Aragorn. "Good and evil have not changed since yesteryear, nor are they one thing among Elves and Dwarves and another among Men. It is a man's part to discern them, as much in the Golden Wood as in his own house."[115]

Our task in youth ministry is to be faithful to the Faith, true to the Truth, tellers of the Story that gives meaning to all others. This approach—and only this approach—will reflect the very deepest understanding of the culture, and the best hope for doing youth ministry within that culture.

---

[114] Kreeft, *C. S. Lewis for the Third Millennium*, 60–61.
[115] Ibid., 76.

JOURNEYING DEEPER: IS SANTA CLAUS REALLY REAL?

Meditations on the Way by Helen Musick

Do you remember the first Christmas that you knew for sure Santa Claus was indeed none other than your Mom or Dad? (I hope at this point I am not blowing the secret for some of you!) I was nine years old. I remember reading the "Made in China" printing on the side of the Barbie (with bendable legs) box. "Now let me see, I thought Santa was from the North Pole." My suspicions were confirmed. My heart was disappointed.

Christmas was a lot more fun when Santa existed. I think it is because within us all there is this hope that at least one time a year, the magical exists, that there is someone who "knows if we've been bad or good" and still fills our stockings with treats that make us smile.

There is something reassuring about a large, jolly man consistently appearing every year to personally deliver those goodies. There is stability in Santa, not just because he is a generous, giving guy, but also because we can see him. We have years and years of photographic proof that he lives in the mall every December.

Do we realize that we have one on our side who does not wait until a certain time of year to make a grand appearance? Maybe not! After all, we cannot see him. Is he really there?

Some 2,000 years ago, a young betrothed couple, a few wise men, and one brilliant star testified to the reality of God Incarnate. One account of this event can be found in Matthew 1:18–2:12. "'The virgin will be with child and will give birth to a son, and they will call him Immanuel' which means, 'God with us' (1:23). God with us!

Think about that for a moment. This is the most foundational, fundamental, and profound truth of the Christian life. We serve a God who chose to appear on earth through the human body of his only Son. Make no mistake about it, God's definition of Christmas blessing and hope is a much more accurate picture of giving and surprise. The eternal mystery of the Immaculate Conception is much more powerful than the temporary magic of Santa. Do you believe it?

In ministry we have opportunities and a calling that urge us to give those around us a true vision of who God is. Through the birth of his son, we see that he is not invisible. In fact, he made himself visible. We may not see him walking the earth now, but we have a powerful account of his life in the Word of God—the Bible. Do you believe its truth?

We may not have boxes full of pictures in our houses as proof that we sat on God's lap as we do with Santa, but we do have snapshots of his presence within the depths of our hearts. These are the albums we need to share. These are the memories that will cause people to believe. What vision of Christmas hope are you casting with your life?

chapter ten

INTRODUCING THE CHURCH:
HOLY GROUND OR UNHOLY GRIND?

During the years you have been a Christian, how often have you thought of what God really seeks? Have you ever thought of the Church? Or is it that what you ponder about is how to pray, how to overcome sin, how to lead sinners to Christ, or how to study the Bible well? Do you consider these matters or the Church? Since what God aims at is having the Church, then whatever falls short of it falls short of His aim. I do not say that these various matters mentioned are not significant and good. I only say that whatever comes short of the Church does not fulfill God's purpose. It is well to have Sunday schools, orphanages, "endeavor societies," and gospel preaching. Nevertheless, such activities and establishments cannot be compared to the Church of God and must never be a substitution for it. God desires and greatly loves the Church. The Lord Jesus even died for the Church. And the Holy Spirit has been outpoured for the Church.
—Watchman Nee[1]

Can he have God as his father, before he has had the church for his mother?
—Cyprian of Carthage, martyred bishop of the early church[2]

For there is no other way to enter into life unless this mother conceive us in her womb, give us birth, nourish us at her breast, and lastly, unless she keep us under care and guidance until, putting off mortal flesh, we become like angels (Matt. 22:30). Our weakness does not allow us to be dismissed from her school until we have been pupils all our lives.
—John Calvin[3]

The church is like manure. Pile it together and it stinks up the neighborhood; spread it out, it enriches the world.
—Luis Palau[4]

---

[1] Watchman Nee, *The Church and the Work*, vol. I (New York: Christian Fellowship Publishers, 1982), 3.

[2] Cyprian, *The Epistles of Cyprian*, quoted in Christopher Hall, *Learning Theology with the Church Fathers* (Downers Grove, Ill.: InterVarsity Press, 2002), 224.

3 John Calvin, *Institutes of the Christian Religion*, in *The Library of Christian Classics*, vol. 21, ed. John T. MacNeill and trans. Ford Lewis Battles (Philadelphia: Westminster, 1960), 1011–1012.

[4] Quoted in Philip Yancey, *Church: Why Bother?* (Grand Rapids, Mich.: Zondervan, 1980), 33.

It did not look like much that day, February 25, 2000, in the late afternoon, as it was being towed out of the harbor of Arica—just a floating bundle of vegetation being pulled to the open sea off the coast of Chile. The *Viracocha* was, in fact, nothing more than totora reeds harvested from the shores of the Peruvian-Bolivian Lake Titicaca, 1.5 million of them, tied together by 5,000 feet of sisal rope into a marvel of nautical design. This odd boat, loaded with drinking water, food, equipment, and crew, weighed in at approximately 25 tons, and it stretched from bow to stern for 64 feet. It might have been a great novelty craft for a sunset cruise or a party boat. But this strange bundle of hand-cut reeds was launched that February afternoon by its crew of eight men and two ducks with the absolutely serious intention of sailing 2,500 miles from the western coast of South America across open water to Easter Island in the south Pacific Ocean.[5]

If the ship looked odd and out of place on that February afternoon floating out of Arica's harbor, one can only imagine what it must have looked like on April 9, 2000, when it sailed into the harbor of Rapa Nui on Easter Island almost three months later. "Each time the boat pitched sideways, the entire roof of the cabin shifted across with a crackling noise oddly reminiscent of someone delving into a bag of Scrabble tiles. It was the sound of cut bamboo splintering . . . "[6]

The structure beneath the steering platform was slowly collapsing.

The kitchen wall of woven bamboo . . . was warped and crumpling under the descending roof . . . The rail had pulled itself loose at one corner leaving a dangerous weakness and a mess of empty rope loops in mid-air. The long rudder shaft . . . seemed looser too, thudding up and down against the rearmost flank of each wave . . .[7]

Cleaning up the boat was "no small task."

Imagine your average bachelor pad, then shake it up and down a bit, and you get the general idea. The kitchen, predictably, was the worst. The floor didn't so much need scrubbing as excavating . . . Even the walls had a pebbledash effect left over from the day the pressure cooker had sprayed Greg's bean hotpot all over him . . .[8]

The floor of the cabin area was flooded by waves splashing over the sides of the boat. It must have been truly disgusting. Bobbing in the mix was a "pathetic inventory of dented pans, orphaned lids, and scuffed plates"[9]—the flotsam and jetsam of eight human beings who had lived through days of sunshine and days of

---

[5] Nick Thorpe, *Eight Men and a Duck* (New York: Free Press, 2002), 65, 233, 207. Sadly, at the journey's end, there were only eight men and *one* duck (Pedro). Pedro's duck sailing companion broke free of its cage somewhere around the halfway point of the journey. As you might imagine, the duck soon found the exhilaration of freedom from the cage overshadowed by the difficulties with finding a dry place to land. What eventually happened to the duck is unknown, but it is not likely he flew all the way back to South America. Perhaps this would be an appropriate moment for you to stop reading and pause for memorial reflection, and perhaps as well, to contemplate the true meaning of freedom.

[6] Ibid., 186.

[7] Ibid., 189.

[8] Ibid., 191.

[9] Ibid.

storm, and who had been utterly, closely together for three months. It was no doubt a water-logged, littered, funky ship.

But not one of the men, even once, ever contemplated the foolish notion that they should abandon this boat. They were under no illusions. The ship, and the other fellows sailing with them, was all they had. They had to cling to that ship as they would cling to life. Because that ship—as bad as it was—was their only hope of surviving this adventure, their only hope for ever making it back home again.

The Ugly and Amazing Fellowship That Is the Church

What those men experienced on the voyage of the *Viracocha* is not unlike normal everyday life in a local church. Sailing together on an amazing adventure of grace, sometimes through good times and sometimes through storms, the church is a collection of believers who understand that it will not always be pretty, and that there will be plenty of messiness along the journey, but our only hope for long-term survival as disciples of Jesus Christ is to stand together and stay together in that ugly, amazing vessel that is Christ's church.

There should be no delusions about this. Sometimes the voyage is magnificent and inspiring. Sometimes we are given glimpses of the wonder of lives interdependent and woven together in trust, affection, and necessity. But sometimes, like the kitchen of the *Viracocha*, we look around the sanctuary, or sit in on meetings, or walk the halls of our local church, and all we can see are people who are dented, orphaned, and scuffed. Hopefully, in the middle of the mess, if we look hard enough, we might also see, first, that God has brought us all together in this fellowship as part of an amazing adventure; and second, that apart from this motley crew of believers that is Christ's church, we cannot long survive. As has been wryly noted, "The church is like Noah's Ark; if it weren't for the storm on the outside, nobody would tolerate the smell on the inside."

It is little wonder that the apostle Paul, grasping for images that would capture the wonder and the importance of the church, used in 1 Corinthians 12:12–27 the metaphor of a *body* (the Greek word *soma*). This was Paul's way of reminding us that "belonging to Christ means becoming like a limb, part of an organism in which each part has its own special function."[10] Consider how long a limb would last if it finally resolved "to be free of this smelly, clumsy, old, unfit body." It would last about as long as eight men bobbing up and down in the Pacific without their boat.[11]

---

[10] Lothar Coenen, *Dictionary of New Testament Theology*, ed. Colin Brown (Grand Rapids, Mich.: Zondervan, 1975), 300, s.v. church.

[11] Or about as long as a small eastbound duck paddling for the coast of South America from somewhere out in the Pacific. See note 5 above.

Paul was not under any delusions about the body being free from disease, discomfort, dysfunction, and disagreement. Indeed, he used this *body* metaphor when writing to what some scholars consider his least healthy and mature church, the church at Corinth. He knew, of course, that the church was not all that it could be or will someday be. But the church is the vessel to which we cling until Jesus one day brings us home.[12] It is a body in which neither our need nor our role can be ignored.

> Now the body is not made up of one part but of many. If the foot should say, "Because I am not a hand, I do not belong to the body," it would not for that reason cease to be part of the body. And if the ear should say, "Because I am not an eye, I do not belong to the body," it would not for that reason cease to be part of the body. If the whole body were an eye, where would the sense of hearing be? If the whole body were an ear, where would the sense of smell be? But in fact God has arranged the parts in the body, every one of them, just as he wanted them to be. If they were all one part, where would the body be? As it is, there are many parts, but one body. (I Cor. 12:14–20)

"Outside the Church, No One Is Saved"

Origen (c. 185–254), one of the early theologians, felt so strongly about the importance of the church that he wrote, "Let no one therefore be persuaded or deceived: outside this house, that is outside the church, no one is saved."

With the kind of allegorical interpretation so typical of his biblical exegesis, Origen draws a parallel between the church and the house of Rahab the prostitute. The Israelite spies promised Rahab protection in gratitude for her willingness to allow them to use her house as a safe house when they were scouting out Jericho before battle. When Jericho fell, Rahab identified her house to the invading Israelites by hanging a scarlet rope from her window. Origen saw this as a picture of the house of God by which we enter through the scarlet blood of Christ.

> If anyone wishes to be saved, let them come to this house, just as they once came to that of the prostitute. If anyone of that people wished to be saved, they could come to that house, and they could have salvation as a result. Let them come to this house [the church] where the blood of Christ is a sign of redemption.

It may not be a traditional way of interpreting Joshua 2, but you have to admit, it clearly underlines the importance of church, and that parallel between the house of God and the house of the prostitute sure grabs your attention!

Origen, Homilia in Iesu Nave, *cited in McGrath,* The Christian Theology Reader *(Oxford: Blackwell, 1995), 402.*

---

[12] This is not just a turn of phrase. Although the metaphor is slightly different, it was Augustine who wrote that the church "is being trained by the stings of fear, the tortures of sorrow, the distresses of hardship, and the dangers of temptation; and she rejoices only in expectation, when her joy is wholesome . . . Many reprobates [nonbelievers] are mingled in the Church with the good, and both sorts are collected as it were in the dragnet of the gospel; and in this world, as in a sea, both kinds swim without separation, enclosed in nets until the shore is reached." Augustine, *City of God*, cited in Hall, *Learning Theology with the Church Fathers*, 243.

What Is the Church?

The best way to begin framing an understanding of the church is to take a quick survey of what the Scriptures tell us about the church. What follows is an abbreviated summary of basic truths:[13]

1. The purpose of the church is to glorify God (Eph. 3:10,21; 5:27).

2. The promise to the church is that Jesus will build and bless it (Matt. 16:18).[14]

3. The purchase of the church came through the blood of Christ (Acts 20:28, 1 Cor. 6:19, Eph. 5:25, Col. 1:20, 1 Pet. 1:18, Rev. 1:5).

4. The people of the church *are* the church. In his book *People-Centered Evangelism*, John Havlik explains:

   > The church is never a place, but always a people; never a fold but always a flock; never a sacred building but always a believing assembly. The church is you who pray, not where you pray. A structure of brick or marble can no more be a church than your clothes of serge or satin be you. There is in this world nothing sacred but man, no sanctuary of man but the soul.[15]

   The church is a fellowship of believers united in an organic, spiritual fellowship with one another and with Christ (1 Cor. 12:12–30; Eph. 1:22–23; 2:20–22; Heb. 10:22–25; 1 John 1:3,6).

5. The program of the church is the nurture and edification (building up) of the believers (Acts 20:32, Eph. 4:11–16, 2 Tim. 3:16–17, 1 Pet. 2:1–2, 2 Pet. 3:18).

6. The proclamation of the church is the apostolic faith (1 Cor. 15:3–5; 1 Tim. 3:15; Titus 2:1,15).

7. The preaching of the church extends to the whole world (John 17:18, 20:21).

8. The practice of the church is to be saturated with authentic love and concern (Acts 2:40–44, 1 Thess. 1:1–3, 1 John 4:12).

---

[13] Adapted from material by John MacArthur Jr., *Rediscovering Pastoral Ministry* (Waco, Texas: Word, 1995), xiii. Please forgive the alliteration. I would like to blame it on the source material, but it is my own doing.

[14] Commenting on this passage, Theodore of Mopsuestia (c. 350–428) writes, "This means that [Jesus] will build his church upon this same confession and faith . . . This then is what he says, that in the church would be the key of the kingdom of heaven. If anyone holds the key to this, to the church, in the same way he will also hold it for all heavenly things. He who is counted as belonging to the church and is recognized as its member is a partaker and inheritor of heaven." From *Ancient Christian Commentary on Scripture*, ed. Manlio Simonetti (Downers Grove, Ill.: InterVarsity Press, 2002), 46.

[15] John F. Havlik, *People-Centered Evangelism* (Nashville, Tenn.: Broadman, 1971), 47.

Watch Out for the "Edifice Complex": Nice Facilities Are Great, But . . .

Theologically, the church does not need temples. Church buildings are not essential to the true nature of the church. For the meaning of the tabernacle is God's habitation, and God already dwells within the human community of Christian believers. The people are the temple and the tabernacle, a tabernacle "not made with hands," a "greater and more perfect tent" of which the Mosaic tabernacle was but a copy (Heb. 9:11) . . . They are not needed for priestly functions because all believers are priests and all have direct access, at whatever time and place, to the one great high priest . . . Theologically, church buildings are at best unnecessary and at worst idolatrous.

—Howard A. Snyder, The Problem of Wineskins (Downers Grove, Ill.: InterVarsity Press, 1975), 66-67.

The virtuous soul that is alone . . . is like the burning coal that is alone. It will grow colder rather than hotter.
—**St. John of the Cross**

Worship ought to kill us. It ought to go against the "character" of a culture that makes commodities of God and worship, that deals with God and humans in terms of chumminess and folksiness, but never with awe—and thus seldom with power to liberate worshipers from the bonds of a binding and dulling culture.
—**Marva Dawn**

Perhaps John Wesley's definition of *church* is as good and as workable as any. The church, said Wesley, is:

a body of men compacted together, in order, first, to save each other in working out their own salvation; and afterwards, as far as in them lies, to save all men present and future misery, to overturn the kingdom of Satan, and set up the kingdom of Christ. And this ought to be the continued care and endeavor of every member of his church; otherwise he is not worthy to be called a member there, as he is not a living member of Christ.[16]

Saying essentially the same thing but a bit more succinctly is Karl Barth, who in his classic

[16] From John Wesley's sermon, "The Reformation of Manners," quoted in Howard Snyder, *The Radical Wesley* (Downers Grove, Ill.: InterVarsity Press, 1980), 85.

John Calvin on the Nature of the Church

We have identified that the distinguishing marks of the church are the preaching of the Word and the observance of the sacraments. These can never happen without bringing forth fruit and prospering through God's blessing. I do not say that wherever the Word is preached there will be immediate results, but that wherever it is received and takes root, it shows its effectiveness. When the preaching of the gospel is reverently heard and the sacraments are not neglected, there for the time being no false or ambiguous form of the church is seen; and no one is permitted to ignore its authority, flout its warnings, resist its counsels, or make light of its chastisements—much less to break away from it and wreck its unity. For the Lord values the fellowship of his church so highly that all those who arrogantly leave any Christian society (provided that it holds fast to the true ministry of Word and sacraments) are regarded by him as deserters. He so values the authority of the church that when it is violated he believes that his own authority has been diminished.

—*John Calvin, cited in Alister McGrath,* The Christian Theology Reader *(Oxford: Blackwell, 2001), 482-483.*

statement on the church said, "The Church exists . . . to set up in the world a new sign which is radically dissimilar to [the world's] own manner, and contradicts it in a way which is full of promise."[17]

The Church: *Holy, Catholic and Apostolic*

The early creeds spoke of the church in terms of three words: "*holy*,"[18] "*catholic*,"[19] and "*apostolic*"[20] church. Like so many words we say in the course of a Sunday morning, they can easily become simply words we speak ("Here I raise my Ebenezer"), or sounds we vocalize, without any sense of awareness of what the words actually are or what they actually mean. It is like the child who prays the Lord's prayer: "Our Father who art in New Haven, how do you know my name . . . lead us not into temptation, but deliver us some e-mail." These creeds become sounds we make with our mouths rather than truths we affirm with our minds. But, in using these words to describe the church—*holy*, *catholic*, and *apostolic*—we are making statements that bear some careful reflection.

[17] Karl Barth, quoted in Yancey, *Church: Why Bother?* 40.

[18] The Nicene Creed.

[19] Both the Nicene Creed and the Apostles' Creed.

[20] The Nicene Creed.

Holy

It is easy to be cynical when looking at the church—to look around on Sunday mornings with that knowing suspicion that "these people are hypocrites," to see their feet of clay, to see that those gathered in the sanctuary are little more than a collection of very earthy earthen vessels—dented, scuffed, and orphaned pots. It is, of course, all true. That local congregation you visited last Sunday morning is permeated with unholiness. So how then can we claim that the church is *holy*, a union set apart from the world, and acting differently from those in the world?

It is in response to that question that we tend to talk in terms of the church visible and the church invisible. We are trying to account for something that God promises to be doing in his church[21] and is doing in his church (Eph. 3:4-12; I Pet. 2:5,9), but that is not always so evident in his church.

Frederick Buechner, in his typically tart terms, puts it this way:

> The visible church is all the people who get together from time to time in God's name. Anybody can find out who they are by going to look.

> The invisible church is all the people God uses for his hands and feet in this world. Nobody can find out who they are except God.

> Think of them as two circles. The optimist says they are concentric. The cynic says they don't even touch. The realist says they occasionally overlap.[22]

It was precisely this kind of realism that led the early church elders to use the word "holy" in the early creeds of the church. In Augustine's day, there were two views of the church. One model was that of the Donatists,[23] who saw the church "as a pure, holy society inhabited only by genuine believers." Augustine, on the other hand, argued for a second model, one that sees the church as a *permixta ecclesia*, "a mixed society of both genuine and false believers."[24] He conceded that the desire for a pure and holy church in the present age might lead genuine believers to abandon the church in a wrong-headed quest for a church that is totally pure and holy.

> If you do not wish to be deceived and if you want to continue loving each other, be aware that each way of life in the church has hypocrites in her ranks . . .

[21] See Philippians 1:6 and Ephesians 5:27.

[22] Frederick Buechner, *Wishful Thinking: A Theological ABC* (New York: Harper and Row, 1973), 15.

[23] The Donatists were a group of Christians, most of whom lived in North Africa, who took their name from one of their early leaders (Donatus). One of their primary concerns was with the purity of the church, specifically whether those who had denied their faith under threat of persecution (during the reign of Decius in the middle of the third century) could be received back into full fellowship with the church. There were some such as Cyprian, the bishop of Carthage (c. A.D. 248–258) who felt that these lapsed believers could be allowed back into the fellowship, although their lapses and apostasy should be taken seriously, and the church should be cautious and unrushed in allowing them to return. But there were others, whose primary spokesperson was a Roman presbyter named Novatian, who argued that only God could forgive the lapsed, and that the call of the church was to be separate and holy from those who had lapsed so tragically. It was in pursuit of that purity and separation that Novatian broke off from the rest of the church and formed his own schismatic body. The Donatists were of the same separatist mindset as the Novatians, hence their strong disagreement with Augustine. Hall, *Learning Theology with the Church Fathers*, 236, 241.

[24] Ibid., 242.

There are bad Christians, but there are also good ones. At first glance you see a number of bad Christians, who as a thick layer of chaff prevent you from reaching the good grains of corn.[25]

> Throughout the New Testament we can find ... that everything is for the church: "Christ also loved the church, and gave himself up for it" (Eph. 5:25) ... He is to be "head over all things to the church" (Eph. 1:22). Indeed, the Lord is building the church upon this rock. The work of the Holy Spirit in these past two thousand years has been to establish the church. God saves sinners and gives them victory in order to build the church. He bestows apostles, prophets, evangelists, pastors, and teachers upon the church for its edification. It is also declared that Christ is to sanctify the church, "having cleansed it by the washing of water with the word, that he might present the church to himself a glorious church, not having spot or wrinkle or any such thing; but that it should be holy and without blemish" (Eph. 5:26-27). All this too is for the church. The final goal of God is to have the New Jerusalem, which is a type or figure of the church. The entire Bible, in fact, is centered upon this ultimate end.
>
> —Watchman Nee, The Church and the Work, vol. I (New York: Christian Fellowship Publishers, 1982), 4.

Augustine's understanding of the church's holiness holds in balance two equally important truths that help us understand the church and take it seriously. First of all, Augustine's view affirms that sin is an offense, not only against God, but against the church. If one part of the body is sick, the whole body suffers in some way. We must not act as if sin is no big deal (see Rom. 1:32 and 1 Cor. 5:1–11). God takes sin in the church seriously (see Acts 5:1–11), and so must we.

On the other hand, Augustine reminds us that any misguided notion that the church in this present age could be rid of all sin vastly underestimates the human capacity for pride and self-deception. If we keep drawing smaller and smaller circles to exclude the impure, we will find in the end, if we are honest, that we ourselves are left with no place to stand. In Acts 5:1–11, God struck down Ananias and Saphira for lying to the church. Had he that day struck down everybody in the room who was guilty of sin, there would have been nobody left to carry out the bodies and blow out the candles.

Why is this so important for people who are exploring a call to youth ministry—especially youth ministry in a local church setting? Because we must understand that this vessel on which we sail, this fellowship in which we work, is not going to be a place of perfect, smooth sailing. The church leaks. The boat is indeed "holey." If we are so naive as to overlook this truth, we will make three grave errors:

[25] Augustine, *Enarrations on the Psalms*, cited in Hall, 242.

1. We will undervalue the church and forget that the church, imperfect though it is, is still Christ's church.

> "God never establishes missions; he only establishes the church" . . . Yet people today create mission boards, set up evangelistic organizations, establish schools and hospitals, open orphanages and "endeavor" societies to help the needy ones. Are these undertakings good? They are all good. But if these are erected as substitutes for the church, God will not be satisfied. Can we not see the cunning hand of the enemy in all this? Satan cleverly entices people to substitute the church—which God has prepared in his eternal will to establish—with the work he will use. How we need to have our eyes opened so that we may focus our attention on the church, since God's aim is the life of the church—which is the body of Christ.[26]

> If, in our disgust with the smell and the disarray, the grime and the all too familiar shipmates, we leave that ship that is the church for the freedom of the open water, we will not long survive the storm. It is true. We do not see a perfect church, presently holy. But it is the body of Christ, and it is the only church there is. We do a grave disservice to ourselves and to our students when we dwell on our disappointment with this ship called the church, and downplay the simple fact that without it, floating all by ourselves, it is especially difficult to keep one's head above water.[27]

2. If we lose a realistic perspective on the church's holiness we will underestimate the impact of program design and good administration.

> We think the church is already the kingdom of God and, if only better organized and motivated, can conquer the world. But nowhere in Scripture or history do we see a church synonymous with the kingdom of God. The church in many instances is more worldly than the world. When we equate the church and the kingdom and the identity turns out to be false, we feel "taken in."[28]

> This is, no doubt, why the church is so obsessed with new paradigms and new models. We think that we can improve our systems, update our methods, and teach more clearly, and the church will just naturally blossom into a holy place.

> There is the untested assumption that the congregation is close to being the kingdom already and that if we all pull together and try a lit-

---

[26] Nee, *The Church and the Work*, 2.

[27] Those who leave the church because they are "fed up" with ———— (fill in the blank) might well be asked this question: "What if everyone in the church thought and behaved exactly like you? What if we all inherited your faith tomorrow? Would there still remain any impurities in the body? Would there be any blind spots?" We might end up like Pedro's unfortunate duck friend. Before we fly off from the church, we might well consider where we would land. Sad to say, this is a mistake commonly made by those who are in some type of parachurch ministry. It probably accounts, as well, for the not altogether encouraging proliferation of "independent" churches. Limbs that amputate themselves to be free from the body's disease find that the operation does not always bring the healing they expected, and it causes a lot of pain and bleeding. We need to be cautious about taking lightly the ministry of the local church.

[28] Eugene Peterson, *The Contemplative Pastor* (Carol Stream, Ill.: Christianity Today, 1989), 44.

tle harder, it will be. Pastors especially seem to assume that everybody, or at least a majority, in a congregation can be either persuaded or pushed into righteousness and maybe even holiness, in spite of centuries of evidence to the contrary.[29]

3. If we lose a realistic perspective on the church's holiness we will become paralyzed by discouragement. It is little wonder that so many people in ministry become cynical and disillusioned with the church. We thought the church was supposed to be holy; and so it *is* (the invisible church), and so it *will be* (the visible church). Someday. But today it is a *permixta ecclesia* (Latin, roughly translated 'mixed bag'). Were we honest enough to admit it, we would understand this condition, as the result of the bag—or boat—containing sinners like us and sinners who are us.

Drawing from Augustine, Christopher Hall summarizes this notion of a *holy* church:

Surprisingly, the kingdom of heaven includes both the good and the wicked, "the man who breaks what he teaches, and the man who practices it, though one is the least and the other is great in the kingdom, while in another sense it is a kingdom into which there enters only the man who practices what he teaches . . ." The pilgrim, journeying church encompasses both the good and the evil person. The church that has reached its destination, the church which at the end of this present age arrives at its heavenly home, will encompass "only one kind . . . when no evil person will be included." Our view of the kingdom, then, and who inhabits that kingdom, depends on our viewpoint. If we view the church in its present state, it is a mixed society. If we view the church in its final, glorified state, it is a holy society composed of genuine Christians. Even in its present state, however, it is "the kingdom of Christ and the kingdom of heaven. And so even now his saints reign with him, though not in the same way as they will then reign."[30]

Catholic

What this means, of course, is that all of you reading this textbook must take a vow of lifelong celibacy if you want full credit for the course. Only kidding. Again, confusion arises here because we tend to think of this word *catholic* in the familiar and specific terms of Roman Catholicism. In fact, historically, the creeds provide us with a larger and richer vision of this notion of *catholicity*. Martin Luther's close colleague, Philip Melanchthon (1497–1560), explained it this way:

What does "catholic" mean? It means the same as universal. [The two Greek terms] *kath' olou* mean . . . "universally" and "in general" . . . Why is this term added in the article of the creed, so that the church is called catholic? Because it is an assembly dispersed throughout the whole world and because its members, wherever they are, and however separated in place, accept and externally

---

[29] Ibid., 45.

[30] Christopher A. Hall, *Learning Theology with the Church Fathers.* Downers Grove, IL: InterVarsity Press, 2002, p. 245.

profess one and the same utterance or true doctrine throughout all ages from the beginning until the very end . . . It is one thing to be called catholic, something else to be catholic in reality. Those are truly called catholic who accept the doctrine of the truly catholic church, i.e., that which is supported by the witness of all time, of all ages, which believes what the prophets and apostles taught, and which does not tolerate factions, heresies, and heretical assemblies. We must all be catholic, i.e., accept this word which the rightly-thinking church holds separate from, and unentangled with, sects warring against that Word.[31]

The Foundation of Ministry

For no one can lay any foundation other than the one already laid, which is Jesus Christ. If any man builds on this foundation using gold, silver, costly stones, wood, hay or straw, his work will be shown for what it is, because the Day will bring it to light. It will be revealed with fire, and the fire will test the quality of each man's work. If what he has built survives, he will receive his reward. If it is burned up, he will suffer loss; he himself will be saved, but only as one escaping through the flames. Don't you know that you yourselves are God's temple and that God's Spirit lives in you? If anyone destroys God's temple, God will destroy him; for God's temple is sacred, and you are that temple.

—I Corinthians 3:11–17.

Not only is this catholicity a statement of the church's geographical breadth—it extends across the whole world—it is also a statement of the church's depth to include every walk of life, and its length, because it reminds us that the church will last into eternity.[32]

It is a huge concept, but a vital one. If we do not understand that the church is catholic, we will be left with a church that is either larger than it should be, or much smaller than it should be. Of course, the greatest danger of all is that without an understanding of a catholic church, we will be thinking of *ourselves* as much larger than we should be. We will forget that we are part of a worldwide, humanity-deep, eternity-long body of believers that is wider, deeper, and longer than our local fellowship. And in the world of youth ministry—where issues so often seem to get flattened to the present, shrunken to the local, and limited to the urgent—this is a great risk.

Apostolic

---

[31] Philip Melanchthon, *Corpus Reformation*, cited in Alister McGrath, *The Christian Theology Reader* (Oxford: Blackwell, 1995), 479. McGrath adds the comment that the Greek phrase *Kath'olou* could literally be translated "according to the whole." Cyril of Jerusalem (c. A.D. 315–386) makes this same point: "The church is called 'catholic' because it extends through all the world, from one end of the earth to another; and because it teaches completely and without any omissions, all the doctrines which ought to be known to humanity concerning both things that are visible and invisible, and things that are earthly and heavenly; and because it brings all kinds of people—whether rulers or subjects, learned or ignorant, under the influence of true piety; and because it universally treats and cures every kind of sin, whether committed by the soul or the body; and possesses in itself every kind of virtue which can be named relating to words, deeds or spiritual gifts of every kind." Ibid., 465.

[32] An adaptation of material from Thomas Aquinas, *In Symbolum Apostolorum*, cited in McGrath, 471.

Novelty may fix our attention not even on the service but on the celebrant. You know what I mean. Try as one may to exclude it, the question, "What on earth is he up to now?" will intrude. It lays one's devotion waste. There is really some excuse for the man who said, "I wish they'd remember that the charge to Peter was 'Feed my sheep'; not 'Try experiments on my rats,' or even, 'Teach my performing dogs new tricks.'"
—C. S. Lewis

If the word *holy* tells us something about the promise of the church, and the word *catholic* tells us something about the scope of the church, it is this word *apostolic* that tells us something about the foundation of the church. One of the absolutely vital marks of the church is its faithful adherence to apostolic teaching.

Martin Luther, writing in 1539, enumerated seven marks of a true Christian church: (1) the sacrament of baptism, (2) the sacrament of communion ("the sacrament of the altar"), (3) ordained leadership, ("office of the keys and ministry"), (4) proper public worship, (5) the bearing of the cross, and finally (6) the preaching and (7) hearing of the Word. It is quite clear in the following statement which ones he felt were the most important marks.

> First, this holy Christian people . . . is to be recognized as having possession of the holy word of God, even if all do not possess it in equal measure, as St. Paul says (1 Cor. 3: 12–14). Some possess it completely purely, others not so purely. Those who possess it purely are those who "build on the foundation with gold, silver, and precious stones"; those who do not possess it purely are those who "build on the foundation with wood, hay, and straw," and yet will be saved through fire . . . This is the main thing, and the most holy thing of all, by reason of which the Christian people are called holy; for God's word is holy and sanctifies everything it connects with; it is indeed the very holiness of God (Rom. 1: 16) . . . For the Holy Spirit himself administers it and anoints or sanctifies the Christian church with it . . .
>
> We are speaking of the external word, preached orally by people like you and me, for this is what Christ left behind as an external sign, by which his church, or his Christian people in the world, should be

recognized.

Now, anywhere you hear or see such a word preached, believed, confessed, and acted upon, do not doubt that the true *ecclesia sancta catholica*, a "holy Christian people," must be there, even though there are very few of them.[33]

There are points in every adventure where a wrong trail can lead to disaster, or at the very least, to grave disap-

> Some years ago, a British evangelical alliance produced a report containing a basic truth worth repeating: "In the last analysis there is only one distinction to be made; that is, between those who believe in the essentials of the Gospel and those who do not. This fundamental distinction is drawn sharply in the New Testament as sharply as the difference between darkness and light, death and life."
>
> —*Thomas Reeves,* The Empty Church: The Suicide of Liberal Christianity *(New York: Free Press, 1996), 181.*

pointment. This emphasis on the apostle's teaching is such a point in the journey of ministry. Turn away here, and the compass is gone, the map is abandoned, the global positioning system (GPS) has lost touch with its guiding signal. In our present cultural context, in which old is bad and new is good, in which relevance is valued sometimes more highly than revelation, we need to peruse these words carefully.

Red Sky in Mourning[34] tells the tragic story of Tami Oldham Ashcraft, whose husband was literally washed off the deck of their sailboat *Hazana* and lost at sea during a violent storm in the middle of the Pacific Ocean. She found herself alone on a vessel for 41 days with every means of navigation gone except for her sextant, the stars, and a *1983 Nautical Almanac*. She understood, even in the midst of her grief and shock, that her survival would depend on strict and careful adherence to those charts and stars. This was not a time for innovation, a time for drifting, or following the sun, or simply leaving one's course to be set by the current. A one-degree mistake in navigation today could mean that she would be hundreds of miles off course in the days to come.

It is in just such a situation that we find ourselves on the deck of ministry. We cannot allow ourselves to drift with the currents of popular opinion, or abandon the course for more agreeable winds. As the church fathers remind us over and over again,

> The church . . . is an inherently conservative institution . . . Whatever the church chooses to say must find its root in apostolic sources . . . Thus teachers in the church must never place themselves above apostolic teaching. They are not free to undercut the apostolic tradition through appeals to further revelation, however secret, mysterious or elevated such revelation might appear to be.[35]

---

[33] Martin, Luther, *On the Councils and the Church*, cited in ibid., 474–475.

[34] Tami Oldham Ashcraft, *Red Sky in Mourning* (New York: Hyperion, 2002).

[35] Hall, *Learning Theology with the Church Fathers*, 230.

the comment of Duke University Divinity School professors Stanley Hauerwas and William H. Willimon that the "roller coaster of clever new theologies has subjected clergy to one fad after another and has misled pastors into thinking that their problem was intellectual rather than ecclesial . . . [As clergy] we have no stake in saying something new. That is a favorite game of academia and is of little use to *a church more interested in saying something true than something new*."[36]

Of course, in the current climate of sometimes modernity, sometimes postmodernity, there is a sense in which all of this "doctrine business" seems overplayed, perhaps even a little heavy-handed. In those immortal words of pop culture, "Can't we all just get along?" David Mills is quite right in observing that there are many of us uncomfortable about saying

> in public anything exclusively Christian. Like those who boast of their belief in the authority of Scripture but are so afraid of being thought of as a fundamentalist or literalist that they rarely quote a word from the Bible, these Christians believe in a gracious God who loves mankind, but they do not talk about how grace is given to men, or who exactly this Jesus is who gives it, or how he is related to the Father and the Spirit, or (especially to be avoided) how those who have received God's grace are supposed to live, or (even more to be avoided) what actions will separate us from that grace, or (most to be avoided) why he is the only Savior of men.[37]

It is an unfortunate trait of much modern youth ministry that we are often cavalier, or perhaps even timid, about theology. No doubt that is in part because so many youth workers are theologically undertrained. We are like chimpanzees rummaging through an automobile engine looking for something edible or something useful.[38] Because our knowledge of the subject is sometimes limited, so may be our appreciation of it. In fact, the engine has a great deal to do with how the car moves, and what makes it a profitable means for the journey. We better not too quickly discard anything without understanding why it was there in the first place.[39]

When C. S. Lewis wrote *The Problem of Pain*, he began his prologue by saying, "I have believed myself re-stating ancient and orthodox doctrines. If any parts of the book are 'original,' in the sense of being novel or unorthodox, they are against

[36] Thomas Reeves, *The Empty Church: The Suicide of Liberal Christianity* (New York: Free Press, 1996), 17 (emphasis added). Mark Galli, in a wonderfully concise article, puts it well: "In fact, nearly every agent of church renewal began by comparing the church or himself not with intellectual and cultural trends but with the faith of the ages, particularly with biblical teaching. The monastic movement began when Anthony of the Desert heard Matthew 19:21 read in church. The Reformation began when Luther, after years of internal struggles, finally understood Romans 1:16. The Pentecostal movement took off because people believed they were living again in 'apostolic' times, in which Acts 2 was a living reality. Indeed, all these reformers adapted their biblical insights to their day—but *not until they had thoroughly wrestled not with their church or culture but with Holy Scripture*. They knew that there is nothing so fresh and incisive for every era as the so-called stock phrases of Scripture." Mark Galli, "The Virtue of Unoriginality," *Christianity Today*, 46, no. 4 (April 1, 2002): 62 (emphasis added).

[37] David Mills, *Necessary Doctrines, Ancient and Postmodern Christianity*, ed. Christopher Hall and Kenneth Tanner (Downers Grove, Ill.: InterVarsity Press, 2002), 107.

[38] Okay, that may be a *little* harsh. But you get the idea.

[39] While I have some concerns about Tony Jones's apparent embrace of so many of postmodernism's premises, I appreciate very much his comment: "The word *doctrine* may carry a great deal of baggage for you. Many Christian youth workers will say, 'All that matters is you love and follow Jesus.' But that statement itself is doctrine, and it's a good doctrine! While this sentiment should always be primary in our ministries, we must broaden our discussion if we are to teach and defend our faith in the postmodern era. Doctrine, in fact, is the way we use words to communicate the whole Christian life . . . While much of the emphasis on discipleship has been well placed, youth ministry has lacked a focus in the area of doctrinal content." Tony Jones, *Postmodern Youth Ministry* (Grand Rapids, Mich.: Zondervan, 2001), 150-151.

Adding "a Spoonful of Sugar" to Biblical Truth

If the church is to be faithful to apostolic teaching, there need to be pastors and youth workers who are willing to explain boldly and clearly and expound apostolic teaching—even when it might make people uncomfortable. In her book *All is Forgiven: The Secular Message in American Protestantism*, Martha Witten documented how most modern preaching and teaching is long on therapeutic emphases (self-image issues, guilt issues, dependency issues, and so on) and short on theological emphases (sin, obedience, righteousness, God). In a qualitative study of 47 sermons preached in Southern Baptist and Presbyterian churches on the parable of the prodigal son (Luke 15:11–32), Witten focused specifically on how preachers dealt with the portion of the passage in which the son admitted to himself that he was utterly guilty, and unworthy of his father's benefits (Luke 15:18–19).

Among her observations, perhaps the most interesting was the creative way that preachers were able to touch on the delicate subject of sin without actually making anyone in their audiences feel that, well, you know, that they were guilty of sin.[1] A majority of the pastors used

> adaptive devices ... that rhetorically buffer listeners from the harshness of direct identification, as if to suggest that the preacher is saying, "When I talk about sinners, well, yes, you're probably included, but I'm not particularly pointing the finger at you." First is the device of depersonalization, which flattens out and defuses the force of the idea of the "sinner." In naming the doctrine, preachers speak generally of "we," or even more weakly of "all men," instead of saying things that could personalize the accusation of sin. The finger of accusation thus swings loosely and vaguely, far above the head of any individual.
>
> Second, the doctrine of the universality of sin loses some of its bite through the device of rhetorical selectivity, in this case the omission of causality. Specifically, the doctrine is incompletely explained, since little note is taken of the source of human beings' tendency to sin: Adam's fall, the generation of original sin. The idea of original sin appears only once here, and there is no mention of anything that directly relates to this doctrine. The notion of original sin might, of course, appear particularly distasteful to modern listeners, as it assumes that human beings lack control over their behavior when it comes to their inherited tendency to sin.[2]

Marsha G. Witten, All Is Forgiven: The Secular Message in American Protestantism *(Nashville, Tenn.: Abingdon, 1988).*

[1] The strongest, most direct speech about sin occurs in sermons by Southern Baptist pastors, as they describe the moral character of the prodigal son himself. The son is frequently pictured in the throes of adolescent revolt against the will of his father. Demanding his inheritance before it is due, leaving home to seek his own life, and living riotously in the "far country" are taken as clear examples of sin in its biblical sense of rebellion. "In contrast, the sample sermons from Presbyterian pastors are less likely to depict the parable characters in terms of sin (only half of them do so, compared with all of the Southern Baptist sermons). In addition, Presbyterian talk about sin is far less vivid and forceful than that of Southern Baptist sermons. For Presbyterians, it is the dutiful, religiously obedient, yet joyless, older brother who tends to serve as the emblem of sin. He is full of self-righteousness about his own dutiful behavior, and he lacks sufficient charity to welcome his errant brother home." Witten, *All Is Forgiven*, 82.

[2] From her summary of the book in "Preaching About Sin in Contemporary Protestantism," *Theology Today* 50, no. 2 (July 1993): 243–253. In an unpublished article, James Singleton did a similar qualitative study in which he examined 200 sermons, half of which had appeared in *Pulpit Digest* (January–February 1981 and March–April 1991) and half of which appeared in *Preaching* (July–August 1985 and January–February 1991). For those unfamiliar with these periodicals, they are published as collections of *model evangelical sermons*. That is what makes Singleton's findings so discouraging. He found that for 39 percent of the sermons there was no attention given either in content or organization to a passage from the Bible, although the substance of the sermon did vaguely reflect a theme that was identifiably Christian. And 14 percent were not discernibly biblical at all. Of the 200 "model evangelical sermons," only 22.5 percent of the sermons reflected explicit attention to a biblical text. Cited in David Wells, *God in the Wasteland* (Grand Rapids, Mich.: Eerdmans, 1994), 149.

my will and as a result of my ignorance." He said much the same in *Mere Christianity*: "For I was not writing to expound something I could call 'my religion,' but to expound 'mere' Christianity, which is what it is and was what it was long before I was born whether I like it or not."[40]

In the realm of youth ministry, there are critical reasons why we cannot afford to underestimate the importance of a church's faithfulness to apostolic teaching:

1. **It is our source of unity.** There are at least four alternative ways that churches have sought to maintain unity in recent times: a common ethical standard ("We may not like Jesus, but we both dislike war"), a common religious experience ("We both have experiences of an 'ultimate being,' a 'wholly other,' we just describe it in different terms"), a common ecclesiastical process ("We are united not by our answers, but by our questions, and we are united through our dialogue"), or a common institution ("Even if we don't agree on the divinity of Jesus, at least we're all good Methodists").

   None of these means of shoring up pseudo-unity typically can hold together the people of a church. "Without a common doctrine, a common ethic simply does not exist; a common experience produces behaviors too diverse to call unity; a common process leads to disagreement and division, if it leads anywhere; and a common institution is not unified in any meaningful sense. Mainline Christians, and Anglicans especially, now know from painful experience that none of these can hold a church together."[41]

   Apostolic teaching is the source of unity because it is the source of authority. Members of a church staff, members of a volunteer team, even members of a church board—all might disagree on ministry methods, worship styles, management techniques, and short-term program emphases. But if there is mutual allegiance to Scripture, and to the authority of apostolic teaching, there is a true common ground for fruitful discussion.

2. **It will have an impact on the church's vitality.** As we observed in our survey of culture in previous chapters, people no longer attend church or religious services as a matter of tradition or habit.

   In a thorough research project, sociologist Benton Johnson and his colleagues Dean Hoge and Donald Ludens sought to find out why the church has faced such a decline in attendance and influence over the past six decades.[42] There are several assumptions normally put forth: (1) the notion that people who grew up in the 1960s and 1970s were put off by the

---

[40] C.S. Lewis, *The Problem of Pain* (San Francisco: Harper SanFrancisco, 2001), Prologue; *Mere Christianity* (New York: Touchstone-Simon and Schuster, 1996), Introduction.

[41] Mills, *Necessary Doctrines*, 115. For a thorough review of each approach, I strongly recommend *Necessary Doctrines* and Hall, *Learning Theology with the Church Fathers*, 106-119.

[42] Benton Johnson, Dean R. Hoge, and Donald A. Luidens, "Mainline Churches: The Real Reason for Decline," *First Things*, 31 (March 1993): 13-18.

churches' supposed indifference to the plight of the oppressed; (2) the highly popular theory among religious conservatives today, which makes the opposite argument, that people have left the mainline churches in protest *against* the support that denominational officials and agencies have given to left–wing causes such as abortion rights and Third World revolutionary movements; and (3) a notion advanced about 35 years ago by Dean M. Kelly in his controversial book, *Why Conservative Churches Are Growing*, that churches had simply grown weak and anemic through lack of conviction and low levels of required commitment.[43]

More than 500 surveys of baby-boomers who had been confirmed in the Presbyterian Church (USA)[44] found little support for most of the traditional assumptions about why people leave the church.[45] What they did find was the importance of faithfulness to apostolic teaching:

> The underlying problem of the mainline churches . . . is the weakening of the spiritual conviction needed to sustain a vigorous communal life. Somehow, in the course of the past century, these churches lost the will or the ability to teach the Christian faith and what it requires to a succession of younger cohorts in such a way as to command their allegiance . . .
>
> . . . Many of them have reduced the Christian faith to belief in God and respect for Jesus and the Golden Rule, and among this group a growing proportion have little need for the church.
>
> Perhaps some now unforeseen cultural shift will one day bring millions of baby boom dropouts back to the mainline churches. But nothing we discovered in our study suggests the likelihood of such a shift. If the mainline churches want to regain their vitality, their first step must be to address theological issues head on. They must . . . provide compelling answers to the question: "What's so special about Christianity?"[46]

---

[43] "Since careful tests of these theories have never been made, no consensus has emerged as to which, if any, of them best explains why mainline churches have lost members." Ibid., 14.

[44] Research was taken from interviews with a national sample of baby boomers who had been confirmed in mainline Protestant churches during the 1960s. It chose to concentrate on a single denomination, the Presbyterian Church (USA), formed in 1983 by merger of the nation's two largest Presbyterian bodies. It drew samples of names from confirmation lists of churches in six states and then sought to make contact with those people. It completed 500 Gallup-style telephone interviews and 40 face-to-face follow-up interviews. Ibid., 14.

[45] "We found that fully 75 percent of our baby boom confirmands had dropped out of church at one time or other, typically around age 21, and that about half of the drop-outs are now active again in some church. In all, 52 percent of the baby boomers are currently 'churched' by our definition, that is, they attend some church at least six times a year and are enrolled members. Six percent of the confirmands have become self-styled fundamentalists, 10 percent have joined other mainline denominations, 7 percent are active members of Catholic, Baptist, or other churches outside the Protestant mainline, and 8 percent are agnostics or atheists who have severed their ties with organized religion completely. Of the remainder, the largest categories are people who are still active Presbyterians (29 percent), people who either belong to a church but do not attend or attend but are reluctant to join (19 percent), and people who describe themselves as religious but who neither belong nor attend (21 percent)." Ibid., 15.

[46] Ibid., 18. Their findings echoed the conclusions of others who have done some work on this question. William McKinney concluded in 1987 that "careful analysis of membership trends shows that the churches hardest hit were those highest in socioeconomic status, those stressing individualism and pluralism in belief, and those most affirming of American culture." In 1992, sociologists Roger Finke and Rodney Stark concurred: "To the degree that denominations rejected traditional doctrines and ceased to make serious demands on their followers, they ceased to prosper. The churching of America was accomplished by aggressive churches committed to vivid other-worldliness." Reeves, *The Empty Church*, 32.

3. **It will have an impact on the church's youth ministry.** First of all, the research by Johnson and his team indicated *a strong* correlation between evangelical churches where people were taught orthodox faith and the willingness of church members to serve the church community through their giving or as volunteers.[47] Why should people give up their time to serve as club leaders or youth ministry volunteers when there is really no urgency or overriding necessity to help people become Christians?

Secondly, they observed a strong correlation between baby-boomer parents, whose own faith is only coolly embraced, and the unlikelihood that their children would become serious about the Christian faith. Johnson explains:

> In the distant past, good Presbyterians held regular devotions at home and instructed their children in the [truths of the Christian faith]. Judging from our interviews, however, in many Presbyterian families today religion is not a common topic of conversation . . . Given the reluctance of so many baby boomers to talk about religion or to instill their own views in their children, the prospects that their offspring will make a serious Christian commitment are even dimmer than their own prospects turned out to be. And among the "religious" dropouts the prospects are dimmer still. They are virtually unanimous in wanting their children to have a religious education, but less than a third with children at home have actually enrolled them in Sunday School. Many hesitate to do so for fear of getting "roped in" to a round of church activities themselves. They are "too busy," and they have a myriad of other commitments. Above all, they see no real point in getting involved.[48]

4. **It is the foundation on which is built any biblical youth ministry.** "In our study, the single best predictor of church participation turned out to be belief—orthodox Christian belief, and especially the teaching that a person can be saved only through Jesus Christ. Virtually all our baby boomers who believe this are active members of a church."[49]

It was the Apostle Paul who affirmed the church is a "household, *built on the foundation of the apostles and prophets*, with Christ Jesus himself as the chief cornerstone" (Eph. 2:19–20, emphasis added).[50] Any attempt to build a ministry based on any other than apostolic teaching—whether it be a wonder of purpose-driven architecture, soil-friendly design, or cutting edge technology—is to build on a foundation that is faulty and uncertain.

---

[47] Johnson characterizes American folk-religion as a "liberal lay theology." It is not typically drawn from the normal buffet of liberal theologies (feminist theology, liberation theology, etc.). It is more of a pick-and-choose Christianity that allows the believer maximum flexibility and convenience. Writes Johnson, "One indication that lay liberalism is not an energizing 'faith' is the fact that its advocates told us they rarely attempt to convert anyone to their point of view. They believe that missionaries should not try to convert people who already have a religion, and they have a strong aversion to the aggressive evangelism of Jehovah's Witnesses, Mormons, fundamentalists, and certain Baptists," Johnson, Hoge, and Luidens, 16.

[48] Ibid., 18.

[49] Ibid., 17. "Among those who do not believe [that a person can be saved only through Jesus Christ], some are active in varying degrees; a great many are not. Ninety-five percent of the drop-outs who describe themselves as religious do not believe it. And amazingly enough, fully 68 percent of those who are still active Presbyterians don't believe it either."

[50] See also I Timothy 3:15.

The Church in Trouble?

Now that we've underscored the importance of the church and the nature of the church, it would be foolish to deny the fact that the North American church is in serious decline. The research of Tom Clegg and Warren Bird presents us with sobering and provocative data—in their piquant phrase, "seven deadly statistics."[51]

1. The percentage of adults in the United States who attend church is decreasing. "U.S. churches are growing, but not enough to keep pace with the population. Of the nearly 280 million people in the United States today, only 40 percent of the adults said they went to church last week. That's down from 42 percent in 1995 and quite a slide from 49 percent in 1991. Other research indicates that only about half as many people *actually go to* church as *say* they do."[52]

2. "Roughly half of all churches in America did not add one new person through con-

The Good News

While the North American church faces a serious decline, the church in China (both organized and underground) is growing faster than the overall population. The same holds true for South Korea; for many African countries, from Mozambique to Nigeria; and for many countries south of the (U.S.) border, from Guatemala to Brazil.

According to *Missions Frontiers* magazine:

▸ Every week 3,000 new churches are opening worldwide.

▸ The church in Africa is increasing by 20,000 people per day on the average.

▸ Worldwide, Christianity is growing at the rate of 90,000 new believers every day.

▸ More Muslims in Iran have come to Christ since 1980 than in the previous thousand years combined.

▸ In 1900, Korea had no Protestant church; it was deemed impossible to penetrate. Today Korea is 35 percent Christian with 7,000 churches in the city of Seoul alone.

▸ In Islamic (Muslim) Indonesia, the percentage of Christians is so high the government won't print the statistic—which is probably nearing 15 percent of the population.

▸ After 70 years of oppression in Russia, people who are officially Christians number 85 million—56 percent of the population.

And *Religion Today* notes that:

Every day in India 15,000 people become Christians.

Tom Clegg and Warren Bird, Lost in America: How You and Your Church Can Impact the World Next Door *(Loveland, Colo.: Group Books, 2001), 26.*

---

[51] Tom Clegg and Warren Bird, *Lost in America: How You and Your Church Can Impact the World Next Door* (Loveland, Colo.: Group Books, 2001), 25–35.

[52] Ibid., 25. All data are from surveys conducted in 2000.

I confess that I have come to feel that the primary reality of which we have to take account in seeking for a Christian impact on public life is the Christian congregation. How is it possible that the gospel should be credible, that people should come to believe that the power which has the last word in human affairs is represented by a man hanging on a cross? I am suggesting that the only answer, the only hermeneutic of the gospel, is a congregation of men and women who believe it and live by it . . . Evangelistic campaigns, distribution of Bibles and Christian literature, conferences, and even books such as this one . . . are all secondary, and . . . they have power to accomplish their purpose only as they are rooted in and lead back to a believing community. Jesus . . . did not write a book but formed a community.
—**Leslie Newbigin**

version growth in the year 2000." That is not to say the churches received no new members in the year 2000. It is simply to say that most of the new membership resulted from what Reginald Bibby describes as the "circulation of the saints."[53] To put it another way, "in the part of the world that stretches west from Poland across western Europe, crosses the northern United States and Canada, and includes Japan, 'there are 3,000 fewer Christians now than twenty-four hours ago.'"[54] Having said that, we can celebrate the fact that in sub-Saharan Africa, there are now 16,000 more Christians than there were just 24 hours ago.[55]

3. No matter how you do the math, current conversion rates still point to one horrible conclusion: lost people lose. In America, it takes the combined efforts of 85 Christians working over an entire year to produce one convert.[56] If this is true, the vast majority of Americans will never get the opportunity to hear the gospel from someone they know in a way that they can understand.

4. Some researchers claim that more churches are closing than opening every year. Somewhere in the neighborhood of 3,750 American churches are closing their doors each year. That is almost three times the 1,300 churches that are starting up each year. In 1900, there were in the United States 27 churches for every 10,000 people. By 1990, the church to population ratio had dropped

[53] Reginald Bibby and Merlin B. Brinkerhoff, "Circulation of the Saints Revisited: A Longitudinal Look at Conservative Church Growth," *Journal for the Scientific Study of Religion* 22, no. 3 (1983).

[54] Martin Marty, quoted by Jane Lampman, "New Thirst for Spirituality Felt Worldwide," *Christian Science Monitor* (November 25, 1998).

[55] Ibid.

[56] Clegg and Bird, *Lost in America*, 29. The authors cite Thom S. Rainer as the source of this data. Rainer is the author of *The Formerly Unchurched* (Grand Rapids, Mich.: Zondervan, 2001). I admit to skepticism about these kinds of statistics, dramatic though they are. But it is hard to deny the basic idea that the American saved are not reaching the American lost at a rate sufficient to encompass the population.

to 12 churches per 10,000 people.[57] Now, to be sure, as church growth expert Lyle Schaller notes, congregations tend to be larger than they once were.[58] Frankly, as we have already noted, some of these churches are dying because they have ceased to be faithful to the apostolic message, in which case their death is less to be mourned (see Rev. 2:2–7). But the data are still cause for dismay.

5. Conversions to other religions and dropouts from Christianity are escalating. As Johnson demonstrated from his studies on the decline of North American Christianity, Christianity without truth is like a deli without food: people might still drop by, but the essential substance that keeps them coming back is missing. It is little wonder that as churches tinker with the menu, by adding seasoning, more sweets, and going light on the staples, the American population sees God as more of a hobby—a possible Sunday option if Starbucks is crowded. As Justin Long notes, "Christianity's . . . biggest competitors are not religious at all. From one million in 1900, the nonreligious have grown to 26 million today . . . Even more startling, atheists have grown from 2,000 in 1900 to 1.4 million today . . ."[59] Churches in the United States are losing nearly three million people a year to secularism, materialism, consumerism, and nominalism.

6. The decline in Christianity has been going on for nearly 50 years. Because we hear so much about growing mega-churches and large youth groups, we might mistakenly draw the conclusion that churches are bursting at the seams. In fact, in the past 50 years, churches in the United States have not even gained an additional two percent of the population. Sociologist Robert Putnam, lamenting the increasing breakdown of community, points out in his book *Bowling Alone: The Collapse and Revival of American Community* that church attendance and membership has declined by as much as 10 percent since the 1960s.[60]

7. Too many churched people believe and behave identically to their unchurched counterparts. George Barna's research among church lay leaders found a disappointing lack of robust and informed faith.

  ‣ Only 43 percent believe that there are absolute moral truths,

  ‣ as many as 33 percent believe that Jesus was not physically raised from the dead,

[57] Ibid. Clegg and Bird note that Charles Arn, in an article for the *Journal of the American Society of Church Growth*, estimates that between 3,500 and 4,000 churches will close and between 1,100 and 1,500 churches will open. Similarly, Lyle Schaller predicts that 100,000 to 150,000 congregations will dissolve in the first half of the twenty-first century. In any case, the picture is not encouraging. Lyle Schaller, *Tattered Trust: Is There Hope for Your Denomination?* (Nashville, Tenn.: Abingdon, 1996).

[58] For example, the average size for many congregations, even among mainline churches, has tripled in the past 100 years.

[59] Justin D. Long, *North America: Decline and Fall of World Religions, 1900–2025*, cited in Clegg and Bird, *Lost in America*, 30.

[60] Robert D. Putnam, *Bowling Alone: The Collapse and Revival of American Community* (New York: Simon and Schuster, 2000). Cited in Clegg and Bird, *Lost in America*.

▸ about 43 percent deny the reality of the Holy Spirit, and

▸ about 19 percent deny that Jesus lived a sinless life when he walked on earth.[61]

Some of these same findings are manifest in Barna's study of "born again" teenage believers as well.

▸ About 40 percent believe that when Jesus lived on earth, he committed sins like other people, compared to 60 percent of teenagers not born again;

▸ some 42 percent believe that Muslims, Buddhists, Christians, Jews, and all other people pray to the same god, even though they use different names for their god; and

▸ about 44 percent believe that a person can lead a full and satisfying life even if he or she does not pursue spiritual development or maturity.[62]

Examining the Body: Diagnosis and Prescription

Perhaps more important than documenting these various areas of decline are the questions behind the decline.[63] Why is it so easy for so many people to find church more bother than it is worth? Why is it that among self-described Christian teenagers only 52 percent attend a church service, only 40 percent attend a Sunday School class at church, and only 36 percent attend a youth group activity or event (other than a small group or Sunday School class)?[64]

There are all of the usual answers, of course, some of which have merit.

Hypocrisy

A high school junior tells his parents that he is fed up with church. "All they are

---

[61] From Barna Research Group press release "Church Lay Leaders Are Different from Followers". Cited in Clegg and Bird, *Lost in America*, 34.

[62] George Barna, *Real Teens* (Ventura, Calif.: Regal Books, 2001), 132.

[63] In 1992 John Seel surveyed 25 prominent evangelical leaders to ask their assessment of the state of the evangelical movement within the church. In compiling their answers, eight themes emerged as key issues the church must address in the twenty-first century:

·Uncertain identity: general confusion about what *evangelical* means;

·Institutional disenchantment: the institutional church is perceived as irrelevant and ineffective;

·Lack of leadership;

·Pessimism about the future of the evangelical movement;

·Growth up, impact down: More people consider themselves Christians, but the impact on society at large seems to be decreasing;

·Cultural isolation: We are living in a post-Christian era (that is, secularization, see chapter 9);

·Political and methodological response: Trying to apply secular solutions to spiritual problems; and

·Shift from truth and orientation to "market-sensitive" ministry: Trying so hard to be culturally relevant that we are biblically unauthentic. John Seel, *The Evangelical Forfeit* (Grand Rapids, Mich.: Baker, 1993), 48–65.

[64] Ibid., 133.

is a bunch of hypocrites!" As Friedrich Nietzche, the atheist philosopher, put it when asked what made him so negative toward Christians, "I would believe in their salvation if they looked a little more like people who have been saved."[65] To be sure, there is much hypocrisy in the church. We are clearly not the holy union we are called to be. Recall Augustine's characterization of us as *permixta ecclesia*—a mixed society of genuine and less-than genuine believers. As the poet Anne Sexton put it,

> *They pounded nails into his hands,*
> *After that, well, after that everyone wore hats . . .* [66]

We can and must concede the charge. Nevertheless, youth workers need to remember that the allegation of hypocrisy cuts both ways. Eugene Peterson's observations are particularly insightful:[67]

> I don't think . . . that simply because adolescents sometimes speak in moral tones they suddenly acquire moral authority. Their insights do not suddenly catapult them into a position of superiority. Finding stupidity, intransigence, and evil where they did not expect it . . . is only the beginning of their moral education. Someday they will find it in themselves; and when they do they will no longer be kids . . . Youths use the pejorative *hypocrite* quite indiscriminately and often inaccurately. Sometimes they simply use it as a synonym for *sinner*—someone who is not perfect, a Christian who forgets and gets irritated and makes misjudgments. In such cases, some elementary instruction in the nature of hypocrisy is in order. For the hypocrite is not a person who claims to be a Christian and who at the same time sins. All of us do that. The finest of the saints did that. Hypocrites are those who spend their time

> *I disliked very much their hymns, which I considered to be fifth-rate poems set to sixth-rate music. But as I went on I saw the great merit of it . . . I realized that the hymns (which were just sixth-rate music) were, nevertheless, being sung with devotion and benefit by an old saint in elastic-side boots in the opposite pew, and then you realize that you aren't fit to clean those boots. It gets you out of your solitary conceit.*
> —C. S. Lewis.

---

[65] Yancey, *Church: Why Bother?* 20.

[66] Cited in Yancey, *Church: Why Bother?*, 20.

[67] Eugene Peterson, *Like Dew Your Youth: Growing Up with Your Teenager* (Grand Rapids, Mich.: Eerdmans, 1994), 69–70. When Peterson originally wrote these words, he was not addressing directly the issue of hypocrisy in the church. He was advising parents about how they might respond when their children charge them with hypocrisy. But his thoughts are just as relevant with regard to a church family.

ritualizing the religious life, but with no intention of living it, ever. They are the people who are not concerned with working out the life of faith in intimate relationships and personal actions. Hypocrites do not sin more than others, they pretend more. They don't fail more often; they do, though, fake it more often.

Church Weirdness[68]

Flannery O'Connor, the Christian writer, observed that one of her in-laws started attending church because the service was "so horrible, he knew there must be something else there to make people come."[69] Unfortunately, there are a lot of folks who can appreciate the truth of this back-handed compliment. Annie Dillard speaks for many of us when she writes:

> Week after week I was moved by the pitiableness of the bare linoleum-floored sacristy which no flowers could cheer or soften, by the terrible singing I so loved, by the fatigued Bible readings, the lagging emptiness and dilution of the liturgy, the horrifying vacuity of the sermon, and by the fog of dreary senselessness pervading the whole,

Church exists primarily not to provide entertainment or to encourage vulnerability or to build self-esteem or to facilitate friendship but to worship God; if it fails in that, it fails. I have learned that the ministers, the music, the sacraments, and the other "trappings" of worship are mere promptings to support the ultimate goal of getting worshipers in touch with God. If I ever doubt this fact, I go back and read the Old Testament, which devotes nearly as much space to specifications for worship in the tabernacle and the temple as the New Testament devotes to the life of Christ. Taken as a whole, the Bible clearly puts the emphasis on what pleases God—the point of worship, after all. To worship, says Walter Wink, is to remember who owns the house.

—*Philip Yancey,* Church: Why Bother? *(Grand Rapids, Mich.: Zondervan, 1980), 23–24.*

which existed alongside, and probably caused, the wonder of the fact that we came; we returned; we showed up; week after week, we went through with it.[70]

The oddness of church, particularly in a culture that values entertainment, titillation, glamour, novelty, and hipness, is often identified as a stumbling block for teenagers. Ironically, as we have already noted, it is the church's attempt to become more entertaining, more titillating, more glamorous, more novel, and more hip that may well be leading to the church's decline. Indeed, Barna's

[68] This encompasses everything from the ugly buses to the lousy music, to the hokey wall hangings, to the bland little classrooms, to the weird people who show up week after week.
[69] Yancey, *Church: Why Bother?* 21.
[70] Ibid., 22.

research indicates that "how friendly the people in the church are to visitors" and "how much the people seem to care about each other" are much more important to teenagers than any of these "seeker-sensitive" emphases[71] when they describe what they might look for in a church. They care about the quality of the preaching (66 percent termed it "very important," and 27 percent as "somewhat important"), and the quality of the music (27 percent deemed this "very important," and 46 percent as "somewhat important"). But 96 percent of the students identify the relational factors as key.[72] What we celebrate in the oddness of the church is the fact that young and old, cool and uncool, rich and poor, singer and nonsinger, likely and unlikely, yuppie and skater, all of us can come together in a fellowship for the express purpose of worshiping God. Will that be weird? You bet! There is nothing else *on earth* like it.

Hypocrisy and the peculiarity of church culture are the two factors cited by most people on the street when they try to explain the church's lack of appeal (*peculiar* is defined in *Merriam-Webster's Collegiate Dictionary* as "distinctive, different from the usual: odd,

You Shall Know the Truth, and the Truth Shall Make You—Odd

Oddness is the consequence of following the one who made us unique, different, and in his image!

In C. S. Lewis's *The Lion, the Witch and the Wardrobe*, the White Witch has turned many of the inhabitants of Narnia into stone, but Aslan, the Christ figure, jumps into the stone courtyard, pouncing on the statues, breathing life into them.

> The courtyard looked no longer like a museum; it looked more like a zoo. Creatures were running after Aslan and dancing round him till he was almost hidden in the crowd. Instead of all that deadly white, the courtyard was now a blaze of colors; glossy chestnuts, ides of centaurs, indigo horns of unicorns, dazzling plumage of birds, reddy-brown of foxes, dogs and satyrs, yellow stockings and crimson hoods of dwarfs; and the birch-girls in silver, and the beech-girls in fresh, transparent green, and the larch-girls in green so bright that it was almost yellow. And instead of the deadly silence the whole place rang with the sound of happy roarings, brayings, yelpings, barkings, squealings, cooings, neighings, stampings, shouts, hurrahs, songs and laughter.

C. S. Lewis's summary of what is happening in Narnia is a brilliant description of what the church should look like: "The courtyard looked no longer like a museum; it looked more like a zoo."

—*Michael Yaconelli,* Messy Spirituality *(Grand*

---

[71] I do not intend this phrase pejoratively. To be seeker-sensitive is not, in and of itself, a bad thing at all. There is important biblical precedent for seeking the lost (Luke 15), and, obviously, to do so requires sensitivity. But there is a type of seeker-sensitivity that dumbs down the gospel and dumbs down worship so that it is more palatable for people who do not believe in God. It is that type of seeker-sensitivity that sometimes betrays the God-sensitivity that should be at the heart of the church. For a very thorough and helpful discussion of this issue, see Marva Dawn, *Reaching Out Without Dumbing Down* (Grand Rapids, Mich.: Eerdmans, 1995).

[72] Barna, *Real Teens*, 141.

curious, eccentric, queer"). But there are other factors—less apparent, more subtle—that leave the church, if not in decline, as least being less than it should be.[73] These factors are much intermingled with the way we think of youth ministry. We need to give them some careful thought.

Word-Centeredness

In our completely appropriate zeal for teaching the Word, we have allowed sacraments such as the Eucharist[74] to become marginalized and trivialized. I must myself confess that as a person who came to Christ through a parachurch ministry, I have faced life liturgically impaired. Because, like me, so many youth workers are less comfortable with the liturgical elements of church life, we tend to treat the sacraments as a nice add-on to the preaching and teaching, something that might be good to do if we can fit it in somewhere before everyone leaves.[75] Chuck Smith argues persuasively that one of the keys to reaching postmodern adolescents, who yearn for and embrace mystery, is through a recovery of sacred ritual. "The postmodern church will very likely see a revival of rituals, ceremonies and sacraments."[76]

Parachurch-Centeredness

No one can deny the wide and strategic impact that parachurch youth ministries have had in reaching high school and middle school students for Christ. As one of those reached, I will be eternally grateful for the impact of ministries such as Young Life, Youth for Christ, Student Life, and so many others. Their role has been significant.

But just as apparent is the fact that there are many communities in which parachurch ministries just such as those named above are a deterrent to, and in competition with, local church youth ministries. The rhetoric of the parachurch ministry is that "we are here to help the local church," and so they should be. But, there is an abundance of anecdotal evidence that this is not always the case. J. I. Packer was not speaking specifically about parachurch *youth* ministries, but this comment about parachurch ministries in general certainly still applies:

> Sadly, . . . these same agencies of God's kingdom draw interest, prayer, enthusiasm and money away from the wider-ranging, slower-moving, less glamorous realities of congregational life, so that the parachurch body comes to have pride of place in supporters' affections and in effect to be their church.[77]

---

[73] I have borrowed here from an article by J. I. Packer, "A Stunted Ecclesiology, Ancient and Modern Christianity," in Hall, *Learning Theology with the Church Fathers*, 120–127. Packer's article lists five elements in all, some of which I have mentioned and some of which I have not. The full article is well worth further study.

[74] Another name for Holy Communion or the Lord's Supper.

[75] Hall, *Learning Theology with the Church Fathers*, 126.

[76] Smith, *The End of the World as We Know It*, 134–135. This point is also made by Tony Jones, *Postmodern Youth Ministry*, 94ff. See also Brian McLaren, *The Church on the Other Side* (Grand Rapids, Mich.: Zondervan, 1998), 73–86.

[77] Packer, "A Stunted Ecclesiology," 127.

A parachurch ministry comes into town and launches its club in a new high school by recruiting students out of *and away from* a local church youth ministry that is already doing relational ministry, seeking to be a presence on the local high school campus. In doing so, this parachurch ministry often causes long-term harm to the church outreach as well as to the students themselves. The unfairness of such an approach is compounded by the tragedy that when we wean students away from the local church to a parachurch program, we are weaning them away from the one ministry that will continue to be available to them *after* they graduate from high school and college.

This is not a call for the abolition of parachurch youth ministries. They are far too important. But it is a plea, for the good of the church, that our brothers and sisters in these ministries live up to their stated mission.

Self-Centeredness

Evangelical preaching and teaching have always emphasized the importance of *personal* responsibility. This is a biblical emphasis (see 2 Pet. 1:5–9). But we have so often emphasized with our students the importance of *personal* response, *personal* commitment, *personal* growth, that we have communicated by default an unbiblical *de*-emphasis on community, interconnectedness, and growth of the larger congregational body. Yet, from what we read of the church's life in Acts 2:42, it is quite clear that the Christian life is about much more than just a personal response to Christian truth. "They devoted themselves to the apostles' teaching *and* to the fellowship [*koinonia*], to the breaking of bread and to prayer" (emphasis added).[78]

That emphasis on the personal to the neglect of the communal has left us with a loss in ways that are both personal and communal. In his short treatise, *Church: Why Bother?*, Phil Yancey makes precisely this point.

> Christianity is not a purely intellectual, internal faith. It can only be lived in community. Perhaps for this reason, I have never entirely given up on church. At a deep level I sense that church contains something I desperately need. Whenever I abandon church for a time, I find that I am the one who suffers. My faith fades, and the crusty shell of lovelessness grows over me again. I grow colder rather than hotter. And so my journeys away from church have always circled back inside.[79]

Not only is this deficit in our emphasis counter to the Scripture's repeated attention to community life, it is especially unfortunate in an age in which adolescents so seem to long for community. The Barna Research Group asked a national sample of teenagers to imagine that they had just moved to a new state

[78] Howard Snyder provides a good summary of what is suggested by this phrase "fellowship (or *koinonia*) of the Holy Spirit" (see Acts 2:42 and 2 Cor. 13:14). "The church should provide structures in which (1) believers gather together, (2) intercommunication is encouraged, (3) an informal atmosphere allows the freedom of the Spirit, and (4) direct Bible study is central." Howard A. Snyder, *The Problem of Wineskins* (Downers Grove, Ill.: InterVarsity Press, 1975), 98. See also 89–99.

[79] Yancey, *Church: Why Bother?* 23.

We must reassert the value of community and rekindle the experience of it.
—Brian McLaren

It is unfortunately possible for people to attempt to build the church out of every imaginable human system predicated on merely worldly wisdom, be it philosophy, "pop" psychology, managerial techniques, relational "good feelings," or what have you. But at the final judgment, all such building (and perhaps countless other forms, where systems have become more important than the gospel itself) will be shown for what it is: something merely human, with no character of Christ or his gospel in it. Often, of course, the test may come this side of the final one, and in such an hour of stress that which has been built of modern forms of sophia *[wordly wisdom] usually comes tumbling down.*
—Gordon Fee

and that they were looking for a church to attend. "What key factors would determine whether or not they would return to a church they had visited?" The most common replies were related to the overall feel of the ministry atmosphere—a positive, upbeat, welcoming attitude, "the ministry ambiance."[80] But, significantly, the second most numerous category of responses related to the sense of community.

> Teens identified this by listing concerns such as a desire for genuine relationships, a focus on creating real community, the hope of being with people who are serious about their faith and about each other, wanting to belong to a place that was family oriented and seeking a congregation in which the people truly supported each other.[81]

As Tony Jones rightly observes, "Postmodern students want real more than relevant. The church needs to be what it is: a sacred community of persons who follow a mysterious and demanding Lord."[82]

Living in "fellowship" is not just drinking juice and eating donuts between services. Marva Dawn reminds us that authentic community is a strength born out of weakness:

> Since the root meaning of the Greek word for *fellowship* is *having in common*, it means sharing deeply in each other's needs and carrying one another's burdens.

> True weakness—that is, a genuine fulfillment of the Church's true vocation as a power—is found, for example, in vulnerability to our brothers' and sisters' needs (Rom. 12), openness to each other's rebukes (1 Thes. 5:12,14), genuine hospitality to the needy (Matt. 25) and to other saints (2 and 3 John).[83]

---

[80] Mentioned by almost half of the respondents. Barna, *Real Teens*, 138.

[81] Mentioned by more than a fourth of the respondents. Ibid., 138.

[82] Jones, *Postmodern Youth Ministry*, 90.

[83] Marva Dawn, *Powers, Weakness, and the Tabernacling of God* (Grand Rapids, Mich.: Eerdmans, 2001), 95. Chuck Smith Jr. notes Paul's use in 2 Corinthians 6:1 of the Greek word *sunergo* ("fellow workers") from which we get our word *synergy* or *synergism*. Synergism is defined by Funk and Wagnall's online dictionary as "the interaction of elements that when combined produce a total effect that is greater than the sum of the individual elements, contributions." Smith goes on to make the point that one of the main features of the postmodern church will be its experience of synergism, "collective muscle." But is this really a new postmodern paradigm for ministry? Perhaps it would be more accurate to say that this is the postmodern church finally coming to realize the power in being the community it is called to be, a unified body with Christ as its head (Eph. 2:19–22). Chuck Smith Jr., *The End of the World as We Know It* (Colorado Springs, Colo: Waterbrook Press, 2001).

It is kind of exhilarating to talk that way, of course. But building that kind of community within a group of teenagers, or more accurately, helping them to build such a community among themselves, is just plain hard, messy work. It is "eight men and a duck" in a small place, on a long voyage together, in true fellowship, with all of the ugly, wonderful possibilities such a journey entails. We have all heard the parody of the hymn:

To dwell above with saints we love,
O that will be glory;
but to dwell below with the saints
we know; that's another story!

It is little wonder that the senior demon character Screwtape, in C. S. Lewis's *The Screwtape Letters,* makes just this point in counseling the rookie demon Wormwood:

> One of our great allies at present is the church itself. Do not misunderstand me. I do not mean the Church as we see her spread out through all time and space and rooted in eternity, terrible as

> North American religion is basically a consumer religion ... Pastors [and youth pastors—DR], hardly realizing what we are doing, start making deals, packaging the God-product so that people will be attracted to it and then presenting it in ways that will beat out the competition. Religion has never been so taken up with public relations, image building, salesmanship, marketing techniques, and the competitive spirit. Pastors who grow up in this atmosphere have no awareness that there is anything out of the way in such practices.
>
> *Eugene Peterson,* Under the Unpredictable Plant *(Grand Rapids, Mich.: Eerdmans, 1992), 35; I have taken the liberty of slightly amending Peterson's statement.*

an army with banners. That, I confess, is a spectacle which makes our boldest tempters uneasy. But fortunately it is quite invisible to these humans. All your patient sees is the half-finished, sham Gothic erection on the new building estate. When he goes inside, he sees the local grocer with rather an oily expression on his face bustling up to offer him one shiny little book containing a liturgy which neither of them understands, and one shabby little book containing corrupt texts of a number of religious lyrics, mostly bad, and in very small print. When he gets to his pew and looks round him he sees just that selection of his neighbors whom he has hitherto avoided. You want to lean pretty heavily on those neighbors. Make his mind flit to and fro between an expression like "the body of Christ" and the actual faces in the next pew. It matters very little, of course, what kind of people that next pew really contains. You may know one of them to be a great warrior on the Enemy's side. No matter. Your patient, thanks to Our Father Below, is a fool. Provided that any of those neighbors sing out of tune, or have boots that squeak, or double chins, or odd clothes, the patient will quite easily believe that their religion must therefore be somehow ridiculous. At his present stage, you see, he has an idea of "Christians" in his mind which he supposes to be spiritual but which, in fact, is largely pictorial. His mind is full of togas and sandals and armor and bare legs and the mere fact that the other people in church wear modern clothes is a real—though of course an unconscious—difficulty to him. Never let it come to the surface; never let him ask what he expected them to look like. Keep everything hazy in his mind now, and you will have all eternity wherein to amuse yourself by producing in him the peculiar kind of clarity which Hell affords.[84]

Consumer-Centeredness

Perhaps the most subtle factor (and therefore the most dangerous) that has weakened the church and diminished its witness over the past several decades is our tendency to think of the Christian faith in general, and the church or a youth ministry in particular, as a product to be packaged, marketed, and sold. Note these words from the evangelical research guru George Barna in the early section of his book, *Marketing the Church*: "So for the next ten chapters let's suspend any attachments to traditional thinking about church growth. Let's also enter this journey with a common perspective on the local church. *Think of your church not as a religious meeting place, but as a service agency—an entity that exists to satisfy people's needs.*"[85]

No one is doubting Barna's intention here. The goal of books such as these is to help churches better reach their local communities with the gospel. His work is extremely appealing and surely well-motivated. But consider carefully the mindset that's implied. Is the church primarily an "entity that exists to satisfy people's needs?" Is the church merely a product to be marketed? What happens to the church when we seek to package it for a broader appeal? Is there not something inherently dishonest about presenting the church as primarily "an entity that exists to satisfy people's needs"?

One of the growing trends in ministry—in youth ministry in particular—is an ongoing discussion about how to make church more palatable to an uninterested and disenchanted culture. There are frequent suggestions about how we can "do church in a new way"; there are conferences and books that call us to a "new kind of Christianity."[86] How can we make the service more "seeker-sensitive"?[87] How can we help our students "get more" out of church?

There are two polarities in tension here: one is a dead traditionalism that keeps raising the sail on the boat even though it sits on dry land; the other is an

---

[84] C.S. Lewis, *The Screwtape Letters*. San Francisco, CA: Harper SanFrancisco, 2001.

[85] George Barna, *Marketing the Church* (Colorado Springs, Colo.: NavPress, 1988), 37 (emphasis added).

[86] See, for example, Brian McLaren's *A New Kind of Christian: A Tale of Two Friends on a Spiritual Journey* (San Francisco: Jossey-Bass, 2001) or *The Church on the Other Side* (Grand Rapids, Mich.: Zondervan, 2000), a revision of his book, *Reinventing the Church.* I personally find McLaren's writing thoughtful and helpful, for the most part. But why for example, does he suggest that these four values "move to the forefront of the new church's mission": "(1) more Christians; (2) better Christians; (3) authentic missional community; (4) for the good of the world"? The values are great, but in what sense are they really new? This sounds to me a lot like the Church in Thessalonica (see 1 Thess. 1:5–8).

[87] Marva Dawn talks about congregations "replacing the invocation with a casual greeting by the pastor or priest in a false attempt to create 'community' and make worshipers feel comfortable." Dawn, *Reaching Out Without Dumbing Down*, 78.

infatuation with technique[88] and novelty that suggests we abandon the sail altogether for a boat that is more "land-lubber-sensitive." Both polarities are flawed.

The traditionalism that continues to raise the sail even though the boat is on dry land has long since forgotten that the sails were raised to catch the wind; and yes, that may cause the boat to lean, it might cause some spray, and the flapping sails could get loud, but—guess what?—that is why it is called *sailing*.

The infatuation with technique, on the other hand, is an approach that says, "People would like sailing better if we didn't ask them to help out on the deck." Or, "You know, if we used the motor instead of the sails, we could get in and out to sea faster, and that would better suit people's needs." But, of course, the problem with that approach is that—guess what?—*it is not sailing.*

Is hoisting a sail and waiting for wind the most practical way of getting from point

It will usually be argued that it is a question of mediation, of bridging the gap between those outside and those inside, of works of "sincerity" on the one side and serious and necessary attempts to win the world for Christ on the other; or that it is a question of the translation of the Christian into the secular at the command of love; or conversely of a translation of the secular into the Christian, of a kind of baptism of non-Christian ideas and customs and enterprises by new Christian interpretations and the giving of a new Christian content, or of a minting of Christian gold on behalf of poor non-Christians. And it is all very fine and good so long as there is no secret respect for the fashion of the world, no secret listening to its basic theme, no secret hankering after its glory; and, conversely, no secret fear that the community cannot live solely by Jesus Christ and the free grace of God, no secret unwillingness to venture to allow itself to live and grow simply from its own and not a worldly root as the *communio sanctorum* [communion of saints] in the world (not against the world but for it, not in conflict but in what is, rightly considered, the most profound peace with it). Where there is this respect, this listening, this hankering, this fear and unwillingness, it always means the secularization of the community.

—*Karl Barth,* Church Dogmatics, *vol. IV (Edinburgh: T.&T. Clark, 1958), 668.*

A to point B? Probably not. Will there be long times of sitting in still water waiting for the wind? Yes, quite likely. Are there other types of boating that might be more attractive to people who don't particularly like the open water? Uh-huh. Are there other boating approaches that would allow us to carry a bigger crowd of passengers? No doubt. But there are certain elements of sailing that simply cannot be discarded without qualitatively changing the experience of sailing.

---

[88] It was one of the favorite themes of the Christian sociologist Jacques Ellul that technology has become a God in modern culture. Marva Dawn argues persuasively that the idolatry of Technopoly has thoroughly infiltrated the church—one of the main casualties being the way the church worships. For more on this, see Ibid., 42–44.

And so it is with the church. Philip Kenneson and James Street, in their provocative work *Selling Out the Church: The Dangers of Church Marketing,*[89] make the point that if we treat people like customers, they will tend to act like customers. This seems a strange environment to nurture teenagers in the way of the cross, to walk with them in the crucified life (see Gal. 2:20). In his blistering and straightforward critique of the consumer-centered church, Doug Webster asks,

How do we present Christ to a consumer-oriented, sex-crazed, self-preoccupied, success-focused, technologically sophisticated, light-hearted, entertainment-centered culture? How do we strategize, as Jesus did with the disciples, to distinguish between popular opinion and Spirit-led confession? And how does the confessional church, as a community of Christian disciples, engage the world?

Many respected church consultants are offering straightforward, unambiguous answers. They are promoting strategies that encourage churches to establish a market niche, focus on a target audience, meet a wide range of felt needs, pursue corporate excellence, select a dynamic and personable leader, and create a positive, upbeat, exciting atmosphere.

But are the Christian marketers asking the right questions? Is the issue for the American church authenticity *or* attractiveness, integrity *or* excitement?[90]

When Paul described the preaching and ministry of the church in I Corinthians 1–2, he used words such as *foolishness, weakness,* and *stumbling block* (Greek, *scandalon,* literally "scandal")—words that make us squirm in our eager-to-please sensitivities. We must never forget that we are ambassadors of an upside-down kingdom (see Matt. 10:39), and if we try to invert the values of that kingdom so that it looks "right" to those on the outside, we have betrayed our vocation as the church.

Remember that the church was born back in Acts 2 through a most unsightly scandal involving accusations of public drunkenness. While the explosion of God's presence that day at Pentecost made a lasting impression on many, there were others who simply "didn't get it." Three times in Acts 2 we read about people being "bewildered" (v. 6), "perplexed" (v. 12), or just out and out amused (v. 13). It is stunning really. Here is God at Pentecost making himself known in a vivid and dramatic way—different languages, howling wind, tongues of fire for crying out loud! And a lot of people who saw it just thought, "These followers of Jesus are odd."

[89] Philip D. Kenneson and James L. Street, *Selling Out the Church: The Dangers of Church Marketing* (Nashville, Tenn.: Abingdon, 1997). This is an excellent book. It provides a very thorough critique of the type of marketing associated with Barna's various books, articles, and seminars.

[90] Doug Webster, *Selling Jesus: What's Wrong with Marketing the Church?* (Downers Grove, Ill.: InterVarsity Press, 1992), 20–21. Another provocative warning about consumer-centered churches comes from David Wells in his book *God in the Wasteland* (Grand Rapids, Mich.: Eerdmans, 1994), 68–87:

How can I make it? How can I maximize my potential? How can I develop my gifts? How can I overcome my handicaps? How can I cut my losses? How can I increase my longevity and live happily ever after, preferably all the way into eternity?" Most of the answers to these questions include the suggestion that a little religion along the way wouldn't be a bad idea.

In our eagerness to please, and forgetful of the penchant for idolatry in the human heart, we too readily leave the center of worship and, with the freely offered emotional and religious jewelry the people bring, fashion a golden calf-god and proclaim a "feast to the Lord" (Exod. 32:5).

Wells also provides a thoughtful and critical look at what became known in the 1970s as "the church growth movement" (Donald McGavran, Peter Wagner, and Alan Tippett being some of its best known proponents).

Thoughtful youth workers will recognize that many of these same issues that arise in the church as it wrestles with its authentic identity show up as well in local youth ministries. Being warned and watchful is half the battle. As in so many areas of life, "an ounce of prevention is worth a pound of cure."

Church Structures

Of the many other topics that might be addressed in an "introduction to the church," one practical issue seems to demand our attention. That is the issue of church structure. Much of what has been written so far in this chapter has been an attempt to think about who the church is called to be, and how we might better fulfill that vocation in a culture that, like those onlookers that day in Acts 2, often think of the church as bewildering, perplexing, and out-and-out amusing. At the heart of this discussion has been the struggle to match up the reality of the church visible with the calling of the church invisible.

The question posed here is this: How might the church visible best be structured to make its mission viable? It is an important question—as important to a youth worker as is the design of the operating room for the surgeon, the layout of the kitchen for the chef, or the boundaries of the field for the athlete.

Howard Snyder[91] suggests that there are four implications for church structure that can be drawn from Scripture (see, for example, 1 Cor. 5,12; 2 Cor. 5:18; Eph. 3:10; Heb 10:24-25):

1. The church must meet together in a way that encourages and expresses the fact that we are the people of God.[92] Any viable church structure will have to provide opportunities for people to come together to provoke one another to love and good works. This might be through cell groups, house meetings, or any number of other means. But what is important is that each part of the body has the sense that it is connected to other parts of the body.

2. The church must meet together as a larger congregation. Not necessarily a large congregation, but a larger congregation. Snyder argues that small groups, as vital as they are, are not enough. "The individual cells of the body of Christ must see and feel their unity with the larger body."[93]

3. The church needs periodic festivals that have covenant significance. The church must be called to remember its covenant heritage, a heritage that both the ancient Hebrews and the early Christians kept alive through spe-

---

[91] Snyder, *The Problem of Wineskins*, 106ff.

[92] The phrase "people of God" is not just a nice turn of phrase. The Greek term, *laos* "people" occurs 140 times in the New Testament, and it is one of the favorite words of both Paul and Peter to describe the church. "It serves to emphasize the special and privileged position of this people as the people of God." Ibid., 102. For a more thorough discussion of *laos*, see 102–106.

[93] Ibid., 107.

cific acts of covenant remembrance. Whatever form these acts of remembrance might take, there are at least four functions they might fulfill:

▸ Rejoicing and giving thanks for the acts of God among his people (2 Sam. 6:1–5, Col 3:16);

▸ Recalling and reaffirming God's covenant with his people (Exod. 23, 34; 2 Chron. 35; Ps. 100: 1–5; 1 Cor. 11:23–26);

▸ Reevaluation and repentance for those ways in which we've missed the mark of God's calling (Ps. 95, especially 8–11; Heb. 10:19–25); and

▸ Renewal of vision and reaffirmation of purpose (Eph. 4:11–15).

4. The church must structure itself in such a way that its unique existence as a people of God is kept central. While it is not always politically correct to think of the church as a people set apart, a distinct people, this is a biblical reality. And that distinct identity must be maintained, by rites of membership, baptism, even church discipline, if the church is to maintain its unique sense of peoplehood.

While Snyder's four values affirm some important elements of church life, a broader and deeper picture is offered by Marva Dawn in *Powers, Weakness, and the Tabernacling of God*[94] in which she describes seven essential practices of the church:

1. the apostles' teaching,
2. fellowship,
3. the breaking of the bread,
4. prayer,
5. signs and wonders,
6. economic and social mercy, and
7. worship.

A wide variety of church structures have evolved over the years, some of them providing a more thorough affirmation of these values than others (and some seeming to affirm none of these values at all). Leonard Sweet identifies four basic church structures:[95]

1. **Mission churches:** these are movement-oriented and mission-minded churches, and they have a community like the early church at Antioch (Acts 11).

2. **Ministry churches:** these are more focused on ministry within the church than on the mission outside the church. These churches may affirm the

[94] Dawn, Powers, *Powers, Weakness, and the Tabernacling of God*, 81–117.

[95] Leonard Sweet, *Soul Tsunami* (Grand Rapids, Mich.: Zondervan, 1999), 308–309.

value of connectedness and celebration, perhaps even the sense of separateness. But they have no sense of vision or reaffirmation of purpose.

3. **Maintenance churches:** these are well-run, well-organized, efficient "church machines," growing perhaps in breadth and prosperity, but not necessarily in obedience and faithfulness. These churches have all the pieces in place to affirm all four values, but they use those pieces to simply maintain the organization instead of mobilizing a body. These churches are best likened to a wisely managed country club and are sadly typical of many (but by no means all) large, affluent mainline denominational churches.[96]

4. **Museum/Monument churches:** these are churches that are living off of old memories, a cherished heritage. These are churches that, as they should, recall and celebrate what God has done in the past. Unfortunately, they do not also structure themselves in expectation of what God might intend to do in the future. These churches tend to be all history—no present, no future.

Sweet's taxonomy of structures is similar, but not identical, to the description of church structures provided by Anthony in the chart below (Table 10-1).

In some cases, as is apparent in the chart below (Table 10-2), churches are structured with a special emphasis on one value that sometimes leads them to neglect another value altogether.

Brian McLaren's insights regarding church structure are worth noting in this regard:[97]

1. One of the sure signs that a church's structure is no longer adequate to its mission is when good people (normally predisposed to congeniality and community) start fighting and acting badly. No need to spiritualize or demonize the conflict. Look for a structural or systemic problem.

2. Any structure that promotes growth will eventually become obsolete. With structures, there is no such thing as one size fits all. "Churches, like snakes and lobsters, need to shed their organizational skins as they grow."[98]

3. Every trade-up in structure will require some sort of compromise, perhaps in terms of priorities, almost certainly in terms of power. In the biological realm, these are known as growing pains.

---

[96] Bishop Richard Wilke of the United Methodist Church, in a book intended to shake up and wake up some of his episcopal and pastoral colleagues, observed, "Our structure has become an end in itself, not a means of saving the world." Richard Wilke, *And Are We Yet Alive?* (Nashville, Tenn.: Abingdon, 1986), 119.

[97] McLaren, *The Church on the Other Side*, 101–105.

[98] Ibid., 101. Here is a deep thought: Is it just me, or does it worry anybody that McLaren's two metaphors for the church are a snake and a lobster? One is an animal that bites with venom; the other is an animal that scavenges garbage from the bottom of the sea and then pinches anybody that tries to hold its hand. The subtle suggestions are a little unsettling.

Table 10–1.
Anthony's Paradigms of Ministry Philosophy

Stage	Spiritual Day Care	Fitness Center	Cathedral	M*A*S*H*
Focus	● Self-absorbed ● Problem-solving ● Meet felt needs	● One another ● Spiritual growth ● Desires development	● Corporate worship ● Worship setting ● Formal liturgy	● Reach out to the lost ● Evangelism/missions ● Teamwork
Attitudes	● Service station ● School of doctrine ● Manufacturing company	● Responsibility for another ● Expect to give ● Mutual trust and love	● Reverence for God ● High respect for God ● Self-reflection	● Proclaim redemption ● Seek the lost ● Bring in the lost
Motivation	● Need for belonging ● Needs reassurance ● Homogeneous groups	● Stage 1: Belonging ● Stage 2: Participation ● Stage 3: Leadership	● Responsible to God ● God's attributes ● Emphasis on symbols	● Love of God ● Love for people ● Bank of eternity
Values	● Always being right ● Success-oriented ● Solutions to problems	● Other Christians ● Deep relationships ● Use of one's gifts	● God's holiness ● Personal humility ● Privatism	● Justice, mercy, faith, salvation, stewardship, and reconciliation

Source: Michael Anthony, *Foundations of Ministry: An Introduction to Christian Education for a New Generation* (Wheaton, Ill.: Bridgepoint Books/Victor Books, 1992), 66.

4. Good organization should neither be ignored nor idolized. The Holy Spirit is the one guide and resource who can help the church to restructure and reengineer in such a way that it loses neither its identity or its edge.

5. There is no single prescribed church structure given to us in Scripture.

6. There is no one "right" size for a church community. Both large congregations and small congregations face issues that must be addressed if they are to be true to their calling. The types of issues they face are the main difference. "Sufficient to the size are the problems thereof, so churches of whatever size should focus on the beam of their own structural problems rather than the splinters of other churches."[99]

7. Like wombs and cocoons, structures must often be left behind before the next stage of development can begin. That means that a church may need to actually abandon a structure before it feels comfortable or necessary to do so.

8. In a healthy congregation, wise leadership will face the question of church structure with an intentional effort to allow for a blend of both historical experience (old) and creative genius (new).

9. Every church (and every youth group) will have its own personality. That personality must be considered when thinking through structural questions.

10. Even the best structure cannot guarantee a congregation's constant forward progress. "We need an ecclesiology that acknowledges latent periods

[99] Ibid., 102.

Table 10-2.
Types of American Evangelical Churches

Type of Church	Unifying Value	Role of Pastor	Role of People	Key Emphasis	Typical Tool	Desired Result	Source of Legitimacy	Positive Trait
The Classroom Church	Information	Teacher	Student	To know	PowerPoint™	Educated Christians	Expository preaching	Knowledge of Bible
The Soul-Winning Church	Evangelism	Evangelist	Recruiter	To save	Altar call	Born-again people	Numbers	Heart for lost
The Social-Conscience Church	Justice	Prophet	Agent	To care	Petitions and declarations	Activists	Cause	Compassion for oppressed
The Experiential Church	Experience	Performer	Audience	To feel	Hand-held microphone	Empowered Christians	Spirit	Vitality
The Family Reunion Church	Loyalty	Chaplain	Sibling	To belong	Potluck meal	Secure Christians	Roots	Identity
The Life Development Church	Character	Coach	Ministry	To be	Ephesians 4	Disciples	Changed lives	Growth

Source: Aubrey Malphurs, *Ministry Nuts and Bolts: What They Don't Teach Pastors in Seminary* (Grand Rapids, Mich.: Kregel, 1997), 33.

without guilt." We should not make knee-jerk changes every time we pass through a brief season of slow growth or no growth.

Jesus's Prayer for the Church

Christ's deep concern for the church is manifest in the prayer he prayed on the night before his death in John 17. After praying for himself (vv. 1–5) and for his apostles (vv. 6–19), he prayed for the whole church present and future (vv. 20–26). While there is much to mine in this rich vein of God's Word where we are given an intimate glimpse "into the presence, mind, and heart of God,"[100] what is especially noteworthy is that Jesus prayed for his church to be characterized by four essential marks:

1. Truth (vv. 11–13). This was the first concern expressed by Jesus in his prayer for the church.

2. Holiness (vv. 14–16). Jesus prayed that the church will not fall victim to either the trap of imitation (trying to be like the world) or isolation (completely withdrawing from the world). "Jesus calls us to live 'in the world' (v. 11), while remaining like himself 'not of the world' (v. 14) . . . This is the 'holy worldliness' of the church . . . We are neither to give in, nor to

[100] John Stott, *The Contemporary Christian* (Downers Grove, Ill.: InterVarsity Press, 1992), 259. Among other topics he covers, Stott provides in this book an excellent biblical overview of the church's theology, structure, message, and life (identity). His exposition of Jesus's high priestly prayer in John 17 is especially rich. See also John Stott, *Christ the Liberator* (Downers Grove, Ill.: InterVarsity Press, 1971), 67–89.

opt out. Instead we are to stay in and stand firm, like a rock in a mountain stream, like a rose blooming in mid-winter, like a lily growing in a manure heap."[101]

3. Mission (vv. 17–19). Particularly in v. 18, Jesus made it clear that there is a direct parallel between his mission and the mission of his church: "As you sent me into the world, I have sent them into the world."[102]

4. Unity (vv. 20–26). Three times Jesus referred to the unity of the church:

   ▶ v. 21a: "that all of them may be one,"

   ▶ v. 22b: "that they may be one,"

   ▶ v. 23b: "may they be brought to complete unity."

Can that church you attended last Sunday (or the one you stopped attending a year ago because you were so discouraged) ever become a place perfectly marked by apostolic truth, authentic holiness, Christ-like mission, and genuine unity? Well, that depends. Does God—will God—answer the prayers of his Son? Will we be faithful to be a part of that answer?

To be sure, the church is not there yet. We are still pretty much "eight men (and women!) and a duck." But our effort to be who we are called to be is itself a part of the voyage. Just because we are not yet sounding all the notes of this symphony called the church does not mean we should cease to follow the conductor and play our part. As Earl Palmer so vividly puts it,

When the Milpitas High School orchestra attempts Beethoven's Ninth Symphony, the result is appalling. I wouldn't be surprised if the performance made old Ludwig roll over in his grave despite his deafness. You might ask, "Why bother? Why inflict on those poor kids the terrible burden of trying to render what the immortal Beethoven had in mind? Not even the great Chicago Symphony Orchestra can attain that perfection." My answer is this: The Milpitas High School orchestra will give some people in that audience their only encounter with Beethoven's great Ninth Symphony. Far from perfection, it is nevertheless the only way they will hear Beethoven's message.[103]

---

[101] Ibid., 263.

[102] Granted, the church's mission is not identical to Christ's mission, because he was the only Savior of the world. But, like Jesus, we are sent out into the world to incarnate—to flesh out—the love of God.

[103] Earl Palmer, quoted in Yancey, *Church: Why Bother?* 99–100.

The Perfect Church Structure

I used to think I could find the perfect structure for my church, the right balance of power, terms of service, checks and balances, and so on. But now I realize that the perfect structure is just about any that is flexible enough to become a better structure tomorrow. Conversely, the "perfect structure" that claims to be *the* right one, immune to improvement, is actually one of the worst structures possible.

My search for the perfect church structure was about as promising as the search for a perfect pair of pants or shoes that my children would never outgrow. It is clear to me now that in the same way our closets are full of outgrown clothes, so our church files should be full of outgrown structural diagrams. Those diagrams were not failures; they fulfilled their purpose for their time. We should not feel bad for not "getting it right the first time" any more than we feel bad about having to replace worn-out or undersized clothes. Now this all seems pretty obvious, but that kind of insight comes amazingly hard and slowly for many of us.

The next time you are talking about the need for change in your church structure, get your people to consider a bigger change than they had bargained for. Make it not just a change to a different structure, but a change to a different way of thinking about structures. This may be harder to accept in the short run, but it proves to be so much better over time.

Brian McLaren, The Church on the Other Side *(Grand Rapids: Zondervan, 2000), 107.*

Travel Log:
South Africa

Youth Worker Profiles by Paul Borthwick

Joshua Fake (pronounced FAH-kee) started out as a
volunteer with Youth Alive ministries, serving the
youth of the black residential areas of South Africa
and Zimbabwe. He became a full-time staff member in
1981, and he now serves as director of the ministry
in Bodibe, Soweto, South Africa.

Holistic. Youth Alive's ministry is holistic—
including clubs, on-campus ministry, unemployment
counseling, family intervention, and work with the
police. Fake explains, "The South African context
means that we must care for the whole person. Our
purpose statement reads, 'To reach out to young people with the gospel of Jesus and disciple them to be
agents of change in church and society.'"

Not Your Typical Youth Ministry. Because many
of the youth grow up in tough urban contexts, Youth
Alive starts with six-year-olds because starting at
age 11 or 12 may be too late. "We work with young
people from the age of six years to the time they
get married. The ministry is structured according to
age—one group focuses on 6-to 11-year olds, another
concentrates on 11-to 13 year olds, and the third
focuses on the high school age group. We do our best
to go into their worlds and teach practical discipleship. And in our country, we can minister directly in the schools, so we go to schools and preach at
assembly in the morning and help young Christians to
be effective witnesses for the Lord in the schools
they attend."

What Goes Around Comes Around. Fake notices he is getting older: "It is the youth world that has kept me young. Not that I am young in looks anymore. I have lots of gray hair and half my hair has fallen out." Nevertheless, he concentrates much of his time training younger workers. Why? "I never forget the grace shown to me as a young person. I was led to Christ through a youth worker who came to our very poor home and reached out to us. He spent the night sleeping on the floor at my home with all of us."

A Vision for South Africa. South Africa has gone through massive changes since the early 1990s. What is Fake's vision ahead for Youth Alive? "I desire to see people come out of terrible depressing situations as the gospel frees them and lets them discover their true potential. Then I pray we can see their lives changed as they develop to become useful citizens of the kingdom and South Africa."

UNIT THREE
CHARTING A COURSE
FOR THE JOURNEY

Our trio of pests still invade and obstruct us on all occasions, these are the Musquetoes, eye knats and prickly pears . . . The mountains they still continue high and seem to rise in some places like an amphatheatre one range above another as they recede from the river until the most distant and lofty have their tops clad with snow.

—Captain William Clark, Lewis and Clark Expedition, on or about July 23, 1805[1]

[1] Stephen Ambrose, *Undaunted Courage* (New York: Simon and Schuster, 1996), 256–257; spellings and grammar as in original.

chapter eleven

ADOLESCENT SPIRITUALITY:
THE ODYSSEY OF GROWING FAITH

Experienced mountaineers have a quiet, regular, short step—on the level it looks petty; but then this step they keep up, on and on as they ascend, whilst the inexperienced townsman hurries along, and soon has to stop, dead beat with the climb . . . Such an expert mountaineer, when the thick mists come, halts and camps out under some slight cover brought with him, quietly smoking his pipe, moving on only when the mist has cleared away . . . You want to grow in virtue, to serve God, to love Christ? Well, you will grow in and attain to these things if you will make them a slow and sure, an utterly real, a mountain steptrod and ascent, willing to have to camp for weeks or months in spiritual desolation darkness and emptiness at different stages in your march and growth. All demand for constant light, for ever the best—the best to your own feeling, all attempt at eliminating or minimizing the cross and trial, is so much soft folly and puerile trifling.
—Baron Friedrich von Hugel[2]

The crown is before you; and it is an incorruptible one: so run that you may obtain it . . . Let the Kingdom be always before you; and believe steadfastly concerning things that are invisible. Let nothing that is on this side of the other world get within you: and above all, look well to your own hearts, and to the lusts thereof, for they are deceitful above all things, and desperately wicked. Set your faces like a flint; you have all power in heaven and earth on your side.
—John Bunyan's character Evangelist, speaking to Christian and Faithful, just before they come to one of the most dangerous parts of their journey toward the Celestial City[3]

[2] Baron Friedrich von Hugel, *Selected Letters 1896–1924*, ed. Bernard Holland (New York: Dutton, 1933), 305–266, cited in Eugene Peterson, *Run with the Horses* (Downers Grove, Ill.: InterVarsity Press, 1983), 109–110.

[3] John Bunyan, *Pilgrim's Progress* (Grand Rapids, Mich.: Zondervan, 1966), 72.

Will Willimon, dean of the Chapel at Duke University, has a distinguished ministry of preaching and writing. One day in the supermarket checkout line, however, he was simply perusing the latest issue of *Star* magazine, hoping that before his turn at the cashier he might finish the article "Vanna Says Nude Photo Is Cheap Shot." For the woman standing behind him in line, though, that was not enough. She nudged him forward with her cart and complained, "Either pay for it, buddy, or let me by."

Willimon responded, "Madam, I'll have you know that you are addressing Vanna White's former pastor."

It was true. While Willimon got very little space in her long-awaited biography, *Vanna Speaks*, the ever-smiling, never-speaking beauty who turns letters on the television game show *Wheel of Fortune* was actually a member of his church while she was growing up in North Myrtle Beach, South Carolina. He even recalls the conversation one Sunday in May of her high school senior year when he asked what she might do after graduation, and she replied, in her unfailingly sweet and positive way, that she had dreams of going to modeling school in Atlanta.

Of course, when the impatient supermarket shopper bumping Willimon from behind received this tidbit—that Willimon had been Vanna's pastor—the whole tone of the scene immediately changed. The woman shrieked and asked for his autograph. Everything came to a halt in the supermarket as people crowded around. "Before it was all over, the manager had given me a free copy of *Star* after I had promised always to shop at his store."[4]

It must have been fun.

But it is an episode that also points to a more serious issue: What happens to the students who pass through our ministries? What is the end product of our work? What are the milestones and markers that might indicate we are making progress toward that end? This is *not* the question that is often asked in youth ministry: "What are we *doing*?" Rather, it is the question that must be asked before that question: "What do we *hope to have done* when we have had our opportunity for doing?"

This is not a new question. It was certainly behind Jesus's words when he commissioned the disciples in John 15:16, "You did not choose me, but I chose you and appointed you to go and bear fruit—*fruit that will last* . . . "[5] It was surely Paul's concern when he wrote in 1 Corinthians 3:10–13: "Each one should be careful how he builds . . . If any man builds on this foundation using gold, silver, costly stones, wood, hay or straw, his work will be shown for what it is, because the

---

[4] William Willimon, *The Last Word* (Nashville, Tenn.: Abingdon, 2000), 62.

[5] Emphasis added. Dr. Stott argues convincingly that the *fruitfulness* we are called to in John 15 is the fruit of righteousness. That also accords with other Old and New Testament passages that point to this interpretation (see, for example, Gal. 5:22–23, and Isa. 5:1–23). John Stott, *Christ the Liberator* (Downers Grove, Ill.: InterVarsity Press, 1971), 50ff. Yet, as Barnes comments, this seems also quite clearly to be a commission of sorts that the disciples "should be rich in good works; faithful and successful in spreading [the] gospel. This was the great business to which they were set apart, and this they faithfully accomplished . . . It is to do good, and to spread as far as possible the rich temporal and spiritual blessings which the gospel is fitted to confer on mankind . . . Their gospel was to spread—was to take a deep and permanent hold on people—and was ultimately to fill the world (Matt. 16:18)." *Barnes' Notes*, Electronic Database, c. 1997 by Biblesoft.

Day will bring it to light. It will be revealed with fire, and the fire will test the quality of each man's work."[6]

Inherent in the heart of any responsible steward (Luke 16:1–9, I Cor. 4:1-2, Titus 1:7) is a concern for wise investment and attention to return. As good shepherds (John 10:1–18), any of us in ministry should always be passionate about the welfare of the sheep—not just accumulating a large flock, but protecting them, feeding them, and providing them nurture.

That is why Willimon's story is so noteworthy. It reminds us that a question we must ask ourselves with regard to our students is not "Where are they now?" but "Where will they be 10 years from now, 20 years from now?" Without drawing any conclusions about Vanna White,[7] suffice it to say that all of us in ministry can look back on students who seemed at the time to start fast, but at last report, had not apparently stayed strong. It is a fact of free will that even with the best of ministries there will be some who get turned on, some who get turned off, some who turn over a new life, and some (or, at least, a few) who just turn over vowels and consonants.

One study done more than a decade ago showed that 64 percent of the church youth surveyed had an underdeveloped faith, defined as being low on the vertical dimension of a "deep, personal relationship with a loving God."[8] George Barna's more recent research[9] on American adolescents indicates that only three out of every ten self-described Christian teenagers claim to be "absolutely committed" to the Christian faith. About five out of the ten describe themselves as "moderately committed." Where will they be 10 years from now?

Moderate Commitment to an Extreme Faith

The Christian life has always been about pilgrimage. Spiritual writers of the Middle Ages referred to believers with the Latin word *viator* "wayfarer or traveler".[10] It pointed to a basic truth: as Christians we are not called to be settlers; we are called to be adventurers, explorers, those who maintain pursuit, who seek to cover new ground. There is nothing "moderate" about this journey. As Eugene Peterson quite rightly observes,

---

[6] Commenting on this passage, Augustine wrote, "The fire will try the quality of everyone's work. If his work remains, he will receive his reward. If his work burns, he will lose his reward, but he himself will be saved. In this fire neither man will be lost forever, though the fire will profit the one and harm the other, being a test for both." From *City of God*, cited in *Ancient Christian Commentary on Scripture*, vol. VII, ed. Gerald Bray (Downers Grove, Ill.: InterVarsity Press, 1999), 33.

[7] I am certain, by the way, that the nude pictures were, indeed, a cheap shot.

[8] Vital horizontal faith was defined as a faith marked by actions of mercy, love, and justice. P. L. Benson and C. Elkin, *Effective Christian Education: A National Study of Protestant Congregations: A Summary Report on Faith, Loyalty , and Congregational Life* (Minneapolis, Minn.: Search Institute, 1990).

[9] George Barna, *Real Teens* (Ventura, Calif.: Regal Books, 2001), 121. Barna reports that typically six out of ten teenagers will say they have made a personal commitment to Christ, and among that group, roughly six out of ten believe they will have eternal salvation because of their faith commitment.

[10] Alister McGrath, *The Journey: A Pilgrim in the Lands of the Spirit* (New York: Doubleday, 1999), 9.

The Christian life is not a quiet escape to a garden where we can walk and talk uninterruptedly with our Lord; not a fantasy trip to a heavenly city where we can compare our blue ribbons and gold medals with others who have made it to the winners' circle. To suppose that, or to expect that, is to turn the nut the wrong way. The Christian life is going to God . . . Christian discipleship is a process of paying more and more attention to God's righteousness and less and less attention to our own; finding the meaning of our lives not by probing our moods and motives and morals but by believing in God's will and purposes; making a map of the faithfulness of God, not charting the rise and fall of our own enthusiasms.[11]

The Tragedy of Unfinished Adventure

The following is from the journal of Robert Falcon Scott, preparing to report on his doomed 1912 expedition to the South Pole that endured two and one-half months of misery and cold only to discover that Roald Amundsen of Norway had arrived first:

> I shall inevitably be asked for a word of mature judgment on the expedition of a kind that was impossible when we were all up close to it . . . On the one hand, Amundsen going straight there, getting there first, and returning without the loss of a single man, and without having put any greater strain on himself and his men than was all in the day's work of polar exploration. On the other hand, our expedition, running appalling risks, performing prodigies of superhuman endurance, achieving immortal renown, commemorated in august cathedral sermons and by public statutes, *yet reaching the Pole only to find our terrible journey superfluous, and leaving our best men dead on the ice.* To ignore such a contrast would be ridiculous: to write a book without accounting for it, a waste of time.

—*Apsley Cherry-Garrard,* The Worst Journey in the World *(New York: Carroll and Graf, 1989), 562.*

In Company with Viators

Those of us in youth ministry cannot assume that all of our students will complete this journey. But we can prepare them and nurture them with forward motion (the process) and destination (the promise) in mind. This task of preparation and nurture has been known in the church for centuries as *spiritual formation.* Shaped by Old Testament patterns of life-on-life transference (see Deut. 6:6–9) and rooted in Christ's mandate to "go and make disciples of all nations" (Matt. 28:18–20), spiritual formation is, to paraphrase the apostle Paul, the process of proclaiming, admonishing, and teaching "with all wisdom, so that

[11] Eugene Peterson, *A Long Obedience in the Same Direction* (Downers Grove, Ill.: InterVarsity Press, 1980), 128.

The frequency with which the word *spirituality* occurs these days is more likely to be evidence of pathology than health. I am not dismissing current interest in spirituality as sick. The interest itself is *not* sick, but sickness *has* provoked the interest. There is considerable confusion regarding the appropriate treatment, but virtual unanimity in the diagnosis: Our culture is sick with secularism.

But deeper and stronger than our illness is our cure. The Spirit of God that hovered over the primordial chaos (Gen. 1:2) hovers over our murderous and chaotic cities. The Spirit that descended on Jesus like a dove (Matt. 3:16) descends on the followers of Jesus. The Holy Spirit that filled men and women with God at nine o'clock in the morning in Jerusalem during Pentecost (Acts 2:1–4) fills men and women still in Chicago and Calcutta, Moscow and Montreal, around the clock, 365 days a year.

—*Eugene Peterson,* Subversive Spirituality *(Grand Rapids, Mich.: Eerdmans, 1997), 32.*

we may present everyone perfect in Christ (Col. 1:28)."[12] Dallas Willard defines spiritual formation as "the process through which those who love and trust Jesus Christ effectively take on his character."[13] It is a "process concerned with the holistic growth and development of the individual," not just "postconversion maintenance," but an "ongoing path of developmental learning and experience."[14] Simply put, spiritual formation helps our students become aware of their true identity in Christ and then helps them toward consistently letting Christ live his life in and through them.[15] It is calling them and nurturing them so that they might become *viators* on the journey, and then helping them in the journey to deepen their intimacy with the Christ who walks with them each step of the way (Phil. 2:12–13, Heb. 12:1–2).

Because youth ministry is about this divine odyssey, we must explore it in some depth. With that in mind, this chapter will embrace three objectives.

▸ We begin first with an overview of Christian spirituality. What is it? What does it look like? Is there any such thing as false spirituality?

▸ Secondly, we will turn our attention to how faith grows and changes over the human lifespan with an introduction to what has become known as faith development theory.

▸ And then, finally, as we explore some of these questions throughout the chapter, we will try to draw some conclusions and highlight implications about Christian spirituality in the life of an adolescent.

[12] See also 2 Thessalonians 31:3, "We ought always to thank God for you, brothers, and rightly so, because your faith is growing more and more, and the love every one of you has for each other is increasing."

[13] Dallas Willard, *The Spirit Is Willing: The Body as a Tool,* in *The Christian Educator's Handbook on Spiritual Formation,* ed. Kenneth O. Gangel and James C. Wilhoit (Wheaton, Ill.: Victor Books, 1994), 225.

[14] Nick Taylor, "Spiritual Formation: Nurturing Spiritual Vitality," in *Introducing Christian Education: Foundations for the Twenty-First Century,* ed. Michael Anthony (Grand Rapids, Mich.: Baker, 2001), 91.

[15] This is an adaptation of a definition of spiritual formation offered by James Bryan Smith, "Spiritual Formation in Adolescents," in Gangel and Wilhoit, *The Christian Educator's Handbook,* 248–250.

True Spirituality: Beyond Goosebumps, Chicken Soup, and Oprah-ism

Because there is so much talk in pop culture about spirituality and because so much of that spirituality is divorced from biblical substance, we must begin our exploration of adolescent spirituality by identifying some general axioms of Christian spirituality.

Axiom Number One:
True spirituality requires our intention, but it is not solely a matter of human effort.

Unlike regeneration, the work by which God acting alone brings us from death to life, sanctification is a work that requires us to cooperate with God's purposes. God works it in, but we must work it out. "Continue [our part] to work out your salvation with fear and trembling, for it is [God's part] God who works in you to will and to act according to his good purpose" (Phil. 2:12–13). "In view of God's mercy, [our part] . . . offer your bodies as living sacrifices . . . Do not conform any longer to the pattern of this world, but be transformed [God's part] by the renewing of your mind" (Rom. 12:1–2).

> ### Definition of *Axiom*
>
> Function: noun. Etymology: Latin *axioma*, from Greek *axima*, literally, something worthy, from *axioun* to think worthy, from *axios* worth, worthy. 1. a maxim widely accepted on its intrinsic merit; 2. a statement accepted as true as the basis for argument or inference; 3. an established rule or principle or a self-evident truth.
>
> Merriam-Webster's Collegiate Dictionary, 2000, s.v. *axiom*.

Having affirmed this, we must also understand that spirituality on the basis of human effort alone, no matter how well-intentioned, will be little more than half-filled people trying to overflow. It requires our intention, but it is not solely a matter of human effort. Jesus affirmed both elements of true spirituality when he said to his disciples, "I am the Vine, you are the branches. When you're joined with me and I with you, the relation intimate and organic, the harvest is sure to be abundant. Separated, you can't produce a thing" (John 15:5, *The Message*).

Axiom Number Two:
True spirituality requires attention to process, but it cannot be reduced to a method.

With only a quick glance at the landscape around us we see evidence everywhere that God's forming work is immensely varied. Any random acre of creation is ample evidence that God can think of more than one way to skin a cat. It should be no surprise then that Scripture gives us no step-by-step template for spiritual formation. The gallery of characters who stare out at us from the pages of Scripture prove that God's sanctifying means are many and diverse. God calls us to walk, but he does not call us all to march in lockstep.

> **Principle of Teenage Spirituality—The No Sequel Principle:**
> **No matter how amazing his stories and plots are, God never makes a sequel.**

His work in every student's life is unique. What he uses to move one student may have no impact on another student. But that does not mean that student is not being affected. It may just mean God is moving through other means. Richard Peace explains:

> Each pilgrimage is unique. Each person is at a different point, arrived at in his own special way. This is important to bear in mind. Since no two pilgrimages are alike, our only concern can be with our own path. What someone else's pilgrimage looks like is not our problem . . . We get into trouble when we start comparing our path to that of someone else. "Why did he have it so easy," we ask and we are envious. Or we seek to model our pilgrimage after that of a person we admire and so we lose our own distinctiveness. Or we compare where we have arrived in our pilgrimage to the point at which another person is, and we feel superior (or depressed). None of these attitudes is healthy. Each story is unique. Each has its own inner logic. Each is in God's hand. In the end, our only concern is to follow faithfully the way God has marked out uniquely for us.[16]

Having said that, the pursuit of true spirituality is not "instantaneous or haphazard," a do-it-yourself buffet of dishes and disciplines that sound tasty. As Ken Boa reminds us, "The spiritual life is progressively cultivated in the disciplines of the faith; you and I will not wake up one morning to find ourselves suddenly spiritual."[17] For centuries before us, believers have practiced spiritual disciplines that have aided them in building up and living out their faith, and we can gain much from the insights and musings they logged along the trail. As Eugene Peterson warns,

> Spirituality is not the latest fad but the oldest truth. Spirituality, the alert attention we give to a living God and the faithful response we make to him in community, is at the heart of our Scriptures and is on display throughout the centuries of Israel and the church. We have been at this a long time. We have nearly *four* millennia of experience to draw upon. When someone hands you

---

[16] Richard Peace, *Pilgrimage: A Handbook on Christian Growth* (Grand Rapids, Mich.: Baker, 1976), 43.

[17] Kenneth Boa, *Conformed to His Image: Biblical and Practical Approaches to Spiritual Formation* (Grand Rapids, Mich.: Zondervan, 2001), 76. "This is why Paul uses the metaphors of an athlete, a soldier, and a farmer to illustrate the discipline of the Christian life (see 1 Cor. 9:24–27, Eph. 6:10–18, and 2 Tim. 2:3–6)." Ibid.

a new book, reach for an *old* one. Isaiah has far more to teach us about spirituality than Carl Jung.[18]

Axiom Number Three:
True spirituality requires attention to our walk, but it does not come from watching our feet.

In middle school I lived for gym class. It was a break from the "sit-still," "be-quiet," "why-didn't-you-prepare-that?" environment of the classroom that ushered us into the activity, laughter, and friendship of the athletics field. Sweet freedom!

Except on those dreadful days when we were all herded into the gym, along with the girls' class, for instruction in ballroom dancing. This was anything *but* sweet. This was torture and coercion. First of all, this was a waste of a perfectly good gym class. We could have been gainfully involved in a game of Ultimate, or character-building games such as "Murder the Man with Ball." But no, we were dancing! What is worse, we were dancing *with girls*. I am sorry, but in seventh grade I thought girls had cooties. I thought the

Five Ignorances That Frustrate Fruitfulness

Francis Schaeffer said that one of the reasons that Christians lack fruitfulness in their lives is because of ignorance. He cited five different "ignorances," each of which is related to true spirituality—and the understanding that God works in what we are called to work out:

> *First*, the Christian may have been taught how to be justified but never taught the *present* meaning of the work of Christ for him. *Second*, he may have been taught to become a Christian through the instrumentality of faith, but then he may have been left, as though from that point on the Christian life has to be lived in his own strength. *Third*, he may have been taught the opposite. That having accepted Christ, in some antinomian way it does not now matter how he lives. *Fourth*, he may have been taught some kind of second blessing, which would make him perfect in this life when he receives it. This the Bible does not teach. And therefore he just waits hopelessly, or tries to act upon that which is not. *Fifth*, he may never have been taught a reality of faith to *be acted on consciously* after justification ... Because of any of these ignorances, the Christian may not "possess his possessions" in this present life.

Francis A. Schaeffer, True Spirituality *(Wheaton, Ill.: Tyndale, 1971), 83–84.*

cool thing to do around girls was to burp loudly and make noises by cupping my arm under my armpit. Now I was being asked to stand close to one.

---

[18] Eugene Peterson, *Subversive Spirituality* (Grand Rapids, Mich.: Eerdmans, 1997), 40.

Every Story Is Different

And as Shasta gaped with open mouth and said nothing, the Voice continued. "I was the lion who forced you to join with Aravis. I was the cat who comforted you among the houses of the dead. I was the lion who drove the jackals from you while you slept. I was the lion who gave the Horses the new strength of fear for the last mile so that you should reach King Lune in time. And I was the lion you do not remember who pushed the boat in which you lay, a child near death, so that it came to shore where a man sat, wakeful at midnight, to receive you."

"Then it was you who wounded Aravis?"

"It was I."

"But what for?"

"Child," said the Voice, "I am telling you your story, not hers. I tell no one any story but his own."

C. S. Lewis, The Horse and His Boy *(London: Geoffrey Bles, 1954), 147.*

> **Principle of Teenage Spirituality—The Ballroom Dancing Principle:**
> In nurturing teenage spirituality, focus on the fellowship, not on the feet.

Then of course, as if this were not bad enough, the person who taught us ballroom dancing was our gym teacher, Coach Welch, who was also the football coach. You can imagine his expertise on the dance floor. I am sure the first time he heard "ballroom," he thought it referred to where we store the athletic equipment. He had a knack for making a waltz sound like calisthenics. "Hut-two-three-slide." You were just sure that one wrong step and he was going to bellow, "Robbins, give me 30 push-ups!" or "Sally, take a lap!" All the while, they kept telling us how graceful this was, how wonderful and romantic. To us, it just felt like fear and intimidation. I remember thinking, "I wish this girl would just leave me alone and let me try to get these stupid steps right."

Which, of course, was precisely the point we missed. Ballroom dancing is *not* just about getting the steps right; it is about a growing relationship with your partner. It is about moving together in an embrace of openness and developing a growing intimacy with your partner.

It is important to savor this picture from middle school gym class because it reminds us of where we have often gone wrong in understanding true spirituality, and in explaining it to our students. We have implied that true spirituality is about getting "the steps" right, when in fact, true spirituality is about a growing relationship with Jesus, the Lord of the Dance. It is defined not by a focus on the feet, but by a focus on fellowship (see Heb. 12:1–2). Remember Isaiah's words, "The Lord says, 'These people come near to me with their mouth and honor me with their lips, but their hearts are far from me. Their worship of me is made up only of rules taught by men (29:13)."[19]

How many times in youth ministry do we encounter students intimidated and discouraged, well aware of the sloppy steps and awkward movements of their relationship with Jesus? What we describe as wonderful and glorious, they experience as frustrating and exhausting. "I just can't do it; I don't blame God for getting ticked off with me. I want to do it right, but I just keep screwing up." Yet the great news of the gospel is that there is a God full of grace, even for those of us who are ungraceful, that true spirituality begins with change in the heart and leads to change in the feet. We must help students nurture a spirituality that begins with fellowship, and then matures into fruitfulness (John 15:4–9).

What Are "the Spiritual Disciplines"?

Using Richard Foster's typology, there are three main types of spiritual disciplines: inward disciplines, outward disciplines, and corporate disciplines:

▸ Inward Disciplines: meditation, prayer, fasting, and study;

▸ Outward Disciplines: simplicity, solitude, submission, and service; and

▸ Corporate Disciplines; confession, worship, guidance, and celebration.

Richard Foster, Celebration of Discipline (San Francisco: Harper and Row, 1978). For other books that explore the disciplines, see John Ortberg, The Life You've Always Wanted (Grand Rapids, Mich.: Zondervan, 1997), and Dallas Willard, The Spirit of the Disciplines (New York: HarperCollins, 1988), 158. Willard divides the disciplines into two groups. Disciplines of Abstinence are solitude, silence, fasting, frugality, chastity, secrecy, sacrifice. Disciplines of Engagement are study, worship, celebration, service, prayer, fellowship, confession, and submission.

Axiom Number Four:
True spirituality requires a giant step of faith, but it is always marked by short steps of obedience.

Getting all the steps right is not nearly as important as a growing relationship with our Partner. But getting the steps right is an important fruit of that growing partnership. Jesus implied that the more we grow in our intimacy with him, the more we will move in his steps (John 14:15,23; 15:10).

One of my all-time favorite movies is *What About Bob?* This is a movie about a character named Bob who is plagued by a long list of psychological disorders, chief of which is his fear of going out in public. During an appointment with his

---

[19] Michael Anthony affirms this principle when he writes, "Spiritual formation begins first in changes of the heart, where being begins. These changes primarily bring about relational depth with God and others. The by-product, not the goal, is secondary change in behaviors and attitudes. Rules cannot create worship. Relationship can." Michael Anthony, *Foundations of Ministry: An Introduction to Christian Education for a New Generation* (Wheaton, Ill.: Bridgepoint/Victor Books, 1992), 92.

> As long as you notice, and have to count, the steps, you are not yet dancing but only learning to dance. A good shoe is a shoe you don't notice. Good reading becomes possible when you need not consciously think about eyes, or light, or print, or spelling. The perfect church service would be one we were almost unaware of, our attention would have been on God.
>
> —C. S. Lewis, Letters to Malcolm, Chiefly on Prayer (New York: Harcourt, Brace, and World, 1964), 4.

therapist (Richard Dreyfuss), Bob finally makes a breakthrough when he realizes that his wholeness will come not through giant steps but through little baby steps of change. *If he can get to the hallway, he can get to the elevator. If he can get to the elevator, he can get to the street. If he can get to the street, he can get to the corner. If he can get to the corner, he can get to the store, and so on.* With that insight, Bob begins an odyssey, touching and fun, that leads to his regaining emotional stability.

Principle of Teenage Spirituality—The Baby-Step Principle:
Genuine commitment is usually marked by baby steps and not by giant steps. They may not seem as dramatic, but that does not mean God is not acting.

What About Bob? is especially intriguing because the basic principle of the movie is profoundly biblical. True spirituality is not about big, dramatic giant steps; it is about consistent, faithful baby steps.

In the Old Testament conquest of Canaan the people of Israel wanted God to give them the entire land of Canaan in a quick surge—no struggle, no trials, no muss, no fuss, just one big splash into "milk and honey." But God explained that he was not going to operate that way. First of all, because of the possible threat from wild animals, it was not smart (Deut. 7:22). Second, God understood human nature enough to know that a half mile of progress usually leads to five miles of pride (Deut. 8:17, 9:4–5). So he told the people that the conquest would come a step at a time. "Every place where you set your foot will be yours: Your territory will extend from the desert to Lebanon, and from the Euphrates River to the western sea" (Deut. 11:24).

It is a pattern of step-by-step progress reflected over and over again in the New Testament, where Paul writes, for example, "Just as you received Christ Jesus as Lord, *continue to live in him*, rooted and built up in him . . . " (Col. 2:6–7, emphasis added). The words *rooted* and *built up* are obvious metaphors here for step-by-step, stage-by-stage growth. Or, in Philippians 3:13–14, "One thing I do: Forgetting what is behind and straining toward what is ahead, I press on toward the goal to win the prize for which God has called me heavenward in Christ Jesus."

True spirituality may begin with a giant step of faith—by an altar, or by a campfire, or at a table in Starbucks. But its authenticity is measured from that point by consistent baby steps of growth:

> ▶ a student decides to stop cursing,

> ▶ a student writes a note of apology to a teacher in whose class he cheated,

> ▶ a student seeks reconciliation with another student about whom she gossiped,

> ▶ a student offers to help out around the house by washing the dishes,

Satan is at work ... dismantling the Sacred Romance—the Larger Story God is telling—so that there is nothing visible ... "to take our breath away" ... He replaces the love affair with a religious system of do's and don'ts that parch our hearts and replaces our worship and communion services with entertainment. Our experience of life deteriorates from the passion of a grand love affair, in the midst of a life-and-death battle, to an endless series of chores and errands, a busyness that separates us from God, each other, and even from our thirstiness.

John Eldredge and Brent Curtis, The Sacred Romance *(Nashville, Tenn.: Thomas Nelson, 1997), 108. "Instead of a love affair with God, your life begins to feel more like a series of repetitive behaviors, like reading the same chapter of a book or writing the same novel over and over. The orthodoxy we try to live out, defined as 'Believe and Behave Accordingly' is not a sufficient story line to satisfy whatever turmoil and longing our heart is trying to tell us about." Ibid., 30.*

> ▶ a student agrees to assume some responsibility at an upcoming outreach event, or

> ▶ a student agrees to seek counsel for a drinking problem.

This is a crucial observation in a youth ministry culture that prizes overnight, giant-step spirituality. We love to see students make the dramatic once-and-for-all, cataclysmic commitment to Christ, and there is something wonderful and powerful about a student having an "Ebenezer experience."[20] But the danger is that we may mistake slow movement for *no* movement, or that we so cultivate giant-step decisions that we forget to celebrate the undramatic baby steps of obedience.

There is no thrill in walking; it is the test of all the stable qualities. To "walk and not faint" is the highest reach possible for strength . . . When we are in an unhealthy state physically or emotionally, we always want thrills. In the physical domain this will lead to counterfeiting the Holy Ghost; in the emotional life it leads to inordinate affection and the destruction of morality; and

---

[20] A monumental encounter with God: see I Samuel 7:12.

and in the spiritual domain if we insist on getting thrills, on mounting up with wings, it will end in the destruction of spirituality.[21]

Helping students make progress in this flow of onward movement is one of the major tasks of spiritual formation. We meet students where they are, and then help them from that point to move toward where God wants them to be. One way to think about these baby steps is to liken them to Four Levels of Learning as illustrated in Table 11-1.

We must understand that this is an ongoing process. It is not a matter of ushering each student through the four levels, and then giving them a high five, a WWJD bracelet and The New VeggieTales Bible. When students get to the fourth level in this learning process, our intention should be through teaching, admonishing, counseling, and shared experiences to open their eyes to new areas of blindness and disobedience, so God can lead them once again from Level One to Level Two and so on. This is how he moves us toward healing and wholeness one step at a time. This ongoing movement of growth into Christlikeness is what the Bible refers to as *sanctification*—being conformed into the image of Jesus.

Axiom Number Five:
True spirituality requires a change of mind; but it is always coupled with a change of heart and a change of lifestyle.

Dion Rich is one of most successful individuals in professional sports—not because he plays *in* the games, but because he has an uncanny knack for successfully *sneaking* into games—and not just into the games, but often onto the fields, into the locker rooms, into postgame parties. That was Dion helping to carry former Dallas Cowboys coach Tom Landry off the field after Super Bowl XII. That was him standing on the podium with former Washington Redskins coach Joe Gibbs after his victory in Super Bowl XVII. He has posed, postured, and impostored his way into World Series games, title fights, America's Cup races, Kentucky Derbies, 14 Olympic games, 33 different Super Bowls, and eight Academy Awards. He even has a snapshot of himself with his arm around Gwyneth Paltrow after she won her Oscar.[22] Dion Rich is a man who has perfected the art of pretending to be someone he is not.

In the mid-1700s, pastor and theologian Jonathan Edwards, author of the classic *Religious Affections*,[23] looked out across the religious landscape of his day and saw what many observers have noted in our own: there are lots of people talking about spirituality, but there is a sad lack of authentic spiritual fruit. Like Dion Rich, we look the part and talk the part and show up in the right places, but much of what passes for modern spirituality is pretense.

---

[21] Oswald Chambers, *Workmen of God* (London: Marshall, Morgan, and Scott, 1937), 202.

[22] Rick Reilly, "In Like Flynn," *Sports Illustrated* 96, no. 6 (February 11, 2002): 108.

[23] Jonathan Edwards, *Religious Affections* (New Haven, Conn: Yale University Press, 1959). Edwards insisted that our religious experience is centered in what he called the "*affections*," described by Gerald McDermott as "strong inclinations of the soul that are manifested in thinking, feeling, and acting." Gerald McDermott, *Seeing God* (Downers Grove, Ill.: InterVarsity Press, 1995), 31. Embedded deeper than either a person's thoughts or feelings, affections are the strongest motivators of the human self and ultimately determine everything the person is or does.

Table 11-1.
Levels of Learning

Levels of Learning	Description
Level One: Unconscious Incompetence	Students are so ignorant of the truth to be obeyed that they do not even realize their ignorance. They do not know how much they do not know. They are unconscious of their incompetence. The Bible refers to this as blindness (see Rev. 3:17). It is an arrogance that says, "I've seen it all" without even realizing that our eyes are not yet open.
Level Two: Conscious Incompetence	Students realize something is wrong. Maybe it is because of guilt, maybe it is a longing, maybe it is a nagging question, maybe it is through trial—but there is a willingness to seek.
Level Three: Conscious Competence	Students now know the truth but must really concentrate to apply the truth in their life—to get the steps right ("focus on the feet"). It is not yet a part of who they are. This is better than Conscious Incompetence, but it is not where we want them to stop. As long as they are watching their feet, they are not enjoying the romance of the dance. The goal is fruit of the Spirit, not works of the flesh (see Gal. 5:19–25).
Level Four: Unconscious Competence	Finally, students have woven the truth into the fabric of their everyday life so completely that they are no longer really conscious of being obedient. It is just who they are.

Source: It is difficult to know who first identified these four stages. The model is described as the Process of Instructional Improvement by Kenneth Feldman and Michael Paulsen in their book, *Teaching and Learning in the College Classroom* (New York: Norton, 1979), 629. Gretchen L. Zimmerman, Cynthia G. Olsen, and Michael F. Bosworth refer to the model as the Transtheoretical Model of Change in "A 'Stages of Change' Approach to Helping Patients Change Behavior," *AFP Bulletin* (March 1, 2000). I explore these four levels much more thoroughly in my book, *Ministry of Nurture* (Grand Rapids, Mich.: Zondervan, 1990), 122–129.

It is interesting to read through a sampling of Edwards's *unreliable* signs of true spirituality written more than 200 years ago, and consider how they might be relevant to today's youth ministry.[24]

▸ **Intense Affections.** Some saw signs of emotional intensity as an indication that God was at work, but Edwards was skeptical. He noted that some of the same people who cried "Hosannah" when Jesus rode into Jerusalem cried "Crucify him" only a few days later (see Matt. 21:9, 27:22–23). He felt that intense affections, in and of themselves, were no indicator of true spirituality.

▸ **Knowledge of Scripture.** Others felt that a ready knowledge of Scripture was a sure sign of spiritual maturity. But, as Edwards pointed out, Satan demonstrated a pretty good knowledge of Scripture when he tempted Jesus in the wilderness (see Luke 4:10). Indeed, Jesus reminded his disciples that the rocky-ground hearers of the Word will receive it with joy when they first hear it, but the Word will not take root (Mark 4:5,16–17).

▸ **Visible Physical Signs.** Some in Edwards's day looked to physical signs that God was truly at work in a person. But Edwards explained that bodily

---

[24] McDermott, *Seeing God*, has done a wonderful job of reinterpreting and translating the ideas from Edwards's original *Religious Affections* so that they might be heard and heeded in today's Christian culture.

Brothers and sisters, it is woefully possible that our fancied love for the Lord is little more than sentimental attachment. Our emotional reactions to his love are not necessarily so deep or so pure as we think. We feel we love him utterly, but we live so much in the feeling realm that we think we are the kind of people we feel we are. We feel we want to live for him alone and want to die for him if he so wills; but if the Lord does not shatter our self-confidence as he shattered Peter's, we shall go on being deceived by our feelings and life will be one of endless fluctuations . . . The measure of our ability to follow the Lord is not assessed by the measure of our desire to follow him.

—Watchman Nee

effects are no sure sign of spiritual life. King Saul, moved by the Spirit of God, stripped naked and lay prostrate for a full day and night (see 1 Sam. 19:23–24)—but there is no evidence that this experience led to any vital spiritual renewal in his life.[25]

▸ **Frequent and Passionate Praise to God.** "Passion" and "praise" are currently the buzzwords in youth ministry circles, but how often do we see the nation of Israel singing praise to God and then disregarding him altogether (see Ps. 106:12–13, 1 Sam. 15:22)?

▸ **Being Convinced That One Is Saved.** Edwards did *not* teach that assurance of salvation was a sign of deception—indeed, he taught that assurance is a wonderful blessing of God's grace. But he *did* teach that assurance is not a sure sign of regeneration—it could just be false presumption (see Matt. 23:13).[26] He was saying, in effect, "Just because these affections are present in your life, don't assume that you have a right relationship with God."

Edwards's words are uncomfortable for us, but more uncomfortable still is the realization that some facets of the current youth ministry culture may be breeding a kind of false spirituality, a Dion Rich brand of Christianity.

How can we avoid nurturing in our students a false spirituality that has all the right sights and sounds—the God-talk, the Christian T-shirts, the cross jewelry, the religious tattoos, the memorized verses, the "I love youth group" attitude—but is somehow lacking in real life-transforming power (see 2 Tim. 3:5)?

---

[25] Although for the servants who walked in and out of the king's chambers that day, we might expect that the sight of the king in his "altogether" brought for them sobering glimpses of divine judgment!

[26] See also 1 John 5:1–13.

Principle of Teenage Spirituality-The 3-D Principle: True spirituality will affect all three dimensions of a student's life: knowing, being, and doing.

Buechner on Sanctification

In *Beauty and the Beast*, it is only when the Beast discovers that Beauty really loves him in all his ugliness that he himself becomes beautiful.

In the experience of St. Paul, it is only when a person discovers that God really loves him in all his unloveliness ... that he himself starts to become godlike. Paul's word for this gradual transformation of a sow's ear into a silk purse is *sanctification*, and he sees it as the second stage in the process of salvation. Being sanctified is a long and painful stage because with part of himself the sinner prefers his sin, just as with part of himself the Beast prefers his glistening snout and curved tusks. Many drop out with the job hardly more than begun, and among those who stay with it there are few if any who don't drag their feet most of the way.

But little by little—less by taking pains than by taking it easy—the forgiven man starts to become a forgiving man, the healed man to become a healing man, the loved man to become a loving man. God does most of it. The end of the process, Paul says, is eternal life.

—*Frederick Buechner,* Wishful Thinking *(New York: Harper and Row, 1973), 85-86.*

In part it begins with our understanding that true spirituality flows from a balance of knowing, being, and doing (see Figure II-I). Rick Dunn, in his book, *Shaping the Spiritual Life of Students*,[27] states that true spirituality in the life of a teenager will be manifest in "the student learning to balance his or her whole self with God . . . increasingly able to submit thoughts, emotions, and choices to the *mind, heart, and will* of God. The desired outcome is a *mind* that is being transformed to think with a 'God view,' a *heart* transformed in its capacity for sharing emotions and affections with God, and a *will* being transformed into loving obedience to his leading (emphasis added)".

Axiom Number Six:
True spirituality requires a first-person commitment, but it almost always involves a second person.

The goal of maturing students in the faith is to help them to embrace a faith of their own. However, what we cannot ignore in the life of a teenager is the shaping power of a faith that is shared by a caring adult.

Of particular importance to adolescents is friendship with an adult who sees in them potential they do not necessarily see in themselves. Studies consis-

[27] Rick Dunn, *Shaping the Spiritual Life of Students* (Downers Grove, Ill.: InterVarsity Press, 2001), 59.

Subverted Spirituality

In his book *Subversive Spirituality*, Eugene Peterson offers these guidelines as a corrective to much of what is currently considered "spirituality":

1. Discover what Scripture says about spirituality and immerse yourself in it . . .

2. Shun spirituality that does not require commitment . . .

3. Embrace friends in the faith wherever you find them. This may mean friends across town in another church, on another continent, or through books from another century . . .

4. But then return home and explore your own tradition. Hunger for a deeper spirituality, a Christian life in which God is authenticated in everyday circumstances and personal relationships, is almost always accompanied by a sense of deprivation; we suspect we were not provided our rightful heritage by our church or pastor or family, that we were not guided and nurtured in the ways of robust holiness . . . Angry over our impoverishment, we cannot help noticing churches or movements that look better. We see places and people who are risking themselves in love and God, and we know we would flourish if we could only live among them . . . We get ready to jump ship . . . [But] our wisest counselors usually tell us to stay put. Every place, every congregation, every denomination, has a rich spiritual tradition to be discovered and explored . . . Recover what is yours by right by going *deep*, not away.

5. Look for mature guides; honor wise leaders . . . Because an appetite for God is easily manipulated into a consumer activity, we need these wise, sane friends as guides and companions. There are entrepreneurs among us who see the widespread hunger for spirituality as a marketplace and are out there selling junk food. The gullibility of the unwary who bought relics from itinerant monks in the Middle Ages—splinters of wood from the true cross, finger bones from the saints, a few pieces of thread from Jesus's seamless robe—is more than matched by North Americans in matters of spirituality.

Eugene Peterson, Subversive Spirituality *(Grand Rapids, Mich.: Eerdmans, 1997), 32ff.*

indicate that a relationship with such an "adult guarantor" during adolescence outweighs all other forms of youth ministry in terms of positive influence on youth development.[28]

We see this progression of influence in the ministry of Paul as he helped first-century believers move from being followers of Paul (I Cor. II:I), to imitators of God (Eph. 5:I), to becoming examples for others to follow (I Thess. I:7).[29] Indeed, we see the whole process telescoped

Figure 11-1.
Three Elements of Balanced Spirituality

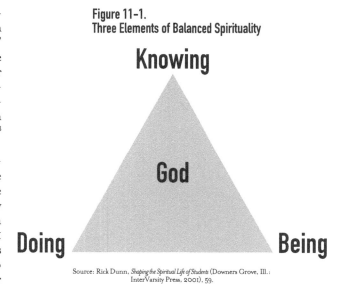

Source: Rick Dunn, *Shaping the Spiritual Life of Students* (Downers Grove, Ill.: InterVarsity Press, 2001), 59.

in Paul's ministry to the church at Thessalonica: "You became *imitators of us* and *of the Lord*; . . . And so *you became a model* to all the believers in Macedonia and Achaia." (I Thess. I:6–7, emphasis added).

Jesus often used illustrations from the natural world to point out realities in the spiritual realm: "Look at the birds of the air" (Matt. 6:26). "See how the lilies of the field grow . . ." (Matt. 6:28). He referred to salt, fig trees, mustard seeds, light, water, and even grains of wheat. If he were preaching today, he might proclaim, "Consider the penguins"—because the solicitude of emperor penguins provides a wonderful parable of this life-on-life process. When the female lays her egg, she gingerly rolls it onto the feet of the male Emperor Penguin who then stands there without moving, incubating that egg for up to two months until it finally hatches! Note well that image: *A close relationship and patient waiting.*

---

[28] Kenda Creasy Dean, *The God-Bearing Life* (Nashville, Tenn.: Upper Room Books, 1998), 27. In support of this assertion, Dean cites her research, "A Synthesis of the Research on, and a Descriptive Overview of, Protestant, Catholic and Jewish Religious Youth Programs in the United States," working paper, Carnegie Council on Adolescent Development, Washington, D.C., 1991, 51.

[29] James Bryan Smith comments, "There are two primary ways young people develop a sense of who they are: *imitation* and *integration*. Imitation is the process of adapting to one's surroundings by patching together the beliefs and behaviors of others. Adolescents try to develop a sense of who they are by attempting to look, act, think, and sound like someone else. "On the other hand, integration is the process of testing, separating, and discriminating between several types of beliefs and behaviors until one discovers that which is genuine and real . . ." James Bryan Smith, *Spiritual Formation of Adolescents*, in Gangel and Wilhoit, *The Christian Educator's Handbook*, 251.

True spirituality cannot survive on "a second hand faith in a second hand God . . . There has to be a personal word, a unique confrontation . . ."
—**Allen Jones**

Principle of Teenage Spirituality—The Emperor Penguin Principle:
The ministry of nurture requires long-term commitment and up-close companionship.

Many is the youth worker who has come to see the power of a first-person faith nurtured and matured by a second person's faith. It is a central element of youth ministry. Rick Dunn describes this as "pacing, then leading":

> Adolescents need spiritual caregivers who will (1) pray for God's Spirit to work in their lives, (2) pray for their spiritual battles in the midst of a perverse world, (3) guide them to a meaningful engagement of the truths of Scripture, and (4) walk with them into a personal encounter with the living God . . . In sum, adolescents need to be paced with and then led by spiritual caregivers who are able to perceive and engage a whole-life spirituality.[30]

In thinking of the responsibility that caregivers bear in such a role, the Christian mystic Baron Friedrich von Hugel suggested that this life transference process should always be based on four premises:[31]

- That God is "present and operative and laying siege to every soul before, during, and after any spiritual director might come upon the scene";

- That we ourselves are needy (it is not *we who are complete* helping *those who are incomplete*);

- That souls are never dittos (we are called to reproduce, not replicate); and

- That spiritual guides should work intentionally not to perpetuate unhealthy dependency (we must be careful that we are not doing ministry to meet our own needs).

[30] Dunn, *Shaping the Spiritual Life of Students*, 56–57.

[31] E. Glenn Hinson, *Spiritual Preparation for Christian Leadership* (Nashville, Tenn.: Upper Room Books, 1999), 173.

True spirituality requires personal commitment, but it is not just solitary growth.

True spirituality and discipleship cannot be fully experienced or expressed apart from community. This emphasis is affirmed repeatedly in the literature on faith development, but it is a biblical principle as well.

For example, in the Book of Acts, the plural form *disciples* is almost always used. Indeed, there are only four instances in the entire Book of Acts in which *disciple* is used, and in each case it is with reference to a particular person (Acts 9:10,26; 16:1; 21:16). The singular form *disciple*, although frequent in John where it always refers to a particular person (for example, John 9:28; 18:15,16; 19:26–28; 20:2-4,8; 21:7,20,23,24), never occurs at all in the gospel of Mark. In Matthew and Luke, the singular occurs only on Jesus's lips, where it is used in teachings about the nature of discipleship (Matt. 10:24-25,42; Luke 6:40; 14:26-27,33). All of which points to an important point: "Individual disciples are always seen in conjunction with the community of disciples, whether as Jesus's intimate companions or as the church."[32]

> Polar exploration is at once the cleanest and most isolated way of having a bad time which has been devised. It is the only form of adventure in which you can put on your clothes at Michaelmas and keep them on until Christmas, and save for a layer of the natural grease of the body, find them as clean as when they were new. It is more lonely than London, more secluded than a monastery, and the post comes but once a year ... Take it all in all, I do not believe anybody on earth has a worse time than an Emperor penguin.
>
> *Apsley Cherry-Garrard,* The Worst Journey in the World *(New York: Carroll and Graf, 1989), vii.*

Axiom Number Seven:
True spirituality requires a great work of God, but it doesn't always look particularly grand.

It was the first pregnancy for my friend and his young wife, so it caught him a little off guard. He never even suspected she might be pregnant. But then came the morning when he awoke to the sound of his wife in the bathroom throwing up. That shook him a little, but what really caused his head to spin was when he stepped into the bathroom. Stumbling through the door, prepared to be caring and sympathetic, he saw his wife look from her kneeling position in front of the toilet. With all of the splendor of someone who had seen the face of an angel staring up from the bowl, she gushed, "We're pregnant!"

He said that his first reaction was just complete bewilderment. He wanted to be supportive and affirming. "But it's hard, when your wife is throwing up, to sort of smile and say, 'This is beautiful,'" he said. "I didn't know what to do. It was just a total what's-wrong-with-this-picture, and I sure wasn't going to kiss her!"

---

[32] Michael J Wilkins, *Following the Master : Discipleship in the Steps of Jesus* (Grand Rapids, Mich.: Zondervan, 1992), 40.

> **Principle of Teenage Spirituality—The Morning Sickness Principle:**
> **The process of spiritual growth does not always look like progress.**

But of course what his wife was observing that special morning was something insightful, and very important. She was saying to her perplexed husband, "I know what you think you see. I know that all the signs are to the contrary. But guess what? Right now, right in our midst, new life is stirring right before our very eyes!"[33]

It was an amazing moment for my friend, the rookie dad. But it is also a moment that gives us a glimpse into what is both the frustration and splendor of nurturing new birth and spiritual life in the heart of a teenager: *The process does not always look like progress.* We see the hassles, the pain, the grief, and the mess of youth ministry, and it is easy to get discouraged. It is easy to overlook the fact that beneath this process is a work of splendor. It may not look like it right now, but God is at work! Even in the midst of the trauma, new life is stirring! When part of us wants to say, "Oh, this is awful," part of us needs to remember, "Wow, this is awesome!"

It is probably significant that when Paul writes to the immature Christians in the church at Galatia, his exasperation takes on the tone of an expectant parent: "My dear children, for whom I am again in the pains of childbirth until Christ is formed in you! . . . I am perplexed about you" (Gal. 4:19). It would be wonderful if youth ministry were only about those great breakthrough moments of new birth and recommitment. But that is not the story of true spirituality. True spirituality is about miracles of God and pushing hard, pains of labor and moments of wonder, first steps and occasional falls. It is a great work of God, but it doesn't always look particularly grand.

Faith Development: The Mystery of Growing Belief

It was Easter weekend during my freshman year of college. I came off the beach, and as I cleared the dunes, I saw this band and a singing group doing an open-air concert right in front of the most popular beer joint in Ocean Drive, S.C. A new Christian myself, I was especially intrigued because they seemed to be singing about Jesus. That is when I saw her on stage, this great-looking girl with an awesome smile and long blonde hair. I knew in a heartbeat that I *really, really* wanted to share my faith with this girl!

I walked up and met her after the concert, and that five-minute encounter began a relationship that grew over the next several weeks. Every time the group

---

[33] The good news is that she did not roll the egg over and place it on his feet for the next two months.

performed, I made sure to be there, taking every opportunity to get to know this girl. Finally, after about two months, I asked her out on a date, and she said yes. I know it sounds crazy, but by this time I was completely smitten by her, and by that late May evening on our first date, I *knew* that I loved her. But, of course, I did not want to tell her that on our first date because I knew that would freak her out. So, I waited until the following night when we were on our second date, and that is when I told her for the first time that I loved her.

I continued to date that girl for almost three years, and then on May 20, 1973, I married her. Now, more than 30 years later, I am still married to that girl, and I still love her very much. In fact, just before I came to my desk to begin typing this chapter, I told her again, one more time, how much I love her.

My purpose in sharing this fairy-tale story of romance ("Beauty and the Beast") is so that we might understand one of the most basic axioms of true spirituality: *True spirituality requires an unchanging commitment to Jesus, but what "commitment to Jesus" looks like will be a matter of consistent change.*

When I told that girl 33 years ago that I loved her, I really meant it. When I told her this morning that I loved her, I really meant it. But *what I really meant when I meant it more than 30 years ago is a lot different from what I meant when I really meant it this morning.* How could it be otherwise? I have gotten to know her better over these years, to appreciate more about her that there is to love. Heck, I have gotten to know myself better over these 30 years. I know more of who I am that I can give to her. That's the nature of genuine commitment. It is consistently changing.

What we must understand about true spirituality is that it is progressive. "Really committed to Jesus" for a 10-year-old will probably look quite different from "really committed to Jesus" for a 17-year-old, and "really committed to Jesus" for a high school student who just met Christ at camp last summer will look different from "really committed to Jesus" for a high school student who grew up in a Christian family and cannot ever really remember *not* being a Christian. All of these people may mean something quite different in saying that they are "really committed to Jesus," but it does not follow that the commitment of any one of them is less than genuine.

Principle of Teenage Spirituality—The Real Love Principle:
Those who are "really committed to Jesus" may not look like your "really committed to Jesus," but that does not necessarily mean they are not "really committed" to Jesus.

One of the ways that we can account for this progression in commitment is through what is known as *faith development*.[34] James Fowler has probably done the

---

[34] For an excellent synopsis of some of the prevailing thinking on faith development, see Joseph A. Modica, "Stages, Styles, or Stories? A Brief Guide to Faith Development," *AFTE Newsletter for United Methodist Seminarians* 25, no. 3 (March 1999). Available through AFTE, 3901 S. Panther Creek Dr., The Woodlands, Texas 77381.

most notable work in this area,[35] basing his research on Jean Piaget's assumptions about cognitive development and integrating as well the work of Kohlberg and Erikson (see chapter 6). To understand Fowler's contribution, we must begin with his definition of "faith" as "a human universal," a capability with which we are all endowed at birth.

> How these capabilities are activated and grow depends to a large extent on how we are welcomed into the world and what kinds of environments we grow in. Faith is interactive and social; it requires community, language, ritual, and nurture. Faith is also shaped by initiatives from beyond us and other people, initiatives of spirit or grace. How these latter initiatives are recognized and imaged, or unperceived and ignored, powerfully affects the shape of faith in our lives.[36]

Fundamental to understanding Fowler's levels of faith development are two additional notions. First, for Fowler, *faith is not the same as belief*. Beliefs are conscious and are often understood in terms of intellectual assent ("I believe that God loves me, and that he sent Jesus to die for me"). For Fowler, faith speaks to something much deeper—something that is conscious, yes, but also unconscious—"something that calls forth our love and devotion and therefore exerts ordering power on the rest of our lives and our attachments."[37] Secondly, related to this deeper understanding of faith is Fowler's understanding of faith as a verb.[38] Faith is not just beliefs we hold, it is how those beliefs, traditions, shared values, and communal influences (family, community, friends, church)[39] hold us and shape our actions.

Fowler argues that just as we move through changes in cognitive development and moral development, we also move through predictable and sequential stages in the ways our faith develops.

He identifies six different stages of faith development (Table 11-2):[40]

[35] Perry Downs notes that Fowler is not the first to write about predictable stages of faith. Perry Downs, *Teaching for Spiritual Growth: Introduction to Christian Education* (Grand Rapids, Mich.: Zondervan, 1994), 124. He cites the writing of Horace Bushnell in the nineteenth century and, back even before that, the twelfth-century work of Bernard of Clairvaux: "As one star differs from another, or as one cell from the next, the spirit of the one making progress and the spirit of the mature can be distinguished. The state of the beginner may be called 'animal,' the state of the one making progress 'rational,' and the state of the more mature 'spiritual.'" Bernard of Clairvaux, *The Love of God and Spiritual Friendship*, abridged ed. (Portland, Ore: Multnomah, 1983), 9.

[36] James Fowler, *Stages of Faith* (San Francisco: Harper and Row, 1981), xiii.

[37] Fowler writes that "as human beings we have evolved with capacities and the need for faith from the beginning. Whether or not we are explicitly nurtured in faith in religious or Christian ways, we are engaging in forming relationships of trust and loyalty to others. We shape commitments to causes and *centers of value*. We form allegiances and alliances with images and realities of power. And we form and shape our lives in relation to master stories. In these ways we join with others in the finding and making of meaning." James Fowler, "The Vocation of Faith Development Theory" in *Stages of Faith and Religious Development*, ed. James Fowler, Karl Earnst Nipkow, and Friedrich Schweitzer (New York: Crossroad, 1991), 22.

[38] As Pazmino describes it, "Faith is a process of becoming rather than something one possesses." Robert W. Pazmino, *Foundational Issues in Christian Education* (Grand Rapids, Mich.: Baker Books, 1997), 208.

[39] Fowler refers to these as *centers of value*. James Fowler, "Stages in Faith Consciousness," in *Religious Development in Childhood and Adolescence*, ed. Fritz Koser and W. George Scarlett (San Francisco: Jossey-Bass, 1991), 32.

[40] To further illustrate Fowler's stages, I make use of Charles McCollough's descriptive terms for each stage, *Heads of Heaven and Feet of Clay* (New York: Pilgrim Press, 1983), 32.

▶ **Stage One:** Intuitive-Projective (4 to 8 years). A child derives images of faith from parents and other significant adults.[41]

▶ **Stage Two:** Mythic-Literal (6-7 to 11-12 years). Child begins to give attention to the rest of his world, begins to distinguish fantasy from the real. God is usually viewed as being both faithful and lawful. The world is still uncertain, but by involving self in belief children gain some sense of security.

▶ **Stage Three:** Synthetic-Conventional (12 years to adulthood). Main characteristic is concern with interpersonal. The student plays different roles around different people. For example, the student acts like a Christian when around youth group, but when on campus and away from youth group, he or she acts like the nonChristian kids at school.

▶ **Stage Four:** Individuative-Reflective (young adult and beyond). Through critique, questioning, reflection, and evaluation, faith becomes one's own. The student is no longer just embracing inherited assumptions but beginning to forge an individual faith.

▶ **Stage Five:** Conjunctive (early midlife and beyond). Through increasing self-awareness one develops a more humble way of seeing reality—"God is much bigger than I realized and my grasp of eternal truth is more limited than I realized." Individual begins to combine faith of Stage Four with honest reflection and open dialogue to deepen understanding of faith and how it applies to real life.

▶ **Stage Six:** Universalizing (midlife and beyond). Individual is wholly committed to principles of love and justice, willing to spend and be spent in the cause of transforming the world, and leading by a sense of guiding authority in all aspects of life.

Because these changes are not exclusively a matter of chronology, it is not automatically true that the older you get, the more fully you develop in your faith. According to Fowler's research, children and adolescents are developmentally unable to attain stages four to six. In fact, most adults in the United States are at stage three or four, and some never get beyond stage two. Fowler's research concludes that the midlife years are important because it will be during those years that the stage is set for stagnation or further development. Few adults over 40 years old ever attain stage five, and stage six is extremely rare.[42]

---

[41] Fowler describes the infant child as being in a *prestage* called Primal Faith—*prestage* because the child in infancy simply is not amenable to the kind of empirical research Fowler used in developing his theory. It is in this stage that the child's predisposition to trust is formed through relationships with parents and others in the child's environment.

[42] James Fowler, "Faith, Liberation, and Human Development," in *Christian Perspectives on Faith Development: A Reader*, ed. Jeff Astley and Leslie Francis (Grand Rapids, Mich.: Eerdmans, 1992), 5.

Table 11–2.
Fowler's Stages of Faith Development

Stage	Level	Age Range	Descriptive Phrase	Comments
Stage One	Intuitive-Projective	4 to 8 years	The Innocent	When a child hears in Sunday School, for example, "God is our Father," intuitively that child projects impressions of his or her own father or mother onto what God must be like.
Stage Two	Mythic-Literal	6–7 to 11–12 years	The Literalist	"Mythic in the sense that it can now capture life's meaning in stories, but literal in that it is generally limited to concrete thinking."[1]
Stage Three	Synthetic-Conventional	12 years to adulthood	The Loyalist	Synthetic—not necessarily in the sense of phony—but in the sense that the adolescent wants to synthesize one's faith with whoever one is around at any given moment. In that sense, one's beliefs are conventional.
Stage Four	Individuative-Reflective	Young adult and beyond	The Critic	As a person matures, there is a growing sense of self, of becoming an individual and being able to reflect on what one's beliefs are apart from the group.
Stage Five	Conjunctive	Early midlife and beyond	The Seer	A faith that brings together various viewpoints and reaches out for new ways of seeing the whole truth.
Stage Six	Universalizing	Midlife and beyond (but exceedingly rare)	The Saint	All matters of paradox ("Can this be true?" and polarity ("That can't be true.") are brought together. "Faith is a universal in which the individual identifies beyond self with God as a felt reality."[2]

Source: James Fowler, "The Vocation of Faith Development Theory" in *Stages of Faith and Religious Development*, ed. James Fowler, Karl Earnst Nipkow, and Friedrich Schweitzer (New York: Crossroad, 1991), 22.

1. Perry Downs, *Teaching for Spiritual Growth: Introduction to Christian Education* (Grand Rapids, Mich.: Zondervan, 1994), 115.
2. Robert W. Pazmino, *Foundational Issues in Christian Education* (Grand Rapids, Mich.: Baker Books, 1997), 209.

Faith Development Theory: Questions and Critique

What are we to make of Fowler's conclusions? Using the *binocular assessment* we discussed in chapter 6, an integrated approach that begins with the theological eye-piece (revealed truth) and brings into focus the scientific eyepiece (discovered truth), what can we gain from Fowler?

1. How trustworthy is Fowler's methodology? Fowler's method of using individual interviews can provide helpful information. But it is a method likely to leave some significant actors and episodes out of the faith drama. An interview subject would have to be remarkably self-aware to give a full account of the complex web of relational and communal factors that have

shaped and are shaping their faith story. Then, of course, the limitations of human awareness prevent even the most self-aware person from knowing the mysterious ways that God himself has played a part in developing that story. We cannot report what we do not know. Unfortunately, Fowler's attempt to use sound scientific method is based on personal report. So

Study Break Recreation Idea

Remember the fun we had back in chapter 7 making up creative names for cognitive stages and levels of moral development? Let's try it again, but this time create your own faux-Fowler stages of faith by using various levels of denominational faith. Examples: Methodistic-inoffensive faith, Southern Baptist Conventional faith, Episcopal-consumptive faith, Mennonite-noncombative faith, Mormonal-bicyclical faith. Grab some hot chocolate and chips, and go crazy.

what we have is a methodology that values "control, prediction, objectivity, numbers, and signs" seeking to understand a faith that values "surrender, surprise, subjectivity and objectivity, words, and symbols."[43]

As Pazmino points out:

Although developmental psychology can provide some intellectual concepts or working hypotheses for dealing with the faith of persons, additional dimensions of faith must be considered beyond Fowler's seven categories. These additional dimensions must recognize the person and works of God and the response of human persons to God which includes surrender, surprise, reverence, awe, and subjectivity. These dimensions are not readily available to scientific inquiry and require . . . a recognition of the mystery and majesty of faith.

2. How biblical is Fowler's view of "faith"? Fowler's understanding of faith is pluralistic, embracing the notion that all religious perspectives are valuable and contribute to a fuller and more mature understanding of God. His approach, affirming Wilford Cantwell Smith's distinction between creed (focused on content) and faith (focused on human interactions),[44] is necessary to draw the kind of universal conclusions he does about human development.[45] But this way of understanding faith is quite different from the Christian understanding of a God who has made himself

---

[43] Huston Smith, "Excluded Knowledge: A Critique of the Modern Mind Set," *Teachers College Record* (February 1979): 419–445, cited in Pazmino, *Foundational Issues in Christian Education*, 210.

[44] Wilford Cantwell Smith, *The Meaning and End of Religion* (New York: MacMillan, 1962), cited in Downs, *Teaching for Spiritual Growth*, 119.

[45] Fowler's understanding of faith is very attractive to the postmodern mindset because it affirms a locus of authority that is internal: less a matter of historic creeds, ancient traditions, and biblical authority (external loci), and more a matter of recognizing that we all bring our perspective and personal background to any understanding of faith. Indeed, for Fowler, without a postmodern mindset, it is virtually impossible to progress beyond a stage three, Synthetical-Conventional faith. James Fowler, *Faithful Change: The Personal and Public Challenges of Postmodern Life* (Nashville, Tenn.: Abingdon, 1996), 161–168.

known uniquely in the person of Jesus Christ. This does not negate Fowler's basic premises of *how* faith develops, but it significantly affects the way we think about what faith is developing *toward*.[46] For Fowler, faith progresses more horizontally: the more one's faith develops, the more one will embrace the perspectives of all people. In a biblical understanding of faith, however, maturity proceeds more vertically: the more one's faith develops, the more one will embrace God and his perspective (revealed specifically in the Word written and the Word Incarnate).[47]

3. One of the interesting implications of Fowler's work is that faith is affirmed empirically as a universal facet of human experience. In other words, we are never working with a faithless teenager. They may not be conscious of their beliefs, or the implications of their beliefs, or even how those beliefs came to be. But we are not trying to start a fire from coals that do not exist. The students who walk into youth group on Friday night have a faith that has been shaped significantly by childhood and community experiences—for good or for ill—and we must meet them at their points of development, and help them progress to the next stage.

4. Fowler's research affirms the importance of community and tradition. While the current youth ministry culture seems to value community, we are not as enthusiastic about tradition. We toss out Christian language and imagery and replace it with a more generic "seeker-sensitive" group culture. In a post-Christian culture like our own, we must do this to some extent. Fowler's research, however, reminds us that this distinctive faith language, and these distinctive faith symbols, *do* have an impact on the development of faith, and that by abandoning these traditions altogether we lose their power to move people to higher stages of faith.

5. Fowler's description of Synthetic-Conventional faith points to both the strengths and the risks of an effective youth ministry. Fowler's research helps us to understand how significant the youth group community can be in helping a student to develop spiritually, especially if there is a strong group inertia toward spiritual growth and excitement about Jesus. On the other hand, it helps us to understand that this is not a stopping place for spiritual development. If a youth ministry is not helping students to develop a faith apart from the group—to move beyond Conventional faith to Individuative faith, then it ceases to be a stepping stone and becomes a stumbling block—a place where unhealthy dependencies are nurtured.

---

[46] This is the same issue we raised in chapter 7 with regard to Kohlberg's designation of justice as the highest moral aspiration.

[47] This may also speak to the question so many rank-and-file youth workers raise about Fowler's assertions: Is it really *impossible* for a teenager to progress to Individuative-Reflective Faith? As youth workers, we agree that most of us have met high school students whose faith is individuative and reflective, so how can Fowler's claim be true? But if, following Fowler's definition, students become more pluralistic as they mature in the faith, then students who are firm in their faith, convinced that Jesus is the only way to God, could be seen as dogmatized and narrow-minded. Fowler would perhaps be uncomfortable with this conclusion. But clearly what we can conclude is that how one defines *what faith is developing toward* will influence how one assesses a student's progress on that journey.

Lord of the Rings

While Fowler's work has been seminal in the discussion of faith development, John Westerhoff,[48] professor emeritus of Theology and Christian Nurture at Duke University, provides what might be a more practical description of faith development.[49] Westerhoff identifies four faith styles that he likens to growth rings on the trunk of a tree. As the tree grows and matures, the old rings remain, but new rings develop (see Figure 11-2).

Everyone who accepts the teaching of St. Paul must have a belief in "sanctification." But I should myself be very chary of describing such operations of the Holy Ghost as "experiences" if by experiences we mean things necessarily discoverable by introspection. And I should be still more chary of mapping out a series of such experiences as an indispensable norm [or syllabus!] for all Christians. I think the ways in which God saves us are probably infinitely various and admit varying degrees of consciousness in the patient. Anything which sets him saying, "Now—Stage II ought soon to be coming along—is this it?" I think bad and likely to lead some to presumption and others to despair. We must leave God to dress the wound and not keep on taking peeps under the bandage for ourselves.

C. S. Lewis, in a letter to Edward Dell, cited in The Business of Heaven, *ed. Walter Hooper (London: Harcourt Brace, 1984), 303.*

▶ **Experienced Faith:** This is the beginning of the spiritual journey—more tactile (sensory) than cognitive. Children experience the faith of significant caregivers who communicate to them a sense of trust and confidence. "A person first learns Christ not as a theological affirmation but as an affective experience,"[50] in the burning candle, the bedtime prayers, the nativity scene, the loving touch.

▶ **Affiliative Faith:** Faith at this point is based on a sense of connectedness to the faith community. The faith of that community, its beliefs and traditions, are reinforced by rites of passage like confirmation and baptism or by rites of worship like the Lord's Table and singing.

▶ **Searching Faith:** Especially typical of late adolescence, searching faith (or struggling faith) is marked by doubt, experimentation, and commitment. It is at this point that young individuals critically examine the faith for themselves and test out this faith identity for their own lifestyles.

▶ **Owned Faith:** This is the point at which genuine conversion occurs (whether "sudden" or more gradual)—when, having wrestled with the questions, one embraces the faith for oneself. Then it is in this ever-growing

---

[48] John H. Westerhoff, *Will Our Children Have Faith?* (New York: Seabury, 1976), 89–91.

[49] Westerhoff defines faith as "an action which includes thinking, feeling, and willing and it is transmitted, sustained, and expanded through our interactions with other faithing selves in a community of faith." Ibid., 91.

[50] Ibid., 92.

ring of faith that one continues to deepen one's relationship with the Lord (through Bible study, spiritual disciplines, community life).

Others have made significant contributions in the dialogue on faith development. Writing from a pastoral perspective, Neill Q. Hamilton draws a distinction between psychological maturing and spiritual maturing: the former is an increasing capacity to love deeply and work productively, the latter is an increasing capacity to love God and neighbor and to be effective in one's God-given vocation. These complementary parallels remind us of the critical work of the Holy Spirit in the full unfolding of the human spirit through the developmental process. We cannot fully account for the psychological maturity of a student without considering spiritual maturity, and we cannot consider the spiritual dimension without considering psychological maturity. Hamilton describes this in terms of three general phases of development (Figure 11-3): discipleship, transition in the Spirit, and maturing in church and mission.[51]

Figure 11-2.
Westerhoff's Styles of Faith

Owned Faith

Searching Faith

Affiliative Faith

Experienced Faith

Source: John H. Westerhoff, *Will Our Children Have Faith?* (New York: Seabury, 1976), 89–91.

Principle of Teenage Spirituality— The Divine Math Principle: God adds up our negative experiences and often uses them in a positive way. Teenagers will often look back on a trial or struggle as one of the most significant milestones in their spiritual development (see Gen. 50:18-20).

Faith Development and Developing Teenage Disciples

Research in faith development is ongoing, and the jury is still out on some of its conclusions. However, a massive longitudinal study was undertaken in 1999 with the incoming class of freshman at several Christian colleges to study how the faith of these students develops and changes over the course of their college years.[52] At

[51] Neill Q. Hamilton, *Maturing in the Christian Life: A Pastor's Guide* (Philadelphia: Geneva Press, 1984), 148, cited in Pazmino, *Foundational Issues in Christian Education*, 213.

[52] The *Faithful Change* research project was conducted under the leadership of Art Nonneman, overall project coordinator, with James Fowler and others serving as co-investigators and consultants. Subjects consisted of 360 undergraduates from nine campuses of the Christian College Coalition, including Azusa Pacific University (Calif.), Eastern University (Penn.), Taylor University (Ind.), Greenville College (Ill.), Korea Nazarene University (South Korea), and Eastern Nazarene College (Mass.). This material is part of the Art Nonneman, Gay Holcomb, and Will Slater paper presented at the CCCU National Assessment Conference, Cedarville University, Ohio, October 2000.

the time of this writing, the research is not complete, but some of the preliminary findings are intriguing and have clear implications for youth ministry:

> **Positive Negatives:** One of the keys to growing faith in adolescence is an honest engagement with trial, crisis, and hardship. Youth workers should see students' trials and crises as an opportunity for growth. Embrace these tough times and the tough questions raised by them.

> **Helping Others Helps Students:** Students were greatly helped by experiences of serving others, being exposed to perspectives other than their own, and learning to see the world through the eyes of others. Youth workers must continually challenge students to commit to a purpose bigger than themselves.

> **Crossing Cultural Boundaries to Higher Stages of Faith:** Students found their faith deepened by international study (not tourism) and prolonged experiences of living in another culture. Also significant was the positive impact of short-term missions projects (international, rural, and urban). Youth workers should try to incorporate these kinds of experiences into their programs.

> **Negative Positives:** Researchers found impeded faith development in students whose faith had been forged by indoctrination rather than through free and open inquiry. That does not mean that youth workers should

Bruce Powers' Stages of Faith

> Nurture (ages 0–6): Primary exposure to and awareness of meaning of life comes from family and church.

> Indoctrination (7–18): Mastering the content of faith—being taught about faith.

> Reality Testing (19–27): Moving from closed system of absolute certainty to a wider system—still with certainties, but now tempered by real-life experiences.

> Making Choices (ages 28–35): Learning to accept personal responsibility for making decisions based on one's beliefs.

> Active Devotion (36 years and up): Choices of previous stage set basic life direction. Individuals can now focus more on active devotion and sharing faith with others.

—*Bruce Powers,* Growing Faith *(Nashville, Tenn.: Broadman, 1982), 14–21.*

Figure 11–3.
Hamilton's Phases of Christian Maturing

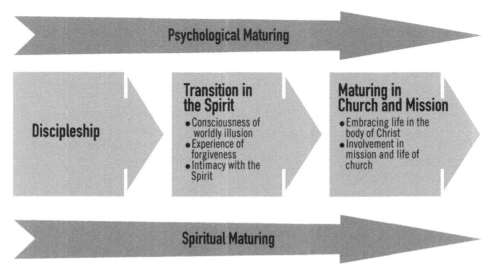

Neill Q. Hamilton, *Maturing in the Christian Life: A Pastor's Guide* (Philadelphia: Geneva Press, 1984), 148.

eschew thinking about answers or teaching about doctrine, but it certainly does mean that we should honestly embrace questions and teach truth in a spirit of open inquiry. Teaching should focus on *what* we believe, and *why* we believe it, but it should be offered in an atmosphere that affirms the legitimacy of an honest search.

▸ **Arrogant Certainty:** The least faith development was found in students whose faith consisted of simple, clear-cut answers, whose faith was characterized more by concrete thinking than by abstract thought. Again, that does not mean truth has no place in a youth ministry. What it does mean is that students develop less spiritually when they are expected to blindly embrace doctrinal truths that they have not struggled with themselves. The struggle itself encourages a humility and openness that leads to deeper growth.

Landmarks on the Odyssey of Grace

Adventurers have long made a habit of marking their journey by significant features of the landscape they travel. Hikers on the Appalachian Trail will occasionally refer to Mahoosuc Notch in southern Maine, considered by many to be the toughest mile on the whole stretch of the 2,100 mile trail from Maine to Georgia.[53] For ancient Native Americans, soldiers, surveyors, emigrants, settlers, and cowboys, that landmark was El Morro, the castle-like natural rock formation that looms from the plateau of scrubby desert plants and junipers of western New Mexico.[54] For Eddy Harris, who canoed alone the entire 2,500-mile length of the Mississippi River, one such place was Hannibal, Missouri.[55] Those who traverse the interior of the Alaska Range will sometimes talk about the dramatic rockscape of Mt. Dickey, the highest granite cliff in North America, referred to by climbers as "the vertical mile."[56]

In the same way, any number of writers have sought to describe some of the landmarks along the way of spiritual maturity.

Practically speaking, most youth workers think of Christian maturity in terms of observable traits and ownable truths. This does not really do justice to the holistic spirituality we have described in this chapter in that it focuses more on the knowing and doing dimensions of spirituality than the being dimension. Having said that, however, there is real value in identifying some developmental and learning goals.

Ruth Beechick, adopting Robert Havighurst's approach of identifying developmental tasks,[57] identified key tasks of spiritual development that a person must accomplish beginning in early childhood:[58]

---

[53] Lynn Setzer, *A Season of the Appalachian Trail* (Birmingham, Ala.: Menasha Bridge Press, 1997), 148.

[54] The sandstone walls of this place have proven so irresistible to hundreds of years of passers-by that it is often called Inscription Rock. "Some of the inscriptions were made on August 23, 1859, when an Army expedition led by Lieutenant Edward Beale passed through, establishing a new route from Texas to California. This group included 25 Egyptian camels being tested as pack animals, an idea that came to nothing. Their wrangler, P. Gilmer Breckinridge, also left his signature on the rock." A photo of the rock is available at http://www.desertusa.com/mag00/jan/stories/photos/emoro6.jpg.

[55] "Mark Twain's town, Home of Huck and Jim. Like a pilgrim arrived at Mecca, I fell to my knees." Eddy Harris, *Mississippi Solo: A River Quest* (New York, Harper and Row, 1988), 111.

[56] In fact, the cliff drops more than 5,000 feet to Ruth Glacier at its base, but then, it extends still beneath the ice of that glacier to a depth no one actually knows.

[57] Robert Havighurst, *Developmental Tasks and Education* (New York: David McCay, 1961), 72–98, cited in Pazmino, *Foundational Issues in Christian Education*, 210. Havighurst sought to identify developmental tasks that arise at or about a certain period in the lives of individuals. If and when they achieve the task, they are able to lead happier, more productive lives, and advance to further tasks. Failure to achieve a task will impede growth to higher levels of development, foster social disfavor, and lead to less personal satisfaction with life. Havighurst specified various roles that persons assume as they move through life: child, friend, organization member, worker, spouse, parent, church member, and user of leisure time. Beechick's work is an adaptation of this idea to the Christian life.

[58] Obviously, many people come to know Christ long after their childhood years. For them the process is truncated, but the sequence would be roughly the same. In other words, a person cannot make life decisions based on eternal Christian values (III-F) without first learning what those basic values are (II-D).

Fran Cosgrove offers these marks of Christian maturity:

▶ A learner who is open and teachable (Prov. 9:8–10, Matt. 4:19, John 6:60-66).

▶ Puts Christ first in all areas of life (Matt. 6:9–13,24,33; Luke 9:23; John 13:13; 2 Cor. 5:15).

▶ Committed to a life of purity and is taking steps to separate from sin (1 Cor. 6:19–20, Eph. 4:22–32, Col. 3:5–10, 1 Thess. 4:3–7, Titus 2:12–14).

▶ Daily devotional time and developing prayer life (Ps. 27:4, 42:1–2; Mark 1:35; Luke 11:1–4; 1 Thess. 5:17–18; James 1:5–7, 5:16).

▶ Demonstrates faithfulness and a desire to learn and apply the Word of God through hearing it taught/preached, reading it frequently, Bible study, Scripture memory, meditation on Scriptures (John 8:31; Acts 2:42, 17:11; Col. 3:16; 2 Tim. 2:15).

▶ Heart for witnessing, gives testimony clearly, and presents gospel regularly with increasing skill (Matt. 28:18–20; Acts 1:8, 5:42, 14:21–23, 22:14–15; Rom. 1:16; 1 Cor. 15:3–4; 1 Thess. 2:4).

▶ Regular church attendance, active in local worship, consistent in corporate worship (Ps. 122:1, Acts 16:5, 1 Cor. 12:12–27, Col. 1:15–18, Heb. 10:25).

▶ Fellowships regularly with other believers, displaying love and unity (John 17:22–26; Acts 2:44–47, 4:31–33; Eph. 4:1–3; Heb. 10:24; 1 John 1:1–3).

▶ Demonstrates a servant heart by helping others in practical ways (Mark 10:42–45, Acts 6:1–4, 2 Cor. 12:15, Phil. 2:25–30, 1 Thess. 2:8,9).

▶ Gives regularly and honors God with finances (Hag. 1:6–9, Mal. 3:10–11, 1 Cor. 16:12–20, 2 Cor. 8-9, Philem. 14).

▶ Demonstrates fruit of spirit by attractive relationship with Christ and fellow man (John 15:1–5).

Fran Cosgrove, Essentials of Discipleship (Colorado Springs, Colo.: NavPress, 1980), 15-16.

Beechick's Outline of Tasks Toward Spiritual Development[59]

I. Preschool Years

A. Experiencing love, security, discipline, joy, and worship
B. Beginning to develop awareness and concepts of God, Jesus, and other basic Christian realities
C. Developing attitudes toward God, Jesus, church, self, and the Bible
D. Beginning to develop concepts of right and wrong

II. Elementary School Years

A. Receiving and acknowledging Jesus Christ as Savior and Lord
B. Growing in awareness of Christian love and responsibility in relationships with others
C. Continuing to build concepts of basic Christian realities
D. Learning basic Bible teachings adequate for personal faith and everyday Christian living:
    1. Prayer in daily life
    2. The Bible in daily life
    3. Christian friendships
    4. Group worship
    5. Responsibility for serving God
    6. Basic knowledge of God, Jesus, Holy Spirit, creation, angelic beings, heaven, hell, sin, salvation, Bible history, and literature
E. Developing healthy attitudes toward self

III. Adolescence

A. Learning to show Christian love in everyday life
B. Continuing to develop healthy attitudes toward self
C. Developing Bible knowledge and intellectual skills adequate for meeting intellectual assaults on faith
D. Achieving strength of Christian character adequate for meeting anti-Christian social pressures
E. Accepting responsibility for Christian service in accordance with growing abilities
F. Learning to make life decisions on the basis of eternal Christian values
G. Increasing self-discipline to "seek those things which are above"

---

[59] Ruth Beechick, *Teaching Juniors: Both Heart and Head* (Denver: Accent Books, 1981), 24–25. This is Pazmino's synopsis of Beechick. Pazmino, *Foundational Issues in Christian Education*, 211–212.

IV. Maturity

    A. Accepting responsibility for continued growth and learning
    B. Accepting biblical responsibilities toward God and toward others
    C. Living a unified, purposeful life centered upon God

For those of us in youth ministry, the question concerns what spiritual maturity might look like specifically in the life of teenager. Might there be specific milestones to watch for in nurturing true spirituality in the life of an adolescent? Mark Senter defines spiritual maturity for a high school student as "that stage in his or her relationship to God when he or she is capable and willing to allow biblical truth to shape his or her values, decisions and actions."[60]

Stuart Hall and Andy Stanley describe maturity in the life of a Christian teenager in terms of seven checkpoints (summarized in Table 11-3).[61] Using a slightly different tack,[62] perhaps we might think of spiritual maturity in the life of a teenager as being marked by five basic characteristics:

1. **First-hand faith:** *Spiritually mature teenagers have begun to embrace the faith for themselves,* not as some sort of secondhand "follow-ship" (see 1 Cor. 11:1) but as a growing and deepening firsthand fellowship (Eph. 5:1).

2. **A faith that affects the heart and the head:** *Spiritually mature teenagers are marked by a faith that endures even when the goose-bumps are gone* (see 2 Cor. 4:16–18, Heb. 11:1). That means nurturing in students a faith that is anchored in the promises of God. Dunn comments:

   > All humans are experiential: we all learn our world through the five senses. Contemporary adolescents do so with a vengeance . . . However, as ends in themselves they can move the student into a false sense of God that will crumble once the sensation has ceased. Intense emotional experiences—whether involving music, drama, or emotional sharing of the heart—must be consistently fastened to the anchor of God's love.[63]

3. **A faith that is real in everyday life.** *A third mark of spiritual maturity in the life of an adolescent is consistency in integrating faith with everyday lifestyle choices and actions.* (James 1:21–24).

[60] Mark Senter, "Axioms of Youth Ministry: The Context" in *Reaching a Generation for Christ*, ed. Richard Dunn and Mark Senter III (Chicago: Moody Press, 1997), 125.

[61] To be completely accurate, Hall and Stanley describe these as principles every teenager needs to know, "the irreducible minimum," and so they are not primarily describing these checkpoints as marks of spiritual maturity. On the other hand, the tone of the book suggests strongly that it would be difficult to describe as "spiritual mature" a teenager who was not growing in each of these seven areas. I think, practically speaking, Hall and Stanley are right on target. "The seven checkpoints are an intentional, systematic approach to student discipleship focused on the content of discipleship." Stuart Hall and Andy Stanley, *The Seven Checkpoints: Seven Principles Every Teenager Needs to Know* (West Monroe, La.: Howard, 2001), 9.

[62] Duffy Robbins, *The Ministry of Nurture* (Grand Rapids, Mich.: Zondervan, 1990). In this earlier work, I discuss each of these five characteristics in much more detail and explore practical ministry strategies by which these traits might be cultivated in the life of a student.

[63] Dunn, *Shaping the Spiritual Life of Students*, 60–61.

4. **A durable faith.** *A mark of mature teenage spirituality is a faith that is strong enough and durable enough to embrace life's questions and struggles without letting go of God* (Jer. 15:15, 17–18; Heb. 12:7–13, James 1:2–8, 12).

5. **A fleshed-out faith.** *The fifth mark of teenage spirituality is the willingness to step out of the adolescent comfort zone and into the risk of fleshed-out faith* (1 Cor. 4:20). It is what Francis Xavier, the Jesuit director of missions in India, China, and Japan in the sixteenth century, described as giving up the rut of "small ambitions." Whether that be the challenge of leading a small group, or being pushed to the limit on a work project, or simply sharing one's testimony some night at a club, a fleshed-out faith is the willingness to take with Peter those halting steps out of the boat and into the waves (Matt. 14:29), or to measure as Caleb did the dangers with the promises and say, "We should go up . . . for we can certainly do it" (Num. 13:30).

Satanic Advice About How to Use Times of Spiritual Dryness

Let him assume that the first ardors of his conversion might have been expected to last, and ought to have lasted, forever, and that his present dryness is an equally permanent condition. Having once got this misconception well-fixed in his head, you may then proceed in various ways. It all depends on whether your man is of the desponding type who can be tempted to despair, or of the wishful-thinking type who can be assured that all is well. The former type is getting rare among the humans. If your patient should happen to belong to it, everything is easy. You have only got to keep him out of the way of experienced Christians (an easy task nowadays), to direct his attention to the appropriate passages in Scripture, and then to set him to work on the desperate design of recovering his old feelings by sheer will power, and the game is ours.

. . . Another possibility is that of direct attack on his faith. When you have caused him to assume that the trough is permanent, can you not persuade him that "his religious phase" is just going to die away like all his previous phases? . . . I assume that the creature has been through several of them before—they all have—and that he always feels superior and patronizing to the ones he has emerged from, not because he has really criticized them but simply because they are in the past . . . You see the idea? . . . Nice shadowy expressions—"It was a phase"—"I've been through all that"—don't forget the blessed word "Adolescent."

C. S. Lewis's character Screwtape giving counsel to his nephew, Wormwood, in The Screwtape Letters *(New York: MacMillan, 1961), 42–43.*

Table 11-3.
Seven Teenage Checkpoints

Checkpoint	Principle	Key Passage	Crucial question
Checkpoint 1: **Authentic Faith**	God will be trusted; he will do all he has promised to do.	Prov. 3:5–6	Are your students trusting God with the critical areas of their lives?
Checkpoint 2: **Spiritual Disciplines**	When you see as God sees, you will do as God says.	Rom. 12:2	Are your students developing a consistent devotional and prayer life?
Checkpoint 3: **Moral Boundaries**	Purity paves the way to intimacy.	1 Thess. 4:3–8	Are your students establishing and maintaining godly moral boundaries?
Checkpoint 4: **Healthy Friendships**	Your friends will determine the quality and direction of your life.	Prov. 13:20	Are your students establishing healthy friendships and avoiding unhealthy ones?
Checkpoint 5: **Wise Choices**	Walk wisely.	Eph. 5:15–17	Are your students making wise choices in every area of their lives?
Checkpoint 6: **Ultimate Authority**	Maximum freedom is found under God's authority.	Rom. 13:1–2	Are your students submitting to the authorities God has placed over them?
Checkpoint 7: **Others First**	Consider others before yourself.	Phil. 2:3–11	Are your students putting the needs of others ahead of their own?

Source: Stuart Hall and Andy Stanley, *The Seven Checkpoints: Seven Principles Every Teenager Needs to Know* (West Monore, La.: Howard, 2001), 10–12.

Photo Finish

What a wonder that God, who brought all creation into being with the words "Let there be light," flashed across the marred face of humanity the light of life, the light of the world, the light of his only Son, Jesus. Then, more wonderful still, that by exposure to God's light, high school and middle school students could become new creatures (see 2 Cor. 4:6), could step out of darkness into life (1 Pet. 2:9). But the drama does not end there. Like a cosmic Polaroid the image is still in the development process. What we see now in that student is only a hint of what is to come. The image is blurred; it is faint; its colors are bland. But, with careful handling and the proper exposure of light, that image is destined one day to look like Jesus.

As youth ministers, that means, in a sense, that we are working in God's "darkroom," assisting in this development process through which we help students grow into the image of God's Son. To be sure, some of them will turn out and some of them will not. Some of them will get turned on, some of them will get turned off, and as Willimon reminds us, some of them may just settle for turning over letters in a game show. But, along the way, it is an awesome privilege and a magnificent journey. By God's grace it will lead to more than catchy headlines and cheap photos at the supermarket check-out. It will lead to a corps of "improbables," "unlikelies," "impossibles," "who-would-have-guessed-she-coulds?" and "I-never-thought-he-woulds" traveling together in an amazing quest—always further, always deeper, always closer.

Even as Mount Doom collapses around them, Sam says, "'What a tale we've been in, Mr. Frodo, haven't we? I wish I could hear it told!' . . . But even as he spoke so, to keep fear away until the very last, his eyes still strayed north, north into the eye of the wind, to where the sky far off was clear."

And so the Eagles espy them, "two dark figures, forlorn, hand in hand upon a little hill, while the world shook under them." They collapse before the Eagles arrive, and do not know that their hope has been rewarded.[64]

True Spirituality: Living with God in the Everyday

As one youth worker put it to me, "When everybody's here at youth group, we're fine. It's when they leave here that they seem to fall into two groups. One group is totally into the emotion of our worship time, but they're like—once the emotion wears off, 'I don't feel God anymore.' Then, the other group is totally into youth group while they're here. But then, on Friday night they go out and party with their friends and they forget all about the commitments they made when they were here at youth group. So, I've got one group that doesn't feel God after the lights come back on, and the other group that forgets about God after the lights go out!"

The test of authentic teenage spirituality is what happens between meetings.

I beheld then, that they all went on till they came to the foot of the hill "Difficulty," at the bottom of which was a spring. There were also in the same place two other ways besides that which came straight from the gate; one turned to the left hand, and the other to the right, at the bottom of the hill: but the narrow way lay right up the hill (and the name of the going up the side of the hill is called Difficulty). Christian now went to the spring, and drank thereof to refresh himself (Isa. 49:10); and then began to go up the hill, saying:

"This hill, though high, I covet to ascend;
The difficulty will not me offend,
For I perceive the way to life lies here:
Come, pluck up, heart, let's neither faint nor fear!
Better, though difficult, the right way to go,
Than wrong, though easy, where the end is woe."

—John Bunyan, Pilgrim's Progress (Grand Rapids, Mich.: Zondervan, 1966), 37.

[64] Mark Eddy Smith, *Tolkien's Ordinary Virtues: Exploring the Spiritual Themes of The Lord of the Rings* (Downers Grove, Ill.: InterVarsity Press, 2002), 124.

LEARNING TO DRIVE

Meditations on the Way by Helen Musick

There has to be no better day in a teenager's life than the day you get your driver's permit. It is like a permit to life and the world of independence. But before getting the "real thing" you have got to learn to operate this vehicle from heaven!

Learning to drive was one of the greatest moments in life but also one of the most stressful times of my life. Why? Because my father was determined that I would learn to drive a "real" car, that is, a stick shift. It was all I could do to estimate the proper ratio between the gas and the clutch. Close friends and family members faithfully coached me. They assured me; they cheered me on. But, despite their votes of confidence, I was convinced I would never learn to get from first to fourth if my life depended on it. My father persevered with me despite the minor whiplash he experienced as a result of me trying to keep the car from stalling every time I had to stop at the top of a hill and gun the clutch so I would keep from stalling the car.

My pessimistic attitude had everything to do with the apprehension and stress I endured during this time. I had it in for myself before I even turned on the ignition. I feared getting into the car; I feared the personal disappointment of stalling; I feared being embarrassed in front of my passengers. The result was extreme stress of mind, body, and spirit. Fear sure has a way of stressing people out!

Look with me at Numbers 13. Here we read of the 12 men selected to explore the Promised Land, Canaan. They received instructions to learn about the area and its inhabitants in order to educate the Israelites about the land that God was giving to them (v. 2). They explored for 40 days (v. 25), and then returned home with a report. Verses 26–33 recount this report given to the Israelites. Two contrasting opinions were shared. Ten of the explorers spread bad reports about taking the land, because they feared the size of the inhabitants. However, the final two, Joshua and Caleb, returned with a much more positive testimony. They believed in the Israelites' ability to take possession of the land.

The Israelites followed majority rule. Numbers 14 goes on to tell about how the community wept and grumbled that night. They even wished for death for themselves! What is that all about? They received a negative report and were motivated by one thing—fear; fear that was completely unnecessary. God had already promised that he was giving them the land (13:2). The exploration of Canaan was never meant to be a feasibility mission! It was intended to finalize the deal through education and preparation. The Israelites did not need to know whether they could take the land. They needed to prepare for how they were going to take it. Do you see the difference?

There is a great price to pay when we allow fear to have dominion over our minds. We lose confidence; we entertain despair; we surrender our spirit. We can't minister in this condition! We lose when we fear!

▶ Why is it that we so readily cling to the negative?

▶ Why do we allow fear to have the final say in our daily lives when we are guaranteed the presence and the promises of God?

▶ What will it take for us to believe the encouraging friends and faithful explorers around us?

▶ Where do you allow fear to keep you from experiencing God's blessings?

chapter twelve

YOUTH MINISTRY ORIENTEERING:
DEVELOPING A PHILOSOPHY OF MINISTRY

Not that the rest of us had much idea what we were supposed to be doing, but at least we had learned to fake it a little . . . In the [boat's] cabin, Marco had perfected a . . . convincing impression of a navigator, standing over the map with a pencil, ruler, and stage frown, making tiny crosses on the chart.

"Where are we, Marco?" I asked.

"Exactly 18 degrees 27 minutes south by 70 degrees 19 minutes west," he said, reading the numbers off the yellow hand-held GPS.

"Oh right . . . what does that actually mean?"

"We're here," he said, showing me a little cross on the chart, barely off the beach. "We've come . . . about twelve miles."

I was grudgingly impressed. Perhaps I had misjudged Marco's competence. The trouble was, I had no way of knowing if he was getting it right or not. And more worryingly, neither did he.

—Nick Thorpe[1]

. . . You might be lost. The best strategy to take at that time, is to stop hiking and think carefully about your next move. The worst thing you can do is keep walking. You may only be just slightly lost; if you keep marching on, you will only make a small problem worse.

—Michael Mouland[2]

A prudent man gives thought to his steps.

—Proverbs 14:15

[1] Nick Thorpe, *Eight Men and a Duck* (New York: Free Press, 2002), 72.

[2] Michael Mouland, *The Complete Idiot's Guide to Hiking, Camping, and the Great Outdoors* (New York: Alpha Books, 1996), 120.

The hike was going great. The scenery was stunning and the weather was beautiful. As the two of them made their way among the tall trees of the old growth forest, they were holding hands, talking together, and enjoying the crisp chill of fall in Washington's Olympic Peninsula. She was impressed with how well he knew the trail. He was impressed with how much she seemed to be impressed.

Perhaps that is why, figuratively at least, the hike started to head downhill. Their circuit trail should have brought them back to the car by mid-afternoon so they could be back on campus that night. But now it was nearly sundown, with no car in sight, and the chill was developing into an uncomfortable cold.

The first time she asked about the map, he pretended not to hear—he acted as if he were too absorbed with the sounds of the forest. When she mentioned it again a few minutes later, adding that it was cold and she was getting tired, he offered a noncommittal "What-do-you-expect-me-to-do-about it?" grunt. When she asked a third time if they might stop to rest and look at the map, she also complained that his pace was too fast. That is when he confessed to leaving the map in the car and explained impatiently that the quick pace was necessary if they were to get back to the car before darkness made it hard to find the trail. When, still again after another half mile, she wondered out loud if they might ask for directions from some hikers at a campsite they had just passed, he was clearly getting angry. First it was too far. Then it was too fast. Now it is "for crying out loud!"

By the time they cleared the fifth major ridge, beyond which he had assured her they would see the car, she was completely exhausted and highly annoyed. That is when the trail got very rocky in more ways than one.

How dare he "be so arrogant" as to assume he needed no direction? Why could she not "just keep walking and enjoy the scenery"? Why could he not "slow down"? Why could she not "talk less and walk more"?

Finally, after about another 50 yards, 20 complaints, 10 rolls of the eyes, and five heated outbursts, he stopped walking, turned to face her on the trail, and then, with a mixture of embarrassment and fatigue he could not admit, and rage he was barely able to control, he spat out the words: "Will you stop nagging me? Okay! You're right! We're lost! . . . But you've gotta admit, *we're making great time!*"

Lost Adventurers

What you have just read in this cautionary tale of romance on the trail to nowhere is, in fact, a parable that vividly portrays one of the classic mistakes of youth ministry: beginning the journey with no clear sense of where it should lead. Ministries spend their money, their people, and their time trying to build good youth programs without giving careful thought to two key questions: *Where do we want to go?* and *Where are we now?* More attention is given to scenery, distance, and speed than to ultimate destination.

The current youth ministry culture provides several different paradigms of response for the "Lost Adventurers Syndrome." Some of them are impressive. None of them are particularly effective.

▶ **Bigger is Better Approach.** Probably the most common response is the one we see in the hapless, heavy-footed boyfriend who is more preoccupied with impressing his traveling companion than he is with questions about destination. "We've got all these kids walking with us in the youth program. We've had record numbers join us on the journey. Why worry about where we're headed? We must be doing something right!" This is youth ministry led astray by the tendency, when large numbers of students are involved, to forget important questions such as "Where are we leading them?"

▶ **Just Say "Mo" Approach.** A second type of response commonly seen in the current youth ministry culture is this sort: "You're right, I think we are lost. Let's just keep on walking, faster and faster, taking each new trail, until we see something that will get us back on track." This is youth ministry based on momentum and more "ministry"—the hope that more money, more effort, and more activity will turn a program around. It is an approach that searches frantically through each new promotional mailing, resource packet, or youth ministry magazine hoping to find signs of the right route or just the right resource to get back on the trail of "successful" youth ministry. The fallacy of this approach is that a ministry that lacks a clear destination or a clear awareness of location, even when it is turned around, is still lost—only now from the opposite direction. There is not much virtue in turning from "we-don't-know-where-we're-going" to "we-don't-know-where-we've-been."

▶ **Follow the Letter Approach.** A third response that is all too common in youth ministry is exhibited by this statement: "Well, we can't be lost. This is a well-traveled trail. If it's working for them, it ought to work for us. Let's just keep going." This is youth ministry orienteering based on mailings received from denominational or regional offices or publishers who mass mail maps to the latest must-have resources. The hype and promotion obscure the need to ask if we really want to go to the same destination as the others using this route. Or whether others who have walked this same trail were just as lost as we are. It never fails: when someone claims to have discovered a hot new youth ministry passage, there are usually lots of takers.

▶ **The Highway and Buy-Way Approach.** Another typical youth ministry response to the "Lost Adventurers Syndrome" is represented by a fourth statement: "You're right. We are lost. We don't know where we're going. We've got to do something drastic! Let's buy a new backpack!" In this scenario, the youth worker senses that the program is not connecting or the strategy is not working, so the response is to build a new building, shop for a new program, purchase new software, or go to a new camp property. But if a ministry is "lost on the trail," buying new equipment doesn't solve the problem. It just means that the ministry—which was lost before—is still lost. But now it is lost in a "dynamic," "creative," and "cutting-edge" way.

▶ **Follow the Star Approach.** Still another common response to the "Lost Adventurers Syndrome," this approach to youth ministry focuses neither on the gear, nor the trail, nor the destination. This is youth ministry that focuses on the guide. It is sometimes referred to as the Bright Light Approach because it is based on the notion that the brightest lantern attracts the most bugs. After all, if we want students to swarm the ministry, it stands to reason that we must find a young, ultra-hip, dynamic "bright light" to guide the journey. The weakness in this approach is that there will always be a flashier youth program or school program or sports program with a brighter light, and many a youth worker has burned out trying to crank up the candlepower. It takes more than flash and fireworks to keep students burning for the long haul. There is only one real Light of the world.

Stop, Study, and Stare

"If you have completely lost your bearings, try to get to a high vista and look around."[3]

There is only one response that makes much sense when lost on the trail, only one response that prevents aimless wandering for an unknown, undetermined destination. The youth workers who avoid this response risk running out of trail, running out of energy, running out of people willing to hike with them, and perhaps even being run out of town! It is a response that can be summed up in three words: *Stop, Study, and Stare:*

▶ **Stop wasting energy.** There is not a great deal of value in making good time when we're getting nowhere.

---

[3] Joshua Piven and David Brogenicht, *The Worst-Case Scenario Survival Handbook* (San Francisco: Chronicle Books, 1999), 129.

Suppose one of you wants to build a tower. Will he not first sit down and estimate the cost to see if he has enough money to complete it? For if he lays the foundation and is not able to finish it, everyone who sees it will ridicule him . . .
—**Luke 14:28–29**

Once you communicate God's purpose for your ministry, you won't have to ask the why question again. The new question will be how: How do we accomplish what God has called us to do? The why must be answered before the how can make sense to others.
—**Doug Fields**

▸ **Study the guidebook.** Look to Scripture to develop a clear sense of purpose or vision.

▸ **Stare at the map.** Develop the program with that purpose in mind. *How do we get from where we are to where God calls us to be?*

In Jesus's Upper Room discourse (John 13–17) when he gave his disciples their final words of instruction, he gave them this clear statement of purpose: "You did not choose me, but I chose you and appointed you to go and bear fruit—fruit that will last" (John 15:16). It was a reminder of a principle he had often stated: "Each tree is recognized by its own fruit" (Luke 6:44).[4]

It is a simple concept but extremely vital. Jesus did not say a tree would be known by how large it is (Bigger is Better Approach), or by the variety of its fruit (Just Say "Mo" Approach), or by whether a lot of folks showed up to admire the gardener who planted the tree (Follow the Star Approach), or by whether the landscaping was new and edgy (The Buy-Way Approach), or by whether the tree was the same planted in other gardens on the same street (Follow the Letter Approach). Jesus said it all comes down to the quality of the fruit.

It is a statement that brings us to the importance of a ministry philosophy.

Beginning with the End in Mind

If I had been reading this book in my early years of youth ministry, I would have read through that last sentence and decided right away that this was a section of the book that could be ignored. "That's just philosophy, and what counts when you're working with kids is not a lot of philosophical, academic mumbo-jumbo; it's what you *do*." Confident that my two years of

---

[4] For further reflection on this passage, see the notes in the preceding chapter on the meaning of "fruitfulness" in John 15:16.

Following the Wrong "Experts"

Like the current youth ministry culture, there was no shortage of experts willing to help adventurers and pioneers make their way west to California in the mid-1840s. One of those experts, a "handsome, strong-faced" man, "quick and intelligent of speech" was Lansford Hastings, an opportunist and political adventurer who hoped to endear himself to westward immigrants by offering them a shortcut through the Rockies. "There is a nigher route," he promised, "and it is no use to take so much of a roundabout course."

What was described as the Hastings Cutoff captured the attention of George Donner and his party of 20 wagons and 73 people, who saw the opportunity to shave as much as a month off what would already be a grueling journey.

Unfortunately, it was not to be. What promised to be a cutoff ended up being a dangerously difficult trail that led through salt deserts and rugged mountain passes. Three months into their journey, exhausted and near starvation, the party stopped to rest only three miles from the summit of the Sierra Nevada on November 1, 1846. It was a deadly delay. The snow that fell that night and the days thereafter made progress even more difficult. By the time the Donner Party realized they had been caught in winter's trap, their temporary camp and cabins were surrounded by nine feet of snow. It was the beginning of a nightmare that involved horrific hardship, cannibalism, and unimaginable grief as one after another of the party died. It was the classic Greek tragedy, "moving one to pity and terror."

The story of the Donner Party offers a metaphor for those of us in youth ministry who are constantly looking for the new route, and are often persuaded by the latest ministry adventure: it is an empty hope that follows the advice of experts without asking if the experts themselves might be lost. Going the right direction on the wrong map can have serious consequences. Beware the shortcut. The easiest route is not necessarily the best.

Source: Irving Stone, Men to Match My Mountains *(New York: Berkley Books, 1982), 104–115.*

> I believe it's true that the difference between great people and everyone else is that great people create their lives actively, while everyone else is created by their lives, passively waiting to see where life takes them next.
>
> —Michael Gerber, The E-Myth *(New York: Harper Business, 1986), 85.*

vast (part-time) experience had taught me all I needed to know about youth ministry, I would have laid this book aside in favor of the newest "how to" programming resource. Looking for new trails and exciting views, I would not have taken the necessary time to ask myself where my program was or where it was headed. Like most rookie youth workers, my ministry philosophy was summarized in the battle cry: "Ready! . . . Fire! . . . Aim!"

But over time, I began to ask bigger questions. What was I *really* accomplishing when I left my wife and children at home on Friday nights so I could spend the evening with somebody else's kids? What was the *real* source of joy and satisfaction in my ministry? Would the short-term goals that occupied me now be big enough to sustain me long-term in youth ministry? In the words of Eugene Peterson, I was haunted by the possibility that I was forfeiting my calling as pastor to become a program director:

> The program-director pastor is dominated by the social-economic mindset of Darwinism: market-orientation, competitiveness, survival of the fittest. This is a shift in pastoral work away from God-oriented obedience to career-oriented success. It is work at which we gain mastery, position, power, and daily check on our image in the mirror . . .
>
> The spiritual-director pastor is shaped by the biblical mindset of Jesus: worship-orientation, a servant life, sacrifice. This shifts pastoral work from ego-addictions to grace-freedoms.[5]

Don't get me wrong. I loved the youth in our group. We had some super times and our group was growing larger. The parents were supportive and the congregation was impressed. The journey was a blast, the scenery was beautiful, the company was great. But deep down I knew: we were making great time—with no real sense of where we were going.

In his book *Education in the Truth*, Christian educator Norman DeJong proposes a ladder of issues (illustrated in Figure 12-1) that are critical in forging a philosophy of ministry (expanded in Table 12-1):[6]

---

[5] Eugene Peterson, *Under the Unpredictable Plant: An Exploration of Vocational Holiness* (Grand Rapids, Mich.: Eerdmans, 1992), 176.

[6] Norman DeJong, *Education in the Truth* (Nutley, N.J.: Presbyterians and Reformed, 1974), 61–63. DeJong was addressing the issue of educational philosophy, but his philosophical ladder is quite helpful in shaping a philosophy of ministry as well. Youth Specialties, arguably one of the foremost youth ministry training organizations, has broken down its training curriculum into three stages that roughly parallel the stages of DeJong's Ladder: CORE Realities (Rungs 1 to 2), CORE Values (Rungs 3 to 4), and CORE Skills (Rung 5). If there is any criticism to simplifying the approach this way, it is that it may not take seriously enough the important theological questions inherent in the first two rungs of DeJong's ladder (see Table 12-1).

1. **Basis of authority.** What is the basis of authority for the ministry philosophy?

2. **Nature of persons.** What does it mean to be human, and how does this understanding of full humanity shape a ministry philosophy?

3. **Purposes and goals.** This is the all-important question of destination. Where should this journey take us?

4. **Structural organization.** Regardless of scenery, popularity, or degree of difficulty, which trail is most likely to take us where we need to go? What provisions will we need for such a journey?

5. **Implementation.** How can we use the resources God has provided, material and human, to step out in pursuit of the goal?

Figure 12-1.
DeJong's Ladder of Philosophical Elements

Evaluation

Implementation

Structural Organization

Purposes and Goals

Nature of Persons

Basis of Authority

Source: Norman DeJong, *Education in the Truth* (Nutley, N.J.: Presbyterians and Reformed, 1974), 61–63.

6. **Evaluation.** Can we stop periodically to look again at the map, and measure the progress of the ministry against the goals of the ministry?

These six issues may seem theoretical or even irrelevant to the world of real-life youth ministry. But they are in fact important, for three reasons.

First of all, DeJong's ladder reminds us that every ministry activity (whether it be a Sunday night program, a Tuesday afternoon small group, a game of Chubby Bunny,[7] a skit, a Bible study, a retreat, a leadership recruitment effort) is a reflection of a youth ministry program. Every programming model is rooted in a ministry purpose (or lack of purpose). Every ministry purpose is a manifestation of a basic understanding of what it means to be called human, and what it means to be called the people of God. Every notion of what it means to be fully human is anchored in some understanding of ultimate truth (or authority). That means every what, how, who, why, and when of a local youth ministry is born of a ministry philosophy. This ministry philosophy may be clearly defined (an *articulated* philosophy), or it may simply be a set of un-expressed assumptions that provide a

---

[7] Not one of my favorite games, because it is plainly dangerous and places participants at risk of choking. I know that it is a youth ministry classic, but I do not think a few laughs are worth the risk of asphyxiation and death.

Table 12-1.
DeJong's Six Elements of Ministry Philosophy

Element of Philosophy	Description	Relevant Practical Questions[1]
1. Basis of Authority	What is the basis of authority for the ministry philosophy? Is this ministry philosophy based on congregational preferences, felt needs of teenagers, youth ministry experts? Whose map is being used to determine location and destination?	• While it may go unstated (and sometimes, unfortunately, even unconsidered), a ministry philosophy will reflect a view of God. Who is he? How does he make himself known, and who does he show himself to be? • Implied in a ministry philosophy will be one's view of Scripture, its truthfulness, the measure of its authority, and its relevance to speak to everyday human affairs. • Beneath the surface of any ministry philosophy is also an understanding of reality (metaphysics). Is this world all there is? Is there a reality beyond what can be accessed through the five senses? Is there only the dimension of time that we know, or is there an infinitely wider, deeper dimension called eternity? • A ministry philosophy will in some way even reflect a view of knowledge (epistemology): How do we know what we think we know? Do we know through personal experience, rational logic, scientific verification, or through a combination of faith and reason? Or through some other means altogether?
2. Nature of Persons	What does it mean to be human, and how does this understanding of full humanity shape a ministry philosophy?	• Among the questions implicit in our understanding of personhood will be questions about how people learn. • With youth ministry in particular, how do teenagers mature and develop into whole persons? • What does whole personhood look like in the life of an adolescent?
3. Purposes and Goals	This is the all-important question of destination. Why does this ministry exist? Where should this journey take us?	• Inherent in purposes and goals will be assumptions about pastoral ministry and about ministry itself. • Embedded in a purpose statement will also be some hint of a rationale: Why is youth ministry important and how does it fit into the overall mission of the church? • Which values (community, creativity, contemplation, fun, digestion of biblical truth, etc.) will shape our processes and structures?
4. Structural Organization	How can we best structure our ministry to accomplish the purposes to which God has called us? Regardless of scenery, popularity, or degree of difficulty, which trail is most likely to take us where we need to go? What provisions will we need for such a journey?	• It is at this point that a philosophy of ministry will manifest some understanding of leadership and of leadership roles. What is the relationship between youth leaders and their volunteer staff, any potential student leaders, or even their other colleagues on staff who might not be directly involved in the youth ministry? What style of leadership best reflects this understanding? • How can the articulated values (creative, edgy, fun, etc.) be inculcated in ongoing ministry programs and practices?
5. Implementation	This is using the resources God has provided, material and human, to step out in pursuit of the goal.	• This is the actual execution of the plan: specific elements of the program (Sunday night meeting, drop-in center, tutoring ministry, worship time, backpacking trip), as well as systems of planning, resourcing, staffing, publicizing, and evaluating.
6. Evaluation	This is the pattern of stopping periodically to look again at the map, and to measure the progress of the ministry against the goals of the ministry.	• It is at this point the process begins again—stop, study, and stare. • Program evaluation: What are the strengths and weaknesses of the program? • Personnel evaluation: What growth, needs, gifts, etc., are visible in the students and in the volunteer leadership? • Personal evaluation: Is there growth or stagnation—or areas of mismanagement in terms of one's family, or devotional, physical, or relational health?

Source: Norman DeJong, *Education in the Truth* (Nutley, N.J.: Presbyterians and Reformed, 1974), 61–63.

1. These questions are adapted from John Dettoni, *Introduciton to Youth Ministry* (Grand Rapids, Mich.: Zondervan, 1993).

tint to all facets of the ministry (an *operant philosophy*).[8]

One might object that a youth worker shouldn't have to go through all the head-work of hammering out an articulated philosophy of ministry "when we already know our mission is to help kids get to know Jesus." But this objection underestimates the problems that follow from a ministry philosophy that hasn't been articulated. If the operant philosophy assumed by some in the leadership differs much from that assumed by others, it won't be long before the ministry suffers the confusion of two or more guides supposedly hiking together, but each taking a different trail. In such circumstances, it is only a matter of time before various factions begin to fight about who leads the students (program issues) and who gets the gear (budget issues). That can get ugly.

It is for such reasons that the writer of Proverbs cautioned, "Where there is no vision, the people perish" (Prov. 29:18).

Anthony's Four Philosophical Foundations

Michael Anthony, professor of Christian Education at Biola University, suggests some basic components essential to any ministry philosophy. Not surprisingly, they parallel those mentioned by DeJong, but they are broader and a bit more inclusive.

1. Focus: Who is being served by this ministry? What is the ultimate purpose?

2. Attitude: How does one view those being targeted and served? What are their needs?

3. Motivation: What is one hoping to accomplish with these people? What is the dream or vision that motivates the work?

4. Values: What values will be cultivated in the process of pursuing this vision?

How would you respond to these questions in developing your personal youth ministry philosophy?

Michael Anthony, Introducing Christian Education: Foundations for the Twenty-First Century

Secondly, DeJong's six issues point to questions that must be posed in an assessment of any ministry philosophy or ministry model. Whether it is described as traditional, biblical, cutting-edge, multiethnic, emergent, student-led, extreme, new, contemplative, Sonlife, Young Life, Wyld Life, family based, Jesus-focused, seeker-sensitive, purpose-driven, Youth Specialties-centered, Group-oriented, Harry Potter-inclusive—it will be by the standard of these six issues that any ministry philosophy will stand or fall.

---

[8] Michael Anthony, *Introducing Christian Education: Foundations for the Twenty-First Century* (Grand Rapids, Mich.: Baker, 2001), 54.

Finally, DeJong's six elements of ministry philosophy provide a template that could be used in forging and articulating one's own philosophy of youth ministry.[9]

Operant and Articulated Philosophy

Quite often, a discerning youth worker coming into a new ministry situation will realize in due course that the ministry has a clear and succinct *articulated* philosophy. However, the philosophy by which the group actually operates (*operant* philosophy) is quite different. It all looked good on paper, but the words never became flesh—the philosophy never became program. In such a case, the problem is not a faulty map, but a faulty effort at following the trail. When that happens—and it happens far too often—the ministry does not stand or fall, it just seems to limp and stagger unless someone gets it back on a proper footing.

Learning how to evaluate the operant philosophy in a ministry situation is an important skill to develop because often one can tell more about an organization's philosophy of youth ministry from how it operates than by what its vision statement articulates. There are four common philosophies extant in the current youth ministry culture. Table 12-2 describes the elements of these four common youth ministry philosophies.

Developing a Philosophy of Ministry

Which of these common philosophies is best? Are any of them worthy? Which most closely approximates a biblical philosophy of ministry? Hammering out an answer to these questions is vital. The task of forging such an answer is encompassed in a four-phase process (see Figure 12-2) of what Aubrey Malphurs describes as "*foundational ministry concepts*":[10]

▶ **Phase One:** Mission—the "Why?" question. Why does the ministry exist?

▶ **Phase Two:** Core Values—the "How?" question. How will the ministry conduct its mission?

▶ **Phase Three:** Vision—the "What if?" question. This provides a mental picture of what this organization or ministry should look like.

---

[9] For an extremely helpful account of the process of developing one's philosophy of ministry, see also Doug Fields, *Purpose-Driven Youth Ministry* (Grand Rapids, Mich.: Zondervan, 1998), 55–69.

[10] Aubrey Malphurs, *Ministry Nuts and Bolts* (Grand Rapids, Mich.: Kregel, 1997), 9–10. In fact, Malphurs suggests that Values come before Mission. I tend to favor the approach of others who suggest that strategic planning must begin with a purpose or mission statement. Doug Fields writes, for example, "Once you communicate God's purpose for your ministry, you won't have to ask the why question again. The new question will be how: How do we accomplish what God has called us to do? The why must be answered before the how can make sense to others." Fields, *Purpose-Driven Youth Ministry*, 56.

On the other hand, Malphurs is quite right in suggesting that core values often shape the ministry's purposes. For example, in the story that opens this chapter, Tarzan and Jane (not their real names) did not simply begin the hike that day so that they could get back to the car. If that had been the sole objective, they could simply have stayed at the car and saved time, effort, and, perhaps, their relationship. They were pursuing deeper values: the enjoyment of God's creation, the importance of expanded time and space for communication, the value of exercise, the importance of fun. Surely, at the deepest level, there was more to the date than locating and walking to a car. In short, their values shaped their mission. I still prefer beginning with the mission or purpose. But there is certainly some merit to the suggestion that it is a bit of a "chicken or the egg" question.

▶ **Phase Four**: Strategy—the "What now?" question. How can we accomplish this mission?

Carefully and prayerfully thinking through these four concepts is essential to developing a personal or corporate philosophy of youth ministry.

> In *Leadership's* study of pastors who were "forced out" of their positions, "pastors indicated that conflicting visions for the church were their greatest source of tension and the top reason they were terminated or forced to resign.
>
> *David L. Goetz, "Forced Out," Leadership 17 (Winter 1996): 42.*

Phase One: Mission—Getting a Fix on the Ministry Purpose

A mission statement is a statement of a ministry's purpose that is broad enough to encompass all that ministry defines as its mission, but brief enough[11] to be stated in a single sentence.

Typically, a mission statement combines a verb and one or more infinitives in a statement that is compelling, concise, meaningful, and action-oriented.[12]

Here are some examples:[13]

Figure 12-2.
Malphurs's Four Phases of Developing a Ministry Philosophy

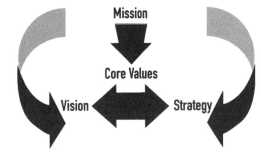

Source: Aubrey Malphurs, *Ministry Nuts and Bolts* (Grand Rapids, Mich.: Kregel, 1997), 9–10.

▶ **Crossroads Church**: "Our youth ministry mission is to win lost teenagers and enable them to become growing and fruitful followers of Christ."

▶ **Wooddale Church**: "The purpose of Wooddale Church is to honor God by making more disciples for Jesus Christ."

▶ **Salvation Army**: "Our mission is to make citizens out of the rejected."

---

[11] Management consultant Peter Drucker argues that a mission statement should be brief enough to fit on a T-shirt. Malphurs, *Ministry Nuts and Bolts*, 65.

[12] Fields, *Purpose-Driven Youth Ministry*, 65.

[13] From Malphurs, *Ministry Nuts and Bolts*, 82–86; Fields, *Purpose-Driven Youth Ministry*, 57; and the Eastern University catalogue.

Table 12-2.
Four Common Operant Ministry Philosophies

	Pragmatist (Focus on ideas and strategies)	Realist (Focus on being culturally relevant without being biblically relative)	Idealist (Focus on faithfulness to ideals)	Traditionalist (Focus on connection to denomination or movement)
How does this philosophy view youth ministry essentials?	Does it meet the needs or wants of our students?	Can we do this, while remaining faithful to our biblical mandates, and attentive to our ministry context?	Is it right? Is this what God calls us in his Word to do?	Is this in keeping with our tradition? How does this line up with others in our denomination or organization?
What are the apparent criteria for starting a new program?	Students would probably attend if we do this.	Sure, we can get students there, but will it meet our goals?; or, yes, it will meet our goals, but we won't get any students to show up.	Scripture calls us to this, so we'll do it, and whatever happens is what happens.	This is a part of our tradition to which we have not been faithful so we need to begin doing it. Other congregations (areas, districts, dioceses) are doing this and we have been requested to join them by organizational or denominational headquarters.
What are the apparent goals for ministry?	To see the program grow (in numbers, budget, popularity).	To see people grow from where they are to where God calls them to be.	Faithfulness to God as he has made himself known in the Scripture.	To help people be faithful to our mission, tradition, etc.
What are the apparent criteria for evaluating the program?	Is the program growing?	Are we seeing fruit?	Are we being faithful to the truth?	Are we maintaining union with those in our denomination, with our organization?
What are the apparent criteria for ending a program?	A better way is found that attracts more people.	It no longer seems to meet needs.	That is one of the problems of this approach. Once everyone agrees this is what God wants us to do, people are unlikely to be open to change (such as changes in hymnody, worship style, Sunday School scheduling, midweek prayer service, missions conference, etc.).	Ministries end only when there is a change at the broader level, which is very seldom. That is why large institutions tend to develop their own momentum.
What is this philosophy's underlying assumption?	Our job is to reach people, the more the better.	It does little good to reach people if we cannot help them know God's embrace. On the other hand, it won't do any good to talk to people about God's love if they are unwilling to listen.	God's Word does not return void (Isa. 55:11). It is his work and he will bless it (1 Thess. 5:24).	There is strength and balance in unity.
What is the inherent strength of this approach?	While there is wide and justified criticism for a ministry that focuses only on numbers, there is the obvious fact that numbers represent individual human beings for whom Jesus died. To dismiss the focus on numbers as shallow and irrelevant overlooks the obvious fact that a youth ministry without any youth is not a very effective youth ministry.[1]	This approach is sometimes maligned as being too purpose-driven, too much based on the notion that "the end justifies the means." This is not entirely fair. The emphasis in this philosophy is not "the end justifies the means" so much as it is that every method and program (means) must be measured by its contribution toward the final goal (ends).	Some would criticize this approach as being too inflexible and unrealistic, and of course it could be. But one person's "inflexibility" is another person's conviction. At least with firm ideals, a ministry is prevented from being too market-driven—or so culturally relevant that it ceases to be biblically faithful.	The word *tradition* has gotten a bad rap in a culture marked by immediacy and the arrogance of the now. But in fact tradition can be an important corrective that allows the iron of one generation to sharpen the iron of another generation (see Prov. 27:17).[2]

Source: This is an adaptation of material offered by Michael Anthony, *Introducing Christian Education: Foundations for the Twenty-First Century* (Grand Rapids, Mich.: Baker, 2001), 56–57. For another delineation of four operant philosophies, a bit more theoretical but with very practical implications, see *Four Views of Youth Ministry and the Church*, ed. Mark Senter (Grand Rapids, Mich.: Zondervan/Youth Specialties, 2001).

1. One of the pithy phrases circulating in the youth ministry world is this brief proverb: "Small is better than big." While we all understand the thrust of this axiom—that size without quality is of little value—it would be more accurate to say "Deep is better than wide." Large or small, the real question is not one of numbers. It is a question of fruitfulness and depth. The key question is not how wide is the ministry, but how deep it is. The hard fact is that some ministries—by no means all—are small because they are doing a lousy job (and maybe also a lazy job) of youth ministry. They are perhaps shallow in their expectations or unfaithful in their teaching. Some large ministries are large because they are doing good, thoughtful youth ministry. One of what Youth Specialties calls its CORE Values is "Small works better than big." This is a different statement from the one above, and more easily defended because it points to the simple fact that working with a small group of students offers advantages (logistical arrangements, personal attention, etc.) that simply are not possible when working with a larger group. (For more on this, see Rich Grassel, *Help! I'm a Small Church Youth Worker* (Grand Rapids, Mich.: Zondervan/Youth Specialties, 2002). Indeed, the first thing most large groups do when they convene is to break up into smaller groups. Wise youth leaders will constantly be thinking about how to design a ministry that acts small even as it grows large (see Robert Waterman and Thomas Peters, *In Search of Excellence* (New York: Warner, 1988), 156ff.

2. For an excellent and timely article on the importance of tradition in the life of the church, and the arrogance that dismisses such tradition, see Wilfred M. McClay, "Tradition, History, and Sequoias," *First Things* (March 2003): 41ff.

▸ **Saddleback Church Youth Ministry:** "Our youth ministry exists to REACH non-believing students, to CONNECT them with other Christians, to help them GROW in their faith, and to challenge the growing to DISCOVER their ministry and HONOR God with their life . . ."

▸ **Eastern University:** "Eastern University exists to equip students to engage and live the whole gospel for the whole world in diverse vocations and locations."

▸ **The U.S. Marine Corps:** "Our mission is to attack the enemy and defeat him."[14]

Because this first phase is so critical to the process it bears closer attention.

Sample Infinitives Often Used in Mission Statements

to assist	to reach	to equip	to produce
to create	to develop	to connect	to promote
to craft	to empower	to establish	to provide
to convert	to energize	to help	to share
to prepare	to challenge	to lead	to nurture

Many of these have been taken from a listing in Aubrey Malphurs, Ministry Nuts and Bolts *(Grand Rapids, Mich.: Kregel, 1997), 83.*

Charting a Biblical Position

One of the most advanced technologies is the global positioning system (GPS). A system of satellites circling above the earth makes it possible to find your precise location any place on the planet within 15 meters (49.2 feet), 24 hours a day. "You can mark a starting point such as a car or a campsite and use the *Goto* feature to find your way back from wherever you end up, or you can pick a point off your map and use the receiver to find your way to it."[15]

A GPS receiver is lightweight, inexpensive, and about the size of a pocket knife. It is invaluable for back-country navigation. Its one limitation is that it will not function accurately if it cannot get a reading from at least four satellites simultaneously. It will often get readings from seven or eight, but there will occasionally be inadequate satellite coverage in dense forests or deep gorges, near high rocks, or inside buildings.[16]

---

[14] Do not even think about adopting this mission statement for your middle-school ministry.

[15] Lawrence Letham, *GPS Made Easy* (Seattle: Mountaineers, 2001), 5.

[16] Ibid., 6.

There is no one biblical philosophy of youth ministry. There are many satellite passages by which we might fix our position. But, as DeJong points out, every philosophy must begin with an anchor of truth and authority. The key for any youth ministry philosophy is that it be rooted and anchored in the Word of God.[17] For a basic starting point, we will take our reading from four fixed points set out by the apostle Paul in Ephesians 4:11–15:

> It was he who gave some to be apostles, some to be prophets, some to be evangelists, and some to be pastors and teachers, to prepare God's people for works of service, so that the body of Christ may be built up until we all reach unity in the faith and in the knowledge of the Son of God and become mature, attaining to the whole measure of the fullness of Christ. Then we will no longer be infants, tossed back and forth by the waves, and blown here and there by every wind of teaching and by the cunning and craftiness of men in their deceitful scheming. Instead, speaking the truth in love, we will in all things grow up into him who is the Head, that is, Christ.

In this passage, provided by Paul as a manifesto for the church at large, we are able to draw some conclusions about essential elements of a ministry to teenagers in particular.[18]

Essential Number One: Focused on God in Christ

We will in all things grow up into him who is the Head, that is, Christ (Eph. 4:15b).

Fundamental to any biblical philosophy of youth ministry is a focus on God as he has made himself known through Jesus Christ. The number one goal of youth ministry is not tithing, church membership, voter registration, political mobilization, retreat attendance, recruiting students to invite their friends, denominational involvement, or T-shirt (light bulb, candy, spaghetti, cookie, Christmas card, or glow-in-the-dark posters of the pastor) sales. It is helping students develop a love relationship with God. Our Lord said, "'Love the Lord your God with all your heart and with all your soul and with all your mind.' This is the first and greatest commandment" (Matt. 22:37–38).

There must be an intentional commitment to help students love God and to develop a relationship with him of growing, deepening intimacy. In a youth ministry culture where program direction is more common than spiritual direction,

[17] For example, Kenda Creasy Dean seats her philosophy of youth ministry on Luke 1:26–38. Kenda Creasy Dean, *The God-Bearing Life* (Nashville, Tenn.: Upper Room Books, 1998), 43–53. Barry St Clair commends Matthew 9:35–38 as the basis for what he describes as "Jesus-focused youth ministry." Barry St Clair, *Jesus-Focused Youth Ministry* (Norcross, Ga.: Reach Out Youth Solutions, 2002), 14. In his very helpful book *Purpose-Driven Youth Ministry*, Doug Fields draws from two passages: Matthew 22:37–40 and 28:19–20. Fields, *Purpose-Driven Youth Ministry*, 46.

[18] Obviously, how these essentials are spelled out and articulated depends on the biblical passages used as a basis. For example, Fields (*Purpose-Driven Youth Ministry*, 46), drawing from Matthew 22:37–40 and 28:19–20, identifies five basic ministry purposes: Honor (Worship), Discover (Ministry), Connect (Fellowship), Reach (Evangelism), and Grow (Discipleship).

Are our churches' goals set by slogans of the culture around us, or by biblical texts? Do our congregational programs find their source in the way sociology defines the present "needs" of consumers (should that read "their wants"?) or from the Scriptures? What decides the doctrinal content of the worship service—one who is theologically trained, or the results of a survey asking people what they want? How much are the doctrinal foundations of a parish's work recognized in the decisions of the church board or council?

For many years Jacques Ellul wrestled with this problem of adopting the methods of the culture around us as we seek to dispense the gifts of the church. In his *False Presence of the Kingdom* he pointedly asks, "Given the fact that you are constantly immersed in this bath [of the world's methods, powers] what can being a Christian in it possibly mean?" He outlines the problem thus:

> Christians who are conformed to the world introduce into the Church the value-judgments and concepts of the world. They believe in action. They want efficiency. They give first place to economics, and they think that all means are good. They are defined by their sociological milieu. The Protestant thinks to adopt the means which the world employs. Since he finds those means useful in his profession, or in his leisure time, they stand so high in his estimation that he cannot see why he should not introduce them into the Church and make the things of the spirit dependent upon them.

> He never faces the problem of these means. They are effective. Hence they are good. Since they are in a sanctified world and are effective, why not make use of them in the Church? The criteria of his thinking as a Christian are so vague, and the demands of his faith are so "inward," that he is unaware of any contradiction between the world's means and the life of faith.

Marva Dawn, Powers, Weakness and the Tabernacling of God *(Grand Rapids, Mich: Eerdmans, 2001), 84-85.*

Eugene Peterson's earnest challenge to pastors has a haunting relevance for youth pastors as well:

> What [youth] pastors do, or at least are called to do, is really quite simple. We say the word God accurately, so that congregations of Christians can stay in touch with the basic realities of their existence, so they know what is going on. And we say the Name personally, alongside our parishioners in the actual circumstances of their lives, so they will recognize and respond to the God who is both on our side and at our side when it doesn't seem like it and we don't feel like it.

Don't Leave Home Without Your Map! Essential History for Youth Ministers

By Tom Bergler, associate professor of Youth Ministry, Huntington College

When I was a boy, my church sponsored its own version of the Boy Scouts called "Royal Rangers." One of the skills we learned was how to use a map and compass to find our way through the wilderness. The map was especially handy for finding trails and figuring out where they led. Sometimes youth leaders think they are blazing a new trail when they are really walking a well-trodden path that may not be taking them where they want to go. The map of history just might help.

During the past 300 years, all Christians hoping to minister to youth have had to find a path over two huge obstacles: the mountain of modernity and the swamp of youth culture. This rugged terrain has made it hard for Christians to provide necessary protection for young people while at the same time mobilizing them to change the world.

Youth ministry as we know it is a response to the transition from traditional to modern societies. This transition began in the seventeenth and eighteenth centuries in Europe and is still going on in parts of the world today. So what changed? Throughout human history, most people have not lived in cities or suburbs. They have worked out of their homes, rather than in factories and offices. They have been relatively poor and have never gone to school. They have held the same religious beliefs as their families, neighbors, and friends. Their families have had significant input into their choices about work and marriage. They have not been divided between middle-class and working-class populations. Finally, they have assumed that religion should shape public affairs, not just private choices. When all these things changed, the transition was so dramatic that people coined a new word: modernity.

Some Christians tried to travel over the mountain of modernity by reaching out to poor or unprotected young people who were suffering the ill effects of these changes. In 1780, William Raikes founded the first Sunday School in England. His school taught young factory workers and street kids how to read and write using the Bible as the text. Similarly, the Young Men's Christian Association (YMCA) was founded in 1844 to evangelize and protect young men drawn to the cities in search of jobs.

These youth groups faced some forks in the road during the next 100 years. First, these experiments could bring renewal to the church at large. For example, Sunday School has spread to nearly every Protestant church, where it helped form generations of people in the Christian faith. Unfortunately, Sunday schools often upheld the segregation between rich and poor, black and white, in America.

One spin-off of the YMCA was the Student Volunteer Movement that inspired more than 20,000 college students to become missionaries between the 1880s and the 1920s. In this case, an organization founded by adults to protect young people spawned a student-led movement that changed the history of the church and the world.

Another fork in the road led to expanded social services, but weaker Christian identity. During World War I, the federal government asked the YMCA to oversee recreational services for American soldiers. In order to serve more people, many YMCA chapters in the United States dropped their emphasis on evangelism and Bible study. This first wave of youth ministries demonstrated how difficult it could be to keep on a path that combined service to the poor, evangelism, and protection of middle-class Christian young people.

Other Christians tried to climb the mountain of modernity using the path of local church youth societies. In 1881, a minister named Francis Clark founded the first Christian Endeavor Society. The movement mushroomed into an international, interdenominational network of youth societies. These student-led chapters required their members to take a rigorous pledge demanding holiness of life and commitment to the church. Christian young people were asked to avoid the evils of alcohol and the theater, and these young people learned leadership skills as society officers. Most Protestant denominations soon copied this model but usually weakened or eliminated the pledge. The first youth ministry professionals were hired by the denominations to train leaders and provide other support for these local youth societies. Most youth societies served only the children of middle-class church members. Even worse, Christian youth societies sometimes degenerated into social clubs, a danger that continues to plague youth ministry today.

The first half of the twentieth century brought two world wars, a Great Depression, and numerous race riots. Concerned about these and other social problems, some Christians forged a new path over the mountain of modernity, the path of social activism. Leaders of denominational youth departments dreamed of mobilizing young people to build a "Christian social order." For example, in the 1930s and 1940s, a few young Methodists in the South staged protests to demand racial integration of their summer camps. These same Christians pioneered work camps and summer service projects—the sort of activities now labeled "mission trips." Along the way they made a difference in society and provided powerful leadership opportunities for young people. Yet as these examples show, young people often did their good deeds in artificial environments rather than engaging the "real world." Even worse, when the bottom fell out of youthful social concern in the 1950s (at least among white, middle-class teenagers), the social activist youth leaders were at a loss. Mistaking the ups and downs of teenage social concern for something more substantial, they had built the second story of social concern without laying the foundation of Christian formation.

It was probably unrealistic to assume that young people could fix modern social problems all by themselves, but things got even tougher with the rise of youth culture. In the 1920s, the "jazz age" hit American college campuses. Students shocked their parents by dancing to jazz music, going to movies, wearing skimpy clothing, drinking heavily, and attending what they called "petting parties." What began among a few older youths soon spread to millions of young Americans.

The twentieth century also saw a steady rise in juvenile crime as the problems of poverty, unemployment, and family breakdown hit young people especially hard. One response was the passage of laws requiring all teenagers to attend high school. But as often happens, by lumping teenagers together to fix them, or at least to keep them busy, adults unintentionally provided them the opportunity to fight back by creating their own peer culture.

During the 1940s and 1950s Americans started using the term "teenager," and businesspeople started actively marketing their products to the young. The rock 'n roll of the 1950s and the political protests, drug use, and other youth rebellions of the 1960s created a further sense of distance between adults and young people. Although the styles of youth culture continue to change rapidly, the underlying themes remain the same: sex, rebellion, and the search for identity, all exploited by some marketers to get rich.

During World War II, a group of Evangelical entrepreneurs chose the path of youth culture revivalism as a way through this swamp. Torrey Johnson, Billy Graham, and many other young evangelists founded Youth for Christ, which sponsored Saturday night youth rallies around the country. About the same time, Jim Rayburn founded Young Life, which used clubs in high schools and homes to try to reach the kids who never came to church. In the name of reaching nonChristian teenagers, they created an alternative Christian youth subculture, complete with its own movies, music, clothing, yearbooks, sports, and even banquets to replace the school prom. Yet this Christian youth subculture often kept

Christians and nonChristians apart, undermining evangelism. These groups did win many Christian converts, but they largely failed to serve working-class or delinquent youth. Even worse, because they had to appeal to white middle-class teenagers and parents, these groups could do nothing about the greatest social evil of their day: racial segregation. These groups tamed youth culture but did not escape the modern prison of privatized faith.

During the 1960s and 1970s, it became much more common for churches to hire a professional youth minister. In the absence of other forms of training, many of these pioneers modeled their work on Youth for Christ or Young Life. Between 1970 and 2000, the new music, entertainment, evangelistic strategies, and social service techniques pioneered by youth ministers entered adult church life, sparking both positive changes and heated controversy. For example, Bill Hybels, senior pastor of Willow Creek Community Church, discovered and tested his methods of church growth as a youth leader in the 1970s. Youth ministry as we have inherited it today still struggles to balance the same competing goals of protecting and mobilizing young people.

One of the most important lessons of our history is that every youth ministry path both closes down some possibilities and opens up new opportunities to renew the church. Choose your path with eyes wide open, and do not get discouraged if the going gets rough and you cannot do it all. Helping some young people traverse the mountain of modernity without falling and get through the swamp of youth culture without drowning is a great victory for the kingdom of God, even if you do not get to visit every scenic spot along the way.

For Further Study

Mark Cannister, "Youth Ministry's Historical Context: The Education and Evangelism of Young People," in *Starting Right: Thinking Theologically About Youth Ministry*, ed. Chap Clark, Kenda Dean, and Dave Rahn (Grand Rapids, Mich.: Youth Specialties/Zondervan, 2001), 77–90.

Jon Pahl, *Youth Ministry in Modern America: 1930s to the Present* (Peabody, Mass.: Hendrickson, 2000).

Grace Palladino, *Teenagers: An American History* (New York: Basic Books, 1996).

Mark Senter, *The Coming Revolution in Youth Ministry* (Wheaton, Ill.: Victor Books, 1992).

Why do we have such a difficult time keeping this focus? Why are we so easily distracted?

Because we get asked to do a lot of things other than this, most of which seem useful and important. The world of religion generates a huge market for meeting all the needs that didn't get met in the shopping mall. [Youth] pastors are conspicuous in this religious marketplace and are expected to come up with products that give customer satisfaction. Since the needs seem legitimate enough, we easily slip into the routines of merchandising moral advice and religious comfort. Before long we find that we are program directors in a flourishing business. We spend our time figuring out ways to attractively display god-products. We become skilled at pleasing the customers. Before we realize what has happened, the mystery and love and majesty of God, to say nothing of the tender and delicate subtleties of souls, are obliterated by the noise and frenzy of the religious marketplace.

> Youth ministry sets out to introduce teenagers to a *particular* relationship—namely, a relationship with Jesus Christ. In a culture where young adolescents say the ideal youth program is, among other things, physically "safe," wholesome activity has much to commend it. But ministry seeks more than wholesome activity.
>
> Kenda Creasy Dean, The God-Bearing Life *(Nashville, Tenn.: Upper Room Books, 1998), 27.*

But then who is there who will say the name God in such a way that the community can see him for who he is, our towering Lord and Savior, and not the packaged and priced version that meets our consumer needs? And who is there with the time to stand with men and women, adults and children in the places of confusion and blessing, darkness and light, hurt and healing long enough to discern the glory and salvation being worked out behind the scenes, under the surface? If we all get caught up in running the store, who will be the [youth] pastor?[19]

It is in the interest of maintaining this emphasis that Kenda Creasy Dean refers to youth workers as "God-bearers" (see Figure 12-3). Drawing from Luke 1:26–38,[20] she suggests we conceptualize youth ministry in terms of Mary's awesome and wonderful privilege of bearing Christ for the students with whom we have contact. For that reason Dean suggests that youth ministries should be redefined in language that is not just *relational* (an encounter with a caring adult or a caring community), but *incarnational* (an encounter with God).[21]

---

[19] Peterson, *Under the Unpredictable Plant,* 172–173, material in brackets added.

[20] The angel went to her and said, "Greetings, you who are highly favored! The Lord is with you." Mary was greatly troubled at his words and wondered what kind of greeting this might be. But the angel said to her, "Do not be afraid, Mary, you have found favor with God . . . The angel answered, "The Holy Spirit will come upon you, and the power of the Most High will overshadow you. So the holy one to be born will be called the Son of God. . ." "I am the Lord's servant," Mary answered. "May it be to me as you have said" (Luke 1:26–38).

[21] Dean, *The God-Bearing Life,* 27.

There is an important facet of this first ministry essential that is vastly under-played in youth ministry culture, and that is the value of theological instruction. A common assumption is often framed in these terms: "Knowing God is more important than knowing about God."[22] To be sure, intimacy with God is more important than cold theological knowledge. But where this maxim fails us is that it presents a false dichotomy between *knowing* and *knowing about*. In truth, it simply is not possible to *know* God without *knowing* something *about* God.

If someone asks, "Do you know Duffy Robbins?" and the answer is "Yes," the assumption is that they know certain facts *about* Duffy Robbins: he is a Caucasian male who lives in Valley Forge, Penn.; he teaches Youth Ministry at Eastern University; his hair style favors a large three-inch part; he has two daughters, a son-in-law, and a grandson; he has the diet of a nine-year-old; and he speaks a lot to teenagers and people who work with teenagers. Of course, one could know all of those things about Duffy Robbins and *have no relationship with him* at all. And hopefully, knowing Duffy Robbins is much more than knowing those facts *about* Duffy Robbins. But to claim to know Duffy Robbins without knowing anything about him simply makes no sense. To that extent, we cannot divorce the mandate of helping students know God from the necessity of helping students know about God.[23]

Figure 12-3.
Dean's The God-Bearing Life

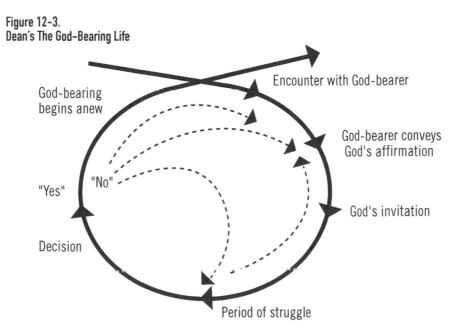

Source: Kenda Creasy Dean, *The God-Bearing Life* (Nashville, Tenn.: Upper Room Books, 1998), 27.

[22] This is CORE Value I, Youth Specialties, The CORE.

[23] See also Amy Jacober's article, "A Bowl of Beans for Your Birthright: Trading Away Theology," in the *Companion Guide*.

A mind given to exhaustive foresight and the mechanical provision of routine wants is rarely attracted to dangerous enterprises, hence the usual arrangement of a learned society or a cautious committee to plan and equip an expedition, and a daring fellow to carry it out under the restraint of prudent instructions. The best explorer, however, is the man who can both "conceive and dare"

—H. R. Mill, friend and mentor of Antarctic explorer, Ernest Shackleton

Another note of caution to be raised here relates to the fact that often youth workers do a better job of nurturing their students' commitment to the youth group than nurturing their commitment to the Lord. Presumably, this is unintentional. It begins with encouraging students to come to youth group as middle schoolers. In those middle school years before they get their driver's licenses, we remind them how much fun youth group is and how critical it is that they have weekly fellowship with Christian friends. We do that partly at least because we know it is true, and we do it partly because we want them to come back to youth group next week!

I can remember one occasion as a youth minister in Rhode Island when I had the pleasure of having a student approach me and say with complete sincerity, "You know, I haven't been in youth group the last five weeks and I have got to be honest that in that time my spiritual life has just gone right down the tubes!" Deep down inside, a part of me thought, "You bet it has, kid. And don't you forget it. You better never miss a week with this youth group again!" Of course, the subtext of such an attitude is this: "You better believe your spiritual life tubed out when you missed youth group these last five weeks, because without this youth group, all you have is . . . God!" We tend to forget that within a few years, they will *not* have the youth group. All they will have is God.

It is almost as if we have forgotten that our main purpose in youth ministry is to help students move forward on that pilgrimage of growth through which they become progressively dependent on God and intimate with God. If we are building students whose faith is dependent primarily on a weekly skit, a creative Bible study, or a summer camp that is "the best week of your life," we are building Christians who simply are not going to last beyond the high school years.

Mark Yaconelli puts it well:

> All youth ministries engage youth in practices; however, not all practices within ministries with youth are beneficial or even Christian. For example, a youth ministry that engages youth solely in forms of entertainment may train youth to relate to God in passive observance. If discipleship only involves lectures on moral living, then youth may relate to God only through how well they are able to live moral lives. If youth ministry revolves around study and memorization, then God may only be known in the intellect. A youth ministry grounded in Christian practices will pay attention to the whole way of life promoted in the content and activities of the ministry. It will seek to offer youth tools and give them opportunities to practice life lived in imitation of Christ.
>
> How do we determine if a practice is Christian? All Christian practices begin in *prayer*, invite personal *confession*, take place within the *worshiping community*, and bear fruit in *solidarity with the poor* in communion with the Spirit of Jesus Christ. It is our availability to love within these four relationships—God, ourselves, the faithful, and the poor—that is the hope of all faithful practices.[24]

A biblical philosophy of youth ministry must be fixed by the clear priority of helping students to know, embrace, and enjoy God.

Essential Number Two: Calling Students to Service

To prepare God's people for works of service25 (Eph. 4:12).

When Jesus cited love for God as the essence of the first and greatest commandment (Matt. 22:37–38), he went on to connect it with a second commandment: "The second is like it: 'Love your neighbor as yourself.' All the Law and the Prophets hang on these two commandments" (Matt. 22:39–40).

Cyril, the great fifth-century Patriarch of Alexandria comments:

Therefore the first commandment teaches every kind of godliness. For to love God with the whole heart is the cause of every good. The second commandment includes the righteous acts we do toward other people. The first commandment prepares the way for the second and in turn is established by the second. For the person who is grounded in the love of God clearly also loves

---

[24] Mark Yaconelli, "Focusing Youth Ministry Through Spiritual Practices," in *Starting Right*, ed. Chap Clark, Kenda Dean, and Dave Rahn (Grand Rapids, Mich.: Youth Specialties/Zondervan, 2001), 157.

[25] Vincent points out that *diakonia* or "ministry" in the New Testament is "spiritual service of an official character." (See Acts 1:25, 6:4, 20:24; Rom. 11:13; I Tim. 1:12; and 2 Tim. 4:5.) Cited from *Vincent's Word Studies in the New Testament*, Electronic Database, © 1997 by Biblesoft.

his neighbor in all things as himself. The kind of person who fulfills these two commandments experiences all the commandments.[26]

The plain fact is that God has called all Christians to do the work of ministry (Eph. 2:8–10, Col. 3:23–24, I Pet. 2:9–10). This is as true for teenage Christians as it is for older Christians. Any definition of spiritual growth that does not include some progressive understanding that God has called each of us to a life of ministry in some shape or fashion is a definition of spiritual growth that is foreign to the clear teaching of Scripture.

Unfortunately, our general unwillingness to call students to a commitment of ministry and service to neighbor—to accomplish something bigger than themselves—lives right down to the low expectations that students generally have for themselves. We do not challenge them to attempt very much because we do not expect that they will be willing to accept the challenge. Students often are reluctant to accept the challenge because they assume they will be incapable.

I remember one ninth-grade girl in our youth group who seemed so quiet and shy that I really could not see her in any kind of leadership role. Owing in part to my own insecurity, I dared not trust her to lead a small group for our youth program. I just did not think she had the stuff. Her poor self-image and low profile in the youth group may have been a reflection of my unwillingness to give her a shot at a leadership position, because, when I finally worked up the nerve to give her a try, she was brilliant far beyond my hope. Kids actually began requesting her as a small group leader. Her personality blossomed. The group discovered her, and she continued as a strong student leader throughout her high school years.

These kinds of experiences suggest that the only way to convince either the students or the leaders that they have underestimated their abilities is by cultivating a climate of challenge, opportunity, and service. Researcher Merton Strommen comments that a major imperative in youth work is to help youth into a sense of mission, of being sent for a purpose and a task, so they will come to know the sense of purposefulness that grips the person who has responded to God's love.[27] This is closely akin to Paul's admonition to the young man Timothy: "Don't let anyone look down on you because you are young, but set an example for the believers in speech, in life, in love, in faith and in purity" (1 Tim. 4:12).[28]

---

[26] Cyril of Alexandria, Fragment 251, *Matthaus-Kommentare aus der griechischen Kirche*, ed. Joseph Reuss (Berlin: Akademie-Verlag, 1957), cited in *Ancient Christian Commentary on Scripture*, ed. Manlio Simonetti (Downers Grove, Ill.: InterVarsity Press, 2002), 157–158.

[27] See Merton Strommen, *Five Cries of Youth*, 1st ed. (New York: Harper and Row, 1979), III.

[28] "Youth need to know how to give away their faith and help others in society to receive social justice. They also need to recognize that . . . they are the continuity of the Great Commission . . . Youth also need to know that missions are an option for their calling from God to service. Finally, and most importantly, they need to know that they are persons called to mission, they have a vocation from God to service in the name of Christ regardless of where they work and live; to serve is the requirement of being a Christian." Dettoni, *Introduction to Youth Ministry*, 34.

A biblical philosophy of youth ministry must embrace an intentional effort to help students understand that a growing, active love for God will always be manifested by a growing, active love for one's neighbor.

Essential Number Three: Building Disciples

. . . so that the body of Christ may be built up . . . (Eph. 4: 12b)

Jesus's followers were commanded, "*Go and make disciples* of all nations, baptizing them in the name of the Father and of the Son and of the Holy Spirit, and teaching them to obey everything I have commanded you" (emphasis added). Over the years the church has called this command "the Great Commission." In reality, as one preacher noted, it should be called "the Great Omission"! Like much of the church, we in youth ministry have forgotten that our number-one priority is not to build big youth groups, growing clubs, or flashy youth programs. We are called to build people.

In his letter to the Ephesians, Paul uses a combination of two Greek words, *katartismon*, which in classical Greek could refer to anything from refitting a ship to resetting a broken bone, and *oikodomeen,* a term used for construction, as in erecting a building. The combination of these terms remind us that ministry is about a building process—mending that which is broken and making stronger that which has been built. In short, Paul is calling the church to outfit a human being as a shipbuilder might outfit a ship to assure that it is seaworthy (see Eph. 4:12–14). This is the work of building disciples.

Paul uses the word *until*, by definition a word that suggests a design, a goal, or perhaps, a destination—for the church, the end goal is to help people "*become mature*" disciples of Christ (Eph. 4:13). That is the essential notion of the Greek words *teleios* and *teleiotes*, translated "mature" and "maturity." God clearly has in mind an end purpose for his people (Phil. 1:6).

It is equally clear from Paul that *disciple-building is an ongoing work—a process*. As with the proverbial exercise of moving half the distance to an object, and then half again, and then half again, we never fully arrive at maturity (Phil. 3:12–14). We grow toward it with the knowledge that God will complete in us the work he has begun. It is not so much a question of *position* as it is a question of *direction*.

Biblically, that goal of building up, that ministry of edification,[29] is both individual and corporate. This is a fact too often neglected in youth ministry, particularly in an increasingly individualistic Western culture. We are not just building individual teenage disciples: we are building the church, the body of Christ: "until we *all* reach unity in the faith and in the knowledge of the Son of God . . . " Each body part must be strong for the body to be strong, but strong individual body

[29] A term related to Latin *ædificare*, from which we get *edifice*—"building."

parts will still suffer the consequences if the body itself is sick. That is why it is so vital that we focus on assimilating students into the church, the larger body of Christ. Essentially, what Paul is speaking of here is what Jesus prayed for in John 17:20–23, that the church might be one. Indeed, Paul fleshes out this vision in Ephesians 4:15–16 when he describes a body of believers as those who, "speaking the truth in love, will in all things grow up into him who is the Head, that is, Christ. From him the whole body, joined and held together by every supporting ligament, grows and builds itself up in love, as each part does its work."[30]

Christian Maturity: Morphing into the Image of Christ

Of course, maturity is often defined by its context. Talk to a football coach and maturity might be understood as capability on both offense and defense. Talk to a backcountry outfitter and maturity might be competence to lead-climb. Talk to a programmer and maturity might be understood as being literate in the language of DOS, Windows, and MAC. Whenever maturity is discussed in the context of adolescence, there are any number of possible interpretations.

What most people probably think of when they think of teenagers growing into maturity is teenagers beginning to behave like adults. This is misleading for two reasons: (1) There is far too little anecdotal evidence to conclude that age has anything whatsoever to do with maturity, let alone a biblical notion of maturity. (2) Teenagers who are mature will still be mature *teenagers*. That is to say, youth ministry is not about domesticating adolescents so that they begin acting *like adults*—wearing their parents' clothing, disavowing body piercings, preferring quiet evenings, and asking if somebody could turn the down music. These common notions of maturity miss the mark.

Paul is quite clear in his definition of maturity: biblically speaking, it is growing into the likeness of Jesus, "attaining to the whole measure of the fullness of Christ" (Eph. 4:13). This is a process called *spiritual formation*, and it is based on the stunning assertion that "we . . . are being transformed into [Christ's] likeness with ever-increasing glory" (2 Cor. 3:18), "that those God foreknew he also predestined to be conformed to the likeness of his Son . . . " (Rom. 8:29).

Spiritual formation describes the continuing work of the Holy Spirit in the life of a believer which conforms the child of God more and more to the image of Christ (2 Cor. 3:18). This work of the Spirit is possible only as we cooperate with God by walking "in the light as he is in the light" (1 John 1:7); by setting our hearts "on things above" (Col. 3:1); by ridding ourselves of the deeds of the flesh (Col. 3:8); and by putting on a heart of "compassion, kindness, humility, gentleness, and patience" (Col. 3:12). God does not treat His people as robots. He does not force His desires or His ways upon us. The necessity of human response to God's gracious invitation to walk with Him hand in

[30] See also Ephesians 4:4–6.

hand, to obey Him, to live according to Scripture, appears everywhere throughout Scripture. In these ways God makes us more and more like His Son.[31]

The key Greek term at the heart of spiritual formation comes from the root word *morphe*, a word suggesting not just shape, but essence—a word that refers "not to the external and transient, but to the inward and real."[32] It is a small word that grasps at the huge idea that God is at work in believers making us into new creatures—creatures like himself. We do not yet fully see what we shall become, but we know that Christ is in us, and that confirms for us the hope of glory (Col. 1:27). It is this "morphing" into Christ-likeness—what is referred to in theological terms as *sanctification*[33]—that is a key element of true spirituality.

Central to any biblical philosophy of youth ministry is an intentional commitment to nurture spiritual formation—not just building programs, but building people.

What Is Spiritual Formation?

Formation . . . suggests the inner being of the person is radically altered so that he or she is no longer the same. Information alone will not make the difference. The person who has taken in the information has been reshaped, remolded, and significantly altered by the active transformation of the data into meaning for oneself. God is remaking Christians; our very central core of being is transformed into something quite different. It is not just an outward change but a metamorphosis from one creature to a new and better one. We are being changed from the "old" to the new who is "in Christ" being conformed to his image.

Formation is not concerned merely with passively receiving the information, even true information. Formation requires knowledge of specific data as well as integrating those data within the larger whole of one's life. It requires prizing that information for one's own value system. Formation also requires that there be a change in behavior based on the knowledge acquired and willingly valued. Ultimately, knowledge, valuing, and behavior lead to a change in one's inner being, the existential core of personhood. Thus, continual transformation occurs (2 Cor. 3:18).

—*Kenneth O. Gangel and James C. Wilhoit,* The Christian Educator's Handbook of Spiritual Formation *(Wheaton, Ill.: Victor Books, 1994), 15.*

---

[31] Kenneth O. Gangel and James C. Wilhoit, *The Christian Educator's Handbook of Spiritual Formation* (Wheaton, Ill.: Victor Books, 1994), 39.

[32] W. E. Vine, *An Expository Dictionary of New Testament Words*, vol. II (Old Tappan, N.J.: Fleming Revell, 1966), 124.

[33] Sanctification, like the Greek *hagiasmos*, means "the act of setting apart or being set apart"—that is, holiness. It is a word that applies to believers on two levels, one that speaks to our *standing* and the other that refers to our *state*. Our *standing: we are made holy* (clean before God) in a legal sense by the perfect sacrifice of Jesus on the cross (Heb. 9:28, 10:10). Our *state: we are being made holy* in life pattern as we allow ourselves to be transformed by God's word and God work in us (John 17:17,19). One has happened, and one is happening. We have been saved by Christ's death (Rom. 5:9), but we are being saved by his life (Rom. 5:10). For more on this, see Lawrence Richards, *A Practical Theology of Spirituality* (Grand Rapids, Mich.: Zondervan, 1987), 22ff.

Two Marks of Spiritual Maturity

Paul crystallizes still further this notion of moving from immaturity to maturity:[34] "Then we will no longer be infants, tossed back and forth by the waves, and blown here and there by every wind of teaching and by the cunning and craftiness of men in their deceitful scheming" (Eph. 4:14).

Mark of maturity: Putting away childish concepts about God.

It is too bad that real life is not a flannelgraph. It would be so much easier if we could reduce all the hassles, temptations, and questions of life to a few cut-out felt figures. But real life does not always match the Sunday school simplicity of four or five figures clinging to a flannel background. When children are young and thinking in a concrete way, it is a fairly simple matter to get them to sing, "Jesus loves me, this I know; for the Bible tells me so." But as these children begin to move into early teen years, new questions emerge. It is a jungle out there. We hack a path around some of these questions during their younger years, and rightly so. But there comes a point at which the questions and dangers of the adolescent jungle are too many and too thick.

Doubt is a predictable part of adolescence. As young people begin to think abstractly (see chapters 5-7), life becomes less "safe and protected." They encounter episodes of struggle and doubt. These questions are intensified by different events like the breakup of the family, the loss of a friend, or the emergence of faith questions that do not fit so neatly on the flannel board. Some young people make it through this storm of questions. Others end up getting "tossed back and forth by the waves, and blown here and there by every wind of teaching" (Eph. 4:14).

Table 12-3.
Childlike Faith and Childlike Faith

Childish Faith	Childlike Faith
Really good Christians do not have pain and disappointments.	God uses our pain and disappointment to make us better Christians.
God helps those who help themselves.	God can only begin to help those who admit their own helplessness.
God wants to make us happy.	God wants to make us holy.
God always answers prayers.	Sometimes he answers with "No" or "Wait."
The closer we get to God, the more perfect we become.	The closer we get to God, the more we become aware of our sinfulness.
Mature Christians have all the answers.	Mature Christians can wrestle honestly with tough questions because they trust that God has the answers.
Good Christians are always strong.	Our strength is in admitting our weakness.

[34] This is the apparent intention of Paul's use of the Greek word *ina* (*then* or *that henceforth*).

Perhaps one of the reasons that so many of our students seem to "graduate" from the faith as they graduate from high school is that they have been nurtured in a nice, clean, childish flannelgraph faith instead of the childlike trusting faith to which Jesus calls us[35] (see Table 12-3). This is no doubt what Paul is referring to in I Corinthians 13:11: "When I was a child, I talked like a child, I thought like a child, I reasoned like a child; when I became a man, I gave up childish ways."

"Putting away childish reasoning" means nothing less, and nothing more, than helping students to forge a path through this jungle. The path is marked not by simple, easy half truths but by durable, biblical hard truths. Some youth workers mistakenly seek to correct childish reasoning by throwing out precious theological babies (biblical miracles, the virgin birth, the sense of a real and active God) with the bath water of immature thinking (a God who helps those who help themselves, a God who always promises physical health and well-being to his people, or some kind of "name-it-and-claim-it" God). That is not putting away childish reasoning so much as it is putting human reasoning above childlike faith.

A biblical philosophy of youth ministry values the nurture in students of a tough, enduring faith that stands under God even when it lacks understanding.

Mark of maturity: Putting away childish thinking in the way life choices are made.

My daughters used to crack me up when we went to the ice cream store. I watched them, little girls, faces pressed against the glass as they stared into this wonder world of ice cream-filled tubs. When I finally asked what flavor they wanted," the answer would inevitably be, "Daddy, I want the stripe" or "Daddy, I want the green." I would have to explain, "Green is not a flavor." "Stripe is not a flavor." I knew what was happening. They were being little kids, and little kids make choices on the basis of appearances: rainbow-speckled ice cream, toys that look like characters they see on TV, candy colorfully packaged. It is an approach that works fine for a little girl choosing ice cream.

Some 15 years later, when that same young woman is making serious choices about lifestyle and faith, it will be important for her to put away that childish approach. Paul observes in Ephesians 4:14b that spiritual immaturity is marked by a childish gullibility that can leave us "tossed back and forth by the . . . cunning and craftiness of men in their deceitful scheming." Primarily, it is a deceit of appearances, an error rooted in an overdependence on the eyes (Ps. 119:37, Prov. 4:25, Isa. 33:15, Matt. 5:29, 2 Cor. 5:7). Sin, after all, entered into human experience because someone saw a tree and it was "pleasing to the eye" (Gen. 3:6).

To be sure, childish thinking is not solely an affliction of the young. But in an adolescent culture that lives the credo "image is everything," teenagers are extremely vulnerable to and easily victimized by the *beautiful lie*. It looks like *freedom*; it

---

[35] "Then little children were brought to Jesus for him to place his hands on them and pray for them. But the disciples rebuked those who brought them. Jesus said, "Let the little children come to me, and do not hinder them, for the kingdom of heaven belongs to such as these"(Matt. 19:13–14).

Effective leaders, at all levels of leadership, maintain a learning posture throughout life . . . Leaders must develop a ministry philosophy that simultaneously honors biblical leadership values, embraces the challenges of the times in which we live, and fits their unique gifts and personal development if they expect to be productive over a lifetime.
—**Robert Clinton**

turns out to be *bondage*. It looks like *cool*; it turns out to be *foolish*. It looks like *love*; it turns out to be *lust*. It looks like *life*; it turns out to be *death*.

A biblical philosophy of youth ministry must be shaped by the necessity of teaching discernment—equipping teenagers with a grid of biblical truth and Christian teaching through which they can sift out the propaganda and deceit of the culture to make wise decisions about their lives.

Building Disciples

Discipleship is a term that figures prominently in the lexicon of modern youth ministry, but what exactly does that word mean? Everyone seems to agree that the end goal of our teaching, nurturing, maturing, and building[36] is to make disciples of Jesus Christ (Matt. 28:19). However, there is precious little reflection in current youth ministry literature about the meaning of discipleship.

The Greek word *mathetes* is rooted in the word *manthano*, to "learn." In the late Hellenistic period, when the New Testament was written, *mathetes* was used to refer to an adherent or follower of a great master—this was not a mere teacher-student relationship.[37] Confusion has arisen, however, over what implications that adherent-follower relationship might have for disciples of Jesus.[38] Of the more prominent views:

▸ Some have suggested that disciples of Jesus are *learners*, and *not necessarily Christians at all*. In fact, Livingston Blauvelt takes this one step further by saying that "the terms 'disciple' and 'Christian' are not synonymous is clear from John's Gospel.

[36] Rick Warren has noted the three present participles in Matthew 28:19—*going, baptizing,* and *teaching*—as elements of disciple-making. The apostle Paul uses two related present participles in Colossians 1:28: *admonishing and teaching.* "We proclaim him, admonishing and teaching everyone with all wisdom, so that we may present everyone perfect in Christ" (Col. 1:28).

[37] Michael J. Wilkins, *Following the Master: Discipleship in the Steps of Jesus* (Grand Rapids, Mich.: Zondervan, 1992), 75–78.

[38] Just think of the many different youth ministry entities described as "discipleship groups"—some intentional about serious commitment, some little more than social groups who just occasionally meet and chat. Are they all really "discipleship" groups, and what does that mean?

'From this time many of his disciples turned back and no longer followed him' (John 6:66). Then there was Judas, an unsaved disciple."[39]

> There's a way of life that looks harmless enough; look again—it leads straight to hell.
>
> —*Proverbs 14:12*, The Message.

▸ Others, concerned about dulling the New Testament edge of discipleship, have suggested that the word *disciple* should be reserved only for *those committed Christians who have made a commitment to follow Jesus and obey his radical demands.*[40] Dwight Pentecost comments that "there is a vast difference between being saved and being a disciple. Not all men who are saved are disciples, although all who are disciples are saved."[41]

▸ Still others suggest that *it is wrong to consider discipleship a second step in the Christian life*—sort of an elective course for those who wish to go beyond conversion—because such a view cheapens God's grace and voids the meaning of Christian commitment. "Cheap grace is grace without discipleship, grace without the cross, grace without Jesus Christ, living and incarnate . . . Happy are they who know that discipleship means the life which springs from grace, and that grace simply means discipleship. Happy are they who have become Christians in this sense of the word. For them the word of grace has proved a fount of mercy."[42]

This view sees discipleship as *synonymous with the Christian life, a process that begins at conversion when one becomes a disciple of Jesus, and then continues in an ongoing process of growth.*[43]

While each of these positions can be supported on biblical grounds, one fact quite clear is that by the time of the Book of Acts "disciple" was the name given to those who were *true believers in Jesus.*[44] Although there is ample room for flexibility, perhaps, on what might be construed by "true believer," James makes it vividly clear in his epistle that true belief will always be manifested by works of love and

[39] Livingston Blauvelt Jr., *Does the Bible Teach Lordship Salvation?*, 143, cited in Wilkins, *Following the Master*, 26.

[40] "What is a disciple? A disciple is one who follows Jesus Christ. But because we are Christians does not necessarily mean we are his disciples, even though we are members of his kingdom. Following Christ means acknowledging Him as Lord; *it means serving Him as a slave.*" Juan Carlos Ortiz, *Disciple* (Carol Stream, Ill.: Creation House, 1975), 9, cited by Wilkins, *Following the Master*, 27.

[41] J. Dwight Pentecost, *Design for Discipleship* (Grand Rapids, Mich.: Zondervan, 1971), 14.

[42] Dietrich Bonhoeffer, *The Cost of Discipleship*, trans. R. H. Fuller (New York: MacMillan, 1963), 47, 60, cited in Wilkins, *Following the Master*, 31.

[43] "Discipleship is not a supposed second step in Christianity, as if one first becomes a believer in Jesus and then, if he chooses, a disciple. From the beginning, discipleship is involved in what it means to be a Christian." James Montgomery Boice, *Christ's Call to Discipleship* (Chicago: Moody, 1986), 16, cited in Wilkins, *Following the Master*, 32.

[44] Wilkins notes that Luke speaks of the multitude of "believers" in Acts 4:32 and then, in Acts 6:2, refers to the multitude or congregation of "disciples." Moreover, in Luke's writings the expressions "those who believe" and "the disciples" signify the same group of people (see Acts 6:7, 9:26, 11:26, and 14:21–22). He observes also that "disciple" was one of the earliest synonyms for "Christian" (Acts 11:26). Wilkins, *Following the Master*, 37.

obedience (James 2:14–24). That does not equate with perfection, but it certainly does suggest intentional and fervent pursuit (Phil. 3:12–16).[45]

A biblical philosophy of ministry will be shaped by the mandate to form and nurture students into Christlikeness, to encourage, guide, and accompany teenagers in that intentional and fervent pursuit called _discipleship_.

Essential Number Four: Building One Another in Love

From him the whole body, joined and held together by every supporting ligament, grows and builds itself up in love, as each part does its work (Eph. 4:15b).

> The discipleship words of the Synoptic Gospels, and others like them, have always been either a fascination or an embarrassment to the church. For the hermit or the monastic, for the prophet and even for the mystic, they have exercised an irresistible attraction. For some of the greatest names in Christian biography—Benedict, Francis of Assisi, Jacob Boehme, William Law, Soren Kierkegaard, Dietrich Bonhoeffer—here lay the key to the mystery of Christian existence. But for the church in general, they have always constituted a problem. If the words are to be taken literally, then there can be but few who can be disciples. If they are to be taken symbolically or spiritually, then they plainly mean something different for us than they meant for those who were first called.
>
> —John James Vincent, "Discipleship and Synoptic Studies," Theologische Zeitschrift *16 (1960): 456, cited in Michael J. Wilkins,* Following the Master: Discipleship in the Steps of Jesus *(Grand Rapids, Mich.: Zondervan, 1992), 25.*

The great privilege of this construction process is that we as youth workers are not building alone. God uses the whole body to nurture the parts of the body. That amazing truth must be a cornerstone of any biblical youth ministry philosophy. We cannot really understand Christian growth and maturity if we do not understand that the Christian life is lived within the context of relationships. The Christian life is not a solitary adventure. It is not a solo climb. New Testament Christianity involves genuine community—not just sardines packed in the same can, but people "joined and held together" (Eph. 4:16) through a process of "speaking the truth in love" (Eph. 4:15).

---

[45] John records three positive statements Jesus made about disciples, each of which suggest what a portrait of Christian discipleship might include: (1) John 8:31-32 points to *faithfulness* to teaching—that is, obedience; (2) John 13:34-35 points to *love for others*; and (3) John 15:1-8 points to *fruitfulness* and intimacy of relationship.

A biblical philosophy of youth ministry will take seriously the communal nature of discipleship, recognizing that a life worthy of Christ is marked by humility, gentleness, patience, forbearance, "making every effort to keep the unity of the Spirit through the bond of peace" (Eph. 4:1–3).

> ## Acts 2:42–46
>
> They devoted themselves to the apostles' teaching and to the fellowship, to the breaking of bread and to prayer. Everyone was filled with awe, and many wonders and miraculous signs were done by the apostles. All the believers were together and had everything in common. Selling their possessions and goods, they gave to anyone as he had need. Every day they continued to meet together in the temple courts. They broke bread in their homes and ate together with glad and sincere hearts.
>
> —*Acts 2:42–46.*

What that means is that an emphasis on Christian community is not only a matter of pragmatic programming, it is a matter of survival. Research has shown that one of the greatest predictors of a teenager's ongoing growth in Christ is membership in, and commitment to, some sort of Christian fellowship.[46] This emphasis on relationships must sift into every nook and cranny of a youth ministry. It will determine what programs we develop, how we execute those programs, and who we recruit as volunteers to lead those programs. Relationships are the context in which Ephesians 4:11–15 becomes a living, breathing reality—a growing, healthy body.

Phase Two: Core Values—Guidelines for the Venture

Core values are an organization's (or person's) "foundational set of convictions on which it premises all of its actions and policies."[47]

The second phase of developing a sound ministry philosophy is the clarification of *core values*, the priorities that undergird every facet and every enterprise of the ministry. As Malphurs[48] points out, for example, the first-century church in Jerusalem was shaped by at least six core values that are represented in Acts 2:42-46:

1. Apostolic teaching (Acts 2:42–43).
2. Fellowship (Acts 2:42).
3. Prayer (Acts 2:42).

---

[46] Strommen, "Cry of the Joyous," in *Five Cries of Youth*, 99.

[47] Malphurs, *Ministry Nuts and Bolts*, 25.

[48] Ibid., 167. This list reflects some slight amendments to Malphurs.

Four Views of Youth Ministry and the Church

By Mark H. Senter III, professor of Christian Education, Trinity Evangelical Divinity School

What is the church? For some youth ministers this is a silly question for to ask. The answer is so obvious. We are.

Right! But who is the "we"? Are we the church spread out through all time and space, rooted in eternity, or a local group of worshipers? Are we focused primarily on community, mission, or worship? Is there any such thing as a parachurch ministry, or are all ministries expressions of local churches? Must the church be intergenerational, or could it be age group-specific?

Youth for Christ (YFC), like most other paraparochial youth ministries, expresses a desire to see the students reached through its ministry become active participants in a church in their community. "As part of the body of Christ, our vision is to see every young person . . . become part of a local church." Yet YFC has yet to establish a formal strategy to bring its vision to reality.

Bill Hybels reports the same problem at Willow Creek Community Church. In a conversation with a friend of his daughter who had come to faith through the church's Student Impact ministry, Hybels discovered that during high school she never went to church. Just Student Impact. When she graduated and went away to school, the pattern continued. Church and youth ministry were not connected.

Unlike most Christian teachings, the doctrine of the church has never received the kind of attention and debate that resulted in a clear definition and explanation of the nature of the church. Millard Erickson comments:

The doctrine of the church has hardly passed its pretheological phase. By contrast, Christology and the doctrine of the Trinity had been given special attention in the fourth and fifth centuries, as had the atoning work of Christ in the Middle Ages, and the doctrine of salvation in the sixteenth century. But such concerted attention has never been turned to the church.

Youth ministry has been filled with "pretheological" thinking. From its beginning in the late eighteenth century, youth ministry has had an inside-out and outside-in relationship to the church. Christian people went out to where young people were in an effort to bring them to faith (inside-out). Living in cultures where the Christian faith was closely associated with church attendance, young people who came to faith were expected to identify with the local church. Frequently, but far from universally, this happened. De facto sociology linked with a pretheology of the church allowed youth movements to flourish and churches to assimilate new converts.

As a distinct youth culture emerged, youth ministry professionals took on the challenge of ministering to an increasingly secular group of adolescents. A new sociology shaped the church's ministry to youth. As popular culture separated youth from adults, youth ministry increasingly did the same thing. Teenagers found churches to be foreign territory. Separated by musical preferences, relational patterns, public speaking styles, and differences in vocabulary, many young people felt as if they were in a foreign culture when they entered the doors of traditional churches.

Two key contrasts came into focus. The first contrast was programmatic. Should youth ministry place its primary emphasis on fellowship or on mission? The second contrast was developmental. Should teenagers, with all their developmental issues, be full participants in shaping the church right now or merely in the future?

When we consider the fellowship or mission of youth ministry in relation to the developmental issues, four patterns begin to form. These patterns form the structure for understanding youth ministry and the church. In *Four Views of Youth Ministry and the Church*, we define these four distinctive approaches to youth ministry as they relate to the church. For each approach, there are strengths and weaknesses.

Inclusive Congregational Approach

This approach, characterized by friendly relations between youth, children, and adults, integrates youth into every aspect of congregational life. Teenagers are seen as full partners in every aspect of God's coming to the faith community. Just as healthy families need occasional baby-sitters but never foster care, inclusive congregational youth ministry needs occasional age-appropriate discipleship but not fully developed youth ministries that isolate youth from the life of the congregation.

The strengths of the Inclusive Congregational approach include the fact that it is holistic, family-oriented, and nurture-oriented, and it can maintain continuity of ministry throughout life. This approach finds its greatest effectiveness in smaller churches. Its weaknesses include a lack of emphasis on evangelism or engagement with peer culture. Because of its emphasis on inclusion, the approach tends to be weak in responding to developmental needs. Consequently it is hard to explain and implement.

Missional Approach

This approach views youth ministry as mission. Using responsible evangelism to disciple young people into established churches, youth and youth ministers are missionaries. Their responsibility is to communicate the gospel to the current generation of high school students, especially those who are disenfranchised or alienated from the primary flow of school and church life.

The strengths of the Missional approach include a Great Commission orientation, a determination to reach the 75 percent of high school students normally missed by other approaches, and a strong relational orientation. The Missional approach attracts gifted young adult leaders. Its weaknesses include a low emphasis on Christian nurture, a limited relationship to other generations, and softness in grounding converts in the faith community. In that most forms of Missional approach youth ministry require a high ratio of staff to students and frequent use of special facilities, this approach tends to be expensive to maintain.

Preparatory Approach

This approach is a specialized ministry to adolescents that prepares them to participate in the life of existing churches. Students are viewed as disciples in training with opportunities for service both in the present and the future. Developmental dynamics suggest the youth ministry be viewed as a laboratory in which disciples are permitted to grow in a culture guided by spiritual coaches.

The strengths of the Preparatory approach include a responsiveness to developmental needs, a relational component providing adult role models for Christian living and, to a lesser degree it, Great Commandment orientation. For this approach there are an abundance of materials and training available. Its weaknesses include a discontinuity of relationships and discipleship after high school. This approach tends to be program-driven and lacks consistent efforts to evangelize the 75 percent of the high school population with whom church kids have little natural contact. It is also isolated from intergenerational involvement.

Strategic Approach

This approach prepares the youth group to become a new church (that is, church plant). Using a continuity in discipleship between youth minister and youth, leadership is nurtured to assume responsibility for roles in evangelism and fellowship. The youth pastor becomes the pastor of a new church with the blessing of the mother church.

The strengths of the strategic approach include a responsiveness to the idealism and faith of youth, a context for Great Commission and Great Commandment living, and a continuity of holistic discipleship. The approach also provides a healthy career path for aging youth pastors. Its weaknesses can include a lack of emphasis on the evangelization of the other 75 percent of the high school population, a potential weakening of the mother church, and a tendency to be more task-oriented than need-responsive. The mobility of young adults may leave the Strategic approach vulnerable to leadership loyalty and turnover.

4. Community (Acts 2:44–46).
5. Worship (Acts 2:47).
6. Acts of mercy and proclamation (Acts 2:43,45).

Core values impact goal-setting, team-building, program execution, resource allocation (people and money), decision making, and more.

One of the best ways of defining core values is simply by thinking through a response to this question: "What are 5 to 15[49] adjectives that you would like people to use in characterizing your ministry?"[50] Most ministries will have several core values, but often there will be one overriding value that adds a particular texture to the whole ministry portrait. For example, in the statement of Core Values for the student ministry at Saddleback Church (Orange County, Calif.) there is a clear emphasis on relationships:

Relational approach
Encouragement
Laughter
Acceptance
Transparency
Involvement of students
Outreach orientation
Numerical growth
Spiritual growth
Homelike feeling
Intimacy
Professionalism
Strategic followup[51]

Adapting some of the same categories we used in chapter 10 to describe different types of congregations, Table 12-4 demonstrates how one key youth ministry value can flavor the youth group's total programming.

Phase Three: Vision—Imagining the End of the Journey

A vision statement is a word picture of what the ministry or organization will look like as the mission is achieved. It should be a statement that is clear enough, and provides enough of a sense of urgency, that others will hear it, understand it, and be enticed to embrace the same dream.

---

[49] This number will vary. Willow Creek Community Church (Barrington, Ill.) is committed to 10 core values. Wooddale Church (Eden Prairie, Minn.) has crafted a list of seven core values. Collins and Porras remark that the visionary companies they studied typically have from three to six core values. James Collins and Jerry Porras, *Built to Last* (New York: Harper, 1994), 219.

[50] For good approaches to stimulating the imagination, consult Malphurs, *Ministry Nuts and Bolts*.

[51] Fields, *Purpose-Driven Youth Ministry*, 235.

The third phase of the process of developing a youth ministry philosophy involves clearly defining a vision. Is this just a rehashing of Purpose or Mission? It should not be. Mission and vision are two ways of thinking about the same purpose. One is a statement, the other is more of a snapshot. One is rooted in the head, the other is rooted in the heart. One is informational, the other is inspirational. Malphurs draws sharp distinctions between the two (see Table 12-5).

When asked, as often I am, what major principle I would convey to someone just starting out in youth ministry, I find myself consistently coming back to the Vision question: "Do you have a dream for what God has called you to do with students?" To be sure, we need to be clear on mission. But to remain passionate we need to be vivid in our vision. It is the absolute essential for someone who wants to stay fresh and enthusiastic about youth ministry over the long haul. It is the chief prevention for burnout. I suspect that, most of the time, what we hear described as "burnout"—when people run out of steam—is more likely "blur-out"—when people are without a clear vision in ministry and simply do not have anything to get "steamed up" about!

Table 12-4.
Youth Ministry Values Affect Youth Group Programming

Type of Youth Ministry	Unifying Value	Role of Pastor	Role of Youth	Key Emphasis	Typical Tool	Desired Result	Source of Legitimacy	Positive Trait
The King James Youth Group	Knowledge	Teacher	Student	To know	Bible study	Informed Christians	Emphasis on truth	Knowledge of Bible
The Outreach Youth Group	Evangelism	Evangelist	Recruiter	To save	Midweek outreach meeting	New believers	Results	Heart for lost
The Boot Camp Youth Group	Missions	Prophet	Agents of change	To serve	Work project	Students with social conscience	Cause	Compassion for oppressed
The Experiential Youth Group	Experience	Facilitator	Participants	To feel	Worship, candles, music	Feelings	Spirit	Vitality
The Family Reunion Youth Group	Loyalty	"Parent"	Siblings	To belong	Sharing groups	Secure Christians	Roots	Identity
The Life Development Youth Group	Character	Trainer	Learner	To be	Accountability groups	Disciples	Changed lives	Growth
The Spring Break Youth Group	Strong program	Ringmaster	Consumer	To be active	Games	Participants	Increased attendance	Enticing

A Vision for Planning

When we talk about a vision for youth ministry, we are speaking in one sense about a vision for plans—the ability to look ahead and see what God might want to accomplish. But we are talking about more than just foresight: we are talking about insight.

Table 12-5.
Mission and Vision—How Do They Differ?

	Mission	Vision
Definition	Statement	Snapshot
Application	Planning	Communication
Length	Short	Long
Purpose	Informs	Inspires
Activity	Doing	Seeing
Source	Head	Heart
Order	First	Second
Focus	Broad	Narrow
Effect	Clarifies	Challenges
Development	Deductive (Taught)	Inductive (Caught)

Source: Aubrey Malphurs, *Ministry Nuts and Bolts* (Grand Rapids, Mich.: Kregel, 1997), 113. I have made some slight adaptations to Malphurs's chart.

Dave began his work in inner-city Chicago with unusual optimism and expectancy. He dared to believe that God could raise up some new growth out of the burned-out stumps of inner-city blight. His vision was contagious. He started getting students excited, and then the students' parents, and then other people around the neighborhood.

Before long, Dave was offered a chance to reclaim and renovate an old abandoned movie theater in the neighborhood. The place did not look like much. It reeked from the garbage of neglect, vandals, drug users, and homeless people seeking shelter. What most people saw as a time capsule of dust, garbage, and destruction, Dave saw as a potential drop-in center and ministry headquarters.

Finally, during the course of several months, Dave mobilized those kids and that neighborhood to make that vision a reality. Together, folks in one Chicago neighborhood transformed an abandoned building into a youth activity center. It happened because one youth minister dared to dream big dreams for God. That is vision.

A Vision for People

But vision is more than seeing what God can do with mortar and drywall. Effective youth ministries are stoked by men and women who have a vision for what God can do with real flesh and blood—the kind of youth worker who can hear a kid sitting in the back of a van reciting the alphabet through a burp, and still believe that this same kid may one day be a missionary on a distant continent sharing his faith in an equally amazing way.

Futurist and theologian Leonard Sweet muses what might happen if ministries, "instead of working on vision or mission statements, establish what could be called 'QSL' ratios—'Quality of Spiritual Life Standards': 'What would the spirit of a church 'thoroughly equipped for every good work' (2 Tim. 3:17) look like? ... Itemize how the energy of each 'spirit' would issue in specific 'matterings' in the Body of Christ."

Sweet offers "a suggestion of 12 QSLs, which you can adapt for your unique setting." On a scale of 1 to 10, how would rank them in order of importance for a youth ministry?

▸ Confidence
▸ Humility
▸ Prayer
▸ Reverence for Scriptures
▸ Repentance
▸ Compassion
▸ Passion
▸ Endurance
▸ Joy
▸ Openness to diversity
▸ Adaptability
▸ State of being out of control

Leonard Sweet, Soul Tsunami *(Grand Rapids, Mich.: Zondervan, 1999), 259.*

It is not naiveté or fluffy optimism. It is the kind of Christ-centered realism that can look at the dust and decay of an abandoned student and trust in God's transforming power—the same power that took the Peter of the Gospels (brash, impulsive, inconsistent, and timid about his faith) and molded him into the Peter of Acts (faithful, bold, and outspoken). It is realism rooted, first of all, in a biblical appraisal of who God is, and, second, in a fair-minded recollection of what God has done in our own lives through the years. Without this vision for what God can do in the lives of our students, we will be kicking Peters off the youth council because of one night's denial (John 18:15–27), or sending home a John or Mark because of one instance of timidity (Acts 13:13, 15:39).

My friend Jack has that kind of vision. As a youth pastor, he was willing to take some risks with a young college intern named Derek. At first, it did not look like a promising wager. Derek's attitude was not that great. He had a knack for saying the wrong thing at the wrong time, and he cultivated a generally sloppy personal appearance that made it hard for people to see beyond the externals.

I have to admit that, as Derek's college professor, I was not hopeful either. When Jack accepted Derek on his ministry team, my response was along the lines of, "Well, if you're really sure." I fully expected the arrangement to last no more than a few months. To be honest, there were several times when it seemed even that projection might have been optimistic. Jack would occasionally call my office, exasperated, with another "Derek story."

However, the amazing thing is that every time Derek was corrected he would respond. No matter how often he was taken down by rebuke, he always came back for more. Slowly but surely, miraculously and painstakingly, Derek began to change. Jack discovered that Derek had a remarkable gift of service. Given a task, no matter how small, he would get it done. In addition, the guy turned out to be a computer genius. He reprogrammed and debugged every computer in the church. He began to show an ability to draw close to students.

In time Derek became a valued, well-respected, and appreciated member of Jack's ministry team. His story is a story of vision—the story of how one youth minister dared to take a chance on a student, looking behind the negatives to glimpse the positives that only God could truly see.

In putting together a Vision Statement the principal task through prayer and brainstorming is to question: *What will this mission look like when it is fleshed out in this ministry?*

▶ **Is it clear enough to be grasped and owned by people within the ministry?** By people outside the ministry? Will this help others in the congregation embrace the dream of this youth ministry? Will this help potential supporters understand and buy into the vision of this youth ministry?

▶ **Does it offer a clear challenge?** Have we embraced a vision that is big enough to inspire, or have we shrunk our dreams to fit what would probably happen anyway?

▶ **Does it offer a picture?** Peer evangelism is a concept; students sharing their faith with friends is a picture. Christian community is a concept; students meeting in covenant groups on a weekly basis, committed to sharing faith and life—that is a picture. Servanthood is a concept; students willing to give a week of their summer to serve God in a work project is a picture. Outreach is a concept; unchurched kids who feel welcomed and embraced by the church is a picture. "Win the war" is a concept; "Take that hill" is a picture. People are much more willing to go for a picture than for a concept.

▸ **Is it future-oriented?** Does it describe where the ministry is, or where the ministry is going? Position informs; direction inspires.

▸ **Is this vision feasible?** Will our students buy into this vision? Will the parents? The board?

▸ **Is there firm commitment to this vision?** If it is big enough to inspire, it will likely be hard enough to demand. Is there a clear resolve to make this vision a reality? Followers are galvanized by a leader committed to going somewhere.

Phase Four: Strategy—Getting from Here to There

Strategy is the plan for accomplishment. It is process-oriented: How will we get from where we are to where we believe God is calling us to be?

Finally, after establishing clear notions about what the ministry should look like and where the ministry should go, it is time to put brush to canvas and boot to trail. This is the place where we begin to think in terms of ministry models and strategies. It is here that we move to hands-on ministry planning:

▸ **Programming components:** Will our ministry environment include small groups, Sunday night meetings, midweek gatherings, a breakfast club, etc.?

▸ **Resource allocations:** Do we spend the money on a missions trip or a half-pipe for skateboarders, a winter outreach or a fall leadership weekend? How do we best use the leaders we have?

▸ **Ministry activities:** How do we schedule an average month of programming? Will we do outreach every week, once a month, or only during certain "seasons" of our youth ministry year?

▸ **Program structure:** Will middle school and high school meet together? How will we coordinate the various components of the program so that there is coherency? (That is, we do not want to plan a huge Sunday School outreach on the same weekend as the Discipleship Retreat.)

These are some of the questions to be considered in the next chapter as we think about a philosophy of youth ministry programming.

"TELEPHONE"

Meditations on the Way by Helen Musick

Have you ever played the game "Telephone"? A group sits in a circle, knee to knee. The leader thinks of a sentence and whispers the message to the person sitting to the right. The object of the game is to see if the message can make it around the circle unharmed. The fun part of the game is hearing what the message becomes by the time it hits the leader again. Inevitably, something is distorted. "I really like hot dogs and milk shakes" becomes something like "On the really hot day we had an earthquake."

One of the main reasons why these messages are almost always different in the end is because the listener is not allowed to ask questions of the speaker. The outcome of the entire game is dependent on the players' abilities to listen and then transmit. Most definitely, if anyone were able to ask questions of clarification along the way, the message would have a much greater chance of coming full circle without any alterations.

As it goes with "Telephone," so I believe it can go during our communication with God, especially when we hit our college years. Pressured to decide about a major, we consistently ask, "What is it that you want for my life, Lord?" Then we stick our ears up toward heaven and wait. One person speaks, the other listens, and we hope that what is heard is accurate.

In the account of Jeremiah's call to prophetic ministry (Jer. 1:4–19), note the dialogue that takes place between God and Jeremiah throughout the passage. A brief synopsis: God initiates; Jeremiah voices hesitation; God acknowledges his fear and touches Jeremiah's mouth; God provides a vision; they discuss its meaning; God reassures Jeremiah; Jeremiah hears it all and is then ready to obey. Jeremiah has much to teach us about the importance of having *all* of our senses awakened and accessible to God. Note how speech, touch, sight, and hearing are all used to communicate with Jeremiah, and note Jeremiah's responsiveness to each one. It is as if each step in the process gets him more prepared to obey, and God is able to speak reassuring words of peace with every hesitation. This is the true beauty of their dialogue.

Do you long for such an encounter with God? Are you desperately seeking his direction for your life? Perhaps this class is an attempt to decipher his leading. God longs to address all your senses, so he can communicate ever so powerfully to you that special calling he has for you. Once you have completely surrendered them to the Lord, you can be confident he will be able to reach you. He longs to dialogue with you—the interaction will allow God to address your fears, reassure your heart, and empower you for service. When in true communication with God, you too will be able to realize and believe you can be as strong as iron and as durable as bronze (v. 18), no matter what.

Travel Log: Greece

Youth Worker Profiles by Paul Borthwick

Dimitris Boukis is lead pastor of the "Evangelical Youth Movement," a branch of the Greek Evangelical Church, in Thessaloniki, Greece.

Building on Local History. Boukis explains about his work: "The youth work of the Greek Evangelical Church as a separate organized entity of the Church Synod was founded in 1950. Its beginnings were the byproduct and desire of the youth in the churches to celebrate their unity in Christ and to serve their generation in a country rebuilding itself after the devastation of World War II and the Greek Civil War that followed. Because of the political surroundings and the small number of Greek Protestants (less than 1 percent of the total population) Greek youth ministry developed a unique character in that it serves ages 15 to 35 simultaneously."

Building on Diversity. "The diversity of ages calls for a number of different ministries. Seminars, rallies, and conferences are held year round, and special interest groups eventually developed their own programs: teenage programs for ages 13 to 17 (started in 1986); student ministry for ages 18 to 24 (started in 1970s); young adults ministry for ages 18 to 35 (1983); and young couples ministry (1985)."

Building on God's Grace. "By the grace and call of God, I served in these ministries from 1987-1991 as an elected youth officer of the Evangelical Youth Movement, and since 1996 as a copastor first, then as the sole pastor following the retirement of my colleague in 2000.

The duties of the position encompass national supervision of the ministry, including support and advice for the elected lay national youth committee, co-organizing and running national and local youth activities, programs and conferences, as well as teaching, counseling, and preparing future leaders and workers of the church. In addition, I have frequent Sunday service responsibility in Greek Evangelical congregations lacking a pastor."

Battling Through Struggles. "We struggle because most churches misunderstand the value of the full-time youth minister (I estimate that fewer than 25 percent understand the importance of having one). This misunderstanding from current church leaders, coupled with the diverse character and scattered characteristics of Youth Ministry in Greece, has proven to be a challenge overcome only through the grace, promises, and provisions of God. God has provided us with an accountability group of fellow pastors, elders, and friends for prayer, encouragement, and spiritual and emotional support and advice. A national network of coworkers, parents, and transformed youth, all with a genuine and sincere heart to serve the younger generation, gather together regularly. They provide assurance of the imperative nature of the ministry."

Building on an Ancient Dream. "An anonymous Christian defender of the second century wrote in *The Letter to Diognetus*, 'In a word, what the soul is to the body, Christians are to the world.' My dream is to see the Christian youth become the soul, the thermostat rather than the thermometer, of the Greek community. In order for them to reach their potential to influence their generation, we ought to equip them through programs and events to develop a Christian ethos that defeats the unrighteousness of the existing world order as we provide them with solid role models and create opportunities to challenge themselves and exercise their gifts. In so doing they will learn through failures and

chapter thirteen

A BIBLICAL PHILOSOPHY OF MINISTRY:
A JOURNEY WITH COMPASS AND COMPASSION

By your words I can see where I'm going; they throw a beam of light on my dark path.
—**Psalm 119:105,** *The Message*

By the grace God has given me, I laid a foundation as an expert builder, and someone else is building on it. But each one should be careful how he builds. For no one can lay any foundation other than the one already laid, which is Jesus Christ. If any man builds on this foundation using gold, silver, costly stones, wood, hay, or straw, his work will be shown for what it is, because the Day will bring it to light. It will be revealed with fire, and the fire will test the quality of each man's work.
—**1 Corinthians 3:10–13**

Anyone who saw the 1997 movie *Jerry Maguire* will remember that the whole plot grew out of the first two minutes of spoken dialogue. In the opening scene, we see Jerry McGuire, played by the actor Tom Cruise, awake and restless in the middle of the night. He sits down at his computer terminal:

> Jerry Maguire: "I began writing what they call a mission statement. Not a memo; a mission statement. You know, a suggestion for the future of our company.
>
> "A night like this doesn't come along very often. I seized it. What started out as one page became 25.
>
> "Suddenly, I was my father's son again. I was remembering the simple pleasures of this job; how I ended up here out of law school, the way a stadium sounds when one of my players performs well on the field, the way we are meant to protect them in health and in injury. For so many clients we had forgotten what was important.
>
> "I wrote and wrote and wrote and wrote, and I'm not even a writer. I was remembering even the words of the original sports agent, my mentor, the late, great Dickey Fox who said, 'The key to this business is personal relationships.'
>
> "Suddenly it was all pretty clear. The answer was fewer clients. Less money. More attention. Caring for them. Caring for ourselves. The games too. Just starting our lives, really.
>
> "Hey, I'll be the first to admit it, what I was writing was somewhat touchy-feely. I didn't care. I had lost the ability to BS; it was the me I've always wanted to be. I took it in a bag to a copymat in the middle of the night and printed up 110 copies. Even the cover looked like *Catcher in the Rye*. I entitled it, 'The Things We Think and Do Not Say: The Future of Our Business.'"

The scene changes and Jerry Maguire enters an all-night copy shop where he hands the clerk his mission statement.

> Copymat Worker: "That's how you become great, man."

It was an intriguing scene in a moderately intriguing movie because it underlined in two minutes of film an important starting point and an important stumbling block both of which are often overlooked in ministry. The starting point, of course, is the mission statement—why are we here? The stumbling block is forgetting that in ministry, the reason we are here is people—God cares for people. "It was he who gave some to be apostles, some to be prophets, some to be evangelists, and some to be pastors and teachers, *to prepare God's people*."[1]

---

[1] Ephesians 4:11-12, emphasis added.

The key to this business is personal relationships.
—*Jerry Maguire* **fictional character Dickey Fox, sports agent and mentor**

Combined, the two ideas invite us to an adventure of compass and compassion, mission and relationships, intention and incarnation. We focused in the preceding chapter on the compass of mission. In this chapter, we must look more closely to where that compass points us.

A Ministry of Incarnation

In the last century, a Korean artist (a refugee from North Korea to South Korea) completed a remarkable piece of art depicting the standing figure of Jesus with arms outstretched. Surrounding the figure of Jesus, around the border of the picture, are 27 angels symbolizing the 27 books of the New Testa-ment. Even if it were a traditional painting, it would be an amazing work of art.

But what makes this piece even more incredible is that this Korean's artistry did not come through sketch work or drawing or brush strokes, but through writing out the entire New Testament with a fine-point pen, making some parts of some letters dark and some parts of other letters light so that through the shaded letters and words the image of Jesus and the angels are clearly visible on the scroll. Remarkably, the figure of Jesus is not superimposed over the text of Scripture; it is actually the words themselves. It was a labor of love that took the artist two years in which he meticulously wrote out the entire 185,000-plus words of the New Testament, shading each letter in just such a way that the detailed portrayal of Jesus and the angels would be clearly visible on his six-by-four-foot scroll.

In his devotional book, *The Word Became Flesh*,[2] E. Stanley Jones explained that the artist, through his painstaking and tedious work, was

[2] E. Stanley Jones, *The Word Became Flesh* (Nashville, Tenn.: Abingdon, 1963), 1–2.

offering powerful testimony to the miracle that John spoke of when he wrote in John 1:14, "The Word became flesh." It was a vivid portrayal of what Christians refer to as the *incarnation*, a word that draws from the Latin word, *carnalis*, and means literally "in flesh." Significantly, John's original usage of the phrase in John 1:14 is followed by this statement: "and dwelt among us." Literally, the phrase could be translated, "He pitched his tent among us."[3] It is a short phrase in which we see, all at once, the genius, the wonder, and the mystery of the gospel. Jesus was Immanuel, "God with us."

Somewhere between the sketches of that old drawing and the words of this familiar passage in the Gospel of John is a truth that takes us right to the heart of youth ministry—a passion to flesh out the life of God and the love of God to the students with whom we are working—to consistently, creatively, and obediently live out the Word of God in their presence. Kenda Dean explains,

> Youth ministry focuses on relationships, not only because of who teenagers are but because of who God is. God is a relationship—Christian tradition uses the relational language of Father, Son, and Holy Spirit to describe the persons of the Trinity—and this God's love is so generous the Godhead alone cannot contain it. Significant relationships with other Christians matter because they teach us something about what God is like—the One who can love us in spite of ourselves and who loves us passionately enough to suffer willingly on our behalf.[4]

Such an approach to ministry will be reflected in at least two critical respects, our personhood and our pursuit. The first focuses on *who* we seek to be as faithful reflectors of Jesus, God's Son. The second focuses on *how* we seek to do ministry that reflects Jesus, the Good Shepherd.

Our Personhood

> Your attitude should be the same as that of Christ Jesus: Who, being in very nature God, did not count equality with God something to be grasped, but made himself nothing, taking the very nature of a servant, being made in human likeness. And being found in appearance as a man, He humbled himself and became obedient to death—even death on a cross! (Phil. 2:5-8)

In *The Wounded Healer*, Henri Nouwen's wonderful little book about Christian leadership, Nouwen identifies three essential roles for the leader of the future. But in so doing, he also provides for us a substantial picture of incarnational ministry leadership.[5]

---

[3] A. T. Robertson, "Notes on John 1:14," *Word Pictures in the New Testament*, Electronic Database, PC Study Bible version 3.3A for Windows, © Biblesoft.

[4] Kenda Creasy Dean and Ron Foster, *The God-bearing Life: The Art of Soul Tending for Youth Ministry* (Nashville, Tenn.: Upper Room Books, 1998), 27.

[5] I hope this is not putting words in Nouwen's mouth. The context of Nouwen's book leads me to this conclusion, and his description of these three traits only confirms in my own mind this assumption. Indeed, the very image of a "wounded healer" is an image of incarnate leadership.

The incarnational leader must be an articulator of inner events.

We live in a culture that simply has no lexicon for the deep, inner longings of the soul. We borrow from the language of mysticism. We baptize the phrases of the therapeutic culture. We have dulled down our God-given taste for the eternal in the hope that it might be satisfied by *Chicken Soup for the Soul*. One of the qualities essential for incarnational ministry is the ability and willingness to speak the language of the spirit. Nouwen defines this in terms of communication and vulnerability.

> In this context, pastoral conversation is not merely a skillful use of conversational techniques to manipulate people into the Kingdom of God, but a deep human encounter in which a man is willing to put his own faith and doubt, his own hope and despair, his own light and darkness at the disposal of others who want to find a way through their confusion and touch the solid core of life.

> This is . . . the careful and sensitive articulation of what is happening . . . so that those who listen can say, . . . "You express what I vaguely felt, you bring to the fore what I fearfully kept in the back of my mind."...When a listening man is able to say this, then the ground is broken for others to receive the Word of God.[6]

The incarnational leader must be a person of compassion.

Compassion, as Nouwen defines it, is neither simply a case of warm fuzzies nor a posture of tough love. It is one's ability to avoid either the "distance of pity" or the "exclusiveness of sympathy." "Compassion is born when we discover in the center of our own existence not only that God is God and man is man, but also that our neighbor is really our fellow man."[7]

Compassion is the ability to look on our students' longings and needs, and recognize that all of us, in our own ways, are no less needy and no less fervent in our longings:

▶ that the middle school kid who is disrupting youth group is perhaps using a tactic that I wouldn't use, but in truth he is only responding to a need that *both* of us deeply feel and understand: a desire for acceptance and approval.

▶ that the teenage girl who tries to dress (or should it be *un*dress?) like her pop idol does not really want to be in a music video any more than I want to be Mick Jagger or Ozzy Osbourne. But what she does want—what we both deeply want—is to be loved and admired.

6 Henri Nouwen, *The Wounded Healer* (New York: Bantam Doubleday, 1979), 39.
7 Ibid., 41.

In short, compassion is recognizing that I am no less sinful, no less needy, no less lost than the most sinful, most needy, most lost person in my youth group. What's more, because God can look on me with clear assessment and unconditional acceptance, I am free (and by gratitude obliged) to look on my teenage neighbor with that same grace and forgiveness.

The incarnational leader must be a contemplative critic.

The incarnational leader must be able to look behind the actions, beneath the surface and beyond the present, to listen and watch for what God is doing in our midst. This requires a contemplative habit, a refusal to be caught up in the flow of cultural traffic and media hype, a habit of not pulling out of the race in some sort of holy isolationism but of pulling over long enough to remain "in contact with what is basic and central and ultimate." Be warned: this is not easy to do in youth ministry, where speed and style sometimes eclipse direction and where our work with teenagers tempts us always to watch for the newest, latest, and hippest.

The contemplative critic "constantly invites his fellow man to ask real, often painful and upsetting, questions, to look behind the surface of smooth behavior, and to take away all the obstacles that prevent him from getting to the heart of the matter . . . More than anything else, he will look for signs of hope and promise in the situation which he finds himself."[8]

Our Pursuit

Suppose one of you has a hundred sheep and loses one of them. Does he not leave the ninety–nine in the open country and go after the lost sheep until he finds it? And when he finds it, he joyfully puts it on his shoulders and goes home. Then he calls his friends and neighbors together and says, "Rejoice with me; I have found my lost sheep." (Luke 15:4–6)

The incarnation was a marriage of theology and geography. Jesus was not just God; he was God with us, God dwelling among us. As Eugene Peterson paraphrases in *The Message*, "The Word became flesh, *and moved into the neighborhood*" (John 1:14, emphasis added). This huge fact points us to a youth ministry that reaches beyond the safe walls of a church building plastered with Christian posters, and calls us out *among* students, on their turf, on their terms.

It is sad to say, too often the church's model has been less the Good Shepherd who goes "after the lost sheep" and more along the lines of Little Bo Peep. "Leave them alone and they'll come home, wagging their tails behind them." And while we are back at the church waiting for the kids to flock to our meetings, they are lost and wandering, some of them seduced by phony shepherds, some of them ravaged by wolves.

---

[8] Ibid., 45.

A critical facet of incarnational youth ministry is centered on the notion of being present where the sheep are. "The Son of Man came *to seek* and to save that which was lost" (Luke 19:10, emphasis added). Jeff Johnson tells the story of a high school counselor named Mary:

> She seemed unable to reach a certain group of girls at her high school and in deep frustration finally asked one of the girls what the problem was. The girl blurted out, "Well, just look where you are!" Mary was sitting behind her desk in the air-conditioned office, across the hall from the Dean of Women where these girls regularly visited for disciplinary reasons. So Mary did some research and discovered that this group hung out around the cafeteria door that led to the parking lot. It was hot and unpleasant, but being near the boiler room, they could smoke and skip classes easily.
>
> Over the summer, Mary moved her office . . . to the boiler room! She had to work through all sorts of red tape with her principal and school board members who assured her it was very unprofessional, but she did it. Relationships started clicking as kids realized she was serious about being their friend. Her nickname soon became "Moms," even though she was the same concerned person as before. All that had changed was geography, but it convinced those girls that she would do what was necessary to have a relationship with them.[9]

That is a ministry of presence, a ministry of seeking. One can almost hear Paul writing (Phil. 2:5–8), "Though being in very nature faculty, Mary did not consider air-conditioning something to be grasped . . . but humbled herself even to the level of the boiler room!"

Dwelling Among Them

When I first began doing youth work, I was an intern with a parachurch mission whose primary vision and focus was to reach out to unchurched high school students. I spent many a lunch hour walking (and sometimes stalking) a campus trying to develop relationships with students who not only did not know me, but apparently did not often feel any great desire to know me. It was some of my scariest youth ministry.

I thought to myself, "Will they wonder why I'm here on their campus? They know I'm not a student. They know I'm not a faculty or staff person. They know I'm not a parent. That only leaves 'narcotics officer,' 'sex criminal,' or 'axe murderer.'" It was a genuine cross-cultural outreach and I was not at all sure how the natives of this culture were going to respond.

Not the least of the obstacles faced in doing incarnational youth ministry is

---

[9] Jeff Johnson, unpublished monograph.

the skepticism and suspicion of students. They are not exactly used to having adults seek them out for the purpose of friendship. More often than not in the world of adolescence, if an adult wants to talk with you, that is usually a bad sign. Most of us remember the forbidding "oooooohhh" that followed the public address announcement that someone "should please report to the office." Such an invitation almost always spelled trouble. There was the intuitive assumption that the person was not being invited to the office simply because the principal was lonely.

But incarnational youth ministry calls us to move beyond our intimidations. As I continued to spend time with students, one truth came back to me over and over again: kids are open to, and will find time for, genuine, sincere love. It will not be easy for most of us, but here are some practical guidelines to remember.

Incarnational witness will be based more on the signpost model and less on the salesperson model.

The difference between the two is basic: signposts point the way; salespeople try to close the deal.[10] Incarnational youth ministry is very similar to what Moses talks about in his charge to parents.

Love the Lord your God with all your heart and with all your soul and with all your strength. These commandments that I give you today are to be upon your hearts. Impress them on your children. Talk about them when you sit at home and when you walk along the road, when you lie down and when you get up. Tie them as symbols on your hands and bind them on your foreheads. (Deut. 6:5–8)

One of the basic principles at the heart of incarnational ministry is that God often works better *between* lessons, *after* club is over, *beyond* church property.

It is intriguing to read the words of those disciples on the road to Emmaus. "They asked each other, 'Were not our hearts burning within us while he talked with us on the road and opened the Scriptures to us?'"(Luke 24:13–33).

One of the hallmarks of Jesus's ministry is that his style of witness was not some canned, rehearsed sales pitch. It was a consistent lifestyle of living out and talking about the kingdom of God. Much of the time, Jesus's greatest work was done "on the road," in transit while he was walking with his disciples, boating with his disciples, ministering with his disciples, praying with his disciples, or eating with his disciples.[11]

That is a hallmark of incarnational ministry. It is a ministry marked by shared life. Newer youth workers often worry that they will be ineffective at their task because they will not have the right answers or come up with the right phrases. But

---

[10] This metaphor comes from John Wesley White, *The Fight* (Downers Grove, Ill.: InterVarsity Press, 1977), 59–76.

[11] Some of you are greatly encouraged by this last phrase.

incarnational ministry is about being *among* the students, spending time with them, and living life in such a way as to become a consistent signpost pointing to Jesus. Quite often, that happens not because someone has just the right words but simply because someone was in the right place at the right time.

One of my most memorable "Emmaus discussions" with a group of students took place around a campfire one night along the Appalachian Trail after a delicious dinner of Spam, rice, and cream of mushroom soup.[12] It seemed like the least likely place for heavy-duty spiritual conversation, but somehow we began talking with each other about what it meant to be a Christian, and it was amazing. I heard questions and shared in discussions that night that I had not experienced in a year of Sunday School and youth meetings.

Why *then*? Why *that* night? We did not have enough light to read a Bible. Most of the kids had carefully packed their Bibles in the very bottom of their packs. We did not even have Power Point! There was no good reason for that night—except for the fact that my group decided at that particular time and place that it was time to talk.

Resist the temptation to be the "Answer Man."

Even the most cursory study of Jesus's teaching in the Gospels will show that he taught more often by asking questions than by giving answers. It is noteworthy that on the road to Emmaus that day (Luke 24:13–33), Jesus never identified himself to the two disciples during the entire trip. It is true that he "explained to them what was said in all the Scriptures concerning himself (Luke 24:27)", but that was not till after they had thoroughly aired their questions and doubts.

Our tendency as youth workers is to want immediately to correct wrong statements about God, to make sure that we point out areas of sin and error in a student's life. Unfortunately, that is a quick way to close down communication. The average teenager is not that interested in playing "Ask Mr. Spiritual." That does not mean we must be silent about our faith or about our feelings. It does mean that we may need to walk awhile with our students and hear their questions before we start "explaining" everything.

One of the oldest principles of incarnational ministry is that we must "earn the right to be heard." As one preacher put it: "No one cares how much you know until they know how much you care." Sometimes the most powerful testimony comes from a mouth that is closed long enough to listen to a heart that is open.

Contact work is not about "acting like a teenager."

The key to contact work is not acting like a teenager. Teenagers do not need more peers. They have plenty of peers.

Nor do they need more parents. It is rare that a teenager comments, "Dude, my life would be so much better if I, like, had two or three more parents."

---

[12] Our hearts were "burning within us" too!

The incarnational youth worker is neither a peer nor a parent, but a priest—someone who will share like a peer and care like a parent, but whose great desire is to bring a student into a closer relationship with Jesus. Teenagers do not need adults who act like teenagers. They need adults who will not have a seizure when teenagers act like teenagers.

You cannot build an in-depth relationship with every student on every campus in your community.

Focus your time on building relationships with a few students. No matter how much compassion we have, it is impossible to hug a group of 30 people. They must be embraced one at a time. The genius of team ministry (see chapter 14) is that it allows different people with different personalities and different interests to build real friendships with individual students instead of one person trying to befriend a mob.

Do not be threatened because you seem to be able to relate to some students better than others.

This is normal. The students themselves relate to some students better than to others. A youth worker who is athletic is likelier to have an affinity with students who are more athletic. Likewise, the leader who has musical ability will have a natural rapport with students who are musical.[13] This is nothing to feel weird about. Again, that is why a team of leaders can embrace more students than someone working alone can.

Every conversation does not have to be an in-depth proclamation of the gospel.

The freedom of incarnational ministry is that we are living out our message, fleshing out the Word in the presence of students. That might mean spending an entire afternoon with a group of students and never once directly mentioning Jesus, sin, the Trinity, or hypostatic union.[14]

To be sure, there will be times for specific conversation about spiritual matters. But it is not a lost opportunity or a betrayal of calling simply to be present without making a presentation. Talking with students about their life, their concerns, their areas of interest—that may be the kind of vital ministry that prepares the ground for later sowing of the seed. Of his own incarnational style, Paul wrote, "We loved you so much that we were delighted to share with you not only the gospel of God but our lives as well, because you had become so dear to us" (I Thess. 2:8).

---

[13] Personally, I relate better to kids who are experiencing premature hair loss.

[14] Although this sounds like some hot tip from Dr. Ruth, it is simply a theological phrase used by some to describe the relationship between members of the Trinity.

Learn to love the sinner, even while hating the sin.

Dick was a Young Life leader in the Southeast who had a knack for getting close to students. As we led club together, I was continually amazed at his ability to befriend the kid that everybody else deemed undesirable and—unreachable.

It took me about a year before I realized why I did not seem to be enjoying the same success: it was as if I expected these guys to act like Christians or I was not going to share Christ with them. I wanted students to come to our group, but I wanted them to come on my terms. I had let these kids know verbally and non-verbally that I did not approve of their lifestyle, so their natural assumption was that neither I nor my God could accept someone as sinful as they were. I had to learn how to love these guys without feeling that I was somehow condoning their behavior.

One of the most common barriers to our incarnational ministry among students is that we cannot get beyond their music, their appearance, and their language to see hurting and lonely people who need to be shown the love of Jesus. We cannot embrace someone we are unwilling to touch. This means taking the first step of unconditional love and outreach.

When Jesus approached the Samaritan woman for a drink of water that hot afternoon (John 4:1ff), she was disarmed and surprised. She asked, "'How can you ask me for a drink?' (For Jews do not associate with Samaritans)"(v.9). If we are reaching out to the lepers and outcasts of the high school, we will probably be met with the same skepticism and suspicion. And yet, if we are willing to be flexible enough to accept students as they are, we are likely to find an openness and thirst that runs much deeper than their unattractive behaviors.

An Embrace That Speaks Louder Than Words

Luke offers us a parable of incarnational ministry in an obscure episode we witness from Paul's ministry:

> Seated in a window was a young man named Eutychus, who was sinking into a deep sleep as Paul talked on and on. When he was sound asleep, he fell to the ground from the third story and was picked up dead. Paul went down, threw himself on the young man and put his arms around him. "Don't be alarmed," he said. "He's alive!" Then he went upstairs again and broke bread and ate. After talking until daylight, he left. The people took the young man home alive and were greatly comforted (Acts 20:9–12).

So often discouragement in youth ministry comes through those students who sleep through the sermon, make inappropriate body noises during the Bible study, and giggle during the prayer time. The all-too-common response is to take them "for dead."

This passage reminds us, though, that sometimes a warm hug is more power-ful than a hot talk. Paul's preaching put Eutychus to sleep, but his embrace brought him back to life. That is a principle of which we must never lose sight if we want to disciple teenagers. Sermons and Bible studies and talks are important parts of the nurture process, no doubt about that. But even the most effective preaching is still the Word become word. The triumph of the gospel of Christ is that it is the Word become flesh.

A Ministry of Intention

Undergirding the ministry of Jesus was a clear sense of purpose. As Watchman Nee points out,

> Jesus did not just come to make contacts with men; He came to seek them out and to save them Some Christian workers seem almost devoid of any sense of responsibility; they do not realize the vastness of the field; they do not feel the urge to reach the uttermost ends of the earth with the gospel; they just do their little bit and hope for the best.[15]

Incarnational youth ministry is not just showing attention to students. It is attention to students with an intention for the students. It is building relation-ships with the intention of building disciples.

Dawson Trottman, founder of the Navigators and widely respected as a man effective and fruitful in ministry, recounts an incident that underlines the inten-tion of incarnation—not just seeking, but seeking "to save" (see Luke 19:10). Trottman recalled an incident when he was interviewing prospective candidates for the mission field. Over the course of five days, he spent several hours inter-viewing these candidates, all of them graduates of universities or Bible schools or seminaries. In the course of the interview, Trottman asked what he considered to be a pivotal question: "How many persons do you know by name who were won to Christ by you and are living for him?"

> The majority had to admit that they were ready to cross an ocean and learn a foreign language, but they had not won their first soul who was going on with Jesus Christ. A number of them said they got many people to go to church; others said they had persuaded some to go forward when the invitation was given.

[15] Watchman Nee, *The Normal Christian Worker* (Fort Washington, Penn.: Christian Literature Crusade, 1971), 17.

I asked, "Are they living for Christ now?" Their eyes dropped. I then continued, "How do you expect that by crossing an ocean and speaking in a foreign language with people who are suspicious of you, whose way of life is unfamiliar, you will be able to do there what you have not done here?"

This is not for missionaries and prospective missionaries only. It is for all of God's people. Every one of his children ought to be a reproducer.[16]

Born to Reproduce

Admittedly, Trottman's language may offend some as a bit archaic. We seldom hear this kind of language in the current youth ministry environment where the language of "winning souls" has been replaced by terminology more suited to postmodern sensibilities. Obviously, all of us do not possess the gift of evangelism that so seemed to mark Trottman's ministry. Too, it should be affirmed that no human being can make a Christian. God makes Christians. The best that we as Christians can do is to make disciples. But at the heart of Trottman's question was a central agenda: we are born to reproduce. We are called to fruitfulness, "to bear fruit that will last"(John 15:16).

In his commentary on Matthew 28:19, Matthew Henry remarks,

The treasure of the gospel was committed to them, first, that it might be propagated: "that you should go," *hina hymeis hypagete*—"that you should go as under a yoke or burden, for the ministry is a work, and you that go about it must resolve to undergo a great deal; that you may go from place to place all the world over, and bring forth fruit." They were ordained, not to sit still, but to go about, to be diligent in their work, and to lay out themselves unweariedly in doing good. They were ordained, not to beat the air, but to be instrumental in God's hand for the bringing of nations into obedience to Christ . . . Secondly, that it might be perpetuated; that the fruit may remain, that the good effect of their labors may continue in the world from generation to generation, to the end of time. The church of Christ was not to be a short-lived thing, as many of the sects of the philosophers, that were a nine days' wonder; it did not come up in a night, nor should it perish in a night, but be as the days of heaven.[17]

This is ministry with an intention—not just activity, but productivity.

Several years ago, the *Providence Journal* ran a story under the headline "Big Names to Have Dirty Linen Aired." The article detailed the results of a study done by the state of Massachusetts examining cases in which state funds may have been poorly used. Ironically, the study itself, a two-year project by a special commission,

---

[16] Dawson Trottman, *Born to Reproduce* (Colorado Springs, Colo: NavPress, 1975), 11-13.

[17] Matthew Henry, *Matthew Henry's Commentary on the Whole Bible*, New Modern ed., Electronic Database, c. 1991 by Hendrickson Publishers.

This excerpt is from Dawson Trottman's *Born to Reproduce:*

Twenty-three years ago, we took a born-again sailor, spent some time with him, showing him how to reproduce spiritually after his own kind. It took time, lots of time. It was not a hurried, 30-minute challenge in a church service and a hasty good-bye with an invitation to come back next week. We spent time together and taught him not only to hear God's Word and read it, but also how to study it. We taught him how to fill the quiver of his heart with the arrows of God's Word so that the Spirit of God could lift an arrow from his heart and place it to the bow of his lips and pierce a heart for Christ.

He found a number of boys on his ship, but none of them would go all out for the Lord . . . they were "also-rans." He came to me after a month of this and said, "Dawson, I can't get any of these guys on the ship to get down to business."

I said to him, "Listen, you ask God to give you one. Ask God to give you a man after your own heart."

One day he came to me and said, "I think I've found him." . . . Three months from the time I started to work with him, he had found a man for Christ . . . He worked with this new babe in Christ, and those two fellows began to grow and reproduce. On that ship 125 men found the Savior before it was sunk at Pearl Harbor.

Men off that first battleship are in four continents of the world today as missionaries. The work spread from ship to ship, so that when the Japanese struck at Pearl Harbor, there was a testimony being given on 50 ships of the U.S. fleet. When the war closed, there was work by one or more producers—I'm not talking about mere Christians—on more U.S. fleet ships and at many army camps and air bases.

—*Dawson Trottman,* Born to Reproduce *(Colorado Springs, Colo.: NavPress, 1975), 31.*

cost the state $1.5 million. The results were almost amusing.[18] By the time the report came out, there were a lot of red-faced public servants running for cover.

Among literally hundreds of case studies were these highlights:[19]

> ▶ "The Boston State College 13-story tower, one of the largest buildings ever built by the Commonwealth. Its top five floors, intended as a library, have been shut off since 1976 because the designer failed to include any centralized security checkpoints. Accordingly, the five floors have been

---

[18] Unless, of course, you are a Massachusetts taxpayer.

[19] Loring Swain, "Massachussetts—Big Names to Have Dirty Linens Aired," cited in *Providence Journal, passim.*

heated, air-conditioned, and unused for four years. The college's auditorium is so constructed that one cannot see the stage from the balcony."

▸ "The Haverhill (Mass.) parking deck. It is so poorly designed it can only be demolished and rebuilt." Apparently, part of the problem here was in fitting some cars up the ramp of this magnificent structure!

▸ "The multimillion-dollar University of Massachusetts power plant. It was built too far from the buildings it services—and never used." Given a limited background in civil engineering, it is difficult to imagine what might have gone wrong here. But the imagination leaps at the thought of the architects trying to explain these problems to a university's trustees board.[20]

What diminishes the amusement value of these state-sponsored gaffes is that they are tragically reflective of what goes on consistently in youth ministries everyday. Large amounts of time, money, and energy are spent on programs and structures so that someone can say, "It's the largest ever built." Half the time, however, the finished product cannot even be used. Youth ministry in its current state witnesses far too many "power plants" not delivering power. We are born to reproduce, but we are tragically impotent.

Immediately following some very serious statements about discipleship, Jesus said, "For which one of you, when he wants to build a tower, does not first sit down and calculate the cost, to see if he has enough to complete it? Otherwise, when he has laid a foundation, and is not able to finish, all who observe it begin to ridicule him, saying, 'This man began to build and was not able to finish'" (Luke 14:28–30).

To build the kind of youth ministry program that will accomplish the purpose for which it was built, serious consideration needs to be given to the agenda, the "blueprint." This entails a philosophy of program design.

Philosophy of Programming

How might we develop a youth ministry program that will flesh out the vision to which we have been called? How might we, having taken our reckoning from the compass of mission, chart a course that will lead us to the desired destination? These are questions of *program design*.

In terms of youth ministry, the answer to these questions is predicated on two important concepts, *systemic thinking* and *targeted programming*.

---

[20] Do you go in humble, and say something such as, "Hey, we kind of screwed up a little bit on your power plant . . . and . . . uh . . . er . . . well, we were wondering if you'd mind moving your university over a little bit?" Or do you go in lighthearted, try to sell it as a blooper? "Hey, d'you guys want to hear something funny?" Or do you take a more constructive approach: "What would you guys think about just having your night classes during the day when it is still light outside?"

Systemic Thinking: Youth Ministry as Wind Chime

It may seem strange to think of wind chimes as a metaphor for youth ministry programming, but in fact, the parallels are intriguing. When wind chimes are hung carefully and in proper balance, the notes blend together. But when the chimes are hung carelessly or out of balance, there will likely be a malfunction. There may be sound, but it will be cacophonous—disharmony where there was intended to be harmony—or perhaps monotonous—one note where there were intended to be many. Each chime must be sounded to strike the proper chord. And wind chimes must be positioned where they can catch the breeze, or there will be no sound at all.

Attacking Richmond

Lorne Sanny, one-time president of the Navigators, recounts that back during the Civil War there was a bit of confusion in the high command of the Union Army. It seems that President Abraham Lincoln could not dissuade his generals from launching an attack on Richmond, Virginia. Why the generals had this obsession to capture Richmond is unclear, but Lincoln's generals persisted. Finally, the story goes, Lincoln challenged his strategists with this observation: "Gentlemen, the Confederate Army is not in Richmond! Even if you win in Richmond, all you will do is gain geography." Lincoln continued, "Sirs, I remind you, we are not out to gain geography, we are out to win a war."

Lorne Sanny, Laborers: the Navigators' Mission, and Navigators Daily Walk Devotional Guide *(unknown date and publisher).*

Like a wind chime, any youth ministry program will comprise several different components: programs for outreach, programs for nurture, programs for leadership, and so on. Each of these elements of the program is essential. If any one of them is missing in a program, the result can be monotony (stagnation) or disharmony (lack of unity among the people or the programs involved). The elements must also be in proper balance: a program with all outreach and little nurture leads to a large, shallow ministry; a program of all nurture with little outreach can breed a small, ingrown ministry. Most important, even the most dynamic and balanced youth ministry makes no "joyful noise"—no noise at all, in fact—without the fresh breeze of God's Spirit stirring it to life.

This balance and interdependency of these various elements of a youth ministry program is best described as a system of relationships. Thinking about youth ministry programs this way is called *systemic thinking*.

Systemic thinking is described by Peter Senge as:

a discipline for seeing wholes. It is a discipline for seeing interrelationships rather than things, for seeing patterns of change rather than "static snapshots."

It is a set of general principles distilled over the course of the twentieth centu-ry, spanning fields as diverse as the physical and social sciences, engineering and management . . . And systems thinking is a sensibility—for the subtle intercon-nectedness that gives living systems their unique character. Today, systems thinking is needed more than ever because we are becoming overwhelmed by complexity. Systems thinking is the cornerstone of how learning organizations think about their world.[21]

What insights relevant for youth ministry programming can be gained from the discipline of systems thinking?[22] There are many. Consider these simple principles.

We need to see each facet of the youth ministry program as interconnected.

Individual elements of a program may be complementary, competitive, synergis-tic, or even destructive. Thinking of the program as a system of interconnected elements prevents one facet of the program from working against another.

▸ The discipleship program may be so demanding, or so insular, that it iso-lates the committed students from the very students they need to reach for Christ.

▸ The overall youth ministry programming environment may be so packed and busy that it actually prevents active students from building a healthy relationship with their families.

▸ The demands on members of the youth choir, in effect, may make it almost impossible for those same students to be involved in the regular youth ministry of the church.

▸ A small-group program being planned during the Sunday School hour may begin to compete with the ongoing small-group program developed for the overall youth ministry program.

▸ The Young Life Campaigner meetings on Sunday night might preclude students from being involved in local church youth ministries that osten-sibly are the goal of the Young Life outreach.

Even within a single meeting or ministry event, wise programming seeks to consider how the individual elements combine to build a unified whole.[23] I recall speaking at one weekend event during which the Saturday morning schedule

---

[21] Peter Senge, cited in Brian McLaren, *The Church on the Other Side* (Grand Rapids, Mich.: Zondervan, 2000), 45.

[22] I am indebted for much of what follows to the work of Brian McLaren. See his *The Church on the Other Side*, 45-49.

[23] For example, I've spoken at countless weekend retreats where the Saturday night schedule looked something like this:

7:30–9:00	Large group meeting: Session #3
9:15–9:45	Cabin time/small groups
10:00–12:00	Dance

Now, I am not antidance per se. But when I hang out in the room during these dances I see much that seems to encourage just the opposite ethos from what was created earlier in the evening session. One has to ask: Are these elements of the pro-gram in harmony? Maybe yes, maybe no. But more often than not, my observation of these dances is they sound a completely different chord than the one that was struck by the earlier session.

offered a camp-wide forum on issues of sex and dating. The intent of the session was to look at some of these issues from the standpoint of a Christian worldview. The session took place as scheduled and there was a time of question and answer to wrap it up. But as the group dismissed, the person running the sound cranked up as "walk out" music a song that celebrated—blatantly—values exactly the opposite of those we had been discussing in the session. The last thing students heard as they walked out of that meeting was a message that completely disregarded the message of the meeting. Was the music fun to listen to? Yes. Did the students seem to enjoy the music? Yes. Was it counterproductive to play that music? Absolutely. I was reminded of the fiery preacher railing against alcohol and exhorting his hearers to dump all of their booze in the local stream, who then closed with the old hymn "Shall We Gather by the River."

Wise programming decisions begin by recognizing that every chime must be held in balance to maintain the proper harmony.

The growth of a program can be limited by the program system.

McLaren comments,

> A mouse can grow only to a certain size. Even an elephant can grow only so large. However, both mice and elephants can multiply, so the total biomass of each species has nearly unlimited growth potential. Churches [and youth groups] are a lot like mice and elephants. Some are small; others are big. The potential for growth is unlimited. But as with mice and elephants, sometimes no amount of coaxing can cause a church [or youth group] to grow beyond a certain size. To get more growth, you must either exchange one type for another or have the church [or youth group] multiply, reproducing after its own kind.[24]

One of the common frustrations of growing youth ministries is that they are seeing consistent numerical growth up to a point, but then they seem to hit a wall. There are a number of reasons why a youth ministry might diminish in size or be stagnant in numerical growth[25]. But a systems approach suggests that we look beyond those factors to see if there are systemic issues that prevent further growth. For example,

> ▸ *The program is driven by a charismatic leader who bases his ministry on relationships with key students.* His "success" with the ministry thus far has allowed him to neglect the priority of cultivating a team of adult leaders who can extend the web of relationships. But when the program grows beyond a certain point, it is impossible for the leader to maintain these relationships that have been so central to the program's growth. So the numbers begin to decline.

---

[24] McLaren, *Church on the Other Side*, 46.

[25] For an excellent look at plausible factors, see Len Kageler, *How to Expand Your Youth Ministry* (Grand Rapids, Mich.: Zondervan/Youth Specialties, 1996), especially 43–45.

Imagination and Ministry

By C. McNair Wilson

A man went down from Jericho to Jerusalem and he fell among thorns that sprang up and choked him—or something like that. Were the characters in Jesus's parables real people? Did he know them personally or just make up all those stories?

Doesn't matter.

Those listening had to use their imaginations to see those stories in their mind. They did not have to imagine very hard. Jesus talked to farmers about an ill-fated seed and he told fishing stories to fishermen. To church leaders he related stories about—what else?—money.

Imagination. We all have one. It is in full flower by age three and anthropologists have observed it in every culture they have ever studied. No parent ever had to encourage a child to play or to make up stories with dolls, trucks, or other toys. Jesus's storytelling and flights of imagination continue to this day in virtually every sermon preached that uses illustrations and stories both real and imagined.

The human imagination has propelled humankind to the surface of the moon and the depths of the oceans. Grand scientific breakthroughs have resulted from acts of imagination. In 1956, a year after Jonas Salk invented a vaccine for polio, Albert Sabin had the harebrained idea to put polio in a sugar cube for children to suck on, and Sabin's vaccine is still used worldwide. Albert Einstein imagined riding on a beam of light. This led to his general and special theories of relativity—and shattered all previous notions of space and time.

The invention of photography brought painters the freedom to render their subjects less precisely and ushered in the Impressionist movement. Claude Monet's reimagined "Water Lilies" may be more real than a photograph of the same pond. Monet imagines them, floating but not still, in a shimmering pool. Where photography freezes life, capturing only a fraction of a second, Monet gives us movement, life itself, floating off the canvas and into our minds.

Peter walked on water toward Jesus, an avid water-walker. But when Peter took just a second to think about what he was doing as an act of faith, he couldn't imagine being able to walk on water. His imagination and his faith failed him.

Imagination can be a weapon. Distraught over the ravages of Hitler's evil, J. R. R. Tolkien set out to stand against those horrors. Rather than retelling the particulars of the Nazi war machine, Tolkien crafted a saga that imagined the forces of good in the persons of the Fellowship of the Ring in his epic trilogy *The Lord of the Rings*. Tolkien taught his friend C. S. Lewis that truth can be taught powerfully through works of imagination—fiction and fantasy—Lewis's Chronicles of Narnia were the splendid result. In our day, evil has been imaginatively attacked on Broadway as *The Producers*, Mel Brooks's hilarious and inventive musical comedy that ridicules Hitler in the play-within-a-play "Springtime for Hitler."

Adjectives make the written word more colorful. So, too, the well-practiced sermon comes alive with stories and characters if we will allot time to prepare on our feet and practice out loud. Words alone will not suffice. Friends who pass Chuck Swindoll's office on his study days share that it is not unusual to see him on his feet practicing in front of a large mirror to achieve the precise gesture or facial expression to support and illustrate a key point.

It has long confused me that seminaries do not offer and require courses in acting, oral interpretation, mime, and dance. We are short-changing preachers and teachers of tomorrow in their effectiveness. Along with mandatory chapel attendance, Christian colleges should also require attendance at theatre and dance productions as well as student art gallery offerings and music presentations. Our high schools are largely bereft of the arts, even though students who participate in band, choir, and theatre do better in math than those who don't participate.

As more and more churches enlist their performing artists—especially the growing movement of Christians in theater arts—we can capture the imagination of a world that watches far more than it reads.

Church can never be MTV, but neither should it be a lecture hall for Greek and Hebrew verb tenses. Growing up all my life in a church-going family (I'm an adult child of evangelicals), I went outside the church to be involved in theater as a kid. When I began to doubt some of the "stuff" of what Will Campbell calls "churchianity," I made up stories to illustrate my questions and performed them for friends. My search focused on the incarnation. "What if God became human and walked among us? What if it has already happened?" So began my first one-man play, *The Fifth Gospel*, in which we experience Jesus's life as recounted by those who were there. A woman at a well, a blind man, a boy with a small lunch, and his closest students. At universities from Berkeley to Biola, students laugh, cry, and think hard about a man they only thought they knew. Since 1972, equipped with only a trunk and a broom, I have asked nearly 1,500 church, conference, college, and theater audiences to imagine God come among us. Imagine a hot day in Galilee. The characters stop to cool off in the river and a wonderful water and mud fight erupts, and Jesus, God among us, doesn't win the battle.

The first human being in Scripture to whom God gave the Holy Spirit was not Moses. (I'm certain your Old Testament professor could make a case for Moses having had the Holy Spirit.) No, the first record is in Exodus 31. The person in question was Bezalel. Moses writes that Bezalel was given the Holy Spirit of God for his craftsmanship in working with gold, bronze, and other materials. God also gave the Holy Spirit to Bezalel's two assistants. They were to oversee the building of God's house, the tabernacle in the wilderness. They were artists and not all that they made was symbolic. Much of it was "just" decorative and beautiful.

As ministers, if we do not encourage the imagination of our fellow believers, we will still their spirits, render passions powerless, and make imaginations impotent.

Church buildings should be open around the clock, filled with book and play reading clubs, art classes, dance and drama groups, and Bible studies that are discovering the Truth in Shakespeare, Dickens, and even Harry Potter. The halls of worship should be the home of imaginations at play. Jesus implored us to love our Creator with heart, soul, and imagination. To do less is, well, unimaginable. Think of it—a place where you can go when you can't go anywhere else, and they accept you just as you are.

A man went down from Minneapolis to Chicago, and he had no place to sleep. Seeing a light on in a church and hearing music—though it didn't sound like church music—he poked his head inside. They gave him a cup of hot tea and a grilled cheese sandwich.

"We're baking cookies later," they said. But first, they asked him to grab an instrument and join in their playing. "Welcome, friend. We're the Joyful Noise Music and Baking Club. We meet Monday nights 'cause every room is full the rest of the week."

Imagine that!

▸ *A ministry grows because it is attentive to the needs of individual students.* However, as the ministry grows to a larger size, there is necessarily more focus on "the group" than there is on individuals in the group. As program maintenance takes priority over people maintenance and meeting needs, the numbers begin to decline.

These are all common systemic issues in youth ministry, and a systems approach suggests that unless there is a change in the way a ministry operates—a different "species" of program—there will be the same barriers to growth.

Effective programming requires a consistent infusion of energy.

Entropy, the loss of heat or energy, is a basic law of life. If a system is to be maintained, it needs to be nourished. In a youth ministry, that nourishment might come through innovation, training, financial help, affirmation, new leadership, new students, or all of the above. The key is that nourishment is required for maintenance. The common problem in youth ministry programming (and in other organizations as well) is that, as a group grows, program maintenance becomes more important than program nourishment. That is why numerical growth in a program can be both a bane and a blessing. Yes, the growing group opens up new possibilities and brings in new personnel, both of which provide new infusions of energy. But the growing group also requires more energy, just as an elephant eats more than a mouse. In addition, the tendency of larger groups is to become self-satisfied so they lose their hunger. Or they start to play it safe with regard to creativity and innovation, and so they lose their edge. As one youth minister explained, "When we only had 20 kids, I was more willing to try stuff. If it bombed, it was only a small bomb. When we grew to 150 kids, I became much more cautious, more prone to playing it safe, because if we bombed then, it felt nuclear. There was more fallout." That is the trouble with big animals such as elephants: it is hard to get them to alter their course when necessary, and it can be risky for anybody who gets in the way.

Systems often benefit from diversity.

A wind chime with only one chime, or with eight chimes that all sound the same note, is not going to offer the same harmony as a wind chime properly balanced that sounds eight different notes. Systems thinking reminds us that diversity can bring the kind of strength and flexibility that fosters growth and survival.[26] Amphibious is better than land-only or sea-only. Crop rotation is better for the field than the same crop planted repeatedly every year. Surely this is part of what Paul was referring to in this passage:

---

[26] This is not about seeking diversity simply for the sake of diversity. Diversity in and of itself is not necessarily worth seeking. As I have said before, nobody wants to seek diversity when it comes to landing an airplane. Christian diversity is not about saying that all ideas and approaches are equally valid. It is about saying that within the worldview that sees Christ as Lord of all, there are people of all types, sizes, colors, and ethnicities, and there is much room for variation in styles of worship, music, recreation, art, etc. That is why Paul emphasizes in Galatians 3:28, "There is neither Jew nor Greek, slave nor free, male nor female, for you are all one in Christ Jesus." What the Scripture really celebrates is not diversity, but *university*—different people becoming one in Christ Jesus.

Now the body is not made up of one part but of many. If the foot should say, "Because I am not a hand, I do not belong to the body," it would not for that reason cease to be part of the body. And if the ear should say, "Because I am not an eye, I do not belong to the body," it would not for that reason cease to be part of the body. If the whole body were an eye, where would the sense of hearing be? If the whole body were an ear, where would the sense of smell be? But in fact God has arranged the parts in the body, every one of them, just as he wanted them to be.(1 Cor. 12:14–30)

A youth program with a diversity of leadership (young, old, quiet, rambunctious, athletic, musical, good listener, good speaker, and so on), a diversity of program elements (variations in worship, music, teaching approaches, gaming and recreation, small group meetings, large group meetings), even a diversity of students (skaters, jocks, geeks, church kids, unchurched kids, kids who are new to the ministry, kids who've grown up in the ministry) will probably have greater strength and flexibility than a program that is completely homogeneous and monotone.

A systems approach understands that the youth ministry program is itself a part of a larger system.

This is a critical factor often lost in the single-minded focus of a youth worker.

▸ The congregation's program for elementary-aged children can have a direct impact on the middle school program.

▸ The Young Life leader must recognize that students will graduate from her ministry; she cannot afford *not* to look beyond club.

▸ The congregation that places a strong emphasis on high school ministry must ask, "Where will we assimilate these students *after* high school?"

The danger is that we will be microscopic in our thinking, forgetting that this youth group is part of the larger system of the church, or that this parachurch ministry is part of the larger system of the body of Christ or that this Sunday School ministry is part of a larger program of Christian education that begins with young children, or that this youth ministry is only one facet of this student's larger world that includes family, school, and other outside interests.

As Paul put it,

The eye cannot say to the hand, "I don't need you!" And the head cannot say to the feet, "I don't need you!" On the contrary, those parts of the body that seem to be weaker are indispensable, and the parts that we think are less honorable we treat with special honor. And the parts that are unpresentable are treated with special modesty, while our presentable parts need no special treatment. But God has combined the members of the body and has given greater honor to the parts that lacked it, so that there should be no division in the body, but that its parts should have equal concern for each other. If one part suffers, every part suffers with it; if one part is honored, every part rejoices with it. (I Cor. 12:21–26)

Targeted Programming: The Youth Ministry as a Pyramid

Several years ago, *The Philadelphia Inquirer*[27] ran a profile of an eccentric artist scheduled to exhibit at the Philadelphia Museum of Art. In its portrait of "power artist" Jonathan Borofsky, the reviewer noted that in Borofsky's early years, before his career really become established, he spent day after day in his New York loft apartment doing nothing but counting. That's right; counting: "One, two, three, four," and so on. Borofsky explains that it was an act of near desperation, an attempt to bring some order into his life: "Like a mantra . . . I'd bring all my thinking down to one thought . . . reducing the noise in my head to one simple, clear, poetic, mathematical noise." As time went on, Borofsky became more ambitious in his counting, filling sheets of graph paper with numbers, one number to a square, 200 to 300 numbers to a page, with numbers on both sides of the paper, changing pen colors occasionally to add the artistic touch.

But, alas, as any youth worker surely knows, all creative people face adversities and skepticism, and the Borofsky counting project was no different. At one point, during an argument with his girlfriend, sheets with the first 20,000 numbers were destroyed—four months of artistic genius trashed in a flash of temper. On another occasion, a spasm of creative insight led him to begin affixing minus signs to the numbers, a whim that took him all the way back to minus 12,000 before he regained his forward motion.

The most interesting part of this portrait of Borofsky was one comment made by the artist himself. Reflecting on the moment that he had passed a million after two years of counting, he said, "I thought maybe something would happen in my mind, but nothing. I just kept counting."

What is most remarkable about that statement, other than Borofsky's apparent surprise at this discovery, is that it is a perfect illustration of the kind of frustration and disappointment that comes about when the sole focus of one's ministry is numbers—higher attendance, bigger crowds, constant counting. The tragedy is that this is precisely the focus of many youth ministries. As with David

[27] Edward J. Sozanski, *Philadelphia Inquirer*, October 7, 1984, H01.

Extending McClaren's material to a local youth ministry program, the following are the kinds of questions that might arise from a systems approach:

1. Think of a total youth ministry program as being analogous to a physical body. If we were to categorize the various facets of that youth ministry—outreach, teaching, discipleship, small groups, leadership development, family ministry, administration—using the various systems within a physical body, which would be the muscular system, the nervous system, the skeletal system, the circulatory system, the reproductive system? For example, leadership development might be described as the reproductive system, administration as the skeletal system, teaching as the muscular system, relationships as the circulatory system, etc.

2. Which of these systems are essential for a body to function properly?

3. Using this approach, survey the organs of your specific program, categorizing each element of the program by its system. That is, a Web site that provides calendar information and a vessel for communication might be part of the circulatory system, or the Parents Advisory Board might be part of the skeletal system.

4. Are any of these systems missing, underdeveloped, or overdeveloped in our programming? Which of these systems are the strongest? Which is weakest?

5. Think of an element of the program that had been effective for some time and then ceased to be as effective. In systemic terms, brainstorm about why that program became weak.

6. Think of examples of other program ideas that thrived in other youth ministries, but failed in your own, or vice versa. Why did this happen?

7. Are there any elements of your program where you see real synergy—or competition? Is it clear how the programs are interconnected?

8. How could the elements of your program be better coordinated?

9. What signs of health and wholeness can we celebrate? Are there any symptoms of sickness or dysfunction in this body that need to be addressed?

Brian McLaren, The Church on the Other Side *(Grand Rapids, Mich,.: Zondervan, 2000),* 211-212.

and the army of Israel (2 Sam. 24:10), the troops are numbered, hoping for a sense that certainly God is blessing the enterprise. Like Borofsky, we vainly hope that at some point something will happen. "But nothing." Even more tragically, like Borofsky, a lot of youth ministries "just keep counting."

There is a certain attraction to the kind of program that draws big crowds and features week after week of fun, high-visibility events. Once the machinery is in place, these programs assume their own momentum. As Borofsky puts it, you reduce it all down to "one, simple, clear, poetic, mathematical noise." But this approach demonstrates a clear contrast between what might be described as a *program-oriented* approach and a *person-oriented* approach.[28] The primary difference between the two might be described in terms of focus: the emphasis with one approach is building a program; the emphasis with the other is building people.[29] Consider the following chart (Table 13-1).

Table 13-1.
Contrast Between Program-Centered and People-Centered Approaches

Program-Centered Approach	People-Centered Approach
Goal is a good program	Goal is building disciples
Starts with ideas	Starts with needs of kids
Success judged by attendance	Success judged by spiritual growth
Success judged by activity	Success judged by productivity
Produce faster results	Produces lasting results

Sound programming begins with a thorough assessment of the target group. This is a step often neglected at great expense in time and energy. Group profiles can be assessed by preparing surveys that the youth respond to, or through one-on-one conversations, or by providing opportunities for group members to collectively evaluate themselves. The key here is to listen. Keep the proverbial ear to the ground. Probe. Watch. Talk with parents, volunteer leaders, and church officials. Almost as important as clarity of destination ("Where are we going?") is clarity of departure point ("Where are we now?")

Larry Richards, in his classic work *Youth Ministry: Its Renewal in the Local Church*,[30] refers to three broad categories of involvement[31] that can be helpful as criteria for evaluating a youth group: *Bible*, *Life*, and *Body* (see Figure 13-1). They can be

---

[28] These terms have been around for a long time. One of the first to make this distinction in these terms was Pat Hurley, *Penetrating the Magic Bubble* (Wheaton, Ill.: Victor Books, 1982), 12–17.

[29] This distinction may sound a bit caricatured. It is not meant to suggest that those with a more program-oriented approach are not interested in building disciples. But there is a clear difference between the two in basic programming methodology. I was interviewing one time for a position at a large evangelical church with a relatively well-known pastor. When I told him that I wanted to model my ministry on Ephesians 4:11–15 and focus on spiritual reproduction, he said simply, "Yeah, that's a great passage, but that won't work here." It is a comment reminiscent of Eugene Peterson's complaint that we have given up being pastors to become program directors. Eugene Peterson, *Under the Unpredictable Plant: An Exploration of Vocational Holiness* (Grand Rapids, Mich.: Eerdmans, 1994), 172–173.

[30] Larry Richards, *Youth Ministry: Its Renewal in the Local Church* (Grand Rapids, Mich.: Zondervan, 1970).

[31] Richards refers to these as "process elements." Ibid.

depicted as three overlapping rings of programming, each spotlighting a broad area of concern and focus.

Bible. What is the group's exposure to and comprehension of biblical truth: its main themes, the basic flow of its redemptive story, its general layout (history, poetry, wisdom literature, didactic writing, pastoral epistles, apocalyptic literature) as well as its content? Part of the assessment here will be students' abilities to read and discern Scripture for themselves.

Figure 13-1.
Richards' Three Process Elements

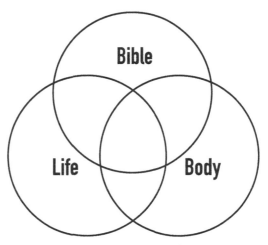

Source: Larry Richards, *Youth Ministry: Its Renewal in the Local Church* (Grand Rapids, Mich.: Zondervan, 1970).

Life. The second area of concern is the task of building disciples who can take Truth into their marketplace, into their schools, on their dates, into their interpersonal relationships, into their evaluations of media messages through video, TV, movies, and music. Responsible discipleship means taking seriously the mission implications of the gospel. In what sense are they taking responsibility for bringing healing to their world at hand, as well as to the world at large?

Body. This third area assesses the group's response to the communal dimensions of the gospel—affirming one another, holding one another accountable, encouraging one another, stimulating one another to love and good works (Heb. 10:24–25).

What this assessment admits is that, within any given youth ministry setting, the students involved will be at varied levels of commitment and spiritual maturity. Ideally, they would all be eager disciples, ready to grow, thirsty for Bible study, asking if they could please borrow your Bible dictionary and concordance for the weekend. But realistically there will be some students who are truly committed, some who are moderately committed, some who are neutral in their commitment, some who are moderately uncommitted, some who are radically uncommitted, and some who just need to be committed before they harm someone. As missiologist Richard Peace rightly observes, "There are various levels of Christian commitment."[32]

Commonly, missiologists describe these levels of commitment in terms of the Engel Scale (see Figure 13-2).[33] This is a scale that James Engel developed, in part to understand how and why people respond to the gospel. Essentially, it is an assessment tool because it codifies and defines levels of spiritual response so that the message and programming will scratch where the target audience itches.

Richard Peace has offered a variation of this same idea by dividing the spiritual pilgrimage into three phases: The *Quest Phase*, the *Commitment Phase*, and the *Integration Phase* (see Figure 13-3).[34] While these phases are self-explanatory, for the most part, the following is a description of how just one phase—the Commitment Phase—might be fleshed out in a youth group setting:

Shane is committed to Breakaway (the Friday night Senior High outreach). He wouldn't think of missing it. But neither would he miss the Saturday night party circuit every week. He is committed to an event on Friday nights, but his behavior on Saturday nights indicates less of *a commitment to Christian ethics*. Jill would never think of going to the Saturday night parties. She thinks the casual sex is stupid and that drugs are dangerous. Anyway, she wouldn't feel right lying to her Mom and Dad if they asked where she has been all night. It has nothing to do with a relationship with God; she just feels this is a matter of love and integrity. In other words, *she affirms some elements of Christian ethics, but she is not, in any sense, affirming Christian doctrine about Jesus's Lordship*, and so on. Jamal is committed to the doctrines of Christianity. The doctrines are "truth" for him. But he manages to compartmentalize those beliefs so that *they have little impact on his personal life* through the week. Erica, a volunteer leader, is deeply compassionate, very involved in the ministry, and *cares deeply for the students, but she really feels no sense of urgency with regard to Christianity*. For her, it all comes down to just trying to love people. Finally, there is Juan, one of those kids who holds Christian beliefs, tries to live by Christian ethics, is active in the youth group and involved in the monthly work projects, but he *seems to have no real personal relationship with Jesus*.

Here are five individuals. Surely God is at work in all of them, but clearly each of them is at a different place in terms of commitment and noncommitment.[35] Targeted programming takes these differences seriously.

---

[32] Richard Peace, *Pilgrimage: A Handbook on Christian Growth* (Grand Rapids, Mich.: Baker Books, 1976), 65.

[33] See James Engel and Ted Ward, *What's Gone Wrong with the Harvest?* (Old Tappan, N.J.: Fleming H. Revell, 1975), 45.

[34] Peace, *Pilgrimage*, 39.

[35] Peace goes on to add that "No matter how the process takes place, Christian pilgrimage demands commitment in at least five areas. There is commitment to Christian ideas, to Christian ethics, to the Christian community, to people in general, and to Jesus as a Person. If there is a lack of commitment in any one of these broad areas, this could well be the obstacle that is stymieing further Christian growth." Ibid., 65.

Figure 13-2.
The Engel Scale

God's Role	Communicator's Role		Man's Response
General Revelation		-8	Awareness of Supreme Being
Conviction	Proclamation	-7	Some Knowledge of Gospel
		-6	Knowledge of Fundamentals of Gospel
		-5	Grasp of Personal Implications of Gospel
		-4	Positive Attitude Toward Act of Becoming a Christian
	Proclamation	-3	Problem Recognition and Intention to Act
		-2	Decision to Act
		-1	Repentance and Faith in Christ
Regeneration			**New Creature**
Sanctification	Follow-up	+1	Post-decision Evaluation
		+2	Incorporation Into Church
	Cultivation	+3	Conceptual and Behavioral Growth
			• Communion with God • Stewardship • Internal Reproduction • External Reproduction
		•	
		•	
		•	
		Eternity	

Source: James Engel and Ted Ward, *What's Gone Wrong with the Harvest?* (Old Tappan, N.J.: Fleming H. Revell, 1975), 45.

Six Levels of Commitment

One of the common ways of conceptualizing these levels of commitment is in terms of a pyramid-type concept (see Figure 13-5).[36] Essentially, each level in the pyramid depicts varying levels of Christian commitment: the higher the level on the pyramid, the higher the level of commitment. What follows is a short profile of each level of commitment.

Pool of Humanity. This level of the pyramid represents the teenage population in general, the teenagers within a given geographical area. A particular group may not, in fact, have any influence on those students at the present time. Indeed, the vast majority of this population probably does not even know the ministry exists. The ministry, however, cannot afford to be unaware of these students. This is the field in which the seed is to be planted. It is out of concern for these students that a wise youth worker must begin the programming task with a careful exegesis of the local youth culture, an assessment of the local pool of humanity.[37]

Come Level. Jon is one of those students who never shows up for prayer breakfast or Sunday School and always seems to have unavoidable conflicts that prevent his helping out with fund-

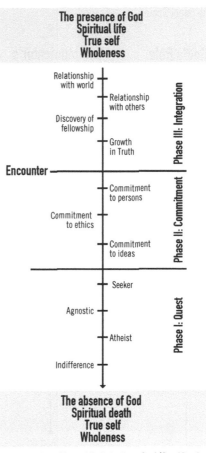

Figure 13-3.
Peace's Three Phases of Christian Pilgrimage

Source: Richard Peace, *Pilgrimage: A Handbook on Christian Growth* (Grand Rapids, Mich.: Baker Books, 1976), 65.

raisers and work projects. The picture is not completely negative, though. There are two areas for which Jon has shown tremendous interest and zeal: one is food and the other is girls. Whenever a youth group activity allows for a large selection of either, you can count on Jon to be there! Jon does not make any pretense about it. He does not have any real commitment to Christ, but he does have a strong commitment to having a good time.

---

[36] Despite the pyramid shape that suggests biblical, Near-Eastern origins of this model, it is not clear who was the first to develop this model. For a classic examination of the ministry of multiplication as it was played out in Jesus's ministry, see Robert Coleman, *The Master Plan of Evangelism* (Old Tappan, N.J.: Fleming H. Revell, 1963). Coleman describes Jesus's ministry as an intentional process that involved seven stages: Selection, Association (Incarnation), Consecration, Impartation, Demonstration, Delegation, and Supervision.

[37] See chapter 9. This information, and other social and religious data about the local youth population, will affect programming decisions. Sometimes, precisely these factors are at play when a programming approach which may have been very effective in Tacoma or Tallahassee bombs when it is used in Topeka (and vice versa).

The figure below shows the organizational structure of The Navigators, the parachurch ministry founded by Dawson Trottman. The Navigators' cycle of ministry is organized in slightly different terms, but with the same general emphasis on targeted programming (note the training objectives and ministry focus specified for each stage).

Figure 13-4.
The Navigator's Cycle of Ministry

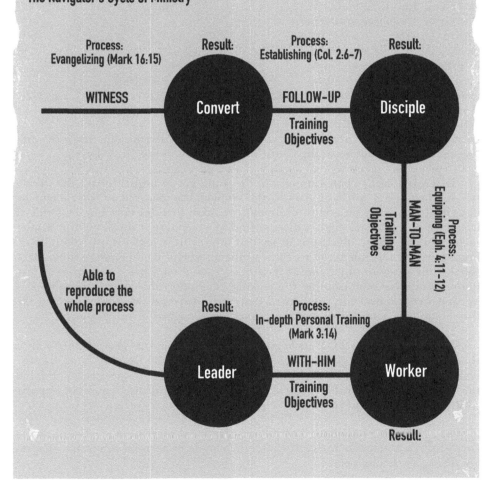

There are students like Jon in the orbit of virtually every youth ministry. Their commitment might be best described as a Come Level commitment. Their only commitment to the group is to *come* when the group is doing something they like—something fun or entertaining.

Grow Level. Students at the Grow Level are students within the program environment who are willing to submit themselves to, or at least tolerate, spiritual growth. These are those students who take part in a youth activity, even if it involves them in some amount of Bible study or spiritual input. Essentially, that is the difference between students at the Come Level and kids at the Grow Level.

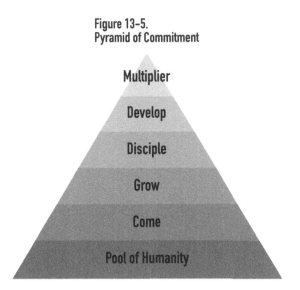

Figure 13-5.
Pyramid of Commitment

Multiplier

Develop

Disciple

Grow

Come

Pool of Humanity

Disciple Level. When a student in the youth group begins to take the initiative for his or her spiritual growth, this student has matured to what might be described as a Disciple Level commitment. We have already examined the kinds of characteristics that one might expect to find in a teenager at this level of commitment (see chapter 4). Suffice it to say that the key here is the word "discipline." Students at the Disciple Level are those willing to discipline themselves—to do personal Bible study on their own, practice spiritual disciplines on their own, take upon themselves responsibility for seeking out opportunities for fellowship and worship. Programmatically, the role of the youth worker at this stage is to provide instruction and tools for students to pursue their spiritual development.

Develop Level. As students begin to advance in spiritual growth, they will in time move into the next level of commitment. Teens at the Develop Level are students willing to take the initiative not only for their own spiritual growth, but for the spiritual growth of others as well. In short, they are willing to own the responsibility of spiritual reproduction.

Why is this so important? For the very simple reason that the goal of the ministry is to reach students for Christ, and the people best suited to reach teenagers are teenagers themselves.

▸ First of all, this is a notion rooted in sound theology (the priesthood of all believers).[38]

▸ Secondly, it is rooted in common sense. Were I, for example, to walk into the lunch room at Connestoga High School, near Eastern University, and sit at a table of eleventh graders, the students would immediately recognize me as an adult. It is highly unlikely they would point in my direction and say, "Who's the new kid? And what happened to his hair?"

That does not mean adults cannot be on campus or hang out with teenagers. They can and they should. That is incarnational ministry. But what it does mean is that when those adults are around teenagers they are automatically suspect *because they are adults*.[39] In that sense, teenagers have one less barrier to cross. It is what missionaries refer to as *indigenous ministry*, ministry done by members of the population that is targeted by the ministry.

▸ There is also the very pragmatic consideration that any nonteaching adult may have difficulty gaining access to the campus, whereas the students themselves have to get permission to get off campus.

▸ Students involved in a youth ministry will also be in daily contact with teenagers who otherwise would likely have no other contact with any person, program, or place related to that ministry.

▸ Finally, there is the simple mathematical reality that one adult and one student (or two or three) can reach more people than one adult. This is why Paul directed Timothy to a *ministry of multiplication* (see Figure 13-6). "And the things you have heard me say in the presence of many witnesses entrust to reliable men who will also be qualified to teach others" (2 Tim. 2:2).

One of the tragic mistakes of youth ministry has been to focus on a ministry of addition, falling into the trap of "Borofskyism"—counting and adding, when the call is to multiplying.[40]

Multiplier Level. The final level of commitment is that point at which students begin to catch a vision for going back into their own middle and high schools to start the process over, reproducing it in the lives of their friends or classmates. When students are moved to this level of commitment, the ministry has been multiplied in much the same way that Paul multiplied his ministry by pouring himself into Timothy and other early church leaders.[41]

---

[38] See chapter 12, particularly the section "Essential Number Two: Calling Students to Service."

[39] Kids look at a guy like me and think, "Of course, you're interested in God. You're old; you're going to die soon. When I get to be your age, I'll be interested in the afterlife too!"

[40] It is very important to mention here that the Develop Level of any lasting youth ministry must include both youth and adults. These youth and adults are people with whom the youth worker can begin to do a focused work of training and equipping for ministry. Equally important, the Develop Level comes after the Disciple Level, and not the reverse. We already have far too many youth and adults in church leadership who, perhaps unwittingly, have assumed responsibility for the spiritual growth of others, but have not demonstrated any willingness to take responsibility for their own spiritual growth. That is not the pattern we are given in 1 Timothy 3 and other passages where Paul writes about spiritual leadership. This is a particularly easy trap to fall into in youth ministry because we are occasionally confronted with students and would-be volunteers who have all kinds of leadership ability but little spiritual maturity. One of the basic laws of biology is that *like begets like*. If the hope is to reproduce growing Christians, reproduction must be done by growing Christians.

[41] These same levels are described with slightly different nomenclature by Kurt Johnson, *Controlled Chaos: Making Sense of Junior High Ministry* (Cincinnati, Ohio: Standard Publishing, 2001), 80-81.

Grow Level Commitment: Two Important Observations

First, willingness to grow is not the same thing as commitment to growth. Students at the *Grow Level* are not seeking spiritual growth on their own initiative. They will come to Club on Wednesday night, or take part in Sunday evening meetings, but only because it requires little more than their passive involvement. We should not assume that a teenager at a weekly Young Life club or a midweek Bible study is hungry for spiritual food and willing to take the initiative to get it.

That is an important consideration with regards to programming. That is not to say Bible study should be dismissed in favor of "fun and games." It is to say that attention must be given to providing Bible study opportunities that incite student interest and invoke active participation. Being in the same room is not the same as being on the same page.

Second, consistent attendance is not an indication of consistent commitment. I did not understand the *Grow Level* commitment early on in my ministry with students. I misinterpreted a student's strong commitment to me or to the program as being a strong commitment to Christ. That was a delusion clearly exposed when one of my most active students graduated from high school, went away to college, and almost immediately made an apparently conscious decision to abandon all principles of Christian living.

A common mistake of youth ministers is to assume that just because students are involved in spiritual activity, they are personally involved in spiritual growth. It is wonderful that students are willing to submit themselves to spiritual growth, but one should not mistakenly assume that this means they will automatically, of their own initiative, develop a pattern of continued growth and fellowship following graduation.

For a glimpse of this process being played out in the ministry of Paul and the apostles, consider the diagram in Figure 13-7 created by missiologist David Hesselgrave.

To think more practically about how these levels of commitment play out in a youth ministry program, it may be helpful to invert the pyramid, to conceptualize it as more of a funnel (see Figure 13-8). Conceptualized this way, the intentionality of programming becomes more visible. For a youth program to be well-balanced, able to accomplish the purpose for which it was designed, there must be some type of formal or informal programming that will meet the needs of students at each of these various levels of commitment (see Figure 13-9). There need to be Come Level programs, geared to the student who is "not into God at all,"

Figure 13-6.
Chain of Multiplication

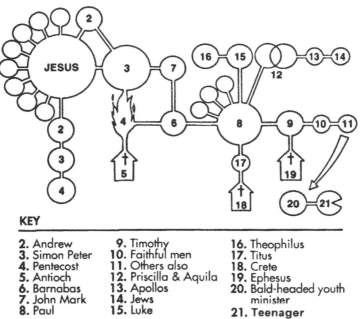

KEY

2. Andrew	**9.** Timothy	**16.** Theophilus
3. Simon Peter	**10.** Faithful men	**17.** Titus
4. Pentecost	**11.** Others also	**18.** Crete
5. Antioch	**12.** Priscilla & Aquila	**19.** Ephesus
6. Barnabas	**13.** Apollos	**20.** Bald-headed youth
7. John Mark	**14.** Jews	minister
8. Paul	**15.** Luke	**21.** Teenager

Source: Waylon B. Moore, *Multiplying Disciples: The New Testament Method of Church Growth*, Colorado Springs: Navpress; (June 1, 1981)

and there need to be programs that will motivate the forward progress and growth of those at the Grow, Disciple, and Develop Levels.

There are numerous variations of this way of conceptualizing a youth ministry program. Probably the most prominent is the configuration designed by Doug Fields in his book *Purpose-Driven Youth Ministry*. In Fields' design (see Figure 13-10), he makes the same distinctions between various levels of commitment and demonstrates the same clear intention of moving students to deeper places of involvement and spiritual maturity.[42]

The necessity of this kind of evaluation is that it exposes where a particular youth program is overweight and where it is underweight, for what kinds of students programming has been sufficient, and perhaps, what levels of commitment have been inadvertently ignored. This is where the hard decisions of person-oriented ministry are played out. This is where the calling impacts the calendar, where mission meets ministry, where purpose shapes program.

With the pyramid and funnel concepts clearly in view, three important programming implications become apparent.

[42] Doug Fields, *Purpose-Driven Youth Ministry* (Grand Rapids, Mich.: Zondervan/Youth Specialties, 1998), 96–97.

While there are any number of ways to highlight the different impact of two approaches, consider this one. A poor college student was offered the choice between a one-time gift of $1,000,000 or the gift starting at one penny on the first day and doubling every day over a 30-day period. Because the college student was poor, desperate, and not particularly astute at accounting, he took the $1,000,000. Not a bad deal, but had he been patient enough to wait, he would have had $10,734,699.99!

The No Target-Low Aim Principle. When there is no intended target group, the tendency is to program for the lowest common denominator.

Everyone is familiar with this expression: "If you aim at nothing, you will hit it every time." This principle is a corollary of that statement as it is played out in youth ministry programming. What typically happens in a youth ministry not targeted and intentional in its programming is that there is one meeting a week, and that meeting is open to every student willing to show up. But therein lies the problem: a program that is targeted at no one is likely to meet no one's needs.

Consider the following case study:

Jake showed up for Sunday night youth group prepared to lead the group in a program that consisted of a snack, a brief game or ice-breaker, worship, and a short Bible study with small-group discussion. Had all of the students in attendance been Grow Level or deeper in commitment, that might have worked out. But, after only a few minutes of worship, it was clear that the Come Level students had no intention of owning Jake's agenda. During the Bible study, the disruptions and discipline problems grew worse. Jake did not want to ask these students to leave—after all, these were the students he and his team wanted to reach. On the other hand, some Grow and Disciple Level students were really eager to learn and participate, and the disruptions were making that impossible.

After several friendly and not-so-friendly pleas for the Come Level students to cease being disruptive, Jake reasoned that he would really have to play to the Come Level students. He knew that if the Disciple Level students were bored, they would at least be bored politely. He was concerned that if he bored the Come Level students, they might begin taking hostages. So he decided to dumb down the study, making it shorter and more shallow than he had planned. By the time he was nearing the end, he decided to cut the discussion time altogether.

The evening ended with the Come Level students feeling bored and disenfranchised, the Grow and Disciple Level students feeling frustrated, and

Figure 13-7.
Hesselgrave's Pauline Cycle of Ministry

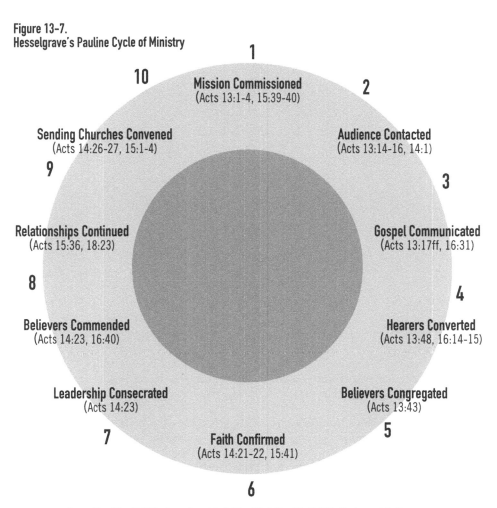

1
Mission Commissioned
(Acts 13:1-4, 15:39-40)

10

2

Sending Churches Convened
(Acts 14:26-27, 15:1-4)

9

Audience Contacted
(Acts 13:14-16, 14:1)

3

Relationships Continued
(Acts 15:36, 18:23)

Gospel Communicated
(Acts 13:17ff, 16:31)

8

4

Believers Commended
(Acts 14:23, 16:40)

Hearers Converted
(Acts 13:48, 16:14-15)

Leadership Consecrated
(Acts 14:23)

Believers Congregated
(Acts 13:43)

7

5

Faith Confirmed
(Acts 14:21-22, 15:41)

6

Source: Adapted from David Hesselgrave, *Communicating Christ Cross-Culturally* (Grand Rapids, Mich.: Zondervan, 1978), 58-59.

Jake considering a career in telemarketing. He had just wasted a night trying unsuccessfully to entertain one group of students and trying unsatisfactorily to nurture another group of students. Because he had not targeted his programming carefully, he was playing to the lowest common spiritual denominator. He had aimed at nothing, and he had hit it dead on.

The writer of Hebrews 5:12-13 implies that people at different stages of spiritual maturity require different types of spiritual nutrition (that is, programming). Programming should be designed in such a way that both leaders and students understand what level of nutrition is on the menu. This can be addressed:

Figure 13-8.
Funnel of Programming

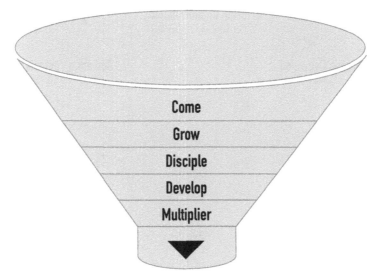

▸ in the way events and activities are publicized (see the Covenant Group Handout in Figure 13-11);

▸ by making the students aware of these various levels of commitment and explaining that every program, every activity has an intention; and

▸ by building requirements into certain upper-level programs so that less-mature students *exempt themselves*[43] from involvement.

Programming for spiritual growth is not one size fits all. Intentional programming will design an event, activity, weekend retreat, or lesson for a target group—and then will work hard to make certain that those students are the ones who attend.

The Law of Spiritual Commitment. *As commitment increases, attendance decreases.* One of the intriguing marks of Jesus's own ministry is that the more he asked in terms of commitment, the fewer people responded to his call. Five thousand people came out to get fed by Jesus (Matt. 14:14–21), but considerably fewer were willing to follow him to Jerusalem, or ultimately to Golgotha. If this was true of Jesus's

---

[43] This is very important. This is *not* the youth leader telling some students that they are not suited to a program. It is designing the program intentionally in such a way that only students to whom it is targeted will want to be there. Having said that, if a Come Level student comes to a Grow Level activity and becomes disruptive, the youth leader must assume the responsibility of (1) not allowing that student to deter the growth of other students, and (2) not catering to that lower common spiritual denominator—even if it means lower numbers in attendance. See the Covenant Group Handout (Figure 13-11).

Figure 13-9.
Targeted Programming Addresses Every Level of Commitment

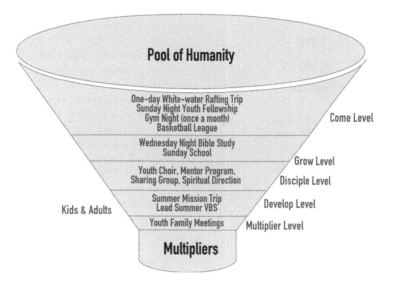

ministry, it will quite likely be true of any ministry faithful to him. The more asked of students in terms of commitment, the fewer students will respond.

I am amazed, and mildly amused, when youth workers question me with genuine sincerity complaining, "I don't understand it. We got 40 kids out to our swim and ski party at the lake last week. But then we followed up this week with a Bible study about Jesus walking on the water, and only four kids showed up—and two of them thought we were going skiing again." I want to say, "Welcome to the world! Kids like swimming better than they like studying the Bible!" That is reality. That is why the funnel is shaped like a funnel—wide at the top, narrow at the bottom (see Matt. 7:13–14).

Why is this such an important programming concept? Because if programming is solely evaluated on the basis of attendance, as is so commonly the case, there will almost always be a tendency to cultivate the shallow. It is axiomatic: if a ministry aims for big, it will almost never grow deep, because *deep does not draw a crowd*—at least, not initially. A Disciple Level program that is really helping to build stronger believers may not draw the crowds that a high visibility Come Level program will. But in reality the Disciple Level program may be a much more vital part of the youth ministry environment. That is why the multiplication concept is so important. It affirms that by going deep with "a few faithful" people, many more can be reached in the long term.

Figure 13-10.
Fields' Top-Down View of the Funnel

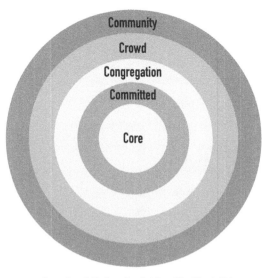

Source: Doug Fields, *Purpose-Driven Youth Ministry* (Grand Rapids, Mich.: Zondervan/Youth Specialties, 1998), 96–97.

That is why, although at first glance it may not seem so, good stewardship would suggest that investing money and time in a small number of committed students will be a wiser investment that money invested in a large number of uncommitted students. These students and programs at the Disciple and Multiplier Levels are the bread and butter of ministry. That does not mean the Come Level program should be neglected. It does mean that when a ministry is putting a huge amount of energy into programs that bring in large numbers and high visibility, it may be "capturing Richmond"—and losing the war.[44]

The Importance of the "Unspiritual." When I was a youth pastor, a parishioner in one of my congregations invariably complained whenever we did an activity that she considered "unspiritual." There was no activity she felt was more unspiritual than our Sunday afternoon Ultimate Frisbee extravaganzas. She felt it was a waste of time, a violation of the Sabbath, and she complained that when I played without my shirt on I was frightening some of the neighborhood children.

The showdown finally came one Sunday morning following worship when she cornered me in the hallway and said, "Duffy, you didn't go to seminary to learn how to throw a Frisbee."[45] Of course, what she was really saying was, "This congregation did not call you as youth pastor so that you could teach kids in the community how to throw a Frisbee." While she was absolutely correct in that assumption, she was mistaken in her basic premise—that somehow one activity (teaching kids to throw a Frisbee) was completely disconnected to the other activity (helping students to live for Christ).

Had this dear woman understood the funnel of programming, she might well have been able to understand that, in the right program environment, even the "unspiritual" activities have very legitimate spiritual goals. After all, the most

[44] Lorne Sanny recounts that during the Civil War, President Abraham Lincoln could not dissuade the Union generals from attacking the Confederate capital, Richmond. Finally, the story goes, Lincoln challenged his strategists: "Gentlemen, the Confederate Army is not in Richmond! Even if you win in Richmond, all you will do is gain geography... Sirs, I remind you, we are not out to gain geography, we are out to win a war." Lorne Sanny, *Laborers: The Navigators' Mission, and Navigators Daily Walk Devotional Guide* (publisher and date unknown).

[45] Technically, this was true. I really honed my Frisbee skills in college. In seminary, I worked more on racquetball.

Figure 13-11.
Covenant Group Handout

THE

Covenant

GROUP

Covenant *(Kuv'e-nant)*, n. a written agreement; a deed; a free promise of God's blessing; a solemn agreement of fellowship and faith between members of a church.

YOU ARE INVITED to be part of an experiment in spiritual adventure . . . not something for everybody . . . a challenge . . . an exercise in commitment and faith . . . a solemn agreement of fellowship and faith between members of Christ's body!

The **COVENANT GROUP** is simply a group of people who are willing to make a 13-week agreement or covenant with each other that they will genuinely seek to (a) grow in their relationships with Christ individually, and (b) grow in their relationships with each other as a group. In the last year there have been a number in our UMYF who point to the Covenant Group as the most meaningful experience they have had in their walks with Christ.

The Covenant Group *IS NOT* some kind of "spiritual Green Berets" or "Superheroes"—it is a group of people serious about making a 13-week commitment to maintain certain disciplines. Basically, those in the Covenant Group are 9th-12th-graders who are willing to make a "solemn agreement" to:

(1) Consistently attend *CORNERSTONE* and *BREAK-AWAY* each week. In addition, Covenanters must attend a special retreat (no cost to you) on May 11-12, 1984.

(2) Attend a weekly Tuesday morning breakfast at church before school beginning at 6:30. The first breakfast will be on Tuesday morning, January 24. You will be expected to be at the breakfast consistently and *ON TIME* (please note this).

(3) Practice the discipline of a daily Quiet Time *and* bring with you each Tuesday morning an entry into a Quiet Time Diary or personal spiritual journal to be kept during the nine weeks.

(4) Enroll in the "Onward Bound" Program. Information available from Youth Office.

If you wish to make such a commitment or covenant, sign here and return this entire sheet to Duffy. It will be returned to you at our first prayer and sharing breakfast on Tuesday morning, January 24, 6:30.

_____
NAME

spiritually intensive program in the world does not do anyone any good if students will not take part in it. Students cannot become multipliers if they cannot be developed, and they cannot be developed if they cannot be discipled, and they cannot be discipled if someone does not help them to grow. It is impossible to help them to grow if they are not first willing to come. We cannot embrace those who remain beyond our reach. Which is why, sometimes, the most spiritual activity we can do with a student is something apparently *un*spiritual—building the relationship and breaking down the defenses.[46]

> J. C. Ryle, an Anglican bishop of the eighteenth century, observes,
>
> The ways by which the Holy Spirit leads men and women to Christ are wonderful and mysterious. He is often beginning in a heart a work that shall stand for eternity, when an onlooker observes nothing remarkable.
>
> In every work there must be a beginning, and in spiritual work that beginning is often very small.
>
> Do we see a careless brother coming to church and listening to the gospel after a long indifference? When we see such things let us remember Zacchaeus.
>
> Let us not look coldly on such a person because his motives are at present very poor and questionable. It is far better to hear the gospel out of curiosity that not to hear it at all.
>
> Our brother is with Zacchaeus in the tree! Who can tell but that one day he may receive Christ just as joyfully? . . . It may be difficult to see how salvation can result from a man climbing a tree. That's because you see a man in a tree, but God sees a man lost and searching.[47]

Methodology Without a Method

It may strike some as disappointing to meet the end of a chapter on programming without having been exposed to a specific programming approach. But, this is based on three important summary principles:

---

[46] Theologically, this notion of an *un*spiritual activity is suspect to begin with. To suggest that some activities are spiritual while others are not is to breed an unholy compartmentalization between everyday discipleship and everyday life. Paul's exhortation in Colossians 3:23 suggests that all of our activities should be done with the end in mind of God's glory.

[47] J. C. Ryle, cited in *Daily Walk* (Atlanta, Ga.: Walk Thru the Bible, 1993).

Declining Numbers of Those Responding to Jesus's

5,000	Jesus fed them (Matt. 14:14–21).
70	Jesus commissioned others to go out in twos in preparatory ministry (Luke 10:1–17).
12	Jesus appointed twelve (Mark 3:14).
3	Peter, James, and John, appear to be ad hoc inner circle (Matt. 17:1, Mark 5:37, Mark 14:33, and with Andrew, Mark 13:3).
1	Only one disciple is mentioned on the scene at the Cross (John 19:26).

When it comes to programming for ministry, there is no one right way.

Programming strategies[48] continue to evolve and emerge as youth workers seek to reach teenagers for Christ. There are more than ample means for accessing these excellent ideas and strategies.[49] There is no *one* right approach.

There are foundational principles that seem to recur in sound programming philosophies, and many of the programming approaches that have proven themselves fruitful seem to share a number of common elements.[50] But as Paul noted (1 Cor. 12:4–6), "There are different kinds of gifts, but the same Spirit. There are different kinds of service, but the same Lord. *There are different kinds of working, but the same God works all of them in all men* (emphasis added)."

No method is sacred.

We are called to be faithful to a message. How we communicate that message changes continually. The apostle Paul commented "To the Jews I became like a Jew, to win the Jews. To those under the law I became like one under the law (though I myself am not under the law), so as to win those under the law" (1 Cor. 9:20).

David tried to fight in Saul's helmet and breastplate and "could not, for he was not used to them" (1 Sam. 17:38–39). Sometimes, when we try to take someone else's program and use it in our ministry, it just does not work because we are trying to fight in someone else's armor. Some fight with armor, and some fight with a sling. But all of us are called above all to be faithful to the fight in whatever way God has equipped us.

---

[48] Mark Senter's article, "Is the SonLife Strategy the Strategy of Jesus? Replicating Dann Spader's Study of a Harmony of the Gospel," *Journal of Youth Ministry* 1, no. 1 (fall 2002): 23–48; and Spader's Response, "A Response to Senter's 'Is the SonLife Strategy the Strategy of Jesus?' *Journal of Youth Ministry* 1, no. 1 (fall 2002): 49–56, provide a wonderful and stimulating discussion of just this point.

[49] For links to several hundred Web sites with widely ranging programming resources, go to www.youthspecialties.com.

[50] Many of these principles have been addressed in this chapter.

In his book *Don't Sleep Through the Revolution*, Paul Rees put it well:

The changeless message (of the gospel of Jesus Christ) in terms of its communication, must take account of the radically altered context in which communication is being made. This is biblical, Pauline, Christian . . . If you are centrally sound in message and motive, you can afford to be unorthodox in methodology. You can afford to break with old patterns. You can afford to innovate.[51]

The danger of promoting a programming approach is that it may lead to idolatry, and a focus on mechanics over the Master.

Consider these wise words from Richard Halverson, a man whose experienced was seasoned by years of pastoral experience before he went on to become chaplain of the U.S. Senate:

God calls a man . . .
Gives him a vision . . .
Anoints him for its fulfillment.
Obedient to the call in the light of the vision and the power of the anointing—his labors are blessed with unusual results.
Others take notice.
Want to get in on the act.
They ask the man how he did it (the assumption being that if they did as he did, they would achieve as he achieved).
He begins to analyze what he did . . . comes up with the methods which were born out of the call, the vision and the anointing.
If enough people ask him how he did it—he'll publish a manual setting out the methods he used.
Then anybody can buy the manual—apply the methods—and get the same results . . . or so the idea goes.
Somehow the call—the vision—and the anointing are forgotten or ignored or subordinated to the mechanics.
As though God could not do another thing with another man.
As though God had run out of calls or vision or power.
As though God had no new ways to do what had never been done before.
How distinct the servants of God in the Bible—how different their ways of doing things.
How incredible their effectiveness . . .
When each was himself as God called and envisioned and anointed him to be.
God has not changed.
He wants to do the same today with those who will yield to him—to be led by Him and allow Him to teach them His ways.[52]

---

[51] Paul Rees, *Don't Sleep Through the Revolution* (Old Tappan, N.J.: Fleming H. Revell, 1957).

[52] Richard Halverson, *Perspective*, November 10, 1971.

Travel Log: Philippines

Youth Worker Profiles by Paul Borthwick

Anne de Jesus Ardina is the faculty and program coordinator of the Youth Ministry Program of the Alliance Biblical Seminary in Manila, Philippines.

Taking a Professional View of Youth Ministry. "As faculty for Youth Ministry, I teach Youth Ministry courses to youth ministers/workers taking their MA or MDiv in Youth Ministry. Because I am still studying full time for my doctorate, I only teach a few subjects such as Filipino/Asian Youth Culture, Filipino/Asian Family and Adolescent Sexuality. I also teach extension modules in the provinces."

Taking a "Hands-On" Approach to Youth Ministry. "In addition to teaching, my 'Volunteer Work' includes being on the Board of the National Alliance Youth Philippines (NAYP) of the Christian and Missionary Alliance as Representative for Luzon.
The NAYP comprises 60,000-plus youth of the 2,000-plus Christian and Missionary Alliance churches in the Philippines. Although the NAYP is 52 years old, the concept of professional (paid and long-term) youth ministers is relatively new."

Handling the Administrative Side of Youth Work. "As one of the adults and advisers on the NAYP Board, I help plan for the national congress (every other year), make policies, do youth ministry training for youth ministers and youth leaders around the country."

Motivation—for Ministry. "My calling to full-time ministry at the age of 10 has kept me going for the past 15 years that I've been in Christian service. Believing that God has chosen me to be his servant has propelled me even through difficult times. My life verse is Matthew 6:33, thus my goal is to seek God's kingdom and expand it on earth, knowing that the blessings I will receive are not material and temporal but eternal: the lives of those I have influenced for him. I have also been affected deeply by the example and ministry of my family—grandparents, uncles/aunts and parents—we're a modern priestly tribe! They have inspired me not only to follow their footsteps but also to stick it out whatever comes my way as they have done/are doing."

Motivation—Specifically for Youth Ministry. "I am in youth ministry today because of people who have believed in me as a youth. Because of the investment they have made in my life, I want to invest in youth as well. I persevere despite the lack of results and discouragements because I know that if God could change me using significant adults to mold and shape me, then no youth is a 'hopeless case.'"

Longevity. "I have also been deeply affected by the example of my mentors—like the youth ministry visiting professors who have come to Alliance Biblical Seminary. Many of these have been in youth ministry for decades, and this has encouraged me to commit to youth ministry for life. They have also continued to believe in me, mentor me, and encourage me."

A Dream for the Youth of the Philippines. "My belief in youth and in their potential keeps me in youth ministry. Knowing that they look up to me and that I've made a difference in their lives has kept me from giving up altogether. My dream is to see the youth affected by my ministry become leaders among their peers—at church, school, and in society. I pray that they would be examples of Christlikeness (in life, speech, faith, love, and purity). From among them, I desire that there would rise excellent youth ministers to lead and disciple the generation after them."

chapter fourteen

THE CORPS OF DISCOVERY: WORKING WITH A TEAM

The Crew . . . bore a close resemblance to a band of rough, experienced camping buddies in pursuit of the ultimate outdoor adventure. The very factors that would have sent more prudent men scurrying toward hearth and home drew these men on. Territory unknown? Death a possibility? Good! When do we start?
—Edward Dolnick, describing John Wesley Powell's party of men who made the first successful boat trip through the entire length of the Grand Canyon.[1]

We have here a room full of rag-tag, foolish, unsophisticated, unfinished, work-in-progress, wandering, weak, disrespected ragamuffins who have been called to work with a group of rag-tag, foolish, unsophisticated, unfinished, work-in-progress wanderers called young people. Adults come up to us and say, "What's going on with this youth group? You've got all these scary people coming in here with tattoos and earrings and all kinds of strange clothes. They're loud; they're rowdy; they laugh a lot . . ." And you say, "Oh, yeah, well, that's our volunteer staff."
—Mike Yaconelli, CORE Seminar 2003[2]

Developing leaders is the best mix of blessing and burden that I know of in the church. It is a blessing to watch adults minister to students, and it is a burden to find the adults, train them, and motivate them.
—Doug Fields[3]

When morning came, he called his disciples to him and chose twelve of them.
—Luke 6:13

---

[1] Edward Dolnick, *Down the Great Unknown* (New York: HarperCollins, 2001), 12.

[2] The CORE is a youth ministry training event based on nine CORE realities taught by Youth Specialties in three one-day events during a three-year cycle.

[3] Doug Fields, *Purpose-Driven Youth Ministry* (Grand Rapids, Mich.: Zondervan/Youth Specialties, 1998), 272.

We are to ascend the Missouri River with a boat as far as it is navigable . . . The party consists of 25 picked Men of the armey [sic] and country and I am So happy as to be one of the pick'd Men . . . We are to Receive a great reward for this expedition, when we Return.[4]

These words, scrawled hurriedly in the journal of Sergeant John Ordway on April 8, 1804, just 10 days before Lewis and Clark's Corps of Discovery launched out for what surely would be the adventure of a lifetime, could be used almost as fittingly to describe the thoughts and expectations of the thousands of volunteers all across the church who every week explore together the adventure that is ministry with teenagers. Counselors, coaches, tutors, mentors, friends, Bible teachers, worship leaders—this corps of youth ministry volunteers surely has some sense of the fear, the exhilaration, the anticipation, and the vivid hope that stirred Ordway that spring day two centuries ago. Like Ordway, they pursue the adventure with the anticipation of great reward.

No introduction to youth ministry could be complete without giving thought to this wonderful, rag-tag, marvelously diverse crew of people. They are the heart and soul of youth work. As any experienced youth worker knows, they are all that stand between a successful venture and the perils of a solo voyage.

Burden and Blessing

Three weeks before I was scheduled to speak at a winter retreat for the youth group at a suburban church in a large city,[5] I received a letter from the youth minister telling me about his group. As it happened, I found out much more than I wanted to know:

The general that will command an army alone may as well say, "Let it be destroyed for lack of command." The schoolmaster that will oversee or govern all the schools in the county by himself may as well say, "Let them all be ungoverned." The physician that will undertake the care of all the sick people in a whole nation, or county, when he is not able to visit one hundredth of them may as well say, "Let them perish."
—**Richard Baxter**

---

[4] Stephen Ambrose, *Undaunted Courage: Meriwether Lewis, Thomas Jefferson and the Opening of the American West* (New York: Touchstone, 1996), 131 (spelling and capitalization as in original).

[5] This letter is genuine, but I withhold the actual name of the church.

When I came to [this church], the youth group was about 100 strong and had a group of 12 leaders. During a four-month interim between my arrival and my predecessor's leaving, the youth leaders formed a very close bond with each other and ran the program themselves—and they did it very well. They gave me the impression that they expected me to be responsible for the program and to take on much of the responsibility myself because they had jobs and families of their own. But when I did things my way—not theirs—we had constant conflict.

These volunteer leaders were very dedicated Christians, but they were not supportive of the church as a whole. The youth group had become a sanctuary for disgruntled adults; they did their own thing in the youth group, and weren't real happy with the church, which, in fact, supported the youth group strongly. The senior pastor wasn't very happy with these leaders because of their lack of support for the church, so there was some open antagonism between himself and our volunteer leaders.

My first year and a half was one of conflict. The conflict became open and obvious in February when I had a program that several of the leaders opposed. Those leaders moved to organize a counter-meeting in one of their homes where we were already having a midweek group meeting sponsored by the church. We were able to resolve the conflict before the counter-meeting so that it never happened, but the stage was set for an exit.

One of the volunteer leaders decided to leave the church, which meant that he would no longer be able to serve as a youth leader—my rule and the church's. When he insisted on continuing to be involved in our weeknight program as a leader, I asked him to stop. The Pastor-Parish Relations Committee backed me up on this. If he did not stop, we were going to cause the group to cease meeting.

In August/September we had a mass resignation of 10 leaders and college students in protest against our not allowing this one person who left the church to continue serving as a youth leader. The whole group went to another church of our same denomination a mile from us and set up shop, involving that minister in their planning, beginning a Sunday night youth program, and setting plans for a fall retreat that would take place two weeks before ours. They actively recruited youth from our youth program, sometimes coming into our own church to do so. It has caused a great deal of heartache and stress in the church, with the youth, the youth group, and for me personally.

As this letter demonstrates, working with volunteers can be a "blessing" and a "burden." There is also little doubt which one had been the experience of this beleaguered youth minister. He must have wondered if it would not just be a lot easier to lead the youth program without any ministry team. After all, it is better to be a sailor on a solo voyage than the captain of a mutinous crew. But, blessing or burden, these crew members who set sail with us in ministry are not just coworkers: they are fellow members of the body of Christ. They bring to the journey gifts and skills that we will need. We risk the mission when we launch out on our own, or demand too hastily that unpleasant crew members walk the plank.

Why Team Ministry?

Frustrations are a normal part of any team effort: miscommunication, hurt feelings, botched plans, lack of dependability, lack of coordination, too many coxswains,[6] and not enough rowers. But there are also in team ministry deep satisfactions: the friendships melded through shared memories, the allegiance forged by standing shoulder-to-shoulder in ministry, the privilege of watching God use your combined efforts to do together what you could not have done alone, and the pleasure of being with fun, resourceful Christians who are just crazy enough to want to work with teenagers. What it amounts to is blessing indeed!

Despite the fact that his ship, the *Endurance*, and its crew were in the vise grip of ice in the Weddell Sea of Antarctica, Thomas Ordes-Lee wrote in his journal, "We seem to be a wonderfully happy family ... Considering our divergent aims and our differences of station it is surprising how few differences of opinion occur."

In their book *Shackleton's Way: Leadership Lessons from the Great Explorer*, Margot Morrell and Stephanie Capparell describe how the men even made a game of trying to get the ship out of the ice, running "from side to side on the ship's deck trying to rock it free. The deck was so crowded with dog kennels and supplies the men had to squeeze through a tight aisle. 'Each falls over the other amidst much laughter and merriment but without much effect on the ship ...'

"Whatever was ahead, the men were behind their leader, prepared to brave the ordeal together. 'We are now six months out from England and during the whole of this time we have all pulled well together and with an almost complete lack of friction,' Capt. [Frank] Worsley wrote just after the ship became stuck. 'A more agreeable set of gentlemen and good fellows one could not wish for shipmates.'"

Margot Morrell and Stephanie Capparell, Shackleton's Way: Leadership Lessons from the Great Arctic Explorer (New York: Penguin Putnam, 2001), 99.

But the basic premises of volunteer youth ministry are theological and not experiential. Preparing God's people for works of service is at the heart of the Church's mandate (Eph. 4:12).

---

[6] The coxswain is the helmsman of a racing shell who gives orders to the rowers.

Theological Foundations

The model of Jesus: Server of the servants.

One of the last and greatest lessons that Jesus gave his disciples as he concluded his earthly ministry took place in an upper room as his disciples arrived for the evening meal. Stripped of his outer clothing, and with a towel wrapped around his waist, Jesus "poured water into a basin and began to wash his disciples' feet, drying them with the towel that was wrapped around him" (John 13:14–16).

It was a vivid lesson, stunning for at least two reasons. First of all, the social convention of Jesus's day was that foot-washing was a task relegated to the lowliest of the servants in the household. Second, within rabbinical culture it was always the student who served his master, and not the other way around.[7] The clear message, both implicit and explicit (see John 13:12-17), is that leadership is about servanthood, and that those of us in leadership are called to serve Christ's disciples. Kenneth Gangel writes, "Thus the first step in building our theology of volunteerism lies in recognizing that those who carry leadership positions in the church also carry—first and foremost—the responsibility of serving those volunteers in whatever lowly manner may be necessary."[8]

Gathered for God's purposes.

Of course, the burden of youth ministry leadership is that "foot-washing" is exhausting work. Many a youth worker, hunched over with towel in hand, has burned out trying to meet the needs of an expanding group of both teenagers and adults. Little wonder that volunteer ministry is so often neglected. Who needs more feet to wash?

At the heart of this exhaustion is a misunderstanding of servant-leadership. It is true, service is sometimes exhausting, and, as Jesus's example showed, it can be costly. But the key is in our theological reconfiguration of resource and supply. Ministry with volunteer youth workers is not primarily about volunteers bringing refreshment to students, nor about youth pastors bringing refreshment to volunteers. It is about creating a space wherein people can find refreshment from Christ—an upper room—holy ground where disciples can encounter Christ and be washed and refreshed by *him*.

In Numbers 11, we catch Moses in a moment of deep frustration. He is clearly tired of looking at dirty feet, and nearly washed up. Moses, approaching God, is angry and frustrated, burned out and bushed—because, despite his best intentions, he does not have the resources to serve the people of God.

---

[7] See Elisha's relationship with Elijah (1 Kings 19:21) or Joshua's relationship with Moses (Exod. 33:11).

[8] Kenneth Gangel, "Four Images of Ministry" in *Leadership Handbook of Practical Theology*, ed. James D. Berkley (Grand Rapids, Mich.: Baker, 1994), 268. Notably, this is also the only place in the whole of Scripture where the word *apostle* is used in a general sense with reference to all the disciples of Jesus. "I tell you the truth, no servant is greater than his master, nor is a messenger [*apostolos*] greater than the one who sent him (John 13:16)." It is a reminder that, at least in this one sense, all believers are messengers or apostles, and that those of us in leadership are servants to the servants.

Moses asked the Lord, "Why have you brought this trouble on your servant? What have I done to displease you that you put the burden of all these people on me? Did I conceive all these people? Did I give them birth? Why do you tell me to carry them in my arms, as a nurse carries an infant, to the land you promised on oath to their forefathers? Where can I get meat for all these people? They keep wailing to me, 'Give us meat to eat!' I cannot carry all these people by myself; the burden is too heavy for me. If this is how you are going to treat me, put me to death right now—if I have found favor in your eyes—and do not let me face my own ruin." (vv. 11-15)

Moses's complaint is real: Doggone it, he wants God to provide some volunteers to share his workload. "Do not let me face my own ruin." God, on the other hand, has something quite different in mind.

The Lord said to Moses: "Bring *me* seventy of Israel's elders who are known to you as leaders and officials among the people. Have them come to the Tent of Meeting, that they may stand there with you. I will come down and speak with you there, and I will take of the Spirit that is on you and put the Spirit on them. They will help you carry the burden of the people so that you will not have to carry it alone." (Num. 11:16–17, emphasis added)

There are two distinct promises in this passage. And, as Kenda Dean observes in *The God-Bearing Life*, youth pastors are apt to cling to the latter promise—"*They* will help you carry the burden" (v. 17)—and ignore the promise of the first part: "I will come down and speak with you there, and I will take of the Spirit that is on you and put the Spirit on them." Unfortunately, that neglect led Moses—and often leads us—to forget that it is not about *Moses's* ministry or our ministry; it is about God's ministry. "Numbers 11 calls us back to a form of ministry in which we gather people for God so that God can give them what we cannot: a share of God's spirit, the spirit that empowers ministry."[9]

God-bearing youth ministry gives volunteers sacred space, "meeting tents" where God calls their myriad talents into service for the sake of all Israel. This form of leadership development represents a significant shift in our usual thinking about volunteers . . . What if we approached potential elders on the basis of God's invitation instead of ours? What if we called them and said, "We've noticed that you have gifts for teaching; and because of that, we'd like to offer you some sacred space in your life. We want to give you room to listen to God's word to you and to experience God's nearness and what that might mean for you. That's why we're gathering people to a 'meeting tent' (or retreat, small group, class meeting, or spiritual direction session with a qualified director), where we will listen to what God . . . has to say to us, remain open to God's presence, and consider how God seems to be equipping us for ministry."[10]

---

[9] Kenda Creasy Dean, *The God-Bearing Life* (Nashville, Tenn.: Upper Room Books, 1998), 90.

[10] Ibid., 91. "The solution for the burned-out Moses consists neither of letting go of the people nor of abdicating his position of leadership. God instructs him to gather the elders *for God*—not for himself, not for the sake of easing his schedule or relieving his weekend responsibilities, although the upshot of Moses's obedience may indeed lighten his pastoral load. Moses is to gather a cadre of volunteers for *God's* sake, and God will spread the spirit given to Moses throughout the community for the good of all Israel." Ibid., 90.

Leaders must make team life a primary commitment in ministry. The primary ambition of a leader should be to enable his or her team members to achieve their fullest potential under God. We must dream about them, dream dreams for them. We must pray for them. As Paul said to Timothy, "Night and day I constantly remember you in my prayers."
—Ajith Fernando, Youth for Christ, Sri Lanka

The priesthood of all believers.

Earlier in this book[11] we affirmed the notion that all Christians share a common dignity, privilege, and calling before God. Stevens observes that this calling is threefold:[12]

▸ the call to belong to God (1 Pet. 2:10)[13],

▸ the call to be God's people in life by living a lifestyle of holiness,[14] and

▸ the call to do God's work through service in both the church and the world.[15]

Paul makes it quite clear that one of the central responsibilities of those in ministry leadership is to equip the people of God to do the work of God, to equip the saints for the work of ministry. This shared labor is implicit in Paul's frequent use of the Greek preposition *syn* (meaning "with" or "together"), which he uses more than 14 times in his letters. Paul attaches *syn* as a prefix to several verbs and thereby creates compound words that are found nowhere else in the New Testament. Paul's clear intention is to communicate that ministry is a work all of us as Christians must do *together*.[16]

For a youth leader to neglect this priority would be like a football coach taking the field by himself because he didn't want to face the difficulties of recruiting and training a team. By definition, such a coach is no coach at all. Regardless of what may be great skill on the field, youth pastors who are so caught up with the game that they neglect the recruitment and training of a team are neglecting a central feature of what it means to be called *pastor*.

[11] See chapters 3 and 12.

[12] R. Paul Stevens, *The Other Six Days* (Grand Rapids, Mich.: Eerdmans, 1999), 88.

[13] See also Hosea 11:1–2,17; Matthew 9:13; Mark 2:17; Luke 5:32; Acts 2:39; Romans 1:6-7, 8:28, 9:24; 1 Corinthians 1:24,26, 7:17,20; Ephesians 1:18, 4:1; Philippians 3:14; 1 Thessalonians 2:12, 5:24; and 1 Timothy 6:12.

[14] See 1 Corinthians 1:8–9, 7:15; Galatians 5:13; Ephesians 4:4; Col. 3:15; 1 Thessalonians 4:7; and 2 Timothy 1:9.

[15] See Exodus 19:6; Isaiah 41:2,4; 42:6; Matthew 4:21; Mark 3:14; Ephesians 4:1; and 1 Peter 2:9–10.

[16] Gangel, "Four Images of Ministry," 269.

We are one body with many parts.

> Now the body is not made up of one part but of many . . . If the whole body were an eye, where would the sense of hearing be? If the whole body were an ear, where would the sense of smell be? But in fact God has arranged the parts in the body, every one of them, just as he wanted them to be. If they were all one part, where would the body be? As it is, there are many parts, but one body. (I Cor. 12:14,17–20)

Paul's use of the "body" metaphor clearly emphasizes the corporate nature of God's calling—that all parts of the body are essential to do what God calls us to do. No one is omni-gifted. The worship leader cannot sing to the gifted speaker, "I do not need you." The soft-spoken, gifted counselor cannot say to the jock, "Do you ever feel that you're not needed? Because you aren't." The contemplative leader cannot say to the wild and crazy game leader, "I do not need you (and I don't want to play your stupid games)." There is almost always an "and" in God's plan: Moses *and* Aaron; Elijah *and* Elisha; Jesus *and* the disciples; Paul *and* Silas; Paul *and* Luke; Paul *and* Barnabas; Peter, Paul *and* Mary.[17]

Pragmatic Considerations

Aside from the theological roots of volunteer ministry, there are the pragmatic considerations.

Continuity

Ecclesiastes 4:12 reminds us that "a cord of three strands is not quickly broken." A youth ministry that wisely incorporates volunteers in shared leadership is a youth ministry that is not hanging by the tenure of one or two leaders. It is a ministry that stays even when the youth minister moves on.

Take, for example, volunteers Darrell and Erlene, who had been working with their church's senior high group for two years when the paid youth minister left for a new position. Because Darrell and Erlene had been equipped as part of a team ministry—trained to plan retreats, do Bible studies, and work closely with students—they ably sustained the work during the year-long search for a replacement.

Dunn and Senter remark that one of the axioms of youth ministry is that "long-term growth of a youth ministry is directly dependent on the ability of the youth worker to release ministry responsibilities to mature and qualified lay leaders."[18]

---

[17] These last three are not actually biblical characters, but a folk-singing trio popular when your professor was in college. It should be noted, though, that Noel (Paul) Stookey is a committed believer. Here is a study group idea: see if anybody knows the words to the song "Puff the Magic Dragon."

[18] Richard Dunn and Mark Senter III, ed., *Reaching a Generation for Christ* (Chicago: Moody Press, 1997), 150.

Diversity

Just as it is difficult to play a Mozart concerto on a piano with only half the piano keys, or write a romantic e-mail on a keyboard with only a few letters, so it is difficult to give full expression to the Christian life through the lens of only one personality. The beauty of working with a diverse group of volunteers—young and old, athletic and musical, quiet and outgoing, and so on—is that it gives students opportunities to see what Christian commitment looks like when it's shaded by different types of personalities. That opens up wider opportunities for rapport with a more varied group of students, and it helps to break the power of negative Christian stereotypes.

Longevity

One of the most common types of backcountry emergencies is hypothermia, a condition in which the core body temperature falls below 96 degrees. It is a serious condition and can be fatal. But one of the oldest first-response remedies is to lie down next to the hypothermic victim so that the body heat of the rescuer can restore some of the heat of the victim.

Sadly, youth ministry sees far too many "hypothermic" youth workers: they started out with a warm heart, but in working alone have simply lost their fire and passion for the journey. The best way to protect and prolong the ministry of youth workers is to recruit other youth workers who will "lie down beside them."[19] Doug Fields comments, "Understaffed youth ministries are often overburdened, stressed, and too tired for new vision. They fall into maintenance mode and stagnate."[20]

Two are better than one, because they have a good return for their work: If one falls down, his friend can help him up. But pity the man who falls and has no one to help him up!

Also, if two lie down together, they will keep warm. But how can one keep warm alone? (Eccles. 4:9–11)

People Are the Plan

Several years ago, Ronald Wilson wrote an article for the journal *Leadership* that ought to be required reading for any people recruiting volunteer leaders.[21] Entitled "Letter from an Ex-Volunteer," this imaginary letter has an important message for us.

---

[19] It would be unwise to take this metaphor too literally.

[20] Fields, *Purpose-Driven Youth Ministry*, 271.

[21] Ronald Wilson, "Letter from an Ex-Volunteer," *Leadership* (summer 1982): 50, 53.

Dear Pastor Potter:

You and some others are down in Finney Hall in the church basement stuffing 20,000 envelopes for the Madison County Deeper Life Campaign at the fairground. I guess I should be there. You asked for volunteers last Sunday, and I had my hand halfway up when you announced hymn number 263, "Work, for the Night is Coming."

As you probably guessed, I'm feeling a little bad about that and about not getting to choir practice and dropping off the planning committee and canceling the literature distribution training session scheduled for our house last month.

How Many Volunteers Are Needed?

When I'm asked about the best student-to-leader ratio, I often point to Jesus's example. He was God and he had a twelve-to-one ratio. Because of his relationship with Peter, James, and John, I could even suggest that his ratio was more like three to one. While I do not believe there is one answer for every youth ministry setting, I do know the magic number is definitely less than twelve. At Saddleback, we try to set our goal at a five-to-one ratio for our small groups, but most of our leaders still have a difficult time trying to invest in and care for five students.

—*Doug Fields,* Purpose-Driven Youth Ministry *(Grand Rapids, Mich.: Zondervan/Youth Specialties, 1998), 273.*

For one thing, pastor, I think I'm burned out—spent, pooped, empty. I've been hearing about it lately, and they say that if you're not careful, it can lead to dropout. I always used to say I didn't mind burning out for the Lord, but lately, I've been afraid I might go up in one big poof.

. . . I haven't dropped out. Maybe I just need to hear you say it once more: "Wilson, it's the ninth inning, and we're two runs behind. We've got two outs and no one on and you're up. We're counting on you to hit. So go get 'em!"

Your brother in the Lord, Ronald Wilson

Change a few of the activities in that letter, and it could have been written by almost any youth ministry volunteer. One hears in its words the three most common plot lines of the volunteer story: cop out, help out, and burn out. But somewhere between "the greatest story never told" and "Curious George goes AWOL" there is another story to be told about volunteer youth ministry. That story is a story that puts people at the heart of the mission, and a mission in the heart of the people. Effective volunteer youth ministry boils down to people with a purpose.

In his classic study of Jesus's ministry, *The Master Plan of Evangelism*, Robert Coleman remarks, "[Jesus's] concern was not with programs to reach the multitudes, but with men whom the multitudes would follow . . . Men were to be his method of winning the world to God."[22] In light of this fact, Paul J. Loth articulates a list of seven "attitude competencies" that are essential for anyone who recruits ministry volunteers:[23]

1. Vision for potential volunteers to serve,

2. belief that people are more important than positions and programs,

3. willingness to work with volunteers to see them reach their full potential,

4. love for the volunteers,

5. belief in the importance of the youth ministry,

6. desire to help volunteers develop, and

7. a willingness to trust in the gifts of others.

The whole scope of effective volunteer youth ministry is shaped by a mindset that sees people at the heart of God's purpose. Doug Fields puts it this way: "I prefer the word *leader* over *volunteer*. I like *leader* because it connotes action and affirms the value of the leader. *Volunteer* communicates that someone is needed to fill a slot no one else wants; it isn't as positive as *leader*. Your ability to find volunteer leaders begins with how you view them."[24]

The Environment of Recruitment

Sir Ernest Shackleton, the great Antarctic explorer, was said to have a rather unorthodox way of screening his crew. First of all, applications of potential candidates were dropped into one of three desk drawers, "Mad," "Hopeless," and "Possible."[25] Then, the "Possibles" were brought in for a personal interview—again, by all accounts, a rather unusual encounter. Reginald W. James, selected by Shackleton as the on-board doctor for the expedition, describes his interview:

Shackleton asked me if my teeth were good, if I suffered from varicose veins, if my circulation was good, if I had a good temper, and if I could sing. At this

---

[22] Robert E. Coleman, *The Master Plan of Evangelism* (Old Tappan, N.J.: Fleming H. Revell, 1963), 27.

[23] Paul J. Loth, "How to Involve Volunteers in Church Ministry," *Christian Education Today* (Fall 1985): 9. I have made some slight changes to Loth's list only to better fit the youth ministry context.

[24] Fields, *Purpose-Driven Youth Ministry*, 274.

[25] Here is another study break idea: It can be fun to divide up your friends in youth ministry by using Shackleton's categories. Write all three categories at the top of the page and begin listing names in their appropriate column. Because you are, after all, dealing with youth workers, do not be surprised that categories one and two grow lengthy.

question I probably looked a bit taken aback, for I remember he said, "Oh, I don't mean any Caruso stuff; but I suppose you can shout a bit with the boys?"[26]

One assumes that medical skill really was Shackleton's first priority for the ship's doctor. This would be absolutely essential for the mission. if a doctor was unable to provide medical care, it is hard to imagine his patients finding comfort in his ability to sing a good tune. But the crew of the *Endurance* worked well together. So, though Shackleton's recruitment techniques might be questioned, clearly they succeeded according to this basic principle: *Every approach to recruitment must be measured by the recruits it yields.*

To put it another way, the measure of any approach to recruitment will always be based on certain criteria, defined or undefined. Those criteria, taken together, combine to create what might be described as the *environment of recruitment*—basic values, related to one another, that shape the search for and selection of volunteers. Obviously, for Shackleton those values were bigger, and more musical, than mere medical considerations.

What are some of the values that might shape the environment of recruitment in a ministry with teenagers (see Figure 14-1)?

Figure 14-1.
The Environment of Leadership Search and Selection

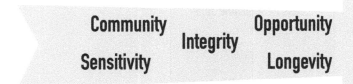

Community

Does the recruitment approach affirm the value of all people in the community while recognizing that not all people in the community are equally valuable to a particular ministry (I Cor. 12:14–31)? All Christians have been gifted by God's Spirit to serve him in the church. But they have not all been gifted to serve in the same ways or to ply the same tasks (see I Cor. 12:4–6). Does that mean there are some God-loving, Jesus-serving, Spirit-filled people who probably just should not be doing ministry with teenagers? Yes. But it means more than that. It means that a wise youth worker will explore options beyond *direct* student ministry whereby willing people can be involved. In fact, one of the ways we can be better stewards of those who are in direct student ministry is by being stewards of those who

---

[26] Margot Morrell and Stephanie Capparell, *Shackleton's Way: Leadership Lessons from the Great Antarctic Explorer* (New York: Penguin Books, 2001), 61.

are *not* in direct student ministry. Doug Fields comments, "Many of us lose potential leaders because we limit our serving opportunities to two positions—*All* or *Nothing*. Everyone in your church is a potential youth worker if you provide serving opportunities that are more simplified and less threatening than working directly with students."[27]

Volunteer management consultant Marlene Wilson, demonstrates this progression of responsibility by using a funnel (see Figure 14-2).[28] Not only does this model reflect the progression of responsibility, it clearly shows as well that volunteer supervision decreases as a volunteer's level of responsibility increases.

Doug Fields, in his ministry at Saddleback Church, reflects this same progression by dividing his field of ministry involvement into four types of positions

Figure 14-2.
Wilson's Funnel Showing Progression of Volunteer Responsibility

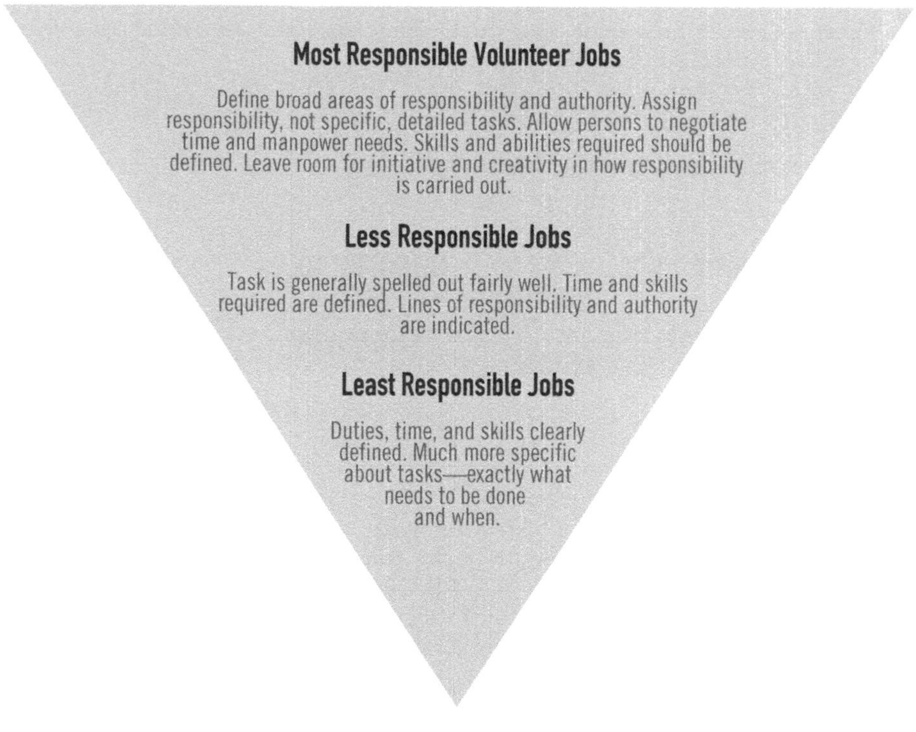

Most Responsible Volunteer Jobs

Define broad areas of responsibility and authority. Assign responsibility, not specific, detailed tasks. Allow persons to negotiate time and manpower needs. Skills and abilities required should be defined. Leave room for initiative and creativity in how responsibility is carried out.

Less Responsible Jobs

Task is generally spelled out fairly well. Time and skills required are defined. Lines of responsibility and authority are indicated.

Least Responsible Jobs

Duties, time, and skills clearly defined. Much more specific about tasks—exactly what needs to be done and when.

Source: Marlene Wilson, *The Effective Management of Volunteer Programs* (Boulder, Colo.: Volunteer Management Associates, 1976), 108.

[27] Fields, *Purpose-Driven Youth Ministry*, 277.

[28] Marlene Wilson, *The Effective Management of Volunteer Programs* (Boulder, Colo.: Volunteer Management Associates, 1976), 108.

(see Figure 14-3).[29] The deeper the level of involvement, the more difficult it becomes to fill the position. But, by using the will and the gifts of those in the upper levels of involvement, it is possible to protect and better use the gifts of those at deeper, more direct levels of involvement.[30]

Table 14-1.
Ministry Involvement Chart

Level of Commitment	Type	Example	Time Commitment	Location	Pre-service Training Commitment	In-service Training Commitment
Low	Support	Staff annual bike rodeo	1-2 hours per week for three months leading up to event; 3-6 hours per week in final month	Typically, most of this happens on the church property.	Orientation session as needed for involvement	None
		Food committee van driver	Service time can vary depending on tasks; usually no more than 1-4 hours a week			
		Parent-support team	Parent-support team meets quarterly; annual leaders' retreat (optional)			
		Prayer support team	Daily	On your knees!		
High	Teaching	Sunday school teacher	3-5 hours per week for planning, program and relational ministry	Church property	Four 3-hour training sessions	
		• Small Group Leader • Onward Bound • Ministry Teams (drama, missions, worship, fine arts, graphic arts)	3-5 hours per week for planning, program and relational ministry	Varies depending on area of involvement	Four 3-hour training sessions	Weekly leadership team meeting; reading resources
		Coach: sports program	Annual leader's retreat			

The Ministry Involvement Chart (see Table 14-1) demonstrates the way one ministry sought to cultivate the gifts of those who might be neither temperamentally inclined nor gifted for direct student ministry. Statistically, the vast majority of volunteers give only a few hours a week, and only 14 percent have been estimated to volunteer five or more hours a week.[31] What it basically says to members of the community is, "Just because you can't do everything doesn't mean you can't do anything." Not only does this incorporate broader-based support and com-

[29] Fields, *Purpose-Driven Youth Ministry*, 277–282.

[30] For specifics on how this plays out, see especially the Resource Inventory used by Doug Fields and his team at Saddleback Community Church. Ibid., 280.

[31] V. A. Hodgkinson and M. S. Weitzman, *Giving and Volunteering in the United States* (Washington, D.C.: Independent Sector, 1992). This data is based on a broader study of volunteerism, and not specifically youth ministry.

Figure 14-3.
Fields' Breakdown of Volunteer Involvement

Church Body

Cheerleading Team

Resource Team

Prayer Team

Hands-on Team

Source: Doug Fields, *Purpose-Driven Youth Ministry* (Grand Rapids, Mich.: Zondervan/Youth Specialties, 1998), 277–282.

munity involvement for the youth ministry, it lightens the load for those leaders who are both inclined and gifted for direct student ministry, and sets them apart to do what they have been called and gifted to do.

Sensitivity

Does this recruitment approach take into account the concerns of the recruited? There are at least four concerns that commonly make people reluctant to do volunteer ministry.[32] Each of these concerns is played out vividly in the realm of youth ministry.

Concern Number One: Having inadequate knowledge.

One fear often voiced by volunteer leaders is that they simply lack the biblical knowledge that they need. They fear that a student will ask a question they cannot answer, or that their answer to the question will be wrong. Then someday, 10 years down the road, James Dobson will be in a prison interviewing a serial killer and asking where he thinks he went wrong, and the unfortunate prisoner will think carefully and then point back to misinformation he received in his Sunday School class.

Remedy. Bible knowledge is important, and obviously, it can be a wonderful asset in a volunteer leader. But leaders also need to be assured that their lack of knowledge will be supplemented by both user-friendly curriculum and ongoing in-service training.

Volunteers also need to understand that students are rarely attracted to someone based solely on theological expertise. Teenagers do not respond to Christ by listening for knowledge from the leader's head, but by experiencing care and friendship from the leader's heart. As Paul knew from his ministry, the most powerful teaching comes through a life that embodies the message.

When I came to you, brothers, I did not come with eloquence or superior

---

[32] Mark Senter, *Recruiting Volunteers in the Church* (Wheaton, Ill.: Victor Books, 1990), 24. Senter actually identifies three concerns. I have taken the liberty of adding the fourth.

wisdom as I proclaimed to you the testimony about God. For I resolved to know nothing while I was with you except Jesus Christ and him crucified. I came to you in weakness and fear, and with much trembling. My message and my preaching were not with wise and persuasive words, but with a demonstration of the Spirit's power, so that your faith might not rest on men's wisdom, but on God's power. (I Cor. 2:1–5)

Concern Number Two: Fear that the job will be never-ending.

People have an intuitive fear (often verified by experience) that any volunteer commitment in ministry is a lifetime enlistment—that any leader who attempts to retire prior to death and decomposition will be considered a flagrant slacker and seriously AWOL.

Remedy. An open-ended commitment is beneficial neither for the volunteer nor for the ministry. Any leadership position description should define a set length of tenure, followed by review, after which the leadership responsibilities can be reaffirmed, downgraded, or ended.[33] There are good, sound reasons why both parties might wish to end or downgrade the commitment in time.

For example, the volunteer leader may have had a change in circumstances—related perhaps to family or work or both. People do not want to be "tied down." Research done by the YMCA found that people were more willing to work 50 hours during a four-week period than they were to work that same number of hours spread over a four- or five-month period.[34] That means that we need to find ways to use volunteers for short-term service.[35]

One youth leader did this in his Sunday School program by dividing each quarter of the year into two segments. One large segment is for teaching a standard curriculum in which students are divided into age-graded classes. The remaining four weeks are a special segment for which short-term volunteers are recruited to teach special elective courses based on student interest. These courses are offered to any middle or high school student irrespective of age. The long-term Sunday school teachers may take an elective course or take off for four weeks up to four times a year. The unexpected benefit has been that some of the short-term teachers so enjoyed their experience that they offered to make a more long-term commitment.

For the youth pastor, the predetermined length of service protects against rapid turnover on the one side, and *no prospect of turnover on the other*. Sometimes the latter problem causes the greater pain. The only thing harder than getting good leaders on the team is gracefully getting bad ones off the team. A preservice agreement on tenure can make that process a bit easier.

---

[33] Probably more informal than formal.

[34] Cited in Senter, *Recruiting Volunteers in the Church*, 23.

[35] Obviously, in youth ministry, there will always be a need for a long-term commitment by some leaders. Short-term commitment simply is not the kind of soil that breeds a ministry of nurture and trust. But a wise youth leader will think of ways to use short-term leaders in such a way that their brief stints of service take some of the pressure off the long-term volunteers.

Lewis and Clark had welded the Corps of Discovery into a tough, superbly disciplined family. They had built an unquestioning trust in themselves, and knew the strengths and skills of each of their men intimately . . . In extremely trying conditions—"We suffered everything Cold, Hunger & Fatigue could impart," Lewis later wrote, as well as "the Keenest Anxiety excited for the fate of [our] Expedition in which our whole Souls were embarked"—the captains managed to keep morale from collapsing. The men never sulked, lashed out, demanded to retreat, or insisted on some alternative route."
—**Stephen Ambrose**

You got gaps, and I got gaps. Let's fill each other's gaps.
—**Character Rocky Balboa, from the film *Rocky***

Concern Number Three: Fearing teenagers, period.

Many adults are intimidated by the assumption that all teenagers are barbarians, incorrigible, just a step above lower primates, and that to go into a room or meeting alone with them is to risk being taken hostage.

Remedy. Again, as with the previous concern—let us be honest—these assumptions are occasionally verified by experience. But experience also paints quite another picture as well. In that picture, the privilege of sharing life and Jesus with an adolescent far overshadows the potential hassles.

Often, this concern can be addressed by a pre-service period of observation. For example, a youth worker in San Antonio invites her prospective leaders to tag along for a weekend retreat as guests of the youth ministry, or to sit in for a few weeks of youth group, so that they might see firsthand what goes on. Looking from the outside in, before they are fully inside, gives them a more realistic picture of both the challenges and the joys of ministry with students.

Concern Number Four: Isolation from the fellowship and nurture of the larger congregation.

Twenty years ago adults were only too happy to pass up their own adult Sunday School program, bailing on curricula they perceived to be outdated and irrelevant. Now an adult volunteer who misses Sunday School may be passing up, for example, anything from a creative class on Christian financial management to a video by one of Christendom's greatest teachers. As more and more congregations move to Sunday School-based fellowship groups, some adults fear that the heavy involvement necessary for youth ministry may cut them off from the broader life of the community. A growing

How to Fire a Volunteer

In his book *Recruiting Volunteers in the Church*, Mark Senter provides these insights for what can be one of the most difficult tasks of leadership:

Preparation
1. *Prayer.* Focus prayerfully on the best interests of the ministry and the person.

2. *Documentation.* Document the issues raising concern.

3. No *surprises.* Some type of ongoing volunteer performance review (formal or informal) will keep the leader from being caught off guard. For guidance on bringing a complaint before the church, see Matthew 18:15–17.

Timing
1. *Don't rush.*

2. *Don't renew.* If possible, rather than dismissing a volunteer, it is always better simply not to renew the relationship. But, as Senter points out, "Absence of renewal does not mean absence of communication."

3. *Don't delay.* Where moral or theological problems have arisen, do not let procrastination and wishful thinking overrule leadership responsibility.

Procedure
1. *Private appointment.* Obviously, the dismissal should not be public. There should be one other third party available as a witness and mediator (if needed), but any more than that can feel like an ambush.

2. *Self-evaluation.* The supervisor should first ask the volunteer for an appraisal of the situation. Sometimes, the volunteer will acknowledge a problem without the supervisor having to say too much.

3. *Confront if necessary* (see Gal. 6:1).

4. *Affirm positive qualities.*

5. *Allow resignation.* After the problems have been defined, ask what the volunteer thinks might be the best course of action for the ministry.

6. *Redirect talents.* If possible, try to help the volunteer leader get plugged in elsewhere.

7. *Follow-up.* Even in the midst of a difficult situation, the goal is redemption of the individual and the relationship.

number of adults are unwilling to forgo the nurture and care of their Sunday school classes to work with teenagers on Sunday mornings.

Remedy. First of all, this is less a problem in parachurch ministries like Young Life, where a larger proportion of the volunteer force is made up of college students or 20-somethings. They are not as likely to feel the close connection to a local congregation anyway. For them, the Young Life or Campus Life leadership team may represent their best source of nurture and fellowship.

For parish-based youth ministries, it will be important to provide adult leaders opportunities for personal growth and fellowship. This may come through the sort of staggered teaching schedule described earlier in this chapter or, at the very least, by making available for-loan videotapes of special Sunday School courses that leaders can take home and view on their own time.

It is also vital that volunteer leaders perceive the others on the team as friends, not just as coworkers. People are far more likely to remain committed to relationships than they are to a job. One writer, in commenting on the uncanny loyalty British soldiers show to their regiments, observed that there is a strong emphasis on regimental unity and continuity. "Men may enlist to serve their country, but they will fight hardest to protect their friends."[36]

Some of the best experiences I have had with volunteer teams have happened when we were out together as friends (with no students) for a day of whitewater rafting. Those afternoons paddling the Big South Fork of the Cumberland River melded our volunteer team into a fellowship of friends who laughed together, helped each other, sweated together, faced death together (!), and reminisced together.

It is hard to leave teams like that. It is like leaving friends and family. Whether it is a potluck dinner or a yearly backpacking trip, volunteers need to experience team-building, praying together, dreaming, and bonding that shows them they are important even when no adolescents are around.

Integrity

Does this recruitment approach find the "right" people for the ministry and screen out the "wrong" people (1 Cor. 4:2)?

Are there *right* people and *wrong* people for youth ministry leadership? Based on considerations that are biblical, legal, and practical, the answer is clearly: Yes. And, whatever else might be said of the *wrong* people, the *right* people should share these three essential traits:

---

[36] Andrew Stuttaford, "Lancers, Fusiliers, Rats," *National Review*, April 21, 2003: 32.

A Love for Christ. As I've said before, the most basic law of reproductive biology is "like begets like." Humans give birth to baby humans, not to baby aardvarks. The implications in the spiritual realm are obvious. If the intent is to reproduce growing disciples of Jesus, the process must begin with growing disciples of Jesus Christ—not people who are perfect, but people who are in pursuit (see Phil. 3:12–17). Paul wrote to the church of Corinth that his life was an incarnation of the gospel, that he sought to live his life as a living letter (2 Cor. 3:1–3). He encouraged the Corinthians to imitate him as he imitated Christ (1 Cor. 11:1). The writer of Hebrews echoed the same idea: "Remember your leaders, who spoke the word of God to you. Consider the outcome of their way of life and imitate their faith" (Heb. 13:7). The number one criterion for selecting prospects for a role on the youth ministry team should be the fruit of their relationship with Jesus.

Table 14-2.
Two Types of Service

True Service	Pseudo-Service
Does not distinguish between large and small tasks.	Enjoys the spectacular.
Is willing to serve behind the scenes. Not afraid to be out front, but neither seeking the limelight.	Likes the spotlight. Motivated by the attention and admiration of others.
Finds contentment in the service. Leaves the results in God's hands.	Is results-oriented. Has score-keeper mind-set. Wants to measure own performance by comparison with others.
Is servant of all.	Picks and chooses when and how to serve.
Is consistent in service. Motivated not by mood swings or short-term passions.	Motivated by the moods and affections of the moment.
Service is fruit of the Spirit.	Service is work of the flesh.

Source: Richard Foster, *Celebration of Discipline* (New York: Harper and Row, 1978), 112–113. I have reworded Foster's distinctions.

A Love for Students. At the heart of any effective youth ministry is a love for teenagers. In referring to his ministry, Paul wrote, "As servants of God we commend ourselves in every way: in great endurance; in troubles, hardships and distresses; in beatings, imprisonments and riots; in hard work, sleepless nights and hunger; in purity, understanding, patience and kindness; in the Holy Spirit *and in sincere love* (emphasis added)"(2 Cor. 6:4-6).

It should be said that a love for teenagers is quite different from a love for the front of the room, or a need for teenagers. In Table 14-2, Richard Foster[37] offers some guidelines for discerning the difference between service rightly rendered and service wrongly rendered.

In her book *Letters to Scattered Pilgrims,* Elizabeth O'Connor remarks:

Many of God's flock go about looking at his world through clouded lenses, using church projects to build up wobbly self-esteem. Enlisting dependent people to foster their phony selves, passing off a neurotic need for affection

[37] Richard Foster, *Celebration of Discipline* (New York: Harper and Row, 1978), 112–113. I have reworded Foster's distinctions.

> The selection process should be looked upon as just that—a selection process. It should not be simply a process of getting "warm bodies" or filling a sheet with names.
>
> —Jack L. Giles, "Recruiting Volunteers," Lutheran Education (March-April 1982): 227, cited in Mark Senter, Recruiting Volunteers in the Church (Wheaton, Ill.: Victor Books, 1990), 160.

as a loving, caring nature, or the compulsion to be ever active must be a priestly concern. Such persons have within themselves all kinds of conflicts that produce dissension in the groups to which they belong. Their vulnerability, excessive demands, expectations and criticisms make genuine community impossible.[38]

A Love for the Church. As happened with the congregation in the letter at the beginning of this chapter, the youth ministry can often become a gathering place for a congregation's disgruntled adults. When that happens, they will likely transfer to the students their own dissatisfaction with the church.

The problem is that when disenchanted adults wean teenagers from a local church, they seldom help them to find nurture in another congregation. That is not healthy for the student, and it is not responsible Christian leadership. This is not a plea for phoniness or unthinking approval. It is an appeal to the fact that while no church is perfect, the church is Christ's body,[39] and one of the best predictors of a teenager's long-term commitment to the faith is assimilation into a local church.[40] Volunteers who cannot or will not nurture that commitment should not be working with teenagers.

Having identified these three essentials for the "right" kind of youth ministry volunteer leader, it is worth asking if there are issues or conditions that might describe the "wrong" kind of volunteer leader. It feels uncomfortable to talk about *right* people and *wrong* people, but biblical teaching, legal mandates, and common sense dictate that extreme care be given in placing people in a role of ministry leadership.

Inclusiveness is wonderful, but nobody wants the fox to guard the hen house.[41] Doug Fields suggests these "red flags" to watch out for:

▶ a brand new Christian or a person new to your church;

▶ a history of short-term commitments;

▶ a critical spirit;

[38] Marlene Wilson, *How to Mobilize Church Volunteers* (Minneapolis, Minn.: Augsburg, 1983), 121.

[39] See chapter 10 for more on the importance of the church.

[40] Merton Strommen, *Five Cries of Youth* (New York: Harper, 1979), 99. "Our analysis shows that the most powerful predictor of youth who see faith as 'very important' is participation in the life of a congregation. Contrariwise, the most powerful predictor of youth for whom faith is not important is little or no participation in the life of their congregation. In other words, dropping out of congregational life is strongly associated with a diminished interest in religious faith."

[41] See also the discussion of ministry leadership in chapter 4.

▸ going through major life crisis or transition (for example, death of a family member, divorce or separation, major career change);

▸ high expectation for staff to be best friends or for ministry to provide personal experiences (for example, a 39-year-old need-a-life single);

▸ hidden agendas—desires and expectations that are counter to your values and goals;

▸ not committed to a lifestyle above reproach; or

▸ unsupportive spouse.[42]

Marlene Wilson notes that this kind of vigilance is important for at least four reasons.[43]

The welfare of the students is at stake. This is not just a question of a leader's integrity: it is also a question of the students' safety. The ministry is first and foremost for the students. Therefore, care must be taken to provide for them a place where they will be protected from spiritual, physical, or emotional injury.[44]

Richard Hammar, coeditor of the *Church Law and Tax Report*, cites research indicating that "70 percent of churches are doing absolutely nothing to screen volunteer youth workers."[45] Hammar goes on to say:

Trust, but verify. Church leaders tend to view the church differently than other institutions in society. It's an institution predicated on trust. It's a sanctuary. It bothers people to have to go through metal detectors or have their fingerprints taken in a church setting . . . But the courts in this country have ruled that what is needed is very minimal. We're talking about an application process that includes reference checks. Starting this year, the Boy Scouts are doing criminal-records checks on all new volunteers.

In my church, we perform criminal record checks on paid employees and male volunteers with minors. More churches are performing these checks, which are being used more often by nonreligious charities. At some point, a court may say they are necessary in screening youth workers.[46]

The ministry's reputation is at stake. The apostle Paul wrote (2 Cor. 6:3), "We put no stumbling block in anyone's path, so that our ministry will not be discredited." He understood that in ministry, trust, and credibility are paramount

---

[42] Fields, *Purpose-Driven Youth Ministry*, 295.

[43] Wilson, *Effective Management of Volunteer Programs*, 122.

[44] Jesus's words in Mark 9:42 make it quite clear that he takes very seriously the welfare of the young and vulnerable: "And if anyone causes one of these little ones who believe in me to sin, it would be better for him to be thrown into the sea with a large millstone tied around his neck."

[45] "Law and Disorder: An Interview with Tax and Law Expert Richard Hammar," *Christianity Today* 47, no. 5 (May 2003): 48.

[46] Ibid., 48–49. The whole subject of legal issues might well be a book of its own. For further reading and study on specifically the issue of volunteer leaders and legal liability issues, see these resources: Thomas F. Taylor, *Seven Deadly Lawsuits* (Nashville, Tenn.: Abingdon, 1996); Carl F. Lansing, *Legal Defense Handbook for Christians in Ministry* (Colorado Springs, Colo.: NavPress, 1993); Jack Crabtree, *Play It Safe* (Wheaton, Ill.: Victor Books, 1994); Cynthia Mazur and Ronald Bullis, *Legal Guide for Day-to-Day Church Matters* (Cleveland, Ohio: United Church Press, 1994); and, especially, William T. Stout and James K. Becker, *The Good Shepherd Program* (Fort Collins, Colo: Nexus Solutions, 1996). Available at http://www.nexus-solutions.com.

(see 1 Thess. 2:10). For that reason, carelessness in recruiting volunteer leaders can bring grave harm to a ministry, and worse yet, to the name of Christ.

The morale of other team members is at stake. The self-perception of other volunteer leaders already on the team can be adversely affected by careless recruiting. All of the pep talks about the importance of the work and the quality of the team ring hollow when it is clear to everyone that the qualifications for service are minimal.[47]

The welfare of the misplaced volunteer is at stake. Pushing volunteers into positions for which they are not spiritually, emotionally, or temperamentally equipped is like trying to build a tree house in a small tree. It is bad for the tree house, yes, but it also crushes the tree—a tree that, in time and with proper nurture and care, might have provided a sturdy and capable support. Despite the fact that the first concern of a youth ministry must be the youth, there must also be concern for the potential leader as well.

Opportunity?

Does this recruitment approach provide the widest possible pool of good candidates? Whether the context is parachurch ministry or congregational ministry, there will always be a pool of potential volunteers. Hersey and Blanchard[48] observe that this pool is made up of four types of people at various stages of *readiness*. They define readiness in terms of two variables: *ability and willingness*.[49] This produces four groups: (1) the able and willing, (2) the able and unwilling, (3) the unable and willing, and (4) the unable and unwilling (see Table 14-3).

One of the implications of Hersey and Blanchard's insights is that any search process must be broad enough to include those who might be possible volunteers but are simply at a much lower state of readiness. Too many recruitment efforts are limited only to those in Quadrant 1—able and willing. The other clear implication is that various means of recruitment are needed to reach those at various levels of readiness. Both are important observations, and they affirm the value of building a youth ministry leadership team from the widest possible pool of good candidates.

For example, as Doug Fields points out, many potential leaders exclude themselves (or are excluded by short-sighted youth workers) from the realm of the willing and able (Quadrant 1) simply because they are perceived as unable. Often

---

[47] Interestingly, in their study of 510 volunteers in 105 nonreligious human service organizations (HSO) such as Big Brother/Big Sister, Cnaan and Cascio found that volunteers who were required to fill out an application form for service scored higher in commitment (hours spent in service) than those who did not. On the other hand, filling out an application form had a negative correlation in terms of tenure (length of service for an organization). Cnann and Cascio offer no explanation for this apparently confusing finding. Could it simply be that the people who work more hours per month (high commitment) tend to serve a shorter period of time because they burn themselves out? In other words, we might predict this result with or without the application variable being thrown into the mix. This may say more about burnout and leader care than it does about administrative red tape. Ram A. Cnaan and Toni A. Cascio, "Performance and Commitment: Issues in Management of Volunteers in Human Service Organizations," *Journal of Social Science Research* 24, no. 3/4 (1999): 23.

[48] Paul Hersey and Ken Blanchard, *Management of Organizational Behavior*, 5th ed. (Englewood Cliffs, N.J.: Prentice-Hall, 1988), 174–181. I have made some minor changes in the presentation of their work.

[49] Ibid., 174–175.

this is solely because they appear to fall short of inaccurate youth ministry stereotypes: "young, funny, athletic, good in front of crowds, strong teacher, has Bible knowledge, outgoing personality, charisma, understands youth culture, owns a van."[50] Just as important are volunteers who are "senior citizens, introverts, young marrieds, musicians, high school dropouts, bowlers, bikers, new Christians, parents, ex-cheerleaders, blue-collar workers, artists, old marrieds, college students, mechanics, single parents, accountants, mature Christians, people with rough pasts, computer nerds, athletes, entrepreneurs, busy people, cooks, administrators, professional wrestlers."[51]

Questions for Possible Consideration

▸ Do team members have to be active members of our church?

▸ Do our team leaders exhibit the evidence of spiritual leadership?

▸ What kind of standards will we have with regard to theological beliefs?

▸ What will be our stance toward team members who become pregnant outside of marriage?

▸ Do we want to establish any guidelines relative to age?

▸ Will we have any special expectations about team members' personal habits (smoking, using alcohol, and so on)?

In fact, as Joseph Galbo discovered in his research,[52] when asked to identify the significant[53] adults in their lives, excluding their own parents, the adults selected were usually older than 24 years of age—and in one study, at least 9 percent were older than 66 years old.[54] That fact in and of itself dispels one of the chief myths that make adults reluctant to work with teenagers—that they are too old to work effectively with teenagers. In fact, in one study of the relationships between adults and various gang and nongang youths, the students were asked to provide no more than four names of adults other than family members with whom they regularly interacted. "The ages of these adults ranged from 35–47. No young adults were mentioned."[55] Students also typically chose as significant adults

[50] Fields, *Purpose-Driven Youth Ministry*, 275.

[51] Ibid., 276. Fields's comment about "busy people" is a little ironic because one of the hindrances occasionally cited in recruiting is that the increased number of working women shrinks what was once a larger pool of willing volunteers. See Senter, *Recruiting Volunteers in the Church*, 21. In fact, employment status does seem initially to have an impact on who volunteers. Demographic research on volunteers in human service organizations, however, indicates that an individual's available amount of free time has almost no impact on *how long* (tenure) or *how much* (commitment) they volunteer. "Those who worked full-time or part-time and those not in the work force volunteered more or less equally." Cnaan and Cascio, "Performance and Commitment," 17–18.

[52] Joseph J. Galbo, "Adolescents' Perceptions of Significant Adults: A Review of the Literature," *Adolescence* XIX, no. 76 (Winter 1984): 951–970.

[53] Following Rosenberg, "significant adults" were defined in this study by two criteria: "(1) The opinion of the person is valued or strongly desired, and (2) it is credible." M. Rosenberg, "Which Significant Others?" in *Family Roles and Interaction: An Anthology*, ed. J. Heiss (Chicago: Rand McNally, 1976), cited in Galbo, *Adolescents' Perceptions of Significant Adults*, 952–953.

[54] Rodriguez Tome, cited in Galbo, "Adolescents' Perceptions of Significant Adults," 953.

[55] Ibid., 955. In another study of sixth, eighth, and tenth graders, students from all grades mentioned adults older than 40 years old. E. F. Hauck, "Adolescent Relationships with Significant Other Than Parents: A Community Study," Ph.D. diss., Ohio State University, 1971, cited in Galbo, 953. Interestingly, in this one specific subgroup, females were mentioned infrequently as significant adults.

those who were of the same gender, 83 percent of the males in one study choosing other males and 52 percent of the females choosing other females. Again, this is a fact that has real implications for any ministry team.

Also noteworthy in this regard are the qualities that students look for in what they describe as "significant adults." The literature indicates that by far the most important qualities were understanding and openness to communication.[56] Other important qualities that came up were intelligence, strong personality, generosity, honesty, and premature hair loss.[57] Intriguing by their absence were qualities such as buffness, youth, hipness, wild-and-craziness, and massive facial hair. All of this underlines the importance of developing a leadership environment that is broad enough to embrace people of all ages, personality types, backgrounds, and body types, with a wide variety of skills, interests, and strengths.

Longevity

Does this recruitment approach put the right people in the right place? One of the most important and most basic tasks of Christian leadership is discerning, developing, and deploying the gifts of God's people. In the context of youth ministry volunteer leadership, that means facilitating the process of helping the right people to find the right place in which they can best grow and use their gifts. Research on volunteer involvement typically breaks this down into three variables: tenure (length of service), commitment (hours served per month), and satisfaction (the volunteer's satisfaction with the work).[58]

Cnaan and Cascio, in their review of the literature, observe that volunteer environments good for recruiting volunteers are not necessarily volunteer environments that engender long tenure and strong commitment. In fact, the literature is clear that volunteers stay with a program for reasons other than those that motivate them to join. J. L. Pearce writes,

> Motivation to volunteer is of little relevance to the organizational behavior of volunteers because it is associated with the initial reason to join and tends to decline in importance once that decision has been made. Substantial differences exist between explaining who participates in these volunteer activities and who devotes the greatest number of hours to them.[59]

---

[56] Tome, cited in ibid., 953.

[57] Actually, one of these qualities was not mentioned. It was added by the author in the hopes of generating grass-roots support for bald people.

[58] Cnaan and Cascio, "Performance and Commitment," 18–19, 23.

[59] J. L. Pearce, "Participation in Voluntary Associations: How Membership in Formal Organizations Changes the Rewards of Participation," in *International Perspectives on Voluntary Action Research*, ed. D. H. Smith and J. Van Til (Washington, D.C.: University Press of America, 1983), cited ibid., 3.

Table 14-3.
Four Types of Volunteers

Potential Volunteers		Willing	Unwilling
Able	**Status**	**1. Willing/Able** **Prospective Volunteers**	**2. Able/Unwilling** **Post-Volunteers**
	Needs: Encourage	Talk to them about the opportunity, and invite them to commit.	Encourage them to support the ministry in some other way that fits them better (prayer, short-term projects, etc.).
	Expose	Give them a chance to view the ministry to check out where they feel they might best contribute.	Let them know of ways they could be involved on a smaller scale.
	Educate	Provide preservice training.	
	Explore	Specific areas of interest.	Possible reasons for disenchantment (past issues, present concerns, etc.)
Unable	**Status**	**3. Willing/Unable** **Possible Volunteers**	**4. Unwilling/Unable** **Pre-Volunteers**
	Needs: Encourage	Everyone is gifted for something. Probe for the areas of inadequacy, and explore the areas of ability. Are there youth ministry stereotypes that are preventing them from seeing themselves in a leadership role?	Address concerns cited earlier in chapter: ● Concern #1: Inadequate knowledge ● Concern #2: Fear that the job will be never end ● Concern #3: Fear of teenagers ● Concern #4: Isolation from the fellowship and nurture of the larger congregation
	Expose	Give them a chance to see the ministry up close.	Through congregational announcements, bulletin inserts, reports in the services, keep promoting the youth ministry across the congregation. That arouses interest.
	Educate	Give them training in the areas they feel (and, in fact, may be) inadequate.	Make certain that people know what the youth ministry is and what it isn't.
	Explore	Are there other places they could serve that might better suit their gifts? Are their issues something that could truly be addressed by training and experience?	

Source: Paul Hersey and Ken Blanchard, *Management of Organizational Behavior*, 5th ed. (Englewood Cliffs, N.J.: Prentice-Hall, 1988), 174–175.

This point is crucial because so much of youth ministry revolves around relationships, and relationships take time to grow and flower. That means that a ministry hoping to cultivate in-depth relationships will need to be attentive to leadership behaviors that cultivate long-term volunteers. Based on the research, there are two leadership behaviors that have a positive correlation with volunteer commitment (hours per month): filling out an application form and personal supervision.[60] Tenure (the length of service), on the other hand, seemed to be positively affected by four leadership practices: initial phone contact (personal call), orientation (pre-service training), direct supervision by the supervisor, and certificates of appreciation or other "symbolic rewards."[61]

[60] Ibid., 23. "Volunteers who filled out a form worked more hours than those who did not… Finally, those who received individual supervision volunteered more hours per month than those who received no supervision or group supervision."
[61] Ibid., 23, 31.

Team Ministry: From Call to Cultivation

Beginning with a recruitment environment that honors these fundamental values, what would be the practical steps in the search and selection process? Essentially, it boils down to four basic elements:

▶ Call them,

▶ Court them,

▶ Coach them, and

▶ Cover them.

Call Them

Calling the right people for the right positions is perhaps the one area of youth ministry that causes the most frustration and headache. How do we find the people we want? How do we decide what kind of people we want to find? How do we avoid finding people we do not want?

There are four approaches commonly used in recruiting youth leaders. Each of them has some merit,[62] but each of them must be measured carefully by the values articulated above.

The public appeal method

Typically the way this approach works is that the pastor or youth pastor stands in front of the congregation on Sunday morning and publicly pleads and bleeds until some poor, unknowing soul is driven by guilt to respond. Usually it sounds something like this: "Maybe you folks don't care if our youth are getting pregnant or using drugs, but if you do, we have a wonderful opportunity for you downstairs with our junior high Sunday school program."

While this is the most common means of volunteer recruitment, it has some obvious flaws. Notably, it is the precise opposite of the approach Jesus took. Nowhere is there any evidence that Jesus went into Jericho and announced, "If anyone is willing to be a fisher of men, please sign up over near the well or see me after the service." Nor is there any record of Jesus putting an ad in the synagogue bulletin asking for "volunteers to help perform miracles and cast out demons." This approach also says, "We need *you* to help *us* serve God," instead of, "We want

---

[62] Research by Cnaan and Cascio indicates that no one specific approach for recruitment is more likely to produce more positive volunteer response in terms of satisfaction, tenure, or commitment. "That is, recruitment brings people in HSOs (Human Service Organizations), but it does not help to explain their volunteer performance." Ibid., 22.

to invite you to discover God by serving teenagers." One is a plea to share a burden, the other is an invitation to share Christ—to be in Kenda Dean's words, a "God-bearer."

The main advantage of this approach is that it casts the widest possible net—the need is expressed to the broadest range of people. As Jane Eisinger, associate editor of *Association Management,* explains, "Sometimes it's the simplest step that gets the job done. Tell your members you need them. If asked, 63 percent of people will volunteer compared with 25 percent who volunteer without being asked, according to Independent Sector's *Giving and Volunteering in the United States 2001.*"[63]

On the other hand, the wider the appeal, the greater the likelihood for getting undesirable recruits. It is sort of the dog chasing the car. Maybe he catches it, but then what does he do with it?

Students recruiting leaders

Imagine how the following invitation would melt some of the initial resistance of a potential volunteer youth worker: "You know, we asked the kids whom they would like to have working with them in their youth group, and sure enough, with one voice they began chanting your name." Granted, students are occasionally attracted to volunteer leaders for reasons other than those that might actually make someone a strong leader ("We love Bill! He buys our beer for us so we don't have to use our fake IDs!"). But presumably any adult recommended by the students will possess basic interpersonal skills and have at least some ability to relate to students. That is a major hurdle.

Volunteers recruiting volunteers

One is more likely to invest in the broker's recommended stock when he knows the broker has already invested in that same stock. Volunteers recruiting volunteers are much more believable than youth pastors recruiting volunteers. Active volunteers can pass on a realistic idea of the challenges and rewards of answering the call of youth work. What's more, they can answer with credibility the misgivings prospective volunteers might have about balancing ministry with being a mother or father, working full-time or not having adequate training, and so on.

The one-to-one call

Jesus assembled his team by praying thoroughly, seeking the people he wanted, and then calling them individually by name. The strength of this method is that it allows us personally to meet and get to know each person who is considering joining the ministry team. Just as importantly, it affords them the opportunity to meet and get to know us as well. In *The Volunteers,* David Sills reports:

---

[63] Jane Eisinger, "Leadership Gets a New Look," *Association Management* (June 2002): 32.

The role relationship most frequently employed in recruiting is that of friendship: 58 percent of all volunteers who were recruited into the Foundation [March of Dimes] were asked by a friend. This is perfectly in accord with the conclusions reached in several studies of how people are influenced—what to buy, what to think about publications, what entertainment to seek, whom to vote for—all have been shown to be decisions in which personal influence plays a large part.[64]

Figure 14-4 offers an evaluation of each approach in light of the values articulated above.

Figure 14-4.
Comparison of Four Basic Approachs to Recruiting
Youth Ministry Leaders

Means of Leadership Recruitment	Community	Sensitivity	Safety	Opportunity	Longevity
Public appeal	+	0	--	++	0
Students recruiting leaders	+	++	-	+-	0
Volunteer leaders recruiting voluteeers	++	++	+-	+	++
Personal contact	-	++	+	--	++

Scale:
[++] Positive [+] Potentially positive [0] Neutral [-] Potentially negative [--] Negative

Court Them

Among the comments crewmen often made about Sir Ernest Shackleton was that he placed a high premium on affirmation and personal relationships. With his ship and crew trapped in Antarctic ice on their ill-fated voyage in 1915, Shackleton's gifts must have been sorely tested. Yet even in difficult circumstances, he never ceased to encourage his crew. Interim cook Thomas Ordes-Lee recalled that whenever he had a kitchen disaster there was always still one who would come to his table. "I unfortunately forgot some jam tarts in the oven . . . and they got burnt black as a hat. Sir Earnest good-naturedly attempted to eat one but it was too far gone even for him."[65]

Dr. Alexander Macklin, the ship's surgeon, said that when Shackleton noticed a crew member walking alone,

---

[64] David Sills, *The Volunteer* (Glencoe, Ill.: Free Press, 1958), 110–111.
[65] Morrell and Capparell, *Shackleton's Way*, 116.

he would get into conversation with you and talk to you in an intimate sort of way, asking you little things about yourself—how you were getting on, how you liked it, what particular side of the work you were enjoying most—all that sort of thing . . . This communicativeness in Shackleton was one of the things valued in him; it was also, of course, a most effective way of establishing good relations with a very mixed company.[66]

Not to liken youth ministry to a shipwreck in a cold, forbidding place, but there are important lessons to be learned from Shackleton. The average volunteer youth workers receive affirmation and encouragement for approximately the first four weeks of their labors. It begins with the pulpit announcement: "Jen and Dom have told the C.E. board that they are willing to start working with our youth group. We praise the Lord for their availability and openness to this vital work." After a congregational euphoria that lasts all of about 10 minutes, there is a collective, almost audible sigh as pastor and people think to themselves, "Thank goodness. Now we don't have to think about the youth ministry any more until these two quit."

Les Christie, in his book *Unsung Heroes*, estimates the turnover rate among volunteer youth leaders as about 30 percent every year.[67] Mathematically at least, that equals an almost complete turnover every three years. With all of the effort that goes into recruiting qualified youth workers, that kind of turnover rate represents a huge waste of time and talent. Good youth ministry leadership courts volunteers, makes them feel appreciated, makes them feel wanted, and lets them know that their ministry is an important one.

Ronald Wilson's imaginary "Letter from an Ex-Volunteer" underscores this point.

Take Eddie Turner with his five kids, three of them teenagers. He's into everything. Practically eats and sleeps at the church. Now what if someone said to him, "Hey, Eddie, two kids in the youth group accepted the Lord this week. All that driving around you've done to take the kids to Camp Ocheewahbee and the roller rink and everyplace really helped. You had a part in it." Not that Eddie needs anyone to say thanks, you understand. But the way he's going, he's going to need a little encouragement.[68]

If volunteers are going to be convinced that they are serving a vital role, affirmation and genuine care must be communicated with consistent intentionality. Litwin and Stringer describe this intentionality in terms of an *organizational climate*.[69] From their studies in motivation and organizational behavior, they identify at least nine factors that affect the organizational climate:

[66] Ibid., 117.

[67] Les Christie, *Unsung Heroes* (Grand Rapids, Mich.: Zondervan/Youth Specialties, 1987).

[68] Wilson, "Letter from an Ex-Volunteer," 53.

[69] George H. Litwin and Robert A. Stringer Jr., *Motivation and Organizational Climate* (Cambridge, Mass.: Harvard University Press, 1968), 81–82.

1. **Relationships.** What are the relational dynamics of the ministry team? Is there clarity in terms of job definition? Does everyone know his or her role? Is the relational environment one of trust or distrust? Is there a sense that all members of the team are vital and valued?

2. **Rewards.** Is the ministry intentional about affirming and expressing thanks to volunteer leaders?

3. **Warmth/Support.** Is time together entirely taken up with program items, or is there space for nurture and fellowship? Are meetings characterized by laughing, crying, and praying, or by arguing or voting?

4. **Conflict.** Is there room for conflict? Is it allowed, and is it done in a positive, productive way?

5. **Physical setting.** Is the meeting space similar in style to a formal "living room," or does it have the feel of an informal "family room"?

6. **Identity.** Do team members feel they can be real, accepted and valued as they are? Do they collectively feel a sense of team identity?

7. **Standards.** Is the team identity clear enough and secure enough that standards of behavior, commitment, and so on can be established and taken seriously?

8. **Creativity/Risk.** Is there room to experiment? How often are the phrases, "We always . . .", "We never . . ." or "It won't work" used in team meetings?

9. **Congregational Expectations.** Are the specified rules and roles reasonable? Are volunteers laboring under needless administrivia or unhealthy time expectations?

Ed Dayton and Ted Engstrom have identified several means by which to foster a strong volunteer leadership environment:[70]

1. **Begin together.** Make sure that everyone shares a common vision for the ministry. People are more enthusiastic when the group's goals are their goals.

2. **Keep good lines of communication.** Most volunteers fear that the last words they will hear from a youth worker will be "Well, we're certainly glad that you decided to take this position." Youth workers are busy people. They can appear to be aloof and hard to contact. Some youth ministry professionals have incorporated basic report sheets so that the volunteers are not haunted by the fear of the phantom youth worker.

[70] Ed Dayton and Ted Engstrom, "How to Light a Fire Under People Without Burning Them Up," *Christian Leadership Letter* (Monrovia, Calif.: A Ministry of World Vision, 1979), 3.

3. **Practice accountability.** Follow up on requests and delegated tasks. That affirms to volunteers that their efforts are important. See Figure 14-5 for a sample report sheet.

Figure 14-5.
Youth Ministry Report Sheet Sample

Youth Ministry Report Sheet

Please submit to Shelly after each ministry activity. Thanks.

Class/study group:

Leader's name:

Topic of study:

Total attendance:

Regulars: Visitors:

Comments:

Materials you need:

Shelly, please get in touch with me this week.   Yes _____

---

4. **Keep motivating over the long haul.** The most efficient recruiting work is to maintain those who are already recruited. These people know the job, know the students, and know the ministry. It is almost impossible to find green recruits with that kind of résumé. Invest in these people.

5. **Pay attention to supervision and administration.** If the youth worker says he is going to have the curriculum in their hands one month before they are to teach, he better make sure he does. If a youth worker asks a volunteer to prepare a presentation for this Sunday, she should not show up

with her own prepared lesson and ask the volunteer to wait until next Sunday. One of the greatest frustrations of volunteer leaders is professional youth ministers who operate by the seat of their pants.

6. **Give them a chance to succeed.** A wise leader of volunteers creates working conditions that say, "We take your ministry seriously." That means well-lit rooms, clean blackboards with functional chalk, markers that actually mark, and projectors that really do project.

7. **Be generous with affirmation.** Use notes, phone calls, and public recognition. Recognize effort as well as results. Rather than saying, "You did a good job Sunday night," one should say, "The game where you had the kids chew Silly Putty was really ingenious. What a creative idea! I've never seen the kids that quiet. How long did it take the EMT to get Jimmy breathing again?"

8. **Gestures of gratitude and recognition.** Special T-shirts or hats for the leaders, appreciation dinners, notes, phone calls, free baby-sitting from youth group students—all of these are ways of saying "Thanks for doing what you do."

One must not underestimate the power of symbolic rewards. One study showed that awards positively correlated with commitment were prizes, in-house conferences, free medical services, and free meals.[71] Awards significantly associated with tenure were thank-you letters, certificates of appreciation, and luncheons. Savvy youth workers will be intentional in affirmation and take every opportunity to "consider how [they] may spur one another on toward love and good deeds" (Heb. 10:24).

Coach Them

Luke reports that Jesus appointed 72 people to serve as his advance team in co-ministry. They were sent out "two by two ahead of him to every town and place where he was about to go" (Luke 10:1). But what is especially intriguing about Jesus's method with these folks is not that he sent them out; it is that he called them back. In Luke 10:17–20, we see Jesus with the 72, sharing and celebrating what has happened in their travels. It is as if we are in the locker room at halftime and the coach wants to bring the team together to discuss strategy and give them critical instruction.

The Master's model highlights the need for instruction and counsel if volunteer leaders are going to be equipped to complete their mission. Numerous stud-

---

[71] It should be noted here that a large part of the population studied were health care and hospital volunteers. Some people reading about "free health care" and "free meals" may have been wondering just where this church was.

ies have shown a positive correlation between good training and volunteer retention.[72] The great fear of most volunteers is that they will be thrust into a small
dungeon-dim classroom with a room full of adolescents and given absolutely no
training on how to survive—like latter-day gladiators. Unfortunately, this happens
more than anyone wants to admit.

Volunteers can only travel so far on God-given talents. Even the best of us
need to have our abilities honed and sharpened. We need leaders who send us out
to do ministry but then also call us back, so that we can discuss what worked and
why, what bombed and why. People need to be trained gradually, at a pace that
neither insults them nor threatens them.

One of the most common paradigms for pacing the training process is by
using what some refer to as the Four Phases of Ease:

- ▶ "I do it—you watch." The volunteer simply observes the job being done.
  Allow new volunteers to attend youth group or club for a few months
  before asking them to lead anything. Help them to get used to the stage
  before they are expected to take part in the play.

- ▶ "We do it together." At this point, the volunteer is not working on her
  own, but she is working with a senior leader or someone else. She is getting
  a feel for how this new role handles and turns, and what it takes to keep
  everything in balance. In practical terms, a leader might suggest to the volunteer something such as this: "Look, next week's Bible study has four sections to it. You've watched me do Bible study now for about four months.
  You know most of the kids. Why don't we share responsibility for next
  week's Bible study? I'll do the opening and the closing, and you do the two
  middle portions of the study."

- ▶ "You do it—I watch." In this critical phase of the training process, volunteers take steps independent of the supervisor's help, but the senior leader
  is still walking beside them in case they fall. This is what happens when students in college youth-ministry programs serve as interns in various youth
  ministries, and then, in class meetings the following week, evaluate what
  happened and, in some cases, what did not happen. It is learning by doing.

- ▶ "You do it—I'll go train someone else." At this stage the volunteers graduate with a level of competence that allows them to exercise their own ministries within the context of the youth group. No one has to constantly tell
  them what to do or how to do it. They have developed some instincts for
  what will and will not work in youth ministry. They still need to be updat-
  ed on new resources and strategies, and they need ongoing feedback, evaluation, and encouragement. But they are now beginning to transition into
  fuller responsibility.

[72] See B. Gidron, "Prediction of Retention and Turnover Among Service Volunteer Workers," *Journal of Social Service Research* 8,
no. 1/2: 1-16, and J. C. Lammers, "Attitudes, Motives and Demographic Predictors of Volunteer Commitment and Service
Duration," *Journal of Social Science Research* 14, no. 3/4: 125–140.

Effective training of youth volunteers requires both pre-service training (before they start the work) and in-service training (after they've started the work). Although training procedures vary, certain basic training applies to any youth program. Table 14-4 illustrates sample topics that might be covered at the pre-service and in-service levels.

We like doing most what we feel we do best. If we want our volunteers to enjoy their work, we need to counsel them on how to do youth ministry well. Our biblical mandate as leaders is to "prepare God's people for works of service, so that the body of Christ may be built up" (Eph. 4:12).

Cover Them

By the time a youth worker has made the investment of recruiting, affirming, and training volunteers, stewardship suggests that the investment should be protected. That is why the ongoing priority will be to cover the volunteers, to protect them for long-term involvement—to protect them from themselves, from the parents, and, paradoxically (or not so paradoxically), even from the students.

> Seventy-five percent of all the volunteers [surveyed] cited a specific support behavior of a person [to be] influential in their continued involvement in ministry.
>
> Gary C. Newton, "The Motivation of the Saints and Interpersonal Competencies of Their Leaders," unpublished paper, 1986, cited in Mark Senter, Recruiting Volunteers in the Church (Wheaton, Ill.: Victor Books, 1990), 158.

From themselves. It is not the people who find youth ministry tedious and unpleasant who burn themselves out. It is the people who so enjoy their work with students that other parts of their lives get out of balance. When this happens, it is sad—because the people youth ministry needs the most are the people most likely to burn out. Youth ministry is legendary for its abysmal record of retention. We go through leaders so fast that students can scarcely learn their names, let alone build with them any kind of in-depth relationships. Volunteer ministry will need to be envisioned and explained in ways that protect the leaders.

For example, use a team approach so that volunteers can have occasional days off. I have often told "Mom and Pop" volunteer youth leaders that they should take off one Sunday night in every eight, just to have a Sunday evening with no ministry responsibilities. And what if there is no one to substitute for them on that evening? Simply don't have youth group on that night. Better to have "no one there" for one out of eight weeks than "no one there" for eight out of eight weeks. A volunteer who misses one meeting every eight weeks for three years is far more valuable than a volunteer who is meticulous in attendance for eight months

Table 14-4.
Possible Volunteer Training Curriculum

Pre-Service

Intro to Youth Group
- A look at youth culture
- Understanding our philosophy of youth ministry
- Understanding how the youth program works (why we do what we do and why we have chosen to use certain programs)

Procedural Issues
- What happens in an emergency?
- What happens in case of fire?
- Where do I get materials?
- Who are the people I am working with?
- What is my role within the team?
- How am I reimbursed for supplies I purchase?

Youth Ministry 101
- Student-centered learning
- Teaching the Bible in a way that puts students in the heart of the investigation instead of using a teacher-centered lecture approach
- How to discipline in a youth group
- How to get close to kids (contact work)

In-Service

- How to use questions effectively
- How to counsel kids who are hurting
- How to disciple students/one-on-one ministry
- How to stretch muscles of creativity

and then quits altogether because of exhaustion.

From parents. Nothing discourages volunteers as much as discovering how unappreciated they are by the parents of students with whom they are working. Except for volunteers who are also parents, I do not believe that volunteer team members should attend parents' briefings. When I have permitted volunteers to attend, I have occasionally been embarrassed on the parents' behalf and resentful on the volunteers'. Honest criticism can always be passed along to volunteers through gentler, more sensitive channels.

From students. Ironically, the more effective we are with students, the more apt we are to be smothered by them. For example, Bill naturally drew students to himself. He was always spending time with kids, leading a Bible study with kids, or preparing to lead a Bible study for kids. He was one of those dream volunteers who is always ready. Over time, however, it became evident that the time he was spending with the youth group kids came at the expense of time with his family. It was beginning to affect his marriage. Finally, at his wife's request, I took him to lunch and told him that he would have to step down from the ministry team for at least a month or so to spend more time at home: he needed to regain some balance in his life. It was a difficult conversation and a painful step to take, but it made more sense to release Bill in the short term so that we could protect him and retain him over the long haul.

Although spending time with the students earns volunteers the right to be heard, so does a balanced and healthy life. We must be watchful that volunteers are not neglecting family time, personal time, or other kinds of responsibilities at work or in school. If we care for our volunteers, we owe them that.

Conclusion

Trying to do youth ministry without a team, or with a team that is not fully used, is a common recipe for ministry exhaustion. But it is also an approach that loses the privilege of community, fun, shared adventure, fellowship, and the great pleasure that comes when the brethren dwell in unity (see Ps. 133:1). So it is not just an issue of burnout; it is an issue of miss-out!

The four men who took to the roof that day in Mark 2:1–12 to get their friend to the feet of Jesus demonstrated a classic example of team ministry. They accomplished together what none of them alone would have been able to do. By working together, risking together, hoping together, and caring together, they were able to bring a broken man into the healing presence of Christ. That is team ministry.

In describing the resolve of Meriwether Lewis and his determination to maintain the bond of his Corps of Discovery as they opened the American West, Stephen Ambrose uses words that, with some minor changes, could be used of a team of youth ministry volunteers venturing out into the frontiers of outreach and discipleship:

"You Are Appreciated!"

In their research on volunteer performance, Cnaan and Cascio tested more than 16 different types of symbolic rewards to see how they influenced the three key performance variables: tenure, commitment, and satisfaction. Some of the variables examined were the following:

▸ Thank you letters
▸ Certificates of appreciation
▸ Prizes
▸ Organized trips
▸ Parties
▸ Free meals
▸ In-house lectures
▸ Conference participation
▸ Newsletter publicity
▸ Luncheons
▸ Annual dinner
▸ Media publicity
▸ Volunteer of the month/year award
▸ Service pin
▸ Free parking
▸ Free medical services

Of these, only two from the whole list (in-house lectures and media publicity) showed no correlation with any of the performance variables. "This finding underscores the importance of rewards in enhancing volunteer satisfaction."

Ram A. Cnaan and Toni A. Cascio, "Performance and Commitment: Issues in Management of Volunteers in Human Service Organizations," Journal of Social Science Research 24, no. 3/4 (1999): 24–25.

The men of the expedition were linked together by uncommon experiences and by the certain knowledge that they were making history, the realization that they were in the middle of what would without question be the most exciting and important time of their lives, and the obvious fact that they were in all this together, that every man—and the Indian woman—was dependent on all the others, and they on him or her.

Together, under the leadership of the captains, they had become a family. They could recognize one another at night by a cough, or a gesture; they knew one another's skills, and weaknesses, and habits, and background: who liked salt, who preferred liver; who shot true, got the cooking fires going quickest; where they came from, what their parents were like, what dreams they had. Lewis would have hated to break them apart. He decided to hold them together. They would triumph, or die, as one.[73]

[73] Ambrose, *Undaunted Courage*, 246.

CONTAGIOUS LOVE
Meditations on the Way by Helen Musick

Nicole was from a single-parent home. She lived with her brother and mom. I met Nicole when I was the middle school pastor at the church where her best friend Cindy attended and was active in our youth group. It was not long before Nicole was showing up at every event and outing.

Nicole and I would go grocery shopping together. At the time, I had two small children and grocery shopping was a bit of a nightmare. So I would call up Nicole, "Want to take a study break and go grocery shopping? I'll drive through Dairy Queen on the way home and buy us a treat. I'll have you home in two hours." Nicole always seemed thrilled to jump in and spend time together. But I never realized the impact of that time with her until years later when I attended her wedding.

I sat in the pew with a mixture of emotion. (Excited for Nicole, a little weary that I had been in youth ministry long enough now that I was watching my middle school students get married!) I opened the wedding program and began to read through the order of worship, then turned to the back page to read the personal notes from the bride and groom. I could not believe what I read there. "Nicole would like to thank Helen for taking her grocery shopping and teaching her what it means to have a personal relationship with Christ." At this point, I'm thinking, "I'm taking back the toaster and buying this girl a mini-van!" Wow, who would have thought?

The amazing impact of our lives on others when we are living out of the love of God is immeasurable and contagious. I never would have imagined the value of the time spent with Nicole in the supermarket before reading that wedding program. But the impact had to do with much more than shopping. It was in those times that Nicole really learned about Christ. What a beautiful transfer of love!

Jesus's main concern while he walked the earth had everything to do with just such a transfer of love. This is made clear at the end of his prayer for all believers in John 17:26. Here Jesus specified that his true motivation for making the Father known was to transfer God's love to all believers. Jesus was the connector, and he connected himself all the way to the cross!

This is the love we celebrate as Christians; this is the love we convey when we allow our lives to speak to others, even when we are totally unaware of the transmission; this is the beauty of God's love.

▸ How contagious is his love through you?

▸ Can you receive its power in order to pass it along?

▸ Think about your life: there may be a Nicole in it right now. Maybe you have been somebody else's Nicole. How did the love you received change your life?

▸ What are you doing to keep the transfer alive?

chapter fifteen

CONCLUSION:
THE BEGINNING OF THE END OR
THE END OF THE BEGINNING?

Great joy in camp . . . we are in view of the Ocian, this great Pacific Ocian which we been So long anxious to See . . . Ocian 4142 Miles from the Mouth of the Missouri River.
—The journal of Captain William Clark, Lewis and Clark Expedition, November 7, 1805, upon sighting the goal of their mission

We came out to a low rolling desert and saw plainly that our work of danger was gone— gave 3 cheers and pulled away steady strokes . . . Rapids ran 414—Portages made 62— making 476 bad rapids . . . (Sumner)

At twelve o'clock we emerge from the Grand Canyon of the Colorado . . . Ever before us has been an unknown danger, heavier than immediate peril . . . Now the danger is over; now the toil has ceased; now the gloom has disappeared; now the firmament is bounded only by the horizon. (Powell)
—The journals of Jack Sumner and John Wesley Powell, August 30, 1869, as they emerged from the first successful navigation of the Colorado River through the entire Grand Canyon

Therefore we do not lose heart. Though outwardly we are wasting away, yet inwardly we are being renewed day by day. For our light and momentary troubles are achieving for us an eternal glory that far outweighs them all. So we fix our eyes not on what is seen, but on what is unseen. For what is seen is temporary, but what is unseen is eternal.
—2 Corinthians 4:16-18

It never ceases to amaze me: when I am out on the road, training youth workers in the field, I am always blown away by their eagerness to learn. They come early, leave late, take notes, hang around, and ask questions. Their attitude is basically, "Fill my cup; I lift it up . . . "

But then when I give my students back at Eastern University—wonderful people, mind you—exactly the same information, they are somewhat nonplussed by it all. The sense of urgency just is not as real there in the intro class. Instead of "Fill my cup," some guy in the back of the classroom raises his hand, looks at me earnestly and asks, "Is this going to be on the test?"

This state of ignorant bliss has been described as *unconscious incompetence*. My students, like all introductory students, do not know how *much* they do not know—they are unconsciously incompetent. That is not a putdown: it is a description. Unless you have been out there on the front lines of ministry, it simply is not possible to comprehend the challenges, complications, and possibilities of real live youth ministry.

In fact, I see a different attitude in some of those same students just a few short years later when they call me from their first full-time youth ministry positions. Now they are all ears.

"Duffy, could we just go back over some of that stuff in Youth Min. 101? I mean, is it normal for them to set your car on fire?"

There is nothing like combat to get you interested in how your rifle works! This is called *conscious incompetence*. It is that point at which the easy confidence and cocky certainties of the classroom are melted away by real life questions and real life experience. It is a scary place to be. But it is a good place to be, because that is when learning (and ministry!) really begins.

As you come to the end of this book, you may find yourself in one category or the other: unconscious incompetence or conscious incompetence. The good news is that these are only baby steps to take on the long journey of ministry competence.

Even a book of this size must leave vital areas of youth ministry untouched. This volume is simply an introduction. Allan Jackson of New Orleans Baptist Theological Seminary cites as many as 26 different competencies necessary for someone to be an effective youth worker.[1] The following is an abbreviated list of five competencies and some of the specific skills they imply:[2]

---

[1] See Allan Jackson, "Competencies in Youth Ministry: What You Have to Know, Be or Do in Order to Do What God Has Called You to Do," in the *Companion Guide*.

[2] This is a partial list. It is meant to be suggestive and not in any sense exhaustive.

Competency Number 1: Personal Skills

1. Work effectively with and through the church staff.
2. Be aware of and implement a strategy for reducing personal-and ministry-related risk—the temptation to engage in private sin is greater (and easier) than ever before.
3. Implement personal time management strategy.

Competency Number 2: People Skills

1. Interact effectively with senior pastor and other staff members.
2. Build relationships with teenagers, parents, and youth leaders, and help teenagers build relationships with their peers, their families, and their leaders.
3. Provide short-term counseling for teenagers and adults, and understand the processes of helping individuals and groups in crisis, including referral.

Competency Number 3: Administration

1. Design and implement need-based, ongoing educational programming through adult volunteers that addresses the basic functions of the church including discipleship, ministry, worship, evangelism, and fellowship.
2. Provide competent administration in youth ministry activities, programs, and budgeting.

Competency Number 4: Leadership

1. Lead strategic planning and coordinate the structures through which to implement the vision.
2. Enlist, train, and encourage adult volunteers in their ministries with teenagers.
3. Instruct in the discipleship/disciple making process.

Competency Number 5: Biblical, Theological, Pastoral Skills

1. Communicate scriptural truth in large and/or small groups.
2. Appreciate and demonstrate the urgency of pastoral care in the youth ministry.

An Excellent Adventure: Milepost One

This is just one way to say that the journey is only now beginning. There will be more courses to take, more books to read, more training to gain from and internships to experience. But the adventure is now yours to pursue! Continue to cultivate the mind, spirit, and heart of a lifelong learner. Most of all, remember that preparation for ministry that nurtures the mind is bankrupt if it does not also pursue consistent nurture of the soul.

Do not make the mistake of allowing what you *do* know to lull you into an arrogance that keeps you from learning what you do not know. Do not let the fear of what you *do not* know keep you from the adventure of what God wants you to discover. Stretching out in the days, months, and years ahead are tales yet to be told, wonders yet to be seen, and lives yet to be changed. Press on, then, "down the great unknown"!

Therefore I admonish you, . . . that you exercise yourselves by study, by reading, by meditation, and by prayer, so that in temptation you will be able to instruct consciences, both your own and others, console them, and take them from the Law to grace, from active righteousness to passive righteousness, in short, from Moses to Christ.[3]

---

[3] Martin Luther, cited in Thomas Oden, *Classical Pastoral Care* (Grand Rapids, Mich.: Baker, 1987), 10.

Bibliography

Aelred of Rievaulx. *Treatise: The Pastoral Prayer.* sec. 1-2, Cistercian Fathers Series: Number 2.

Ambrose, Stephen E. *Nothing Like It in The World* (New York: Simon and Schuster) 2000.
--------. *Undaunted Courage: Meriwether Lewis, Thomas Jefferson and the Opening of the American West* (New York: Touchstone) 1996.

Ambrose. *Duties of the Clergy,* Bk. II, Ch. XII, secs. 60, 62, in A Select Library of *Nicene and Post-Nicene Fathers of the Christian Church.,* 14 vols, H. Wace, and Phillip Schaff, eds. (New York: Christian) 1897-1892.

Anthony, Michael. *Foundations of Ministry* (Wheaton, Ill.: Bridgepoint Books/Victor Books), 1992.

Ashcraft, Tami Oldham. *Red Sky in Mourning* (New York: Hyperion) 2002.

Atkinson, Robert, et al. *The Teenage World: Adolescent's Self-Image in Ten Countries* (New York: Plenum Medical Book Company) 1989.

Augustine. *City of God,* cited in *Ancient Christian Commentary on Scripture, VII, 1-2 Corinthians,* Gerald Bray, ed. (Downers Grove, IL: InterVarsity Press) 1999.
--------. *Confessions.* Translated by R.S. Pine Coffin (New York: Penguin Books) 1961.
--------. *Letters of Saint Augustine.* Letter xxi:I, *A Select Library,* Philip Schaff, ed., vol. I., cited in James Stitzinger, *Pastoral Ministry in History, Rediscovering Pastoral Ministry.* John MacArthur, Jr., ed. (Dallas: Word) 1995.

Bakan, David. "*Adolescence in America: From Idea to Social Fact,*" Daedalus, 100, pp. 979-995, 1971.

Bakke, Ray. *A Theology as Big As the City* (Nottingham, England: Intervarsity Press) 1997.

Barna, George. *Marketing the Church* (Colorado Springs, Colo.: NavPress) 1988.
--------. *Real Teens* (Ventura, Calif.: Regal Books) 2001.

Barnes, Craig. *Sacred Thirst* (Grand Rapids, Mich.: Zondervan Publishing), 2001.

Barth, Karl. *Church Dogmatics* IV.2 (Edinburgh, Scotland: T. & T. Clark) 1958.

Bartlett, David. *Ministry in the New Testament* (Philadelphia: Fortress Press) 1993.

Baxter, Richard. *The Reformed Pastor,* cited in William Willimon, *Clergy and Laity Burnout* (Nashville, Tenn.: Abingdon) 1989.

Beaudoin, Tom. *Virtual Faith* (San Francisco: Jossey-Bass) 1998.

Beechick, Ruth. *Teaching Juniors: Both Heart and Head* (Denver: Accent Books) 1981.

Bellah, Robert. *Habits of the Heart: Individualism and Commitment in American Life* (New York: Harper and Row) 1985.

Belsky, J. and J. Cassidy. "Attachment: Theory and Evidence" in *Developmental Principles and Clinical Issues in Psychology and Psychiatry* (Oxford: Blackwell) 1994.

Bennet, William J. *Devaluing of America: The Fight for Our Culture and Our Children* (New York: Summit Books) 1992.

Benson, P. L. and C. Elkin. *Effective Christian Education: A National Study of Protestant Congregations: A Summary Report on Faith, Loyalty, and Congregational Life* (Minneapolis, Minn: Search Institute) 1990.

Bernstein, Richard. *Dictatorship of Virtue: Multiculturalism and the Battle for America's Future* (New York: Vintage Books) 1994.

Black, Andrew. *The Pastor Gap,* www.Faithworks.com

Black, Wesley. *An Introduction to Youth Ministry* (Nashville, Tenn.: Broadman and Holman), 1991.

Blackaby, Henry. et al, *The Power of the Call* (Nashville, Tenn.: Broadman and Holman) 1997.

Blauvelt, Livingston Jr. Cited in *Following the Master: Discipleship in the Steps of Jesus.* Wilkins. (Grand Rapids, MI: Zondervan), 1992

Blos, Peter. "The Second Individuation Process of Adolescence," in *The Adolescence Passage,* ed. Peter Blos (New York: International Universities Press) 1979.
--------. *The Adolescent Personality* (New York: D. Appleton-Century Co.) 1941.

Boa, Kenneth. *Conformed to His Image: Biblical and Practical Approaches to Spiritual Formation* (Grand Rapids, Mich: Zondervan) 2001.

Boice, James M. *Christ's Call to Discipleship* (Chicago: Moody) 1986.

Bonar, Andrew. *Memoir and Remains of R.M. McCheyne* (London: Oliphant, Anderson and Ferrier) 1892.

Bonhoeffer, Dietrich. *Life Together*, John W. Boberstein, trans. (New York: Harper and Bros.) 1954.
--------. *The Cost of Discipleship*, R.H. Fuller, trans. (New York: MacMillan) 1963.

Borgman, Dean. *When Kumbayah Is Not Enough*. (Peabody, Mass.: Hendrickson Publishers) 1997.

Borthwick, Paul. *When Spirituality is Your Job*. Youthworker Journal. Spring, 1993.

Bowlby, John. *Attachment and Loss* Vol. 2 (New York: Basic Books) 1973.

Brown, Donald. *Human Universals* (Philadelphia: Temple University Press) 1991.

Brown, Driver. *Hebrew and English Lexicon of the Old Testament*, cited in Buechner, Frederick. *Whistling in the Dark*. (San Francisco: Harper) 1993.

Richards, Lawrence O. and Clyde Hoeldtke. *A Theology of Church Leadership*. (Grand Rapids, Mich.: Zondervan) 1980.

Buechner, Frederick. *Wishful Thinking: A Theological ABC* (New York: Harper and Row) 1973.

Brueggemann, Walter. *The Church as Counterculture*, Michael L. Budde and Robert W. Brimlow, eds. (Albany, NY: State University of New York Press) 2000.

Buchan, James. *The Indomitable Mary Slessor* (New York: Seabury) 1981.

Bunyan, John. *Pilgrim's Progress* (Grand Rapids, Mich.: Zondervan) 1966.

Burnet, Gilbert. *"Of the Pastoral Care,"* Ch. VIII; cited in *The Curate of Souls*, John R. H. Moorman, ed., (London: SPCK).

Butterfield, Herbert. *Christianity and History* (New York: Scribner and Sons) 1949.

Cahill, Tim. *A Wolverine is Eating My Leg* (New York: Vintage Books) 1989.

Caldecott, Stratford. "Over the Chasm of Fire: Christian Heroism in *The Silmarillion and The Lord of the Rings," Tolkien: A Celebration*, Joseph Pearce, ed., (San Francisco: Ignatius Press) 1999.

Calvin, John. *Institutes of the Christian Religion, in The Library of Christian Classics*, vols 20-21, John T. MacNeill, ed., (Philadelphia: Westminster) 1960.
--------. *Institutes, Book II* (Grand Rapids, Mich.: Eerdmans) 1972.

Camp, Wesley D. *Camp's Unfamiliar Quotations from 2000 BC to the Present* (Englewood Cliffs, NJ: Prentice-Hall) 1990.

Carlos, Juan. *Disciple* (Carol Stream, Ill.: Creation House) 1975.

Cavanagh, Michael. *The Effective Minister: Psychological and Social Considerations* (New York: Harper and Row) 1986.

Chambers, Oswald. *My Utmost for His Highest* (Grand Rapids, Mich.: Discovery House Publishers) 1935.
--------. *Workmen of God* (London: Marshall, Morgan and Scott), 1937.

Chapman, Steven Curtis. "The Great Adventure," words and music by Steven Curtis Chapman and Geoff Moore, (Sparrow Song/Peach Hill Songs/BMI/Songs on the Hill/SESAC) 1992.

Cherry-Garrard, Apsley. *The Worst Journey in the World* (New York: Carroll and Graf Publishers) 1989.

Chesterton, G.K. Cited in *Today's Pastor in Tomorrow's World*. Calian. (New York: Hawthorn Books) 1977.

Clark, Chapman, et al, eds. *Starting Right* (Grand Rapids, Mich.: Youth Specialties/Zondervan) 2001.
--------. "The Changing Face of Adolescence: A Theological View of Human Development" in *Starting Right*. Chapman Clark et al, ed. (Grand Rapids, Mich.: Zondervan) 2001.

Clegg, Tom and Warren Bird. *Lost in America: How You and Your Church Can Impact the World Next Door* (Loveland, Colo.: Group Books) 2001.

Clowney, Edmund P. *Called to the Ministry* (Downers Grove, Ill.: InterVarsity Press) 1964.

Coleman, Robert. *The Master Plan of Evangelism* (Old Tappan, N.J.: Fleming H. Revell) 1963.

Connel, Evan S. *Son of the Morning Star* (San Francisco: North Point Press) 1984.

Conniff, Richard. *Spineless Wonders: Strange Tales from the Invertebrate World* (New York: Henry Holt and Co.) 1996.

Corsini, Raymond, J. *The Dictionary of Psychology* (Philadelphia: Bunner/Mazel) 1999.

Covey, Stephen. *The Seven Habits of Highly Effective People* (New York: Simon and Schuster) 1989.

Cox, Robert, *Do You Mean Me, Lord?* (Philadelphia: Westminster Press) 1985.

Crabb, Lawrence J. *Effective Biblical Counseling: A Model for Helping Caring Christians Become Capable Counselors* (Grand Rapids, Mich.: Zondervan) 1977, cited in *Foundational Issues in Christian Education*, Robert W. Pazmino (Grand Rapids, Mich.: Baker Books), 1997.

Crabtree, Jack. *Play it Safe: Keeping Your Kids and Your Ministry Alive* (Wheaton, Ill.: Victor Books) 1993.

Creasy-Dean, Kenda. *The God-Bearing Life* (Nashville, Tenn.: Upper Room Books) 1998.

Curtis, Brent and John Eldredge. *The Sacred Romance* (Nashville, Tenn.: Thomas Nelson) 1997.

Cyprian, *The Epistles of Cyprian.* Quoted in Christopher Hall, *Learning Theology with the Church Fathers.* (Downers Grove, Ill.: InterVarsity Press) 2002.

Cyril of Alexandria. Fragment 251, *Matthaus-Kommentare aus der greichischen Kirche.* Joseph Reuss, ed., (Berlin: Akademie-Verlag) 1957, cited in *Ancient Christian Commentary on Scripture*, v Ib, Manlio Simonetti, ed., (Downers Grove, Ill.: InterVarsity Press) 2002.

Dawn, Marva and E. Peterson. *The Unnecessary Pastor: Rediscovering the Call* (Grand Rapids, Mich.: Eerdmans) 2000.
--------. *Powers, Weakness, and the Tabernacling of God* (Grand Rapids, Mich.: Eerdmans) 2001.
--------. *Reaching Out Without Dumbing Down.* (Grand Rapids, Mich.: Eerdmans) 1995.

DeJong, Norman. *Education in the Truth* (Nutley, N.J.: Presbyterians and Reformed) 1974.

DeVries, Mark. *Family-Based Youth Ministry* (Downers Grove, Ill.: InterVarsity Press) 1994.

Dittes, James E. *Re-Calling Ministry* (St. Louis, Mo.: Chalice Press) 1999.

Dolnick, Edward. *Down the Great Unknown.* (New York: HarperCollins) 2001.

Downs, Perry. *Teaching for Spiritual Growth: Introduction to Christian Education* (Grand Rapids, Mich.: Zondervan) 1994.

Dunn, Richard R. "Putting Youth Ministry in Perspective," *Reaching a Generation for Christ.* Richard Dunn and Mark Senter III, eds., (Chicago: Moody Press) 1997.
--------. *Shaping the Spiritual Life of Students* (Downers Grove, Ill.: InterVarsity Press) 2001.

Edelwich, Jerry. *Burnout: Stages of Disillusionment in the Helping Professions* (New York: Human Sciences Press), 1980.

Edward, Gene. *A Tale of Three Kings* (Wheaton, Ill.: Tyndale) 1992.

Edwards, Jonathan. Cited in *The Philosophy of Jonathan Edwards from his Private Notebooks*, ed. Harvey G. Townsend. (Eugene, Ore.), 1955.
--------. *Religious Affections* (New Haven, Conn.: Yale University Press) 1959.

Ekstrom, Reynolds. *Access Guide to Pop Culture* (New Rochelle, N.Y.: Salesian Society) 1989.

Eldredge, John. *Journey of Desire* (Nashville, Tenn.: Thomas Nelson Publishers) 2000.

Elkind, David, *The Hurried Child: Growing Up Too Fast Too Soon* (Reading, Mass.: Addison-Wesley) 1984.
--------. *The Disappearance of Childhood* (New York: Dell Books) 1984.
--------. *All Grown Up and No Place to Go: Teenagers in Crisis* (Reading, Mass.: Addison-Wesley) 1984.

Elliot, Elisabeth. *Shadow of the Almighty* (Grand Rapids, Mich.: Zondervan) 1958.
--------. *A Chance to Die: The Life and Legacy of Amy Carmichael* (Old Tappan, N.J.: Fleming H. Revell) 1987.

Ellul, Jacques. *Propaganda* (New York: Knopf) 1965.

Engel, James, and Wilbert H. Norton. *What's Gone Wrong With the Harvest?* (Grand Rapids, Mich.: Zondervan), 1975.
-------- and Ted Ward, *What's Gone Wrong With the Harvest?* (Old Tappan, N.J.: Fleming H. Revell) 1975.

Ephron, Delia. *Teenage Romance or How to Die of Embarrassment* (New York: Ballantine Books) 1981.

Erickson, Millard J. *Postmodernizing the Faith* (Grand Rapids, Mich.: Baker, 1998).

Erikson, Erik, "The Life Cycle Epigenesis of Identity/Identity Confusion in Life History and Case History," *Social and Personality Development: Essays on the Growth of the Child.* William Damon, ed. (New York: W.W. Norton and Co.) 1983.
--------. *Identity: Youth and Crisis* (New York: W. W. Norton and Co.) 1968.

Ernest, J. B. *Theological Lexicon of the New Testament*, 3 vols. (Peabody, Mass.: Hendrickson) 1994.

Farrar, Steve. *Finishing Strong.* (Sisters, Ore.: Multnomah Books) 1995.

Fee, Gordon D. *The First Epistle to the Corinthians*, The New International Commentary on the New Testament (Grand Rapids, Mich.: Eerdmans) 1987.

Feldman, Kenneth and Michael Paulsen. *Teaching and Learning in the College Classroom* (New York: W. W. Norton) 1979.

Fields, Doug. *Purpose-Driven Youth Ministry* (Grand Rapids, Mich.: Zondervan) 1998.

Fisher, David. *The 21st Century Pastor* (Grand Rapids, Mich.: Zondervan) 1996.

Flannery, Tim. *Throwim way leg: Adventures in the Jungles of New Guinea* (London: Weidenfeld and Nicholson) 1998.

Ford, Leighton, "Hour of Decision" Broadcast, March 9, 1975.

Fore, William. "Television's Mythic World," *Access Guide to Pop Culture* (New Rochelle, N .Y.: Don Bosco Multimedia) 1989.

Foster, Richard. *Celebration of Discipline* (San Francisco: Harper and Row) 1978.

Fowler, James. "Faith, Liberation, and Human Development," *Christian Perspectives on Faith Development: A Reader*, Jeff Astley and Leslie Francis, eds., (Grand Rapids, Mich.: Eerdmans) 1992.

Fowler, James. *Faithful Change: The Personal and Public Challenges of Postmodern Life*, (Nashville: Abingdon) 1996.
--------. *Stages in Faith Consciousness in Religious Development in Childhood and Adolescence*, Fritz Koser and W. George Scarlett, eds., (San Francisco: Jossey-Bass) 1991.
--------. *Stages of Faith* (San Francisco: Harper and Row) 1981.
--------. *The Vocation of Faith Development Theory in Stages of Faith and Religious Development*, James Fowler, et al, eds., (New York: Crossroad) 1991.

Freud, Sigmund. *A General Introduction to Psychoanalysis* (New York: Washington Square Press) 1917.

Frye, Northrup. *The Great Code: The Bible and Literature* (Toronto: Academic Press) 1981.

Fryling, Bob. *Being Faithful in This Generation: The Gospel and Student Culture at the End of the 20th Century.* (Downers Grove, Ill.: InterVarsity Press) 1995, cited in Brian McLaren, *The Church on the Other Side* (Grand Rapids, Mich.: Zondervan) 2000.

Gaede, Stan. *When Tolerance Is No Virtue: Political Correctness, Multiculturalism, and the Future of Truth and Justice.* (Downers Grove, Ill.: InterVarsity Press) 1994.

Gangel, Kenneth O. and James C. Wilhoit. *The Christian Educator's Handbook of Spiritual Formation* (Wheaton, Ill.: Victor) 1994.

Gerber, Michael. *The E-Myth* (New York: Harper Business) 1986.

Gilligan, Carol. *In a Different Voice: Psychological Theory and Women's Development* (Cambridge, Mass.: Harvard University Press) 1982.

Goldschmidt, Walter. *Comparative Functionalism* (Berkeley, Calif.: University of California Press) 1966.

Goodrich, Frances and Albert Hackett. (dramatizers of) *Diary of Anne Frank* (New York: Random House) 1956.

Grenz, Stanley and Roy D. Bell. *Betrayal of Trust* (Downers Grove, Ill.: InterVarsity Press) 1995.
--------. *Primer to Postmodernism* (Grand Rapids, Mich.: Eerdmans) 1996.

Grunlan, Stephen A. and M. Mayers. *Cultural Anthropology: A Christian Perspective* (Grand Rapids, Mich.: Zondervan) 1988.

Guinness, Os. *The Call* (Nashville, Tenn.: Word) 1998.

Habermas, Ronald and Klaus Issler. *Teaching for Reconciliation.* (Grand Rapids, Mich.: Baker) 1992.

Hale, J. Russell. *Who Are the Unchurched? An Exploratory Study* (Washington, D.C.: Glenmary Research Center) 1977, cited in Harvie M. Conn, *Evangelism: Doing Justice and Preaching Grace* (Grand Rapids, Mich.: Zondervan) 1982.

Hall, Stuart and A. Stanley. *The Seven Checkpoints: Seven Principles Every Teenager Needs to Know* (West Monore, La.: Howard) 2001.

Hamilton, Myrlene L.J. *All I Needed to Know About Ministry I Learned from Fly Fishing* (Valley Forge, Penn.: Judson Press) 2001.

Hamilton, Neill Q. *Maturing in the Christian Life: A Pastor's Guide* (Philadelphia: Geneva Press) 1984.

Hands, Donald R. and Wayne L. Fehr. *Spiritual Wholeness for Clergy: A New Psychology of Intimacy with God, Self, and Others* (Bethesda, Md.: Alban Institute) 1993.

Hansen, David. *The Art of Pastoring* (Downers Grove, Ill.: InterVarsity Press) 1994.

Hare, David. *Racing Demon* (Faber and Faber) 1990 Cited in Stott, *The Contemporary Christian.* (Downers Grove, Ill.: InterVarsity Press) 1992.

Harvey, David. *Condition of Postmodernity* (Cambridge, Mass.: Basil Blackwell) 1989.

Havighurst, Robert. *Developmental Tasks and Education* (New York: David McCay) 1961.

Havlik, John F. *People-Centered Evangelism* (Nashville, Tenn.: Broadman) 1971.

Henry, Matthew. *Matthew Henry's Commentary on the Whole Bible: New Modern Edition*, Electronic Database. Copyright © 1991 by Hendrickson Publishers, Inc.

Hesselgrave, David. *Communicating Christ Cross-Culturally* (Grand Rapids, Mich.: Zondervan) 1978.

Hiebert, Paul G. "Anthropological Tools for Missionaries" (Singapore: Haggai Institute) 1983.
--------. *Anthropological Insights for Missionaries* (Grand Rapids, Mich.: Baker) 1985.

Himes, J. *The Study of Sociology* (Glenview, Ill.: Scott) 1968.

Hinson, E. Glenn. *Spiritual Preparation for Christian Leadership* (Nashville, Tenn.: Upper Room Books) 1999.

Holmes, Arthur F. "Toward a Christian View of Things," *The Making of a Christian Mind*, Arthur F. Holmes, ed., (Downers Grove, Ill.: InterVarsity Press) 1985.

Howe, Neil and William Strauss. *Millennials Rising* (New York: Vintage Books) 2000.

Hunter, James Davison. *The Death of Character: Moral Education in an Age Without Good or Evil* (New York: Basic Books) 2000.

Jacober, Amy. *Bilingual Conversations in Youth Ministry: Speaking the Language of Theology and Psychosociology*

Jenkins, Daniel. *The Protestant Ministry* (New York: Doubleday and Co.) 1958.

Johnson, Darrell W., *Ordination, The Leadership Handbook of Management and Administration*, ed. James D. Berkley (Grand Rapids, Mich.: Baker Books with Christianity Today Inc.) 2000.

Johnson, Kurt. *Controlled Chaos: Making Sense of Junior High Ministry* (Cincinnati, Ohio: Standard Publishing) 2001.

Johnson, Luke Timothy. *The Real Jesus: The Misguided Quest for the Historical Jesus and the Truth of the Traditional Gospels* (San Francisco: Harper) 1997.

Johnston, Robert K. *Reel Spirituality: Theology and Film in Dialogue* (Grand Rapids, Mich.: Baker Academic) 2000.

Jones, Allen W. *Journey Into Christ* (New York: Seabury Press) 1977.

Jones, E. Stanley. *The Word Became Flesh* (Nashville, Tenn.: Abingdon) 1963.

Jones, Karen. "Setting Ministry Goals: Personal and Interpersonal" in *Starting Right*, Karen Jones, et al. (Grand Rapids, Mich.: Zondervan) 2001.

Jones, Tony. *Postmodern Youth Ministry* (Grand Rapids, Mich.: Zondervan) 2001.

Joy, Donald M. "Kohlberg Revisited: A Supra-Naturalist Speaks His Mind," *Moral Development Foundations* (Nashville, Tenn.: Abingdon) 1983.
--------. *Parents, Kids and Sexual Integrity* (Waco, Tex.: Word Books) 1988.

Junger, Sebastian. *Fire* (Harper Audio, 2001).
--------. *The Perfect Storm* (New York: Harper Torch) 1997.

Kageler, Len. *How to Expand Your Youth Ministry* (Grand Rapids, Mich.: Zondervan/Youth Specialties) 1996.

Keating, Charles J. *Who We Are Is How We Pray: Matching Personality and Spirituality* (Mystic, Conn.: Twenty-Third Publications) 1987.

Keating, D. "Adolescent Thinking," in *At the Threshold*, S. Feldman and G. Elliot, eds., (Cambridge, Mass.: Harvard University Press) 1990.

Kennedy, Gerald, ed. *The Best of John Henry Jowett* (New York: Harper and Bros) 1948.

Kenneson, Philip D. and James L. Street, *Selling Out The Church: The Dangers of Church Marketing* (Nashville, Tenn.: Abingdon) 1997.

Kesler, Jay. *Being Holy, Being Human* (Dallas: Word) 1988.

Kilpatrick, William. *Why Johnny Can't Tell Right From Wrong* (New York: Touchstone-Simon and Schuster) 1973.

Kohlberg, Lawrence. "Moral Stages and Moralization: The Cognitive-Developmental Approach" in *Moral Development and Behavior*, Thomas Lickona, ed., (New York: Holy, Rhinehart and Winston) 1976.

Konzelman, Robert G. *Marquee Ministry: The Movie Theater as Church and Community Forum* (New York: Harper and Row) 1971.

Kotesky, Ron. "Adolescence as a Cultural Invention," *Handbook of Youth Ministry*, Donald Ratcliff and James Davies, eds., (Birmingham, Ala.: Religious Education Press) 1991.

Kotter, John. *A Force for Change: How Leadership Differs From Management* (New York: Free Press) 1990.

Kraft, Charles. *Anthropology for Christian Witness* (Maryknoll, N.Y.: Orbis Books) 1996.

Krakauer, Jon. *Into Thin Air* (New York: Random House) 1997.

Kreeft, Peter. *C. S. Lewis for the Third Millennium* (San Francisco, Calif.: Ignatius Press) 1994.

Kwast, Lloyd. "Understanding Culture," in *Perspectives on the Christian World Movement*. R. D.Winter and S. C. Hawthorne eds., (Pasadena, Calif.: William Carey Library) 1981.

Lapsley, D. K., et al, "Moral and Social Education" in *Adolescent Development: Issues in Education* J. Worrell and F. Danner, eds., (New York: Academic Press) 1986.

Larson, Gary. *The Pre-History of The Far Side* (New York: Andrews and McMeel) 1989.

Larson, Knute. *In Need of a Good Reputation, Measuring Up*, Stuart Briscoe, et al, eds.,(Sisters, Ore.: Multnomah Books) 1993.

Leno, Jay. *More Headlines* (New York: Warner Books) 1990.

Letham, Lawrence. *GPS Made Easy* (Seattle: The Mountaineers) 2001.

Lewis, C. S. *Letters to Malcolm: Chiefly on Prayer* (New York: Harcourt, Brace and World) 1964.

Lewis, C. S. Letter to Edward Dell. Cited in *The Business of Heaven* Walter Hooper, ed., (London: Harcourt Brace) 1984.

--------. *Mere Christianity.* (New York: Touchstone-Simon and Schuster) 1996.
 --------. *The Business of Heaven: Daily Readings From C. S. Lewis*, Walter Hooper, ed., (New York: Harcourt, Brace and Company) 1984.
--------. *The Chronicles of Narnia: Prince Caspian* (New York: Iverson-Norman Assoc. for Religious Books Club) 1973.
--------. *The Great Divorce* (New York: Touchstone-Simon and Schuster) 1996.
--------. *The Horse and His Boy* (London: Geoffrey Bles) 1954.
--------. *The Problem of Pain* (San Francisco: Harper SanFrancisco, 2001)
--------. *The Screwtape Letters* (New York: The MacMillan Co) 1959.
--------. *The Weight of Glory* (Grand Rapids, Mich.: Wm. B. Eerdmans) 1973.

Lightfoot, J. B. *The Christian Ministry, in St. Paul's Epistle to the Philippians* (Grand Rapids, Mich.: Zondervan) 1953.

Loder, James E. and W. Jim Neidhardt. *The Knight's Move: The Relational Logic of the Spirit in Theology and Science* (Colorado Springs, Colo.: Helmers and Howard) 1992.

London, H.B. and Neil Wiseman. *Pastors at Risk* (Wheaton, Ill.: Victor) 1993.

Lothar, Coenen. *Dictionary of New Testament Theology* Colin Brown, ed., (Grand Rapids, Mich.: Zondervan) 1975.

Louth, Andrew, ed. *Ancient Christian Commentary on the Scriptures, vol I, Genesis* (Downers Grove, Ill.: InterVarsity Press) 2001.

Lugo, J. O. *Infant Development, Encyclopedia of Psychology* Vol. 2, Raymond J. Corsini, ed., (New York: John Wiley and Sons) 1984.

Luther, Martin. "Sermon on John 8:46-50,1528," *What Luther Says.* 3 vols. E. Plass, ed.,(St. Louis: Concordia) 1959.
--------. *Luther's Works*, 55 Vols., T. G. Tappert, ed.; (St. Louis: Concordia) 1955-86.
--------. *The Babylonian Captivity, Works of Martin Luther II*, Philadelphia Edition. 6 vols. (Philadelphia: Muhlenburg Press) 1943.

Lyman, Tom and Bill Riviere. *The Field Book of Mountaineering and Rock Climbing* (New York: Winchester Press) 1976.

Lyotard, Jean-Francoise. As summarized by Steven Connor, *Postmodernist Culture: An Introduction to Theories of the Contemporary* (Oxford: Basil Blackwell) 1989.

John MacArthur, Jr. *Rediscovering Pastoral Ministry* (Waco, Tex.: Word) 1995.
-------- *Pastoral Ministry in History*, James Stitzinger, ed., *Rediscovering Pastoral Ministry* (Dallas, Tex.: Word) 1995.

MacAulay, Susan Schaeffer, *How to Be Your Own Selfish Pig* (Elgin, Ill.: Chariot Family Publishers) 1982.

MacDonald, Gordon. *Ordering Your Private World* (Nashville, Tenn.: Oliver-Nelson) 1984.

Malinowski, Bronislaw. *A Scientific Theory of Culture and Other Essays* (Chapel Hill, N.C.: University of North Carolina Press) 1944.

Mallone, George. *Furnace of Renewal* (Downers Grove, Ill: InterVarsity Press) 1981.

Malphurs, Aubrey. *Ministry Nuts and Bolts: What They Don't Teach Pastors in Seminary* (Grand Rapids, Mich.: Kregel) 1997.

Manning, Brennan. *The Boy Who Cried Abba* (Berkley, Calif.: Page Mill Press) 1997.

May, Rollo. *Power and Innocence* (New York: W.W. Norton and Co.) 1972.

McCollough, Charles. *Heads of Heaven and Feet of Clay* (New York: The Pilgrim Press) 1983.

McDermott, Gerald. *Seeing God* Downers Grove, IL: InterVarsity Press, 1995.

McDowell, Josh. *The New Tolerance.* (Wheaton, Ill.: Tyndale) 1998.

McGrath, Alister. *The Journey: A Pilgrim in the Lands of the Spirit* (New York: Doubleday) 1999.

McLaren, Brian. *A New Kind of Christian: A Tale of Two Friends on a Spiritual Journey* (San Francisco: Jossey-Bass) 2001.
--------. *The Church on the Other Side* (Grand Rapids, Mich.: Zondervan) 2000.

Medved, Michael. *Hollywood vs. America,* (New York: HarperCollins) 1992.

Melanchthon, Philip. *de appellatione ecclesiae catholicae*, in *Corpus Reformation*, cited in Alister McGrath, *The Christian Theology Reader* (Oxford: Blackwell) 1995.

Mendez, Antonio. *Master of Disguise* (New York: Perennial-Harper Collins) 2000.

Merton, Thomas. *The Seven Story Mountain* (New York: Harcourt, Brace and Co.) 1948.
-------- *Thoughts in Solitude* (Garden City, N.Y.: Image Books) 1958.

Mickey, Paul A. and Ginny W. Ashmore. *Clergy Families: Is Normal Life Possible?* (Grand Rapids, Mich.: Zondervan) 1991.

Miller, Donald E. "The Developmental Approach to Christian Education," in *Contemporary Approaches to Christian Education*, Jack L. Seymour and Donald Miller, eds., (Nashville, Tenn.: Abingdon) 1982.

Miller, Samuel. *Letters on Clerical Manners and Habits Addressed to a Student in the Theological Seminary at Princeton*, N.J. (New York: G&C Carvill) 1827, Letter III, "Offensive Personal Habits."

Mills, David. *Necessary Doctrines, Ancient and Postmodern Christianity*, Christopher Hall and Kenneth Tanner, eds., (Downers Grove, Ill.: InterVarsity Press) 2002.

Moore, Waylon B. *Multiplying Disciples: The New Testament Method for Church Growth* (Colorado Springs, Colo.: NavPress) 1981.

Mouland, Michael. *The Complete Idiot's Guide to Hiking, Camping, and the Great Outdoors* (New York: Alpha Books) 1996.

Mueller, Walt. *Understanding Today's Youth Culture* (Wheaton, Ill.: Tyndale) 1994.

Myers, David. *The Human Connection* (Downers Grove, Ill.: InterVarsity Press).

Nanus, Burt. *Leaders Who Make a Difference* (San Francisco: Jossey-Bass) 1999.

Nash, Robert N. Jr. *An 8-Track Church in a CD World* (Macon, Ga.: Smyth and Helwys) 2001.

Nee, Watchman. *The Church and the Work*, Vol I (New York: Christian Fellowship Publishers) 1982.
--------. *The Normal Christian Worker* (Ann Arbor, Mich.: Servant Publications) 1985.

Neuhaus, Richard John. "C. S. Lewis in the Public Square," *Ancient and Postmodern Christianity: Paleo-orthodoxy in the 21st Century*, Christopher A. Hall and Kenneth Tanner, eds., (Downers Grove, Ill.: InterVarsity Press) 2002.

Newbigin, Leslie. *The Gospel in a Pluralist Society* (Grand Rapids, Mich.: Eerdmans) 1996.

Nicholls, Bruce. "Towards a Theology of Gospel and Culture," *Down to Earth: Studies of Christianity and Culture.*, Robert Coote and John Stott, eds., (Grand Rapids, Mich.: Eerdmans) 1980.

Niebuhr, Richard, et al. *The Purpose of the Church and Its Ministry: Reflections on the Aims of Theological Education* (New York: Harper and Brothers) 1956.
--------. *Christ and Culture* (New York: Harper and Row) 1956.

Nielsen, Linda. *Adolescence: A Contemporary View.* (Philadelphia: Harcourt, Brace College Publishers) 1996.

Nouwen, Henri. *Name of Jesus: Reflections on Christian Leadership.* (New York: Crossroad) 1993.
--------. *The Wounded Healer* (New York: Bantam Doubleday) 1979.

Oden, Thomas C. *Pastoral Theology: Essentials of Ministry* (New York: HarperCollins) 1983.
--------. *Classical Pastoral Care* (Grand Rapids, Mich.: Baker) 1987.

Olford, Stephen. *Camping With God* (Neptune, N.J.: Loizeaux Brothers) 1971.

Origen. *Homilia in Iesu Nave III*, 5; in McGrath, Alister, *The Christian Theology Reader* (Oxford: Blackwell Publishers) 1995.

Ortberg, John. *Confessions of a Lazy Pastor.* Cited in John Ortberg, et al, *Dangers, Toils and Snares* (Sisters, Ore.: Multnomah) 1994.
--------. *The Life You've Always Wanted* (Grand Rapids, Mich.: Zondervan) 1997.
--------. *Love Beyond Reason* (Grand Rapids, Mich. Zondervan) 1998.
--------. *Orthodoxy* (London: The Bodley Head) 1957.

Oswald, Roy M. *Crossing the Boundary: Between Seminary and Parish* (Washington, D.C.: Alban Institute) 1980.

Palmer, Parker. *The Courage to Teach* (San Francisco: Jossey-Bass) 1998.

Parker, Percy Livingston, ed. *Journal of John Wesley* (Chicago: Moody Press) 1974.

Parkes, C. et al. *Attachment Across the Life Cycle* (New York: Tavistock/Routledge) 1991.

Parrott, Les. *Helping the Struggling Adolescent: A Counseling Guide* (Grand Rapids, Mich.: Zondervan) 1993.

Pascal, Blaise. *Pensées* (New York: Random House), 1973.

Pat Hurley. *Penetrating the Magic Bubble* (Wheaton, Ill.: Victor) 1982.

Patterson, Ben. *Is Ministry a Career? The Leadership Handbook of Management and Administration*, James D. Berkley, ed., (Grand Rapids, Mich.: Baker Books with Christianity Today, Inc.) 2000.

Patty, Steven. "A Developmental Framework for Doing Youth Ministry," in *Reaching a Generation for Christ*, Richard Dunn and Mark Senter III, eds., (Chicago: Moody Press) 1997.

Pazmino, Robert W. *Foundational Issues in Christian Education* (Grand Rapids, Mich.: Baker Books) 1997.

Peace, Richard. *Pilgrimage: A Handbook on Christian Growth* (Grand Rapids, Mich.: Baker) 1976.

Pelikan, I and H. T. Lehmann, eds. *Luther's Works.* 54 vols. (St. Louis: Concordia), cited in *Classical Pastoral Care*, Thomas Oden (Grand Rapids, Mich.: Baker) 1987.

Pentcost, J. Dwight. *Design for Discipleship* (Grand Rapids, Mich.: Zondervan) 1971.

Peterson, Eugene. *A Long Obedience in the Same Direction,* (Downers Grove, Ill.: InterVarsity Press) 1980.
--------. *Like Dew Your Youth: Growing Up With Your Teenager* (Grand Rapids, Mich.: Eerdmans) 1994.

--------. *Subversive Spirituality* (Grand Rapids, Mich.: W. B. Eerdmans Publishing) 1997.

--------. *The Contemplative Pastor* (Dallas, Tex.: Word Publishing) 1989.

--------. *The Message* (Colorado Springs, Colo.: NavPress) 1993.

--------. *Under the Unpredictable Plant* (Grand Rapids, Mich.: Eerdmans) 1992.

--------. *Working the Angles* (Grand Rapids, Mich.: Eerdmans) 1987.

Phillips, Derek L. *Authenticity or Morality? The Virtues: Contemporary Essays on American Character.* (Belmont, Calif.: Wadsworth Publishing Co.) 1987.

Phillips, J. B. *The New Testament in Modern English* (London: Geoffrey Bles) 1967.

Piaget, Jean. *Piaget and His School*, B. Inhelder, et al, eds., (New York: Springer-Verlag), cited in "Adolescent Thinking and Understanding," Gary L. Sapp, *Handbook of Youth Ministry*, Donald Ratcliffe and James A. Davies, eds. (Birmingham, Ala.: Religious Education Press) 1991.

--------. *The Moral Judgement of the Child* (New York: Harcourt, Brace, Jovanovich) 1932.

Pippert, Rebecca. *Out of the Salt-Shaker.* (Downers Grove, Ill.: InterVarsity Press) 1979.

Piven, Joshua and David Brogenicht. *The Worst-Case Scenario Survival Handbook* (San Francisco: Chronicle Books) 1999.

Pomerantz, Gary. *Nine Minutes and Twenty Seconds: The Tragedy and Triumph of Flight 529* (New York: Simon and Schuster Audio) 2001.

Postman, Neil. *Amusing Ourselves to Death* (New York: Viking Penguin) 1985.

Powers, Bruce. *Growing Faith* (Nashville, Tenn.: Broadman) 1982.

--------. *Primitive Culture* (London: J. Murray) 1971.

Putnam, Robert D. *Bowling Alone: The Collapse and Revival of American Community* (New York: Simon and Schuster) 2000.

Rainer, Thom S. *The Formerly Unchurched* (Grand Rapids, Mich.: Zondervan) 2001.

Rayburn III, Jim. *Dance, Children, Dance* (Wheaton, Ill.: Tyndale) 1984.

Rees, Paul. *Don't Sleep Through the Revolution* (Old Tappan, N.J.: Revell)

Reeves, Thomas. *The Empty Church* (New York: The Free Press) 1996.

Richards, Larry. *Youth Ministry: It's Renewal in the Local Church* (Grand Rapids, Mich.: Zondervan) 1970.

--------. *A Practical Theology of Spirituality* (Grand Rapids, Mich.: Zondervan) 1987.

Robbins, Duffy. *Ministry of Nurture* (Grand Rapids, Mich.: Zondervan) 1990.

Robertson, *Word Pictures in the New Testament*, Notes on John 1:14

Romanowski, William D. *Eyes Wide Open: Looking for God in Popular Culture* (Grand Rapids, Mich: Brazos Press) 2001.

--------, et al. *Dancing in the Dark* (Grand Rapids, Mich.: Eerdmans) 1991.

Rower, Samuel. "Testing Validity: Moral Development and Biblical Faith" in *Moral Development Foundations* by Donald Joy (Nashville, Tenn.: Abingdon) 1983.

Ryle, J. C. Cited in *Daily Walk* (Atlanta, Ga.: Walk Thru the Bible) December 1993.

Sanford, John. *Ministry Burnout* (New York: Paulist Press) 1982.

Sanny, Lorne. "Laborers: The Navigators' Mission" in *Navigators Daily Walk Devotional Guide* (date unknown).

Santrock, John. *Adolescence* (Dubuque, Iowa.: Brown and Benchmark) 1996.

Schaeffer, Francis A. *True Spirituality.* (Wheaton, Ill.: Tyndale) 1971.

Schwartz, Sherwood. "Send Help Before It's Too Late," *Parent's Choice*, Winter, 1984, cited by R. Ekstrom, *Access Guide to Pop Culture* (New Rochelle, N.Y.: Salesian Society) 1989.

Selman, Robert. *The Growth of Interpersonal Understanding: Clinical and Developmental Analyses* (New York: Academic Press) 1980.

Senter, Mark, ed., *Four Views of Youth Ministry and the Church* (Grand Rapids, Mich.: Zondervan/Youth Specialties, 2001).

Setzer, Lynn. *A Season of the Appalachian Trail* (Birmingham, Ala.: Menasha Bridge Press) 1997.

Shackleton, Sir Ernest, C.V.O. *South: The Endurance Expedition* (New York: Signet) 1999.

Simonetti, Manlio, ed. *Ancient Christian Commentary on Scripture*, v Ib (Downers Grove, Ill.: InterVarsity Press) 2002.

Skelton, Tracey and Gill Valentine. *Cool Places: Geographies of Youth Culture* (London: Rutledge) 1998.

Smith, Chuck, Jr. *The End of the World As We Know It* (Colorado Springs, Colo.: Waterbrook Press) 2001.

Smith, Efrem. From roundtable discussion, San Diego, Calif., May 31, 2002.

Smith, Gordon. *Courage and Calling* (Downers Grove, Ill.: InterVarsity Press) 2002.

Smith, Mark Eddy. *Tolkien's Ordinary Virtues: Exploring the Spiritual Themes of The Lord of the Rings* (Downers Grove, Ill.: InterVarsity Press) 2002.

Smith, Wilford Cantwell. *The Meaning and End of Religion* (New York: MacMillan) 1962.

Snyder, Howard A. *The Problem of Wineskins* (Downers Grove, Ill.: InterVarsity Press) 1975.

Spurgeon, Charles. *Lectures to My Students* (Grand Rapids, Mich.: Zondervan), 1954.

Steere, Douglas V. *On Beginning from Within* (New York: Harper Brothers) 1943.

Stevens, R. Paul. *The Other Six Days* (Grand Rapids, Mich.: Eerdmans) 1999.

Stone, Irving. *Men to Match My Mountains* (New York: Berkley Books) 1982.

Stonehouse, Cathy. "Moral Development: The Process and the Pattern," *Counseling and Values* 24, October 1979, cited in Shelton, Charles, *Adolescent Spirituality* (Chicago: Loyola University Press) 1983.

Stott, John R. W. "Our Motives and Message," *Change, Witness, Triumph* (compendium of addresses from Urbana '64 (Downers Grove, Ill.: InterVarsity Press) 1964.
--------. *Christ the Liberator* (Downers Grove, Ill.: InterVarsity Press) 1971.
--------. *Down to Earth: Studies in Christianity and Culture* (Grand Rapids, Mich.: Eerdmans) 1980.
--------. *Guard the Gospel* (Downers Grove, Ill.: InterVarsity Press) 1973.
--------. *The Contemporary Christian* (Downers Grove, Ill.: InterVarsity Press) 1992.
--------. *The Preacher's Portrait* (Grand Rapids, Mich.: Eerdmans) 1961.

Strommen, Merton, et al. *Youth Ministry That Transforms* (Grand Rapids, Mich.: Zondervan) 2001.
--------. *Five Cries of Youth* (New York: Harper) 1970.

Sumner, William Graham. *Folkways* (Boston: Ginn) 1906.

Swain, Bernard. *Liberating Leadership* (San Francisco: Harper and Row) 1986.

Sweet, Leonard. *Soul Tsunami* (Grand Rapids, Mich.: Zondervan) 1999.

Taylor, Nick. *Spiritual Formation: Nurturing Spiritual Vitality, Introducing Christian Education,* Michael Anthony ed. (Grand Rapids, Mich.: Baker) 2001.

Tejada-Flores, Lito. *Wildwater: The Sierra Club Guide to Whitewater Boating* (San Francisco: Sierra Club Books) 1978.

Tertullian. "Testimony of the Soul," *Fathers of the Church.* R. J. Deferrari, ed., 74 vols. to date. (Washington, D.C.: Catholic University Press) 1947.

Thieleke, Helmut. *A Little Exercise for Young Theologians* (Grand Rapids, Mich.: Eerdmans) 1968.

Thomas, W.H. Griffith, *The Work of the Ministry* (London: Hodder and Stoughton) 1910.

Thorpe, Nick. *Eight Men and a Duck: An Improbable Voyage in a Reed Boat to Easter Island* (New York: The Free Press) 2002.

Tolkien, J. R. R. *Fellowship of the Ring* (Boston: Houghton Mifflin) 1965.
--------. *The Lord of the Rings* (1968).
--------. Quoted in A. N. Wilson, *C. S. Lewis* (New York: Fawcett Columbine) 1991.

Tozer, A. W. *Knowledge of the Holy.* (San Francisco: Harper) 1961.

Trottman, Dawson. *Born to Reproduce* (Colorado Springs, Colo.: NavPress) 1975.

Trueblood, Elton. *Your Other Vocation* (New York: Harper and Row) 1952, cited in Gordon MacDonald. *Facing Turbulent Times* (Wheaton, Ill.: Tyndale) 1981.

Vitz, Paul. *Psychology as Religion* (Grand Rapids, Mich.: Eerdmans) 1977.

von Hugel, Baron Friedrich. *Selected Letters 1896–1924.,* Bernard Holland, ed. (New York: E.P. Dutton) 1933.

Wagner, Peter, *Ministries Today*, Nov/Dec, 1992, cited in H. B. London, Neil Wiseman. *Pastors at Risk.* (Wheaton, IL: Victor Books) 1993.

Wangerin, Walter Jr., *As for Me and My House* (Nashville, Tenn.: Thomas Nelson) 1990.

Ward, Pete. *God at the Mall* (Peabody, Mass.: Hendrickson Publishers) 1999.

Ward, Ted. *Moral Development Foundations* (Nashville, Tenn.: Abingdon) 1983.

Warner, Greg. *Job Insecurity Leaves Young Ministers Wary*, www.Faithworks.com

Webster, Doug. *Selling Jesus: What's Wrong With Marketing the Church?* (Downers Grove, Ill.: InterVarsity Press) 1992.

Wells, David. *God in the Wasteland* (Grand Rapids, Mich.: Eerdmans) 1994.

Wesley, John. *Journal of John Wesley* (Chicago: Moody Press).
--------. Sermon: "The Reformation of Manners," *Works, VI*, quoted in Howard Snyder, *The Radical Wesley* (Downers Grove, Ill.: InterVarsity Press) 1980.

Westerhoff, John H. *Will Our Children Have Faith?* (New York: Seabury) 1976.

Wilcox, David. "That's What the Lonely is For," *The Very Best of David Wilcox*, A&M Records, 2001.

Wilke, Richard. *And Are We Yet Alive?* (Nashville, Tenn.: Abingdon) 1986.

Wilkins, Michael J. *Following the Master: Discipleship in the Steps of Jesus* (Grand Rapids, Mich.: Zondervan) 1992.

Willard, Dallas. Mars Hills Audio tapes, Volume 36, January/February, 1999, Side One, "Dallas Willard on Discipleship".
--------. "The Spirit is Willing: The Body as a Tool," in *The Christian Educator's Handbook on Spiritual Formation*, Kenneth O. Gangel and James C. Wilhoit, eds., (Wheaton, Ill.: Victor) 1994.
--------. *The Spirit of the Disciplines* (New York: Harper Collins) 1988.
--------. *Calling and Chacter* (Nashville, Tenn.: Abingdon) 2002.

Willimon, William, *Pastor* (Nashville, Tenn.: Abingdon) 2002.

Wilson, Earl D. *Steering Clear* (Downers Grove, Ill.: InterVarsity Press) 2002.

Wolfe, Alan. *One Nation, After All* (New York: Putnam Penguin Books) 1998.

Wolterstorff, Nicolas. *Educating for Responsible Action* (Grand Rapids, Mich.: Eerdmans) 1980.

Yaconelli, Michael. *Messy Spirituality* (Grand Rapids, Mich.: Zondervan) 2002.

Zacharias, Ravi. *Deliver Us From Evil: Restoring the Soul in a Disintegrating Culture* (Waco, Tex.: Word Books) 1996.

Periodicals

Arn, Charles. "The Growth Report," *Ministry Advantage* 5. July-Aug 1994.

Bates, Stephen, *Religious Diversity and the Schools*, The American Enterprise 4, no. 5 (Sept/Oct, 1993).

Bibby, Reginald and Merlin B. Brinkerhoff. "Circulation of the Saints Revisited: A Longitudinal Look at Conservative Church Growth," *Journal for the Scientific Study of Religion* (vol. 22, no. 3, 1983).

Corliss, Richard. "The Medium is the Message," *Film Comment* 19 (July-August, 1983)

David, Donald M. "Nihilism in Music Television," A paper presented to the Mass Communication Division of the Speech Communication Association at its annual meeting, Chicago, November 1984.

Derrida, Jacques. "Limited, Inc, abc," *Glyph* 2 (1977)

Fineman, Howard. "One Nation Under Who?" *Newsweek*, July 8, 2002, Volume CXL, No. 2.

Galli, Mark "The Virtue of Unoriginality," *Christianity Today*, vol. 46, no. 4, April 1, 2002.

Goetz, David L. "Forced Out," *Leadership*. #17 Winter, 1996.

Grenz, Jonathan. "Factors Influencing Vocational Changes Among Youth Ministers." *The Journal of Youth Ministry*, vol 1. no. 1, Fall, 2002.

Gretchen L. Zimmerman, Psy. D., et al, "A 'Stages of Change' Approach to Helping Patients Change Behavior," *AFP Bulletin*, March 1, 2000.

Halverson, Richard. *Perspective*, November 10, 1971.

Hart, Archiblad D. "Being Moral Isn't Always Enough," *Leadership*, Spring, 1988.

Hassan, Ihab. "The Culture of Postmodernism," *Theology, Culture and Society*, 2 (1985).

Hayden, Thomas. "Gotcha," *U.S. News and World Report* (August 26, 2002).

Johnson, Benton, et al. *Mainline Churches: The Real Reason for Decline*, First Things, 31 (March 1993).

Kotesky, Ron. "Growing Up Too Late, Too Soon" *Christianity Today*, March 13, 1981.

Long, Justin D. "North America: Decline and Fall of World Religions, 1900-2025," from *The Global Evangelization Movement's Monday Morning Reality Check* (no. 5, 1998).

Marshall, Shelley. "The Character Question," *Leadership Journal*,

Marty, Martin. Quoted by Jane Lampman, "New Thirst for Spirituality Felt Worldwide," *Christian Science Monitor*, November 25, 1998.

McClay, Wilfred M. "Tradition, History, and Sequoias, First Things," (March, 2003, No. 131).

Meadows, Susannah, "In Defense of Gamma Girls," *Newsweek*, June 3, 2002, vol CXXXIX, No. 22

Modica, Joseph A. "Stages, Styles or Stories?: A Brief Guide to Faith Development," *AFTE Newsletter for United Methodist Seminarians*. Vol. 25, no. 3., March, 1999.

Neuhaus, Richard John. "While We're At It" *First Things* 54 (June/July 1995).

Peters, George W. "Is Missions Homesteading or Moving?" *Mennonite Brethren Herald*, April 15, 1977.

Poston, Larry. "The Adult Gospel," *Christianity Today*, vol. 34, no. 11, August 20, 1990.

Reilly, Rick. "In Like Flynn," *Sports Illustrated*, vol. 96, no. 6, February 11, 2002.

Rupert, Hoover. *Not What I Had in Mind*, Presbyterian Outlook, vol. 162, no. 7, Feb 18, 1980.

Searle, John. "Reiterating the Differences: Reply to Derrida," *Glyph* 1 (1977)

Senter, Mark. "Is Son Life Strategy the Strategy of Jesus?" Replicating Dann Spader's "Study of a Harmony of the Gospel," *The Journal of Youth Ministry*, vol. 1, no. 1, Fall, 2002.

Simon, William. "The Missing Issue," *National Review*, March 15, 1993.

Smith, Huston. "Excluded Knowledge: A Critique of the Modern Mind Set," *Teachers College Record* February 1979.

Snyder, Howard A. "Study of a Harmony of the Gospel," *The Journal of Youth Ministry,* vol I, no. I, Fall, 2002.

Spader, Dan. "A Response to Senter's 'Is the SonLife Strategy the Strategy of Jesus?'" *The Journal of Youth Ministry,* vol I, no. I, Fall, 2002.

Stott, John R. W. "The World's Challenge to the Church" *BibliothecaSacra* 145 (578), 1988.

Swaim, Loring. "Massachusetts - Big Names to Have Dirty Linen Aired," *The Providence Journal.*

Thomas, Karen. "The Kids Are Alright: Social Norming May be the Way to Keep Them That Way," *USA Today,* May 28, 2002.

Twain, Mark. "Old Times on the Mississippi," *Atlantic Monthly,* 35, no. 209 (March 1875).

Vincent, John James. "Discipleship and Synoptic Studies," *Theologische Zeitschrift* 16 (1960).

Woodward, Kenneth with Patrica King. "When a Pastor Turns Seducer," *Newsweek,* August, 1989.

Wuthnow, Robert. "Youth and Culture in American Society: The Social Context of Ministry to Teenagers" and "Christ and the Adolescent: A Theological Approach to Youth Ministry," From the 1996 *Princeton Lectures on Youth, Church and Culture* (Princeton, N.J.: Institute for Youth Ministry, 1996).

Wyshak, Grace and Rose Frisch. "Evidence for Secular Trend in Age of Menarche," *New England Journal of Medicine,* April 29, 1982.

Index